FROM

*The Morgenthau
Diaries*

BY JOHN MORTON BLUM

FROM

# The Morgenthau Diaries

## Years of Crisis, 1928–1938

ILLUSTRATED WITH PHOTOGRAPHS

The Riverside Press Cambridge

HOUGHTON MIFFLIN COMPANY BOSTON

1959

# *Preface*

I AM DELIGHTED that this book based on Henry Morgenthau's diaries is being published. One of the things which came to my mind most strongly as I read it was the fact that for so many years, both as friends and as workers, my husband and I were closely associated with Mr. and Mrs. Henry Morgenthau, Jr. They were much younger than we were but the difference in age seemed to matter very little. They were our neighbors in the country and we enjoyed them as neighbors and friends before politics and work for different social aims came into our relationship. It is interesting to know that my husband never held a political office from the time of his governorship of New York State without having Henry Morgenthau, Jr., in some way in his official family. My husband no doubt often treated Henry as a younger brother, they differed and were annoyed with each other and probably said things neither of them meant on occasion, but there was an underlying deep devotion and trust which never really wavered.

It was a fortunate thing that Henry Morgenthau's wife and I also had a close relationship in our working interests as well as in our enjoyment of the theatre, art and literature.

This book is, of course, one that will provide material of an essential kind for future historians, but there is also much of the human side as well as the technical. From it emerges the existence of basic trust and respect between two men who lived in strenuous and exciting times which required great qualities and, I think, fostered great friendships.

ELEANOR ROOSEVELT

# Foreword

"I WANT someone," Mr. Morgenthau said at luncheon five years ago, "who will work with me on my biography. I want an historian to go through my Diaries and write an account of my years with Franklin Roosevelt. I want him to explain what happened and why it happened. I want him to tell the whole story. I am willing to let the chips fall where they may."

That statement provided the chart and compass for this book. Professor Arthur M. Schlesinger, Jr., had introduced me to Mr. Morgenthau, who had asked him to propose an historian for the task, and after a few preliminary conversations, Mr. Morgenthau and I went to work, profiting continually from Mr. Schlesinger's advice. At first we planned only one volume, but the richness of the Morgenthau Diaries persuaded us to write two, one focusing on the years 1933–38, a period during which Mr. Morgenthau's continuing concern was with the problems of the depression; a second, to be published at a later date, on the years 1939–1945, a period during which Mr. Morgenthau was preoccupied by the problems of World War II. A model for our book was, as Mr. Morgenthau had suggested, Henry L. Stimson and McGeorge Bundy, *On Active Service in Peace and War* (New York, 1948). That volume, as Mr. Bundy noted, was "an attempt to substitute a joint effort for . . . singlehanded autobiography . . . to present Mr. Stimson's actions as he himself understood them." Ours has been a similar attempt. It is not autobiography. It appears under my name alone because I have written all of it. Yet it is more than "authorized biography," for Mr. Morgenthau has participated intimately and continuously in its construction. He has given it its flavor.

Our method of operation needs explanation. I worked initially from the Diaries and other related manuscript materials. On the basis of my research, I wrote a draft which I reviewed word for word with Mr. Morgenthau. He then suggested three kinds of changes. First, he recommended many simplifications of language, for he believes now, as he always has, in making himself understandable to adults who have no special knowledge of the techniques and the vocabulary of finance. Second, he helped me recast descriptions of his associates so that those descriptions would conform to his best memory and judgment of the men in and out of the Treasury with whom he worked for a dozen years. Third, he expressed his present views on many past episodes. I have incorporated those expressions in this book, differentiating them from statements Mr. Morgenthau made while he was in office.

My references to and quotations from the manuscript sources, especially the Diaries, are of course unaltered. Mr. Morgenthau has fully respected the record of the past, even when it is critical of him or when conversations in which he took part reveal spontaneous ideas, roughly expressed, rather than polished statements of considered opinions. At his suggestion, I deleted two references, both personal remarks made two decades ago by a man still alive about another man still alive. Otherwise nothing has been deleted. If, then, there are any serious omissions in this book, the fault is entirely my own, and it is inadvertent, for I have tried to execute the mandate Mr. Morgenthau gave me — to tell, within reasonable limits of space but without reserve, what happened and why it happened.

To that end, I have attempted to include descriptions of the significant attitudes and ideas of those who advised Mr. Morgenthau and of those who disagreed with them and with him. I have not, however, anticipated developments that occurred after 1938, the last year this volume covers. It will fall to the second volume to discuss such controversial matters as the preparedness campaign, the financing of World War II, the Bretton Woods Conference, the Morgenthau Plan, the American program of aid for China, and the question of Communist influence in government. Neither Mr. Morgenthau nor I intend to minimize any of those issues, but we both believe they should be handled in their historical context, and none of them arose within the Treasury until after 1938.

This volume covers the issues that concerned Mr. Morgenthau through 1938. It is by no means a history of the New Deal or even of the Treasury as a whole, but of his activities, within the Treasury and without, and of his relationship with the President. For the sake of clarity, I have organized the material, for the most part, topically rather than chronologically. Mr. Morgenthau's early life and his career in the government of New York State fall into Chapter I; his months in the Farm Credit Administration, into Chapter II; his administation of the Treasury's miscellaneous functions, into Chapter III; his gold and silver policies — domestic and foreign — into Chapters IV and V; his fiscal policies, into Chapters VI and VII; and his banking and credit policies into Chapter VIII. Chapter IX deals with the recession of 1938, which raised new questions about all of Mr. Morgenthau's domestic policies; Chapter X treats the developments of his foreign economic policies in response to events in Europe and Asia in 1937–38.

The Morgenthau Diaries contain an extraordinary record out of which to reconstruct the past. Mr. Morgenthau kept fragments of a diary in his youth, an intermittent diary while he was in Albany, and a much fuller diary while he was Governor of the Farm Credit Administration, but these differ in scope and type from the celebrated Diaries relating to his years in the Treasury. The Morgenthau Diaries for the period 1934–1945, in all more than eight hundred bound volumes of several hundred pages apiece, are not "diaries" at all, though they occasionally include the kind of reflective, personal observations of which "diaries" are ordinarily made. Rather, the Morgenthau Diaries are a collection of the papers that crossed the Secretary's desk, letters and memoranda, incoming and outgoing; of verbatim minutes of meetings held in his office; of stenographic transcripts or condensed summaries of other meetings he or his subordinates attended; and of verbatim conversations he had on the telephone. At their fullest, the Diaries provide a minute-by-minute account of his days in office.

In his first years as Secretary of the Treasury, Mr. Morgenthau recorded and preserved less than he later did, and particularly for 1934 and 1935, his miscellaneous papers are indispensable as a supplement to the Diaries. For all his years in office, the records of press conferences, the public documents, and the newspaper clippings that he saved and had bound are of great value. So also are drafts of essays about various phases of his career which a number of historians prepared for him before I went to work. All these and other pertinent materials are on deposit with the Diaries in the Franklin D. Roosevelt Library, where there is also, of course, useful information about Mr. Morgenthau in the manuscript collections of the President, of Harry Hopkins, and of other New Dealers. But the Diaries were the source of most of the important data on which I have relied, as the notes at the end of this book indicate. The Diaries are still closed except to Mr. Morgenthau or his agent, but they will be made available gradually to qualified scholars, according to a schedule calling for the opening of the papers for each succeeding Roosevelt term after twenty-five years have elapsed from the end of the term.

The sheer bulk of material on which this volume is based — I suppose I have examined at least a million pages of manuscripts, newspapers, periodicals, government documents, memoirs, biographies, and special studies — would have been beyond my power to locate or to use had I not had the benefit of the wise, tireless cooperation of Mr. Herman Kahn, Director of the Franklin D. Roosevelt Library, and his staff. Dean John E. Burchard and Professor Howard R. Bartlett of the Massachusetts Institute of Technology, and Professor George W. Pierson of Yale University devised ways for me to find time for research and writing. Mesdames Mary Lou Joyner, Helen M. Smelser, Suzanne Kernan, and Miss Patricia Watlington worked diligently and carefully for small reward. As I struggled to understand economic problems about which I was markedly ignorant, I profited especially from the thoughtful explanations of my former colleagues, Professors E. Cary Brown and Eli Shapiro, both at one time employees of the Treasury Department. Miss Dorothy Borg kindly corrected some of my misconceptions about China. I am even more indebted to Professor Arthur M. Schlesinger, Jr., and to Mr. Craig Wylie, who read and criticized the entire manuscript to the great benefit of its content and readability. None of them, of course, bears any responsibility for any errors of interpretation, economic or otherwise, for any mistakes of fact, or for any awkwardness of prose that I have neglected to remedy. I owe a special debt, as I have often before, to my uncomplaining wife, who cheerfully disposed of the chores I should have handled while instead I worked on this volume. Most of all, I am grateful to Mr. Morgenthau for his patience, his encouragement, his incomparable hospitality, his considerate friendship, and his unfailing honesty.

JOHN MORTON BLUM

*Yale University*

# A Personal Note by
# Henry Morgenthau, Jr.

DURING MY LIFETIME, Franklin Roosevelt threw me into completely new ventures which demanded original thinking. I certainly enjoyed them. I have been asking myself where I got my desire to help people. It seems to me that in the first instance my father and mother taught me to participate in charity in order to bring better living conditions to the masses of people. My father retired from all business activity at fifty in order to devote himself to the public good.

I was very fortunate in marrying Elinor Fatman in 1916. We lived happily together for thirty-three years until she died after a long illness. My inclination as a young man was to hop from one venture to another. It was Elinor more than anybody else who kept my nose to the grindstone. She had a brilliant mind and insisted that I, having selected farming as a way of life, stick to it. I am deeply indebted to her for her help and advice during our married life.

I also owe a great deal to Miss Lillian D. Wald of the Henry Street Settlement for having brought me in touch with the less fortunate people in greater New York.

I want to explain that I am indebted to many people who were experts in their fields and who assisted me in solving the many problems presented to me by Mr. Roosevelt. During the first two years that Mr. Roosevelt was Governor of New York, I had at my elbow William I. Myers, Professor of Economics at Cornell, to help me on the rural tax and school problems. He continued to assist me later in Washington. When I was Conservation Commissioner, my deputy was Carl Ladd, and I also had help from George Warren, one of the great conservationists of the East. Together we worked out experimental programs which subsequently became the basis of national programs to create work for the unemployed.

Mr. Roosevelt asked me to go to Washington with him to get the Farm Credit Administration started. On the day the President was inaugurated, Edward S. Greenbaum, who assisted me in many different ways, introduced me to Herman Oliphant, who in my opinion had one of the finest legal brains in Mr. Roosevelt's Administration. I suppose Oliphant worked out more original programs for the President and for me than did anybody associated with me.

At Farm Credit I also had the assistance of Herbert Gaston, a Farmer-Labor reformer from Minnesota, who was most useful during my entire stay in Washington. Also in Farm Credit was William McReynolds, formerly a post office inspector, who was extremely helpful then and later. He was one of the ablest of the civil service administrators.

Six months went by and I found myself the acting head of the Treasury, a position so complex that it seemed almost impossible to master it, although my training in Farm Credit was very useful. I was able right at the beginning to secure the services of four other men, all outstanding: two economists, Walter Stewart and Jacob Viner, and two financiers, Earle Bailie and Randolph Burgess. Those four men served their country well at an all-time low ebb, and assisted me in restoring the confidence of the people in their Treasury. At the Treasury I also found Daniel Bell, whom I considered the number one civil servant in the United States. Later Harold Graves built the war bond organization state by state, and I am equally indebted to George Haas, Roswell Magill, Roy Blough, Henry Murphy, Randolph Paul, Elmer Irey, and Harry White, who under my direction helped give birth to the World Bank and the Monetary Fund. My secretary, Mrs. Henrietta Klotz, who came to work for me in 1922, was not only very able but also grew with the opportunities that the position offered her. Her loyalty and extreme honesty provided a barrier insurmountable for the many people of questionable character who tried to reach me. In the Procurement Division, which was a dangerous spot for possible graft, Admiral Peoples, an old friend of Mr. Roosevelt, held forth.

When I worked on foreign monetary and economic policies I was fortunate to have Merle Cochran in Paris, on loan from the State Department. He was a great help in the years of the Tripartite Pact. Later in the pre-Lend-Lease period, Arthur Cox and Philip Young were important figures on the Treasury's side, and Sir Frederick Phillips directed British personnel in Washington extremely well. For the British, Arthur Purvis did a wonderful job. He was by far the ablest of their representatives whom I ever worked with, and the only foreigner who ever had access to my house twenty-four hours a day. It was a tragedy when he was killed in an airplane accident.

Louis McHenry Howe, the secretary to the President, was a mighty useful friend to have in the White House. When the going was tough, I found that, if I was right, I could always count on Louis Howe.

It was my good fortune as a man totally inexperienced in politics to have James A. Farley as Chairman of the Democratic National Committee. I cannot remember a single instance that Farley ever asked me to do anything that was not honorable. Farley made my life much easier than it would have been had the National Chairman been an old-time politician.

In the President and Mrs. Roosevelt, my wife and I were favored with a unique friendship which we tried to repay by giving them one hundred per cent service and loyalty.

Mr. Roosevelt often asked me to do things for the government which had nothing to do with regular Treasury work. He would usually ask these things of me after some other Cabinet member had failed, with the result that I made many enemies. Many times Mr. Roosevelt needed a whipping boy and he favored me with that role. But then, he had to run for office and be re-elected and I didn't.

It took me a long time to make up my mind to make use of the Treasury papers. I had saved them in order to make possible a book showing young people what government service is like. It has been pleasant working with John Blum in the preparation of this book, and I feel that Blum and Arthur M. Schlesinger, Jr., who has advised him and me, are trying to tell the truth about the Treasury and the New Deal. I am grateful to them both.

Many people are curious about how I have spent my time since leaving the Treasury, and I shall attempt to tell you a little about it. In a very short period I lost my closest friends and dear ones. The

President died on April 12, 1945. Two months later I resigned from the Treasury. I lost my wife Elinor in September 1949, and shortly after that my mother and father died. The people I was fondest of and leaned on most heavily suddenly disappeared from my life. The emotional shock was tremendous.

Throughout the war years I had burned myself out. My doctor had recommended in 1943 that I resign, but I couldn't while the war was on. In 1949 I found myself a much disturbed person, and I particularly missed the companionship and affection of a wife. It was my good luck to meet Marcelle Puthon in 1950, and after a year's courtship we decided to get married. This was a wonderful thing for me, but for the first few years it was extremely difficult for Marcelle as I had one major illness after another, including two heart attacks. Marcelle, being French-born, had both her feet on the ground, and her constant cheerfulness, and her attitude toward the world and people generally, helped me to establish a new philosophy which is completely free from political concern or ambition. My friend Dr. Harold Wolff also greatly assisted me in tiding over the change from Secretary of the Treasury to apple grower, and Judge Irving Lehman, a man with a beautiful soul, gave me excellent personal advice, as he had in earlier years.

Now my wife and I travel about half of every year, visiting places new to us, learning at first hand in Hong Kong and India and Africa and elsewhere how the rest of the world really live. I find this experience stimulating, doubly satisfying because Marcelle also enjoys it so much. As we travel, moreover, I am constantly buoyed up by the vast affection and esteem that the people we meet everywhere in the world have for Franklin and Eleanor Roosevelt.

HENRY MORGENTHAU, JR.

# Contents

# *Illustrations*

FROM

# The Morgenthau
# Diaries

# I

## One of Two of a Kind

### 1891 - 1932

### 1. The Land and the People

THE SOURCE of the good life was the land. The purpose of the good life was helping those who needed help. The land and the people were the important things, the things the young man cared about. He was a sensitive young man who wanted to strike out on his own. He had grown up with wealth but he had no interest in a career of making money. He had attended an excellent school and college but he had no interest in the professions of law or medicine or management for which excellent schools and colleges train most of their alumni. He found his satisfactions instead in his family, in the bounty and the beauty of the land, and in striving to bring something of the bountiful and the beautiful to the thousands of Americans whose existence was meager and drab. He did not think he knew the secrets of the universe, but he did think he knew good from evil, and he believed the land and people good.

He was a farmer, a reformer, a democrat, one of the children of American plenty whose spirits have transcended the material advantages of their personal inheritances. This transcendence and his independence gave him the equipment for disinterested public service. Friendship with another young man of wealth and independence and high purpose gave him in time the opportunity for public service.

As the close associate of Franklin Delano Roosevelt, Henry Morgenthau, Jr., made his contributions to America. For Morgenthau the young man, the desire to contribute grew out of the definitions of the good life he made in his youth.

Henry Morgenthau, Jr., was born in New York City on May 11, 1891, in the old Beresford apartment house at Central Park West and 81st Street, the only son and the third of four children of Henry and Josephine Sykes Morgenthau. His forebears were German Jews; his paternal grandmother, Babette Guggenheim; his paternal grandfather, Lazarus Morgenthau, a cigar manufacturer who emigrated to the United States in 1866. The senior Henry Morgenthau, starting with little, had become rich by 1891 and was to become increasingly so thereafter. A self-made, self-confident, restless, and forceful man, one of New York's shrewdest investors in real estate, the elder Morgenthau was also a generous and conscientious steward of his wealth who was involved emotionally as well as financially in supporting the Ethical Culture church, the Henry Street Settlement, and the movement "to clear up the slums and the fire traps" that followed the death of over a hundred girls in the Triangle fire of 1911. In the same year he joined the campaign to make Woodrow Wilson President. "Mother felt weak," Morgenthau, Jr., recalled, "when father walked into the room. He was electric, a bundle of nerves and ambition."

Josephine Morgenthau, a woman almost as ambitious and as energetic as her husband, brought to her home warmth, volatility, and a love of beautiful things. For many years she was absorbed by social work, particularly the development of Bronx House and the school of music there. She often listened all day long to rehearsals by the Metropolitan Opera Company, of which she was an enthusiastic patroness. Partly because music gave her a sense of peace and satisfaction, she arranged lessons in music and other creative activities for each of her children. She wanted young Henry, who had a fine deep voice, to learn to sing, but her husband considered singing "sissy," so the boy was taught instead to play the cello, which he never much enjoyed. This was a characteristic development, for the senior Morgenthau claimed and exercised a kind of exclusive proprietorship over the upbringing of his son who found the restrictive intimacy of this relationship at times oppressive.

"Henry Morgenthau, Jr.," his wife Elinor later recalled, "was an average, sturdy, fun-loving youngster, not particularly given to intellectual study. He loved riding, golf, swimming, driving a car, sailing, puttering with a motor boat, rowing and canoeing. For all these things he had a natural aptitude. . . . He was . . . in all things absolutely fearless." But, she went on, he was "an only son with a father who adored him, who made him his constant companion. He adored his father. This undoubtedly had both its good and bad sides. . . . Things his father did and told him come back to him — never to drive such a hard bargain that your customer wouldn't return, never to go on a note, never to become director of a bank controlled by politicians, never to accept a business favor for which you were not able to pay in full. . . . On the other hand, his father tried to regulate his life and to dominate his thoughts — he kept him too much with him and away from companions his own age."

At thirteen Morgenthau entered Phillips Exeter Academy, where he began to keep a diary, a practice which he continued intermittently the rest of his life. For the years at school, the diary recounted briefly the usual student routines. So, on September 19, 1904, "the first check I ever drew from a bank" was to the order of "cash" for $2; on February 9, 1905, "it snowed all day. . . . We had an English Exam and I received B as a mark. In the evening we had a class meeting and Powers was elected track manager."

Morgenthau's grades were ordinarily less than B. He continually fell asleep over his work, not from lack of interest but from the fatigue of his adolescent growth. "He had been robust," Elinor Morgenthau pointed out, "but in one year before he was 14 he grew about 9 inches so that at 14 he had his present height of 6' 1½". This handicapped him all through school and college. A great big gawk, loving sports and naturally good at them, yet in decidedly delicate health, never being allowed to join in organized athletics, and always being so tired that he couldn't quite keep up with his work."

Morgenthau's routines sometimes included a weekend with his father in Boston, where they stayed together at the Parker House, often attended vaudeville, and saw his father's friends. He had friends of his own at school, of course, but the remarks in his diary revealed the nostalgia that punctuated his life at Exeter. "I received a letter from Papa," the last entry of 1905 began, "saying that he had retired from business on Saturday April 1. . . . He is now Vice President of the Lawyers Title Co. I got my trunk up from the cellar, and it makes me feel as if I wish I was home."

After another year at Exeter, Morgenthau returned home to finish preparing for college, first at Sachs Collegiate Institute in New York City and then with a Mr. Kramer in Ithaca. In January 1909 he matriculated at Cornell to study architecture, not because he had any real interest in the subject, but because his father thought it relevant to the future he planned for his son in real estate. Three semesters were enough for Morgenthau, who left Cornell in 1911.

During the following year, he tried three new ventures his father selected: one as a timekeeper with a construction agency, one as a machinist with the Underwood Typewriter Company, in which both Morgenthaus held stock, one as a teller in a bank. The records "Mr. Henry" kept showed the meticulous care with which he checked the hours and wages of the Irish and Italian laborers in his charge. He has observed rather wistfully that he learned a lot as a timekeeper, even began to see large possibilities in the construction business, but could not contemplate pursuing them because any contracting he attempted would have had to be under his father's supervision, which was precisely what he did not want.

Yet everywhere his inheritance seemed to follow him. During one of his first days on the job at Hartford, a fellow employee testing him as every new man was tested, made some sassy remark. Morgenthau, with typical pugnacity, immediately socked his tormentor on the jaw. The victim and his gang would have ambushed him at lunchtime had not the foreman, who knew who Morgenthau really was, refused to let him go out to lunch. Morgenthau, who was rather proud of striking a blow in his own defense, was willing to be spared a drubbing by the gang, but he did not like to think of himself constantly in the role of the protected son of a major stockholder. This reluctance, rather than his immediate physical environment, made him, during his days as a teller in a bank, feel "caged."

At the Henry Street Settlement, New York's equivalent of Hull House in Chicago, he gained the satisfactions his work denied him.

There during the hot weeks of the summer, he nightly pulled his mattress to the roof, daily presided over the boys' table and saw how the indigent lived. It was an unforgettable experience and an awakening apprenticeship. Years later Lillian D. Wald, the head of the settlement, wrote to Josephine Roche, a new Assistant Secretary of the Treasury: "You are associated with my dear friend Secretary Morgenthau. . . . He will understand and appreciate your simplicity and sincerity." Those qualities, she knew, he had early learned to value.

There was much to learn that books did not teach. To convalesce from typhoid fever, Morgenthau in 1911 went to Texas, where he had the leisure to find out something about farming and ranching and a lot about himself. In 1912 he told his father that he had decided to become a farmer. He loved the land, the outdoors, and the companionship of unsophisticated people, and he was determined to be in a business about which his father knew nothing, to stand on his own feet and make his own mistakes. Morgenthau put it directly. "Pop started from the bottom," he commented, "when he was nine years old. From then on his whole life he had all of his family on his neck. He was the only one who was a financial success. Every penny meant something to him. He had to fight every inch of the way. His theory for me was you can start at the top and save all that. That was his philosophy. I had to overcome that. He was crazy to have me in business with him. He would say to my poor mother, 'Josy, you can have the girls, let me have the boy.' In a desperate move to get out from under I moved to the country."

First he enrolled again at Cornell, this time to study agriculture. Impatient as always with books and lectures — he preferred to learn from conversation and observation — Morgenthau left the college after a few months to see for himself what the farmer's opportunities were. With Carl Schurz Scofield, a young expert from the Department of Agriculture, he set out on a trip to the west coast and back in three and a half months. The journal he kept showed the range and direction of his interests. He and Scofield investigated farms producng wheat, potatoes, alfalfa, milk and cream, cattle, sugar, rice, and citrus fruits. He gave special attention to the mechanization of agriculture, to scientific farming, to canning for home consumption, and to rural schools. He returned to New York with new enthusiasm for agriculture as a calling, convinced that better management could result in increased production, wider consumption, and an improved standard of living not for farmers only but for the entire country. He was persuaded also that his own best opportunity lay close to home in Dutchess County. There, in the area of East Fishkill, where the foothills of the Berkshires come within an easy ride of the Hudson River, in 1913 he purchased several hundred acres, many of them orchard, the core of the farm that was thereafter his home and his vocation.

## 2. A Good Start

Morgenthau's progress in his new life caught the attention of the Poughkeepsie *Sunday Courier* in June 1914. "His first venture," a long article explained, "was in the raising of steers and last fall he went to the western market . . . and purchased a carload of . . . fine animals. . . . Already butchers are hastening . . . to secure them. The success of the venture is assured and Mr. Morgenthau has the credit of again starting what may become one of the chief factors in giving our people better meat at cheaper prices. . . . He is an enthusiast over farming for profit. . . . He has no new fangled ideas — he keeps no livery, no high priced chauffeur, or landscape gardeners, or unnecessary help but is directing his time to plain, simple, practical farming. . . . He is using the most modern machinery . . . has . . . become a member of the local Wiccoppee Grange . . . and is fast acquiring a large host of friends. . . . He has been recently made a Deputy Sheriff." This was a lot to show for less than a year in the country.

The year, like the two that followed, was broken by journeys to Turkey, where Morgenthau's father was the American ambassador. On his second visit the young man arrived soon after the Turks entered World War I as allies of the Germans. He left the day before the British and French began to bombard the Dardanelles — the first stage of a military plan of the *enfant terrible* of the British Admiralty, Winston Churchill — and returned home via London where, as private secretary to his father, he delivered a message about conditions in Constantinople to Sir Edward Grey, the distinguished

British Foreign Secretary. In London again in November 1915 he received from Grey for communication to the Turks an official proposal for an exchange of prisoners. After reaching Constantinople, he inspected the tough Turkish lines at Galipoli, where a "perfectly gorgeous" view contrasted with the land pocked while he watched by shells of the British artillery.

At the American embassy German officials disturbed Morgenthau by their outspoken intention to resort to brutality to win the war. They also impressed him in other ways. The new German ambassador had been to luncheon, he wrote home: "It was most interesting. . . . The German is very shrewd, of the old school of diplomacy, by which I mean he always flatters by suggestion and is very suave, etc. . . . it will not be long before he will have great influence here." Like his father, Morgenthau deplored that influence, sympathized with France and England, and hoped and expected that the United States would get into the war on their side.

"I was a little office boy," he recalled. "I never did anything, but it was a thrilling experience. I was there because my father wanted company. What the Turks did to the Armenians made a terrific impact on me. Later on when the Germans did the same things to the Jews, I remembered the feelings I had had in Turkey during World War I. And I also always remembered one Christmas Eve at the Dardanelles. There was a German officer there sitting and talking who didn't know that I understood German. I heard him damning Americans in foul language. This made a great impression on me."

He witnessed some great events and met some famous men, but Morgenthau remained committed to his farm and to Dutchess County. There he took his bride of April 1916, Elinor Fatman, whom he had known since their childhood when they met at play in Central Park. The marriage had been expected. From the farm Morgenthau had written his parents two years earlier about a weekend spent at the home of the Herbert Lehmans, relatives of his wife-to-be: "I was asked to come over the telephone, the bait being Elly Fatman. . . . I bit." He had gone abroad in 1915 primarily to talk with his father about his intentions and immediately after debarking again in New York he had proposed and been accepted.

Elinor Fatman Morgenthau had been born on the same block

as her husband, had been delivered by the same doctor, had been wheeled as an infant along the same paths in Central Park, and had attended the same primary school. Her father was the chairman of the Raritan Woolen Mills of New Jersey; her mother, a Lehman. She graduated in 1913 from Vassar College, where she was a competent and popular student and the president of the dramatic society. Her dark, poised intensity, her quick intelligence, her extraordinary warmth made an immediate and persisting impression upon those who knew her. She had an energetic and informed interest both in creative arts and in social work, a suppressed ambition and a latent talent for a career in the law, a selfless zeal for community service.

Like her husband city-born and city-bred, she nevertheless found, as he did, large satisfactions in country life. From the time they were married it was as a team that they made plans for their farm and their future, made friends, and made a mark in their adopted new home. Thinking back to the beginning of their happy life together and forward across the whole range of his career, Morgenthau without hesitation attributed to her the principal credit for anything worthwhile that he had done.

Their first trying assignment was to mobilize the work of Dutchess County for war. This actually began in 1914 when Morgenthau organized and financed the first local girls' canning clubs. During the war, as chairman of the County Committee on Conservation of Food, he widened the scope of these clubs to include housewives throughout the area. Here was a way, he explained, to preserve food, improve diet, make people more self-sufficient, and give them a sense of identity with the war effort. Their sense of neighborhood and their capacity for self-help profited from the establishment of farmers' cooperatives, which Morgenthau warmly advocated. The canning project itself depended on his arrangement for cooperative purchase of 50,000 glass jars for resale at cost to the canning clubs which would otherwise have failed for lack of equipment and funds. He also worked to set up a public market in Poughkeepsie where townspeople could conveniently purchase the fresh produce of the county's farms, and where farmers could find a direct, professionally managed outlet for their crops. The war gave him a first large laboratory for encouraging more production and better distribution.

The need to increase productivity preoccupied Morgenthau in those years. A plan to send tractors to France grew out of his experiments with their cooperative use in Dutchess County. The lack of agricultural labor had forced the French to leave untilled about one fourth of the acreage in the uninvaded part of the country. This of course accentuated the shortage of foodstuffs for both military and civilian use, a condition that in turn imposed an extra burden on the already insufficient shipping facilities of the Allies. Three thousand tractors, Morgenthau calculated, would permit the cultivation of 2,000,000 acres and increase the harvest by 450,000 tons of wheat and 3,000,000 tons of potatoes. The tractors, furthermore, would tie up far less shipping than would the equivalent of such a harvest. The scheme appealed to Herbert Hoover, then the head of the United States Food Administration, to officials of the American Red Cross, and to André Tardieu, French High Commissioner in the United States. Morgenthau, as Tardieu put it, "kept in touch with the transaction through all stages of allotting contracts, manufacture and shipping by rail and water."

In 1918 Morgenthau followed his tractors, fifteen hundred of them, to France. "Arrived Paris eight o'clock A.M.," he noted in his journal. "Took a taxi to Hotel Crillon. Thought I would not be able to get a room. But there was plenty of room." That night he attended the opera, which struck his wife when he wrote her as very funny, but seemed to him the natural thing to do of an evening in Paris, war or no war. The next day he had difficulty with the Chief of the Culture de Terre, who apparently considered the coming of the tractors a criticism of his agency, but the Minister of Agriculture gratefully took over the project Morgenthau had begun, and within a week he felt free to go back to the farm.

The trip to Paris was his only European service, for the Army continually rebuffed his efforts to enlist because his eyesight was so poor, and the Navy, slow to waive that disability, granted him a commission as a junior lieutenant in Overseas Naval Transport only a few months before hostilities ended.

### 3. New Friendships, New Vistas

After the war, Morgenthau tried his hand at potatoes and cabbages, squash and rye, corn and beef cattle. At last he settled on a dairy herd over which one profit-sharing employee presided, and an apple orchard, which became his own special enthusiasm. "Mr. Morgenthau," the manager of the herd once remarked, "knows his cows." He knew his apples, too; he had to. Apples demand courageous care, being subject to more blights and bugs than children, and enormous patience, for some kinds of trees do not bear commercially useful crops for years. But pain and patience made them pay, and Morgenthau liked to attribute his lasting financial conservatism to his difficult times with a dozen breeds of apples.

The privileged visitor to his farm was sure to be invited to join its owner for an hour or so in the orchards, to learn from him the name and history and bearing habits of each variety of tree, to hear him discuss with his superintendent the latest spray, the irrigation ditches, the machinery, the possible patterns for new planting or annual picking, the condition of the market, the prospects for rain or frost, the special virtues of the McIntosh, the Golden, the Cortland, or the Rome. So it was for twenty years after 1913 — a tall man, heavy but not stout, squinting a little behind pince-nez, seeming therefore to frown, but given sporadically to a wide, slow smile, dressed for his task in soft shoes or rubber boots, a white shirt open at the collar, an old brown hat to cover a hairline completely receded, in some seasons a tweed jacket and in others sun glasses — a man at home on his farm and in the green, rolling cultivated hills in which it sits, not very far from Manhattan Island, but of another world.

The farm during the 1920's had to compete for Morgenthau's time. He had repeatedly to consider, though he usually declined, his father's importunities to join in some venture, in real estate or canned heat or a McClure's publication, in a theatrical production, a jewelry business, an automatic grocery store. He had continually to advise his much traveled parent about their large and complex portfolio of investments, a demanding assignment in the decade of the bull market. He also gave constant attention to, and found great satisfaction in, his three children, Henry III, Robert, and Joan, their education and their play. He went occasionally to Europe. He and his wife, moreover, were involved more and more deeply in the life of the county. They served on the boards of rural schools and state fairs, established for Dutchess County a visiting nurse service and a mobile library, worked with the dairymen's cooperative and the Grange.

Besides all this Morgenthau published the *American Agriculturist*. This weekly, one of two farm papers in New York, had a full-time editor, but Morgenthau guided its policies, deliberately concentrating on the education and protection of its increasing number of subscribers. The *A.A.* instructed them, as it previously had, in the scientific techniques developed at Cornell, but it also began to print "homely hints for good pies and sewing circles." It warned its readers, as in their isolation they had to be warned, against the schemes of fraudulent promoters who traded on their gullibilty, who proposed, for example, that the propensity of rabbits to multiply guaranteed an eternal bonanza to purchasers of a pair of bunnies. The paper's honesty cost it advertising and led to several libel suits, no one of which Morgenthau lost. It also earned him the confidence of farmers. Using the *A.A.* as his platform, he drew attention to the questions that seemed to him most important for the welfare of the farmers of the state. With their growing support, he advocated inexpensive rural credit, lighter rural taxes, rural electrification, reforestation, reclamation, and more efficient utilization of land, construction with state aid of more rural schools, more farm markets, more farm-to-market roads.

Partly to further this program Morgenthau developed an active interest in Democratic party politics. He had had a first taste of politics in company with his father in 1912. It fell to him that summer to serve one afternoon as the unofficial chauffeur for Speaker of the House Champ Clark when that "ol' hound dawg" of the Missouri Democracy visited Woodrow Wilson who had bested him for the presidential nomination. At headquarters in New York City Morgenthau also met the managers of Wilson's campaign and the candidate himself. Two years later, as his father's representative, he attended a Democratic conference at Saratoga to discuss the possibilty of nominating a progressive ticket. "The whole conference," he reported sadly, "was a cooked up . . . performance." Boss Charlie Murphy of Tammany Hall had things his own way. One of those who suffered on that account was the former state senator from Dutchess County, then Assistant Secretary of the Navy, Franklin D. Roosevelt, who in 1914 aspired to the senatorial nomination.

Then in his early thirties, Roosevelt was already something of a celebrity. A tall, slight, handsome young man, a graduate of Groton and Harvard, he had managed his family estate in Hyde Park while practicing law in New York City. In 1910 and again in 1912 he had been elected to the state senate as a Democrat by a constituency previously Republican for twenty-eight years. To politics he brought not only his vibrant voice but also a patrician sense of obligation comparable to that of his distant cousin, Theodore Roosevelt, the uncle of his wife and the hero, in or out of office, of America. Young Roosevelt had won the confidence of the farmers of Dutchess by talking their language, which he understood, and by pleading their cause, in which he believed, against city bossism, Democratic or Republican. The example of his cousin Ted's career and his own enthusiasm for the sea, which he loved as he loved the land, made him welcome his appointment as Assistant Secretary of the Navy. From that post he hoped to move on, as his distinguished cousin had before him, to higher office. Endowed both with an extra nerve of energy common to the Roosevelts and with a special nerve for politics, he was happily active simultaneously within the Navy Department, among the young liberals around Wilson in Washington, in the New York Democracy, and in the affairs of Dutchess County.

Though his father had worked with Roosevelt on behalf of Wilson in 1912, Morgenthau did not meet his Dutchess neighbor until 1915, when Roosevelt at luncheon at Hyde Park tried without success to persuade him to run for sheriff. "He is an awfully nice fellow," Roosevelt judged after this first meeting, "and one who will be a tremendous asset to us in the county. . . . Certainly we ought to do everything possible to keep him interested."

Morgenthau, who was flattered by the offer he declined, had also thoroughly enjoyed his luncheon companion. During the next few years he warmed to the friendship Roosevelt offered. Even Roosevelt's exacting and commanding mother seemed to approve.

"Young Mr. Morgenthau and his wife called this P.M.," Sarah Roosevelt wrote her son from Hyde Park. ". . . We had a pleasant tea, young Morgenthau was easy and yet modest and so nice and intelligent. The wife . . . appeared very well." From Europe later that year Roosevelt instructed Louis Howe — his homely, perspicacious, dedicated political and personal secretary — to ask after the welfare of "Morgenthau, Jr." "I was apparently solicitous about you," he recalled jokingly twenty years later, "but I do not know why!"

When Roosevelt received the Democratic vice-presidential nomination in 1920, Morgenthau served as chairman of the notification ceremonies at Hyde Park. He also helped to direct the unsuccessful Democratic campaign in Dutchess. He attributed its failure there and elsewhere in upstate New York largely to excessive urban influence in the party, an opinion Roosevelt shared.

It was their mutual intention to redress this political imbalance; it was Roosevelt's purpose thereby to enhance his political future; and to his friend's ambition, even when it wandered beyond rural reformism, Morgenthau gave his fond loyalty. This increased during the dreary months when poliomyelitis seemed to have undone Roosevelt's hopes. The Morgenthaus in those years on occasion joined Roosevelt aboard the houseboat *Narooco* on which he sailed in the winter through the Florida Keys. There and at Hyde Park Morgenthau drank without relish or complaint the gin and orange juice his host insisted upon serving and played parcheesi with him hour after hour.

He was much less involved in Roosevelt's politics than was Louis Howe, but he did occasionally see influential Democrats like Senator Carter Glass of Virginia, and he brought to them a point of view about the party in New York that worked to Roosevelt's advantage. The *American Agriculturist,* furthermore, advocated precisely those agricultural policies that Roosevelt held most necessary. Meanwhile Elinor Morgenthau was busy with Eleanor Roosevelt, organizing women voters for social reform and for the Democratic party, keeping the Roosevelt name in that way before potential constituents.

In 1924 and again in 1928 Roosevelt and Morgenthau both supported the presidential candidacy of the Governor of New York, Alfred E. Smith, Tammany's finest flower, a child of the Lower East

Side, a Catholic, a "wet," and a reformer. Roosevelt, while he convalesced, needed his identification with Smith, the strongest Democrat in America, and Morgenthau had considerable enthusiasm for many of the governor's policies. The *American Agriculturist* consistently supported Smith, and in return the governor in 1924 conferred about agricultural matters with upstate publishers and farm leaders selected by Morgenthau.

The conference accomplished nothing tangible, but at other times Morgenthau met Smith in more relaxed situations. "Elinor and I," he noted, "spent a most enjoyable evening with Irving Lehman at their home in Albany. . . . The governor arrived 45 minutes ahead of time and we had to take turns getting dressed for supper, while one of us entertained Governor and Mrs. Smith. He was in great shape." Smith one day returned a telephone call from Morgenthau and "told me he was very busy, and he was going over to Bell's to try on a suit. I asked him if I could go along. I had the fun of seeing him try on a couple of suits, and also gave Bell hell because his trousers were too short."

Two weeks earlier Morgenthau and his wife, the only husband and wife present as delegates, had gone to the national convention that met in Houston in 1928. There Roosevelt, as he had in 1924, in a "high-bred" speech put the name of the Happy Warrior before the party. "There was very little for us to do at Houston," Morgenthau wrote his father, "as there was no doubt from the beginning that Smith was to be the candidate. I really think that the Smith managers once they got there also had very little to do. . . . Elinor presented planks for the Women's Democratic Union before the Resolution Committee and Senator Wagner . . . the member from New York was extremely kind to her. Elinor made quite a hit with everybody and they were particularly impressed with her ability and knowledge of political affairs."

So it was that the circle of Morgenthau's personal and political friends and acquaintances widened. There were Franklin Roosevelt and Alfred E. Smith. There was Elinor Morgenthau's favorite uncle, Herbert Lehman, who had taught at the Henry Street Settlement, known Roosevelt since the time of the war, and served Smith as a consultant on banking and labor problems. There was Robert Wagner, long Smith's political associate and labor's most ardent spokesman in the state. These were the elect and elect-to-be of the Democracy of New York.

"Franklin," Morgenthau reported, guessing incorrectly as did most observers in 1928, "will definitely not run for Governor. . . . There is quite a little talk about running Senator Wagner. . . . There is also some talk of putting me on the state ticket with Wagner. Elinor and I are not getting excited over the prospect as there is only about one chance in fifty of this coming about. . . . Elinor leaves tonight . . . for a trip upstate to organize clubs. . . . With Herbert and Franklin as members of the Executive Committee, and Eleanor Roosevelt, Chairman of the Women's Advisory Committee, Elinor and I are able to keep in close touch with what is going on in national campaign headquarters."

While Smith, the victim of Coolidge prosperity and corrosive anti-Catholicism, was becoming one of the worst-beaten Democratic nominees in history, Roosevelt, initially a reluctant but already an accomplished campaigner, was carrying New York. Morgenthau contributed both funds and energy to this victory. He helped to plan his friend's tour of upstate cities, he helped to muster among farmers an extraordinary Democratic vote. It was natural, then, for political as well as for personal reasons, that Roosevelt after the election should invite Morgenthau to Warm Springs to discuss New York's agricultural problems. Then and later, when conferring upon Morgenthau some new responsibility or trust, Roosevelt was wont to explain that he was the only man he knew who had made a profit farming. It was equally natural for Morgenthau to hurry south.

## 4. A Program for Agriculture

Speaking at Jamestown, New York, during his campaign, Roosevelt had said that he wanted to see the "farmer and his family receive at the end of each year as much for their labor as if they had been working . . . as skilled workers under the best conditions in any one of our great industries." Morgenthau shared this objective, but like Roosevelt he had in 1928 little conception of the vast apparatus of controls that would one day make parity a reality. He

thought then, as did the governor-elect, of limited and local remedies, at that time untried in New York. He was especially committed
to a plank in the Democratic platform pledging the creation of an
unpaid, nonpartisan commission to study farm taxes and the distribution of farm products, and he emphasized the importance of
these matters during his conversations with Roosevelt, who not only
agreed to appoint the commission but also made Morgenthau its
chairman.

The Agricultural Advisory Commission at once began an "in-
tensive study" of its problems. These involved directly the welfare
of New York's 260,000 agricultural workers and 160,000 farms, of
which almost half were dairy farms. Reflecting the point of view
of the governor, of its chairman, and of his newspaper, the commission concerned itself not with prices only or even primarily, but
with the whole question of rural life, its tribulations, its potentialities, its intimate relationship to the life and health of the entire
state. The group had met, Morgenthau told the press in January
1929, "and decided that we would make a study of the whole tax
situation as it affects . . . highways . . . the rural school situation,
rural health, and the whole problem of making homelife on the
farm more satisfying." The agenda included also the questions of
agricultural marketing and of the retirement of submarginal land.

Before the end of February the commission made a series of recommendations that Roosevelt submitted to the legislature. Supplementary findings were reported later in 1929 and 1930. With no
significant exception, all these recommendations became law. The
state relieved the rural counties, and therefore rural taxpayers, of
almost all their previous expenses for the construction of highways,
for snow removal, and for the elimination of grade crossings; the
state doubled its appropriation for rural roads, a long step toward
Morgenthau's announced goal of "a hard road to every farm."
County taxes for rural schools were reduced but the rural school
program was expanded. The budget for research on fruit and po-
tato blights was trebled. Other appropriations permitted a rigorous
inspection of dairy products, accelerated reforestation, and underwrote surveys of soil, weather, and agricultural possibilities throughout the state. These were impressive accomplishments, especially for
a party which in New York had ordinarily directed its energies to

satisfying the needs of the cities. On the manuscript copy of a speech reviewing the record, so much the fulfillment of Morgenthau's purpose, Roosevelt gratefully wrote: "For Henry himself."

Morgenthau was pleased by the success of his mission and by the governor's response. He also took a kind of retributive glee in the readjustment of road and school expenses which he felt he "put over" on a drowsing Tammany Hall. "Before Roosevelt's governorship, the richer the district, the more state aid it received for schools and roads. We completely reversed this with new legislation," he recalled fondly. "The result was the farmers swore by F.D.R. as their friend."

This had been Morgenthau's intention, for he realized that Roosevelt's small margin of victory in 1928 necessitated the conversion before 1930 of the upstate farmers who ordinarily voted Republican. He had therefore made politics a part of his province. As Chairman of the Agricultural Advisory Commission he had no state office, but he took over a desk in the room outside the governor's office where the clerks worked, and he and his wife rented a suite at the DeWitt Clinton Hotel in Albany. This gave him constant and ready access to Roosevelt and his staff.

He also invariably supported nonpartisan farm organizations. Al Smith had made a deal with the Republican machine that in effect gave all patronage from Westchester County south to the Democrats, all from Putnam County north to their rivals. Roosevelt therefore inherited an upstate Democratic organization that Morgenthau considered the exclusive domain "of crooks and stool pigeons." As others rebuilt the party, Morgenthau reached the farmers through their own associations, sponsoring their preferred policies of which the most popular were the revisions in the tax allocations for schools and roads. While he worked, he compiled statistics showing for each county the increases in state aid granted during Roosevelt's term. These were effective campaign weapons, as were the new, consolidated rural schools. He helped, Morgenthau felt, to accomplish a real revolution in rural life, one in which Franklin and Eleanor Roosevelt were deeply interested. "Doing things for people at the bottom of the ladder," Morgenthau believed, "this is revolution."

Republican editors, however, in 1929 claimed for their own party and its majorities in the legislature the exclusive credit for the farm program. Roosevelt therefore asked Morgenthau whether he thought it wise to initiate a letter-writing campaign to answer these editorials. Morgenthau recommended instead the organization of a Democratic news bureau to prepare articles for circulation among the rural newspapers. Before discussing this plan with Louis Howe, as Roosevelt suggested he might, Morgenthau had one of the staff of the *American Agriculturist* interview ninety-six farmers of whom only thirteen were fully informed about the new laws. He sent the governor this and other statistics, reporting also that he had seen Howe who had the publicity problem in hand. "What hits me most," Roosevelt replied in typical cadence, "is the very high percentage of ignorance . . . sheer, utter and complete ignorance displayed by such a large number of farmers. You are doing a splendid and constructive bit of work with the American agriculturist."

The friendship of Roosevelt and Morgenthau grew constantly closer. They had embarked upon a neighborly rivalry in the cultivation of squash that provoked an exchange of banter while the governor rested and exercised his crippled legs in Georgia. "Please write me any further directions as to how the common stock should be planted," Roosevelt asked in one characteristic squash-letter, "whether it should be watered, whether the distribution should be wide or closely harrowed, whether it carries any bonus (beside bugs)."

"Why don't you take a shot at forecasting the price of squash and pickles next fall," Morgenthau asked at a time when official Washington was blinking away the implications of panic on Wall Street. "I am sure you will come just as close to it as Hoover."

They also exchanged gifts. "A little birdie told me that you lost the raincoat we gave you last year," Morgenthau wrote in 1930. "Elinor and I sent you another . . . and we hope that this will prove to be storm relief against all farm relief."

"You and Elinor are angels," Roosevelt replied. "I have told William that if this raincoat is stolen out of the car, he will never have a chance to lose another!"

During 1930 Morgenthau's work in Albany also brought him close to the governor. As that year began, he was pressing Roosevelt to support various recommendations of the Agricultural Ad-

visory Commission. He especially wanted him to call a conference
of upstate mayors and health commissioners to consider ways to
exclude from New York's cities uninspected milk from the west —
a prospect of equal importance for the health of urban consumers
and the wealth of New York dairymen. Pursuing this end, Morgenthau spent an afternoon with Roosevelt. "We were constantly interrupted," he noted in his Diary, "but it was lots of fun . . . to
watch him run the business of the state." Roosevelt considered it
bad business to invite all the mayors to a conference, for some of
them were notoriously hostile either to the exclusion of western
milk or to the inclusion of Democrats. Morgenthau "discussed this
matter with Eleanor Roosevelt and she thought that the Governor
would make a mistake if he did not invite all of the mayors as some
of them might feel slighted."

After they had together won over the governor, Morgenthau, as
was his habit, consulted every expert he could find, including the
health commissioner of New York City, a public health authority
at the Rockefeller Foundation, the president of the Dairyman's
League, and executives of the Borden Company. He also had "a
lengthy discussion as to just how far the State of New York might
go in excluding western cream" with Samuel Rosenman, Roosevelt's
astute counsel and ghost-writer whose appointment Morgenthau
had urged upon the governor when Al Smith was sponsoring Robert
Moses for the same job.

Although he was well prepared, Morgenthau found the conference at its first meeting "too much . . . to handle," but in talking
with a small group of health officers he made enough "progress"
so that in spite of "a very bad headache" he could direct the proceedings to a successful resolution. A week later, he helped Rosenman and Dr. Thomas Parran, the fearless and imaginative public
health officer whom Roosevelt had called from Washington to Albany, to write the governor's message to the legislature recommending an appropriation, ultimately granted, for the enforcement of
rigorous inspection of milk and cream. The whole matter then
slipped into history, significant largely for the emergent relationships it marked.

So it was also with an appropriation Morgenthau commended
to Roosevelt for the construction at Cornell of a building for the

special use of the Department of Agricultural Economics and
Farm Management. The department's head was Dr. George F.
Warren. He had grown up on a farm in Nebraska, studied agriculture at the university there and then at Cornell, and written several
books on farm management and on prices. Frequently during the
'20's Morgenthau had consulted him about farm problems and
Governor Smith had sought his advice about reforestation. Mrs.
Morgenthau and Mrs. Roosevelt had attended Warren's lectures at
Cornell, where he spelled out his thesis that the price of all commodities varied more or less directly with the price of gold. As an
energetic member of the Agricultural Advisory Commission, Warren eloquently spoke the case for a scientific survey of land-use and
for the development of a comprehensive conservation policy in New
York, objectives that elicited the enthusiasm of both Roosevelt and
Morgenthau. In 1930 the professor was especially anxious to have the
state provide a new building for his students and colleagues, a new
home for work which Morgenthau considered of first importance.
Morgenthau therefore "asked the Governor what time he would be
in the best humor" to discuss the appropriation and other matters.
"He said while he was shaving. So, while he was shaving," Morgenthau "took up the question." Roosevelt agreed to let Cornell have
more money that year on the understanding that the dean of agriculture at Cornell would cut back his requests for the next year, a
solution that eminently satisfied Warren.

There were, as Morgenthau's Diary showed, other kinds of problems. "Elinor and I," read the entry for June 4, 1930, "arrived in
Boston . . . to attend James Roosevelt's wedding. I went up to
Franklin's room at nine o'clock and spent one and a half hours with
him. He told me that he was absolutely opposed to New York City
coming up to Dutchess County for its water supply. He said he
felt that within the next twenty years Dutchess County would become suburban and . . . need all of its water. . . . He told me in
the strictest confidence that . . . he was beginning to be suspicious
of the fact that Alfred E. Smith was working for the nomination for
President in 1932."

Roosevelt wanted that nomination for himself, but first he had
convincingly to win re-election as governor. Morgenthau accompanied him on one major campaign trip. On October 18, 1930, the

governor's party set out from Albany in two cars and two buses, almost "froze to death" at a picnic lunch, and in the afternoon drove on to Binghamton while Roosevelt, Rosenman, Morgenthau, and Basil O'Connor, the governor's law partner, "had a lot of fun joking and teasing one another." As he had two years earlier, Morgenthau that night led the governor onto the stage. The next day they went on to Elmira, where Eleanor Roosevelt joined them temporarily for dinner and went walking with Morgenthau before departing for New York City. Morgenthau then "matched Sam Rosenman to see who would sleep with the Governor and . . . won. Before retiring we had a grand rough house." They all enjoyed the ride to Buffalo for "the Governor was in an excellent mood and made up silly songs." The caravan covered over a thousand miles in the tier of counties north of the Pennsylvania border. Before it disbanded on its eighth day, Roosevelt stopped "at the Poughkeepsie bridge . . . and we said goodbye to him and he turned and said to me — this is the only day that you did not arrange and it is the only one we were late at every meeting."

## 5. Conservation Commissioner

As a reward for services rendered, Roosevelt after his re-election appointed Morgenthau to the office he most desired. "I just want to tell you," Elinor Morgenthau wrote him, "that I feel a tremendous joy and pride in your giving Henry the important post of 'Conservation Commissioner,' for I think that Henry always goes about his work with a real feeling of consecration, but the fact that he is working under you and for you, fills him with . . . enthusiasm. . . . The part which pleases me the most is that while you are moving on in your own work . . . it also gives Henry a chance to grow, so that your friendship can continue to be cemented by a community of interest as well as by the deep affection with which he holds you."

This was also the governor's intention, for he told Morgenthau that he wanted him to gain experience in running a department that would be useful someday in Washington. Roosevelt was "getting ready to be President," and he expected Morgenthau to "get ready" to accompany him. The governor instructed his friend, whose sentiments he knew so well, to shake hands with the head of Tammany Hall. "This was very repulsive to me," Morgenthau remembered years later, "but F.D.R. was insistent."

His new office gave Morgenthau large administrative responsibilities. His department had jurisdiction over lands and forests, water power, fish, and game. Moreover, it controlled patronage that Democratic leaders hoped would "prove useful in the building up of the . . . party." Morgenthau, as the *New York Times* observed, was "very well equipped for the work through his broad knowledge of every part of the state and his thorough familiarity with conservation problems . . . and . . . reforestation." He was also acutely conscious, as he went to work, that his job, like those of the rest of the governor's cabinet, was complicated by two new situations: the depression that engulfed New York and the rest of the nation, intensifying the difficulties of farmers, adding each day to the appalling numbers of unemployed workers and bankrupt firms; and the candidacy of Franklin Roosevelt for the Presidency, which demanded of his associates political and administrative behavior that would persuade Democrats the country over to support him.

Morgenthau showed himself an imaginative administrator. As his wife put it, he had a clear public "philosophy": "if you care enough about seeing a thing go through, work out a plan, get the best people to help you (here again real ability to know who the best people are) then present it to whomever you think has the best chance of putting it through, and forget about yourself. This scheme worked perfectly in New York state." His reorganization of his department revealed his talent in selecting expert advisers, his ability to take their advice, and his willingness to delegate the authority they needed to do their jobs. He began characteristically by appointing an advisory council of distinguished conservationists, of whom Dr. Warren was one. "There will," he announced, "be no time lost in initiating the actual work of investigation and prosecuting it with all possible vigor. I look to the accomplishment of constructive work by the new Council within the next few months."

This prophecy was accurate. Dr. Warren, authorized at last to undertake a scientific survey of land use, made a pilot study of Tompkins County, investigating there the interdependent factors

of soil, climate, population, the potential demand for various products, and the potential availability of hydroelectric power. His
conclusions confirmed Morgenthau's personal enthusiasm for re-
timbering, for withdrawing marginal land from production, and
for developing a long-range, regional program for the use of land
in New York.

To these ends Morgenthau's advisory council worked out a program of reclamation and reforestation which Roosevelt supported
as an amendment to the state's constitution. The council also
helped Morgenthau bring order to his department. Acting partly
on its suggestions, he established an independent bureau to employ
scientific techniques for the protection and propagation of fish and
game; he introduced a system for the distribution of game on a
biological basis, setting quotas according to such factors as the
quality and quantity of food and cover in each of the various areas
to be stocked; he enlisted unprecedented cooperation from sports-
men's clubs, initially suspicious but soon enthusiastic about his
plans. Within the department he established a management section
to analyze and improve administrative techniques and a bureau of
law enforcement under a chief inspector whose staff made life as
grim as possible for poachers, previously little policed. He also
created a division of finance that replaced the haphazard accounting
of earlier years with a carefully constructed and tightly controlled
budget. These achievements demonstrated that Morgenthau could
bring method to government and confirmed Roosevelt's judgment
in appointing his friend.

If those who valued efficiency were pleased, Democratic politicians
were not. "We had," Boss Edward J. Flynn of the Bronx recalled,
"some difficulty with Morgenthau." The commissioner chose as his
deputy a newspaperman, Herbert Gaston, formerly a member of the
staff of the New York *World*. A quiet, serious, fearless Westerner
who was for many years to be a loyal and unselfish member of
Morgenthau's staff, Gaston had been the chief of publications of
the radical farmers' Nonpartisan League. He had crusaded against
gambling and the political protection of gamblers in Minneapolis;
he had further alienated regular Democrats by moving successively
from the Bull Moose to the Socialist to the La Follette Progressive
parties before coming to the support of Smith in 1928. The regulars

were equally annoyed by Morgenthau's appointments to lesser offices, for he ignored party lines so consistently that one Republican
subordinate concluded he was "probably the world's worst politician."

This was nowhere more obvious than in his relations with
Llewellyn Legge, since 1908 the chief protector of fish and game.
Legge had prepared for this career as a barber in Binghamton,
where he developed a benign influence with local lords of creation.
Morgenthau first suspected that Legge's record might not be impeccable when Al Smith asked him, as a personal favor, not to fire
Legge. This seed of doubt planted, Morgenthau ordered an investigation which disclosed that the official used a yacht, authorized for
marine research and operated at public expense, as a pleasure boat,
afloat where New York's rivers ran, replete with food and drink for
man. In the early 1920's it had occurred to Legge that the ruffed
grouse was about to become extinct in New York. He set out therefore to Hungary, proposing to look into the feasibility of importing
and releasing Hungarian grouse, but traveling to his destination by
way of several European capitals where no grouse lived. This, too,
was apparently at the state's expense. His behavior, Morgenthau
discovered, commanded the protection of powerful men because
Legge regularly cruised in his official yacht to the Canadian border,
returning with the stuff to quench the thirst that prohibition imposed. Morgenthau got rid of Legge by abolishing his office. He
established instead the position of Director of the Division of Fish
and Game, and to the dismay of professional Democrats, he filled
it by offering a competitive examination open to men of any party
or state. The victor to whom went the spoils was a Massachusetts
Republican whose opinion about the Eighteenth Amendment Morgenthau did not even ask.

This kind of behavior by Roosevelt's friends provoked Smith to
complain to a newspaperman: "Do you know, by God, that he has
never consulted me about a damn thing since he has been Governor?
He has taken bad advice. . . . He has ignored me!" Even if he
had not felt this way, Smith would have coveted the Democratic
nomination for himself, for as 1931 wore on and the depression
deepened, it became clearer and clearer that almost any Democrat
would defeat President Hoover. Though he denied that he was an

active candidate, Smith opened his campaign at Tammany Hall by attacking a proposed amendment to the New York constitution which Morgenthau's group of experts had recommended and Roosevelt had approved. The amendment was, he suggested, unnecessary, expensive, and contrary to the principles of good government.

In fact the amendment simply provided for a schedule of mandatory appropriations for twenty years, in all for $20,000,000, for reforestation in certain areas outside the Adirondack's forest preserve, areas where abandoned or submarginal farms could be purchased by the state for planting designed both for the conservation of land and water and for the development of recreational facilities. "The human species," Morgenthau told one audience during the fight over the amendment, "requires for a proper habitat something more than farming land, factory locations and urban areas. We need . . . common public playgrounds of wide extent to give us a place fit to live in and to live a healthy, balanced life. The waste spaces of today, the uncultivated areas which we plan to reforest and the existing woodlands form such a natural playground."

The voters approved the amendment, Roosevelt's political stock rose, and New York embarked upon a larger forestry operation than any state had previously attempted. During 1931 and 1932 Morgenthau's department either planted or helped private organizations to plant over ninety million trees of many varieties. These not only had value in themselves. Their leaves in decomposing fertilized the soil, and as they grew they encouraged the proliferation of wild life, protected streams, checked erosion, and added to the pleasure of recreation, all of which enhanced the beauty and the wealth of the state.

Planting, moreover, provided an opportunity for the useful employment of young men unable to find work with private industry. Charity might keep them alive, but in the grim months of 1931 and 1932 they needed desperately to feel wanted and productive. No one understood this better than did Morgenthau and Harry Hopkins, the director of the state's Temporary Emergency Relief Administration. A veteran social worker who had been in charge of fresh-air work and unemployment relief for the New York Association for Improving the Condition of the Poor, Hopkins first met Roosevelt in 1928. As Secretary of the Temporary Emergency Relief

Administration, he impressed Morgenthau who, when the agency's first chairman retired, urged the governor to name Hopkins as his successor. Fond of playing at being a man-about-town, extroverted, exuberant, sometimes even profligate, Hopkins was in personality Morgenthau's opposite, but they had a common background in social work, a common dedication to improving the lot of the underprivileged, and a common loyalty to Roosevelt. Morgenthau, furthermore, from the beginning of their relationship, found to his gratification that Hopkins, when he gave his word, always followed through.

Working together, in the spring of 1932 they directed the state's employment on reforestation projects of ten thousand men. This was the genesis of the New Deal's Civilian Conservation Corps, the federal agency that was to put young men to work on reforestation and related projects. Morgenthau had earlier experimented by using the unemployed to thin out a hundred acres as a wood lot, distributing the cut wood to the indigent in a neighboring village. On the basis of this experience he calculated how many could be employed on each hundred acres to be reforested, and he also accumulated data on how their work assignments could be organized. Because he alone had a plan for assigning labor to worthwhile projects, he was given three-quarters of the state's appropriation for work relief.

In spending this money, Morgenthau insisted on selecting men only from lists of the needy unemployed in the counties where reforestation was carried out. Now and then this could be done through Hopkins's agency. Where it could not, Morgenthau relied upon local committees consisting of one Democratic politician, one Republican, and one representative of a local relief agency, usually the county welfare commissioner or a town supervisor. Soliciting lists of young men from social workers in New York City, Morgenthau also personally organized a precursor of the New Deal's National Youth Administration, the federal agency that was to provide work relief for young people. "We took the gas house gang," he recalled, "the bad boys who were loafing on the streets and getting into trouble, and we put them on the 4 A.M. train that ran up to the Bear Mountain area where they worked all day. Then because there was no housing for them we took them back at night. F.D.R.

was much interested in this conservation of human resources, as in all conservation work."

In the reforestation program, however, politics again intruded. Morgenthau told the chairman of the county committees of both parties that partisanship was not to influence the hiring of relief labor. He intended to feed the hungry, he explained, however they voted. But one influential Rochester Democrat complained because Morgenthau was nonpartisan, and even though the upstate relief officials who selected most of the workers were usually Republican, the Republican State Committee claimed that only Democrats had been given jobs. For sheer inanity this criticism was excelled only by that of Hoover's Secretary of Agriculture who found the purposes and methods of Morgenthau's department "utterly visionary and chimerical . . . ridiculous . . . and absurd."

Unemployment in the state, of course, far outran the capacity of the planting program to provide jobs, but what was done was well done. Roosevelt, always an ardent conservationist, was not only delighted that New York planted more trees than all the other states combined; he was also persuaded of the utility of reforestation as one method of national unemployment relief. The criticism from Hoover's Cabinet simply intensified the governor's convictions.

The planting program, moreover, had equal significance as one facet of the total experience of Roosevelt and his associates in Albany. There the governor assembled part of his future Washington team and gave them a first chance at the work of reconstruction and reform. There, in programs like that over which Morgenthau presided, this team was bound together by a creative approach to problems of government and by humanitarian ideals. Harry Hopkins in handling relief, Morgenthau in agriculture and conservation made vital contributions to each other's and to Roosevelt's understanding.

## 6. Roosevelt and Morgenthau

Outside his department, Morgenthau, like the others, was an avid partisan, anxiously watching Roosevelt's campaign for the presidential nomination. As trouble developed in New York City where the chicanery of several of the grandest tigers in Tammany posed a problem for the governor, Morgenthau urged him to prosecute the corrupt even at the risk of alienating the faithful. Because he understood his friend, he understood why Roosevelt proceeded more cautiously than he advised.

Some of the candidate's maneuvering was good for a chuckle. "I was greatly amused," Morgenthau wrote his father, ". . . to see that there apparently had been a leak in Franklin's plans to meet with Governor Gifford Pinchot [the celebrated Pennsylvania progressive]. I would be willing to bet dollars to doughnuts that the leak was from the Chief Executive himself. . . . He finds it very difficult to keep as good a story as this."

At Roosevelt's request Morgenthau undertook one especially sensitive assignment in the preconvention campaign. Early in May 1932 he set out on a trip through the Middle West and South to survey the opinions of farmers, editors of farm newspapers, and agricultural experts about the continuing agricultural depression and about Roosevelt as a candidate. On one typical day in St. Paul, Morgenthau in six hours met successively with the Farmers' Union Terminal Association, the state conservation commissioner, various organizations of milk producers, and the Governor of Minnesota. Elsewhere he talked with leaders of the Grange and of the Farmers' Union, with professors of agriculture and of economics, and with directors of farmers' cooperatives. In every state he visited farm mortgages were being foreclosed at a frightening rate, farmers were contemplating violent resistance, and commodity prices had dropped to levels which made even subsistence difficult. The stabilization operations of Hoover's Federal Farm Board had obviously failed to put a brake on falling prices; available credit facilities were clearly inadequate for refinancing the huge farm debt.

There was no disagreement among most farm experts about the need for federal action, but there was wide difference of opinion about the forms it should take. Many of those whom Morgenthau saw gave first priority to the establishment of federal agencies to refinance the agricultural debt. Others favored, as farmers had for generations in times of depression, currency inflation of one kind or another. Still others, confusing their situation with that of industrialists who had benefited from high Republican tariffs, thought that tariff protection for agriculture would help them. Perhaps the most controversial issue was the Domestic Allotment Plan which called for government intervention to control production as a means of raising prices and liquidating surpluses.

Speaking to that point, Henry A. Wallace of Iowa, agricultural economist and editor of the influential *Wallace's Farmer,* told Morgenthau at their first meeting that if low prices persisted he expected either revolution or state socialism in the near future. Only by limiting domestic production and insulating the national market, Wallace argued, could prices be raised. He was therefore an advocate of Domestic Allotment, as were other advisers who in 1932 had Roosevelt's ear. The governor had decided by June 1932 to make some version of the Domestic Allotment Plan his own, but Morgenthau, even after hearing Wallace's case, had reservations about any device that put an artificial ceiling on production. Prices, he agreed, had to be raised, but he accepted only reluctantly and tentatively the theory that this could best be accomplished by growing less. He had always believed that the solution had to lie in distributing more.

Yet what he heard and what he saw enlightened Morgenthau. Though the situation was even worse than he had feared, a new and bold Administration would have available various correctives. Farmers, moreover, were "numb," as Morgenthau put it publicly. They wanted "a change" and would "leave the Republican fold." "My trip is going fine," he wrote Roosevelt. "I am meeting a lot of very interesting farm leaders. Most of them are Republicans but are ready to vote for you, if given the opportunity. Our New York story on agriculture has reached them and they all admit New York has done more for the farmer than any other state."

For the long run, Morgenthau recommended the application on a national scale of the New York program, especially a complete soil survey of the United States, the elimination from production of marginal land, and extensive reforestation. More immediately, he told Roosevelt, three policies were particularly important: increased federal aid for cooperatives; federal refinancing of farm debts to reduce interest and amortization payments; and any one of several plans to raise the price of wheat and cotton by restricting either the production or the domestic availability of those crops.

Roosevelt had received similar reports from the West and South, but it was useful to have a personal representative confirm them, and perhaps even more useful to have farmers discover that the agent of the governor of New York was a man who sympathized with their problems, a man they liked. After Roosevelt was nominated, the acquaintances Morgenthau had made were ready at his request to advise him about winning the farm vote. Through him they emphasized the political virtues of supporting inflation, easier credit, and Domestic Allotment. Roosevelt made his major speech on agriculture at Topeka, incorporating in his text a summary of the record in New York prepared by Morgenthau and Herbert Gaston. In its final form the address drew upon the ideas of many of Roosevelt's advisers and advocated, albeit sometimes obliquely, all of the policies demonstrably popular with farmers.

This of course was good politics, but the votes Roosevelt won in normally Republican rural areas reflected not only discontent with Hoover but also the conviction that the governor and his friends were dedicated to the immediate relief of agricultural distress. This conviction derived in no small degree from the impression Morgenthau had made as Roosevelt's subordinate and representative.

Morgenthau was at the Biltmore Hotel in New York with Roosevelt, his family, and some of his closest associates while the returns came in during the evening of November 8, 1932. Like the governor, he was supremely happy as bulletin after bulletin fulfilled the hopes for victory so long and so devoutly nourished. As he left for home at 1:40 A.M., the President-elect said to his mother: "This is the greatest night of my life." Those who had been working intimately with him felt the same way.

To continue to work with Franklin Roosevelt was Morgenthau's only ambition. He was therefore pleased that recognition of his achievements brought him, though he was an Easterner, many endorsements for the position of Secretary of Agriculture. These came from such diverse organizations as the Northwest Seedgrowers' Association of Portland, the Washington Cooperative Egg and Poultry Association of Seattle, the Farmers' National Grange Corporation of Chicago, the Kansas State Farm Bureau, the Texas Wheatgrowers' Association, the Poultry Producers of California, the Dairymen's League of New York, the North Carolina Cotton Growers' Cooperative Association, the Louisiana Cotton Cooperative Association, and the National Farm Bureau. On the last day of 1932 rumors that Morgenthau would be the next Secretary of Agriculture reached Harry Flood Byrd of Virginia, a conservative Democrat influential in his own state, soon to be a power in the Senate. "I cannot imagine any better thing for the country," he wrote, "than for you to extend to the nation what you have already done for the farmers of New York State."

The appointment was not to be Morgenthau's. On several counts Roosevelt decided to give it to Henry Wallace. Wallace was a western man, identified as had been his father and grandfather before him with the western farmer, well-known in the corn and wheat country, a progressive Republican with Bull Moose blood in his veins. It was politically important to have such a man in the Cabinet and especially in the Department of Agriculture. Wallace, furthermore, was in favor of Domestic Allotment. Like-minded men, aware of Morgenthau's hesitation, urged the Iowan upon Roosevelt, causing unnecessary "bad blood," as one observer interpreted it, about the possibilities of Morgenthau's getting the office.

Morgenthau had difficulty, as Roosevelt prepared to leave Albany, in reading his intentions. "I cannot make this a formal letter," the governor wrote him, "but before I go out I want you to know how very grateful I am to you for all the splendid work you have done for the people of this State . . . also for the splendid loyalty you have given me." This was warm, but Morgenthau, sensing his friend's inclination toward Wallace, came to suspect that he had no future in Washington. About a month before his inauguration Roosevelt gave him vague reassurance. He wanted him, he said, "very close." As the senior Morgenthau then remarked, "If F.D.R. wants you 'very close' the only way he can do so is to put you in." Roosevelt did.

"F.D.R. first offered to make me the head of an agency for the unemployed," Morgenthau recalled. "He said it would be the most powerful agency in Washington. He said I would have the Army and Navy working for me. He had thought this out almost to the last detail. But I could not grasp the possibilities and refused it. Later . . . I had the pleasure of telephoning Hopkins that he would get this job." To Morgenthau Roosevelt offered instead the governorship of Herbert Hoover's Federal Farm Board with a broad mandate in the field of farm credit. This Morgenthau happily accepted.

In the early weeks of 1933 Morgenthau's appointment, whatever it portended, was the fulfillment of an accomplished past, of the courage of a young man of parts who broke the patterns of his youth to become a farmer, of his devotion to the soil and its tillers, of his companionable contributions to the career of an ambitious friend. It was a fulfillment, indeed, for both friends, for the man who was appointed and for the man who, knowing his companion well, wanted him "very close."

They meant much to each other. "Slowly," Eleanor Roosevelt wrote, recalling her life before she was mistress of the White House, "a friendship grew . . . with . . . Mr. and Mrs. Henry Morgenthau, Jr. . . . We had many interests in common in the county, and Mr. Morgenthau and my husband were thrown more and more together. Mrs. Morgenthau . . . and I grew gradually to have a warm affection for each other." Morgenthau and a few others, she observed, were men whose "interest was in my husband and in the work to be done. . . . They could be very objective even when their own work was involved." She once commented that Louis Howe and Morgenthau alone dared tell her husband categorically that he was wrong, but to this short list Morgenthau prefixed her name. She was, he knew, the incomparable force for good in Franklin Roosevelt's life.

Morgenthau's bond with her husband was firm. They had, to begin with, the same sense of adventure and of fun. They both delighted in finding simple and direct devices to resolve complex problems. Morgenthau's World War I plan to send tractors to France was just the kind of idea Roosevelt loved. Both for a time were optimistic directors of Photomaton, Inc., a corporation that distributed automatic cameras triggered by slot machines into which customers fed quarters. Both harbored a transient enthusiasm for squash as a cash crop. Both knew better than to take too seriously this kind of gadgetry — it was a form of speculative amusement that might just pay off.

Both hugely enjoyed practical jokes, especially at each other's expense. They found the same stories funny, particularly each other's. They liked their reciprocal banter. This was unrecorded in the '20's, but the documents of the '30's reveal the spirit of both decades. So, for example, at a Cabinet meeting in 1935 Roosevelt passed Morgenthau a note chiding him for sailing home from Europe on a French rather than an American liner. "I paid my own expenses . . . and therefore could choose the fastest ship," Morgenthau scribbled back, differentiating his trip from that of a colleague who had traveled on public funds.

"So glad," the President retorted, "you are so rich and seek speed — more speed."

Or once while Morgenthau was taking a brief vacation from monetary problems, Roosevelt sent him a turgid book on currency, "to read while in swimming," with the comment that "this inspiring detective story will probably cause you to commit suicide."

Roosevelt and Morgenthau had in common also similar backgrounds and habits of mind. Both were the sons of wealthy fathers, both were comfortable, both enjoyed a degree of easy elegance, yet neither really cared for the toys and games of the adult rich. Both loved the land, the trees, the soil itself, all the things that conservation was intended to protect and to develop. Both, in the best sense of the word, were gentlemen, considerate, civilized, decent men who avoided displays of wealth or emotion. Both, furthermore, took their problems one by one, looking for practical solutions rather than for broad concepts about government, society or man. Theirs was a kind of patrician instinct for public service and social welfare, theirs also an inbred attachment to country, to family, to neighborhood, and to private property. Neither was a radical, neither an intellectual, but both had a respect for intellectuals and an open-minded zest for new ideas.

They complemented each other. Morgenthau's diffidence with strangers, his seeming suspiciousness and brusqueness shielded the warmth and generosity that Roosevelt's ways brought out. These qualities Roosevelt had to have in a man who took him for himself, not for what was his to dispense. The celebrated smile, the great "hello" that Winston Churchill somewhere called the most wonderful word in the English language, the spontaneous, contagious laugh — these were also shields of a kind. Franklin Roosevelt revealed to most men very little of himself. But he could and did trust Morgenthau with personal matters of which few others were aware. Morgenthau was never a rival or a sycophant or a scold. He had a quick sympathy for Roosevelt's moods. His worries and his migraine Roosevelt could help him laugh away. His understanding and his dedication helped Roosevelt in those private hours when he did not want to laugh, helped him to bear the lonely responsibilities of high office.

"To Henry," Franklin Roosevelt once wrote across a photograph of himself and Morgenthau riding side by side in an automobile, "from one of two of a kind." Morgenthau was this and more, was that rarest of assets in the lives of great men, a friend.

# II

# *"The Courage to Experiment"*

## *1932-1933*

### 1. The Agricultural Crisis

FOR THOSE who were part of it, the New Deal was a great adventure, "unforgettably thrilling," as Morgenthau attested. The New Dealers were mostly young, many of them in their late thirties or early forties. Though they came into office in a time of trouble, they brought with them a zest for their work, a willingness to share the spirit of their leader whose confidence in himself and in his country was an indispensable qualification for the Presidency. The despondency that attended depression, the terror that accompanied the paralysis of the banking system in the early months of 1933, produced a state of mind in the United States that needed most of all to be told that the only thing to fear was fear itself. What Franklin Roosevelt and his associates intended to do was for many months less important than their determination to do something. They had plans, of course, but none of them proved to be as significant as the underlying belief in the social responsibility of the federal government, or as the commitment to experimentation. The crisis of 1933 was very much a crisis of morale.

It was also a time of want and despair. Long lines of brooding, hungry men formed in front of soup kitchens and employment agencies. Failing businesses and closing banks threatened the savings and the position of the comfortable, introducing them to a new insecurity, a new experience of fear. Need and hopelessness and lost status bewildered urban man.

For rural America the depression was as terrifying. Most farmers, even in the worst of times, could ordinarily produce food enough to prevent hunger, though not necessarily malnutrition. But agriculture had long since ceased to be a self-sufficient occupation. The farmer had to have cash for a multitude of personal essentials — shoes, clothing, fuel, medicine. He needed cash more urgently for his business. The capital equipment vital for an increasingly mechanized agriculture was expensive to buy and to maintain. The fixed costs of the mortgages on this equipment and on land and improvements, moreover, had to be met in bad years as well as in good. Failure to meet them meant foreclosure followed at best by tenancy and dead hopes, at worst by dispossession, migrancy, and abject unemployment.

The depression, furthermore, had come to agriculture first. Throughout the 1920's the farmers' share of the national income decreased. With the onset of general depression, agricultural prices fell further and faster than did the average price level. In 1932 Morgenthau, on his trip through the country for Roosevelt, had seen corn, shelled and delivered in Illinois, selling at twenty-three cents a bushel; milk sold in Wisconsin at about a cent and a half a quart; eggs in Oklahoma at five cents a dozen. Men whose incomes depended upon those prices simply could not pay off debts they had contracted during relatively prosperous years. In 1932 it took roughly three times as much farm produce to earn a dollar as it had in 1921; by 1932 some twenty thousand farms were being foreclosed each month.

The decline in farm income had for several years been a drag on the whole economy. It damaged not only investors in farm mortgages but also, more generally, all producers of manufactured goods. The average city dweller was no more than vaguely aware of the significance for his own life of the increasing inability of the farmer to buy, but urban representatives in Washington, exposed for a decade to the demands of their rural colleagues for federal aid, were coming to see the connection.

Republican policies had afforded insufficient remedy. The Agricultural Marketing Act of 1929 created the Federal Farm Board principally to direct the lending of a $500,000,000 fund to cooperative associations and to supervise the activities of stabilization corporations which were attempting by their purchases to promote an orderly market. The framers of this act intended it for normal times. They expected the Farm Board to sustain farmer-controlled cooperatives and through them to level off fluctuations in the market occasioned by good or bad crops, seasonal variations in deliveries and other such conditions. The crash of 1929, however, altered dramatically the environment which the Farm Board was supposed to control. The remedies it had in hand could not halt the precipitate and continuing decline of agricultural prices. The board did make its resources available to corporations founded to stabilize grain and cotton prices by buying crops and holding them for sale until prices improved. But in the disastrous years after the crash prices did not improve.

The high Republican tariff of 1930, erecting new obstacles to the sale of European products in the United States, intensified the difficulties of marketing crops in Europe, while at home the production of staple crops was inadvertently stimulated by the Farm Board's purchases. In mid-1931, its funds exhausted, the board began to liquidate its holdings. Wheat then fell below forty cents a bushel. A year later, though the government owned three and a half million bales of cotton, the price of that staple had reached the historic low of four and six-tenths cents a pound. Farmers generally valued federal assistance to marketing cooperatives, but the Farm Board was thoroughly discredited by the patent inadequacy of its techniques for combatting depression. Indeed its own economists were among the vast majority of agricultural experts who were fully persuaded that some device to curtail production had to accompany any successful stabilization operation.

The collapse of agricultural prices and income, moreover, so exhausted the savings and the credit of farmers that by 1933 some immediate financial aid had become urgent. Federal agricultural credit agencies established in 1916 and 1923 had not been organized to cope with the conditions of depression, with potential borrowers who neither had assets nor the prospect of profits. The Hoover Administration scarcely touched this problem, adding to existing facilities only regional credit corporations to make relatively small, emergency, short-term loans secured by liens on livestock or crops. While the resources for agricultural credit remained inadequate, interest rates were often inordinately high, especially in districts remote from money centers. From 1929 on the pace of foreclosures and dispossessions quickened. By 1933, loans that banks had made on crops and farm mortgages had lost much of their face value and almost all of their liquidity. Directly in the South and West, indirectly elsewhere, this contributed to the spate of bank failures and, at the time of Roosevelt's inauguration, to the enforced bank holiday.

By that time rural newspapers were seriously advocating a moratorium on mortgage payments. Some also favored nationalization of the banking system, and many proposed that the federal government print paper money to lend to farmers for paying their debts. In Iowa, Minnesota, and elsewhere farmers were attempting to prevent foreclosures by brandishing shotguns or threatening lynchings. In order to raise prices, farmers almost universally urged immediate inflation of the currency. To keep prices from falling any further, some burned their crops; others responded eagerly to the campaign of the National Farmers' Holiday Association for the organization of farmers' strikes. In this, probably the most harassed hour in the whole history of American agriculture, Roosevelt and his advisers had to fashion policy.

On the morning of December 3, 1932, a month after the election, in the office of the Chairman of the House Committee on Agriculture, there met the first of a series of Democratic conferences on farm policy. The group that assembled that first day had been selected by the President-elect according to a formula that was to become characteristic of federal government for the next twelve years. He assigned to the solution of one large problem men of differing points of view with each of which he in part agreed, men of conflicting ambitions whose least common denominator was personal loyalty to him. As they mounted and pursued their several attacks, he could support now one, now another, now two or three simultaneously, until the problem at issue yielded to the energies he had mobilized. This was not a neat and tidy system, but it left ultimate command in Roosevelt's hands. It permitted experimentation on a grand scale when society seemed infected with maladies for which no one had tested remedies, and it put his subordinates much on their mettle. Only the toughest survived.

The men who sat down together on December 3 were to meet often

again. Their host was Marvin Jones, congressman since 1917, truly
a representative of the cotton growers of his native Texas. A drawl-
ing, unobtrusive, considerate man whose integrity Morgenthau respected, Jones had long been fighting to overcome what he considered the raw deal of American farmers. He spoke for the South and
for Congress, and he favored some form of Domestic Allotment* and
of large financial aid from the federal government.

The strongest advocates of Domestic Allotment at the conference
were Henry A. Wallace and Rexford G. Tugwell. Like his father
and grandfather before him, Wallace was identified with the interests
of the corn and hog farmers of Iowa. He believed in social justice
and high agricultural prices, and believed also that both could be
defined, weighed, and administered. Sometimes stubborn, often
disingenuous, he was something of a dreamer, even a mystic, who
had once tried to live on corn meal and milk after reading that this
had been the diet of Caesar's legions in Gaul. Rex Tugwell was also
a dreamer, but of a different kind. This son of a prosperous farmer
had become professor of economics at Columbia and from that post
a member of the "brains trust" that Sam Rosenman recruited to help
direct Roosevelt's campaign. Perhaps the handsomest and certainly
one of the most articulate of the New Dealers, large, vigorous, loose-
moving, accessible, Tugwell put his whole faith in what he called
the rationalization of industry and agriculture under the positive direction of government. Through scientific management and planning he expected to adjust the flows of production and consumption
to each other, to bring order to the economy.

Across the table from Wallace and Tugwell sat Morgenthau and
William I. Myers, then a professor of farm finance at Cornell. Myers,
who had worked closely with Morgenthau in New York, was as quiet
as Tugwell was aggressive. He looked no special part nor did he play
one, and he had no confidence at all in schemes to limit or to plan
production. Suspicious of large bureaucracy, he considered it impracticable to do more than advise farmers about the probable consequences of any given production program. Morgenthau was willing
to consider crop reduction as an emergency measure but he was
"absolutely against it as a permanent solution to the agricultural

---

* That is, government payments to farmers in return for their agreement to
reduce the acreage they planted.

problem." He felt, he recalled years later, "that we could never produce too much so long as there were hungry people at home and
abroad; that the answer lay, not in artificially restricting production,
but in working out better methods of distribution. . . . Above all,
something instinctive within me revolted at the destruction of existing crops."

Morgenthau and Myers, as they realized, fought a rear-guard action. Adjusting accordingly, they proposed modifications in the
plans for production control that Wallace and Tugwell presented,
and they emphasized the importance of a multiple approach to the
agricultural crisis. Morgenthau was especially concerned about
drawing legislation so as to eliminate speculation in commodity
futures. He also argued for giving first priority to the establishment
of an adequate and permanent system for advancing credit to
farmers. There was no meeting of the minds. With Roosevelt's approval, the group agreed only to postpone decisions until after representatives of the national farm organizations conferred in Washington later in the month.

At this second farm conference, Morgenthau, speaking as Roosevelt's personal representative, told the delegates that the Federal
Farm Board had to go, but he assured them that all of its constructive work would continue, particularly its assistance to cooperatives.
He promised them that the new Administration would move as
rapidly as possible to pass a farm relief bill, but he warned that no
bill would be introduced until the farm organizations agreed to support a common program. Speed and unanimity were vital.

The "brightest lights" of the conference, Bill Myers observed, were
Earl Smith of the American Farm Bureau Federation and C. E.
Huff of the Farmers' National Grain Corporation, for "in spite of
the depression both sported ostentatious diamond rings." "The big
wind" was Charles Ewing of the National Livestock Marketing
Association, "who viewed with alarm on any and all occasions." But
the spirit of the conference was solemn, for the delegates without
exception recognized the urgency of their work.

They reached agreement on three points, which became the bases
of the agricultural legislation passed the following May. Unanimously they favored restoration of the farmers' pre-World War I
purchasing power. To this end, with no important dissent, they

approved of reducing production as a means to raise prices. The scheme ultimately worked out was more flexible and less drastic than the original Domestic Allotment Plan, but it incorporated many of its principles. It depended upon agreements between the government and those farmers who volunteered to reduce the acreage on which they planted any one of several staple crops including wheat, cotton, corn, and tobacco. The government was to pay the participating farmers, who were permitted various methods for withdrawing land from production. One of these was the retirement of marginal land, a favorite objective of Morgenthau. A tax on the processing of agricultural products was to be set at a sufficient rate to provide the money to finance the payments. This voluntary allotment plan was the core of Title I of the farm bill that created the Agricultural Adjustment Administration to organize and supervise it.

The delegates to the December conference also unanimously endorsed easier and cheaper credit for farmers. The conference adjourned before considering any precise plan, but during the next two weeks Morgenthau and Myers, working with Marvin Jones, prepared Title II, the Emergency Farm Mortgage section, of the Administration's farm bill.

Finally, the delegates to the December conference were unanimous in approving the resolution of their committee on money. Following the prescription of Dr. George Warren, Morgenthau's agricultural adviser in New York, this resolution called for reducing the quantity of gold in the dollar, or in other words reducing the value of the dollar in terms of gold, as a device to raise prices approximately to the level of 1921–29. This "reflation," the conference believed, would ease the burden of debtors by making money "cheaper." Reflecting the persistent suspicion of farmers toward Wall Street, the resolution also demanded the removal of "control of the monetary system" from "the hands of bankers" by the creation of a bureau within the Treasury Department to be charged with keeping prices steady by varying the gold content of the dollar. This kind of monetary maneuvering was encouraged by Title III of the farm bill.

Thus the conference of the representatives of the national farm organizations fully anticipated the directions of the New Deal's agricultural policy, of which monetary management, involving broad considerations of national and international affairs, was a major part.

But the conference did not settle the differences that existed among the responsible New Dealers, nor did it determine which of them would prove capable of exercising his mandate or of influencing his chief. Wallace and Tugwell on the one hand, Morgenthau and Myers on the other, had just begun to fight — toward the same broad goal, to be sure, for they all had at heart the welfare of American agriculture, but with separate and sometimes conflicting programs. Faced as he was by a severe agricultural crisis, believing as he did in attacking vigorously on many fronts, Roosevelt when he entered office mobilized a team remarkable for its diversity rather than for its homogeneity, poised not for a union of the spirit but for quick and competitive action.

## 2. The Farm Credit Administration

Morgenthau's immediate administrative tasks were to liquidate as rapidly as possible the stabilization operations of the Federal Farm Board, to wind up the affairs of the board itself, and to develop plans for an agency to succeed it. In January, two months before he took office, the first of these obligations took him to Canada, where he represented the President-elect at confidential conferences with Prime Minister Bennett. Both Roosevelt and Morgenthau recognized the common interest of the American and Canadian governments in finding new markets for wheat, in preventing competitive dumping, and in arranging cooperatively for any curtailment of planting. With these issues in mind, Roosevelt instructed Morgenthau to explore the possibilities for a world conference on wheat.

Morgenthau found the Canadian Prime Minister "a real fellow . . . keenly interested in the wheat situation." With characteristic directness, he asked Bennett whether he liked the idea of calling a conference in Washington in March. The Canadian, pleased by this prospect, volunteered to sound out other wheat-producing countries. His preliminary investigations showed that Australia and Argentina were interested in a multilateral agreement to limit production, but plans for a special conference were abandoned when the nations concerned decided instead to make wheat one item on the agenda of the World Economic Conference scheduled for London in July.

Morgenthau in March proceeded independently to get the government "out of wheat." Assisted by Edward Babcock, an accomplished trader whom he had known in New York, he sold the last of the actual holdings of the Farm Board on his fourth day in office, turned then to disposing of over thirty million bushels which the Board had committed itself to buy in the future, and announced that when they were gone the Grain Stabilization Board, a subsidiary of the Farm Board, would be permitted "to die." On April 29, during a twenty-minute conversation on the telephone, he sold in the Chicago pit the last million bushels of wheat futures. This terminated the unsuccessful and unpopular program of the Hoover Administration and also released funds previously tied up in storing and marketing crops.

As Morgenthau pointed out, the uncertainties about the disposition of huge surpluses held by a single agency had irritated merchants on commodity exchanges and had depressed prices. He would continue to accept crops as collateral for loans to farmer-owned cooperatives, but he would also strive to bring representatives of the cooperatives together with commission merchants in order to work out marketing procedures less disturbing to the exchanges and consequently more profitable both for brokers and growers. So it was that early in May federal officials and representatives of the wool industry together sold fifteen million pounds of wool quickly and profitably. Abandoning the Republican policy of holding products off the market for higher prices that never materialized, Morgenthau then and later cultivated "sales mindedness."

This was an early demonstration that a man who most enjoyed the reputation and the role of a reformer realized successful reform depended upon the application to government of efficient methods. A comparable efficiency marked the reorganization of the entire structure for making federal loans to farmers. Morgenthau was responsible for this reorganization which took into account the recommendations of leaders of farm organizations and of congressmen from agricultural states. He drew also on the advice and assistance of Bill Myers and of Herman Oliphant, who was to be his general counsel in the Farm Credit Administration and the Treasury Department until he died in 1939.

Oliphant, the son of a Hoosier farmer, had been a student of philology at the University of Indiana, later a graduate of the Chicago Law School and a professor of law at Chicago, Columbia, and Johns Hopkins. He was an expert on the statistical and quantitative aspects of law, and the first president and creative force of the New York Law Society. A shy man, tireless, acid, one of the keenest and most unselfish New Dealers, he was as little known outside of Washington as he was respected within that city. The day of Roosevelt's inauguration, Oliphant and Morgenthau were introduced; Oliphant agreed to do a temporary job, did it so well that he was urged to stay on, and in remaining brought to the organization of the Farm Credit Administration and later to many other problems, his learning, his imagination, and his unshakable faith in the potentialities of progressive democracy.

Morgenthau, Oliphant, and Myers proposed to centralize farm credit operations in a single agency. Previously five separate agencies (including offices in the Farm Board, the Department of Agriculture, the Treasury Department, and the Reconstruction Finance Corporation) had supervised agricultural credits of one kind or another. The new organization, to be called the Farm Credit Administration, was to be run by four commissioners, all responsible to Morgenthau. Each was to be concerned with one of four kinds of credit institutions. These were the Federal Land Banks, established in 1916 to finance farm mortgages; the Federal Intermediate Credit Banks, created in 1923 to rediscount loans on crops held by cooperatives or warehouses; the Production Credit Corporation, a new agency to make loans for seed and to relieve victims of floods and other natural disasters; and the Central Bank for Co-operatives, also a new agency for financing cooperatives.

After reviewing Morgenthau's plans, Roosevelt by Executive Order on March 27, 1933, set up the Farm Credit Administration. It took over the activities of the Farm Board, the supervision of the Cooperative Research and Service Division of the Department of Agriculture, and, after a transitional period of two months, the control of the regional agricultural credit corporations of the Reconstruction Finance Corporation. Title II of the agricultural bill, which Congress passed in May, gave the Farm Credit Administration the immediate authorizations it needed and an initial appropriation. On June 16 the Farm Credit Act enabled Morgenthau to complete the consolidations and changes that finally made effective the four-way division of credit functions.

With Myers as his deputy governor, Oliphant as his general counsel, and Herbert Gaston as his secretary and special assistant, Morgenthau had meanwhile worked out a system for putting the resources of his agency at the ready disposal of farmers. He established twelve regional districts. In each of these, within a single city, were branches of the four credit institutions, all responsible to a single board of directors and to a district agent who served as their executive officer and as Morgenthau's representative. "Our idea," Morgenthau said, "is to fix the credit structure so that a farmer can borrow money for planting, harvesting and upon his land all in one spot." His practical reorganization effected a permanent improvement in the nation's farm credit system.

In the two months after Roosevelt's inauguration, while Congress dallied over the farm bill, farmers became frantic for help. On May 9 the Governor of Minnesota had telephoned the White House to report that unless something were done at once farmers in his state would resist any attempts at foreclosures. In Iowa they already had. Roosevelt had Morgenthau prepare a statement requesting a moratorium on foreclosures until the pending farm relief bill passed, which it did three days later. Keeping the statement in reserve, the President also asked Morgenthau to explain the government's plans.

On the day the bill became law, Morgenthau, talking on the radio, told farmers and their creditors how they would benefit. First, the Federal Land Banks within sixty days would reduce the interest rate on all mortgages they held from 5½ per cent to 4½ per cent, thus saving some four hundred thousand farmers $55,000,000 during the next five years. For the seven farmers in eight whose mortgages were held by private institutions, the law offered another kind of aid. It authorized the Land Banks to issue $2,000,000,000 of 4 per cent bonds guaranteed by the federal government. These were to be exchanged for mortgages held by banks, insurance companies, and other investors. In making the exchange, the Land Banks would accept no mortgage unless its principal was cut down to twice the appraised value of the farm. Thus mortgages written in boom times were reduced to a nearer approximation of the deflated values of farm properties. In return for this theoretical loss in value, holders of mortgages could exchange their dubious securities for bonds underwritten by the government.

Besides reducing the principal on mortgages, the Land Banks would lower the interest from an average of 6 per cent to 4½ per cent. The new act also provided $200,000,000 for small loans, to be secured by second mortgages, for redeeming land already foreclosed, for repaying miscellaneous debts, and for operating capital.

More radical proposals would have had the federal government subsidize farmers by refinancing the entire agricultural debt at 2 per cent; more conservative proposals would have limited the government to assisting private efforts to reduce the average principal of farm mortgages by pooling them. The policy Morgenthau described permitted an orderly reduction of both principal and interest. It also assured uniform rates for identical loans regardless of the borrower's proximity to the money market.

Morgenthau wanted the farmers to become the proprietors as well as the beneficiaries of FCA. He therefore arranged for those who got mortgages to buy stock in a farmers' association which in turn purchased the stock of the Land Banks. "My hope," he said years later, observing that his plans were changed after he had left the agency and it had become a part of the Department of Agriculture, "was that Farm Credit would eventually become a farmer-owned, farmer-operated credit enterprise, which could borrow from the public on favorable terms and pass on the benefits to farmers by lending at reasonable rates of interest."

The refinancing of farm mortgages not only relieved the anxieties of farmers about dispossession but also rescued many country banks from insolvency. Their depositors and their creditors (including larger, eastern banks and Federal Reserve Banks in districts through the nation) had drawn from them much of their cash and liquid securities during the previous months. Federal conservators, who investigated all banks after the bank holiday of March, could permit only those with adequate funds to reopen. In rural areas, the heavy investments of local banks in farm mortgages of doubtful value delayed or in some cases prevented reopening. When the FCA in June established in Madison, Wisconsin, its first office to deal with this problem, more than $500,000,000 in farm mortgages was locked in closed banks. Funds released by the refinancing of these mortgages during

1933 and 1934 permitted many banks to reopen and to pay in full their depositors, mostly farmers and small merchants who would otherwise permanently have lost their working capital and their savings. This refunding operation had to be conducted with care, however, for some institutions, including many in the South, could not have survived any considerable scaling down of their investments.

The task of the Farm Credit Administration was so complex, the sums of money it handled so large, that Morgenthau needed an honest, efficient and resourceful staff. To obtain one he had to battle for generous salaries and for freedom from political interference in making his selections. In the spring of 1933 Roosevelt was still trying desperately to cut back the expense of government. His devoted subordinate in this mission was his Director of the Budget, Lewis Douglas, a former congressman from Arizona, a veteran both of World War I and preparatory-school teaching, a conservative Democrat whose fiscal standards were those of the Hoover Administration. Personally unfamiliar with and insensitive to the financial problems of most government officials, Douglas disapproved Morgenthau's request for ten salaries of $10,000 each for FCA personnel. In some pique, Morgenthau, during a private luncheon with the President, maintained that so long as he kept within his appropriation, it was his business and not Douglas's to decide about salaries. Roosevelt tried to split the difference, recommending that five salaries reach the figure requested. With so many new agencies coming into being, he told Morgenthau, the precedent of paying $10,000 salaries might become troublesome. Very few men in Washington then earned that much. But he accepted Morgenthau's revised formula which provided for three salaries of $9800 and seven of $10,000.

At the last moment, however, Morgenthau learned that these and other moneys for FCA — in all $42,000,000 — had not been included in the deficiency bill before Congress. With Bill Myers, he set up shop in the office of Vice President Garner, who assisted their energetic lobby. Garner, for many years a congressman from Texas and for two the Speaker of the House, had a proclivity for cigars, poker, and whiskey that matched his incomparable command of salty language. These talents annoyed his critics but endeared him to most of his colleagues who also recognized his genuine interest in farmers' needs. During the long evening that Myers and Morgenthau sat in his office, Garner appeared about every half hour, on each occasion bringing some senator with him. As he hoped they would, most of his companions yielded to Morgenthau's pleading. The next afternoon, while the bill was in conference committee, Morgenthau pressed his gains. "I am not going to pay any cut-rate salaries," he informed the managers of the bill, "and you can tell the President I said so." This adamancy helped him get his way.

Several days later Morgenthau told Roosevelt what he had done, whereupon the President pretended to laugh up his sleeve. But there was one more obstacle to overcome. When Roosevelt asked Miss Marguerite LeHand, his shrewd, competent but sometimes unceremonious secretary, to give him the FCA papers to sign, she protested that Morgenthau would have to wait until she finished drinking a milk shake. "Missy," Morgenthau called through the door, "I will buy you ten milk shakes if you come in." She did, she found the papers, the President signed them, and the episode was closed.

Congressmen who had supported Morgenthau's requests for salaries or helped him find office space expected him in return to look with favor on their candidates for appointments. "The tension here is terrific," Morgenthau had written his father, "on account of the patronage question. Senators and congressmen clamoring for jobs and we withholding them until our bill passes." Nor did the tension ease, for the faithful had an ardent champion in James A. Farley, Postmaster General and Chairman of the Democratic National Committee, one of the effective agents of Roosevelt's prenomination and election campaigns.

Morgenthau made no secret of his distaste for playing politics with important jobs. One highly recommended man so "reeked of liquor" he was never seriously considered. Many others were scarcely more desirable. When the President asked him to help reorganize one disorderly office in Washington, Morgenthau replied: "Franklin, there is no use my looking into it unless you have Jim Farley sitting in this room and the three of us talk over the whole situation. It is all a matter of patronage."

Even Roosevelt put occasional pressure on Morgenthau, who "took care" of several men but laughed off the President's recommendation of two deserving New York Democrats with the comment: "Good heavens, why are you punishing me?" "I made up my mind," Morgenthau wrote in his Diary, "that I am not going to aid the politicians, and I am going to tell them politely, but firmly, that I cannot accept their candidates. I believe, in the long run, they will respect me more for it." They did, and above the clerical level, he made merit the basis for his selections.

He was a polite and considerate but exacting administrator. The problems of recruiting and training a staff were so large that the work begun in May at first went slowly. A temporary, speculative recovery in commodity prices, moreover, made investors hesitate to exchange mortgages at less than their face value, and persuaded government officials that they could take their time. But in the summer prices broke again, farmers resumed their picketing, and western congressmen began to chastise the Administration for inactivity. Morgenthau, as impatient as his critics, had completed the formation of his staff by early September. The recent increase in the number of appraisers of farm properties, he told his subordinates, "means little to the farmer who has been waiting . . . to learn whether he can get a loan. He knows there has been delay. He doesn't know why and it wouldn't help him to pay his debts if he did. He wants action; so do I. . . . This is an emergency. We have been busy, but we've got to get busier."

"Get results," he warned, "or give way to somebody who will." They got results. Between July and November 1933, federal loans to farmers jumped from $3,500,000 to $30,000,000 a month. In that time the Federal Land Banks received more applications for loans than they had in the previous nine and a half years. They made emergency loans to prevent foreclosures at the rate of three hundred a day. In the first year of its life, FCA closed or approved over 540,-000 loans aggregating over $1,356,000,000. In its first year and a half, it refinanced about 20 per cent of the total farm mortgage debt in the United States. This reversed the trend toward foreclosures. In 1937 there were about 300,000 more owner-operators of American farms than there had been in 1933. By the end of 1937, Land Banks held 40 per cent of the total farm mortgages, over three times their holding a decade earlier. The crisis in farm credit had passed.

The figures spoke less eloquently than did the recipients of the loans. Four typical letters to the Farm Credit Administration told the human story. The farmer who received Loan 47485 had been fighting foreclosure: "I was hounded till I was about to lose my mind . . . they were nagging me to death. . . . I appreciate the loan."

"We thank you," wrote a relative of recipient 47609, "a thousand times that my father-in-law's loan went through that saved his farm. . . . Now he sees he can make a go of it where before he knew no way out as this farm he worked and paid for it and it had been his place for 24 years which is a mighty long time and then when a time comes when you are old and no wife, it made him almost insane at times to think of losing it."

"I could write you a book," another said, "on how your loan has helped me but you wouldn't have time to read this from way down in Arkansas." And to the agent of FCA in St. Louis, recipient 47742 confided: "I would be without a roof over my head if it hadn't been for the government loan. . . . God bless Mr. Roosevelt and the Democratic party who saved thousands of poor people all over this country from starvation."

There was another kind of testimony. "Damn you old money-bags," Jack Garner said to Morgenthau one day at Cabinet meeting. "Until you came along Mrs. Garner and I averaged 16 per cent a year on our money, and now we can't get better than 5 per cent." Even more intimately than Garner, Bill Myers, who succeeded Morgenthau as Governor of FCA, realized what his chief had done. "A large part of the progress that has been made," he wrote in April 1934, "was due to your leadership and to the tremendous effort put forth to get the big machine rolling during those discouraging days last fall."

## 3. Prescriptions for "Galloping Palsy"

"The tremendous effort . . . to get the big machine rolling" covered the whole front along which the New Deal advanced. Morgenthau found himself involved not only in the organization of the Farm Credit Administration but also, at Roosevelt's request and some-times as his agent, in a variety of other problems.

Some of these were only indirectly related to agriculture, but one, the administration of the voluntary allotment plan, continued to be the most controversial of the New Deal's policies for farm relief. The speculative rise of commodity prices in the spring of 1933 worried Henry Wallace, for higher prices encouraged farmers to plant larger crops at just the time he wanted them to cut down on production. At his request, the President called a conference about this problem early in May, when Congress was preparing to pass the agricultural bill.

Wallace and Tugwell opened discussion, spelling out their plans for the Agricultural Adjustment Administration. Their organization chart included over three hundred employees who were to work in counties to lease land in order to take it out of production. But George Peek, whom Roosevelt had decided to appoint head of the AAA, disapproved of this program. As he had for many years, Peek still advocated high tariffs on agricultural products and large-scale "dumping" abroad of agricultural surpluses rather than the limitation of crops. He also objected to the tax on the processing of agricultural products — the milling of wheat, the ginning of cotton — which Tugwell and Wallace favored, preferring to use customs receipts to subsidize domestic agricultural prices. Budget Director Douglas feared that a processing tax would produce too little revenue to finance Wallace's leasing program, and Jim Farley considered Wallace's table of organization too complicated. Wallace and Tugwell nevertheless persisted in their recommendations, and Marvin McIntyre, Roosevelt's secretary, urged the President to appeal by radio to farmers to cooperate in the program.

Morgenthau then spoke up. It would be a "terrible mistake," he argued, for Roosevelt to go on the air. He saw "nothing else but" difficulties in Wallace's plan. Indeed, he went on, though Congress was about to pass the farm bill, the officials of the Department of Agriculture had yet to agree among themselves about policy. He personally was exasperated that he had to take time from his own duties to discuss matters that should have been under control. The President, he implied, should not endorse a program as questionable and as nebulous as that which Wallace had presented. Obviously annoyed by this impromptu speech, Roosevelt answered that the bill was going to pass and he was going to sign it. Shortly thereafter the meeting broke up without reaching any decision. In his Diary, Morgenthau observed that the President had forced Peek upon Wallace, who had retaliated by requesting the meeting in order to "drag" the President into disciplining Peek.

Morgenthau's abruptness yielded unexpected fruit. The next morning Wallace thanked him for what he had "done to help him." When Roosevelt heard about this, he remarked to Morgenthau: "I don't see why Wallace thanked you in as much as you kicked him twice." He also explained that his purpose in calling the conference had been simply to acquaint members of the Administration with the difficulties of carrying out the farm program.

Morgenthau, still critical of Wallace, ten days later suggested to Roosevelt that almost any method of financing the leasing of land would, in the long run, be less expensive than the processing tax. That tax, he contended, would produce inadequate revenue and have a harmful incidence. Processors, he predicted, would pass the tax along by increasing food prices, which many Americans could ill afford. Roosevelt's "funny look" conveyed his displeasure with these comments, but Morgenthau stuck by his guns "as I always do with him." Wallace, however, prevailed, even to the extent of soon supplanting Peek, whose influence languished long before his resignation in December.

Convinced as he was that no recovery could be permanent unless production were cut back, Wallace was continually afraid that a premature rise in prices might keep farmers from contracting to reduce their planting. Morgenthau, in contrast, was more concerned with the immediate need for raising prices. The legislation of May had come too late to permit AAA leasing to have much effect on production in 1933, and the checks the farmers received for curtailing their planting did not sufficiently compensate for the persisting thinness of the market. When prices tumbled in the late spring, farmers had increasing difficulty in holding the line between solvency and bankruptcy. Morgenthau consequently looked outside of his own province for devices to bring quick relief.

"The smell of revolution was in the air," he later recalled. "We had to do something about farm prices . . . and we had to act fast. . . . Our activity in the realm of farm credit did not touch the big problem . . . the general level of prices. . . . If we could get farm prices up, we would reduce the weight of debt in terms of purchasing power and thus lighten the debt burden as effectively as direct mortgage relief. But, if prices should fall any further, then the whole farm community would be threatened with bankruptcy, and no one could foretell what violence might ensue."

In this spirit Morgenthau viewed the possibility of making a loan to China to finance her purchase of one million bales of cotton. Roosevelt on May 17 directed him to discuss such a loan with officials of the Department of State and of the Reconstruction Finance Corporation. The State Department objected to the scheme on two accounts. First, the Chinese were using their customs receipts to pay current expenses instead of repaying debts owed to American citizens. More importantly, a loan to China might offend Japan, the largest customer for American cotton. Impatient with this reasoning, Morgenthau replied that even if the loan were never repaid, the sale of the cotton would boost domestic prices, increasing the value of cotton stocks on hand within the United States by as much as $100,-000,000. This, he observed, would put a stop to Wallace's plan to have a portion of the cotton crop plowed under. He also made this point to Roosevelt, who for the first time listened to criticism of Wallace without showing irritation. Indeed the President approved a loan on liberal terms.

Roosevelt's reaction settled any question of foreign policy, but Wallace raised new objections. He had earlier protested against a much smaller sale of the last of the Farm Board's cotton. At a conference on May 26 about the management of the Chinese loan, he contended that, in an unofficial opinion, the Department of Justice had ruled it illegal for the government to sell China cotton acquired as security for loans previously made to farm cooperatives. Morgenthau then suggested the Chinese use their loan to buy cotton in the open market. Wallace replied that he would prefer to see the government's cotton sold. "If you hold it illegal," Morgenthau asked, "why argue about it?"

"Well," Wallace said, shifting his ground, "if you do sell I do not want it announced for at least thirty days, so that the price of cotton will stay down and I can go out and conclude my arrangements to lease land from cotton growers and withdraw it from cultivation, because if the price of cotton goes up now it will make it much more difficult for me to lease the land."

"Henry, I wonder if you realize what you are doing," Morgenthau asked. "You would be withholding information from the farmers and if in a month or two they learn that you knew all the time that this Chinese deal had been concluded the farmers would feel that you had misled them."

"I don't care what they think," Wallace replied, "as long as I can lease their land."

Morgenthau said he would not let the President be put in such a position. "All right," Wallace said, preparing to leave, "make any kind of deal you want but when you get ready to release the publicity let me know." But he later insisted on selling the government cotton domestically, a reversal that outraged Morgenthau.

In spite of the wide differences between them, the Chinese loan was made. It had a negligible effect, however, for the Chinese, reluctant to import either wheat or cotton, used only a small fraction of the $50,000,000 they received.

Before the negotiation with the Chinese began, Roosevelt had asked Morgenthau to help conduct conversations looking toward the recognition of Soviet Russia. The President considered the policy of nonrecognition futile, for whether or not the Soviet government was democratic, it had been for over a decade the established government of Russia, recognized by the major powers except the United States. Roosevelt also felt that continued isolation of Russia would impede his purpose of preventing war in Europe or Asia by organizing the collective moral sense of the nations of the world. He therefore included the President of the Soviet Union among the heads of state to whom he sent a cable in May calling for military and economic disarmament. He viewed Russia, moreover, as a potential ally against Japanese aggression in the Orient or German resurgence in Europe.

Because the Department of State was unfriendly to the idea of opening negotiations with the Russians, Roosevelt turned for assistance to Morgenthau. In and out of government, advocates of recognition expected the Soviet Union to absorb some of the American surpluses of manufactured goods and raw materials, and Morgenthau, engaged in liquidating the holdings of the Farm Board, was especially well placed to discuss the disposition of cotton stocks in which the Russian trading corporation, Amtorg, was interested.

Morgenthau approached Amtorg through two intermediaries, whose first reports revealed the delicacy and the risk of any negotiation with the Russians. If the deal worked out well, he remarked to Roosevelt one day at luncheon, he would be a hero, but if it flopped, he would have to leave Washington. "Well, of course, you know that I stand back of you in these negotiations," Roosevelt replied, "and if you have to leave Washington I will leave with you."

Conversations moved slowly partly because the Russians tried to play off against each other the various Americans who represented Morgenthau, the Treasury Department, and the Reconstruction Finance Corporation, partly because no individual Russian was willing to assume authority or make a commitment. "Gosh," Roosevelt told Morgenthau, "if I could only, myself, talk to some one man representing the Russians, I could straighten out this whole question. If you get the opportunity, Henry, you could say that you believe but have no authority to say so, that the President would like to send some person to Moscow . . . in order to break the ice between the two countries and in that way gradually get the people of the United States used to doing business with the Russians."

This scheme failed, however, and Roosevelt had to continue to work through agents whose activities he supervised. When Morgenthau reported in August that the Soviet Union wanted to buy $75,-000,000 worth of raw materials, the President informed him that through other channels, they were seeking $50,000,000 worth of machine goods. Instructing Morgenthau to set an over-all limit of $100,000,000 on sales to the Russians during the next few months, he suggested making half the sales raw materials, half machinery, all on the basis of a down payment of 15 per cent to 20 per cent. Purchases of this dimension, had they been made, would have given some help to the economy and much more to the morale of the depression-ridden nation.

Such purchases, however, depended upon large loans to the Russians which would have involved considerable publicity. That had to await a decision about recognition. "What would you think," Roosevelt asked Morgenthau late in September, "of bringing this whole Russian question into our front parlor instead of back in the kitchen?" He had in mind writing a letter to the President of the

Soviet Union suggesting formal negotiations to lead to diplomatic relations, but he wanted first to be certain that the Russians would welcome the gesture.

Morgenthau learned about the details of the President's plan the next day at luncheon with William C. Bullitt who was handling Soviet affairs for the State Department and was later to become the first American ambassador to the Soviet Union. Bullitt, a man of "great charm" and "violent" loves and hatreds, had gone to Russia on a mission for Woodrow Wilson during the Paris conference after World War I. He returned convinced that the Western democracies had to overcome their antipathies to Bolshevism and work with the Soviet government. Persisting in this attitude, Bullitt now saw in American aid "the means by which the Soviet Union could break away from its dependence on Germany and could become a bulwark against the aggressive tendencies . . . developing in Japan."

Bullitt ascribed the bias of the State Department against recognition to the concern of Secretary of State Cordell Hull about the religious issue. Hull, a Tennessee Democrat who had been in Congress for many years, brought to his office a controlled and quiet manner that ordinarily hid his large personal ambitions and his jealousy of his prerogatives. He had a veteran politician's educated sense about how to treat senators and about inveterate Democratic sensibilities, and he placed his unshakable faith in the ability of free trade to cure almost all the ills of the world. He believed that Americans in Russia should be allowed to worship as they pleased. He was perhaps also convinced that American Catholics, most of them Democrats, would resent the recognition of a notoriously anti-Christian government. But the Secretary of State also had larger reservations about the recognition of the Soviet Union which he had communicated directly to the President. These pertained to the settlement of the war debt owed the United States by the pre-Soviet government and, more significantly, to interference in American affairs by Soviet-sponsored Communist organizations.

During the last stage of the conflict over recognition, Morgenthau was an informed and sometimes an involved observer. "Bullitt began walking me to work in the mornings," he recollected, "in order to pump me about the latest developments. At first this annoyed the President, on the ground that Bullitt was going over Hull's head. . . . But, as affairs developed, he entrusted the negotiations more and more to Bullitt." Morgenthau helped to bring Bullitt together with the Soviet representative, Boris Skvirsky, in order to arrange the exchange of letters Roosevelt desired. "I have a piece of paper in my hand," Bullitt told the Russian at one point. "It is unsigned. It can be made into an invitation for you to send representatives here to discuss diplomatic relations. We wish you to telegraph it by your most confidential code and learn if it is acceptable. . . . If not, will you give me your word of honor that there never will be any publicity about this proposed exchange of letters and that the whole matter will be kept secret?"

Skvirsky gave his word, the exchange was arranged as Roosevelt had proposed, and in November Maxim Litvinov arrived in Washington to begin the talks that resulted on the 16th of that month in American recognition of the Soviet Union. Morgenthau took part in the early discussions with Litvinov who impressed him then "as a warm, friendly man, sparkling in conversation, abundant in hospitality." But the little Russian, whatever his personal charm, could not depart from his orders from Moscow. These permitted him to give Hull plausible assurances about the religious freedom of Americans in Russia and about the activities of Communists in the United States, but the question of the Russian debt had to be postponed until after the two countries exchanged ambassadors. Discussions of the debt dragged on for years. While they continued, never to be settled, the government-owned Export-Import Bank of Washington would not give the Soviets credits for purchasing raw materials or machinery from the United States.

As in the case of China, so in the case of Russia, Morgenthau's first ventures in foreign policy did not get rid of the cotton glutting the American market. He nevertheless counted the Russian negotiation a success. "Recognition," he observed years later when the memory of Russian-American cooperation to defeat Hitler was fresh, "was one of Roosevelt's first attempts to create a community of good neighbors as the best security against the depredations of the neighborhood roughnecks."

The diplomatic success, however, left commodity prices untouched. Increasingly worried about them, Morgenthau urged Roosevelt to emphasize the distribution instead of the destruction of surpluses. The government, he suggested, could combat falling prices and urban destitution by purchasing 1,000,000 bales of cotton and 100,000,000 bushels of wheat to distribute to the unemployed. Roosevelt declined, answering rather sharply that the machinery for plowing crops under had already been set up. But as the price of wheat dropped to 90 cents at the end of September and then skidded below 70 cents during the next twelve days, even the proponents of plowing under were alarmed.

The President, Morgenthau later noted, "was gravely concerned. The malady threatened much more than just the farm belt: the whole recovery program was jeopardized by this galloping palsy." Roosevelt therefore gave to Morgenthau and Jesse Jones a chance to experiment with the resources of their credit agencies. Jones, a big, breezy, genial man, one of the many Texans in the New Deal, had for many years been a banker in Houston and a money-raiser for the Democratic party. On the recommendation of Jack Garner, Jones's old friend and companion in matters political and spiritual, Hoover had appointed Jones a director of the Reconstruction Finance Corporation in 1932. In 1933 Roosevelt made him chairman.

Partly because of their common objections to Wallace's program, Jones and Morgenthau had worked together on the loan for China. They were allied again in attempting to lift agricultural prices. Jones's RFC in October underwrote the Commodity Credit Corporation, established to prop up prices by offering cotton growers a loan of ten cents for every pound they kept from market, a loan larger than the price they could realize by selling. This induced them not to dump their cotton and push prices still lower, but it also involved the government in the kind of operation which Hoover's Farm Board had tried without success, and it did not help to clothe the urban unemployed. Morgenthau hoped, therefore, to handle wheat a different way. On the night of October 16 a telephone call from Roosevelt gave him his chance.

"We have got to do something about the price of wheat," the President said, his voice registering worry and fatigue. "I can't take it any longer. . . . Can't you buy 25,000,000 bushels for Harry Hopkins and see if you can't put the price up?"

Hopkins was then head of the Federal Emergency Relief Administration, established by an act of Congress of May 12, 1933. The first of the New Deal's relief agencies, it operated largely by providing the states with funds, food, and clothing for the needy unemployed. With Wallace and George Peek, Hopkins drove over to Morgenthau's, where he quickly agreed to take 30,000,000 bushels of wheat. Farm Credit was to lend the money with which to buy it to the Farmers' National Grain Corporation, a private organization that had worked closely with the Farm Board, but Morgenthau "was certain not to get stuck with loads of surplus" because Hopkins's FERA would undertake to process and distribute the wheat.

After checking with Roosevelt, Morgenthau started buying the first thing the following morning. Wheat opened at 647/8, but his first order for 1,000,000 bushels at 72 to 74 held the market up above 70 for about half an hour. In spite of his second order for another 1,000,000 at 741/8, however, the market "busted" down to 68. "I was a pretty sick boy when this happened," Morgenthau confided to his Diary. "It seemed to me that I was trying to hold up not only the commodity markets of the world but also the stock market as everything was sagging."

He fought on, placing a standing order to buy all cash wheat offered that day and reporting this news to the *Wall Street Journal* and the press services. In the end he bought 103 carloads. His purchase, along with the publicity he planted, helped the price of wheat to hit a ceiling for the day of 741/8, up almost ten cents from the opening. The stock market also rallied, and Morgenthau felt he had accomplished what the President wanted. Late in the afternoon he called Roosevelt to say that the firm of Hopkins and Morgenthau was in the wheat business, and to offer him one-quarter interest in the company. "Make it one third," the President said, with the old fight in his voice. "Squeeze the life out of the shorts and put the price up just as far as you can."

The next day, with Morgenthau again buying all cash wheat offered, the market held at its opening and rose two cents before closing. As the purchasing program continued, however, there were some frantic days. On November 4 an early order of 500,000 bushels of corn for Harry Hopkins's account raised the price less than a cent. When the price sagged again in the afternoon, Morgenthau ordered another 500,000 bushels. In the last five minutes before closing, this order put corn up two cents and delighted the President.

The last Saturday in October had been even more worrisome. Roosevelt, learning that wheat was off three cents, told Morgenthau to try to make it recover before the market closed. The effort might involve purchasing two or three million bushels, the President warned, but he wanted to attempt to boost prices in order to lend cheer to the weekend and to the Sunday newspapers' financial sections. Morgenthau began to buy, but, he noted, "evidently the crowd in the wheat pit was laying for me because I made very little headway." About six minutes before closing, he told his agent "to give them the gun and to buy everything that they offered in order to try and reach our objective. When the smoke cleared away we had bought four million four hundred thousand bushels. . . . I felt literally dizzy while the thing was going on. I went home and went to bed for two hours after lunch."

As both Roosevelt and Morgenthau knew, however, not even forays conducted on a grand scale could sustain commodity prices. Just as the huge purchases of the Farm Board had failed to stabilize the market, so Morgenthau's purchases, even though they were not held for resale, could provide only transitory remedy. He could and did on occasion outwit the bears in the wheat pit, but his operations did not touch the basic problem. Nor was the distribution of surpluses to families on relief a promising long-range solution. It was, in Morgenthau's opinion, vastly preferable to destroying existing crops, but there was too much cotton, too much wheat, and too little machinery for its disposal to permit domestic consumption to bring demand up to supply. Furthermore, whatever the remote possibilities of "bridging the gap between domestic surpluses and world hunger," for the immediate future, markets in Europe were closed by a complex of trade barriers, and markets in Russia and China could not quickly be opened. Nevertheless, except as a temporary and, indeed, a sinful expedient, Morgenthau could not accept Wallace's formula. He was therefore especially responsive to the possibility of devaluing the dollar by raising the price of gold, a prospect increasingly attractive after prices broke in June.

## 4. The Price of Gold

Probably the foremost exponent of devaluation, and certainly the man who most influenced Morgenthau's thinking about it, was Dr. George Warren. In his books and articles on the subject, Warren maintained that reducing the gold value of the dollar would have two sure, salubrious results. It would raise the level of prices and restore the balance between the prices of raw materials and consumers' goods. The price of raw materials, he argued, moved faster and further than other prices in times of inflation and deflation. By 1933, he went on, deflation had produced a serious distortion in the price structure, with basic commodity prices relatively lower than industrial prices. Increasing the price of gold, he concluded, would rapidly and directly reinflate commodity prices and thus correct the abnormality of the price structure. He also contended that no effort to restore prices to pre-depression levels could succeed unless the price of gold were first increased. As one of Warren's associates put it succinctly to Morgenthau: "Only as the amount of gold in the dollar is reduced can commodity prices be raised and held. . . . In no case has any country been able to change the course of wholesale commodity prices . . . except by changing the gold content of its money."

Their long friendship naturally helped Warren to convince Morgenthau, but he could not have succeeded had there not been a widespread enthusiasm for inflation and specifically for raising the price of gold. Not laymen and politicians only, but many businessmen and professional economists believed in 1933 that depressions were simply the result of a collapse in prices. Given the insistence of Warren's theory that prices varied directly with the price of gold, the conclusion was inevitably suggested that recovery would follow an increase in the price of gold.

In the temper of 1933 this was not a radical idea. Farmers and other debtors, the most ardent of American inflationists, endorsed all kinds of inflationary devices, including the printing of billions of dollars of paper money, which in recent memory had led Germany down a path of disaster, and the extensive use of silver as a base for

currency, a panacea that had frightened most of the business community for half a century. Increasing the price of gold seemed relatively conservative. Gold had long been the only measure of value
generally accepted by most Americans and Europeans. To abandon
the existing, orthodox gold standard that set the value of gold at
$20.67 an ounce was, to be sure, an adventurous proposal, for that
ratio had existed unchallenged since 1900, but Warren's theory, even
though it involved establishing a new and flexible ratio, did not substitute for gold either silver or paper.

Various European nations, furthermore, including Great Britain,
had already abandoned orthodoxy, shifting to a managed currency
that left gold at a modified ratio which could be manipulated. These
nations had neither resorted to the printing press nor been swept
away by uncontrolled inflation. By devaluation they had obtained
some temporary advantage in competing for trade with the United
States and other countries still wedded to orthodoxy. The physical
movement of gold from the United States during 1931–32 represented in part American payments in an unfavorable balance of
trade. The outflow of gold had serious domestic repercussions, for
by depleting the monetary base, it contributed to deflation.

At the time of Roosevelt's inauguration, orthodoxy still had its
illustrious champions, among them Hoover and most Republicans
of stature, Al Smith, Lewis Douglas, and other right-wing Democrats.
There were also impressive proponents of change. The Committee
for the Nation to Rebuild Prices and Purchasing Power, for example,
numbered among its devotees scores of business executives, and
among its leaders J. H. Rand, Jr., of Remington, Rand, General
Robert E. Wood of Sears, Roebuck, and Frank A. Vanderlip, president of the National City Bank of New York, all of whom pretty
much subscribed to Warren's theory. The new President was under
such great pressure that his real problem was not whether there
should be inflation but whether he could control the direction it
was to take and the dimensions it was to reach.

Roosevelt's initial moves were heterodox but not directly inflationary. To stop the accelerating flow of gold to Europe and to combat the hoarding of gold domestically, both of which helped to bring
on the banking crisis and were in turn accentuated by the panic accompanying that crisis, the President in March suspended the ex-

port of gold except by license from the Treasury. In April he forbade the hoarding of gold and required the delivery of all gold held domestically to the Federal Reserve Banks. These orders were essential preliminaries for currency management or reinflation, but for the time being the United States remained on the rigid gold standard, for the Treasury did license the export of gold to support the dollar in foreign exchange, and the dollar did not immediately depreciate abroad.

Late in April the President went further. The dollar was beginning to sag abroad and New York bankers were applying for licenses to export gold in large quantities. In Congress, moreover, where the farm bill was being debated, senators from agricultural states insisted upon inflationary policies. Only by a close vote did the Administration defeat a proposal for the mandatory coinage of silver at a ratio to gold of sixteen to one, the magical formula of the silver crusade of the 1890's. There were still pending proposals to force the printing of greenbacks in large quantity. The Administration had either to take charge of inflation and manage it or permit Congress to impose by statute an uncontrolled and possibly uncontrollable inflation.

This threat from Congress, coupled as it was with pressure on the dollar, forced Roosevelt's hand. On April 19 he announced his willingness to accept the discretionary powers which Senator Thomas's amendment to the farm bill invested in him. These powers permitted but did not compel him to issue paper money, to provide for the unlimited coinage of silver, to force the Federal Reserve System to expand the credit base, or to reduce the gold content of the dollar. Roosevelt was not ready to use any of these powers, but he did renounce a rigid gold standard. His Executive Orders on April 19 and 20 prohibited the export of gold. At once the value of the dollar in terms of other currencies fell off. Concurrently the prices of commodities and securities in the United States rose, and there began a period of speculative increases in prices that lasted until almost the end of June.

To some, like Lewis Douglas, the abandonment of the gold standard seemed to portend an end to Western civilization, but more perceptive men were less deluded than he was by monetary orthodoxy. J. Pierpont Morgan welcomed the President's action. Efforts to maintain the exchange value of the dollar, he commented, were having a deflationary effect upon already deflated American prices, wages and employment. "The way out of the depression," Morgan said, "is to combat and overcome the deflationary forces." Conservative economists considered the embargo on gold temporarily essential to permit the Administration to initiate measures for domestic recovery, whether by monetary action or by deficit expenditures to stimulate business activity. But in April 1933, even as Roosevelt applied the embargo, there was no certainty that it would continue, and even less certainty about what action would accompany it.

Morgenthau was much concerned about both of these questions. Although he had played no significant part in the decisions already made, he was, as he intermittently indicated to the President, an advocate not only of what had been done but also of supplementing it as soon as possible by reducing the gold content of the dollar. While Roosevelt delayed decision about which, if any, of the powers in the Thomas Amendment to use, Morgenthau pressed Warren's case. "Warren is going to write a story . . . on the subject of 'gold,' " he wrote the editor of the *American Agriculturist,* "which I would like to go on the front page of our next issue. . . . Herbert Gaston will write the press release relating to this story which will be released from Washington." Warren also drew up charts showing weekly changes in prices of agricultural commodities and associating these fluctuations with similar changes in the price of gold on the world market. Morgenthau regularly took the charts to the President, who was impressed.

The test of Roosevelt's intentions came toward the end of June, just before prices had begun their downward plunge. There was then meeting in London the World Economic Conference. One of its crucial problems was currency. Most of the nations of Europe had left the gold standard, but France, Holland, Belgium, Italy, and Switzerland had not, and they wanted the conference to stabilize the gold value of currencies. Great Britain, after depreciating the pound sterling in 1931, was prepared to stabilize at 1933 levels advantageous to her.

For the United States the problem was different. The gold content of the dollar had not been changed. Had the dollar been fixed at the existing level, at its existing gold value and its existing ratio to European currencies, it would have been difficult, if not impossible, to raise domestic prices. On June 17 Roosevelt therefore rejected a stabilization agreement that would have committed him not to use the inflationary powers of the Thomas Amendment. On June 29, at his summer home at Campobello Island, where Morgenthau was visiting, he received a compromise proposal that endorsed the principle of stabilization but did not bind countries not then on the gold standard to work toward stabilization immediately. Those in London who had arranged this compromise fully expected the President to accept it; those at home who favored inflation opposed any international limitation on domestic monetary policy.

After hearing about the compromise proposal from Louis Howe, who was adamantly against it, Morgenthau with his usual candor noted in his Diary that he knew little about the issue, but on principle agreed with Howe. The compromise, Morgenthau felt, would have impeded or even prevented the devaluation he considered necessary. He had, moreover, received gloomy reports about London from his father, a technical expert at the conference, who observed that the prospects were "not at all hopeful . . . unless F.D.R. is very positive and takes leadership in his own hands." With this assessment, as she told Morgenthau, Eleanor Roosevelt by and large agreed.

The President had kept his own counsel, but on June 30 he gave Morgenthau the impression that he wanted first and foremost to raise prices, especially commodity prices, in the United States. Two days later he read to Morgenthau and Howe a message he had drafted for London. This chastised the conference for considering stabilization ahead of "larger purposes" and asserted that "the sound internal economic system of a Nation is a greater factor in its well-being than the price of its currency." The content and tone of the message dispelled any hope for agreement on stabilization at London. Morgenthau was delighted. "We were tied up hand and fist at the London Conference," he later recalled. "We had to break it. He broke it. I really had nothing to do with it."

Just a week after sending his "bombshell" to London, Roosevelt asked Morgenthau to bring to tea Professor Warren and two like-minded economists. Warren had just been in the West interviewing farmers. He felt that Wallace's voluntary allotment plan could not work and was not needed. Monetary action, he believed, could by itself produce "a striking improvement." The continuing decline in prices during the following month persuaded Roosevelt that he had to make some monetary change. At luncheon on August 16, he told Morgenthau that he would like to buy gold in the open market at more than the prevailing price, but he did not know how he could do so.

Late in September Morgenthau first learned that the Attorney General believed the President did not have the power to buy gold. Morgenthau immediately told Roosevelt that the lawyers in Farm Credit disagreed. At Roosevelt's request, he obtained a fuller statement about the issue. Herman Oliphant had already defined a legal basis for action. His fertile intelligence found various sources for the necessary authority, including, among others, two forgotten statutes of 1862 and 1864. After reading the memorandum Oliphant had prepared, Roosevelt commented, in great good spirits: "I have a method of my own to break the law which I think is much simpler." He proposed setting up a corporation under RFC to buy gold. Following his instructions, Morgenthau discussed that possibility with Jesse Jones, and together they suggested forming a new federal corporation to purchase gold, silver, cotton, and other commodities. The Attorney General tentatively endorsed this scheme, but Roosevelt, still uncertain, referred it to a group of lawyers from the Treasury and Justice Departments for further consideration.

While their inconclusive discussions rambled on through the middle of October, prices fell and the sentiment for inflation mounted. On October 16, the day Roosevelt asked Morgenthau to "do something about the price of wheat," Warren prodded them both to do something about the price of gold. "Things . . . are looking worse," he reported. "We have lost time since the middle of July." The longer the delay, he warned, the greater would the reduction in the gold content of the dollar have to be. By open-market purchases or other means, he advised, the price of gold should be raised rapidly to $35.25 an ounce (which would make the new dollar worth 59 cents of the old) and ultimately to $41 an ounce. The Agricultural Adjustment Administration, Warren wrote Morgenthau, was "about 10 per cent useful, 15 per cent political expediency, 25 per cent hot air, and 50 per cent" a measure that would "result in violent reaction unless prices are raised. . . . Rumors are current that members of the Agricultural Department have stated that they wanted the fall of prices . . . so they could be sure to get their plan tried." Morgenthau heartily concurred with Warren's assessment. Tired of talk, he found the President, when next they met on October 19, equally restive. That day the issue was resolved.

Among Roosevelt's advisers the outstanding opponent of Oliphant's memorandum on gold was Dean Acheson, the Under Secretary of the Treasury, whose chief, William Woodin, was seriously ill. Acheson, a dedicated and brilliant public servant, had an impeccable legal and liberal pedigree. A graduate of Yale and of the Harvard Law School, he had been private secretary to Associate Justice Louis D. Brandeis, and he had also been a junior member of the law firm of George Rublee, a prominent T.R. Progressive. But Acheson, like his friend Lewis Douglas, was never comfortable with the pace and the tumult of the early New Deal. Opposed in any case to manipulating the currency, Acheson worried especially about what he considered the ethical implications of embarking upon a policy of devaluation at just the time he was completing the sale of a series of federal securities to the public. If the dollar were devalued, the value of those securities would fall proportionately. That loss, Acheson felt, would violate the obligation of the government to its bondholders. He therefore resisted Roosevelt's importunities. As the President put it to Morgenthau, he had tried for six weeks to get the Treasury to find a way to buy gold, but it was "like punching your fist into a pillow."

Morgenthau and Oliphant were not alone in disagreeing with Acheson. The General Counsel of the Reconstruction Finance Corporation, Stanley Reed, who later became a respected Associate Justice of the Supreme Court, also held that the government could and should buy gold. But at luncheon at the White House on October 19 Acheson still balked. Morgenthau, exasperated by this round in the endless debate, suggested locking all the lawyers who had ideas on the subject in a room together until they reached a decision. "That's fine," the President agreed. "Let them go to the Attorney General's office and do it." They did, and they returned with the decision Roosevelt wanted, for Attorney General Homer Cummings ruled categorically — though he did not put his opinion in writing for some weeks — that the Secretary of the Treasury, with the approval of the President, had the power to purchase gold in the open market.

Roosevelt intended the Reconstruction Finance Corporation to operate as the government's agent in executing this policy, and he planned to finance the purchases by selling short-term obligations of that corporation. At the meeting of the board of the RFC to vote on these sales, Acheson arrived looking "like a thundercloud." "I am opposed to our buying gold," he announced. "The President has ordered me to do it. I will carry out his orders." But he left it to Morgenthau, who attended the meeting as Roosevelt's "watchdog," to work out the details of the program with the Attorney General. Morgenthau, Oliphant, and Warren also assisted the White House staff in drafting the speech which the President delivered Sunday evening, October 22, as his fourth Fireside Chat to the nation.

The RFC, Roosevelt then announced, would buy newly mined gold in the United States at prices that he and his advisers set. Whenever necessary, gold would also be bought in the world market. "The definite policy of this Government," the President explained, "has been to restore commodity price levels" that would enable agriculture and industry to give work to the unemployed, make possible the payment of public and private debts more nearly at the level at which they were incurred, and restore a balance in the price structure so that farmers might exchange their products for the products of industry on a fairer basis. "When we have restored the price level," he added, "we shall seek to establish and maintain a dollar which will not change its purchasing and debt-paying power during the succeeding generation." The permanent welfare and security of every class of the American people, he concluded, ultimately depended on the attainment of those purposes. "I have had the shackles on my hands for months now," Roosevelt told Morgenthau the next day, "and I feel for the first time as though I had thrown them off."

## 5. Gold Buying

Every morning, beginning October 25, Morgenthau, Warren, and Jesse Jones met in the President's bedroom to set the price of gold for the day. Roosevelt "would lie comfortably on his old-fashioned three-quarter mahogany bed. A table stood on each side; on his left would be a batch of government reports, a detective novel or two, a couple of telephones. On his right would be pads, pencils, cigarettes, his watch and a plate of fruit. Hearty and refreshed after a night's rest, he would eat his soft-boiled eggs" while the others reported on the behavior of gold and commodity prices.

The price that the morning conference established on any given day made very little difference. The object was simply to keep the trend moving gradually upward, a little above the world price, in the expectation that commodity prices would follow. To prevent speculators from guessing what the price of gold would be, the conferees deliberately varied the daily increment, choosing figures that sometimes seemed arbitrary but always served their original purpose.

On October 21, the day before Roosevelt announced the new policy, the price of gold in London, the world's largest market, was $29.01 an ounce. On October 25, the first day the RFC bought American gold, the price in London opened at $31.02. At Morgenthau's suggestion, Roosevelt directed the RFC to buy at $31.36. He put the price up another 18 cents the next day. At tea on October 28 he discussed the long-range program. Morgenthau had had a dizzy day buying wheat; there were rumors that France and Great Britain might refuse to permit American purchases of gold in their markets; criticism of the policy at home was increasing. But Roosevelt, imperturbable, set his objectives for January 1, 1934, as 10-cent cotton, 50-cent corn, and 90-cent wheat. To start to reach these prices, he intended during the next week to raise gold to $33.02. His schedule called for putting the price Monday up to $31.98 and then adding daily for five days 28, 12, 28, 20, and 16 cents. He considered this schedule sufficiently erratic to confuse speculators, sufficiently high to affect world gold and commodity prices.

Roosevelt stuck close to this plan, but small deviations from his original estimates for daily increases left him on Friday, November 3, with a range of from 19 to 22 cents to add to the price of gold — the original estimate had been 20 cents. The President that day took one look at Morgenthau, who was feeling more than usually worried about the state of the world, and suggested a rise of 21 cents. "It's a lucky number," Roosevelt said with a laugh, "because it's three times seven." Morgenthau later noted in his Diary: "If anybody ever knew how we really set the gold price through a combination of lucky numbers, etc., I think they would be frightened." But as he later realized, Roosevelt had relieved a tense and gloomy moment by pulling his leg. He had also, his frivolity notwithstanding, hewed close to the plan that he had set almost a week earlier, and he continued daily to raise the price.

At first the RFC bought only gold offered within the domestic market. Soon the price within the United States rose above the world price. Consequently the dollar was worth more (or, in other words, had depreciated less) in London and Paris than at home. Morgenthau on October 27 therefore pointed out that it would be foolish to go much further unless the RFC began to buy gold abroad. Only in this way could the American purchases affect the world price of gold and other commodities. Only in this way could the United States offset any effort of the countries on the gold standard or in the sterling bloc to prevent the dollar from depreciating in terms of their currencies. The President had hoped to confine purchases to newly mined domestic gold, but the persistent gap between the domestic and foreign price compelled him to agree with Morgenthau.

This decision, as they realized, had large implications. They could buy gold abroad only by operating in foreign exchange, traditionally the province of private bankers who bought and sold foreign exchange themselves or worked indirectly through the Federal Reserve Banks, whose policies they governed. By taking over control of foreign exchange the federal government would reveal even more than it already had the President's intention to manage the currency. That was bound to frighten bankers who believed that they alone understood the techniques of their calling. Furthermore, the initiation of foreign exchange operations would surely be considered a declaration of monetary war. American gold purchases abroad would close the gap between the domestic and foreign price and thus bring the exchange value of the dollar down to the levels Roosevelt set. This would appreciate foreign currencies, alarm foreign nations about their potential loss of trade, perhaps set off a wave of competitive international currency depreciation like that which had followed England's departure from the gold standard in 1931.

To take charge of the foreign exchange operation Roosevelt called upon the Governor of the New York Federal Reserve Bank, George Harrison, an urbane, experienced, conservative financier who was conscious and jealous of the traditional powers of his office. Harrison insisted on having full authority over the technical aspects of his job, to which Roosevelt agreed, but the President hesitated to accept the banker's suggestion that the United States talk with the British and French before beginning to trade in gold abroad. "Every time we have taken the British into our confidence," he remarked, "they have given us a trimming."

After further thought persuaded him to let Harrison go ahead, the President thoroughly enjoyed the shocked surprise of the Europeans. The French, Harrison reported, had nearly jumped out of their skins. Governor Montague Norman of the Bank of England, a diehard Tory whom Roosevelt called "old pink whiskers," heard Harrison's news about American plans with incredulity. "This is the most terrible thing that has happened," Norman wailed into the transatlantic telephone. "The whole world will be put into bankruptcy." Harrison's instinct was to reassure Norman, but Roosevelt and Morgenthau, picturing foreign bankers with every one of their hairs standing on end in horror, caught each other's eye and began to roar with laughter. Within twenty-four hours, Roosevelt told Morgenthau, he expected to "see the whites of the eyes of the enemies," and he expected Harrison to shoot.

By November 1, when operations in foreign exchange were bringing the Administration's gold policy into full play, the disciples of orthodoxy were vigorously attacking the President. As the month wore on and the price of gold moved up, the Chamber of Commerce, the American Legion, the American Federation of Labor, and the Economists' National Committee on Monetary Policy condemned gold buying and cheered Al Smith's bitter denunciation of the Roosevelt "baloney dollar." The President also had his defenders.

Spokesmen of the Committee for the Nation and for the Farmers' Union urged him to advance the price of gold even more rapidly, and in reply to Al Smith, Father Coughlin, the Detroit radio-priest and inflationist who was then approaching the crest of his astonishing popularity, gave his national audience their choice of "Roosevelt or Ruin!"

Within the government the conflict of opinion was most serious in the Treasury Department where Dean Acheson and others still opposed the President's policy. On several occasions Morgenthau openly expressed his annoyance with them. Once, after he had criticized Acheson for failing to prepare a formal statement on the price of gold, the Under Secretary snapped back: "Why don't you move into Mr. Woodin's office?" Morgenthau, hurt by this retort, replied: "Dean . . . I live each day for itself. . . . I am neither a schemer nor a plotter." Jesse Jones was unable to resist joining in the raillery. "What other orders have you for us?" he asked Morgenthau, who, again upset, said: "Don't do that to me, Jesse."

As long as Acheson dawdled, Roosevelt had to have someone outside of the Treasury on whom he could rely. On October 27 he had told Morgenthau that he could not decide whether to fire Acheson, who he had reason to believe had told a reporter that the Attorney General doubted the legality of buying gold. Two days thereafter, addressing a meeting of his advisers on financial matters, Roosevelt said that if he had not begun buying gold and other commodities, there could have been "an agrarian revolution in this country." He explained what Jesse Jones was doing for cotton and how Morgenthau was buying wheat for Harry Hopkins. "Gentlemen," he continued, "I have called you together to inform you that the question of buying gold is an administration policy. We are all in the same boat. If any one does not like the boat, he can get out of it." Looking around, the President added that he meant no one in particular but everyone in general. Nevertheless, to Morgenthau Acheson looked "very miserable and very sick through the whole thing."

Acheson's disturbance persisted, partly because the Attorney General had yet to put in writing an opinion sustaining the President's authority to buy gold, partly because economists within the Treasury questioned the wisdom of the policy, largely because on principle the Under Secretary himself still disapproved of it. On November 1

Acheson had a row with Jesse Jones about RFC procedures. About that time he left with Roosevelt a handwritten, undated letter of resignation for the President to accept if and when he wished.

Acheson's hesitancy, Morgenthau observed, was making government especially difficult. The time for contemplation had passed. Like Roosevelt, Morgenthau was engrossed in deciding what policy to pursue and only then with finding a legal foundation for it. While the Under Secretary of the Treasury was searching his soul about the legality and the ethics of buying gold, Oliphant, with Morgenthau's consent, was searching his library for authority to have the RFC buy silver, too. Many inflationists in and out of Congress believed that such purchases would also help raise commodity prices. The plan was not adopted, but in explaining it to Roosevelt, Morgenthau suggested jokingly that instead of taking it up with Acheson, the President first get the Attorney General to rule and then tell Acheson about it. "You devil," Roosevelt replied, "you are just as bad as I am."

"Well," said Morgenthau, "who taught me?" Roosevelt roared.

At the breakfast conference of November 13, the President asked Morgenthau to stay after Jesse Jones left. He said he wanted to talk about Farm Credit, but he began on a different subject. "I had a very interesting and confidential conversation with Mr. Woodin," Roosevelt remarked. "I have suggested to him that he take a leave of absence without pay." "I am going to write him a letter," he continued, "in answer to one which he has written to me suggesting that we get somebody to become Acting Secretary who knows government and knows finance." He paused. Then he said: "I have decided that that person is Henry Morgenthau, Jr."

Morgenthau was "so dumbfounded" that he "broke out in perspiration" while Roosevelt went on: "You made good for me in Albany, and you are one of the two or three people who have made an outstanding success in Washington, so let's you and I go on to bigger things. . . . We will have lots of fun doing it together." Still staggered, Morgenthau, as he recalled, "managed to get something out about how much I appreciated the opportunity . . . walked over and shook his hand."

On November 16 Roosevelt accepted the undated resignation of Dean Acheson, who held the office for which Morgenthau was designated. Later Roosevelt told Morgenthau that he had consulted no one about the appointment. Acheson first heard of the changes, according to his recollection, after the President announced them to the press, but Acheson could hardly have been surprised, for he had made no secret of his discomfort. In years to come he and Morgenthau were to work together effectively on different problems, and Morgenthau was to gain a large respect for Acheson's courage and integrity. In 1933, however, he felt Roosevelt had to let the Under Secretary go.

"The President," Morgenthau recalled years later, "wanted a Treasury Department which would play its proper role in his campaign on prices; he wanted a Secretary who would be loyal and would try to get things done; so he threw me in to plug the hole." Under his direction, the battle to keep prices up continued. The price of gold was raised to $34.01 an ounce on December 1, to $34.06 later that month, to $35.00 in January, a price that has remained unchanged for over two decades. It was not the President alone who was pleased. Walter Lippmann, publishing his column in the Republican New York *Herald Tribune,* derived "a sense of assurance" from the changes in the Treasury. "We are delighted in your appointment of . . . Morgenthau," the president of the American Farm Bureau wired Roosevelt. "We feel he is the friend of we folks and will help give us an honest dollar." "You are fortunate," wrote an officer of the Committee for the Nation, "in having a man like Mr. Morgenthau who will have the strength and courage to carry out the monetary policy."

Gold buying had less dramatic results than its advocates expected. By mid-November, the price of gold in London again lagged behind that set in Washington. The price of wheat did not quite touch 90, Roosevelt's objective, but after passing 89 in mid-November, slumped again to 85. While the government raised the price of gold 17 per cent, the price of cotton rose only 14 per cent, of corn 7 per cent. The general index of all farm products actually fell off a little during November and December in spite of the gold policy, the purchases of cotton, corn, and wheat, and the reduction in planting arranged by the AAA. But the average of thirty key industrial stocks increased in proportion to the price of gold, for the dollar value of these industrials reflected the inflation. Conversely, government bonds fell three points between the end of October and mid-January, for the real income their interest earned shrank as the dollar was devalued. These changes, however, did not restore the balance between agricultural and industrial prices that Warren had hoped to redress.

Yet there were important gains. When prices were falling and threatening to fall further, the President and his advisers reversed the trend. Devaluation ultimately facilitated a considerable rise in prices within the United States. This had been Roosevelt's objective. Devaluation also lightened substantially the burdens of farmers and other debtors. The deflation of 1930–32 had made their debts oppressive. The depreciation of the dollar permitted them, as Roosevelt had intended, to pay their debts "more nearly at the price level at which they were incurred." Devaluation, furthermore, was ultimately followed, as Roosevelt had promised, by stabilization of the gold value of the dollar.

Compared to what Roosevelt might have done — to raising the price of gold to $40 as the Committee for the Nation urged, to printing three billion dollars of paper currency, to remonetizing silver at 16 to 1 — the gold-purchasing program was modest. European nations on the whole resented the policy, but no nation had for several years shown much regard for the economic convenience of others, and in 1933 the pressure on the President was such that he had to do something.

Roosevelt and Morgenthau seized the particular tool that seemed best to them at the time, and they used it boldly. They made the manipulation of the value of the currency an open and admitted instrument of public policy. This in itself signified the intention of the New Deal to free government from the decisions of bankers who, whatever their talents, had fallen into the habit of timorous inactivity. It was a time for action, and only the federal government was at once willing and able to act. Roosevelt and Morgenthau had the courage to make decisions, to declare war on falling prices, thereby to encourage those thousands of Americans to whom further deflation would have brought calamity. They cast aside the monetary orthodoxy which, had it persisted as it did so long in France, would have impeded recovery. As the President put it, they unshackled themselves and the federal government.

This unshackling represented the best spirit of the first ten months of the New Deal, which energized the federal government as it had never been energized before. Some of the policies upon which the President relied in this period were carry-overs from the past. Others had later to be modified or abandoned. But the genesis and the duration of the efforts of the first ten months were less significant than was the determination of the government by positive action to try to improve life and opportunity for the American people.

That determination was the source of the exciting, satisfying, buoyant mood of the New Dealers. For a reporter from the *New York Times* Morgenthau phrased it very well: "There is a new sense of social responsibility and interdependence . . . implicit in the administration's policy. . . . It looks forward toward a more stable social order, but it is not doctrinaire, not a complete cut-and-dried program. It involves the courage to experiment. Behind it is the conviction that no prosperity can be permanent which is not shared with all elements of the population."

Morgenthau had particularly demonstrated a sense of social responsibility in behalf of the farmer, whose lot had been especially unhappy. The agricultural problem was far from solved when he left the Farm Credit Administration for the Treasury. Indeed he was dubious about the policies Wallace and Tugwell were developing. But he had the comfort of knowing that he had tried every remedy that seemed potentially useful to him or to the President. Morgenthau and his associates had bought gold and wheat and cotton, had sought new markets for surplus commodities, had expanded and reorganized the federal machinery for financing the farm debt, and had not only saved thousands of farms from foreclosure but also helped to arrest the deflation farmers could no longer have suffered. Morgenthau did not fancy that they had finished the job. He was happy enough to have begun it well.

As he left Farm Credit, he realized that his new responsibilities in the Treasury — he became Secretary in his own right in January 1935, after the dying Woodin resigned — would involve him in still larger and more complex problems. "When I was thrown into this thing in the middle of November," he reflected seven months later, "I was glad to be able to swim with the tide and not sink." He was never afraid of the water.

As much as his achievement in FCA, his dauntlessness won him promotion. Roosevelt could not afford, in a season of great crisis, to have around him obstruction or even reluctance. The President was not intolerant of dissent (he had permitted Morgenthau constantly to criticize the AAA), but he was impatient with the doubts that stifled action. The luxury of self-searching had to await a quieter time. In 1933 those with power had to use it fast and joyously.

Louis Howe, who knew about everything that happened in Washington and understood and loved his chief, congratulated Morgenthau on his new office. "People have gotten into the Cabinet," he said, "by past performance or by political record, but you are the first man to go into the Roosevelt Cabinet who earned it."

# III

## Miscellany of Office

### 1934-1938

### 1. The Department of the Treasury

As SECRETARY OF THE TREASURY, Morgenthau commanded the most extraordinary department in the federal government. It collected and disbursed billions of dollars a year, borrowed money, bought and sold gold and silver, supervised the national banks, and kept the government accounts. The Treasury did much more than manage the nation's finances. It also administered a multitude of services whose annual operating budget was exceeded only by those of the Army and Navy, and whose combined activities took the full time of the largest police force and one of the largest staffs of lawyers in the federal establishment.

Under the Treasury the Coast Guard patrolled the oceans for icebergs and the coastal waters for smugglers and amateur sailors in difficulties; the Bureau of Narcotics pursued peddlers of cocaine and marijuana from the Bronx to Nob Hill; the Secret Service guarded the President and combatted counterfeiting; the Bureau of Engraving and Printing manufactured dollars, stamps, and bonds; and the Public Health Service examined immigrants for contagious diseases, campaigned against syphilis, and studied American diets. In addition the Procurement Division built post offices and courthouses, arranged competitions for paintings and sculptures, purchased thousands of tons of cement for public buildings and dozens of footballs and baseballs for the recreational use of public servants; the Bureau of Customs examined the baggage of hundreds of travelers, evaluat-

78

ing jewelry, tweeds, pipes, and toys, apprehending both smugglers and petty chiselers; and the Alcohol Tax Unit rooted out moonshiners and bootleggers. Above all, the Bureau of Internal Revenue, a constant companion to every citizen, collected his income and estate taxes and his pennies when he smoked or attended the theater or purchased gasoline.

Over all this and more Morgenthau presided, carrying the final responsibility for what went right or what went wrong, making the final decisions about organization, personnel, and policy, at all times, as he put it, running his own show. His hours were long and intense. As he had for years, he arose at about six in the morning. He began his day by glancing through a few leading newspapers, usually the *New York Times,* the *Wall Street Journal,* and the Washington *Post,* reviewing reports taken home the night before, and often telephoning one or two of his staff who learned not to expect to sleep beyond seven-thirty. After breakfast he ordinarily walked the two miles from his home to his office in company with a colleague, discussing some problem scheduled for further consideration later in the day.

Arriving at his desk by eight forty-five, the Secretary usually checked first on international exchange rates and on the trading that had already begun in London and Paris markets. At nine-thirty he held his morning staff meeting, attended by six to ten of his top advisers. There followed mid-morning conferences with officials of the Federal Reserve Board, or with representatives of the State Department or of foreign countries involved in an international monetary agreement, or with members of any one of the half-dozen committees of which Morgenthau was chairman or of the dozen other committees on which he served. When Congress was in session, he was often on the Hill, sometimes twice a day, testifying on legislation or appropriations. Except on Mondays, when he regularly took luncheon with the President, he ate at his desk, often with a colleague, a congressman, a newspaperman, a banker, an economist, a businessman, or a visitor from abroad. In the afternoon there were more meetings, more telephone calls, more conferences, correspondence to read and to answer. He was fortunate to be home by six, and he gave several evenings a week to homework. Now and then he could fly to his farm for a weekend, but ordinarily his was a six-day week and his Sunday was as much a time for study as for rest. No one in Washington, saving only the President, had more to do; no one worked harder.

At one time when Morgenthau was particularly harassed, a group of college students asked him whether he favored the consolidation within the Treasury of a number of independent agencies. "We've got all the possible responsibility that any human brain can handle," he replied, ". . . and I hate to see any more responsibility thrown on the Treasury. . . . Morning after morning I've got to get up at six o'clock . . . and do my paper work at that time; night after night we have meetings at the house. I mean there's hardly a day that the day doesn't run fifteen, sixteen hours. . . . The human brain can just about assimilate so much and be intelligent. And I think that's the thing you've got to watch. . . . Don't throw too much on any one person."

The essence of good administration was to separate the important from the unimportant, policy from routine, and to delegate the less important and the routine to capable assistants. On this account Morgenthau recruited loyal, expert, and industrious aides to supervise the work of the Treasury's various branches. Four of his key people he brought with him from Farm Credit.

Herbert Gaston, appointed Assistant to the Secretary, took charge of all matters of publicity and public relations. One of Morgenthau's first directives instructed officers and employees of the Treasury Department to submit to Gaston all statements to the press or to the public, all speeches, interviews, and other news releases. Roosevelt had suggested this arrangement out of his impatience with Treasury subordinates who had given to the press stories critical of the Administration's gold policy. But Morgenthau was more interested in long-run efficiency than in short-run censorship. He explained to the Treasury Correspondents' Association, when it objected to the new order, that he was "not trying to keep you men from getting information. . . . You will get as much in the future as in the past." What he was trying to do was to keep track of "what is going on in the Treasury." In order to facilitate the work of the newspapermen, he soon modified his initial order by permitting section heads to give out factual and statistical information.

The Secretary himself met the press twice a week. With Gaston at his side, he usually read a prepared report about matters of current interest and then responded to questions. Although he was rarely really at ease during these conferences, and although he rather frequently went off-the-record, he kept on good terms with the correspondents who regularly covered the Department and, without playing favorites, established useful relationships with the Washington representatives and financial editors of the *New York Times,* the *Herald Tribune,* and the *Wall Street Journal.*

Morgenthau also brought with him Mrs. Henrietta Klotz, who had been his private secretary for twelve years. Long familiar with his methods of work, Mrs. Klotz, as he told the Treasury, had his "complete confidence." She handled his personal correspondence, attended staff meetings with him, and supervised the compilation of the hundreds of volumes of the Morgenthau Diary.

As General Counsel for the Treasury, Morgenthau installed Herman Oliphant, under whom he centralized the legal staffs of the many divisions of the Department. At first those who had become accustomed to the independence of decentralization tended to resist this policy, but the change proved fortunate, for Oliphant set an example of energy and dedication that inspired the Treasury's lawyers to do some of the most useful legal work in Washington.

William H. McReynolds, Morgenthau's Administrative Assistant in Farm Credit, continued in that capacity at the Treasury. A Republican, a product of the stern training of the postal inspection service, a civil servant experienced in the ways of the federal bureaucracy, McReynolds handled all matters of personnel and budget with a nonpartisan efficiency that charmed Morgenthau as much as it irritated Democratic job seekers and congressmen.

Good government remained for Morgenthau a commanding objective. He was doubtful about the mere theorist, the philosopher given only to reflection. As he explained when he was looking for a junior man to help with certain financial operations, "we could have an economist sitting here and he wouldn't be a damn bit of use." He needed instead practical men who had "trading experience."

Seeking talent wherever he could find it, he chastised the Commissioner of Internal Revenue for refusing to appoint one able candidate because she was a woman. There was to be no discrimination against women in his Department. He was determined, moreover, to keep capable people in the Treasury at all ranks by making their conditions of employment as desirable as possible. He personally saw to it that offices were well lighted and well ventilated; he ordered salary increases for groups of workers whom he considered underpaid; and he wrote letters of praise for meritorious service and letters of sympathy in cases of death or illness. An anonymous civil servant of seventeen years' experience and insignificant station told the Washington *Herald* "he knows his employees and has a kind interest in every one of them."

He was not interested in their politics. "I want to say a few words about my political creed which is a very simple one," Morgenthau announced at his very first staff meeting. "If we are going to appoint someone in the Treasury he has to be efficient irrespective of his politics; he has to stand on his own feet. We promote and demote entirely on merit. I will not fire someone because he is a Republican if he is a capable employee." He might have added that he would not keep an ineffective employee because he was a Democrat.

As time passed many of the faithful who had come to the Treasury with the blessing of the Democratic National Committee left, to be replaced by career men whom Morgenthau found in Washington or brought to government from the academic, financial or business world. Even Jim Farley was willing to cooperate as long as he could make the stenographic appointments for every assistant secretary Morgenthau selected. He asked only for three chances to fill any vacant clerical job, promising to stop there if Morgenthau found none of his trio satisfactory. As good as his word, Farley recommended competent Democrats and let the Secretary choose his important staff free from political interference. With the same freedom, Morgenthau consistently rewarded performance. The Treasury, once considered second only to the Post Office Department as a repository for political hacks, became a model of service. Morgenthau's standards, Eleanor Roosevelt observed, "must have seemed alarming to some of the old types."

They did indeed. Because officials in the office of the Collector of Internal Revenue in Philadelphia had violated the law by soliciting political contributions, the Civil Service Commission in 1934 recommended the removal of the Collector and the suspension of some of his subordinates. After Morgenthau had acted on this recommendation, the Collector complained that he had been working for the Democratic party since 1896, and that in 1932 he had led the fight for Roosevelt in the primary against Al Smith. "I think both your letter to me and your letter to Mr. Farley," Morgenthau replied, "reflect a very serious misapprehension on your part of the reasons which led to the request for your resignation. . . . You were asked to resign because the evidence brought before me indicated very clearly that pressure had been exercised by others in your office to compel Civil Service employees . . . to contribute to political funds in violation of the law. My judgment was that if you were ignorant of what was going on in your office, it revealed a woeful lack of capacity on your part to direct the office. . . . If I should be faced again with the same, or a similar set of facts, with respect to any other office under my jurisdiction, I could not act differently."

## 2. Public Health

Like any Cabinet officer, Morgenthau gave most of his time to matters of large policy, but he had to keep informed about detail and to be prepared personally to intervene to direct or to assist his subordinates. He therefore spent many fruitful hours with his colleagues in Public Health, Procurement, and the Treasury's police and enforcement agencies.

Morgenthau was proud of his appointment of Josephine Roche as Assistant Secretary of the Treasury in charge of Public Health. Miss Roche had stumped the West in 1912 for Theodore Roosevelt, served on the Commission for Relief in Belgium during World War I, directed the girls' department of the Juvenile Court in Denver and the editorial division of the United States Children's Bureau in Washington. As president for five years of the Rocky Mountain Fuel Company, she had been one of the few managers in the United States who was consistently a friend of labor. Morgenthau brought Miss Roche to the Treasury, he explained, both to see to it that the Department's employees were properly treated and to give her an

opportunity to apply her enthusiasm for humanitarian causes.
Working closely with the Surgeon General and with the Children's
Service of the Department of Labor, Miss Roche helped organize
emergency and long-range programs for the prevention of disease.
She was also the Treasury's representative on the interdepartmental
committees concerned with social security and with children and
young people. She succeeded in getting money from federal relief
agencies for state health programs, for federal enterprises in the
field of industrial hygiene, and for research on diet. When she temporarily left the Treasury to run unsuccessfully for Governor of
Colorado, Eleanor Roosevelt wrote her: "Of course the President
has told you how sad he was to have you go, and both he and the
Secretary are hoping very much for your return. . . . I want to tell
you how much I personally shall miss the feeling that you are in
Washington."

Miss Roche profited from Morgenthau's support and from his
assistance in finding funds for her use. Late in 1934 she brought to
him a group of state health officers who were requesting $10,000,000.
Morgenthau told them he feared the sum was beyond reach at that
time, but he asked how they would spend it if they had it. They
needed, they said, one million to promote research, one million to
increase staff, and the remainder to match local moneys to develop
state and county health services. The deficiency bill which Congress had passed had provided no funds at all, but Morgenthau
tackled the problem from the point of view of unemployment, put
together data on how many nurses and doctors were out of work,
and from Harry Hopkins's Federal Emergency Relief Administration got a grant to cover emergency medical care and part of the
rest of the suggested program.

A few months earlier he had managed to jolly Marvin McIntyre
into using his influence to persuade Roosevelt to approve an allocation for Miss Roche. On that occasion Morgenthau's vehicle was
a long telegram:

> This is my sad story and not too much to the point. A long
> time ago . . . we conceived the idea that the United States
> Health Service should be allocated a measly sum of one million
> dollars out of an appropriation of some eight hundred million

dollars. Certainly you cannot accuse the Treasury of being pig-
gish about its own money. This request . . . has been kicked
around from the Bureau of the Budget to the State Department
to the Attorney General and then strangely was lost. As a last
resort I called in the Coast Guard and ordered them to make a
search from coast to coast and yesterday I received an S.O.S. informing me that the Coast Guard had picked up a mysterious
bottle with a lost piece of paper in it. . . . Treasury intelligence such as it is informs me that the document is now proceeding by slow freight to the summer White House located
they tell me at a place called Poughkeepsie. Now listen, Mac,
this million dollars can do more good and get quicker results
than any other million dollars I know of because with it the
Health Service can give every member of the stock exchange a
shot in the arm. It can take the gold out of the teeth of the
bankers and remove the decay. Furthermore we will be glad
to furnish free veterinarian service to the whole White House
staff as long as the million dollars lasts. I forgot to say that the
purpose of this telegram is to ask you to personally escort this
much abused piece of paper to Hyde Park with the hope that
the President will affix his signature to the same and thereby
release a million dollars worth of good.

In 1936 Morgenthau gave the public health program a timely
lift by appointing Dr. Thomas Parran as Surgeon General of the
United States. One of the great practical humanitarians of his time,
Dr. Parran had impressed both Roosevelt and Morgenthau by his
work as Health Commissioner in New York State. He was their first
and only choice when the office of Surgeon General fell vacant. Because of the highly specialized nature of his office, Dr. Parran by his
own account frequently operated outside of channels, making his
own excursions to the Hill for authorizations and appropriations
and often dealing directly with executives in various government
agencies. The Social Security Act of 1935 had enlarged the mission
of his service, but he also needed and appreciated the continuing
good will of the Secretary. He got it because he stood for just those
things which Morgenthau most valued.

"The treatment of disease is no longer the concern solely of the individual who is sick; the community as a whole has a financial stake in untreated illness," Parran maintained. ". . . There are sound scientific, social and economic reasons for more aggressive attention to the public health. Yet there are those who would limit Public Health Service to sanitation, quarantine, and the care of the insane and the indigent sick. To accept this view is to ignore the inherent responsibility of government. I think we have reached the stage in our civilization when we must accept as a major premise that our citizens should have an equal opportunity for health as an inherent right." Parran was concerned not only with the prevention of disease, but also with the preservation of physical and psychic health, with the conservation of human resources. During a time of depression, he pointed out, it was incumbent upon government to protect the spirits as well as the bodies of the destitute, especially of the children, to combat malnutrition on the one hand and a sense of helplessness on the other.

Several of Dr. Parran's ventures particularly pleased the Secretary. One was the organization of a medical cooperative for a group of families that the government had relocated in North Dakota. Another was the establishment of the National Cancer Institute, the product of legislation sponsored by ninety-two of ninety-six senators. It set the pattern for all national health institutes by arranging for grants-in-aid to private institutions and individuals who needed funds for training or research. A third was the campaign which Dr. Parran waged against venereal disease. Although he was cut off the air when he attempted to mention the word syphilis on the radio in 1935, he soon succeeded in dispelling the taboos and he prepared the public and the government to understand and then to begin to eradicate V.D. The President, as late as 1938, wanted to restrict the federal effort to providing money for education and publicity, but Parran and Morgenthau persuaded him of the necessity for direct federal grants to match expenditures by local governments for the control of venereal disease. The Treasury's efforts to fight disease and to reduce the private cost of medical treatment were the essence of what Morgenthau considered reform.

## 3. The Division of Procurement

An Executive Order of June 10, 1933, effective four months later, established the Division of Procurement within the Treasury Department. This division was charged with determining policies and methods of procurement, warehousing, and transportation of all equipment and supplies for all federal agencies except the military services. It also assumed control of the Office of the Supervising Architect of the Treasury Department. The executive nominally responsible for the Division when Morgenthau took office was Assistant Secretary of the Treasury Lawrence W. ("Chip") Robert, a dapper Democratic man-about-town and friend of Jim Farley. The operating head of the agency, however, was Rear Admiral Christian Joy Peoples, the Director of Procurement, a regular Navy officer who had risen through the Supply Corps to the office of Chief of the Bureau of Supplies and Accounts. Peoples was a loyal, honest, and dogged man, a representative of the best of the Navy's tradition, and a veteran of many bureaucratic skirmishes. As his own summary of five years of work revealed, he measured his official life in dollars and cents. Its dimensions were not insignificant. Before the end of 1938 the Division of Procurement had purchased over $900,000,000 worth of supplies and spent over $400,000,000 on the construction of public buildings in more than 2400 communities.

By and large the Division of Procurement operated without incident, but on a few occasions it became the object of conflict between Morgenthau and Harold Ickes, the Secretary of the Interior. A Chicago lawyer and reformer, a T.R. Progressive, an avid conservationist, and a self-trained curmudgeon, Ickes was a man of unquestionable honesty, sensitive egocentricity, massive ambition, unblanching candor, and at times undisciplined energy — in Morgenthau's opinion, Washington's "tough guy." He and Morgenthau had a great deal in common, particularly their dedication to reform, to Franklin Roosevelt, and to the eradication of fascism in the world. In time they learned a mutual respect, but in the early days of the New Deal, each often found the other difficult to work with.

Their first important difference arose over the construction of a new building for the Department of the Interior. In his capacity as administrator of the Public Works Administration, Ickes in June 1934 allotted $10,000,000 for the new building. The Comptroller General, however, advised the Secretary of the Treasury that the Division of Procurement had exclusive supervision over the construction of public buildings. Only by specific authorization of the President could the Treasury turn over the job to the Interior.

Determined to spend what he took to be his own money, Ickes in October proposed that Admiral Peoples authorize the National Park Service, a unit of the Interior Department, to act as agent for the construction of the building. Morgenthau, however, hesitated to establish a precedent that might lead to the diffusion of the authority of the Procurement Division. He therefore persuaded the President to endorse an alternative scheme that put Ickes's engineers and architects temporarily on the Division's payroll. "This should clear up the whole situation," Roosevelt wrote both Cabinet officers, "and I see no reason why the work should not proceed . . . in the record-breaking time desired by the Secretary of the Interior." Reluctantly Ickes acceded.

He and Morgenthau had a more serious clash in connection with the letting of a contract for the construction of the Post Office Annex in New York City. In keeping with the administrative patterns established for such projects, Ickes's Public Works Administration allocated to the Post Office Department the funds for the Annex, but the Procurement Division was to supervise expenditures. Through the Division the Post Office requested two sets of bids, one for the entire Annex and one for the Annex with two floors uncompleted. One construction company in New York submitted the low bid for the entire building, another the low bid for the uncompleted building. At this point the Post Office advised the Treasury that the preferred contract was for the completed building. The company that this decision favored, it later developed, had failed to qualify under existing federal regulations until forty-eight hours after submitting its bid. Postmaster General Farley, furthermore, was alleged to have had a political interest in seeing this company get the contract.

Peoples and Morgenthau were totally unaware of these complications until after Ickes had ordered an investigation of the whole affair. The investigation was conducted by Louis R. Glavis, a Progressive martyr to stand-pat Republican politics in 1910 whom Ickes had brought back to Washington as a special assistant. Rather more zealous than reliable, Glavis never informed the Treasury that he was looking into the Post Office contracts, nor did he report his findings, as he should have, through Ickes to Morgenthau, Peoples, or Farley. Instead he turned them over to Democratic Senator Millard Tydings of Maryland.

At once disturbed and alerted, Tydings confronted Morgenthau with Glavis's report. The Secretary was dazed, "driven crazy," he later recalled, because he was "besmudged" for behavior of which he was "entirely innocent." He insisted that Tydings immediately go with him to ask Chip Robert about the contracts. After some delay, they found Robert in a Turkish bath. He unhesitatingly accepted entire responsibility for the negotiation, pointing out that Morgenthau had known nothing about it. Robert had not only cooperated with the Post Office Department in arranging for the letting of the contract but also had returned to that department a letter, subsequently there destroyed, which contained evidence that seemed to substantiate some of Glavis's charges.

Robert's candor dispelled Tydings's doubts about Morgenthau and confirmed Morgenthau's doubts about his Assistant Secretary. With the aid of Louis Howe, who was also outraged by Robert's conduct, Morgenthau urged Roosevelt to give Admiral Peoples the real authority to run the Procurement Division. The President, who had long admired Peoples, let Morgenthau proceed against Robert without interference in spite of the Assistant Secretary's strong political backing. Soon thereafter Robert decided to resign. Immediately after hearing Tydings's story, Morgenthau had instructed Peoples to readvertise for bids for the completed post office, thereby eliminating the possibility of favoritism for any contractor.

The matter did not end there, for in an effort to embarrass the President by attacking Farley, Senator Huey Long, the Louisiana kingfish who made larceny, brutality, and demagoguery the instruments of his power, introduced a resolution calling for an investigation. This resulted in publicity that would have been unnecessary had Glavis from the beginning kept the Treasury informed. Annoyed by this needless appearance of scandal, furious when he found

Glavis's charges against Farley by and large without foundation, Morgenthau was distressed most of all by Ickes's secret investigation of the Treasury Department.

At a Cabinet meeting on February 15, 1935, Morgenthau by his own account "got very excited and demanded of Ickes what he meant by investigating the Procurement Division." Ickes at first denied all knowledge of Glavis's letter reporting the investigation, but he later admitted that he would have to take the blame. While his spirited rejoinder was under way, Roosevelt wrote out a note which he held up to Morgenthau: "You must not talk in such a tone of voice to another Cabinet officer." Then, tearing the note up, the President pounded the table and told Ickes, Farley, and Morgenthau to get together. "I cannot have three Cabinet members disagreeing," he said.

When Morgenthau again insisted that Ickes had been investigating the Treasury, Roosevelt turned on him angrily and said, "Don't you understand, Henry, that Harold says he knows nothing about it and that ends the matter."

"I am afraid I am very dull, Mr. President," Morgenthau said. "I do not understand."

"You must be very dull," Roosevelt replied.

On returning to his office, Morgenthau wrote both Ickes and Farley suggesting a meeting. He also warned Louis Howe that Ickes might send a report to Congress instead of proceeding within the Executive Department. Later that day the President called Morgenthau. "He was most sympathetic and kind over the phone," Morgenthau observed. "I responded to his mood and we must have talked for about fifteen minutes." The Secretary reasserted that Ickes was not telling the truth about what he and Glavis had done, but Roosevelt ended the conversation by saying, "Stop worrying, Henry, go to bed and get a good night's rest." The telephone conversation, Morgenthau felt, came as close to being an apology as the President could offer.

On Sunday, February 17, the principals in the affair met at the White House. During that conversation, Roosevelt again pounded his desk and said: "My Cabinet has to get along with one another or I will ask them all to get out." Morgenthau then replied: "That suits me fine Mr. President but if you want your Cabinet to get along as well as our people do in the Treasury then you've got to tell Ickes to stop investigating other Cabinet offices." Roosevelt agreed, and there the issue was dropped. Unquestionably Ickes had been indiscreet and Morgenthau had let his temper run away with him, but Morgenthau, contrary to the account in Ickes's *Diary,* was innocent of any guilt in favoring one contractor over another.

Ickes did not immediately restrain Glavis, who continued to bring unwarranted charges against the Treasury and other departments, but in 1936 Ickes began to tire of his subordinate. Indeed he came to believe Glavis quite capable of framing people in order to make a convincing case. The ill feeling between the two Secretaries continued for some time, however, reaching a silly peak in January 1936 when Ickes took to sulking "in a very brown mood" because Roosevelt saw Morgenthau for luncheon every Monday. Immediately after Ickes complained about this, Roosevelt excluded Morgenthau just once from a meeting about certain appropriations for agriculture. "It seems so petty," Morgenthau wrote in his Diary that day, "that it really amuses me."

"The trouble with Ickes," he suggested to the President, "is that he likes to step on everybody else's toes but if anybody tries to defend himself he cannot take it." "That," Roosevelt said, "is absolutely true."


## 4. The Treasury Art Program

The controversies with Ickes over the Division of Procurement were infrequent and transient; the contribution of the Division to fine arts in America was persistent and penetrating. It began with the establishment of the Public Works of Art Project in the Public Buildings Branch of the Division in December 1933, as an emergency relief activity to aid qualified artists in need of employment. Edward Bruce originally suggested the project to Harry Hopkins, who willingly furnished funds from his relief appropriations. Bruce, who had practiced law and published a newspaper in the Philippines, became a successful professional painter after his business ventures in the Orient failed. He was an unusual man, combining a capacity for organization, a knowledge of politics, and a determination to help his fellow artists. Among his enthusiastic sponsors was Elinor Morgenthau, who shared his delight in promoting the arts in the United States and recognized his talent for making hard work the handmaiden of a sophisticated esthetic judgment. She awakened her husband's interest, and therefore the Treasury's, in art, and she constantly urged Morgenthau to assist Bruce, who also benefited from his acquaintance with the President.

Bruce's Public Works of Art Project divided the country into sixteen regions and in each appointed a volunteer committee to select and supervise artists. Completed works of art were placed in post offices, courthouses, and other federal institutions to provide decoration and to bring the names of the artists who had created them to the attention of the public. Before his funds ran out, Bruce had uncovered talent that otherwise might never have come to light in depression years, and had given experienced artists hope in a time of need.

Bruce's particular champion within the Treasury was Herman Oliphant, who found New Deal art refreshing after the "meretricious stuff" of the Hoover regime. Oliphant spurred Admiral Peoples to recommend the creation of a permanent section on the arts in the office of the Supervising Architect of the Division of Procurement. In October 1934 Morgenthau accordingly organized the Section of Painting and Sculpture with Edward Bruce as its consulting expert.

The new section had two functions. The Treasury Relief Art Project aided artists on relief by employing them to decorate federal buildings. The larger job involved picking architects and artists on the basis of merit to plan public buildings and to execute murals and sculptures for them. Morgenthau defended the Section from political interference and set the general policy for the architects on the staff of the Procurement Division. He wanted public buildings to be economical, handsome, and utilitarian. There were to be no more mausoleums. In the interest of both cost and beauty, there was to be little outside ornamentation. His instructions encouraged improvements in the design of federal buildings and also resulted in the substitution of cement as the common structural material in place of the limestone and granite which had previously prevailed.

With Bruce's assistance Morgenthau wrote the specific orders under which the Section of Painting and Sculpture operated. The

Section's mandate was to secure art of the best quality in such a way as to stimulate the development of art in America. This meant the employment of local artists so far as it was consistent with high standards, and the use, wherever practicable, of competitions in order to make merit the sole test of selection.

Bruce carried out his orders by inviting experts to form local committees to judge local competitions and by giving these committees complete latitude within specifications of money, space, and time. Only after the selection of a winning design were the envelopes indicating the names of the contestants opened. "I am glad to learn," Franklin Roosevelt said of this practice, "that . . . no attempt was made to seek out for special favor, artists of established name, but that the competitions were open to the unknown, to the young, and to established and famous artists, on exactly the same terms. . . . Youth and experience have had equal opportunities."

In October 1938, when Morgenthau changed the name of the Section of Painting and Sculpture to the Section of Fine Arts, he had a summary made of the work of the Section during the previous four years. It had conducted or was conducting ninety-six competitions for which almost five thousand artists submitted over ten thousand sketches. For the Post Office and Justice Department buildings in Washington alone, a special jury of six painters, three sculptors, and two architects examined over five hundred designs submitted by more than two hundred and fifty painters and sculptors. Seven hundred artists either had finished or were working on projects for which Morgenthau had obligated 1 per cent of building costs, to that time approximately a million dollars. Among the artists who had received commissions were many of America's finest, including Thomas Benton, George Biddle, John Stewart Curry, Reginald Marsh, Henry Varnum Poor, and Boardman Robinson.

The Treasury Relief Art Project had held the artists on its payroll to the high standards Edward Bruce set. There was no starving or skimping. The Project paid, on the average, $89 a month for ninety-six hours of work, and provided $70 to $100 a month for materials. Bruce arranged to exhibit much of the work he subsidized in galleries in Washington and New York, where critics were on the whole favorably impressed. They remarked, among other things, on the "astounding fact" that Bruce had recruited talent from all parts of the country, and on the "general high level of work." Even those who criticized the tying of art to architecture, a condition inherent in the mandate of the Section, praised the Treasury's desire to encourage American art.

Morgenthau made no pretense of being an accomplished critic, but at the opening of one exhibit at the Corcoran Gallery, he expressed his personal pleasure in what Bruce and the Treasury had accomplished. "It seems to me that there is a double gain . . ." he said. "It provides a new opportunity and a new stimulus for artists by permitting them to work on subjects of the broadest cultural interests with the knowledge that if their work is soundly conceived . . . it will form a part of a permanent exhibition. For the public it means a better opportunity to enjoy modern works of art and thus to develop that knowledge of and feeling for works of grace and beauty which is an essential part of a National culture. It means also that this age will be able to leave behind it, along with the achievements of the machine, a record of our art sense and our art progress."

### 5. Let the Chips Fall

As Secretary of the Treasury, Morgenthau had large and varied responsibilities for enforcing the law. Over half of the prisoners in federal institutions in 1934 had been put there by his Department. Some 5700 T-men served as White House Police, as intelligence or narcotics agents, in the Secret Service, as guards at the Treasury, the Mint, the Assay Office, and the Bureau of Engraving and Printing, in the Customs agencies, or in the Alcohol Tax Unit. Schools administered by the Department taught students about customs and tax law, accounting procedures, sleuthing and shooting. As commander of this largest of federal police establishments, Morgenthau demanded efficiency, aggressiveness, and incorruptibility. No statement he ever made carried more conviction and authority than his first and standing directive: "Let the chips fall where they may."

He had to review especially sensitive cases himself. Some of them were pathetic. One judge who had been an important influence for legal reform was married to a sick woman of enormous vanity and uncontrollable kleptomania. As he left with her for Europe in 1938, he asked the Treasury to let her return without going through customs. Customs agents, the judge felt, had been something less than considerate on previous occasions, and to avoid dealing with them, he offered himself to file a full declaration of all purchases his wife made abroad. Morgenthau acceded to his request, but the judge's wife tried to enter the United States with a valuable watch under her glove. She disclosed it and paid a $10,000 fine only after customs officers showed her a photograph of the watch which an informer had supplied.

Morgenthau considered the use of informers an unpleasant necessity. "It is one of the things that you are not so proud of," he told the press. "I once had to meet one of them; he wouldn't tell anybody but myself. . . . Fifty thousand dollars was involved. I went right into the washroom and washed my hands. Until the thing got through I felt soiled. It is not nice business, but it is there." So it was also with wiretapping, which was frequently indispensable for tracking down counterfeiters and narcotics peddlers. Federal law, the Attorney General ruled, prevented wiretapping in the District of Columbia, in interstate work, and within states with statutes specifically forbidding it. The Justice Department and the Treasury agreed to resort to wiretapping in other states only in connection with the most vicious crimes. In keeping with this principle, Morgenthau in 1938 instructed Treasury agents not to supervise lines without his personal approval.

To improve the Treasury's police work, Morgenthau in 1934 established the Committee for the Co-ordination of Treasury Law-Enforcement Activities under Harold N. Graves, his technical assistant. Graves, an extremely competent public servant, had been Superintendent of Insular Audits in the Philippines, Administrative Assistant to the Secretary of Commerce, and Executive Assistant to the Postmaster General. He now held regular meetings of representatives of the Coast Guard, the Intelligence, the Secret Service, the Bureau of Customs, the Bureau of Narcotics, the Bureau of Internal Revenue, and the Alcohol Tax Unit. By bringing together activities which had previously functioned independently of each other, Morgenthau and Graves were able to organize integrated offensives, first against smugglers and bootleggers, and then against international and domestic narcotics rings. In 1937, when Graves went to the West Coast to direct Treasury enforcement activities there, he was succeeded by Herbert Gaston, who in an interim report noted: "the good results which obviously have been secured — improvement in morale, added efficiency of the personnel, increased production and willing co-operation, all of which have brought the organizations . . . to the highest degree of efficiency in their history."

Developments within the separate agencies bore out Gaston's assessment. Elmer Irey, the head of the Intelligence Unit, received from Morgenthau the backing he had long wanted. Encouraged by the Secretary, Irey's unit cracked down on criminals with partners in politics and politicians with partners in crime. Private arrangements with the police had permitted many of America's most vicious gangsters to avoid arrest or conviction. They found it difficult, however, to escape prosecution for their persistent failures to declare their incomes and pay the federal government the taxes they owed.

Before Morgenthau took office Elmer Irey and his agents had dug out the evidence that led to the imprisonment for tax evasion of Al Capone, the lord of the Chicago underworld and the prince of American gangsters. In 1935 Irey's men began to investigate the affairs of four heirs-presumptive to Capone's notoriety. One of them, Johnny Torrio, Capone's predecessor in Chicago, had hidden his profits under a number of corporate aliases while declaring a taxable income for 1933 of only $18,000. In court Treasury investigators showed that this was a colossal understatement. Torrio had to pay $100,000 in taxes and penalties and spend two and a half years in jail. Moses L. Annenberg, who had built his fortune around a national syndicate for distributing race track information, tried to defraud the government by keeping his books in code. Special Agent Samuel Klaus and his staff worked five years to decipher it. They delivered ten hand trucks of records to a federal grand jury that indicted Annenberg, who pleaded guilty on the advice of counsel, accepted an assessment of $8,000,000 — the largest sum any individual charged with tax evasion ever paid, and was sentenced to three years in jail. It took five years and three trials for the Treasury to win the conviction, with a million-dollar settlement and a ten-year sentence, of Enoch L. ("Nucky") Johnson, the Republican boss of Atlantic City, New Jersey, who had made his money in horses, vice, and the

numbers game. His Democratic counterpart, Thomas J. Pendergast
of Kansas City, had collected indirect tribute from bookies, dope
peddlers, prostitutes and procurers while his political hangers-on
controlled local elections. Influential Democrats in Missouri and
Washington exercised "every ounce of political pressure," as Irey put
it, to protect Pendergast and several of his associates from conviction
for income tax evasion, but Morgenthau, undeterred, was "deeply
pleased" when Pendergast pleaded guilty and was sentenced to fifteen
months.

The Secretary pressed most avidly his campaign against Huey
Long and his gang of thieves in Louisiana. Long posed as a friend
to the underprivileged small farmers of that state whom he beguiled
with a "share-the-wealth" program, promising them free bridges, new
roads, free textbooks, and other boons to be paid for by the rich. In
fact, however, the state spent much of its income on projects designed
to enrich Long and some of his friends, and what they did not collect through taxation they gleaned from bribes. Bribing in return,
threatening or damaging those not susceptible to bribes, Long
brought to Louisiana a genial native totalitarianism. He hoped ultimately to extend this to the whole country, and as he bullied his
way through local and national politics, he succeeded for years in
frightening officials in both parties who should have had the courage
to strike back.

In 1932 one of Irey's agents had reported that Long and his associates were delinquent in their federal taxes, but Secretary of the
Treasury Ogden Mills, preferring to leave the issue to the Democrats, ordered Irey to suspend investigation. There the matter remained until Morgenthau's appointment as Secretary of the Treasury was confirmed. Three days later Morgenthau sent for Irey. "Get
all your agents back on the Louisiana job," he commanded. "Start
the investigation of Huey Long and proceed as though you were investigating John Doe." Morgenthau promised to protect the men
on the job from political pressure. In return he expected maximum
efficiency. "I want to see you once a week, from now on," he told
Irey. He meant it literally. After Irey had reported every week for
almost a year, he was short of information and skipped one meeting.
The next morning Morgenthau telephoned. "This is the Secretary,"
he said. "You haven't been to see me in eight days."

The Treasury planned to plead its first case against Joseph Fisher, a state representative who was a lesser member of the Long machine, next to try Abe Shushan, one of Long's intimates, and then, if these convictions were secured, to bring to trial Long himself or one of his two closest associates, either Robert S. Maestri, the Mayor of New Orleans, or Seymour Weiss, that city's official greeter, most conspicuous dandy, and most privileged entrepreneur. The program began well with the conviction of Fisher in April 1935, but on September 8 Huey Long was assassinated on the steps of the State Capitol. His successors in the Democratic command were more concerned with protecting themselves than with grandiose political ambitions. In return for federal patronage and leniency, they were prepared to swing Louisiana to Roosevelt in 1936. Morgenthau feared that some Democrats in Washington might now be susceptible to election-year temptations. Five days after Long's assassination he therefore told Irey not to lay off the Louisiana cases except on personal order from the Secretary.

When Shushan was brought to trial in October, the Justice Department suggested deferring prosecution until after the Louisiana primaries in January. But Morgenthau insisted upon moving the case ahead as rapidly as conditions permitted. Not a day passed, he told the President in November, but that someone tried to keep the Treasury from proceeding. Yet he would not desist, and he was fortified by Roosevelt's explicit approval. In Louisiana, however, the Shushan jury was sentimentally attached to the memory of the martyred Long. Although Elmer Irey thought the government's case was good, the verdict came back "Not Guilty."

The evidence for use in the next set of trials, scheduled for May of 1936, seemed strong. Fifteen gamblers and contractors had already entered pleas of guilty or *nolo contendere,* and the grand jury had returned indictments against Seymour Weiss and a number of others. Nevertheless, Rene A. Viosca, the United States Attorney in New Orleans, argued that the cases were weak because of the change in atmosphere since Long's death. Irey and Morgenthau suspected that this opinion reflected undue solicitude for the Louisiana machine. They tried therefore to have a special prosecutor sent to New Orleans, but the Department of Justice, though Viosca was admittedly soft, would not supplant him.

On May 29 Morgenthau reported sadly to Roosevelt: "Mr. President, I have to tell you something very disagreeable. . . . Within the past forty-eight hours the Attorney General sent a letter to Viosca in New Orleans telling him to use his own judgment in regard to the two Seymour Weiss cases. This morning Viosca appeared . . . and had the cases dismissed and Weiss did not even pay his taxes plus the penalty." Roosevelt was shocked.

Nine members of the grand jury that had indicted Weiss and others in Long's old gang sent a petition to New Orleans newspapers condemning the decision. "As to whether the cases are 'weak,' " the petition read, "this same United States Attorney . . . presented these . . . cases to us for investigation." The newspapers called the affair "the Second Louisiana Purchase." Morgenthau decided to push on. Though the Justice Department had refused to undertake the criminal prosecution, there remained the alternative of civil action. In 1937 he therefore brought suits against Long's associates for tax evasions.

Morgenthau hoped the Justice Department would assign Assistant Attorney General Robert Jackson to the Louisiana cases. A convinced liberal, a forceful speaker, and an able trial lawyer, Jackson had won a national reputation by his aggressive prosecution of the Mellon tax case,* for which Morgenthau had brought him to Washington. But success, Morgenthau came to believe, fed Jackson's ambition and made him cautious where he had once been bold. Before leaving the Treasury for the Justice Department, he had become reluctant to testify in behalf of unpopular tax legislation. He had objected to replacing Viosca in New Orleans. Now he refused to prosecute the civil cases.

Each case, Jackson argued, called for a long investigation of detailed items of profit and loss. Where considerations of graft or gambling were involved, the government's testimony was largely that of accomplices or otherwise unreliable people. The government's evidence, consisting primarily of unexplained bank balances, seemed to Jackson a difficult basis for proof. The Treasury's insistence on a no-compromise policy, he also believed, would mean the trial of between fifty and a hundred cases involving from two hundred to four hundred tax years and certainly not less than five thousand disputed

* See page 324.

items, as well as other matters of fraud and negligence. "Wholly apart from the inconsistency of such an assignment with my government work," Jackson wrote the Attorney General, "I am personally unwilling to spend the month in Louisiana which would be necessary to the trial of these cases, or to be committed to a task of such indefinite duration in the government service. . . . I have confidence that . . . these cases . . . should not be given an exaggerated position in public attention, but should be handled as regular routine."

Perhaps Jackson simply made an error in judgment. The cases were neither weak nor unimportant. Every individual whom the Department of Justice had refused to prosecute admitted guilt in the Treasury's civil actions and paid every cent the Treasury claimed. This was true of Maestri, of Seymour Weiss, even of the Estate of Huey Long. Although a jury had called Abe Shushan innocent, he also paid. In later years further investigations uncovered more frauds and tax delinquency and resulted in more fines and some sentences. The Treasury collected more than $6,000,000 overall. These gratifying results, Morgenthau believed, vindicated his policy.

## 6. T-Men at Work

In 1935 one of Irey's ubiquitous investigators submitted a report on the customs house in Buffalo, where the misuse of government property and the falsification of records had led to conditions which Morgenthau considered "awful." The Secretary immediately discharged the offending officials. He also summoned Thomas J. Gorman, the Deputy Commissioner of Customs, and gave him the choice of putting his house in order or being fired. "If you will tell me what you want," Morgenthau said, "I will see you through hell. . . . You have been here thirty years and I want to give you a chance. Let's get rid of the crooks in customs."

This admonition provoked a "perfectly magnificent" response. Grateful for the Secretary's support, Gorman a few days later submitted a directive which Morgenthau signed authorizing customs agents to conduct examinations without prior approval from Washington. This enabled the agents to disclose irregularities which political appointees in collectors' offices had previously covered up. The new procedure trapped those inclined to be careless with government funds. The increased probability of discovery, moreover, doubtless persuaded many to resist temptations once irresistible. The Customs Service remained, as it had always been, a favorite target of congressional patronage, but under Morgenthau it knew a novel discipline. With his backing Gorman became a first-rate executive.

Morgenthau was also effective in resuscitating the Secret Service, which was troubled not by politics but by the age and inertia of its chief, William H. Moran. At one time an able man, Moran, after forty years in the Service, had become a testy guardian of superannuated practices, resentful alike of change and of criticism. His procrastination and neglect so damaged morale that in 1935 some of the Secret Service men guarding the President took to drinking while on duty. Instead of dealing with this himself, Moran left it to the Secretary, who announced that in the future he would immediately fire anyone guilty of the offense. Understandably anxious about the situation, Roosevelt was pleased both by Morgenthau's action and by his supplementary orders requiring every Secret Service man to take a physical examination three times a year, to have target practice once a week, and to carry tear-gas bombs while on duty.

A year later the increasingly infirm Moran could no longer postpone resigning. Going outside the Secret Service for its new chief, Morgenthau selected Frank J. Wilson, a member of Elmer Irey's Intelligence Unit, who had done an impressive job in securing evidence that led to the conviction of Al Capone. On the basis of plans proposed by Wilson and Harold Graves, Morgenthau in 1937 reorganized the field work of the Secret Service, and Wilson revised the training program. He also called the first general conference in thirty years of all Secret Service supervisory agents.

Following the Secretary's instructions, Wilson began an eminently successful drive against counterfeiting. Besides conducting classes to alert merchants and bankers to dubious money, Secret Service agents in one three-month period called upon over a hundred thousand retail stores in greater New York, held over twenty thousand neighborhood meetings in the same area, and posted more than half a million notices describing the principal counterfeit notes in circulation. The Treasury had a film made called "Know Your Money" for showing at schools, police stations, and business meetings in all cities of over two hundred thousand people. At almost every showing an agent lectured, answered questions, and distributed copies of a folder explaining how to recognize counterfeits. This pamphlet was so good that the Chase National Bank of New York printed and distributed four hundred thousand copies at its own expense. Such activities led to the conviction of important groups of counterfeiters and to the precipitate decline in counterfeit currency.

The Bureau of Narcotics was free from political interference and blessed with a serious-minded chief, Harry J. Anslinger, but it too benefited from the Secretary's continual help. Morgenthau backed Anslinger's generally successful efforts to get the states to make their laws conform to federal narcotics statutes and to penalize offenders. He helped Anslinger's agents resolve jurisdictional disputes with officers of other Executive departments, and he encouraged them to intensify their own attacks on the vicious trade in drugs.

Much of the narcotics entering the United States in 1935 was brought in by passengers or crews on the steamship lines operating between China and Hawaii. Lack of cooperation from officials of the steamship companies had made such smuggling difficult to prevent. But, since the law provided only for a fine against the master of a ship on which opium was carried, company officials were immune from prosecution. While individual smugglers could, of course, be put into prison, Morgenthau saw the only permanent solution in forcing the companies themselves to take action. At a meeting of his staff he therefore proposed that the Post Office cancel mail contracts with the offending steamship lines.

An Anslinger subordinate commented that this might embarrass a bank, currently in receivership under the Treasury's jurisdiction, which had a large interest in the steamship company immediately involved. Morgenthau said that was just too bad: "Narcotics is a much bigger thing than any bank; the money involved just doesn't enter into it. I think it is up to the bank and up to us to know the character of the kind of people we are dealing with. And if the . . . line can't clean its house, we will do it for them."

A week later he sent for the president of the line, told him how a Canadian company had handled a similar situation by firing the whole crew of a suspect ship, and suggested that two or three Treasury men travel back and forth on his ships to stop the traffic in opium. Morgenthau said he wanted to be fair, but that he intended to be "hard-boiled." The president agreed at once to work something out with Anslinger. A few months later Morgenthau was able to report that the company was making a real effort to stop smuggling.

Nevertheless the Bureau of Narcotics failed to produce the results Morgenthau wanted. He hoped for better performance following a reorganization of Treasury enforcement agencies proposed to Congress in 1936. This reorganization would have permitted the consolidation of the existing agencies under a career official responsible to an assistant secretary and through him to the Secretary himself. But the State Department objected that international conventions required the maintenance of a special service with exclusive jurisdiction over narcotics. While Morgenthau felt that a consolidated Treasury agency would meet this standard, Secretary Hull and his advisers insisted that the Bureau of Narcotics had to stand by itself. Whatever the merits of their view, they carried their case in the Senate.

In the interest of efficiency, Morgenthau nevertheless put all investigative work abroad under the Customs Agency Service. At the same time he directed the Bureau of Narcotics to discontinue all contact with the Department of State on aspects of the international drug traffic, placing these negotiations instead in the hands of an assistant secretary. Although Treasury agents continued to report violations of international narcotics treaties by Japan, China, and Portugal, the State Department with frigid unconcern in January 1937 declined a Treasury request that its consular officers furnish regular reports on narcotics. In the absence of such reports, the Treasury had to do its own detective work, and in February 1938 Morgenthau informed Hull that drug smuggling was so serious it required an immediate increase in the personnel of the Customs Agency Service. He begged Hull to see to it personally that consular agents cooperated with Treasury men.

He also sent abroad Lieutenant Commander B. M. Thompson USN (Ret.), as his personal representative. Thompson, a veteran of the Treasury's campaign against bootlegging, stayed on for some time as an attaché at the American embassy in Paris where he concentrated on finding the organizers of the international drug trade. One of his early reports to Morgenthau revealed the nature of his work. "We are all busy as hell around here the last few days, lining up informers and chasing big-shot traffickers here and there as they come into our picture. We are having no trouble getting informers, the big difficulty being in weeding out the chiselers. . . . We have several men already working . . . in Paris and a couple we have sent to other ports. We call these boys the day shift. Then we have inaugurated the night shift, which is composed of women whom we are sending in to associate with known American smugglers. . . . The picking of these operatives has to be done very carefully, as the girls soon get wise to the racket of informing on both sides. . . . The Polish, Austrian and French police have all worked fine with us . . . so far." Thompson and his agents in Europe, and Martin R. Nicholson, the Treasury's effective agent in China, were able substantially to reduce the flow of narcotics at their sources.

Morgenthau personally initiated the most successful roundup of master-peddlers of narcotics within the United States. Impatient with the pace at which Anslinger's men had been working on the Pacific Coast, the worst area in the country for the trade, he sent Harold Graves and Thomas J. Gorman there in the fall of 1936. They discovered two smuggling syndicates, a Japanese group engaged principally in bringing in manufactured drugs like cocaine, and a Chinese group concentrating on opium. The head of the Japanese syndicate was Kanekaichi Yamamoto, a civic leader in Seattle who also controlled a number of gambling clubs. His Chinese counterpart was Lew Kim Yuen of Portland, Oregon, who had operated an opium-smoking den conveniently across the street from the police department, owned several gambling establishments, and made appointments to police vice squads all down the coast.

Graves and Gorman deployed for battle at a conference in October 1936. They sent experienced agents to each port on the Pacific Coast, arranged to install a number of telephone taps and to translate conversations in oriental languages, and assigned two narcotics agents, chosen for their special ability to mingle with the underworld, to communicate relevant information to the Bureau of Internal Revenue. They also had the Coast Guard watch all vessels arriving from the Orient in order to prevent the unloading of narcotics before disembarkation. At frequent intervals after the conference they inspected the activities on the coast, on each occasion bringing aid and exhortation to their corps.

By March 1938 they had routed their enemy. The once powerful Yamamoto had lost his influence, had paid $16,500 in taxes and penalties to the Bureau of Internal Revenue, and had expressed his urgent desire to leave permanently for Japan. Lew Kim Yuen, indicted by a federal grand jury in Portland, Oregon, had fled to China, forfeiting his cash bond of $5000 and leaving the Intelligence Unit with a lien of $40,000 against his assets for evasion of income taxes. In addition to these eminent violators, the Treasury had obtained convictions against twenty-six others and had seized considerable quantities of narcotics.

Perhaps the best test of the success of the drive was the way in which the price of drugs on the Pacific Coast skyrocketed. At the beginning of the investigation, smoking opium brought $50 for a five-tael tin, morphine about $50 an ounce. The price of morphine had gone up to $125 an ounce and smoking opium, when it could be procured, cost from $185 to $230 a tin. Morgenthau took large satisfaction in this accomplishment.

## 7. Postlude to Prohibition

The scope of one of his mandates startled even the Secretary. After a press conference on August 6, 1934, Morgenthau told his staff that the newspapermen "almost got my goat pressing me on the tax on liquor. I went a little bit too far and said that if I can't lick the bootlegger I would be willing to go home. I am afraid this statement will come back to roost sometime — but then I really meant it." No one who knew him could question his sincerity, but in 1934 almost anyone had reason to question his ability to carry through. During the decade and a half of prohibition no one had been able to "lick the bootlegger." As Morgenthau put it himself, "a whole generation

grew up, taking it for granted they could break the law and no one
would punish them." The failure of enforcement and the spread of
bootlegging, rum running, and organized crime had been the major
factors in persuading the American people to forgo their "experiment noble in purpose."

From the time the Eighteenth Amendment went into effect in
1920 until 1930 the agencies for its enforcement were within the
Treasury. In 1930 the Bureau of Prohibition, later renamed the
Alcohol Beverage Unit, was moved to the Department of Justice,
but some of its functions remained behind. On repeal of the Eighteenth Amendment in 1933, bootlegging ceased to be a violation of
moral law and became instead a lucrative form of tax evasion. An
Executive Order therefore transferred the authority for enforcement
back to the Treasury, but Congress in the 1934 and 1935 budgets
made no provision for exercising this authority.

Morgenthau pressed Congress for help. "This is a year to hit and
hit hard," he told the House Committee on Appropriations in 1934.
He would not "sit idly by and permit the illicit traffic to entrench
itself, and at the same time . . . millions of dollars in federal revenues to escape." Estimating that alcohol taxes would yield over
$320,000,000 in 1935, he asked the committee for over $10,000,000
for enforcement. The public would cooperate, he predicted, when
it understood that taxes on liquor would lessen other tax burdens.

Entirely apart from revenue, Morgenthau believed that law had
to be obeyed. While he awaited appropriations from Congress, he
arranged for the Treasury to receive funds originally allocated for
enforcement activities of the Justice Department. He also began
to mobilize field agents of that department. This proved difficult, for
he was obliged to recruit these men through the Civil Service Commission, which needed half a year to make the necessary certifica-
tions. But Morgenthau, refusing to give bootleggers a six-month
holiday, found a way to hurdle the bureaucratic barrier by selecting
men from a certified list of prohibition agents formerly employed by
the Justice Department. The Civil Service Commission approved
each of the seven hundred men who received appointments.

These retreaded veterans gave the Treasury temporary strength.
But in June 1934 Senator Kenneth D. McKellar of Tennessee introduced an amendment to the Emergency Appropriation Act, which

the Congress passed, depriving Morgenthau's agents of their salaries. While conceding that the Treasury had acted in good faith, Mc-Kellar objected because, by his reckoning, all seven hundred inspectors were Republicans. Twenty-six of the twenty-eight appointed in Tennessee, the senator said, had originally been named by President Hoover or by a Republican congressman from Knoxville. Senator Carter Glass of Virginia, speaking to the same point, observed ruefully that of twenty-three "carpet baggers" operating in Virginia, only three were Democrats.

Although he realized that it was "a helluva risk to buck McKellar," Morgenthau could not afford to lose his force or their large accumulation of experience. He therefore asked an opinion from the Attorney General, who ruled that the inspectors might continue in the service "in a duty status without pay." There the Secretary kept them until he was able three months later to get them back on the payroll.

In August an Executive Order concentrated all phases of liquor law enforcement in the Bureau of Internal Revenue. Morgenthau then created within that bureau the Alcohol Tax Unit. One of its two branches supervised the legitimate industry. The other, the enforcement branch, investigated and prosecuted violations of the laws.

The Alcohol Tax Unit worked out the complex regulations governing the sale and use of revenue stamps, the production and licensing of whiskey bottles, and the installation of brewery meters. It deliberately prevented the bulk distribution of alcoholic beverages, for that was hard to police. In 1935, however, the Ways and Means Committee of the House of Representatives proposed legalizing the sale of distilled spirits in wooden barrels or kegs. At least one member of the committee, Congressman Claude A. Fuller of Arkansas, expected this to increase the sale of oak staves made in his district. But the committee's main argument was that the change would bring down the price of liquor and help break an alleged bottle monopoly.

Meeting with the committee on June 24, Morgenthau warned that permitting some two hundred thousand retailers to do their own bottling would invite a new wave of bootlegging. Existing bottling procedures added only nine cents to the retail price. He had no quarrel with Fuller's desire to provide good, cheap whiskey, but it could already be had at $1.25 a quart. When the congressman questioned his figure, Morgenthau sent out three men, who returned in those idyllic days with four quarts of whiskey, one costing $1.00, three $1.25. Oddly no one volunteered to sample the specimens, but the opinion was unanimous that they smelled all right. Although this tactic justified the existing price, the committee abandoned its passion for oak barrels only after Morgenthau agreed to its proposal for placing within the Treasury the Federal Alcohol Control Administration. The Secretary believed that this agency for licensing firms in the liquor business had no place in his Department, but, as he put it to his staff, the issue was not "nearly as important as the sale of bulk liquor."

While the supervisory branch of the Alcohol Tax Unit was developing techniques of regulation, Morgenthau in the summer of 1934 directed the enforcement branch to close in on the bootleggers. It was not worth while, he felt, "from the standpoint of life or money to enforce the . . . laws in the Alleghany Mountains." Revenue agents had been "going out after 5 and 10 gallon stills, which were unimportant, and the people with a suite of rooms at the Waldorf they didn't dare touch." He "just reversed the whole thing." By the end of 1935 Treasury agents had seized 24,000 stills, many of them large plants, arrested 48,000 persons, and obtained 24,000 convictions carrying an average sentence of about a year and an average fine of about $350. Illicit traffic fell off as the government apprehended a much higher proportion of liquor-law violators than during the period of prohibition.

Another phase of enforcement involved the policing of the retail trade. In January 1935 Morgenthau himself opened the campaign, arranging with Mayor La Guardia and Governor Lehman of New York for a "three cornered drive of Federal, State and City" officials against the sale of liquor on which no taxes had been paid. The success of their block-by-block canvass made it easy to persuade Governor Horner of Illinois to cooperate in a comparable effort in Chicago. There followed joint federal-state-local projects in Philadelphia, Pittsburgh, Buffalo, Milwaukee, San Francisco, and Los Angeles, where once every month or quarter Treasury agents inspected "all liquor package stores, and all restaurants, hotels, clubs, and tap rooms." In September 1935 Morgenthau extended the system to almost all cities with populations over a hundred thousand, thereby covering about 40 per cent of the liquor dealers in the country. By March 1936 these municipalities were "virtually free from illicit liquor traffic."

The Secretary recruited the federal agents for all of the joint projects from white-collar workers on relief for whom Harry Hopkins was anxious to find jobs. Choosing unemployed lawyers or accountants or men of similar experience on the basis of their competence and need, the Treasury swore them in as Deputy Collectors of Internal Revenue. They performed admirably, resented only by Tammany Hall, which complained because local Democratic leaders in New York were not consulted about the selections.

Smuggling, which during prohibition had brought into the country as much as twenty million gallons of spirits a year, presented a special problem of enforcement, for the Treasury had to have help in policing the foreign bases from which smugglers worked. Partly by trading concessions in international monetary policy for this assistance, Morgenthau induced France to place an embargo on spirits moving from St. Pierre, and England to take similar action at St. Johns, Newfoundland, and Belize, British Honduras. Cuba and Mexico also adopted regulations which the Treasury recommended.

With the Western Hemisphere effectually closed to them, smugglers hired tramp steamers from European ports to enter the waters adjacent to the United States or Canada for the transfer of cargoes in small boats. In 1936 most of these steamers were sailing from Antwerp. Morgenthau urged the State Department to denounce the trade agreement between Belgium and the United States unless the Belgians were willing to cooperate with the Treasury. "Considerable pressure" would be needed, he observed, because "certain high officials of the Belgian Government were supposed to be members of the syndicate . . . responsible for the illicit traffic." The State Department preferred to discuss the situation with the Belgian ambassador, who promised Morgenthau that Belgium would do her part in return for the Secretary's help in stopping "the disagreeable articles in the newspapers."

Meanwhile the Treasury had acted to prevent smuggling from the Bahamas and from mother ships which lay outside of the customs

waters of the United States waiting to transfer their cargoes to small
vessels. "Franklin," Morgenthau had told the President in 1934,
"this three-mile limit is no goddam good. They sit there till it's dark
and then they run it in." The President, Morgenthau recalled, had
"the War of 1812 at his finger tips — search and seizure and all that.
I'm not a very good historian. He said let's take off all limits. Let's
have the Coast Guard cutters surround the boats and starve the bastards out. Make them go back to the Bahamas and dump their
load."

Morgenthau ordered the Coast Guard to patrol close to the Bahamas and intercept the fast boats that raced from those islands to
the Florida coast. He and Roosevelt also supported antismuggling
legislation which Congress passed in 1935. The new law redefined
customs waters and made hovering more difficult. It also subjected
to fine or imprisonment Americans convicted of smuggling into a
foreign country provided that that country established penalties for
its nationals smuggling into the United States. The Department of
State had looked with some disfavor on this effort "to purify the
seas" by legislation instead of by negotiations, but the Act served its
purpose. By March 1936 the Treasury had broken "the backbone of
the liquor smuggling operations." Volume had been "reduced to a
mere trickle compared with what it was," and close and constant
supervision reduced it still further during the next few years. Morgenthau had no occasion to go home — he had "licked the bootleggers."


## 8. Retributive Justice

Morgenthau had also exacted a kind of retributive justice against
some of the mighty of the Volstead era. There remained at large in
1934 such gaudy figures as Arthur Flegenheimer, alias Dutch Schultz,
one of the most repellent of the racketeers who had grown rich on
prohibition. To Morgenthau, Schultz represented a symbol of gangsterism that had to be erased. He early suggested to the administrator of the Distillers Institute that that organization, as a means of
dramatizing the distinction between business and bootlegging, offer
a reward of $10,000 for the apprehension of Schultz. When this

came to nothing, Morgenthau on November 1, 1934, took action of his own. He telephoned Mayor La Guardia of New York and J. Edgar Hoover of the FBI, pointing out that the Treasury wanted "this fellow" for income tax and other violations, and asking them to forget the differences among the Treasury, the New York police, and the FBI. La Guardia and Hoover promised their full cooperation and agreed to put Schultz down "as kind of public enemy number one secretly."

With the net closing around him, Schultz on November 28 gave himself up to the Department of Justice at Albany, New York. Hoover at once phoned Morgenthau to try to arrange to turn Schultz over to Treasury officials, hoping to set bail at $100,000 but Schultz refused to sign the waiver necessary to permit his transfer to the jurisdiction of the Southern District of New York, where indictments against him had been returned. He was acquitted on two different charges, largely, as Thomas E. Dewey told Morgenthau, because the trials "were so badly handled . . . that they couldn't get a conviction." Dewey, who was then becoming nationally celebrated as special prosecutor for the New York Racket and Vice Investigation, intended to try Schultz a third time himself. But before he could complete his plans, unknown assailants shot the "last of the big gangsters" in October 1935. Dewey did, however, successfully prosecute Schultz's attorney, J. Richard ("Dixie") Davis. Morgenthau then turned the Treasury "inside out" to provide Dewey with the records of agents who had worked on the Schultz case.

Morgenthau was curious about the structure of the liquor industry as it emerged from the prohibition years. He therefore commissioned Samuel Klaus to make a special investigation of the alleged existence of a "whiskey trust." Klaus reported that there was "an effective *entente cordiale*." Fourteen distillers produced 95 per cent of the spirits manufactured in the United States. They had various connections with British and French cartels and Canadian firms, and with manufacturers of industrial alcohol, bottles, corks, and barrels. The Department of Justice, reflecting the indifference of the early New Deal to antitrust problems, blinked at the conditions Klaus criticized, but his findings convinced Morgenthau that would-be monopolists within the United States were working closely and surreptitiously with major firms in the liquor industry in Canada.

He knew in any case that at the time of repeal domestic bootleggers still had forty or fifty million gallons of illicit liquor, much of it produced in Canada. In June 1934 they sent a group of respectable New York attorneys to Morgenthau with an offer to pay the excise on the liquor in order to make it available for distribution; but with Roosevelt's commendation, he refused to legalize any production of the prohibition years. He intended, moreover, to collect the taxes owed the federal government by Canadian distillers who during prohibition had marketed much of their whiskey through American bootleggers.

The distilling industry in Canada, unimportant before the advent of prohibition in the United States, grew rapidly after 1919. There had been only five distilleries in the Dominion; by 1933 there were twenty-one. Some Canadian companies purchased American machinery, appropriated American brand names, and on occasion even counterfeited revenue stamps. To meet the competition of American firms bootlegging liquor produced illicitly within the United States, these Canadians maintained agents across the border, financed operations of American gangs handling their merchandise, and used the ruthless techniques of organized crime to broaden their market.

The Canadian government at first more or less ignored these ventures. The distillers used every stratagem to clothe their operations with the color of legality, and the theory apparently prevailed in Ottawa that they were within the Canadian law. The government in any case was loath to discourage a growing industry even though it was surrounded by corruption.

In 1925, however, Canada signed a treaty requiring her to give notice to American customs officers of all prospective consignments of liquor to points in the United States, and in 1930 Canada prohibited all clearance of liquor for delivery to the United States. Canadian companies then simply changed their methods. Whereas previously they had moved whiskey directly across the border, they now made their shipments to intermediate points like Belize or St. Pierre. As it worked out, they profited from the change, for it exempted them from payment of a Canadian tax of seven dollars a gallon.

At the time of repeal, the Federal Alcohol Control Administration set up a permit system for distillers and importers, granting permits automatically where there was no evidence of conviction for bootlegging. Since Canadian bootleggers by remaining outside the United States had avoided convictions, many Canadian firms easily obtained permits that let them liquidate their stocks of whiskey or re-establish their businesses in the United States. Some concerns disposed of their inventories by sales to American interests, while others simply brought their whiskey over the border to their own warehouses.

These transactions interested the Treasury, which suspected that several Canadian companies had not only violated smuggling and prohibition laws but also evaded income, customs, and excise taxes. As they now began to dispose of their assets, the Treasury pressed its tax claims. The Department faced the problems of obtaining data with which to prove its cases and of acquiring jurisdiction over defendants who were present in the United States, if at all, only through complicated legal aliases of affiliated and subsidiary corporations. The Treasury had also to make sure that if it obtained judgment after the delays of litigation there would be assets in the United States out of which to collect the claims. Merely obtaining a judgment was not enough, for Canadian courts would not impound Canadian assets.

Treasury agents got permission to examine customs and tax records in Ottawa, but after one day the Canadians realized what they were up to and closed the files. Although the Treasury believed Canada had by treaty to make the records available, the State Department would not press the point, and Morgenthau had to negotiate for himself. Prime Minister Bennett proved cooperative. "Henry Morgenthau and I have been friends," he remarked; "we're going to clean up this damn smuggling thing and that's all there is to it." But in 1935 William Lyon Mackenzie King succeeded Bennett as Prime Minister and reversed his predecessor's policy.

At that time the Treasury had prosecuted only one case, a suit for which the available evidence was quite strong. Nevertheless the government settled its $17,000,000 claim for $700,000, of which $200,000 represented the bond forfeited by the defendants, who had been apprehended in the United States on criminal charges but then jumped their bail. They escaped legal attachment in the United States simply by selling their Canadian inventories F.O.B. Vancouver, payment at Vancouver.

To defeat this kind of evasion the Federal Alcohol Control Administration advocated an embargo against the product of any foreign distiller who refused after a suit had been instituted to submit to the jurisdiction of United States courts. The State Department feared this regulation would restrict foreign trade and induce foreign nations to retaliate, but with the endorsement of the Justice Department, the Treasury nevertheless included the embargo in one chapter of the Omnibus Liquor bill, which the House of Representatives passed unanimously in 1935.

Late in August the Canadian Minister to the United States protested. Canada felt that the assistance it had already rendered was sufficient to accomplish the Treasury's purposes. Morgenthau disagreed. He became especially wary in November when the Department of State showed him a draft of the proposed Trade Agreement between Canada and the United States which, among other things, reduced the tariff on whiskey from $5 to $2.50 a gallon, a boon for the Canadian exporters.

Frankly worried about the outcome of the Treasury's claims against the Canadian distillers for $50,000,000, Morgenthau reminded the State Department "that every fancy lawyer in New York and Washington has been hired . . . and all sorts of heavy pressure" had been brought to bear on the matter. Morgenthau therefore "refused to take the responsibility for the loss of the claim until after the . . . Justice Department had a chance to study the matter and until he talked to the President." Roosevelt allowed him to delay decision for forty-eight hours. The Secretary then approved the reduction of the whiskey tariff only in return for an understanding that the Trade Agreement would have no effect upon the claims. In a memorandum to the State Department the Treasury insisted that the agreement was not to be interpreted to indicate the abandonment of pending cases, nor was it in any way to deter the Omnibus Liquor bill from limiting the right of Canadian distillers to export their products to the United States. Before signing the Trade Agreement on November 15, the Canadian Under Secretary of State for External Affairs, according to a report from the State Department, accepted the Treasury memorandum "without question."

In January 1936, however, Canada began to construe the memorandum as a statement by the Treasury and not by the United States government. Adoption of the embargo provision in the liquor bill, the Canadians asserted, might nullify completely the concession on whiskey in the Trade Agreement and effectively prevent the operation of Canadian firms in the United States even if they did submit to the jurisdiction of American courts. Should the Senate pass the bill with the embargo in it, the Canadians would therefore consider recourse to the termination clause in the Trade Agreement.

Now Treasury and State came to a parting of the ways. The State Department, anxious as always about Hull's trade agreements, advised the Senate Finance Committee that it objected to the embargo. The committee therefore postponed further hearings on the bill until the two departments could discuss the possibility of a draft less objectionable to Canada.

The Treasury was prepared to assure the Canadians preferred treatment, though not to abandon the embargo. The State Department at first agreed, but on March 17, while interdepartmental conferences were still going on, the Canadian Parliament again debated the issue. Thereafter the State Department felt "forced to do everything in its power" to protect the Trade Agreement. The Department was "not so much concerned with the exact merits of the . . . proposition as with what the Canadians think about it."

Convinced that the Canadians would in no circumstances abandon the Trade Agreement, since that would mean a return to a $5 duty on whiskey, Morgenthau would not yield. On March 12 he had discussed the affair with Roosevelt, who gave him permission to stick by his guns. But the President also permitted Secretary Hull's associates to express their views to the Senate Finance Committee. Although they asserted that the President wanted the embargo killed, Harold Graves told Morgenthau that the Treasury's friends on the Finance Committee were ready "to carry the question to the floor in the event that the disputed provision was omitted from the bill."

Roosevelt now interceded. At the very least, he suggested to

Hull, the Canadian companies should give some "practical assurance" that they would come into court and pay any judgment that might be obtained against them. In that case no legislation would be necessary. If their representatives would give the Treasury better evidence of their intention to go through with a proper agreement, Roosevelt observed, the matter could be negotiated, but thus far the distillers' lawyers had been vague and elusive.

Informed of Roosevelt's views, Prime Minister Mackenzie King instructed his minister to Washington to urge a conference between the distillers and the Treasury Department. It might have been hard to arrange had not Morgenthau left for Georgia to recuperate from a short illness. It was "very repugnant to him to consider sitting down and talking" with men he considered unscrupulous violators of American law. But he let his subordinates confer, and he followed their progress by talking with his office daily on the telephone.

Canadian Minister Hume Wrong, the lawyers for the distillers, and representatives of the Treasury and State Departments met on March 30. The Treasury faced a virtual alliance of all the others. The Canadians began by objecting to the pending legislation as unjust and discriminatory. They held that they could not be expected to give "practical assurances" until the Treasury revealed what the amounts of the claims would be, and that even then assurances would require the authorization of boards of directors and stockholders. But the Treasury's attorneys were neither prepared nor authorized to discuss policy matters. They wanted instead to hear about the "practical assurances" for which Roosevelt had asked. The Canadians finally offered to negotiate the claims whenever they were made and to "consider" not disposing of assets during that time.

These proposals, Graves and Oliphant agreed, fell far short of the Treasury's demands. After a telephone conference with Morgenthau, they advised Secretary of State Hull that since the Canadians were unable "to suggest any assurances within the scope of the President's instructions," the Treasury was "compelled to request the Senate Finance Committee to proceed with its consideration of the legislation."

Hull immediately sent a long telegram to Roosevelt, who was

then vacationing at sea. The Canadians, he reported, had proposed before leaving Washington that the Treasury Department drop the embargo for a month. In that period the distillers would regulate their exports so that there would be an ample quantity of whiskey against which the Treasury could proceed if necessary. The Canadian government would use its good offices insofar as possible to insure compliance. The distillers, moreover, would discuss with Treasury officials the nature and amount of the claims and try to reach some solution. If the Treasury then still believed the embargo necessary, the Canadian government would not interpose serious objection to it. In any case, the Canadians urged holding up the proposed legislation until the President returned to Washington so that they might present their views directly to him.

Roosevelt on April 3 wired Hull asking him to give Morgenthau the gist of this new proposal. "Tell him from me," the President instructed, "that some form of temporary settlement similar to your suggestion seems advisable and that I hope State and Treasury can agree to a formula. If no such formula can be arranged ask Treasury . . . to hold things in abeyance until I get back." Morgenthau and his associates objected to what they considered the Canadian tactics of delay, but on April 13 they accepted Hull's proposal with minor modifications, as did the Canadian government.

Conferences with the companies began on April 20. These proved fruitless, for the distillers did not consider themselves obligated by their government's negotiations and the Americans felt that the distillers were not proceeding in good faith. Although the matter had become an important political issue in Canada, Morgenthau decided to exercise his prerogatives and advise the State Department of his intention to request the Senate to pass the embargo. On May 11, with the thirty days allowed for negotiation running out, he explained his position to the President. "Cordell Hull will be heart-broken," Roosevelt said, ". . . but don't worry that they will cancel the Canadian Treaty, they never will."

The Treasury's intention to proceed with the legislation had in the meantime somewhat chastened the distillers. During the negotiations they had offered a settlement of about $2,500,000.

The Treasury, claiming over $53,000,000, indicated a willingness to take $6,000,000. On May 12, a day before the end of the truce, the Canadians raised their ante to $3,000,000. The Treasury still wanted more, but Roosevelt put "terrific pressure" on Morgenthau to concede. As the Secretary explained it, "the President said that normally he would say that if they offered us three million and we are asking six . . . million he would want one-half of the difference. . . . On account of the 'good neighbor' policy he will start between zero and what the Treasury wants and split that in half."

Morgenthau would like to have exacted larger punishment, but there was some compensation. Though the companies never admitted any guilt, the Treasury never exonerated them, and the concessions the Secretary made did not seem to him to compromise his moral position. Furthermore, Roosevelt in the spring of 1936 was especially anxious to appease Hull on the Canadian question because he supported Morgenthau's position on a larger issue, one involving the Nazi government of Germany whose current practices were more significant than were the past misdeeds of the distillers.*

The case of the Canadian distillers revealed the intensity of Morgenthau's commitment to his responsibilities. His prosecution of Boss Pendergast in Kansas City and the Long gang in Louisiana had its equivalent in his dealings with the whiskey companies. No federal official during the entire history of prohibition had been more uncompromising toward bootleggers. While Morgenthau's forthrightness complicated Cordell Hull's relations with a good neighbor, the niceties may have been on the side of the Department of State, but with them, Morgenthau believed, there went a kind of appeasement. The boldness was the Treasury's, for Morgenthau would no more appease gangsterism abroad, either that of bootleggers or that of the Nazis, than would he compromise with criminals at home.

The days of hard work that Morgenthau gave to miscellaneous matters — to public health, to procurement, to the fine arts, to the enforcement of law — were days well spent. These issues never absorbed more than a small fraction of his time, but as he shaped

* See discussion of countervailing duties, page 149 ff.

the duties of his department, the routines which preceding secretaries had at times considered beneath their dignity, he gained the loyalty of his subordinates and the confidence of the President. He was, by his own definition, the keeper of the public purse, but he was also a keeper of the public conscience. His own conscience was the handmaiden of his devotion to reform, for helping the underdog often necessitated destroying his oppressors. The Cancer Institute, the Treasury Relief Art Project, the prosecutions of the drug and crime syndicates were all parts of Morgenthau's persistent purpose to bring to the American people good government and a better life. It was his good fortune to serve a President who supported him. Their achievements in these matters revealed the spirit with which they approached larger tasks.

# IV

# The Dollar at Home and Abroad

## 1934-1936

### 1. The Gold Reserve Act

SIMPLY BY VIRTUE of assuming office as Secretary of the Treasury, Morgenthau was forced to look upon familiar questions from a new angle. His commitment to the devaluation of the dollar as a means to raise farm prices had provided the immediate occasion for his appointment. In the first months of his tenure, the demands of the devaluation program absorbed his energies, and he had now to resolve the monetary problems, national and international, related to gold buying. These were troublesome. The exchange fluctuations which the rising price of gold produced could not long be permitted to disrupt international trade. As 1934 began, Roosevelt and Morgenthau therefore wanted to set a relatively permanent price for gold. They had to do so if the government was to realize the profits from devaluation. The increase in the price of gold naturally gave a larger dollar value to the nationalized American gold stocks, but the Treasury could not enter the gain on its accounts until the price of gold was stabilized. The estimated budgetary deficit for 1934 gave this problem immediate importance.

Most significantly, the dollar was again appreciating relative to other currencies. Jacob Viner, the eminent economist and monetary specialist of the University of Chicago, investigated European conditions for Morgenthau late in 1933 and reported that American gold purchases abroad were not on an adequate scale to influence the exchange value of the dollar or to inflate the domestic price level. Morgenthau agreed, but he and Roosevelt also ascribed the failure of the dollar to depreciate abroad to the deliberate policy of the British government. In 1932 the British had created the Exchange Equalization Account, an arm of the Exchequer, equipped with a special fund for trading in foreign exchange. Its purpose was to prevent unwanted fluctuations of the pound sterling. Morgenthau and Roosevelt suspected that the Equalization Fund was operating to keep the pound from appreciating relative to the dollar. As the Secretary later recalled, he became excited when he concluded that the British were "fighting" him, for "it was one thing to devalue, and another to implement it."

Solely to place the British on record, Roosevelt instructed George Harrison of the New York Federal Reserve Bank unofficially to ask Governor Norman of the Bank of England whether the British were still interested, as they had been in June 1933, in setting a stable pound-dollar rate. Norman discussed the question with Sir Frederick Leith-Ross of the British Treasury, who replied that his government was not interested, nor was it willing to commit itself to a rate of stabilization for the immediate future. The British might, however, consider arranging a *de facto* dollar-sterling rate for a temporary period.

In Washington Morgenthau consulted representatives of the New York Federal Reserve Bank, the New York banking community, and members of his own staff, who universally agreed that the only way of making the depreciation of the dollar effective was to establish an American equalization fund comparable to the British. In mid-December Roosevelt wrote Morgenthau that his confidential agents reported that private bankers in New York and political forces led by Ogden Mills, Hoover's Secretary of the Treasury, were arousing sentiment for fixing the gold content of the dollar at a level favorable to the British. Those advocating this policy, Roosevelt went on, asserted that if the United States restored the gold standard, England would follow. But, informed by George Harrison that such was not the case, the President concluded that the British wanted the United States to go back onto gold in order to maintain their own favorable trading position and their own liquidity. With all

this in mind, both Roosevelt and Morgenthau considered it imperative for the United States to have an instrument capable of checking
British influence on international exchange.

On January 15, 1934, Roosevelt sent a special monetary message
to Congress. "The time has come for a more certain determination
of the gold value of the American dollar," he said. He already had
authority to fix the lower limit of revaluation of the pre-1933 dollar
at 50 per cent. He now asked Congress to set an upper limit of 60
per cent. To permit the Secretary of the Treasury "to bring some
greater degree of stability to foreign exchange rates," Roosevelt also
recommended "that, out of the profits of any devaluation, there
should be set up a fund of $2,000,000,000 for such purchases and
sales of gold, foreign exchange, and government securities as the
regulation of the currency, the maintenance of the Government, and
the general welfare of the United States may require."

Congress began at once to consider the necessary legislation.
There was general agreement with the President's proposals, but
opposition developed from two sources. Inflationists, still powerful
in and out of Congress, objected to limiting revaluation. Some of
them also supported the suggestion of Frank Vanderlip of the Committee for the Nation for the creation of an independent, national
authority to assume all the monetary powers of the Treasury and
the Federal Reserve System. Morgenthau helped persuade Congress
to table this plan. As he nursed the legislation through Congress,
he had also to contend with the Federal Reserve System and its
friends, including many private bankers.

Roosevelt had asked Congress to reaffirm the government's title
to the Federal Reserve System's gold, for he intended the profits
from devaluation to go to the Treasury, not to the Federal Reserve.
Officials of the Federal Reserve, while accepting his view about the
profits, held that physical possession of the gold protected them
from political pressure. Congress nevertheless adopted the President's plan for replacing the gold with inconvertible gold certificates,
a solution that cost the Federal Reserve some prestige. The proposed Stabilization Fund threatened its power.

Reserve officials questioned the propriety of authorizing the Treasury to buy and sell foreign exchange and government securities
through a Stabilization Fund. The Treasury, they argued, lacked

the necessary experience and leadership to exercise these functions which were classically the prerogatives of private bankers and privately governed central banks. The friends of the Reserve System in the Senate therefore sponsored amendments to establish a board of directors to administer the Stabilization Fund, to restrict its transactions to foreign exchange, to require public reports of its operations, and to limit its life to two years. Only the last of these amendments survived, and it was modified to permit Congress to renew the Fund. The others fell partly because the Administration had the votes it needed, partly because Roosevelt and Morgenthau were again defending not a radical but a middle position, partly because most congressmen trusted Morgenthau and shared his expressed opinion that "when we go into play this game, we want a fund that will permit us to play . . . as everyone else is doing."

On January 30, 1934, Congress passed the Gold Reserve Act by impressive majorities, the House voting 370 to 40, the Senate 66 to 23. The measure followed the Administration's prescriptions. The next day a presidential proclamation and Treasury regulations put the new law into effect, setting the price of gold at $35 an ounce, thus reducing the dollar to 59.06 per cent of its pre-1933 gold content. That price and that ratio still prevail.

Treasury policy put the United States on a limited gold standard. Acting as the agent of the Department, the Federal Reserve Bank of New York could sell gold to the central banks of foreign nations on the gold standard whenever the dollar reached the gold-export point, the price of $35 plus the cost of transportation. If gold rose above that price, it would profit the Treasury to sell. Such sales would in turn bring the price back to $35, the level the Administration wished to maintain. The law and Treasury regulations permitted American traders to buy gold abroad as they always had, but when they shipped it to the United States, they had to sell it at $35 an ounce to the Treasury. If gold was cheaper than this in foreign markets, private arbitragers were sure to buy it. Alternatively, the Treasury could make direct purchases of its own to hold the world price at the American figure.

The old gold standard, however, no longer existed. Not since April 1933 had Americans been permitted to own gold or freely to convert paper currency into gold. Furthermore, although the government now agreed to take all gold at $35 an ounce, the sale of gold was at the discretion of the Treasury. It could at any time stop sales or change their conditions. The President, moreover, had the right at any time to devalue to 50 per cent of the old parity. The new standard, subject as it was to change, was a matter of convenience. Roosevelt called it the bullion system; Morgenthau described it as "the 1934 model gold bullion standard . . . streamlined . . . air flow . . . and knee action. . . . It's the one which suits our own need."

The question of suitability awaited the test of time, but some economists immediately criticized the Gold Reserve Act for setting limits for revaluation and thereby making monetary policy less flexible. In January 1934, however, Roosevelt and Morgenthau were less worried about flexibility than about their harassment by the Committee for the Nation and affiliated inflationary groups. By establishing a statutory limit on devaluation they were able to escape the lobbying which inflationists had instead to direct at Congress,* and they were relieved of the necessity for reviewing continually the question of the price of gold.

The Gold Reserve Act completed the alterations in the monetary system that had begun with the nationalization of gold. Before 1933 the United States had accepted gold as the standard of value to which the currency had to conform; the Federal Reserve System had maintained the currency in terms of gold. Now the government no longer considered this maintenance desirable. Under the traditional gold standard, flights of capital from the United States, depleting American monetary stocks, might have interfered with cheap money policies or with deficit spending. The new arrangements simplified the pursuit of these policies, which the President and his advisers deemed essential to the public good. The Administration acquired effective control over the exchange and gold value of the dollar, which permitted the protection of the internal credit structure from the influence of foreign monetary changes. Neither the deliberate or inadvertent devaluation of a foreign currency had any longer to affect the domestic value of the dollar or to touch the level of American prices. Perhaps most significantly, as Morgenthau repeatedly noted in retrospect, the Act turned over to the Treasury much of

* See pages 183–88 for an account of the silver lobby.

the authority for the management of credit and currency. This made monetary control an instrument of national policy.

## 2. The Supreme Court and the Gold Clause

As Morgenthau began to exercise the authority the Gold Reserve Act conferred upon the Treasury, he made it his first business to close the gap between the domestic and the foreign price of gold. His heavy purchases established the American price all over the world within about two months. He bought approximately $400 million of gold in February 1934, and $237 million in March. To maintain the $35 price the Treasury during the remainder of 1934 bought another $385 million, during 1935 about $1887 million, and during 1936 $1133 million.

For all of the incoming gold the Treasury issued equivalent, non-circulating, inconvertible certificates to the Federal Reserve System. These increased reserves provided a base for a vast expansion of credit and currency. The expansion made money more available, "easier," precisely as the New Deal intended, for easy money (or low interest rates) helped potential commercial borrowers, and industrial borrowing for the expansion of plant or inventory would put men to work and help move the economy out of depression. However, as Morgenthau realized, easy money, though one condition for revival, was not in itself sufficient. Unless businessmen took advantage of low interest rates, the level of investment would not rise.

The expansion of gold reserves made it possible to market government securities at lower interest rates. This permitted Morgenthau gradually to reduce the carrying charge on the debt and to handle effectively the existing and pending federal deficits, much of which the government spent on essential relief and recovery projects.*

In spite of Morgenthau's aggressive execution of gold policy during 1934, Dr. Warren and his school were dissatisfied. Urging a further increase in the price of gold, they rehearsed their familiar argu-

---

* For a discussion of debt management, see Chapter VIII; for a discussion of the Treasury's role in financing the relief and recovery program, see Chapter VI.

ment that it would directly lift commodity prices. But Morgenthau by 1935 had become skeptical of Warren's thesis. A higher gold price, he knew, would mean even larger American gold purchases, which by further depleting the reserves of countries still on the gold standard, would surely push them off and perhaps lead to unending competitive devaluation. The Secretary was reluctant to disturb the exchange and bond markets which the Treasury was bringing under control. He did not think devaluation had failed, but he and his advisers could see no domestic benefit in pushing it further. Aware of Morgenthau's views, Roosevelt in August 1935 suggested — partly in fun, partly to test him — that he might consider changing the price of gold. "Please do not tease me," Morgenthau replied, dismissing the topic, "it is too early in the morning."

Political rather than economic considerations had persuaded the President, to Morgenthau's dismay, seriously to propose tinkering with the price of gold in January 1935. At that time the Supreme Court was weighing the constitutionality of the Joint Resolution of June 3, 1933, one legal basis for the Administration's gold program. This resolution declared it to be against public policy for contracts to provide for payment in gold or in any particular type of currency. It forbade such provision in the future, and it made all contracts, past or future, payable in whatever coin or currency was legal tender at the time of payment. Many private contracts, especially bonds, had been written in earlier years to provide explicitly for payment in gold dollars of the pre-1933 weight and fineness. Much of the bonded debt of the United States was written in this manner, and many bond holders believed the Joint Resolution unconstitutional, contending that it deprived them of their contractual rights. If the Supreme Court accepted this view, it would jeopardize the New Deal's gold policy.

Against the possibility of an adverse decision, the White House, the Treasury, and the Justice Department prepared proclamations invoking the President's authority during a period of national emergency to regulate currency transactions, and prohibiting for ninety days payments on all contracts except in dollars at the rate of $35 for an ounce of gold. They also drafted a message to Congress recommending the withdrawal of the right to sue the United States for payment of more than the face value of bonds and similar obligations.

The government, however, hoped for a favorable decision. Its brief maintained that the Administration had suspended gold payments and allowed the dollar to fall in order to save the economy by stopping deflation, but that the instability in foreign exchange and domestic prices which inevitably followed the cutting loose from gold was intolerable as a long-range condition. Therefore, the government argued, it had fixed the price of gold at $35 an ounce and established the Stabilization Fund to maintain that price. Throughout the formulation and execution of this twofold policy, moreover, the Administration had been determined that all Americans should suffer or benefit equally. Since the gold clause could not be inserted in private bonds not originally containing it, equality of treatment was possible only by striking the clause from previously existing private and public contracts. For the same reason the government had required all holders of gold and gold certificates to surrender them and accept payment in dollars of the new value.

Herman Oliphant analyzed the government's brief for Morgenthau. If the Administration reversed its position on gold while the judges were discussing their decision in conference, Oliphant concluded, it would weaken the government's case. He believed that the stability in the price of gold, which had remained at $35 for a year, gave the judges confidence in the Administration and might reconcile them to the abrogation of the gold clauses. "Even a hint of possible change," he wrote, "might destroy that confidence."

At luncheon with Morgenthau and Homer Cummings on January 14, Roosevelt seriously questioned this reasoning in what Morgenthau considered one of the most unpleasant hours he had had since coming to Washington. The President said he wanted to keep things in an unsettled state until the Supreme Court handed down its gold decision. The only way the man in the taxicab could become interested in the gold case, he contended, was if the story were kept on the front page. Roosevelt therefore wanted bonds and foreign exchange to fluctuate in such a way as to suggest crisis. If things were in constant turmoil and the case went against the government, the man in the street would say, "For God's sake, Mr. President, do something about it." Then if he did something about it, the country would "heave a sigh of relief and say thank God." Cummings, who was in charge of the presentation of the case, vigorously agreed.

In reply, Morgenthau, as he later noted, "argued harder and more intensely than . . . ever before" in his life. He said that he did not advise Cummings on legal matters and did not expect Cummings to advise him on financial matters. Congress had given him the Stabilization Fund as a trust, and his conscience told him to use it as it was intended. He could not conceivably encourage uncertainty. When he had entered the Treasury a year earlier, Morgenthau reminded Roosevelt, things had been chaotic. Step by step, he felt, he had stabilized foreign exchange and the bond market. He had built up the confidence of the country in himself and in his Department, and he expected to keep that confidence. "Mr. President," Morgenthau said, "you know how difficult it is to get this country out of a depression and if we let the financial markets of this country become frightened for the next month it may take us eight months to recover the lost ground."

Nevertheless Roosevelt pressed Morgenthau "very very hard, arguing all the time for the political effect." Finally Morgenthau began to fear that the President might order him to obey, in which case he would have to refuse and resign. To avoid this, he pointed his finger at Roosevelt and said: "Mr. President, don't ask me to do this."

"Henry, you have simply given this thing snap-judgment," Roosevelt replied. "Think it over."

"Let's all three of us think it over," Morgenthau said, rising to depart. As he left, he asked Roosevelt's consent to buy francs to steady the exchange market. Roosevelt agreed. For the time being, Morgenthau decided, he could continue on the course he preferred.

On the telephone the next morning, Morgenthau considered the tone of the President's voice "particularly nice." He felt that Roosevelt must have slept on the matter and that "my advice was going to prevail." That evening they both attended a dinner at the Vice President's. Roosevelt was at Mrs. Garner's right, Morgenthau on her left. Leaning back in his seat, the President said across his hostess's back: "Well, Henry, I am glad to see that you are smiling again." Then he turned to Mrs. Garner: "You know, Henry was very serious for an hour yesterday. . . . I was arguing with him about the gold case and in arguing I often take the side of the opposition in order to bring out the various points but of course I didn't believe in these arguments." Looking over at Morgenthau, Roosevelt continued: "Henry feels much happier tonight and I see he is smiling." This, Morgenthau wrote in his Diary, was the method Roosevelt took to inform him that he had not meant what he had said the day before, or at least that he had changed his mind. In any case, Morgenthau knew he had won.

The Secretary had now for the first time to test the Stabilization Fund. He had set it up in April 1934, providing it with a working balance of $200 million and setting aside or "sterilizing," as a special item in the Treasury's gold statement, the remainder of the $2 billion Congress had authorized. The Fund's operations remained insignificant until January 1935 when uncertainty about the pending gold cases unsettled the exchange market. Speculators, betting on a decision against the government which would have the result of appreciating the dollar, sold pounds and francs to buy dollars. The franc, which was hit particularly hard, fell below its gold point on January 15. Morgenthau, after consulting his advisers, had decided the previous day that he would have to use the Stabilization Fund to steady the market by buying francs. With Roosevelt's approval, he allocated $10,000,000 to this end.

The speculative raid on the franc infuriated the Secretary. As he put it on January 16, international speculators were willing to sell the government short in order to make a penny. "They haven't got any guts," he said, "they haven't got any backbone and they haven't got any flag that they follow." Determined to fight them, he committed the Fund to further dealings in the franc and the pound.

On succeeding days the Fund continued to operate in London and Paris. During the period January 26 through February 18, it took £28,000,000 to hold the sterling rate steady. Such expenditures prevented any significant appreciation of the dollar. At luncheon with the President on February 11, Morgenthau noted that since January 14 banks and dealers in foreign exchange had practically stopped buying and selling gold; the international bullion standard had ceased to operate automatically. But the Treasury, using the Stabilization Fund, had successfully managed the value of the dollar in terms of foreign currencies. The United States could, therefore, go about its business with the assurance that the Treasury was prepared to continue the operation as long as necessary. This statement pleased Roosevelt who endorsed Morgenthau's proposal for giving it to the press. The newspapers received it well. It dissipated much of the worry about the dangers of an adverse ruling in the gold cases, for it showed that, no matter which way the Court went, the Treasury considered the dollar under control.

On February 18, the day the Court handed down its decisions, Morgenthau and some of his staff awaited word in the executive offices adjoining the White House. Shortly after noon McReynolds relayed a flash from the UP ticker in the Treasury that the Court was in session. Morgenthau rushed into Miss LeHand's office and told her to get the President. In what seemed like less than a minute, Roosevelt arrived smiling to take his regular place at the Cabinet table. His secretaries hovered around him during the tension preceding the final word. From the Treasury news arrived that the pound sterling was going up. It would skyrocket if the Court decided for the government. Morgenthau suggested selling some of the sterling the Stabilization Fund held, but Oliphant very emphatically said no, let it go higher. Morgenthau replied that it would be better to take a profit while he could. The President nodded his head. The Secretary then directed the Treasury to sell sterling every time it went up a little bit.

Minutes later the Supreme Court's decision came over the telephone. By a margin of one vote the judges for all practical purposes favored the government. The majority upheld devaluation for essentially legal rather than economic reasons. In substance the Court concluded that repudiation of the gold clause was constitutional in private contracts but not in government bonds. However, the majority also ruled that the plaintiff in the government bond case had proved no loss and therefore had no remedy. The result, to which the minority entered a stormy dissent, protected the Administration, though Chief Justice Hughes in rendering the opinion scolded the President. The gold policy was safe.

As the group at the White House talked the cases over, Morgenthau saw from the President's questions that Roosevelt knew no more than he about the legal details. Oliphant had to interpret the meaning of the decisions for both of them. The Court's reasoning was complicated and its temper unfriendly, but those around the Cabinet table were none the less grateful. They sat and talked for about an hour with the atmosphere "very jolly." Roosevelt was "very natural, laughing and smiling practically all the time." "It certainly was one of the big moments of my life," Morgenthau later reflected, "and it was an experience to be with him."

### 3. Invitation to Stabilization

The decisions in the gold clause cases, sustaining the Administration's monetary policy as they did, gave Morgenthau freedom to concentrate upon preserving the exchange ratios among the dollar, pound and franc. He had no doubt about the desirability of stabilization. Instability of exchange, as Jacob Viner reported after again investigating European conditions, checked world recovery. Americans, Viner also believed, would not freely invest their funds at home if the dollar was sinking on the world market, and he foresaw no recovery in the United States until private investment was resumed on a larger scale. At best, furthermore, it would be a few years before the American price level fully adjusted to the established gold price. Viner therefore urged immediate *de facto* stabilization. He was a conservative economist, but Herman Oliphant, long an advocate of inflation, by March 1935 had come to agree with him, and their views reinforced Morgenthau's.

It was difficult for the Secretary to show his colors. Early in March, with the pound falling in relation to the dollar and the franc, the Bank of France considered offering a credit to the British. The French wanted the United States to cooperate in the offer, but Morgenthau and Roosevelt held back. "We view the objective with sympathy," Morgenthau told the French, "but would prefer not to participate in a joint offer of a credit to the Bank of England which has not been requested by them and which we understand would not likely be accepted by them and might therefore be both futile and embarrassing. Assuming that what is presently aimed at is an exchange relation among the pound, franc and the dollar at a level substantially where it has been in the past year, we would do nothing to hinder a Franco-British arrangement and would give sympathetic support to this objective whenever possible."

Disappointed, the French decided not to act on their own. Their desire to cooperate, however, seemed to Roosevelt and Morgenthau to contrast sharply with what they took to be the intransigent aloofness of the British. The Secretary on April 9 allocated $5,000,000 from the Stabilization Fund to help support the franc which was then in trouble, jokingly noting that the French had just done us a favor by issuing a decree effectively preventing smuggling from the island of St. Pierre. In a serious vein he explained that he had decided to form a Franco-American entente for stabilization and let the British either come along or flounder. As he put it the next day to French Ambassador Lefebvre de la Boulaye, he was in favor of stabilization at current rates, and he thought that the United States and France, owning between them 70 per cent of the world's gold, could force England's hand; with which the ambassador agreed.

Roosevelt was not opposed to *de facto* stabilization, but neither was he excited about it. He did not believe the United States could get other nations to agree upon stabilization until they had established their internal price levels to their own satisfaction, just as he felt he had now done. However, like Morgenthau, he hoped to avoid another round of devaluation, and he was willing to have the Secretary try.

The State Department, in contrast, was hostile to the new departure. Hull had concluded that the stagnation of British industry would force a further depreciation of the pound. He believed the United States should cooperate, let the dollar appreciate, and adopt conservative monetary policies in order to increase business confidence at home. He went so far as to suggest returning to the pre-1933 pound-dollar ratio, and incorporated his views in a memorandum intended for circulation to American embassies in Europe.

Morgenthau denounced the memorandum to the President as one of the most anti-New Deal broadsides he had seen in a long time. The thought of sending it to the American embassies, the Secretary said, "made my blood boil." Roosevelt was equally angry. "J. P. Morgan has as much influence in the State Department as he ever did," he remarked. He also permitted Morgenthau to remind Cordell Hull of the agreement putting the Treasury in charge of stabilization.

"I was considerably disturbed to learn that your Department had prepared a memorandum on Exchange Stabilization to send out to the foreign embassies," Morgenthau wrote the Secretary of State on April 17. "You will remember our talk with the President, and I feel that any initiative on this subject should come from the Treasury Department. Will you let me know if this is your understandin?" Hull on April 20 explained his interest in exchange stabilization as a factor in international trade but withdrew the memorandum and promised to guard against saying or doing anything that would trench on the Treasury's prerogatives.

His path clear, Morgenthau had to decide how to proceed. Neither he nor Roosevelt was prepared to sacrifice any freedom in monetary policy that domestic developments might require. Neither wanted directly to approach the British or needlessly to offend them. Yet the Secretary thought it essential to make some cautious gesture toward informal and flexible international stabilization. He hit upon the device of a radio speech which he and his staff spent a month drafting for delivery on May 13.

The address reviewed and justified American monetary policy, stated the case for flexibility, and invited discussion of stabilization. "So far from engaging in a competitive race with other nations," Morgenthau concluded, "we hold out to them a currency of such steadiness that the normal tendency may very well be for the rest of the world to move gradually toward practical exchange stabilization." The United States would not declare "that we will not change the present gold content of the dollar," for that would "put us right back where we were in 1932" and tempt others to take advantage of American rigidity by again devaluing, but "the world should know that when it is ready to seek foreign exchange stabilization, Washington will not be an obstacle. . . . We are not unwilling to stabilize."

The newspapers caught the significance of the speech. As the *Wall Street Journal* commented, Morgenthau's willingness to discuss stabilization was something gained. The *Christian Science Monitor* called the address "a beacon in the darkness" of interna-

tional economic relations. Although there were also unfavorable
criticisms, Secretary Hull was so pleased that he requested and received permission from Morgenthau to issue a statement referring
to the timely and clarifying speech of the Secretary of the Treasury.


## 4. First Aid for France

Within the month Morgenthau gave substance to his remarks. Belgium, one of the few countries cooperating with France in attempting to preserve the gold standard, suffered a severe currency crisis
in the spring of 1935. By early May most American observers agreed
that it was only a matter of time before the French would have to
abandon gold and devalue the franc, which had been under periodic
pressure for four years. But in France there was strong sentiment for
remaining on the gold standard, because the French experience with
devaluation in the late twenties had been unhappy. Although
French inflationists and many French progressives considered devaluation a necessary precondition for social reform, the coalition
government of Pierre Flandin and the parties of the Right were
determined to cling to gold.

The political instability and party rivalries that had characterized
French government since World War I contributed to uncertainty
about monetary policy and were in turn complicated by the international tensions produced by Adolf Hitler's accession and gradual
assumption of dictatorial power. The German threat and the possibility of European war that it raised, and persisting unemployment
and gloom within France, persuaded French capitalists to convert
their francs to gold, sell the gold for dollars, and invest them in the
United States, where the government was stable, the economy improving, and the chance of war seemingly small. To a lesser degree,
they also sold francs in order to buy pounds sterling. Thus the
Bank of France was gradually losing its stock of gold and continuing
pressure would ultimately force it to suspend gold payments and
devalue. This might provoke devaluation elsewhere.

Morgenthau had various stakes in the situation. As Secretary of
the Treasury, he recognized his responsibility for preventing competitive international devaluation and the disorder it would involve.

It would also appreciate the dollar which might lead to demands for American counteraction, a prospect he disliked. Finally, he hoped to preserve sufficient stability within France so that Franco-American cooperation might bring the British to *de facto* stabilization.

On May 17, 1935, M. Charles Cariguel, who handled exchange for the Bank of France, informed the Federal Reserve Bank of New York that a crisis in the franc was pending. As he explained within the next few days, the Flandin government would soon have to resign, and a new government would probably be formed by Pierre Laval, who was advocating a deflationary budget and a standpat domestic program. Confidence both in the government and in the franc was shaky, and the Bank of France expected a flight from the franc within the next fortnight unless the political situation changed dramatically.

Cariguel commanded attention. He was a strongly built, red-faced, cool-headed Breton who had studied economics in London for several years, managed the foreign business of the Bank of France for over a decade, and established himself as the most valued adviser of Jean Tannery, the Governor of the Bank. Gifted in evasion when his suspicions were aroused, Cariguel was direct with people he trusted. As Morgenthau realized, Cariguel both trusted and needed the Treasury.

Before coming to the support of the French, Morgenthau wanted to be sure that any francs the Stabilization Fund purchased would be immediately convertible into gold. Were the French to depart from the gold standard, and were he at that time to have large holdings of francs, he might suffer a considerable loss. If the Bank of France could assure convertibility, he was prepared to do his best to cooperate.

Cariguel guaranteed prompt, daily delivery of the gold equivalent of all francs purchased, and on May 29 requested a $200 million credit. With Roosevelt's consent, Morgenthau suggested that the Bank of France ask the British for a quarter of this sum, thereby involving the British in protecting the franc and setting a precedent for democratic cooperation on monetary matters. But while Cariguel promised to raise the question with Governor Tannery, the French were mainly interested in getting dollars, not sterling.

From Merle Cochran in Paris Morgenthau received more information. Cochran, a stocky middle-aged former consular officer, was the specialist in finance on the staff of the American embassy. An experienced trader and an expert on money, the Treasury's liaison to the central bankers of Europe, Cochran had been constantly in the company of Cariguel and by telephone intermittently in touch with Morgenthau who considered him a "magnificent type of public servant." On May 29 he told Morgenthau that England was simply not interested in preserving the stability of the franc. Although the Secretary nevertheless wanted to test the Bank of England, the Bank of France refused to ask them for part of the credit. The British had already bought large amounts of francs on their own account, and since sterling was not linked to gold, the French did not feel warranted in asking for further help. They therefore repeated their request for a $200 million credit from the United States, offering to earmark gold for the Treasury in Paris. If the Americans wished, they were prepared to store the gold at the American embassy, pending shipment by the first available steamer.

Morgenthau then talked with Ambassador Jesse I. Straus at the American embassy in Paris. Straus thought things looked very bad. He was sure the government of France would fall; he suggested the United States exploit the weakness of the franc by withholding purchases until they could be made at a lower price; and he advised Morgenthau to go easy, to offer no more than a $25 million credit. Cochran, however, believed that anything less than $200 million would be inadequate, and Morgenthau, anxious to help the French, decided to offer the full amount. Roosevelt approved, stipulating only that the Treasury make no suggestions about the use of the credit.

When Ambassador Straus on May 30 learned about the credit, he wanted to tell the Paris papers. "In no uncertain language" Morgenthau instructed him to say nothing. The Bank of France, the Secretary said, alone could decide whether publicity would hurt or improve the Paris market. Morgenthau's instructions pleased Roosevelt so much that he made a short speech to the Cabinet about the virtues of silence.

The Bank of France revealed nothing, but acted forcefully. At one A.M. on May 31 the Flandin government fell, and the day began dismally for the franc. But the officials of the Bank, secure in their American support, had slept well for the first time in three nights. They needed their strength as a tremendous rush for dollars and, to a lesser degree, for sterling began. Before the day ended, Cariguel had to use $33,000,000 of the credit. He could not have survived without it. Knowing that he had the dollars he needed, he felt just as if he had won a grand lottery. Although the world expected the franc to fall with the government, Cariguel went onto the floor of the exchange telling stories, joking with the traders, creating the impression that he had no worry under the sun. He offered dollars promptly and fully to every customer, and his air of confidence and his quick action broke the mad rush. It was extraordinary that the purchases remained as small as they did, for powerful French political leaders were agitating in the Chamber for immediate devaluation. If the franc had got out of hand on the exchange, the French government might have had temporarily to embargo gold or establish exchange controls. Cariguel and Tannery reported privately that the United States Treasury had saved the situation.

Also confidentially, Morgenthau then told the whole story to Key Pittman, Chairman of the Senate Foreign Relations Committee, and Charles L. McNary, the Senate minority leader. They were "enthusiastic," especially McNary who considered the Secretary's decision "courageous and statesmanlike."

After the market had remained steady for a fortnight, the Bank of France felt safe enough to acknowledge the American aid publicly. Speaking at Basel to the governors of European central banks, Jean Tannery on June 17 paid tribute to Morgenthau's "broad understanding." In a crisis during which France lost nearly ten billion francs worth of gold, half of it to the United States, Tannery reported, the American Treasury had stepped in and "constantly supplied the market with dollars." The bank governors considered the episode a major development in American policy. If devaluation had to come, they believed responsible legislative bodies should guide it. It should not be forced upon legislatures by any event which might be attributed to faulty management or to a breakdown of exchange mechanisms. By assisting the Bank of France, Morgenthau had let the Chamber of Deputies make the final decision. He had protected the franc from the erosions of fright and the raids of international speculators. He had also, those at Basel believed, taken an encouraging step toward *de facto* stabilization. After polling the bank governors privately, the *Wall Street Journal* concluded that Great Britain remained the only barrier to that end.

Quizzed about Tannery's comments, Morgenthau referred to the credit as representing "common decency among nations." He would not discuss details, past or future, but he did say that the transaction had the approval of the President, Senator Pittman, and Senator McNary. American monetary policy, he reminded the press, remained on a twenty-four-hour basis.

His deeds had already said more than his words. While Ambassador Straus hesitated, Morgenthau had acted. The credit to the Bank of France was the largest amount by far that the Stabilization Fund had yet used for any specific objective. The Treasury was pointing the way to international monetary cooperation.

## 5. Rapport with England

The American credit was at best only a palliative for the French economy. For the long pull the French had to help themselves and to rely upon the United States and Great Britain for further help. On his way home from a brief trip to Europe, Morgenthau stopped in Paris in October 1935 to discuss monetary matters. He had already done what he could to assist France, he told Premier Laval, and he was ready now to listen sympathetically to any plan on which France and England could agree. Laval and his associates objected that France lacked the financial power to motivate the British. Any push in that direction would have to come from the United States. But Morgenthau, reaffirming his interest in stabilization, said he thought that the Europeans should act first.

There was no chance of this while Laval remained Premier. His reactionary domestic policies denied the workers of France hope that the government would intercede to relieve their increasingly miserable conditions. Their mounting dismay foreshadowed a political crisis whose obvious imminence frightened the investors Laval desired to reassure. Laval's foreign policy, moreover, threatened the security of France and shook the confidence of England. His vacillations when Mussolini invaded Ethiopia in September 1935, his flirtations with fascists at home and abroad, weakened the already faltering spirit of the European democracies and helped to nurture German resurgence, setting the stage for Hitler's military occupation of the Rhineland in March 1936.

Even in 1935 Morgenthau sensed Laval's hesitancy, though neither he nor anyone else could fully foresee his perfidy. The Secretary was on sound ground in urging the French to get together with the British, for unless the French were willing to face up to their problems, there was little the United States could do to assist them. A sure instinct had led Morgenthau not to rely upon the French alone. In spite of his own doubts and those of the President, while he supported the franc in May, he also decided to sound out the British about stabilization.

For that purpose he sent to England an able young economist brought into the Treasury by Jacob Viner. Harry White was a man of extraordinary energy and quick intelligence who had already proved useful to the Treasury as a reporter on monetary conditions in Belgium and Holland and as a monetary analyst in the Research Division. On his mission to England in 1935 he succeeded, as he was so often again to succeed, in winning the confidence of economists and bankers who could not help but respect his mastery of his field. His report, moreover, helped to clarify the thinking of Morgenthau and his associates about the possibilities for a rapprochement with the British Treasury.

Most of the British businessmen White interviewed saw no advantage in again fixing the pound sterling to gold; indeed, for better or for worse, they had come to believe that their depression from 1925 to 1931 was caused chiefly by the British adherence to the gold standard. By 1935 British exporters were selling their goods primarily in sterling areas and were therefore unconcerned about fluctuations of their currency in terms of gold or of dollars. On the other hand, neither the business community nor the public was demanding further depreciation, and British economists on the whole opposed it. They considered some kind of stabilization possible if the United States would take the initiative. John Maynard Keynes, the brilliant economist and outstanding British monetary authority, believed strongly that *de facto* stabilization was desirable and

thought that the primary obstacle lay in the difficulty of securing
an informal arrangement with the Un⸳ ⸳d States. He feared that
Congress, subject as it was to inflationary enthusiasms, would destroy any tentative agreement the Executive might make. The way
out, Keynes suggested, might be through the cooperation of the
French, British and American treasuries in a manner which did
not involve any legislative action. This suggestion impressed White,
who himself preferred action through treasuries to action through
banks or treaties. Furthermore, although British Treasury officials
considered the pound overvalued at the existing rate, their desire
for some kind of stabilization encouraged White, as it encouraged
Morgenthau.

Since the devaluation of the pound in 1931, the British had managed sterling in terms of the franc and its gold base. Technically the
franc was a useful anchor. Depreciation of the franc would deprive
the British of a handy measure for exchange operations and confront them, as well as the United States, with the disturbing prospect of another round of competitive devaluation. The treasuries of
both countries were therefore anxious about the renewed flight from
the franc following Hitler's march into the Rhineland.

As French capitalists, afraid both of war and of domestic instability, converted francs to gold, they drained the reserves of the Bank
of France. In April 1936 Morgenthau thought the French would
soon have to devalue or impose controls on the export of gold and
the purchase of foreign exchange. "England," he told Roosevelt, "is
holding up the franc." The time was at hand to define American
policy toward the British.

George Harrison advised Morgenthau to let the British sell gold
directly to the Treasury, and buy it directly from the Treasury, at
$35 an ounce.* The Equalization Fund could in that manner oper-
ate freely in dollars as well as sterling and gold, and if the franc
went adrift, England could manage the pound in terms of dollars
which were stable. This advice suited Morgenthau's inclination
toward internationalism — "I'd rather be looked at as a big
brother," the Secretary had remarked a few months earlier, "than a
big stick." It suited also his growing determination to use monetary

---

* The Treasury by its own order had confined this privilege to nations on the
gold standard. See page 123.

policy to build a united, democratic front to resist Hitler. But Harrison had been notoriously susceptible to British influence, willing in 1933 to establish a dollar-sterling rate that greatly overvalued the dollar, avowedly committed to the gold standard at any cost. His memorandum, moreover, recommended a degree of cooperation with England that Morgenthau suspected the President would not tolerate. The Secretary therefore put it aside for further thought, perhaps for reference to Roosevelt at a propitious time.

While Morgenthau pondered whether and how to approach the British, he watched the London gold market. On April 28, 1936, Poland embargoed gold and established exchange controls, and the price of gold in London dropped for the first time in many months. This was in itself trivial, but it gave Morgenthau a specific subject on which to begin the conversations with the British he had been contemplating, and on April 29 he asked Roosevelt's permission to discuss stabilization with them.

For half an hour the President stressed the importance of having the first move come from the British. Morgenthau reminded him that since 1934 the United States had not done so badly. "You and I, of course," Roosevelt replied, "started with no knowledge of this subject but the two of us have done well and have been able to more than hold up our end. The trouble is that when you sit around the table with a Britisher he usually gets 80 per cent of the deal and you get what is left. Tell them that. Tell them that if we got 45 per cent we think that we would be doing well. As long as Neville Chamberlain is there [as Chancellor of the Exchequer] we must recognize that fundamentally he thoroughly dislikes Americans."

In his Diary Morgenthau observed that the President thoroughly distrusted the British. He did not tell Roosevelt, for he did not want to irritate him, that the British, convinced the President had double-crossed them at London in 1933, had therefore acted peculiarly about stabilization ever since. Morgenthau trusted himself to hold up his end of the argument, and he had the President's permission to open conversations.

Later that day he spoke with T. Kenneth Bewley, the acute, reserved British financial counselor at the Washington embassy. Morgenthau asked Bewley to find out what the British thought about the flurry in the price of gold. "It is perfectly silly," the Secretary said, "for the two countries to be doing business together in the dark with a big wall between us, each country slipping the other country a note under the wall but not being willing to talk. . . . I want to open a channel of communication. I think it is very important."

Bewley promised to talk to his superiors, but for over two weeks Morgenthau heard nothing from him. Meanwhile the victory of the French Left in the May elections assured the formation in June of a coalition government under Leon Blum, the eminent French Socialist. This promised changes in French domestic policy, for Blum's Socialists and their allies were resolved to improve the lot of the French laboring class. The ensuing strain on the French budget and on the franc would surely lead to devaluation, although Blum and his associates were giving lip service to the gold standard. Morgenthau rejoiced in the accession of a progressive government, but he had concluded that it would do no good for the United States to provide the franc with another artificial stimulant. The very urgency of France's plight might at last bring her and England to stabilization.

On May 18 Bewley returned, but he reported only that the British Treasury considered insignificant the brief break in the price of gold in late April. Morgenthau replied that if he had to wait as long as he had for answers to his questions, the information he received was useless. "As far as I am concerned," he continued, "if they cannot use their imagination I am not going to make any more suggestions. . . . I have tried to make a gesture and I have not gotten very far and I will now let the Chancellor of the Exchequer make the next gesture."

"I would like," Bewley said, "to put that to my people."

The United States operated candidly, Morgenthau went on. If it bought or sold sterling, it did so through the Bank of England and left the money on deposit there. This was open and aboveboard, but if the British were not of a mind to reciprocate, Morgenthau was going to alter his ways. He could get any information he wanted from the French government, and he would like to be in the same position with England. "Frankly," he concluded, "you could make your post a really important one rather than just try to interpret the financial news."

On June 1 Bewley had more to report. The general lines of British monetary policy, he said, had not changed since the London Conference of 1933. The ultimate aim of the British government was to go back to the gold standard, but it would have to be a reformed gold standard. The British, furthermore, felt that each country had to make up its own mind about when it could afford to return to gold, and Chancellor of the Exchequer Neville Chamberlain thought Great Britain should keep interest rates low for the time being. The British conceded that if any country felt as they did and discovered that in order to accomplish its purpose it had to lower the value of its currency, then nobody else should have any grievance.

The British did not know what was going to happen to the gold bloc. They hoped the countries still on a gold basis could carry on without devaluation, and especially without applying exchange restrictions of the type that interfered with trade movements. But even if these nations were forced to devalue, the British would hold the pound steady unless gold prices fell substantially. If, therefore, the dollar continued steady, the parity between the pound and the dollar would remain unchanged. If on the other hand there were a considerable drop in gold prices, the British, loath to face the resulting deflation, would have to take more radical steps.

They were in any case anxious for closer cooperation with the Americans. As Neville Chamberlain put it in a letter to Morgenthau which Bewley delivered, "in the difficult times through which we are passing and in the perhaps still more difficult days to come, the closest and most friendly contact between the two Treasuries is desirable."

Bewley's report was encouraging. Obviously the British were reconciled to the American decision of 1933 to avoid stabilization until the dollar was adjusted to domestic conditions. Obviously also they were prepared to work with the United States to sustain the existing dollar-pound ratio. Morgenthau could not immediately reply formally, but he asked Bewley to send word to Chamberlain that he was "very much pleased with this message." He also suggested that only the treasuries discuss stabilization. In 1933, he said, the central bankers had made negotiations excessively difficult, and he did not wish them brought in now.

The Treasury staff agreed with the Secretary that Bewley's report and Chamberlain's letter were everything that could have been hoped for — frank, honest, informative, important. The State Department was also delighted. At the Treasury to help draft a formal reply, Under Secretary of State William Phillips, a Grotonian friend of Roosevelt and an experienced diplomat whom Morgenthau especially liked, spoke for himself and for Hull. "I congratulate you," he told Morgenthau, "on the most important diplomatic step that has been taken. . . . It touches our trade agreement program; it touches everything."

Morgenthau, Jake Viner said, had caught a big fish. "And I am scared," the Secretary replied. He had been out for sea bass and caught a sailfish. Now the British had talked candidly and talked first, and he had to talk candidly in return.

He had also to talk fast, for on June 3, as strikes swept France and the flight from the franc toward gold continued, the Bank of England warned that "we are fighting a rear guard action and we do not know how much longer we are going to be able to do it." That day Morgenthau gave Bewley his friendly reply to Chamberlain. "I am glad to learn," he wrote, "that we are in agreement that full and frank communication between the two Treasuries may well prove to be urgently needed if the currency troubles of a disordered world are to be satisfactorily overcome."

On receiving this message, Bewley said there was one point he had been asked to bring up, although he was not instructed to press for an answer. The British were interested in knowing whether they could buy dollars in the United States and convert them into gold. This, though Bewley probably did not know it, was essentially what George Harrison had proposed.

There was no statute preventing the United States from permitting what the British had asked, Morgenthau said. It was purely a matter of Treasury policy, but he could not decide right away.

Later that day he took the question up with Roosevelt. He hoped, he told the President, to give Bewley a complete answer in a few days. But as the Secretary had feared, Roosevelt objected. He "started on a long harangue that he thought we ought to have a secret commodity price index with which we could manage the dollar. He said that Sweden had been very successful with it and so had the English. He felt that his message to the Conference, in

July 1933, should be our text and bible." Morgenthau, as he noted in his Diary, "told him that I felt that if we could indicate to France that both England and ourselves would not try to devalue further if France would make a clean-cut devaluation at this time, that it might assist France to make up her mind . . . and we might be able to bring about world stabilization between England, France and ourselves within a couple of weeks. He was quite excited and enthusiastic about the idea and realized fully its importance. However, I am going to have quite a time of it until I can pin him down, because every time I have brought up this subject of the discussion of stabilization with England, he always balks."

Overnight Morgenthau resolved to put an end to balking. "The European situation is getting clearer and clearer to me," he remarked. "There is such a thing as being too slow and missing one's opportunity. The time . . . the French need us is when they are making up their mind to devalue. . . . The quicker Blum knows how we feel, the better."

"This European situation is getting steadily worse," he told the President. "I would like to have your permission . . . to send for Bewley. When I saw Bewley yesterday he asked if it were possible for the British to get gold here. My answer was that it was. I cannot work in this roundabout political way. I want to tell him that we have been close friends with the French and that I want to send for them and either alone or in Bewley's presence tell the French what Bewley told me and give them the assurance that unless something unforeseen happens that Great Britain and the United States would not devalue further if the French devalued twenty to twenty-five per cent. If I can do that now and get that to Blum over the week end, he might be able to save his country. To sit here until the catastrophe blows up in our face, I think is stupid."

With Roosevelt's support, Morgenthau later that morning went right to the point with Bewley: "I want to talk to you straight from the shoulder and not diplomatically. The situation is so critical that if we use the usual diplomatic procedure we may have a smash-up in Europe. On the surface people seem far more nervous than the situation seems to justify, but they are very nervous and, of course, this French strike is getting very much worse. . . . I have just had telephone information that the French have advanced their program and will form their Cabinet tonight and go before Parliament on Saturday for approval. . . . The biggest thing that they have facing them is what are they going to do with the franc and if the French could know that your Government and our Government would be willing to sit by and see them devalue twenty and thirty per cent and that we would not try to go under them, they would then have the assurance that they could take this jump from the springboard and would land on solid ground and they must be really in a desperate situation because they do not know what to do and what your Government will do and what we will do."

Bewley explained that he did not know what his government had been telling the French. Morgenthau assured him that he would say nothing without British permission. On the other hand, he thought there was a distinct possibility they might accomplish what everyone wanted if the three governments moved simultaneously. He did not feel they would even have to draw up written papers or memoranda, but "we want the assurances as to what extent the French will devalue, and Great Britain and the United States will, in return, give the French assurances that we will not try to go below them."

As Bewley left to put the case to the British Treasury, he remarked unofficially that it sounded good to him. Morgenthau instructed him to telephone him at home if necessary. "The very fact that they are so nervous without there being a visible reason for it increases my nervousness," the Secretary said. "It was a similar situation that started the march in Rome. The Hitler situation was just like this."

Morgenthau had Oliphant prepare the legal documents he would need if England agreed to his suggestion. He also arranged, as he had a year earlier, to make funds available to the Bank of France. But neither the French nor the British were ready to act.

Premier Leon Blum and his Minister of Finance, Vincent Auriol, were both pledged against devaluation. They were also pledged to reinflate their economy, but they had yet to admit that an increase in domestic prices, including the price for labor, could not be reconciled with a balanced budget and an overvalued franc. They talked about imposing unprecedentedly high taxes, but admitted it would take several months to work this out.

At Morgenthau's direction, Cochran implied that the United States and Great Britain would not retaliate if France devalued, but his hint fell flat. Auriol wanted the United States to negotiate agreements between the dollar and each of the currencies in the gold and sterling blocs, ultimately to conclude an agreement among all the currencies. When this had been completed, he wanted to announce that the leading powers had made an international monetary truce at specified rates. But he considered it impossible for the French to approach the British. He refused even to be quoted as personally favoring devaluation according to any plan, and he suggested tying in international trade and peace with monetary discussions. Cochran pointed out that stabilization was enough to try at one time, but Premier Blum stood behind his Minister of Finance and in his first speech to the Chamber confirmed Auriol's position, denying any intention to devalue.

Morgenthau could interpret the French response only as a rejection of his offer. On two counts, furthermore, neither he nor the President would accept Auriol's counterproposal. Since the London Conference they had been opposed to multilateral negotiation about stabilization. Their insistence upon flexibility at home, moreover, precluded stabilization at specified rates.

The British were of the same mind, and largely on that account unwilling to take the initiative. Furthermore, as Bewley reported on June 8, Chamberlain doubted the wisdom of a *démarche* to France. The new French government had not approached him in any way. So far as London officially knew, the French hoped to remain on gold. Chamberlain feared it might prove embarrassing to make a gesture that could later be represented as a British effort to push the French off gold. He doubted the French would welcome a statement of any sort except for the purpose of shifting the responsibility for devaluation to the shoulders of others. This would only embarrass Great Britain and the United States. Unwilling to act, Chamberlain did not want Morgenthau or anyone else outside the British government to speak for him.

The impasse annoyed Morgenthau. The situation, he told Bewley, was ripe, but his overtures had been rebuked. As for the United States, he said: "We are like the American Indians. We are very good sitters." Bewley asked whether the Secretary thought the

French were so weak that they were afraid to take any steps. Morgenthau did not want to judge that. He was taking everybody at face value, but "everybody who knows the French says that they will only move when they are forced to. People say they will never come through with a clean-cut devaluation. Just as long as we have this thing, it certainly keeps the world in turmoil."

So, of course, did other conditions. William Phillips remarked to Morgenthau that the British had many irons in the fire. Phillips believed England would do nothing about stabilization until France asked for help because she wanted to put France under obligation to her. Things were pretty tense, he felt, with the question of the sanctions imposed against Italy by the League of Nations coming up for discussion on June 16.

Manifestly tense, Merle Cochran telephoned on June 15 to say that Auriol was planning to declare his policy before the Chamber of Deputies. Cochran asked permission to tell the Minister of Finance about Morgenthau's conversations with the British. He felt that if he could make the French see that the British would not move unless the French approached them, Auriol might take the first step. If France had this information right away, Cochran thought it might make a difference in what Auriol said to the Chamber. After some hesitation Morgenthau agreed, and he also gave Cochran permission to tell Auriol if he asked advice, that the United States recommended that France devalue immediately.

Cochran's message did not move Auriol. If it was just a question of an arrangement between "you and the people across the Channel," he told Cochran, it was not enough. It was indeed "absolutely impossible." The French still insisted on a network of agreements. Any action by France, he maintained, had to follow general stabilization and the adjustment of related economic problems.

This was discouraging, but negotiations were not closed, for Auriol was sending a confidential emissary to Washington. With his arrival, Morgenthau might yet create a monetary alliance. The Secretary had already begun to use monetary means to encourage resistance to fascism. He was directing American silver policy to buttress the economy of China, then plagued by Japanese ambitions.* He had also, at the very time he was pressing for Anglo-

* See pages 220–27.

French monetary cooperation, finally succeeded in applying economic pressure against Germany. This maneuver, significant in itself, gave Blum and Auriol increased confidence in the Secretary and in the United States.

## 6. Countervailing Duties

When Adolf Hitler, defying France and England and violating the Versailles Treaty of 1919, ordered German troops to occupy the Rhineland in March 1936, he demonstrated that he meant to pursue the program of conquest which his speeches and writings had long advocated. He had already provided significant evidence for his intentions in the policy of economic aggression of his Minister of Finance, Dr. Hjalmar Schacht. Under Schacht's direction, Germany was weaving a web of bilateral agreements through which she could force her economic will on other nations. Schacht had also developed a system of export bounties. By the use of various devices, including "scrip" marks (marks purchasable from the government at a discount but convertible within Germany at face value), German exporters received large subsidies in their competition for world markets, including the market of the United States.

German currency practices had begun to worry Morgenthau in November 1935. Herman Oliphant, who was an implacable opponent of Hitler and all that he stood for, then told the Secretary that in his opinion the tariff laws of the United States made retaliation mandatory. The Tariff Act of 1930, he held, forced the Treasury's hand. Section 303 of that Act provided that whenever any nation bestowed a bounty on the export of any article which was dutiable upon admission to the United States, the Treasury had to levy an additional duty equivalent to the net amount of the bounty. The Act called upon the Secretary of the Treasury to make all the regulations necessary for the identification of such articles and the assessment and collection of additional duties. Under Section 303, Oliphant concluded, action was mandatory once the Secretary had established the fact that a bounty was being paid.

The crux of the problem in the case of Germany was whether or not currency manipulations constituted a bounty or "grant" within the meaning of the Tariff Act. It was Oliphant's view that the Supreme Court in two decisions had given to the word "grant" the widest possible definition, clearly inclusive of the devices which Germany had adopted to subsidize the export of many commodities to the United States. The Treasury, moreover, had received complaints from American manufacturers and their congressional representatives about German subsidies to various products including, among others, bicycles, plumbing accessories, whistles, cutlery, optical instruments, gloves, aluminum foil, shellac, newsprint, nails, microscopes, and steel tools.

The Executive Committee on Commercial Policy, an interdepartmental coordinating body, disagreed with Oliphant. Currency manipulation, it believed, had to be regarded as a special case of currency depreciation. The application of countervailing duties would tend further to disturb already abnormal international monetary relations. Furthermore, where interpretations of Section 303 were in doubt, the committee felt that general economic considerations should be given weight. The United States both had been a victim of monetary dislocations and had itself contributed to them. It would therefore, in the opinion of the committee, be unfortunate if the United States attempted to take special measures against currency procedures of other countries. The committee noted, among other things, that Germany was experiencing genuine difficulties in dollar exchange, that her purchases of agricultural products from the United States had already decreased, and that much existing German-American trade was possible only because of Germany's currency policies. Furthermore, the Department of State was trying to persuade Germany to remove important discriminations against American trade, and the inauguration of countervailing duties would create an unfavorable atmosphere for the negotiations. This would result in an injury to American economic interests, the committee thought, far more serious than any that German monetary policy produced.

In a letter of April 2 to Morgenthau, Secretary of State Hull strongly endorsed the conclusions of the Committee on Commercial Policy. Assistant Secretary of the Treasury Wayne Taylor, to whom Morgenthau referred the matter, felt that Hull was correct; but Jacob Viner, who at Morgenthau's request also made a special study of the question, on April 10, 1936, recommended the imposition of countervailing duties.

At luncheon with the President on April 14, Morgenthau reported that the Treasury Department was working on the issue of countervailing duties, but that there was a considerable division of opinion within the Department and in any event the Department of State was opposing action. "If it is a borderline case," Roosevelt said, "I feel so keenly about Germany that I would enforce the countervailing duties." He added, however, that because of the difference between the Treasury and the Department of State, he wanted an opinion from the Department of Justice.

Oliphant and McReynolds considered it a bad precedent to shift the decision about tariff matters to the Justice Department, but Morgenthau argued that the importance of the case dictated exceptional procedures. "I want to do the thing that is legally right and ethically honest," he said. Increasingly hesitant after Jacob Viner changed his mind and sided with Hull, Morgenthau declined to proceed until he had a ruling from the Attorney General.

On April 30 Golden W. Bell, the Assistant Solicitor General, completed a memorandum on countervailing duties. The concern of the Department of State about economic policy was so great, Bell observed, that it was difficult for the Department to dissociate policy and law. He found the State Department's fears about foreign trade entirely justified. However, he wrote, if German currency practices fell within the contemplation of the law, the Secretary of the Treasury was under a mandate to impose the duties, and only action by Congress could relieve him. Furthermore, it seemed clear to Bell that German currency manipulation was for the benefit of German exporters. While the Tariff Act of 1930 probably did not anticipate those particular devices, the statute was plainly intended to apply as conclusively as possible to all practices that might be invented to circumvent it, and the Supreme Court had noted that no word could have a broader significance than "grant." Bell therefore did not doubt that the German devices constituted the bestowal of bounties and grants within the meaning of the Act. The law therefore required the imposition of countervailing duties, but Bell recommended that the Treasury, the State Department, and perhaps also the President, consider the question further, for it was so complex and so sensitive that possibly an effort should be made to change the law.

Overruled on the law, the Department of State pressed its interpretation of policy. Assistant Secretary of State Francis B. Sayre on May 4 maintained that the invocation of Section 303 of the Tariff Act against Germany would make it necessary to take comparable action against other countries, both in Europe and South America, that employed multiple currency systems to encourage exports. Hungary, Latvia, Argentina, Brazil, Chile, and Uruguay at the very least would fall within that group. Yet such a widespread resort to countervailing duties, Sayre wrote, would not only engender ill feeling but also result in substantial damage to American export trade. Sayre believed that the questionable currency procedures were designed primarily to overcome price maladjustments resulting from a depreciation of many currencies, including the dollar. Therefore, he argued, countervailing duties were not necessary as a safeguard for American producers. They would, moreover, create new barriers to trade and thus run counter to the whole trade agreement program of the Department of State.

In the case of countervailing duties, as in the matter of the Canadian liquor manufacturers,* the Treasury's understanding of the law clashed head on with Secretary Hull's interpretations of the needs of his trade agreement program. Yet on the question of Germany, as Morgenthau put it to Roosevelt on May 12, he had no choice. "Is that right, Mr. President?" Morgenthau asked. "Yes, that is right," Roosevelt replied.

Ten days later the President directed Morgenthau to confer with the Secretary of State and the Attorney General to "try to find an immediate method of carrying out the law. I am convinced that we have to act. It may be possible to make the action apply to Germany only."

At an interdepartmental meeting on May 29, Attorney General Cummings noted that the Tariff Act was mandatory, and Hull agreed. But Hull then rehearsed the case which the Department of State had already so often made. Yet prodded by Morgenthau, he repeated that there was no question of law. "And there is no question

* See page 115.

of policy," Morgenthau said, "but I have been very careful regarding this whole question and I have considered it from every angle regardless of my personal position."

"The Commercial Policy Committee finds this is a very serious thing," Hull objected. "If this law is carried out it is difficult to see where it will end and I am afraid that it will break down our whole international trade program. . . . Whenever things go wrong, at the present time the tendency seems to be to hit the other fellow in the nose and we do not think this is the right way to proceed. We want to work things out in a spirit of fairness and good fellowship."

"I would like you to get my position very clear on this," Morgenthau replied. "I . . . have held up the decision for a great length of time simply to convince myself that I have looked at it from every possible angle but I cannot see any way out. . . . I am to see the President this afternoon for a few minutes . . . and although my time with him will be limited, I will be very glad to report to him the substance of this meeting . . . which I will endeavor to do as fairly as possible."

With Hull's approval, Morgenthau did so. "As long as the law is clear," Roosevelt said, "there is nothing for you to do but carry it out." He expressed entire satisfaction with Morgenthau's position and with his proposed procedures for giving publicity to the forthcoming order on countervailing duties. Morgenthau was relieved that the question was settled. As he put it to his Dairy: "I thanked him for the backing he had given me and told him that the whole situation had been most difficult for me."

At his press conference on June 4, 1936, Morgenthau released the Treasury decision imposing countervailing duties on Germany only, effective June 30. The press release explained that the decision had the approval of the Attorney General. The amount of duties to be imposed on any particular product was to be determined by an estimate of the subsidy granted that product by the currency practices of the German government. This was to result, for example, in an increase in the duty on cameras, toys, and dolls imported from Germany of 45 per cent, on cotton and rayon gloves of 39 per cent, on surgical instruments of 56 per cent.

German newspapers at once expressed their pained surprise.

Adopting the argument which their government was also to use, German editorial writers argued that the devaluation of the dollar had made it necessary for their government to contrive its own methods for handling currency. The German government officially requested a postponement of the effective date of the order pending discussion of possible adjustments in German-American trade relationships. Indeed German officials talked of applying new protective legislation against the United States unless some satisfactory arrangement could be made to delay the application of the Treasury ruling.

Neither this implied threat nor the objections to the decision from American cotton exporters had any effect, for Morgenthau could not delay enforcing the law. When his ruling became effective, Germany submitted a formal protest to the Department of State. At the same time the German ambassador asked whether the Treasury would discuss ways in which Germany might finance her trade with the United States in a manner which would not violate the Tariff Act. Replying for Morgenthau, Assistant Secretary Josephine Roche said that conversations with German experts about countervailing duties would result in no more than a restatement of the Attorney General's opinion. The Department of State therefore informed the German government that any emissary coming to the United States should have clearly in mind that the law on countervailing duties was mandatory.

In spite of continuing protest from Germany, from American importers of cameras and other German products, and from the Department of State, the Treasury stood firm. Supported by Oliphant's repeated invocations of the law, Morgenthau permitted no exceptions or postponements in the application of the duties. His deliberate intransigency impressed Dr. Schacht's emissary to Washington who advised his government to capitulate. On August 4 Germany abandoned the procedures which had provoked the United States Treasury to retaliate. On August 10 the Treasury announced withdrawal of the duties.

"Contrary to the fears of the State Department and the bluster of the German press," Morgenthau later pointed out, "the Treasury policy worked. . . . It was the first check to Germany's career of economic conquest." It also established a propitious atmosphere for Morgenthau's discussion of monetary cooperation with the confidential agent of Leon Blum and Vincent Auriol.

## 7. The Monick Mission

On June 20, 1936, Auriol's special emissary, Emmanuel Monick, reached Washington. Long a devaluationist, Monick had been at odds with Governor Tannery of the Bank of France, whose tenure had ended when Blum came to office. Tannery's unsuccessful effort to remove Monick from his post as the French Treasury's representative in London created in Blum's eyes an initial presumption in Monick's favor. In several interviews Monick had substantially persuaded Blum of the necessity for devaluation of the franc, but Blum believed that, in order to preserve his coalition, he had to get on with social reform before attempting monetary change. Yet at Monick's suggestion, the Premier had included in his speech in defense of the franc a caveat about possible realignment in the event of an international understanding. In sending Monick to the United States, the French Premier revealed an inclination toward devaluation.

When Monick arrived, Roosevelt was preoccupied by the proceedings of the Democratic National Convention which was meeting to renominate him. Morgenthau therefore set the tone of the conversations. The Secretary did not entirely trust Monick, who had a reputation for unreliability, but he was eager to learn what Blum and Auriol were planning. Monick said at the outset that he was instructed to try to negotiate a currency agreement between France and the United States, if possible to include Great Britain. His mission, however, was highly confidential. Were it to become known that he was in Washington to discuss devaluation, the Premier might have to repudiate him for political reasons.

Repeating what Cochran had already told Auriol, Morgenthau said the United States looked with favor upon a moderate devaluation of the franc. Great Britain agreed but insisted that France approach her directly. What would happen, Monick asked, if the three countries reached an agreement and then Germany devalued more than she already had and began to dump goods? If France,

England and the United States could join hands, Morgenthau replied, they would be so powerful that he doubted any nation could fight them singlehanded in a currency war.

Monick expressed the French concern about the situation in Poland. If economic deterioration in France and Poland continued, he said, the chances of war were large, for Germany would surely exploit her advantage. Suggesting that England alone was keeping the three democracies apart, Monick became, as Morgenthau later noted, quite "French," swinging his arms around and complaining that the British wished to keep the pound independent of any other currency. These considerations underlay the French demand for a network of currency agreements.

Morgenthau in turn, by his own account, became terribly excited at Monick's criticism of the British and at his advocacy of multilateral negotiations. "I would no more sit in on a world monetary conference," he told the Frenchman, "than jump out of this window. I have seen what you can do with the Stabilization Fund and how you can move the thing around. If Germany started a monetary war, in the first place let's be practical. They can do that any time today. And you and England and ourselves would be alone and we would have no method to fight them. . . . In the Treasury, two weeks ago, we set up countervailing duties against Germany. . . . I would like to go into the German thing afterwards, but right now . . . Great Britain . . . will not do anything until your country speaks to them. You do not have to go to London. You can do it here."

Grateful for this statement, Monick talked freely with Roosevelt and William Phillips at the White House on June 23. His real reason for coming to Washington, he admitted, was the European political situation. The small countries surrounding Germany, especially Poland, were collapsing. Holland and Belgium were defenseless. Should Germany attack again as she had in 1914, Belgium would not and could not resist. He drew this dark picture, Monick explained, to emphasize the importance of lending immediate strength to the French government, which was in a precarious state. He sought what it needed, British and American support in a program of devaluation.

Roosevelt reminded Monick that the British government considered London the center of international banking. In dealing with the British, one had always to consider their "amour propre." He felt the British would be extremely reluctant to accede to any French request unless the French went directly to them. In his opinion, three-cornered conversations should be held simultaneously. Endorsing this proposal, Monick suggested beginning at once in Washington.

Roosevelt demurred. The British would consider discussions in Washington to be under American aegis. It would be better for the French to send similar and simultaneous communications to London and Washington. In that event, London would presumably inform Washington that it had received a message and request the views of the American government. A quick exchange would then take place, and in this way the French government would probably achieve its purpose. Monick gave the impression that he would act on the President's advice.

At the Treasury the next day, Monick said that he had begun to realize his mission would not be as empty as he had feared. But the form of the matter was important. Devaluation had to occur in such a way that the French people would accept it. The battle to keep on the gold standard had become for the French a battle of honor, and this was equally true of the other gold bloc countries. If France moved, she would have to answer to the Dutch, the Swiss and the Poles. Morgenthau said that someone had to take the lead. "But we are prepared to take the lead," Monick exclaimed. Things were so bad in France, he said, that there was as yet no agreement about how to inform the public. It would have to be done subtly, in a way that was not humiliating.

Morgenthau observed that "in American language" Monick was saying he wanted "to dress it up and make it look attractive to the French people as a French accomplishment."

"That's not exactly my point," Monick replied. "I want some dressing, but this dressing is not French dressing, I would say."

"As long as it is not Russian dressing," Morgenthau said, "I am satisfied."

"What we want is a dressing of something general," the Frenchman said. "We want a peace dressing. . . . Some months when the political situation will have been cleared, then I hope I shall come

here to talk declaration with you . . . but we want this feeling of
peace and not only to France, but to the world that really this is
monetary peace which is coming now. . . . We must give the feeling in France that the battle is over, and that it is the beginning of
monetary peace and some form of collaboration between the stable
currencies."

Monick then got down to figures. He suggested the pound sterling seek its point of equilibrium between $4.75 and $4.97 (the traditional rate of $4.86 was right in the middle of that spread). This was
essential, he said, for France did not want to make any move that
left the pound completely free to fluctuate. As for the franc, he suggested a range between $0.0475 and $0.0497. France would use the
profit from devaluation, he said, to establish a fund to manage the
franc.

Morgenthau agreed, emphasizing his belief that most of the devaluation profit would have to go to a stabilization fund instead of
going to meet a deficit. "If France has a stabilization fund," the
Secretary said, "England has one and we have one . . . the three
would . . . work together . . . as each one took care of its own
currency."

On June 30, preparing to leave Washington, Monick brought
Morgenthau a cable from Paris expressing the gratitude of the
French. He also thanked the Secretary personally, particularly for
being "extremely frank about everything." Europe, Monick said,
was going to have to choose between democracy and totalitarianism.
Uncertainties, monetary uncertainty not the least, bred fascism, provoked governments "to neglect the liberty and the heart of the people." This was frightening, but now, after his conversations with
Roosevelt and Morgenthau, after hearing the President's stirring attack on fascism in his speech accepting renomination, Monick could
for the first time see a way out for France.

"Your coming here," Morgenthau replied, "made things easier.
. . . It is the exchange of views which gradually will bring about
the stabilization we all hope for, but it takes time."

Indeed it did. Mid-August came and went without results. The
French government, Monick cabled, was delaying because domestic
politics were so tense. For the time being the flight from the franc
had subsided, and Premier Blum was less enthusiastic about taking

the initiative, but the cabinet included several devaluationists and the President was urging the Premier to act. The Minister of National Economy, under pressure from the labor unions to establish a 40-hour week, was afraid to do so before devaluation because he estimated that 20 per cent of French enterprises would close down rather than attempt under existing conditions to bear an added wage burden. Yet as Monick saw it, only a renewed flight from the franc would compel Blum to move.

So Morgenthau waited, convinced that the sooner action came the better, but that sooner or later it would have to come. Meanwhile he discussed with the British the conditions under which it would be possible for the United States to consider selling them gold of which the British Treasury was now especially anxious to have a sure source. British bankers owned gold in France. To withdraw it would further weaken the franc. But a domestic crisis in France, a communist or fascist coup, might result in the freezing of gold stocks, which would leave the British short. Morgenthau's discussions therefore reassured the British, eased pressures on the French, and helped to keep alive the possibility of stabilization.

Because these discussions were obviously also clearing the way for an eventual Anglo-American understanding about gold, Oliphant and others in the Treasury feared they might be interpreted as a repudiation of the gold policy initiated in 1933–1934. The Republicans, they argued, might charge the Administration with abandoning an unsuccessful experiment. Morgenthau disagreed. "I will tell you something, gentlemen," he said. "I have found that the best kind of politics is to do your job well and not think about the political effect on the election. I have done that ever since I have been with Roosevelt and I think I have met with my share of success and to stall this thing because an election is coming I think is just wrong, I just would hate to do it. I don't think in the long run it's good politics — politics in the sense of good Government."

## 8. The Tripartite Pact

During the last days of August 1936, France again suffered serious losses of gold. Blum took them as his cue to maneuver toward devaluation. On September 4 Finance Minister Auriol handed Merle Cochran a provisional draft for an agreement to facilitate French devaluation and to effect international currency stabilization. If the United States and Great Britain found the agreement acceptable, the French intended to ask the Netherlands, Switzerland, and at least two other gold bloc countries to adhere to it. Auriol asked Cochran whether Morgenthau would like to see the draft secretly, previous to its submission to the British, or whether he wanted copies sent simultaneously to both nations. In either case the French hoped to expedite the matter. Through Cochran, Morgenthau replied that he preferred to have the French deal simultaneously with England and the United States. "After months and months," the Secretary told the British embassy in Washington, "something is actually going to happen."

The French draft, which the Treasury received on September 9, was unsatisfactory. It called on England and the United States to maintain the prevailing pound and dollar rates while the franc was lowered. It envisioned cooperation among the three central banks with each assuming the task of holding its own national currency within agreed limits. It cited, as the final objective of the contracting parties, a general return to the international gold standard. The French admittedly had in mind a detailed agreement on monetary rates in the nature of a treaty among the three powers, constructed so as to pertain also to international commerce and inferentially to criticize German and Italian commercial practices. Their plan took a position on the gold standard that Roosevelt had found unacceptable since 1933. It also failed to permit the flexibility which both England and the United States had consistently demanded.

As soon as he received the text of the French draft, Morgenthau asked Secretary Hull to send someone to the Treasury to help draft a reply. Hull selected Herbert Feis. Called to Washington by Henry Stimson, Hoover's distinguished Secretary of State, Feis, a Ph.D. from Harvard, had for some years been the Department's most astute adviser on international economics and finance. He found himself working with men of comparable background and talent. Those who regularly counseled Morgenthau on monetary policy during 1935 and 1936 were Herman Oliphant, Jacob Viner, and Harry White; Assistant Secretary of the Treasury Wayne C. Taylor, a successful banker and financier; George Haas, the veteran head of the Research Division; and Archie Lochhead, a specialist in international exchange who concentrated his trader's talents on interpreting the daily fluctuations in money markets all over the world.

In the end it was Morgenthau who made the decisions and took the responsibilities, and at each consultation he defined the subject for consideration and expressed his own opinions about it. So it was on September 9 at the first meeting to discuss the French draft. The Secretary began by registering his objections. He took exception first of all to setting precise rates which were to remain firm. "We are not ready for that," he said, "because when the United States Government puts its name to it we can live up to it, but the other fellows cannot." As to making a return to the gold standard an ultimate objective, Morgenthau observed, "that is not the Roosevelt philosophy. I cannot say that." He then said what he was ready to do: "I think we ought to agree on very wide points at the beginning — plenty of fluctuation . . . as we gain some experience and find that it is working out successfully then these points can be gradually narrowed down. This will have to be a gentlemen's agreement. . . . England is going to come back and say, well, under these conditions, will you give up gold? And under these conditions the answer is, yes, as between these points. . . . That is how I feel."

Herbert Feis suggested dividing the agreement into two parts, first a public statement of intention, and second, a secret understanding among treasuries about the limits within which the three currencies should fluctuate. Morgenthau concurred, provided the French put "every dollar . . . of profit . . . into the stabilization fund."

"The Blum Cabinet," Feis objected, "is counting on that eight hundred million or one billion dollars to carry them through until the period of devaluation is over. I think I would ask for half of it, knowing what a hole they are in."

"I would ask the whole and probably get half," Morgenthau replied, "rather than ask for a half and get a quarter."

Summing up, Morgenthau repeated "this agreement would have to be a gentlemen's agreement; we would do everything possible to make it successful, but we would have to watch our internal price level just as they would. I would rather put it this way instead of

saying that we will not agree to this and we will agree with that. I
think we ought to make them talk as to how much they would
devalue. We think this is a fine move and this is what we have been
waiting for, for three years, and we will do everything possible to
make it successful."

Morgenthau directed his staff to draft an American reply along
the lines he had set out. These, he learned during the afternoon of
September 9, completely satisfied Cordell Hull. While he awaited
an opinion from the President, Morgenthau asked his advisers to
consider what percentage of devaluation of the franc the United
States should endorse. After some discussion of international price
levels, the Secretary expressed his own opinion that 25 per cent was
too much. It would, he felt, tend to appreciate the dollar dangerously on international exchange. He preferred 15 to 20 per cent
devaluation, to be exceeded only if it became absolutely necessary
for France. Archie Lochhead suggested that a reasonable objective
would be a ratio of five dollars to the pound* and a hundred francs
to the pound. This would leave the franc at five cents. These figures fell outside the percentages Morgenthau favored, but they
suited the President.

Roosevelt, who had been motoring through the Great Smokies,
telephoned at 11:00 P.M. He considered the Treasury's draft "better
than good." Particularly pleased that Morgenthau had deleted all
references to the gold standard, the President had only one recommendation. The draft had preserved the language of the French
proposal suggesting the three central banks cooperate to manage the
currencies. Roosevelt wanted to eliminate the central banks. The
three treasuries, he said, should manage their currencies. This was
more than a matter of vocabulary. It emphasized Roosevelt's conviction, and Morgenthau's, that monetary policy was the obligation
of government, not of private finance.

Morgenthau rushed to cable the American reply to Paris, but the
British delayed several days while Chamberlain completed a holiday
in Scotland. On September 14 the Chancellor of the Exchequer,
taking a position similar to the American, assured the French that
he would take no countermeasures against a reasonable devaluation
of the franc. But Chamberlain was unwilling to link sterling to

* The prevailing ratio then was $5.07.

gold between fixed points, nor would he limit his power of independent action by signing a formal agreement such as that which the French proposed. Like Morgenthau, he wanted to remain on a day-to-day basis, to avoid any declaration that resembled a treaty, and to rely instead upon informal cooperation and international good will.

This reply pleased both Roosevelt and Morgenthau, but in spite of the British and American responses, the French scarcely modified their original proposal. On September 17 they communicated a revised draft which remained unacceptable to the other governments. The preamble called for a simultaneous declaration by the three powers advocating international monetary order for the purpose of safeguarding peace and liberty. The Americans considered a simultaneous declaration as tantamount to a treaty. They objected also to French phraseology identifying the declaration with the improvement of the standard of living of all social classes. As Oliphant said: "We can't talk about social classes in America." The French, furthermore, again made the return to an international gold standard the final objective of the agreement. Their draft remarked, too, that international stability awaited a lasting compromise among the various economies based upon world prices. Roosevelt and Morgenthau much preferred to refer instead to a fair price level within each country. The French, moreover, assigned the maintenance of stability to the treasuries and banks of issue of the three countries, whereas Roosevelt and Morgenthau remained firm in their determination to speak only of the treasuries.

Doubtless aware of how unyielding they had been, the French made a "really beseeching plea" for the acceptance of their second draft; but Morgenthau, as he told his staff, preferred doing nothing to adopting it. He would not proceed further until he knew exactly what degree of devaluation the French had in mind, but they had yet to mention this. He wanted them to get down to business. "This thing is a lot of hooey," he said. "It may be very nice for the French people, but there is nothing in here that the President and I have said on monetary things. . . . If we knew how much they were going to devalue, I think we could get a joint statement very quickly. But as long as we don't know, I think all talks about the statement are useless. . . . I suggest that the French Government read our note very carefully because we have stated our ideas. . . . It goes without saying that we cannot enter into any agreement which will definitely tie our hands or which looks forward to a return to the gold standard." Roosevelt concurred. "It's terrible," he said of the French proposal. "It gives me a pain."

Morgenthau telephoned instructions to Cochran on September 18. Among other things, he told him to ask the French politely whether they would say confidentially what percentage of devaluation they were planning. He appreciated that they had made some concessions, but they would have also to accept his remaining reservations.

One of these produced a rift within the Treasury. Jacob Viner proposed inviting Marriner Eccles, the Chairman of the Board of Governors of the Federal Reserve System, to join the conferences on the stabilization agreement. Morgenthau demurred: "In the first draft of the message from the French they spoke of the three central banks. The President cut that out himself and changed it to read 'the three treasuries.' In the cable which they sent yesterday they again spoke of the banks and the President said again to cut that out. I would not trust half of that Board to keep these negotiations secret."

"I think they ought to be at least informed," Viner argued. "It will be a mark of lack of confidence if the President does not trust his own Federal Reserve Board."

"I just cannot see that," Morgenthau said. "At the London Economic Conference, George Harrison was the mouthpiece and whenever there was anything on international monetary matters George Harrison handled it. Now Harrison is not doing it. I am. . . . I would rather have this thing a success and be technically wrong in history. . . . I am not going to let anybody interfere on this thing."

The Treasury staff had adjourned and reconvened when in midafternoon Friday, September 18, Cochran called from Paris. The French, he reported happily, welcomed changes in phraseology. The Americans could write the agreement as they chose. He also had information on the extent of devaluation, but he was apparently concerned lest a telephone operator overhear that secret.

*"Können Sie Deutsch sprechen,"* Cochran asked.

"What's that?" said Morgenthau, whose German was weak.

*"Können Sie Deutsch verstehen?"*

*"Ja."* (Hopefully)

" *— von vier und zwanzig bis zwei und dreissig —* "

"Yes," Morgenthau said, relieved. "I got that." Then he began to roar with laughter. "Excuse me, Cochran. I suppose nobody else in the world speaks German either. Next time try Turkish."

"Chinese," said Cochran.

Cochran's German meant a devaluation of the franc by from 24 to 32 per cent which in turn meant an exchange rate of from 100 to 110 francs to the pound. The British, Cochran said, could probably stand at least 100, but Chamberlain was not in London, and there would be no decision until he returned.

"In other words," Morgenthau replied, "nothing could interfere with an English week end." But as the Secretary told Cordell Hull a few minutes later, he was "much more hopeful." The French figures on devaluation were not impossible, and he expected the British to accept them.

The Treasury group began immediately to draft a stabilization agreement. Their plan was for each government to issue an independent statement. To protect against misunderstanding, they intended to clear each statement with every participating government and then to have the statements released simultaneously. The Treasury's draft was straightforward. The government of the United States, it read, after consulting with the British and French governments, joined with them to safeguard peace and restore order in international economic relations, to promote world prosperity and raise living standards. All the nations, of course, had to take full account of the requirements of internal prosperity, but the United States welcomed the opportunity to reaffirm its purpose of maintaining the greatest possible equilibrium in international exchange. France had informed the United States of her decision to devalue. The United States as well as Great Britain welcomed this decision and proposed through their own actions to minimize any exchange disturbances resulting from the French readjustment. The three governments would cooperate to that end, convinced that their policy was linked to the development of international trade. They invited the cooperation of other nations and they attached particular importance to an immediate attack on existing systems of trade quotas and exchange controls.

The draft delighted Morgenthau, who reviewed it with his advisers the evening of September 18. "I can't change it," he said. "I think it is swell." But he wondered about adding a warning to countries that might try to damage the agreement. Besides inviting "the collaboration of other nations," he thought they might say: "We feel that the three countries are strong enough to resist the interference of any other nation." As he put it to his staff: "In other words, we ask you to get on board, but look out — don't try to wreck this thing or we will be on your neck. This is a threat to Italy and Germany — don't try to undervalue because you are going to go under. . . . This is a notice to Japan, Germany and Italy that we won't stand any monkey business. . . . This is a notice to the boys — *Achtung!*"

Herbert Feis questioned the propriety of concluding with even a quiet threat. "We have numerous potential causes of war now," Feis said. "I don't like to bring into the arena as another cause of war national action as regards the value of currency and I think if you bring it out in such terms you are directing public opinion to regard these words as so valuable."

Morgenthau interrupted: "Shall we be very frank with each other? . . . There is a difference of approach on these things. I am not saying I am going to do this thing. What I am trying to forestall is particularly Germany and I am thinking also of Japan. It's very easy for them to change their yen rate and the only country that does not suffer through this is Japan. We definitely suffer temporarily and so does England . . . I think we are at an immediate disadvantage until the realignment takes place. Now, why not at this time simply serve notice to any country, but don't let's mention any country, that the three countries who are trying to accomplish something in monetary peace won't brook any interference. . . . And again using Germany, if Germany should immediately devalue forty per cent this is notice to her that we will all get together and take steps to protect ourselves."

"Henry," Feis said, "I don't think I made myself clear. The minute you mentioned the idea of working into the statement something that would have as its purpose the nature of warning against an attempt to disrupt, I agree. It's against the form of presentation because — and this is what I did not make clear . . . that . . . would bring the peoples throughout the world to attach a certain new type of importance to moves in the currencies field — a new type of importance; a sharpening of their feeling that it is a matter of vital interest; the type of vital interest in the defense of which they might be led to use arms. I am dealing entirely with the presentation."

Morgenthau, agreeable to temperate language so long as its meaning was clear, had his staff append to the American statement a sentence that also satisfied Feis. The United States, the addition read, "trusts that no country will attempt to obtain an unreasonable competitive exchange advantage and thereby hamper the effort to restore stable economic relations which it is the aim of the three Governments to promote." This quiet warning exactly suited the Secretary. "After three months," he teased, "I have won against the career diplomats. Three cheers!"

On September 19 Roosevelt approved the completed draft which Morgenthau then transmitted to Paris and London. The initial response from both capitals was favorable, but final word was delayed while Chamberlain, back at his desk on September 21, pondered his own reply to Auriol. Meanwhile the French continued to lose staggering quantities of gold and Morgenthau, as he put it to Hull, was "just a little bit shaky in the knees about the whole thing, because it is so important."

While he waited, Morgenthau decided to prepare the American financial community for the forthcoming declaration. He did so by answering a letter of September 2 from Arthur Vandenberg of Michigan, one of the leading Republicans in the Senate, who had written him questioning the advisability of purchasing gold at $35 an ounce. Vandenberg observed that Europeans had found the means to buy American securities by selling gold to the United States government, but European governments meanwhile continued to decline to pay their war debts. He argued that the Democratic gold purchase program in effect subsidized Europe at the expense of the American people. Morgenthau replied in a public letter of September 22. It was not the price of gold but insecure political and economic conditions, he wrote, that provoked the movement of international capital to the United States. If the political disturbances in Europe and the Orient were to disappear, there would be a reflux of a portion of that capital. "It would be an excellent thing to the United States, as well as for the world," Morgenthau asserted, "if such events should come to pass." Even a relatively heavy outflow of gold would not hurt the American credit base. The Stabilization Fund, furthermore, could now prevent temporary maladjustments in exchange rates, whereas in 1931 that had not been possible. By suggesting that he would be glad to see gold leave the country, the Secretary felt he was setting the stage for the gold policy that would have to accompany the three-power monetary cooperation.

He was also anticipating Republican criticism of the monetary agreement, which worried Roosevelt, too. The President did not want the American public to interpret the agreement as a departure from the basic purposes which he had set for monetary policy at the time of the London Conference. On September 24 he wrote out for Morgenthau a memorandum of what might be said to the newspapers whenever the agreement was announced. "This does not mean [a return] to old gold standard," Roosevelt began, "or an agreement to do so in future. It supports and sustains the American domestic price level. It leaves each country free to act in case its domestic price level is adversely affected. Because we have too much gold bullion for American needs this will provide an opportunity for other nations to acquire a part of the excess thus stimulating world trade. . . . And finally America's position is fully safeguarded while at the same time our action should encourage peace and commerce."

Roosevelt was equally sensitive to criticism from the Coughlinite Union party, whose candidate, Congressman William Lemke, was an ardent inflationist. After talking with the President, Morgenthau said to his staff: "Did any of you see what Mr. Lemke said. . . . He talked about international bankers. Lemke and Coughlin say we have sold out to the international bankers. We have not. We can't just brush this thought aside. What we have done is, we have taken the foreign exchange business and put it in the hands of the countries." He continued, like the President, therefore, to insist that

France and England also make it clear that they would operate through their treasuries rather than their central banks.

Roosevelt's political instincts also influenced the Treasury's thinking about cross rates for the dollar, pound, and franc. The President wanted a five-dollar pound. Sterling was at $5.07. He was willing to let it drop to $4.90, but not to the traditional, pre-1931 level of $4.86. Information from Cochran, however, indicated that the British and French were contemplating a cross rate that would equate the pound with 105 francs. This would set up a pound-dollar ratio of 4.86. Morgenthau therefore informed Cochran that it would not do. The President, he observed, was "keenly interested in this thing," and he had felt it necessary again "to feel his pulse so I could refresh myself as to just how he did feel and, of course, I thought I had his viewpoint — now I know I have it."

When Harry White suggested that a five-dollar rate might be too high for the British, Morgenthau replied that Bewley had several times told him England was satisfied with $5.07. "In this room," the Secretary continued, "we can't do the other thing five or six weeks before election. We can't go out and talk about a 4.86 pound. We didn't pick this time. . . . Five weeks before election and a 4.86 pound are impossible." To his relief, the British, responding to an American statement about cross rates, said they took for granted a five-dollar pound with a ten-cent leeway up or down. Morgenthau's advisers, furthermore, saw no reason why the United States could not maintain that rate. "You have given me the assurance I wanted," Morgenthau told them late in the evening of September 24. ". . . All right, I'm going to bed." It had been a long day.

On the morning of the 25th, Cochran called from Paris with a summary of the British comments on the proposed American text. The Chancellor of the Exchequer accepted it fully. He noted, however, that he had no legal authority to fix the pound within gold points. Furthermore, it was British policy to let the pound find its natural level. Possibly this level was $5; possibly it was lower. The British reply in any case made no precise allusion to $4.86, though it did say specifically that the Chancellor would not deliberately depreciate the pound. The French government, Cochran said, also satisfied with the American text, would request authority to devalue from 25 to 34.35 per cent, with a mid-point of about 30 per cent — slightly more than Morgenthau had expected. The government would use ten billion francs for a stabilization fund and allocate the rest of the profit from depreciation for current expenses. A cable from London confirmed Cochran's report, and in a later message Chamberlain suggested issuing the simultaneous declarations at approximately 9 P.M. British time, or 3 P.M. American time, on September 25.

Morgenthau then called Roosevelt. The President, "sick and tired" because Chamberlain constantly referred to himself as "the Chancellor of the Exchequer" and to Morgenthau by name, recommended the following reply: "The Secretary of the Treasury is glad to have Mr. Chamberlain's note. . . . It is a matter of opinion as to whether under the new circumstances a natural level of the pound would be at five dollars. . . . However, as long as Mr. Chamberlain understands that we believe the five-dollar level to be the appropriate one . . . without agreeing to Mr. Chamberlain's present thought of a lower rate between the dollar and the pound, the Secretary of the Treasury believes that this is not an obstacle that need prevent the issuance of the simultaneous statements in order to carry out their broad, useful and indeed essential objective."

"This is the way I feel," Morgenthau said. "I think the French are going to do it anyway. . . . I can explain that this is not ideal; that the peace of the world is at stake and that for that reason we are going along. Here is the interesting thing. The real big financiers are going to be tickled to death with this; they are going to consider this the real turning point for world peace and there is nobody among the big financial crowd who can criticize you and that is where your real opposition comes from. I am almost dazed. I have the British in the other room. I have tied up the telephone from two o'clock overseas. I hope you have had a good lunch. I have had none."

That afternoon Morgenthau showed Hull the message Roosevelt had dictated, explaining that he had not yet delivered it to the British. It was, Hull said, "much better than I hoped for." With obvious relief, Morgenthau then admitted: "I thought the President might back off and say, no."

Moments later Morgenthau handed the British the reply to Chamberlain substantially as Roosevelt had dictated it. "If this goes through," he commented, "I think it is the greatest move taken for peace in the world since the World War. . . . It may be the turning point for again resuming rational thinking in Europe. It may be just the thing to again bring reason back to these perfectly mad people. Let's hope so. . . . After all, we are the only three liberal governments left. . . . And the beauty of the thing is — there are no signatures. It is good faith. We have confidence in each other, and I would ten times rather shake hands than have all the signatures in the world. Signatures haven't been worth much."

At 4:20 P.M. Morgenthau spoke with Cochran. The earliest hour at which everything could be straightened out, he noted, was midnight Paris time. "Well," Cochran said, "we'll try and keep the President up then, if we can."

"How does one keep the President of France up," Morgenthau asked. "What's going on at the Montmartre tonight?"

At 5 P.M. Washington time, with the end in sight, Morgenthau was ready to tell the Federal Reserve what was going on. He telephoned George Harrison of the New York Federal Reserve Bank, Governor Ransom, Eccles's deputy on the Federal Reserve Board, and also James M. Landis of the Securities and Exchange Commission. He also talked with Marriner Eccles, who was in Utah. Just as he finished, a message arrived from Auriol that the President of France wanted to go to bed and could not wait until he got American approval of the French text. First provoked, Morgenthau was then amused that Cochran's prediction had proved accurate. "As a matter of history," he said to the French attaché, ". . . we have approved the note but we are awaiting for the Chancellor of the Exchequer."

The Secretary then talked again with Roosevelt. "The French," he said, "have accepted our . . . draft in toto without changing a word. I handed this thing to the British around four o'clock, and I told them that I wanted some kind of an acknowledgment from the Chancellor and that they should phone him, but that we would not release the various messages until we heard from the Chancellor, so the French and ourselves are sitting here waiting. . . . Hull is just tickled pink. He thinks it is the greatest thing that has happened. . . . Eccles . . . is delighted.

"Now the other thing which is almost unbelievable is that the British have overlooked . . . the right to get gold from us. . . . This is something they know I would give them. . . . This is something they have been hinting at for months. Your policy, and one you have taught me, is to make them ask."

Waiting for the British was hard for the French. Cochran later described the scene in Paris: "I was seated in the chair of the Minister of Finance. With him and his colleagues and assistants pacing the floor of the magnificent Empire salon, in the old Louvre palace which he occupies, glancing at their watches, grinding cigarette stubs into the marvelous carpets, and listening to the rumble of voices from the press representatives outside their door, made the situation extremely tense. Finally, you told me that the British had arrived at your office. We then waited until you had studied the reply. When you let us know that this was satisfactory and that we were in final agreement, there was great relief on the French side."

That occurred at 6:35 P.M., September 25, Washington time. Chamberlain, taking note of the American views, agreed that they constituted no obstacle to publication of the declaration. He proposed to use the American text and to release it at once. "The British are going to release this now at once," the Secretary told Cochran on the telephone, "so I say it might be all right to release it, and I'd like to try some of my very poor French to congratulate Mr. Auriol." Auriol came to the phone and Morgenthau, first in French and then in English, wished him "great success." He also thanked Cochran for his "splendid work" and suggested that Cochran and Auriol go out and have a drink on him.

The Secretary had one small task left. To Roosevelt he sent a jocular telegram: "A special messenger has just arrived from the French Embassy and wishes to inform me that the President of France wishes to go to bed. Please advise me what I should do in this great emergency."

Just before 8 P.M. he received a reply: "The President says . . . to tell Embassy to employ any American visitor now in Paris. Costs on the French Government — no commissions or liabilities."

The fun added to Morgenthau's ebullience. "I am thrilled —," he told Roosevelt on the telephone, "so thrilled I don't know what to say." Jake Viner thought he had every right to be. "When they build your monument," the economist said, "this will be high on the list of your battles."

The Tripartite Agreement immediately won general applause. Belgium, Switzerland, Holland, even Italy quickly announced their adherence to its principles. The London *Times* expected that it might "prove to be a step, the first of several, towards the ultimate stabilization of the world currencies." The *Times* was especially pleased that it minimized the risk of destructive competition to reduce the purchasing power of currencies. The Manchester *Guardian* expressed the hope that now "the way to European economic cooperation will become easier." American newspapers and commentators were equally enthusiastic. Walter Lippmann, in a column similar to editorials written throughout the nation, called the agreement a "sure foundation" for escaping the "evil results" which had been building up since the collapse of the gold standard in 1931.

Minister of Finance Auriol, perhaps the most relieved of all the negotiators, thanked Morgenthau personally in a letter of October 5: "The French Parliament has enacted our proposal for the realignment of the franc. It is delighted with the agreement of the three great democracies. . . . In turn, I congratulate myself on the adherence of almost all the nations of the world to our common declaration which put the definite end to the monetary war and opened the road toward the 'economic peace' — so essential to peace among nations. . . . I do not know how to find words sufficiently expressive to convey to you the thanks of President Leon Blum and his Government, and of myself, for the energetic, enthusiastic and wholehearted cooperation which you have given us. I hope that this collaboration will continue in the work toward world economic peace which must be achieved if peace among peoples is to be attained."

## 9. A Bearish Interlude

On Saturday, September 26, the day after the announcement of the Tripartite Pact, Morgenthau had to use the Stabilization Fund to sustain the value of the pound. The markets in London and Paris were closed when Lochhead reported at nine in the morning that sterling had fallen to $4.94 in New York. Morgenthau did not want sterling to close low, for that would make it seem as if the Treasury, in spite of the Tripartite Agreement, either could not or would not control fluctuations of exchange. He therefore immediately instructed the New York Federal Reserve Bank to buy $1,000,000 worth of sterling for the Stabilization Fund at the lowest price at which it could be had. Within fifteen minutes the Fund acquired £50,000 at $4.91.

Reporting this purchase, the New York Federal Reserve Bank explained that the Russian government had an order in to sell £1,000,000 at the best price. Morgenthau asked at once why he had not been told that before. Clearly the Russian selling order was pulling sterling down. The Secretary directed the Bank to pull out all buying orders and to tell the Chase National Bank, which was handling the sale for the Russians, that the Federal Reserve Bank would buy the entire £1,000,000. "They are trying to break down this agreement and I am calling the President and will ask him whether I can give this out publicly," the Secretary added.

"I want your permission," Morgenthau told Roosevelt, "to announce that the Russian Government tried to break this thing and that we bought the one million pounds sterling that they had ordered dumped on our market. Before I actually do it, I want to call you back once more. The negotiations are going on right now between the Federal Reserve Bank and the Chase. Those bastards want to break this thing so that Blum cannot get his support. In talking to Paris this morning they said that the only people who were fighting Blum on this is the Communist Party. We are the only market that is open and they are trying to break the market here."

George Harrison objected to making the transaction public, but Morgenthau assured him that he would ask permission from the Chase before he did so and that he would not reveal that the Chase was handling the Russian account. Checking the market, the Secretary discovered that the Federal Reserve Bank had bought £900,000 for the Stabilization Fund from the Chase, but that £100,000 had been sold in the market before the Treasury order was executed. After ordering the Reserve Bank to clean up the market, Morgenthau thanked the senior officer present at the Chase for the Bank's cooperation and told him that he wanted to release a story about the sale. "I cannot help but feel that they did this for political purposes," the Secretary said. "It will have a more healthy effect to announce that they placed this order and I bought it." He understood, he added, that if Chase had not handled the order, some other bank would have. He had nothing against the Chase and would not give it any bad publicity. Only then did the Chase disclose that the Russian order to sell was actually for £1,200,000 of which £300,000 had been sold on the market.

Before calling a press conference "to give notice to the world that we will not let Russia or anybody else wreck this thing," Morgenthau made sure he had Roosevelt's consent. The Treasury had never before revealed exactly how it was using the Stabilization Fund. Now its use, Morgenthau remarked, "answers Hearst" who was accusing the New Deal of being soft on Russia.

The Secretary began his press conference by drawing attention to the part of the American statement on the Tripartite Agreement that expressed the hope no country would attempt to hamper efforts to restore more stable economic relations. He then described in detail how Russian sales that morning had driven the pound down from the previous day's level of $5.02 to $4.91. He had then entered the market. "This is . . . the only instance today," he said, "of any government, any bank, or any individual trying to artificially influence the foreign exchange market in the United States and I point out that both London and Paris are closed and I sincerely hope that this incident will not be repeated."

On September 28 Winthrop Aldrich, the president of the Chase National Bank, telephoned Morgenthau. The Russian transaction, Aldrich insisted, was perfectly ordinary business, necessary because Russia had to pay $6,000,000 to Sweden and therefore had to sell pounds to get dollars. He agreed that the timing was bad and that the sale drove down the market; but he thought Russia, trying to cover as rapidly as possible, had had to act on a Saturday when only the American market was open. He saw nothing sinister in his customer's purpose. "Let's say there was nothing sinister," Morgenthau replied, "but I mean on the other hand they weren't willing to cooperate with every other country in the world and give this thing a chance."

Talking later with his friend Arthur Sulzberger, the publisher of the *New York Times,* Morgenthau mentioned his "particular satis-

faction" in breaking "this idea that there was any relationship between us and Russia." He considered Aldrich's explanation of Russia's behavior stupid. Sulzberger, agreeing, pointed out that the
Russians could perfectly well have used pounds to pay the Swedes.

The Russians were furious about Morgenthau's statement to the
press. It was absurd, the Tass Agency maintained, to get excited
about an ordinary banking transaction "effected by the State Bank
through the Chase Bank in New York." So from the Russians themselves the Chase received the publicity it had been trying to avoid.
The Russians also asserted that they had needed over $6,000,000 for
payments in Stockholm. That was not true. They could have paid
in pounds or, as Morgenthau contended, they could have waited to
convert the pounds until all the money markets were open. The
Secretary had had ample reason for acting and ample grounds for
suspicion.

He also saw the amusing side of the episode. "I have had more
fun," he told Roosevelt. "Aldrich had me on the phone explaining
what a wonderful government Russia is; how we misunderstood
them; that this was a legitimate transaction. I told him that I
would take his word for it, but why did they have to do it on Saturday? That everybody else waited, but they could not. Today the
Chase received a telegram from the Russians which practically says,
we told you to sell the one million pounds sterling at the best. Why
did you sell it at the worst? Aldrich is so worried and Harrison is
so worried. As I told George Harrison today, I just love to hear . . .
Aldrich come to the defense of the Russian government. . . . Here
is Aldrich, close to Landon, and he comes out and makes a statement showing that he is befriending the Russians."

The President suggested Morgenthau slip the story to some newspaperman, but the Secretary said he had never planted a story like
this before and would not now. He had stomach for neither elec-
tioneering nor revenge. But he was pleased. As he put it to Roosevelt: "Aldrich and Harrison have learned by now that they are not
running the Treasury of the United States."

## 10. The Currency Club

To make the Tripartite Agreement fully effective, the Treasury still had two jobs to complete. Morgenthau and his associates had to decide under what conditions the participating nations were to give up gold to each other. They had also to arrange to permit Switzerland, Holland, and Belgium, all of whom had endorsed the agreement, to participate in it.

On October 5 Morgenthau reviewed the gold problem. The United States, he noted, was buying sterling but could not convert it. Sterling was declining partly because England was buying dollars but had no way of converting them to gold. France also was buying dollars she could not convert. All this could be remedied if each nation would quote a daily price at which it would sell gold to the others. Then, if the franc weakened, the United States would be in a position to support it with the foreknowledge that francs purchased on any day could be converted to gold at the price established for that day. All the prices would pivot around the American gold price of $35 an ounce.

Neville Chamberlain welcomed Morgenthau's suggestion for cooperation between stabilization funds for conversion of currency into gold and gold into currency. There was obviously no difficulty in converting dollars into gold or gold into dollars, for this could be done as Morgenthau proposed, with the United States Treasury buying and selling gold at $35 an ounce plus or minus the expenses of transportation and insurance. The conversion of sterling into gold was a little more difficult. Through Bewley, Chamberlain suggested the United States Treasury convert sterling that it acquired into gold in London at a price to be fixed daily by an exchange of cables. If the Treasury were oversold in sterling as a result of control operations, the Bank of England would be willing to buy gold from the Treasury at prices similarly set. These arrangements, which were immediately acceptable to Great Britain, France and the United States, could be extended as other nations subscribed to them.

At a press conference on October 12 Morgenthau announced the new system. "Each country," he said, "operates its own stabilization fund to equalize its own currency by buying and selling exchange in terms of other currencies. . . . In this market we buy sterling or francs; in London they would be buying dollars or francs. No country wishes, through these operations, to accumulate too much paper currency of the other countries, and, therefore, we propose to permit each country to convert the other countries' paper money into gold, the price being fixed each day. This represents a divorcement of the the control of the foreign exchange market from the few individual international speculators. The responsible governments of the people will now cooperate to assure a minimum exchange fluctuation. Businessmen with merchandise to sell abroad, or businessmen who are importing merchandise, will be free to operate through their respective banks in regular and normal exchange operations. The international speculator, responsible to no one, and recognizing no flag in the conduct of his business, will in the future not be able by rapidly shifting his fund from market to market, to reap private advantage through stimulating chaos in foreign exchange."

Morgenthau wanted to bring the smaller democracies into the system — "the currency club," as he came to call it — as soon as possible. They were anxious to participate. Furthermore, England was losing gold to them, and Morgenthau and Bewley believed that it would ease the strain on England if the small democracies could draw directly upon the United States. In the case of Holland and Switzerland there was no problem, for both countries had stabilization funds and were willing to operate on a twenty-four-hour basis. Belgium, however, alone of the Western nations, remained on the old gold standard. She had no stabilization fund and was reluctant to establish one, for her central bank had been a satisfactory fiscal agent for her treasury. American bankers seemed extraordinarily anxious to maintain a separate relationship with Belgium. "Underneath the whole thing is this fight to keep Belgium as she is," Morgenthau told his staff. ". . . That's what Harrison said to me — 'Keep Belgium as she is, so eventually we can go back to the old gold standard.' . . . They want to keep a little piece of sour dough."

As Morgenthau explored the situation, he concluded that he objected only to having a central bank itself set daily gold prices. If the Belgian treasury stood behind the bank, he had nothing against dealing with the bank as its agent. His doubts dispelled, he completed negotiations with Belgium, Holland and Switzerland, and on November 24, 1936, announced that they had adhered to the Tripartite Pact and were entitled to exchange gold on the same daily basis as France and England.

With this announcement Morgenthau fulfilled the promises he had made to the world and to himself in May 1935. He had completed arrangements to make the gold policy of the United States a handmaiden of international monetary stability and thereby of international peace. There was of course a long road ahead. Implementation of the new policies would be both crucial and exacting, but the declarations of September, October and November set the ground rules which were to obtain until the outbreak of war in Europe made them no longer pertinent. The achievement was impressive, significant for both the monetary and the political well-being of the European democracies.

Although in a campaign year Roosevelt preferred not to mention it, the United States had come a long way since the London Conference. As economists pointed out, the Tripartite Agreement of 1936 and the two agreements supplementing it provided an essential means for international monetary exchange. These agreements gave the French government the international endorsement it needed for devaluation. They gave the British a broader base for managing the pound. And they helped the American treasury. It had previously limited gold exports to central banks of nations on a full gold standard. This would have been an untenable position after French devaluation, because only the Belgian bank thereafter met the Treasury's specifications. Furthermore, the new arrangements for sales and purchases of gold provided the Treasury with vital contacts abroad.

These benefits were essentially technical, but technical operations had broad implications. The democracies had accepted the American price of gold as the basis for evaluating their currencies. They had utilized special instruments, stabilization funds or their equivalent, to act as the agencies for this operation. Stabilization funds had originally been considered emergency weapons; now they were recognized as the successors to central banks in international finance. The participating governments, furthermore, had entered into a monetary relationship which acknowledged that the international values of their respective currencies were a matter of mutual interest. They had demonstrated their concern for keeping order in international exchange. Although perhaps tentatively, their agreements established international comity where previously there had been hostility or suspicion.

The old gold standard was gone, as it happened not just for a season but for a long, long time, perhaps for ever. Under its operations money had been as much a measure of value as a medium of exchange. The gradual divorce of Europe from gold after 1931, the gradual divorce of the United States from gold during 1933 and 1934 left money primarily a medium of exchange. The advocates of the old gold standard had often asserted that it was not manipulable. It was presumed to respond mechanically to automatic operations of internal and external economies. But this was not necessarily an asset. Other standards could be manipulated, and in a time of internal stresses and international difficulties, management was in order. Initially the New Deal, like other governments, had conceived of monetary management primarily as a device for solving internal problems. Certainly this had been Morgenthau's purpose in the fall of 1933 when he advocated the gold purchase program. But gradually the United States government, in large part because of Morgenthau's changing ideas and capable direction, came to view the management of money as vital not only for domestic recovery but also for the support of democratic nations in a troubled world.

Morgenthau did not conceive of himself as abandoning the policies initiated in 1933, but rather as expanding and adapting them to the large needs of the Atlantic community. It was cooperation among gentlemen rather than exact stabilization that the Tripartite Agreement assured. None of the participating nations was to abandon its concentration on internal needs, but all of them, conscious of the political and economic dangers of fascism, were resolved thereafter to devise and protect mutually beneficial monetary arrangements. This multilateral thinking had not existed when England gave up gold in 1931 or when Roosevelt in 1933 followed suit, driven by domestic conditions to think first and only of the American economy. As the French faced their crisis of 1936, however, the two English-speaking powers, like the French themselves, had to view their internal problems in conjunction with those of Western Europe.

Roosevelt and Morgenthau had consistently favored placing ultimate responsibility and authority for monetary policy in the Treasury rather than the Federal Reserve System, an agency of the private banks. The internationalizing of the management of money for mutually beneficial purposes reinforced their preference. Money was one factor in international health, and for consultations on international health, the appropriate doctors were the governments of the world. Where money was the issue, the Treasury spoke for the United States. This gave Morgenthau a clear mandate in one sphere of foreign policy. Hull resented this division of authority over foreign affairs, but it served Roosevelt's purposes, for he could rely on Morgenthau to face up to situations that Hull preferred to avoid, and he could in any crisis decide which of his two secretaries to support.

From the beginning there was no question in Morgenthau's mind but that the agreements he was negotiating had large political meaning. His conversations repaired constantly to political themes. He and his associates in the Treasury did not want to see France go the way of fascism. They were disturbed by the German threat to France and to Belgium. The Tripartite Agreement was scarcely an offensive against totalitarianism; Europe was not ready for that. But it was an early reaction to fascism, the first evidence that the Western democracies could profit collectively from mutually acceptable concessions. It was welcomed, as Cochran put it, "most enthusiastically by a world which had almost despaired of international cooperation. For such an agreement to be reached secretly, but cordially, between three great democracies in a time when so many political situations were causing worry, gave ground for much relief and did a great deal to reawaken hope."

"Japan," Morgenthau suggested to Bewley, "thought . . . there would be . . . revolution in France. And while everybody was worried over there, this was the time to jump on China. . . . Japan . . . has backed down. . . . This has caught her unaware as it caught Germany, and this thing has steadied Germany and Japan." There was something in this analysis. The Tripartite Agreement and its supplements, the evidence of friendship among the United

States, England, France and the small democracies, probably did temporarily give pause to Germany, Italy and Japan. Though he knew difficult days lay ahead, Morgenthau could for the moment feel "like the cat that swallowed the canary . . . very pleased."

# V

# Statecraft for Silver

## *1933-1936*

### 1. "Something for Silver"

THE STRUCTURE of congressional politics prevented Franklin Roosevelt from ever forgetting his campaign promise to "do something for silver." He had to do much more than he intended, for the powerful friends of that metal effectively imposed their purpose upon the New Deal. To Morgenthau's dismay, it fell to the Treasury to execute the policy they devised. He never got rid of it, but he did learn to minimize its unfortunate domestic and international effects, even to use it, as he used gold policy, to encourage resistance to fascist aggression. This was political alchemy of a very high order.

Foremost among the agitators for increasing the price of silver were the owners and managers of silver mines and their employees. They had some natural allies. Silver was so often found with other metals that any subsidy it received enriched the producers of zinc, lead, and especially copper. These mining interests, strong in the sparsely populated mountain states of the West, carried great weight in the Senate. There during the 1930's the silver bloc included at least twelve and, in some congresses, up to sixteen men, many of them senior Democrats and skillful tacticians.

Their objective was to commit the government to buy all the silver produced in the United States at $1.29 an ounce, the arbitrary value established by Congress for the silver which the Treasury owned and used as money. The market price of the metal during 1933 was about 45 cents. Obligatory federal purchases at $1.29

would provide a handsome subsidy and, according to the reasoning of the silver bloc, raise the price of silver on world as well as domestic markets. This in turn, the silverites argued fatuously, would increase the purchasing power of China and other countries on a silver standard and thus create a potentially vast market for American goods. In fact, of course, an artificially swollen price would drain those countries of their silver reserves.

Proponents of inflation, sympathetic allies of the silver bloc, wanted to have the government make greater use of silver for monetary purposes, either in coins or as a reserve for paper money. This objective was part of the historic cult that fed on resentment against Wall Street and international bankers who, according to the folklore, used the gold standard to further a sinister conspiracy against farmers. By no means guileless themselves, inflationists and silverites, contriving to enlist other interest groups, proposed using silver to pay pensions to veterans and subsidies to cotton growers.

The farm conferences that Morgenthau attended early in 1933 made demands for the use of silver which the Thomas Amendment to the Agricultural Adjustment Act of that year gave the President permission to satisfy. Roosevelt held back as long as he dared, but he did make a gesture of concession by appointing Key Pittman of Nevada, the Democratic chairman of the Senate Foreign Relations Committee, to the American delegation to the London Conference. In his cups or out of them an ardent and inelegant champion of silver, Pittman directed his energies at London almost exclusively to negotiations in behalf of the metal he loved. The London Silver Agreement, which Roosevelt accepted by proclamation in December 1933, limited the melting and selling of silver coinage and bound silver-producing countries to consume among them 35,000,000, ounces annually. The President's implementing proclamation directed the Treasury for four years to purchase substantially that entire amount. Roosevelt also, however, ordered the Treasury to pay only 64.5 cents an ounce, half the statutory price but still a bonus of about 20 cents an ounce above the prevailing market price. The Treasury took the balance of the statutory price as a book profit for monetizing the silver.

Though Morgenthau felt that Roosevelt had gone too far, the silverites and inflationists, who had expected no deduction for seigniorage, were unappeased. They struck hard in January 1934, during the debate about the Gold Reserve bill. Senator Burton K. Wheeler of Montana, an agrarian Democrat, introduced an amendment making mandatory the purchase of 50,000,000 ounces of silver a month until a billion ounces had been added to the monetary reserve. Although Roosevelt expressed his own and the Treasury's opposition to the amendment, it failed by only two votes. Even that margin was possible only because the President accepted a substitute proposal giving him authority to issue paper money against all silver the Treasury might acquire. These powers were permissive, but it was clear that Congress intended to demand more.

On March 10, 1934, the House Coinage Committee reported out a bill designed by Representative Martin Dies of Texas. It provided for the sale of surplus farm products abroad in return for payments in silver at a premium of 10 to 25 per cent above the world price. It had the support of the Committee for the Nation and of the radio priest, Father Charles E. Coughlin, whose sermons on cheap money were commanding huge audiences every Sunday. In contrast, the Economists' National Committee and 85 per cent of the members of the American Economic Association opposed additional silver purchases at any price. The Dies bill horrified them, the financial community, the President, and the Secretary of the Treasury.

Because Roosevelt was politically vulnerable, Morgenthau led the Administration's resistance. His strategy throughout the spring of 1934 was to try to delay action by proposing further study of silver prices, and, meanwhile to build up public antagonism against a mandatory program by revealing the influence of speculators in silver, concurrently he tried to satisfy producers of silver by sustaining the price of the metal through timely Treasury purchases in the London market. On March 15 he told the press that he had "still . . . to be shown that silver . . . is a cure-all," and he hinted that the Treasury's investigations of speculation implicated some of the champions of silver in Congress.

Both statements backfired. "The Secretary of the Treasury and his expert advisers," said Key Pittman, ". . . know little about silver. . . . They are misadvised by . . . learned professors who know less about silver." Congressional friends of the metal, angered by Morgenthau's remark about speculation, complained so bitterly that the Secretary in another public statement exonerated them. In the House, Speaker Henry T. Rainey, a silverite for four decades, suspended the rules and called up the Dies bill which passed by a vote of 258 to 112.

Morgenthau nevertheless kept trying. He had decided in February to send Professor James Harvey Rogers of Yale, an economist whose ideas about gold were similar to Warren's, to investigate monetary conditions in the Orient. Rogers, he announced in March, would report back on whether or not an increase in the price of silver would foster Chinese imports of American goods. Again the silverites were unimpressed. It was "the height of asininity," they said, for a professor prejudiced against silver to attempt to learn anything by interviewing Chinese coolies. This kind of argument would not yield to reason. Puzzled, Morgenthau asked Senator Henry F. Ashurst, a mild-mannered Arizona Democrat, why he took silver so much to heart. "My boy," Ashurst replied, "I was brought up from my mother's knee on silver and I can't discuss that any more with you than you can discuss your religion with me."

Ashurst's spirit prevailed in the Senate Committee on Agriculture and Forestry which on April 10 unanimously reported out a much amended version of the Dies bill. The measure owed its new form largely to Democratic Senator Elmer Thomas of Oklahoma, one of the most stubborn inflationists in Washington. It now provided for the nationalization of all domestic silver and for the mandatory purchase of 50 million ounces a month in the world market until the price reached $1.29 or until American prices generally reached their 1926 level. The silver chips were down.

At a conference with the silverites on April 21, the President made plain his unyielding opposition to mandatory legislation. Privately he endorsed two defensive maneuvers of Morgenthau. The Treasury sold some of the gold it held in London in order to buy silver there and push up its price. Morgenthau hoped this would gradually ease the pressure within Congress. He expected to get quick relief by "springing" the roster of silver speculators which the Treasury had been compiling for several months. At Roosevelt's recommendation, he stretched out publication of the twenty-six pages of names over three days, beginning April 24. There were no congressmen on the list, but it did include Frank Vanderlip and others of the Committee for the Nation, William Jennings Bryan, Jr., and Miss Amy Collins, the treasurer of Father Coughlin's Radio League, who had speculated in silver with funds the priest had solicited. Coughlin at once denounced Morgenthau and his investigation, but on the Hill the Treasury's list did little good. Congress ignored Morgenthau's recommendation for a complete investigation of silver speculation, and Thomas's bill held the loyalty of what seemed to be a majority of senators.

On April 27 Roosevelt asked the Cabinet whether to compromise or to attempt to prevent all legislation. The consensus was for compromise, especially since a veto would be "most embarrassing for Congressmen at election time." To avoid a veto, the President had to negotiate. In the process, he and Morgenthau endeavored at all costs to prevent Congress from making silver purchases mandatory, for that would challenge the independence of the executive and run counter to national financial needs.

Negotiations reached fruition on May 8 when Roosevelt and the silverites agreed upon phraseology for legislation and for an executive message recommending it. With the President's support, Pittman introduced a bill authorizing the Secretary of the Treasury to buy silver until it constituted one-fourth of the nation's monetary reserve or until its price reached $1.29. He was to make his purchases "at such rates, at such times, and upon such terms and conditions as he may deem reasonable and most advantageous to the public interest."

The compromise won over enough of the silverites, especially those who were concerned primarily with subsidizing the industry, to be sure of enactment. For one of its features Morgenthau was the outstanding spokesman. This was a tax of 50 per cent on the profits from domestic silver trading. Its purpose was to limit the gains of those who had bought silver speculatively and then lobbied for a subsidy. As the Secretary told the press, "we are not going to let fifteen or twenty people clean up twenty-five or fifty million dollars through a monetary program of the Government." Eight or nine of the silver senators were quite enthusiastic about the bill, he added, and he was perfectly satisfied with it himself.

By large majorities both the House and the Senate passed the Pittman Silver Purchase Act, which Roosevelt signed on June 19, 1934.

Its permissive features represented a considerable Administration victory, but Roosevelt had yielded under pressure, and as part of his bargain he conceded even more by committing himself verbally to execute the Act "enthusiastically." Morgenthau made the same promise. The law, he said, was a direct mandate he was obligated to follow.

This, too, was subject to interpretation, for with the stock of gold rapidly increasing in response to the gold purchase program, the amount of silver needed to constitute one-quarter of the monetary base also rapidly increased. When the Act was passed, 1,200,000 ounces of silver would have met the requirement, but before the end of 1934, gold stocks had climbed to the point where 125,000,000 additional ounces of silver were necessary, and each year this figure rose. Alternatively, of course, the Treasury could have put the domestic price of silver at $1.29 an ounce. Morgenthau, however, did not believe that even enthusiastic execution of the law involved granting so gross a subsidy. His mandate, he realized, forced him to serve silver more generously than he would have liked to. He had to go along with the President's part of the compromise. But as he viewed it, it did not permit the easy achievement of either of the alternative goals, and it did not commit the Treasury to inflation. Because the silverites, still strong in Congress, thought otherwise, because he could not overlook them, the Secretary had ahead of him a succession of conflicts about the meaning of the Silver Purchase Act and the Treasury's buying and pricing policies.

## 2. Executing the Mandate

Morgenthau immediately minimized the inflationary dangers of the silver program. Exercising the discretion the law allowed him, he issued silver certificates in one-, two-, five-, and ten-dollar denominations on the basis of the actual cost of the metal, not its statutory price of $1.29. As the Treasury released the certificates, furthermore, it retired Federal Reserve Bank notes and National Bank notes, which prevented any significant increase in the supply of paper currency. Indeed, to the dismay of men like Senator Thomas, between

June 1934 and June 1935 the total monetary stock rose only 11 per cent, the per capita circulation of currency only 3 per cent.

To mollify the silverites who might otherwise have sponsored inflationary legislation, Morgenthau prepared to buy silver aggressively as soon as he could. As a preliminary to nationalization of the metal, on June 28, 1934, he placed an embargo on shipments of silver from the United States except by government license. This order stopped speculators from sending the metal to Europe to protect it from nationalization until it could be resold in America at advanced prices. Roosevelt's confidential instructions directed the Treasury to nationalize as soon as the market price reached 49.5 cents. On leaving Washington for a month's rest, the President ordered Under Secretary of the Treasury T. Jefferson Coolidge, who was Acting Secretary while Morgenthau also was on vacation, to force the price of silver to 49.5 cents by continuing, large purchases.

Jeff Coolidge, a conservative, well-born, Boston banker, was perhaps the most unlikely recruit of the early New Deal. George Harrison had recommended him to Morgenthau, who needed an Under Secretary experienced in marketing bonds. Coolidge had supported Roosevelt in 1932, but he sympathized with very little the President did after 1933. He alone of Morgenthau's staff opposed the abrogation of the gold clause in public contracts. He also persistently and bitterly denounced the Administration's budgets. Distressed by the Silver Purchase Act, Coolidge could not understand the political conditions that produced it. An honest but often indecisive man, insecure about his role and his duty, he disapproved of the President's order to buy silver and lacked the loyalty to execute it.

On July 12 Coolidge wrote Morgenthau that he had been unable to purchase any silver in the New York market. He admitted that if he began buying in London, the price would rapidly go up to 50 cents, but he had decided to sit tight and await Morgenthau's return before operating abroad. When Morgenthau got back on July 30, he discovered the Treasury had bought only 5,100,000 ounces. Coolidge, furthermore, tried to persuade him to postpone the buying campaign.

Persuaded only that Coolidge was "absolutely useless when it comes to being aggressive and taking chances," Morgenthau took charge himself. He instructed the Federal Reserve Bank of New York to buy in London for the Stabilization Fund, and he also cabled Roosevelt that he intended to push the price to the nationalization point. He made it on August 9 and immediately executed the nationalization orders. Roosevelt, delighted, said he believed in thought transference, for he had awakened one night on board the cruiser *Houston* worried about silver, and on the next morning received Morgenthau's telegram announcing that he had begun to buy.

During the next half year the Treasury bought steadily, averaging 24,000,000 ounces a month. These purchases slowly forced up the world price which passed 55 cents in mid-October. The President wanted to drive it to 64.5 cents — the price the government was paying for newly mined American bullion — before Congress met, and although it took a little longer than he had hoped, by April 1935 it had reached that level.

This precipitated a decision Roosevelt felt he could not avoid. Insatiable as ever, armed with the threat of mandatory legislation, the silverites were agitating for a higher domestic price. As the world price touched 64.5 cents, the President could consider their case plausible. The question was how far to go. They favored $1.29. Taking their position, Herman Oliphant argued that that price would shake out the speculators by eliminating hoarding for further raises. The Treasury would save money, he maintained, by giving the silver states what they wanted and thereby removing pressure for elevating the price of silver the world over. But when Morgenthau relayed this opinion, Roosevelt, his voice so strident that the telephone crackled, said: "What has come over Oliphant."

Morgenthau had experienced the same shock, but if Oliphant's formula disturbed him, so too did the President's suggestion for raising the market price a cent a day. As Morgenthau pointed out, that would play right into the hands of the speculators. They knew the Treasury had a mandate to buy. They counted upon the silver bloc to keep pressure on the Treasury to raise the world price and on the President to jump the domestic price above it. They were confidently exploiting a rising market, buying spot and future silver to resell at a profit. Morgenthau hated having to play their game. Worse still, if the market price rose to 72 cents, the silver in the Mexican peso would be worth more as bullion than as coin. That would force Mexico, one of the largest producers and users of the metal, off the silver standard. Morgenthau proposed therefore to set the domestic price at 71.11, to keep the Treasury's market bids below it, and to explain the necessity for this decision to the silver bloc.

With Roosevelt's approval, he immediately did so. His announcement of the new price stimulated a wave of speculation in London where silver skyrocketed on April 12 and continued to climb rapidly thereafter. Speculators, as before, calculated that the Treasury would buy at any price and ultimately readjust the domestic price, starting another upward spiral. Roosevelt told Morgenthau and Oliphant on April 24 that he would change the domestic price again only if the pressure from the Hill made him. Later that day one of the wire services issued an erroneous report that the Treasury would thereafter buy silver only in the world market. The market boomed, but Senator Pittman, "mad as a hornet," interpreted the wire-service story to foreshadow a desertion of domestic interests. To placate the silverites, Morgenthau with Roosevelt's approval at once raised the domestic price to 77.57. At his press conference on April 25 he explained with obvious annoyance that the misleading story and the resulting boom had forced his hand. He recovered his good humor, however, when one newspaperman asked if he always responded that way when he was angry. "If they knew that," the Secretary said, "they would know how to raise the price of silver."

Immediately after Morgenthau proclaimed the new price, silver rose again on the world market. Oliphant considered this confirmation of his case for $1.29, but Morgenthau, feeling as if he were hitched to the tail of a bear, said he would resign "if the price ever reached $1.29."

The developments of the next day, April 26, changed his mind. The world price, still climbing, reached 81. Roosevelt for the first time admitted that the execution of the Silver Purchase Act had mostly benefited the international speculators. Morgenthau then suggested going to $1.29 to shake them out and to head off further silver legislation, but the President demurred. He had the votes to prevent any legislation during the current session of Congress, he said, and he opposed enlarging the subsidy to the mining industry. Morgenthau then proposed holding the domestic price steady for a few months, even though it fell below the world price. Roosevelt approved, leaving it to the Secretary to explain the lag to the silverites.

A few hours later Morgenthau talked with five of them — Pittman, Wheeler, William E. Borah, the eminent, progressive Republican of Idaho, Alva B. Adams, Colorado Democrat, and William H. King, Utah Democrat. The speculators, the Secretary said, "have this thing on the run." He might, he suggested, raise the price of newly mined silver 5 per cent at a time, or go to one dollar immediately, or go to $1.29. Senator King advocated torturing the speculators. For that purpose he was even agreeable to a temporary recession in the domestic price. But the others wanted to go to $1.29, Borah because he thought it would end speculation, Adams because he considered a series of small raises undignified. Borah, however, pleased by Morgenthau's handling of the situation, said he would approve whatever the Secretary decided. Morgenthau then asked how the senators would feel if he occasionally sold some silver to industrial users within the United States who were pinched by the rising price. Pittman almost lost his temper at the thought, but Borah again suggested leaving the matter to the Secretary's discretion. As the conference closed, the senators approved Morgenthau's decision to do nothing for a few days and gave him what he took to be an informal vote of confidence.

Jeff Coolidge showed less faith. "Henry," he said on May 1, "I don't know whether I can go along with you on account of silver."

"Jeff, please never say that to me again," Morgenthau replied. "If you can't go along then resign."

"Do you want me to walk out?" Coolidge asked.

"I do not want you to walk out but please never threaten again," the Secretary said. "I just can't stand somebody around me constantly threatening to resign."

But Coolidge, anxious to clarify his position, restated it on May 3: "I firmly believe that when Congress gives in its law discretionary power to the Administration that an understanding exists between the Administration and the American people to the end that the Administration should use its best judgment to promote the interests of the Country. I can recognize no other understanding. I cannot go along on the higher price for silver. At your request I will naturally give you my resignation at any time."

Containing himself, Morgenthau replied four days later: "Last year as you know I favored a silver bill, which should be discretionary as to power, but Congress . . . placed responsibility upon the President and upon the Secretary of the Treasury to carry out the mandate. . . . I pledged myself to carry out that policy enthusiastically. If a time ever came when I could no longer do so conscientiously I would have . . . to resign. . . . It is a tough job, and in it I need your help. . . . When I was away last summer you felt unable to pursue our silver policy, and therefore on my return I relieved you entirely of that burden. . . . I have now this suggestion to offer — that you once more think over the situation clearly and carefully and tell me whether you feel that you can continue to support the present Treasury policy aggressively and enthusiastically, leaving the administration of the silver policy entirely to the President and me." Coolidge talked with Roosevelt, reconsidered, and remained.

Meanwhile Morgenthau had taken effective steps to bring the market under control. The Silver Purchase Act did not specifically allow the Treasury to sell silver, but the Stabilization Fund had been set up for the purpose of stabilizing currency. Roosevelt agreed with Morgenthau that it was therefore legitimate to sell silver which the Fund had acquired. The Secretary made his first sales on April 30. Silver opened in London that day at 75.45, but fell on May 1 to 74.91. As Morgenthau noted in his Diary, almost no one was aware that the Treasury's sales had worked. On May 14, with the price of silver again jumping, he sold 250,000 ounces. The next day he told Key Pittman what he had been doing. Pittman was satisfied, but, as he said, it was impossible to foretell how his less moderate colleagues, especially Senators Thomas, Wheeler, and Pat McCarran of Nevada, would react.

Senator McCarran, who was a shrewd and immoderate champion of sundry unattractive causes, had already tried to have Congress repeal the 50 per cent tax on profits from silver speculation. Annoyed because he had not been invited to the April conference on the Treasury's silver policy, he attacked that policy in June when silver prices declined. With four other senators he organized a committee to work for $1.29 silver. In a public letter of June 7 he asked Morgenthau whether the Stabilization Fund had sold silver, and if so, how much and at what price. Rumors from markets all over the world, McCarran asserted, predicted the abandonment of the purpose of the Silver Purchase Act.

Replying on June 11, Morgenthau made his familiar point that discussion of the Stabilization Fund would not be in the public interest. He was glad, however, to tell McCarran that in the ten months ending May 31, 1935, the Treasury had purchased 25,647,000 ounces of newly mined domestic silver and 283,000,000 ounces in the market, and by nationalization acquired another 112,850,000 ounces — in aggregate over 421,000,000 ounces. The Treasury had received delivery of two and a half times the silver purchased in the entire history of the Sherman Act of 1890. These data, Morgenthau argued, attested to his efforts in carrying out the letter and spirit of the law. The market price of 81 cents in April 1935, he explained, had been the product of speculative manipulation. It was bound to drop.

Key Pittman took occasion on June 12 to support the Secretary. The silver program was working splendidly, he said. Sooner or later the United States would have to part with some of its gold and silver in order to effect a stabilization of currencies with other nations. If the Treasury were left alone, Pittman believed, it would work out a satisfactory monetary program.

This was a fair assessment, for during the spring and summer of 1935 Morgenthau was trying to execute his mandate. He was also, however, involved in a long guessing game with silver speculators who used every trick they knew to force the Treasury to show its hand. Aware of this, the Secretary let policy follow each day's developments, buying silver as cheaply as he could find it, selling if prices threatened to rise. As one reporter pointed out in July 1935, Morgenthau played a canny game. Speculators had deliberately incited a break in prices to try to smoke out American policy. On the surface they seemed to succeed when the Treasury bought

42,000,000 ounces, but in fact most of the speculators who sold silver had lost money. Since the Treasury had a mandate to buy, Morgenthau's only latitude lay in his method and timing, and he had kept the market guessing and picked up his silver at bargain rates.

The Secretary would like to have been able to fix the market price in order to stop speculation entirely. Senator Pittman, however, advised him against doing so, for Thomas and McCarran were poised to exploit any change in policy. Morgenthau therefore remained on a twenty-four-hour basis.

In mid-August, as London speculators sold "stale" holdings, silver suddenly dropped two cents and the Treasury's critics resumed their attack. Morgenthau bought heavily for three days, acquired 27,000,000 ounces on August 14 (the largest single day's purchase up to that time), and succeeded in holding the price close to 65 cents. But Senators Thomas and McCarran denounced purchases in a falling market as contrary to the Silver Act and insisted on an investigation.

With Pittman's help and advice, Morgenthau headed them off. To dispel confusion, he departed from his usual rule against giving out data about the Treasury's purchases and on August 14 told the press that in one day he had bought more silver than the total production of the United States in 1934. He also telephoned George LeBlanc, a New York banker and speculator who was an intimate of Senator Thomas. The Treasury had been buying amply in a falling market, Morgenthau said, which was the right way to buy. He did not want to reveal details, for that would "tip his hand" to Great Britain and Japan, countries which were also active in the market and intent on using silver policy as a fulcrum for influence in China. He hoped LeBlanc would make this so clear to Thomas that the senator would give up his plans for an investigation.

At LeBlanc's request, Thomas delayed introducing his resolution. That gave Pittman time to get an alternative resolution through the Senate. Without reference to any immediate or particular investigation, it created a Special Committee on Silver. Although in years to come this watchdog of the subsidy was to interfere with the Treasury's policies, in August 1935 the nature of the Special Committee seemed comparatively benign. Pittman rather than Thomas was chairman, which in itself portended moderation, and there was no probing of Morgenthau's execution of the Silver Purchase Act.

As the Secretary, conscious always of the demands of that law and its guardians, continued to buy heavily, he could not avoid draining silver from the Orient and Latin America. In October and November 1935, the Treasury acquired more silver than ever before in a two-month period. The strain on countries attempting to maintain a silver standard was unbearable. In November China gave up and offered to sell the United States 200,000,000 ounces. The British in Hong Kong offered 100,000,000 ounces. Although Morgenthau declined both offers, he could not stop the flood of silver to market. Early in December, Hong Kong nationalized silver and began immediately to sell it in large quantities in London. If the Chinese were also to dump their stock, not even aggressive purchasing would sustain the price.

In his Diary on December 8, 1935, Morgenthau summarized the situation:

> During the past week our silver purchasing policy has seemed to me more and more stupid. It is now clear that exclusive of the newly mined silver we are simply siphoning the silver out of China through two channels — one, Japan and the other England. Going back three or four years I find that the normal exports of silver from Japan are between six and nine million ounces per year. For the first nine months of 1935 they exported sixty million ounces. This silver can only be gotten into Japan by smuggling it out of China and somebody is making the difference between 40.5¢, approximately what you can buy silver for in China, and 65¢ the world price. . . . All week . . . there has been an extra amount of silver pushed on the London market. . . . It must be the Hong Kong monetary reserve silver.
>
> For us to continue to take all . . . silver . . . at a fixed price when we can unquestionably get it for much less than 65¢ so goes against my better judgment that I decided it was time to act . . . because at the rate we are going we will buy

up all the floating silver in the world, drive all the silver-using countries off silver, and for the use of paper money — and then what have we. . . . I telephoned the President . . . and told him what I had in mind and that I wanted to drop silver and told him the reasons why. To my surprise, he readily acquiesced and made the following suggestion. He said, "Why don't you send over word to London that you are ready to buy two million ounces and they should quote you a price and after you have received the price you will let them know whether or not you will accept the offer." . . . I was dumbfounded that he jumped at the idea so quickly because heretofore he definitely wanted to keep up the price of silver. Perhaps he is getting a little tired of it too.

Morgenthau tried out Roosevelt's system on Monday morning, December 9. About two million ounces of silver were offered at the opening in London. Following the customary procedure, the brokers there asked for orders so they could establish their fix. The Treasury, however, instructed the Chase National Bank, which was operating as its agent, to advise the brokers it did not care to put in an order at the fix but would await a firm offer from London. The brokers, stunned, replied that all their sell orders had been received from clients on the basis of previously established practices. They could not retroactively change procedure, and therefore they asked the Treasury to place an order covering the day's business. After some consideration, Morgenthau agreed to take four million ounces, half at 63.85 and half slightly higher, with the understanding that thereafter London would have to adjust to the Treasury's new system.

On December 10 the dealers refused to accommodate. No silver moved in London. This terrified holders of silver as far away as Persia and India who feared the price would collapse out of sight. Rumors flew that the Treasury was getting out of the market entirely, though that was improbable. Yet the Treasury had so eased its support that silver fell five cents on December 10 in Canada and was sure to fall further and faster in all markets in ensuing days.

To the Treasury's monetary experts Morgenthau disclosed that he hoped to see a drop to 40 cents, the price at which there was no profit for anyone smuggling out of China. He foresaw no resistance from Congress, for Senator Pittman had said he did not care what happened to the world price so long as the price for newly mined domestic bullion did not fall. Even Senator Thomas was relaxed. Asked about the panic in silver on December 10, the senator said: "They have made suckers out of us long enough. I think it is a fine thing for both silver and the United States to have this showdown." Beneath the ticker report of Thomas's statement, Morgenthau gleefully wrote, "You see! Just my words!"

The senators' contentment doubtless stimulated the President's aggressiveness. Eager to put the speculators to rout, Roosevelt suggested the Treasury buy silver in all markets in order to take business away from London. In dealing with London, he added, the Treasury was to turn the tables completely and permanently, to say nothing about a price but instead to force the brokers to propose one. This was a mandate Morgenthau could execute with real enthusiasm. As he put it to his Diary on December 12: "I am trying . . . to take the artificial support away from the silver market . . . to get it down . . . where the world will support the price for whatever the intrinsic value of silver is. . . . Our silver program is the only monetary . . . policy that I cannot . . . justify . . . but if I could expose it . . . now it would save us much grief." While preventing any sudden collapse in price, he gradually but relentlessly drove silver down until on January 20, 1936, it reached 45, where it leveled off.

The Administration thereafter abandoned even the pretense of seriously executing the Silver Purchase Act. For over a year Morgenthau, prodded by Roosevelt, had felt that congressional politics compelled him to buy silver aggressively, to push up its market price, twice to raise its domestic price. The results were so devastating that after December 1935 not even politics could persuade him to continue. Silver, he had learned, was a special form of madness.

The President was similarly disenchanted. Congress was sufficiently docile, and the pressure for inflation had sufficiently subsided, to permit him to stand up to the silver bloc. During the campaign of 1936, he said little about silver, referring only to the reemployment of men in the West. That much was politically unavoidable. All that remained of the silver policy, which Roosevelt jokingly called "the forbidden subject," was the lush subsidy to the mining industry. The silverites protected it fiercely. Late in 1937, as the London Silver Agreement was about to expire, Pittman demanded the continuation of large scale domestic purchases. The special silver committee in the Senate was of the same mind. Roosevelt and Morgenthau compared views on December 8. Independently of each other, they had decided at least to drop the domestic price to 64.5, half the statutory price. "See if you can't find some index," Roosevelt said, "which will more or less justify this 64½¢." Morgenthau was sure he could, and there the price settled, back at the level from which it had departed after Congress passed the Silver Purchase Act and sent the reluctant Administration off on a wild and pointless adventure.

## 3. Repercussions in Mexico

American policy created special problems for nations using silver as a basis for their currency or producing the metal in large quantities. Mexico was affected both ways. Much of her circulating media consisted of silver pesos with a bullion value in 1934 of 71.9 cents an ounce in American money. Management of this coinage was to become difficult when the market reached 72. On the other hand, the boom stimulated by American purchases was to benefit the important Mexican silver industry, and rising silver prices to permit Mexico to acquire dollars to redress an unfavorable balance of trade. Indeed the American program ultimately provided an incidental but significant subsidy to Mexico's depressed economy and sometimes shaky government.

In March 1935 Morgenthau warned Mexico that the Treasury's purchases might soon drive silver past 72. To help her readjust, he had already sold her 32,000 ounces of gold, and he was prepared to sell as much more as she needed. The Mexicans, however, failed to respond. As Morgenthau saw it, they hurt themselves by withholding from the market silver which might otherwise have kept the price down. The Bank of Mexico, moreover, bought silver in London on speculation, thus accentuating the boom.

Though he considered the Mexicans partly responsible for their own predicament, Morgenthau wanted to be a good neighbor. Their government, he learned, had known nothing of the bank's transactions. Indeed at his request the head of the bank was removed. In April the Secretary asked Ambassador Don Francisco Najera for specific suggestions for assistance. None were immediately forthcoming. Morgenthau on April 23 therefore offered to buy the silver the Mexican bank had purchased in London. That would permit him, he explained, temporarily to slacken his other purchases, which would ease the pressure on the price and give Mexico more time to accommodate. The ambassador promised to reply that evening, but the Bank of Mexico delayed decision, the market rose, and on April 24 the United States raised the price of domestic bullion to 72.

With the market climbing above that figure, Mexico had to act. Silver pesos were rapidly disappearing from circulation. The government prohibited the melting or export of silver coins, ordered them to be surrendered in exchange for paper notes, and declared an emergency bank holiday. Assistant Secretary of the Treasury Roberto Lopez flew to Washington, where he and Najera asked Morgenthau to give Mexico breathing room by holding the price of silver steady for at least a month.

The Secretary was by no means a free agent. When he explained Mexico's problem to the President, Roosevelt, whose major concern was with the silver bloc, simply replied: "It's just too bad." Senator King frankly wanted to squeeze the Mexicans. Pittman and his colleagues, counting on the world price to pull up the domestic subsidy, had no interest in adapting to Mexico's needs. Morgenthau, as he told the Mexicans, could therefore help only by making available to them American facilities for minting their new, copper fractional coinage and printing their new currency. They could help themselves, he suggested, by selling the silver they owned in London and elsewhere in an effort to hold the market down. Lopez agreed to discuss the suggestion with his government, but he again asked Morgenthau to postpone increasing the price.

If the Mexicans had persisted in their request, Morgenthau, under instructions from Roosevelt, would have had to refuse, but on April 28, Lopez reported that Mexico no longer feared a rise in the price, for the edict calling in coins was working and the crisis had passed. Mexico now offered the United States first option on any of her silver for sale either in New York or London. "That is very nice but it is nothing new," Morgenthau said. "You have been doing this for months. You have been selling to us because we paid you a better price than anybody else would. This has been mutually advantageous." Lopez said his point was that Mexico would positively not speculate in silver.

Promising a reply the next morning, Morgenthau observed privately to Archie Lochhead that the Mexicans were evidently under as much political pressure not to sell silver as were the Americans. That was the only explanation he could find for their rapid reinterpretation of their domestic situation after he had recommended selling. However, on April 29 he told Cordell Hull that he had begun to feel the Mexican mission was a phony, that somebody in the Mexican government was long on silver, and that they were trying to dump their London holdings on the Treasury. Silver dropped two cents that day, and Morgenthau informed Lopez that the Treasury wanted to wait until the market settled before making an offer.

In the next weeks Mexico sustained control of her revised monetary system. During the remainder of the year she prospered. Supplementing her own silver reserves with sporadic purchases of American gold, she managed her currency with ease. With silver selling at high prices, the Mexican government collected large taxes and made a handsome profit by reminting old coins with a smaller silver content. Indeed, once the mechanical problem created by the rise of the bullion price over the monetary price had been resolved, Mexico benefited from the aggressive purchasing which Morgenthau felt bound to continue until December, 1935.

Subsequently the Secretary's decision to permit the price of silver to fall startled the Mexicans, who reported that the move increased the proportion by which the issue of their currency exceeded reserves. Fearing a run on the banks, the Mexican government asked to exchange some old silver coins for gold which would provide a better base for currency and help to persuade the Mexican people that the banks and currency were safe. Secretary of the Treasury Eduardo Suarez, "trembling in his boots," urged a quick reply.

Oliphant, who investigated the question, came up with the startling information that the Mexicans were misrepresenting their situation. They had in fact a 100 per cent bullion reserve for their outstanding currency, whereas under their law they needed only 50 per cent. Their purpose, he concluded, was to maneuver the United States into buying their remaining silver, about 200 million pesos. Obviously angry, the Secretary said the United States was not interested in exchanging gold for silver coins. He would, however, review the matter if Mexico at some later date had real monetary difficulties.

Real troubles developed soon. As the American commercial attaché in Mexico, Thomas Lockett, explained in an emergency telephone call on December 17, the Mexican Treasury did not know how to dispose of the newly refined silver it was buying, about five million ounces a month. With their gold reserves dwindling, the Mexicans wanted to negotiate some kind of an agreement with the United States. "This is a very unsatisfactory way to do business," Morgenthau said. "I don't like to have to do business always on a five minute notice." If Suarez was worried, he had better come to Washington for detailed discussions. "He'd better see me," Morgenthau concluded, "and he'd better approach me through the State Department."

While Suarez was on his way to Washington for conferences that began on December 31, Morgenthau and his advisers prepared a cordial but somewhat skeptical reception. Archie Lochhead ascertained that in 1935 Mexico had sold to the United States not only her newly mined silver but also 14,600,000 ounces of her reserves. Morgenthau was annoyed. He wanted to help Mexico, he told his staff, but he was concerned first with his own country. The Mexicans, he said, "certainly have as much at stake as we have and I think they ought to play ball. They certainly ought to maintain silver as part of their reserve. . . . I think it is proper, inasmuch as they are coming here to sell us their output, to ask them what they are going to do to help."

The Secretary, after explaining the Senate's interest in increasing the use of silver, put his question to Suarez who suggested Mexico might consult all the Latin American countries about their monetary policies. Mexico's own reserves, he said, still contained "a certain amount of gold and a big proportion of silver," but she faced an increasing demand for dollar exchange and wanted to sell some of her silver reserve to meet it.

"If you find yourself in deep water and need dollars," Morgenthau said, "we will find some way of helping you." But, he added, he would "be greatly influenced in deciding about the purchase of the silver reserve if you . . . could encourage the use of the silver peso in Mexico."

Negotiations reached a satisfactory conclusion during conferences on January 2 and 6, 1936. Supported by Senators King, McNary, Pittman, and Thomas, Morgenthau contracted to buy from Mexico five million ounces of newly mined silver each month. "We do not want you to feel that you have to sell us that amount . . . at whatever price we set," the Secretary said, "but we will offer to buy it from you." He also arranged to supply Mexico with dollars. Mexico was to place in escrow the eleven million ounces of silver she had in the United States. Against this deposit, the Treasury would give her up to $5 million. For the time being, however, the Treasury declined to purchase the 20 million pesos of silver reserve that Suarez was eager to sell. Future decisions about that reserve and other matters, Morgenthau noted, would depend upon Mexico's program for increasing her domestic use of silver, upon her initiative in calling an inter-American conference, and upon her cooperation against liquor smuggling.

Before he departed, Suarez made acceptable promises about smuggling, but the other matters dragged. In the summer of 1936 he issued some new silver coins and made some currency redeemable in silver, but he stopped far short of what Morgenthau had urged. The inter-American monetary conference did not materialize. It fell to the United States to negotiate a monthly silver purchase agreement with Canada modeled on the Mexican precedent, and the United States had still to moderate world silver prices. Morgenthau rejected Mexico's repeated offer of her reserve, but his continuing monthly purchases satisfied her needs until the persisting weaknesses in her economy were accentuated by her growing difficulties with the American State Department over the expropriation of oil reserves. Only then, two years after Morgenthau's conferences with Suarez, did Mexico again view American silver policy as a troublesome subject demanding international negotiation.*

During 1934 and 1935 that policy had subsidized Mexico by establishing an inflated price for one of her major exports. The cooperation of the United States had eased Mexico's temporary monetary problems in April 1935, while American purchases thereafter assured Mexican miners and mining interests of generous support. Even after the Treasury let the market drop, Mexico was able to sell her bullion at a better price than that which would have prevailed without the American Silver Purchase Act. Mexico's difficulties were in large part occasioned by the failure of her officials to guard her currency system against rising silver prices and later by their speculative handling of her monetary reserves. Yet with continuing patience, although not without intermittent irritation, Morgenthau helped the Mexicans adjust to American policy. At times they asked for the moon. They were refused. But as they realized, they dealt with a very good neighbor.

## 4. Repercussions in China

The Chinese had valued silver for centuries as a store of wealth and a medium of exchange. Producing none, they imported more than any other nation and consequently benefited from the low prices of 1930–33. Thereafter China's insecure government, weak economy, continuously unfavorable balance of trade, and susceptibility to Japanese aggression, made her especially vulnerable to the dislocations arising from American silver policy. As the price of the metal rose above its value as currency, Chinese na-

* See pages 493–97.

tionals smuggled it out for quick sale in world markets. So also did the Japanese, who found smuggling not only a profitable trade but also a useful device for weakening China and the government of Chiang Kai-shek. Speculation by Chinese bankers and businessmen, some of them closely identified with the ruling Soong family, made matters worse.

In October 1934, alarmed by American purchases, the Chinese asked the United States to confine buying to American silver. Morgenthau, fully aware of Chinese problems, felt sorry for them, but as he told the Department of State, he could not grant their request while Roosevelt insisted on executing the Silver Purchase Act aggressively. After consulting the Treasury and the President, Hull had to tell the Chinese that the mandate from Congress governed American policy. He could only suggest that China sell her silver and use the proceeds to acquire gold.

This answer satisfied neither the Chinese nor Hull nor Morgenthau. Minister of Finance H. H. Kung, obviously harassed, in a cable of December 10, 1934, asked the United States either to lower the price of silver or to provide a credit for Chinese currency reform. Both Morgenthau and Hull wanted to help, but they disagreed about how to do it. The Department of State, taking the view that the Chinese government lacked sufficient administrative control to manage for itself, urged the Treasury to stop buying silver or at least to reduce the price to 45 cents. The State Department also opposed an alternative remedy, American assistance in Chinese currency reform. The Department maintained that any reorganization of China's finances should be an international project. It would be hazardous, the argument went, for the United States to tie the dollar to the devalued Chinese yuan and thus assume responsibility for any untoward consequences growing out of administrative difficulties in China or retaliation from nations with colonies near her.

The position of the Department of State made Morgenthau furious. As he told Hull again and again, no modification of silver policy was politically possible. The United States could best help China, Morgenthau believed, by assisting in the reorganization of her currency. He ascribed Hull's opposition to that course to an undue sensitivity for Japan's opinion. The Department of State was taking pains not to violate the so-called Amau Doctrine, an official Japanese statement of policy that asserted Japan's interest in any developments involving China. Morgenthau was of the opposite mind. Japan's demands on China, unabating after her conquest of Manchuria in 1931, seemed to him to threaten the peace of the Orient and of the world. Impatient with what he considered Hull's appeasement of Japan, Morgenthau was prepared to use monetary aid to China as an instrument of political support. Otherwise, he feared, the United States would lose all influence in the Orient, leaving the area entirely to Japan and Great Britain.

Roosevelt, who seemed to Morgenthau sometimes to share his views about Asian politics, had distinct opinions of his own about Chinese finance. "Please remember," the President wrote Morgenthau in a private memorandum of December 4, "that I have a background of a little over a century in Chinese affairs. . . . China has been the Mecca of the people whom I have called the 'money changers in the Temple.' They are still in absolute control. It will take many years and possibly several revolutions to eliminate them. . . . I am inclined to believe that the 'money changers' are wrong and that it is better to hasten the crisis in China — to compel the Chinese people more and more to stand on their own feet without complete dependence on Japan and Europe — than it is to compromise with a situation which is economically unsound and which compromise will mean the continuation of an unsound position for a generation to come." Roosevelt, unwilling to alter American silver policy for the sake of the Chinese, was obviously not supporting the proposals of the State Department, but he was also clearly less enthusiastic than was the Treasury about helping China reform her currency. He apparently intended for the time being merely to observe.

The conflict over American policy reached a first resolution on December 17, 1934. The State Department then rejected several Treasury suggestions on the grounds that each tended toward bimetallism and would entail administrative commitments in China objectionable to the Japanese. Roosevelt, also opposed to encouraging bimetallism, tempered his usual stand on silver and instructed the Treasury to conclude a purchasing agreement with the Chinese. According to its terms, the Treasury was to buy silver only from the Chinese central bank, and to buy it in sufficient quantity to keep the world price from falling below 55 cents, the highest level to which Morgenthau's advisers thought the Chinese could adjust. This arrangement, which Morgenthau immediately negotiated, suited him completely. He had hesitated to alter his buying policies only because Roosevelt forbade it. Now the President had changed his orders, but not for long. The agreement with the Chinese was terminable on one week's notice. Pressure from the silver bloc forced its cancellation in two weeks. Morgenthau then again began to buy aggressively in London, the Chinese again complained, and the Secretary could only suggest that they appeal to the congressmen who had written the law.

Morgenthau also invited the Chinese to send a financial representative to Washington, but this too came to nothing. While the Chinese delayed, Senator Pittman insisted they should not discuss silver policy but only problems of foreign exchange. Secretary Hull proposed canceling or postponing the visit because he feared that if conversations failed, the effect on the whole world would be bad. In a "very gentle and polite manner," Morgenthau explained that he had told the Chinese to come with some proposal of their own. Hull was agreeable to proceeding on this basis, for it left the initiative with China and freed the United States from potential criticism from Japan. Roosevelt, however, when he learned of Pittman's objections, called off the project. As things stood, he said, as much could be accomplished by cable as by direct talks.

By cable Minister of Finance Kung stated the problem bluntly. Asking for American help to establish a bimetallic currency, he said that American silver purchases and uncertainty about American silver policy were destroying China's foreign and internal trade, sapping her revenues, and embarrassing her efforts to stamp out communism. Kung suggested that China supply all the foreign silver the United States had to buy, provided the quantity, timing and price were mutually agreeable. Gradually China would change from a silver standard to a currency linked to the dollar. During the period of transition, China would need dollar resources, at a minimum a loan or long-term credit of about

$100 million, and a like amount to be advanced against future silver deliveries.

In mid-February 1935, after weeks of delay, Hull's subordinates completed a "tentative draft of the proposed reply" to Kung, who had urgently repeated his plea for help. Their wordy draft called the Chinese scheme impracticable and suggested instead that the United States would cooperate in a program of collective assistance if China would request it simultaneously of several powers. In a memorandum to Morgenthau explaining the reply, the Division of Far Eastern Affairs said that a positive response would be "highly impolitic," presumably because it would offend the Japanese, while a negative response would be "highly inadvisable," for it might throw China into the arms of Japan.

Morgenthau called this reasoning timid, but so long as the State Department considered the issue within its exclusive province, he said he would not officially object. If, however, the State Department later concluded that the question was primarily monetary, the Treasury was ready to proceed vigorously. Meanwhile he counted on the President, to whom he and Hull were both responsible, to coordinate the action of the two departments.

Roosevelt, as Morgenthau interpreted him, now moved toward the Treasury's position. At meetings with both secretaries, the President told Hull either not to answer the Chinese at all, or just to go through the motions, and to tell them that the Treasury would discuss their monetary troubles. He made his point about three times, Morgenthau noted in his Diary, but "made absolutely no headway with Hull." The President also deemed it important to avoid discussing silver policy with foreign powers who would surely oppose it. Here again Morgenthau felt that Hull either did not get the point or did not want to get it. There was certainly some confusion. According to Morgenthau's report of the meeting of February 18, Roosevelt pleasantly but firmly told Hull not to commit the United States to conferring with other nations and to let the Treasury treat the Chinese problem as a monetary matter and handle it accordingly. Yet the State Department's reply to China on February 26 effectively rejected Kung's proposal for American assistance and clearly suggested a preference for internationalizing any operation on Chinese currency.

During the next two months Roosevelt left his subordinates to their own resources. Morgenthau in that period gave considerable time to studying intelligence reports of the Department of State about Chinese affairs. He was shocked, as he was to be frequently during the next decade, by Chinese standards of personal and public morality. In order to combat the Communists in outlying provinces, Chiang Kai-shek's Nationalist government had to depend upon organized bands of brigands who systematically profited from trade in opium, gambling, and prostitution. Some of these guerrillas, moreover, seemed much more adamant in their resistance to Japanese expansion than did the Generalissimo himself. These conditions were hard for Morgenthau to stomach, but he felt he had to, for Japan's intentions were alarming. American agents reported that the Japanese were making extraordinary economic demands. They wanted to have a Japanese appointed chief inspector of Chinese customs, to revise the Chinese tariff to favor the importation of Japanese products, to prevent China from negotiating any foreign loan without Japanese participation, and to standardize the currency of Japan, China, and Manchuria. Japan was reported to believe it would facilitate the last objective if she adopted the silver standard. This intelligence supported a hunch of the President that somehow American silver policy was hurting the Japanese. It obviously hurt China more. Morgenthau could not reverse it, but the spectrum of Japanese purpose increased his desire to assist the Chinese government. The question was still how to proceed.

The State Department responded favorably to a British proposal. Happy to have the English take the lead, the Department favored accepting an invitation of March 28 to send a financial representative to China to work with a British monetary mission. The British objective was obscure, but it apparently envisaged cooperation among England, Japan, France and the United States — precisely the international solution Hull had been advocating. The project gained urgency when soaring silver prices again staggered China in April. It gained prestige when in June the British announced that Sir Frederick Leith-Ross, one of their most eminent Treasury experts, would head their mission.

Morgenthau, however, was wary. Replying in April to a State

Department inquiry about the mission, he suggested asking the British precisely what they had in mind. He wanted to know whether the project was essentially political or essentially monetary. If it was political, the State Department could decide for itself about participation. If it was monetary, the Treasury wondered whether the British contemplated discussing problems other than those peculiar to China. Though he did not say so in so many words, Morgenthau had no intention of permitting American silver policy to become a subject for international decision, nor had the President. They were finding it hard enough without that additional burden to appease Senators Thomas and McCarran.

Though the British did not define their plans, the State Department persisted in recommending cooperation. It argued that monetary and political matters were in any case indivisible. It ignored the Treasury's references to the feasibility of unilateral American action. It urged Morgenthau in June at least to meet Leith-Ross while he passed through Canada on his way to China. With Roosevelt's support, however, Morgenthau stood his ground. In the end the United States sent no representative to join the British mission, largely because the Treasury, sensitive to the mood of the silver bloc, opposed the whole idea, but partly because the State Department also felt the British were forcing the game, and partly because both departments realized that American policy had already put the United States in an unfavorable position for international monetary discussions in China.

As an alternative, Roosevelt approved Morgenthau's appointment of Professor J. Lossing Buck, an economist and statistician, to report periodically from Nanking on monetary questions. Buck was not an envoy. He had no authority to negotiate. "If I were to send a representative . . . ," Morgenthau told Chinese Ambassador Alfred Sze, "your people would just crucify him . . . for our silver policy . . . and you know, as well as I do, that the program is laid out for me and there is nothing I can do." The rigidity of the program probably convinced the Chinese that they could gain nothing by accepting Morgenthau's suggestion to send T. V. Soong, the brother of Madame Chiang and an official in the central bank, to meet him in Portugal for informal conversations.

But for both the Treasury and the Nationalist government, Buck
was a useful channel of communication, and his wife, Pearl, the
novelist, an unofficial but influential cultural envoy.

Through Buck in July, Chiang Kai-shek relayed his familiar
lament: American policy was encouraging smuggling, helping
Japan, forcing China off silver; China needed American aid in
establishing a managed gold standard; China was prepared to
link the yuan to the dollar. For more than a year Morgenthau
had hoped to bring that to pass. Because Roosevelt was at first
dubious and the State Department was continually resistant, he had
singularly little to show for his efforts.


## 5. The Yuan and the Dollar

On October 28, 1935, Ambassador Sze offered Morgenthau 200
million ounces of silver. China had given up. She was leaving the
silver standard, Sze explained, and had to sell her bullion either
directly to the United States or on the world market in order to
acquire foreign exchange for the management of her new currency. Here at last, Morgenthau believed, was a strictly monetary
problem that he could handle without reference to the Department of State.

"It is very amusing to have the Chinese come to us," Morgenthau
said to Roosevelt the next day, "with Leith-Ross sitting in China."
The Secretary had decided on what bases he could do business.
He would buy 100 million ounces at once, and more if the deal
proved successful, provided that China would deposit the proceeds in New York, use them exclusively for stabilization, appoint
two Americans to a stabilization committee of three members, and
tie the yuan to the dollar at the established rates for gold of $35 and
silver of $1.29 an ounce.

Before negotiations could proceed, the Chinese on November
3 nationalized silver, ordered its exchange for legal tender notes,
and tried to stabilize the yuan at the existing level of about 30
cents. The prospect of inflation and of possible Japanese interference caused near panic in Shanghai markets. Alfred Sze hur-
ried to Morgenthau's farm to explain what had occurred. He

carried a note from the Chinese treasury which did not specify how China would use the proceeds from the proposed silver sale, or whether her new currency was to be on a gold or silver basis, or whether it was to be linked with the pound, the yen or the dollar. This communication, Morgenthau told Sze, was vague and unsatisfactory. If the Treasury bought the silver, he said, it would be acting in direct opposition to Congress's intention of enhancing the monetary use of the metal. He had therefore to be exceedingly careful. He had also to treat the matter as a monetary question only, and consequently to be sure that the proceeds from the purchase would not be diverted to military supplies. With Roosevelt's approval, he insisted that China meet his terms.

From Nanking, H. H. Kung now cabled at greater length. He had already established a stabilization committee on a basis somewhat different from that Morgenthau had suggested but nevertheless satisfactory to the Secretary. China accepted all of Morgenthau's other conditions except that tying the yuan to the dollar. As Sze explained, she could do no more than state the level at which she intended to maintain the yuan. She could not link it to any foreign currency.

"We have our politicians and our public and our future to think of," Morgenthau said. "We are not going to invest $65,000,-000 and you tie your money to sterling. . . . You made this move and we want you to succeed. We feel that it is best for both countries to have the yuan quoted in terms of dollars instead of in terms of sterling. You people are playing poker and you are bluffing. . . . Kung could not announce his entire plan because he was waiting for us to buy his silver. . . . You have to pick the kind of money you are going to tie the yuan to."

On November 6 Morgenthau discussed the situation with the President, whose "snap judgment," as he put it, called for accompanying any purchases of Chinese bullion with "some sort of qualifying memorandum" linking the yuan and the dollar. Senator Pittman was of a similar view. The Chinese, however, were unyielding, and the State Department considered a link unnecessary. Morgenthau's own advisers gradually came to agree. If the yuan were tied to the dollar and something went wrong in

China, the United States would be blamed. American intransigency, moreover, might drive the Chinese to the British or even the Japanese. Worried about the political issues at stake, which Sze took pains to emphasize, Morgenthau was also disturbed because, contrary to the purpose of the Senate, China and Hong Kong were leaving silver. If, furthermore, they dumped their bullion in London, the Treasury, as the Secretary saw it, would have to let the market price fall. That in itself would help the Chinese, but Morgenthau wanted also to do more. The time had come to review silver policy with Roosevelt.

At the White House on November 9 Morgenthau told Roosevelt that internal pressure prevented the Chinese from tying the yuan to the dollar. China was also under pressure from Japan. Nevertheless, he had learned, she had announced the reorganization of her currency without consulting the British, and she had come to the United States for help. "The British plans," the Secretary continued, "were evidently prepared with the idea of inducing the silver-using countries to give up the use of silver as a monetary metal. If they can induce China to adopt a plan which does not include the use of silver, Hong Kong will also follow the same procedure. . . . This is . . . apparently what they would like to accomplish."

But the Chinese did not state what they were tying the yuan to, Roosevelt interrupted.

"They have simply said that they are going to stabilize their currency around the present level, which is thirty cents, or one shilling, two and one-half pence, and will buy or sell this exchange to maintain this level," Morgenthau said.

The President thought they could not tie the yuan to two entirely different currencies. Archie Lochhead suggested that perhaps the Chinese left this question open purposely so as to play the British and the Americans off against each other.

One way to prevent China and Hong Kong from selling their silver, Morgenthau went on, was to allow its price to decline to about 40 cents, for then neither China nor Hong Kong would find any advantage in selling it. "One thing that has to be considered," Roosevelt said, with the silver bloc in mind, "is that it may be easy enough to drop the price of silver but a very difficult thing to raise it once such action has been taken. . . . This idea of dropping the price does not seem so good. What is your other idea?"

The other idea, Morgenthau answered, was to buy from China enough silver to help her through her present crisis, though not necessarily one or two hundred million ounces.

The President was apparently dubious. Instead of commenting directly, he said: "Have you ever considered the idea of a trade dollar? You know, if you go back seventy-five years or more you will find that there was a silver American trade dollar coined for use in China."

Herman Oliphant replied that in order for such a trade dollar to be of any real use, the price of silver had to be fixed. Otherwise the value of the trade dollar would fluctuate constantly. Archie Lochhead added that the Chinese, determined to control their own currency, would resist any attempt to introduce a trade dollar containing a foreign imprint.

Still dodging the issue, Roosevelt said: "An idea to be considered is one that would insure the physical distribution of both gold and silver reserves among the various nations of the world. In other words, settlements of trade balances by shipments of both gold and silver combined in some manner."

Oliphant said he had been studying that subject for six months and had had the mint make a sample coin, part gold and part silver. "The idea . . . appears to be entirely feasible," he continued, "but of course in considering this subject careful study must be given to the ratio of gold and silver, and to do this one has to go back over a period of say one hundred years to study the relationship which probably can best be determined by ascertaining the amount of gold and silver produced during this period and fixing a relationship between the two metals in that proportion."

The President laughed. "William Jennings Bryan."

"Of course," Oliphant said, responding to Roosevelt's mood, "you understand that my ideas on this subject are not emotional. . . . The relationship between the two metals as fixed by Alfred Marshall is nearer twenty to one than sixteen to one."

"This is only an idea which has occurred to me," Roosevelt

said, "which I do not care to take any immediate action upon but simply want you to think . . . over as of possible interest. Suppose for instance some country had a favorable balance of trade with the United States." Lochhead suggested Colombia.

"Well, say, for example," Roosevelt went on, "that at the end of some period of time, say a year, or three months, or even one month, Colombia had a favorable trade balance with the United States of $10,000,000. Suppose this balance was not settled from day to day, but was held up until the end of the stated period. At the end of that period we owe Colombia $10,000,000. We might then say we intend to settle this balance by actually shipping you $10,000,000 consisting of both gold and silver. You will have to actually take this metal and hold it in your reserves. In this manner the actual metal would be distributed."

The difficulty, Lochhead said, would be that Colombia had unfavorable balances with other nations. Colombia could not keep the whole amount of gold and silver in her reserve for she had to buy currency, such as the pound and the franc.

"Well," Roosevelt replied, "as I said before, this is only an idea which is not necessary to consider at the present time. The question seems to settle down as to what is the best thing we can do at the present time to help China?"

With the President at last willing to address himself to the problem at hand, Morgenthau suggested buying something on the order of 25 million ounces of silver to tide China over.

"My idea would be 20 million ounces which we may consider as a bet on what may develop in the future," Roosevelt commented. "Yes, I think that is the best thing we can do. That is, to go along without making any radical changes in the price of silver and see what happens."

This was at best a makeshift solution, but the President was not yet prepared to risk offending the silver bloc by dropping the world price, and both Morgenthau and Roosevelt were unwilling to purchase the entire amount China had offered without larger assurances than she would give.

The Chinese were desperate. "The Chinese ambassador is waiting in an outer office," Morgenthau told Roosevelt on November 13, "and he has now agreed to the . . . points which we asked him to submit to Kung and, very briefly, they are: that they will keep the money over here; that they will keep us fully informed; that they will only use the money for stabilization purposes. Yesterday the Yokohama specie bank raided the Chinese currency and China only has about thirty-five or forty million dollars in gold and foreign exchange, and in order to fight it and hold it up, they want a commitment on the one hundred million ounces of silver." Morgenthau wanted to tell the "poor devils" that he would take up to 50 million ounces. Roosevelt said to go ahead.

"I am trying to make it as easy as possible for China," Morgenthau told Sze, "because we want to see you out of this trouble and I am willing to go through with this agreement on my word of honor and yours. . . . The only reason for doing it is that everybody seems to be against you and we will not ask for any trade preferences at this time. I take it that on all of the silver that the Chinese wish to sell, that they will give us the first chance and after we agree to buy these 50,000,000 ounces that you will not turn around and sell 50,000,000 ounces more to the English." Sze immediately agreed and the sale was consummated.

A few days later Morgenthau talked with Kenneth Bewley about conditions in the Orient. Leith-Ross, Bewley said, had no mandate to persuade China to adopt sterling exchange, but should China choose to adopt it, the British would not oppose it. This, however, depended first on the Chinese choosing it and secondly on the other countries concerned, specifically the United States and Japan, whose good will the British sought to retain. The Chinese had asked Leith-Ross about the possibility of a loan, but he had told them there could be no loan unless the United States, Japan, and possibly France were agreeable. At this point the Chinese on their own had adopted a managed currency. The British now felt that success of the Chinese scheme depended on the reserves they could obtain to back their currency. Britain believed that China needed to sell some of her silver and presumably also to procure a loan. The sale of the silver, the British were aware, depended on the decision of the United States Treasury. With regard to the loan, British policy was to come in to some extent if the Chinese wished it; but it would be difficult, if not impossible, for the British to agree to any loan unless it involved linking the yuan in some way to sterling. On any other basis, sterling would have to be sold for dollars or for gold which would weaken it. In any case, Bewley repeated, the British would not approve a loan, if the United States and Japan objected. Indeed the British would prefer all three nations to participate in a loan.

Morgenthau replied that all this was new to him, although probably the State Department had known about it. Though the United States had not said it would not make a loan, Morgenthau had discouraged the Chinese from asking for one, because he thought they had very little chance of success. "I would say," the Secretary continued, "that it would be impossible almost for Great Britain, Japan and ourselves to get together on a joint loan if Great Britain would insist that the currency be tied to sterling. On the other hand, I can understand why you would insist on it." He was not clear, however, on just how far the British would go to help the Chinese.

"Our line has always been that we don't want to do anything unless we have the good will of the Japanese and yourselves," Bewley said. "If it comes to a definite conflict of opinion between the Japanese and other powers, I would not like to say at all what it would be."

"Suppose everybody could get together except the Japanese," Morgenthau asked.

"I would not like to say," Bewley replied, "because it is our policy to work in with the Japanese, if possible. The ambassador talked with the State Department and one of the main features he made was, if possible, to work in everybody."

Morgenthau said he had good reason to believe the Japanese had tried to wreck the new Chinese monetary system. In that case, Bewley asked, did Morgenthau consider it possible for the United States and Great Britain to do much to help?

"I don't know," Morgenthau said. "You can't tell what you can do until you try it. Talking for myself, I would like to see the Chinese succeed."

"I think we all would," Bewley said.

"But," Morgenthau continued, "just saying so and sitting here is not much help."

"Yes; quite," Bewley agreed. "There are two possible lines on that. I don't know it is quite fair to ask you. I don't know whether we would be prepared to make a loan on our own, apart from you and the Japanese. I am putting this purely hypothetically. Would you have any strong objections or feelings on that?"

"You mean if you people made a loan would the United States object?" Morgenthau said. "Oh! No! We would have no right."

"I mean," Bewley said, "if we could only make the loan on condition that they join with sterling. . . . You would have no feeling?"

"Don't misunderstand me," Morgenthau answered, "— not if it was a fair bargain with China; if you people did not drive too hard a bargain. . . . If it was a fair bargain for China, then we could not object. . . . If she does not get some help, it looks pretty gloomy over there."

As his conversation with Bewley revealed, Morgenthau was fully prepared if necessary to let China affiliate with the sterling bloc and to risk the alienation of Japan. He spoke, however, only for the Treasury. Upon learning about his conversation, the Department of State indicated that it believed any loan would have to be from a consortium, presumably including the Japanese. On the other hand, the Treasury's suggestions to Roosevelt during the long White House conference furthered a major State Department objective. When Morgenthau was at last able in December to persuade the President and the silver bloc to let the market drop, Hull rejoiced.* Yet there was still no real meeting of departmental minds, and though the declining price of silver effectively curtailed Japanese smuggling, it did not cure China's ills.

In mid-December Japan again raided Chinese exchange and China asked the Treasury to buy another 50 million ounces of silver. Sze also requested information about future American silver policy. Morgenthau hesitated. As he explained to the ambassador, there was such outright speculation in China (much of it by Chiang's official family), that the Treasury could not reveal its plans for changing prices. Informed by Buck that the Chinese treasury was thinking of selling 200 million ounces of silver in world markets, Morgenthau suspected Kung of contemplating

* See pages 197–98.

some double-dealing. He was disturbed too because the Chinese, contrary to their promise, were not giving Buck adequate data about their monetary policy. Though the Secretary remained sympathetic, he therefore declined China's requests for another silver purchase.

On December 31, 1935, a $3 million Chinese debt to the Farm Credit Administration came due. Characteristically bad communications between Ambassador Sze and the State Department led the Chinese astray. Told too late that they could avoid default by making a down payment, the Chinese repaid the entire amount. Sze was shaken by the experience. "Can you help me?" he pleaded. "When I go to the State Department it is such a long, tedious process. I was put in an awful jam."

Sze's plea moved Morgenthau. "I want to drop a hint," he said. "Before I do anything more about buying any silver, I would like to be able to talk directly with Kung or Soong. I just want you to hint to them."

Sze said the State Department would oppose having Soong, who was avidly anti-Japanese, come to Washington.

"I will take care of that," Morgenthau said. "I will talk to the President. What Soong should do is come over here on the pretense of trying to straighten out the . . . loans. . . . There is no use talking about anything more until I know face to face what they want and what their situation is."

As Sze predicted, Cordell Hull objected to Soong's visit on the grounds that it might provoke Japanese resentment against the United States or England. He preferred to postpone discussions, but was willing to defer if Roosevelt and Morgenthau considered them of major importance. In his Diary Morgenthau called Hull's response typical of State Department philosophy. "Don't do anything that might offend anyone," Morgenthau wrote. "Hull has also put himself on record that if this mission fails, I will be the goat. However, I consider it so important as a part of our silver program that I am willing to take the risk involved. My policy in the Treasury is nothing ventured, nothing gained."

"Informally, I can tell you that it is agreeable to the State Department and to the President of the United States to have Soong come," the Secretary told the Chinese, "and that if Soong did decide to come here, he would get a very welcome reception. . . . No one in the State Department, except Secretary Hull, knows about Soong's proposed coming. . . . We will consider T. V. Soong's coming here as a Treasury matter and not a diplomatic mission. If he is coming, the sooner the better."

China's domestic situation and international relations were so critical that Soong did not feel he could leave the country. The Chinese therefore asked whether the United States would consider K. P. Chen as a substitute emissary. Roosevelt ruled that Morgenthau did not have to consult the State Department about Chen, who was reported to have an excellent reputation in both foreign and Chinese circles. Originally not close to Chiang Kai-shek, Chen had recently become more friendly with the General-issimo. A self-made man, considered the most honest, sincere and dependable of the Chinese bankers, Chen had had much to do with modernizing and westernizing Chinese banking methods. Though he had generally sought to avoid political affiliations, he had a sound knowledge of Chinese politics, and without being anti-Japanese, he was satisfactorily pro-American.

Impressed by these qualifications and determined to clarify the Chinese problem, Morgenthau in February 1936 cabled Kung that Chen would be an entirely acceptable representative. Dealing with China had not been easy, but for the forthcoming mission, the Secretary had measured hopes.


### 6. The Chen Mission

In the weeks preceding K. P. Chen's arrival in Washington early in April, and during the six weeks of conferences that then ensued, Morgenthau and his staff received voluminous reports about China from Buck, from Treasury customs agents, from the State Department, and from Kung. This material was as much political as economic. It had to be, for politics affected China's monetary problems and her interpretation of them. Politics also affected Morgenthau's response. Silver was his fulcrum, but his concern related always to the balance of forces in the Orient.

Kung's cables, Morgenthau remarked, provided "the first comprehensive, complete picture that I have ever gotten out of China." It was discouraging. China had adopted a program to balance her budget within eighteen months in order to avoid inflation, but revenues were falling and expenditures were difficult to cut. The disturbed international situation and the devaluation of the yuan discouraged imports and reduced customs receipts, as did the wholesale smuggling by the Japanese in North China. Too weak to collect direct taxes, the government had found no satisfactory device for raising revenue by indirect taxation. But the communist threat in the provinces and the need to maintain a posture of defense against possible Japanese aggression kept military costs high. Furthermore, loan and indemnity payments were heavy and would remain so through 1940. Meanwhile China found it impossible to convert its obligations but was planning to reorganize its internal loans by spreading principal payments over longer periods. She needed foreign credits to see her through her budgetary difficulties and to give her the exchange to manage her new currency.

Because of the deficit and the international situation, Kung explained, Chinese currency was vulnerable even though its reform had been introduced under technically favorable conditions. China's exchange reserves were too small to insure stability in the event of a prolonged attack by Japanese banks. The reserve, moreover, was largely in silver, and when silver depreciated as it had in the previous weeks, it impaired public confidence. Now that China was off the silver standard, she would welcome higher prices for the metal.

Kung admitted that the banking system needed strengthening. He was planning stricter regulation of commercial banking, the creation of a special farm mortgage bank, and the reorganization of the Central Bank of China. Special difficulties, however, arose from Japanese opposition to the circulation of the notes of the Central Bank in North China.

Very confidentially Kung said that China wanted a back door by rail to British Burma so as to be able to cope with Japanese aggression from the Pacific. The Japanese were already moving heavy artillery into Eastern Hopei in order to replace the loyal ruler of that province with a man friendly to them. China was therefore making all possible preparations for an armed conflict which might not remain localized in the north. Kung believed that "if other countries do not attack the bandits (pro-Japanese) now, the bandits will attack them later and Japan will be in a much stronger position after gaining control of China's natural resources and manpower." On this account he urged the United States and other Western nations to take a firm stand. Specifically he wanted the United States to buy more silver at prices advantageous to China. This would provide the foreign exchange for stabilizing the yuan. The need for financial support, Kung concluded, was imperative, as was the need for a public announcement that the United States was rendering that support.

Morgenthau balanced Kung's assessment against an analysis of April 4 from American customs agents. They reported that there had been no abatement in Sino-Japanese hostility, that Chiang Kai-shek was continuing to refuse Japanese requests for an independent regime for North China, but that he was neither ready nor courageous enough to undertake armed resistance. While he pursued the more compatible goal of finding a compromise, he was also cultivating Russia. He had issued a secret order permitting the publication of pro-Soviet articles in magazines and newspapers, and he was subsidizing General Li Tu who was negotiating privately with Soviet authorities. Many of the northern generals wanted to send an emissary to Moscow, but Chiang hesitated because he thought it might provoke the Japanese. It seemed certain to the Americans that the Japanese were ready to contrive an incident in North China similar to that which had set off the war in Manchuria in 1931. Soon Nanking would have to choose between surrender and resistance.

Morgenthau considered it essential to cultivate the Chinese will to resist. He could do so, he believed, by focusing upon the monetary problem. He therefore refused to permit the State Department to put on his agenda the troublesome question of private debts outstanding between Chinese and American nationals, and he decided not to discuss the outstanding Chinese loans which the Export-Import Bank was willing to handle through Ambassador Sze. "Talking for the United States government," Morgenthau said at his first meeting with Chen on April 8, "the only interest that we have in these financial discussions is to help China. . . . As far as the Treasury is concerned, it is purely monetary. We feel we can be instrumental in helping you and in the long run we will be helping ourselves. We feel it is very important to the world peace to help China strengthen her currency, because the way I see it, that is the center of the whole thing as far as China goes. . . . In discussing this thing, we have no axes to grind."

The Secretary asked Chen whether it was in China's best interest to have four different agencies issuing currency. He could not understand why the so-called Farmers Bank, which Chiang Kai-shek owned, seemed to be able to print any amount of paper money without anything to back it up. He also requested a description of the capital, currency, and metallic reserves of the Central Bank, titularly the most important of the banks of issue.

The government, Chen explained, was trying to reorganize the Central Bank by making it a bankers' bank. The four banks issuing notes had altogether a 75 per cent reserve made up of silver, gold, foreign currency, and government bonds.

Morgenthau reminded Chen that the United States was interested in China's monetizing as much silver as possible. Chen replied that they could not decide on the content of their coins until they knew what American policy on silver prices would be. He was optimistic, however, for not only the Chinese but also all foreigners except the Japanese were turning in their silver for bank notes.

Before pursuing discussions further, Morgenthau wanted his staff to review the information Chen had brought about the Chinese banking system and budget. The next day he received a report from George Haas and Harry White recommending the purchase of Chinese silver. This would help, they wrote, to improve business conditions in China and to keep the yuan from depreciating; it would decrease American gold holdings and increase gold holdings elsewhere; it would provide the United States government with a handsome seigniorage profit. As a reciprocal concession, the Treasury could ask China either to return to a silver or bimetallic standard, or to link the yuan to the dollar, or to dissociate the yuan from sterling. Any one of these would do, provided China also agreed to increase the use of silver in her coinage.

On April 12 Morgenthau decided to offer China a contract for the purchase at the market price of five million ounces of silver each month during the remainder of 1936. This would be in line, he told his staff, with the agreements already concluded with Mexico and Canada. It was so hard to ascertain the real facts about China's situation that he preferred making gradual purchases to consuming immediately a large block of silver. Furthermore, since the Silver Purchase law authorized the Treasury to buy silver until it equaled one fourth of the monetary reserves, continuing purchase of a reasonable amount from China could be construed as fulfilling the terms of the Act.

On the following day, before revealing his intention, the Secretary complained to Chen because the sterling rate in China remained constant while the dollar rate changed. Chen denied that China was tied to sterling, but Morgenthau pointed out that it looked as though she were. He urged Chen to consider a system like that of Canada, whose currency was related to both dollars and sterling. He also suggested the Chinese send silver to the United States with the idea of borrowing against it. He did not want to take a lump sum of silver, the Secretary continued, but he was thinking of buying five million ounces a month for the next eight months. If he did, China would have to use the exchange or gold she acquired exclusively for stabilization. He was in no position, he said, to determine whether silver should be in coinage or in metallic reserve, but he did believe it would be a nice gesture, since the United States had always made Chinese dies, to continue to have them made in America rather than in England. He did not want to give the British a chance to crow.

The meeting then adjourned so that Morgenthau could keep a luncheon appointment with Roosevelt. The President asked a great many questions, especially about Chen's politics. After assuring him that Chen was anti-Japanese, Morgenthau said: "If Hitler can protect himself in Europe so that he will not have any conflict on his hands on either of his borders . . . he is very apt to join hands with Japan and attack Russia." Roosevelt agreed that was a possibility. China was in bad shape, Morgenthau continued, and unless the Japanese were diverted by a conflict with Russia, China's chances of pulling through were poor. This weakness, he suggested, had inspired his plan to buy five million ounces of silver a month. Roosevelt expressed no objections.

After further discussions with the Chinese, Harry White on April 17, at the Secretary's request, evaluated Morgenthau's plan. It would not, he wrote, much increase China's reserves, but it would strengthen the expectation of silver holders that the government could sustain the yuan rate. This salubrious psychological effect could be increased, White suggested, if the Treasury bought more silver, and bought it faster, than Morgenthau had proposed, and if the Treasury loaned China $50 million against silver deposited in the United States.

The Secretary now tested the Chinese. To see whether they were trying to rig the market before making a sale to the United States, he suggested they sell silver when the price reached 46.40. Their consequent disposal of $21½ million worth of the metal in London knocked its price down. This, Morgenthau believed, was a significant indication that China and the United States could regulate the world price by working together. The Chinese had constantly asked about future American policy. On April 20 Morgenthau told Chen that he could not supply a long-range answer, but the present policy was to keep silver at about 45 cents. If it went too high, he suggested, China could sell, and if it went too low, the United States could buy. He calculated that he would buy at about 42 cents if China would sell at about 47 cents. He did not want to draw up a document to that effect, but only to give Chen his word. China, he added, now knew more about American silver policy than did any other nation.

Morgenthau also told Chen confidentially that a Japanese commercial and financial representative, Yutaro Tomito, was arriving from London. Because the State Department had invited him, Morgenthau had to see him. The Secretary thought the Japanese were curious about his negotiations with Chen. "They evidently figure this is so important," he said, "they will try to find out and it's none of their business." Indeed, he added: "I may make a speech and say how fine I think China is coming along and ask them to cooperate." In that case, Chen said, laughing, Chinese bonds would go up two and a half yuan.

On April 22 Tomito visited Morgenthau's office with Stanley K.

Hornbeck of the State Department's Far Eastern desk. The Japanese made a number of technical inquiries about American monetary and fiscal policy, which the Secretary answered by referring to appropriate Treasury and Federal Reserve publications. Tomito then asserted that Chinese monetary reform was failing. Morgenthau said that in his opinion it had gotten on remarkably well. All foreign banks had turned in their silver, he noted, except the Japanese, who were holding out about $10 million worth. Tomito said the Japanese banks withheld the silver because they were convinced Chinese monetary policy would not succeed. At that point the Japanese ambassador, who was also present, terminated the interview. After the Japanese left, Hornbeck expressed his pleasure with what the Secretary had said. Morgenthau replied that he had had to "give it to" Tomito who, as Hornbeck agreed, had "asked for it."

Meanwhile the Treasury staff had continued talking with Chen about conditions for American silver purchases. Chen agreed to recommend the coinage of new silver yuan and half-yuan pieces and to suggest larger allotments of silver to industry and the arts. He was also willing to consider increasing the bullion and foreign exchange in the currency reserve. He admitted that the yuan seemed pegged to sterling because it had been quoted that way. By altering their system of quotation, the Chinese would make it obvious that the yuan was geared to no other national currency.

Completely satisfied, as were his advisers, the Secretary on May 12 submitted a draft of a Chinese-American monetary agreement that Chen accepted. To avoid bringing in the Department of State, Morgenthau made the agreement between the Chinese Ministry of Finance and the United States Treasury, not between the governments. It made no reference to credits or loans but instead to the furnishing of dollar exchange. Only the Chinese and American governments were to know that the United States would provide $20 million against the deposit of 50 million ounces of silver. Morgenthau also proposed to buy 75 million ounces of silver, starting with 12 million ounces for the month ending June 15 and continuing with nine million ounces each month through January 15, 1937. The price was to be the current market price, and the Chinese could elect to have payment in gold. Proceeds from these sales were to be left in New York where the Chinese could use them only for stabilizing the external value of the yuan. The details of this arrangement were also to remain confidential.

With his staff Morgenthau also prepared press releases designed to stimulate confidence in Chinese currency. In the text used in China on May 18, 1936, the Ministry of Finance announced that it had made "definite arrangements" to increase "the gold and foreign exchange of the note issue reserve." It promised "supplementary measures of monetary reform" to assure "the continued maintenance of an independent currency system not linked to any foreign monetary unit and the permanent stability of the Chinese currency which will inevitably lead to greater economic improvement and prosperity of the Chinese people."

From Washington Morgenthau simultaneously made an optimistic statement. "I feel confident," he said, "that the monetary program being pursued by the National Government of China is not only along sound lines, but constitutes an important step toward the desired goal of stability of world currencies. . . . To cooperate with them in their program of monetary reform and currency stabilization, and in accordance with our silver purchase policy, we have definitely indicated our willingness, under conditions mutually agreeable, to make purchases from the Central Bank of China of substantial amounts of silver, and also to make available . . . dollar exchange for currency stabilization purposes." The Secretary denied newspapermen details about the operation of the agreement, but he did tell them that the Department of State approved of it, as did Senators Pittman and McNary.

With the help of the United States, China was able during the next year to manage her currency. The operation of the Silver Purchase Act had forced her off silver, occasioning large distress, but Morgenthau had gradually modified policy enough so that in the end the Treasury provided the assistance that permitted China to enjoy a period of unprecedented stability in both the internal and external value of her money. In that time, in spite of Japan's continuing hostility, Chiang Kai-shek extended the control of his government.

Like the Tripartite Pact with France and England, the silver agreement with China marked the end of an evolutionary phase in American monetary policy. Morgenthau had adjusted the gold and silver programs, instituted essentially for domestic purposes, to international monetary and political conditions. Within the limits of his authority, he had begun to develop technical devices to encourage resistance to fascist aggression. His achievement was timely, for the forces of oppression were on the verge of a great offensive. Monetary diplomacy could not prevent it, but when it came, the Treasury alone of American agencies had established foundations from which to meet it.

The President stood behind his friend. Like the good general in the analogy he so often drew, Roosevelt would not go out too far ahead of his army, but he was not averse to using an adventurous scout. He suffered Hull's hesitancy, but he also gave Morgenthau the opportunity to make stronger commitments across both oceans than did the Department of State, to go farther than most of the American people realized, farther than most of them — had they understood — would probably have condoned. And to his chief's satisfaction, Morgenthau did as much as he could.

# VI

## *Essential Spending*

### *1934-1937*

### 1. A Difficult Job

THE NATIONAL BUDGET had never presented more troublesome or important problems than it did when Morgenthau assumed office. In 1933, as he later put it, "the economy of the country had literally come to a standstill." But Roosevelt's "vision and courage brought a scared and sullen country to life again. He gave people jobs . . . stopped mortgage foreclosures, dared to throw all the resources of the federal government into the battle to save bank deposits, homes, farms and individual self-respect. It was worth every penny it cost. In those early days there was no time for careful planning or for detailed coordination. We were in a race against hunger and revolution, and we had to act fast."

The race permitted no feasible alternative to unprecedented peacetime spending. That spending and the deficits it produced involved Morgenthau in every aspect of federal policy. Charged by the Constitution with making "a regular statement and account of the receipts and expenditures of all public money," the Secretary of the Treasury had to know whether budgetary procedures achieved the objectives of economy and efficiency in the conduct of government. He had to ascertain how new spending proposals related to existing costs and to probable revenues, and whether those proposals served national policy.

Some of these responsibilities fell also to the Director of the Budget. In 1921 Congress had created the Bureau of the Budget, placing it in the Treasury Department, but making it responsible to the President, who appointed its Director. The Bureau was to assist the President in preparing a comprehensive budget and to strengthen his authority over the executive departments. These changes lightened but did not remove the burdens of the Secretary of the Treasury, for his Constitutional obligations remained just what they had always been, as did his official and legitimate concern about public finance and national fiscal policy.

Furthermore, the actual working of government depended less upon blueprints than upon people. The Director of the Budget in 1933 was Lewis Douglas, a former congressman from Arizona, who propounded rigidly orthodox ideas about fiscal policy with ability and insinuating charm. This orthodoxy troubled many New Dealers who thought it held back the battle against depression. As Morgenthau put it, he and Roosevelt "felt that Douglas' policy involved too great a gamble with human lives; that we could not stop the essential spending necessary to keep people alive, to keep the farms producing, to keep the government functioning without doing irreparable harm to the recuperative forces of the country. Yet we differed from Lew Douglas, not over whether a balanced budget was our ultimate goal, but over what sacrifices of relief and reform we were prepared to make in order to get it right away."

With some twelve to fifteen million Americans looking for work, the Administration had difficulty finding enough money for relief. Morgenthau helped the search for funds. In February 1934, at the risk of incurring an additional deficit, he assigned $150 million to the Federal Emergency Relief Administration. He was also reconciled to further deficits. At luncheon with the President on August 13, 1934, he submitted the draft of a speech which said that the Administration looked forward to a balanced budget. Then "a rather dramatic thing happened." The President tried to rewrite the statement, but finally said he did not see how Morgenthau could make it because the budget could not be balanced even in the fiscal year 1936, the period July 1, 1935–June 30, 1936. There had been nothing provided for unemployment or for public works. "Well," Morgenthau replied, "cross it out."

The Secretary did not hesitate. For him, relief and recovery came first, a balanced budget second. Lewis Douglas was of a different

view. He was willing to accept the dole, the cheapest form of relief, but he opposed public works. Already disturbed by the Administration's gold policy, Douglas found the prospect of a budget
in continuing imbalance utterly alarming. On August 30, 1934, he
resigned.

Morgenthau never forgot the episode. "I drove up the winding
road to Roosevelt's house at Hyde Park," he later wrote, "and, at
the door, was told the President would see me upstairs immediately.
He was taking a bath." He sat up straight in the bathtub, looked
Morgenthau directly in the eye, and said: "Henry (with great emphasis), in the words of John Paul Jones — we have just begun to
fight." The previous evening, he explained, Lewis Douglas had
quit. Roosevelt had tried to persuade him to wait until December 1, appealing to him as a patriot and, with the forthcoming Congressional elections in mind, as a Democrat. But Douglas declined.
To Morgenthau, the President seemed "terribly upset and hurt. He
said that he told Douglas that ten years from now he would be very
sorry for what he had done." And he added: "Henry, I give you
until midnight to get me a new Director of the Budget."

Morgenthau was worried about the spending program himself.
In the first place, he recalled,

I wanted all spending for relief and public works to be coordinated under a single head so as to avoid duplication and
administrative confusion. In the second place, I wanted a
scheduled tapering off of spending so that we could look forward to a balancing of the budget.

It was with these two objectives in mind that I asked the
President whom he was considering as Douglas' successor.

He took my breath away by saying, "What do you think of
Tom Corcoran as Director of the Budget?"

This seemed to me absolutely out of the question. Tom Corcoran was a first-class lawyer, a first-class political operator, a
first-class accordion player. But I felt sure he knew very little
about finance and could not be relied upon to keep a tight rein
over the spending policies.

So I hastily suggested Daniel Bell, then my Commissioner of
Accounts and Deposits in the Treasury Department for the

job. Fortunately Roosevelt liked the idea, and Bell was made Acting Director.

That evening, at a clambake at the Morgenthaus', Roosevelt had a cocktail alone with his host. "You could tell," Morgenthau observed, "that he had a great weight off his shoulders. As the evening went on he began to sing songs and you could tell from the way he acted that a great load and worry was off his mind. As a matter of fact the people closely associated with him said that they had never seen him sing and be so jolly as he was that night since he became President."

Morgenthau was also pleased. Dan Bell, who was to remain Acting Director of the Budget for four years, was precisely the kind of dedicated civil servant whom the Secretary found indispensable. Bell had advanced from post to post within the Treasury Department since coming to work as a bookkeeper in 1911. If he had any political affiliation, he never revealed it. A talented and diligent man, unselfishly loyal, he held Morgenthau's confidence and returned it in full. They worked together with singular harmony of purpose and method.

They were determined "to ride herd over the spending program," for they believed, as the Secretary said, that "the various agencies who are doing the spending, their eyes are always bigger than their stomachs." Their appetite and lack of direction fostered extravagance which, as Morgenthau saw it, impeded recovery. "I wanted to see a free private enterprise economy as flourishing as the twenties but operating more soundly and more equitably," he explained years later. "It seemed vital to me that the government try sincerely to build a feeling of confidence in its financial operations so that businessmen would be encouraged to take over their proper role of invigorating the economy. I did not believe in the notion that a large, permanent deficit was necessary to 'compensate' for inadequacies of private investment, or for deficiencies of private purchasing power. Nor, I think, did the President or any of his close advisers in 1933–34."

In September 1934 the Secretary and his staff did believe, however, that Roosevelt was getting "a lot of poor advice." In order to identify and eliminate waste, Morgenthau suggested setting up a double budget, one for the regular expenses of government and the other for extraordinary expenses for relief and recovery. It was also necessary, he told the President, to establish some control over the spending agencies. Douglas had been bitter because Roosevelt in January 1934 withdrew an Executive Order only three days old that put the independent agencies under supervision of the Bureau of the Budget. Morgenthau persuaded the President to let him refurbish the Order for possible use in the future. More immediately, he got Roosevelt to call the spenders together for a series of meetings beginning October 1. At these the Treasury hoped to obtain a coordinated estimate based upon national needs and assets. The Department could then plan its financings for 1936 and work for a balanced budget for the fiscal year 1937 or 1938. "We certainly have a difficult job ahead of us," Morgenthau wrote. "Just where it will all end, heaven only knows."

## 2. Search for a Program

In March 1933 the New Deal had had to improvise a relief program. About twenty-one million people were receiving some kind of public assistance, but the states and localities had practically exhausted their resources for rendering aid. The burden of sustaining life rested upon the federal government, which had neither precedents nor plans for the action that Roosevelt courageously promised. Under these conditions, the New Deal's achievements during the next eighteen months were magnificent but disorderly.

Harry Hopkins brought his indomitable energy to the direction of the Federal Emergency Relief Administration. It disbursed an initial $500 million, largely in the form of grants which the states distributed as dole; but Hopkins, who considered handouts degrading, in the fall of 1933 devised the short-lived Civil Works Administration, which spent about $1 billion during the next half year putting men to work — some four million of them — on small federal projects. Many of these were hastily conceived, some were of little permanent value, but the experience of the Civil Works Administration and the gratitude of those it hired confirmed the belief of Hopkins and Roosevelt that only work relief, as opposed to direct relief, could preserve the spirit of the able unemployed during the distracting months of depression still to come. To provide a system within which work relief could proceed efficiently and constructively, Hopkins and his associates in September 1934 were preparing plans for the President and, with his approval, for Congress.

Morgenthau had no precise knowledge of Hopkins's plans, but he did know that the business community by and large opposed work relief, preferring the dole because it was cheaper and because employers feared that government competition for labor would force increases in wages. Morgenthau, in contrast, shared Hopkins's humane purpose and had no objection to incurring federal deficits in accomplishing it. He wanted, however, to keep expenditures to a minimum, and on that account to re-examine the nature and cost of proposed work relief projects, the capacity of those projects to provide jobs for the unemployed, and the pace at which projects would need financing. These considerations governed the Treasury's response to the competition for federal funds between light and heavy public works — between Hopkins's work relief program and Harold Ickes's Public Works Administration.

That competition had begun in the spring of 1933. The National Industrial Recovery Act then provided $3.3 billion for public works. The advocates of the appropriation expected PWA to stimulate heavy industry by spending the money for projects like dams that called for huge quantities of steel, cement, and other capital goods. But Ickes had criteria of his own. Determined to use his funds for durable projects of permanent social and esthetic value, he pursued his high purpose with maddening deliberation. As Morgenthau recalled, Ickes "was so anxious to keep graft and politics out of the public works program that he practically spent money through a medicine dropper. Ickes's slowness in making decisions was sometimes a real handicap. The important thing was to alleviate unemployment crises but because of insufficient advance planning the public works projects were frequently slow in getting started and therefore expenditures for them were sometimes being made after instead of before the crises had passed their peaks."

Hopkins, in contrast to Ickes, gave first priority to providing as much work as possible, as fast as possible, at as low a cost per man as possible. Morgenthau therefore favored channeling the bulk of federal relief expenditures through Hopkins. Ickes resented this preference, considered Hopkins wasteful and Morgenthau meddling, and fought both with pugnacious obstinacy.

On October 1, 1934, Morgenthau entered the White House for the first of several conferences with Ickes, Hopkins, and Roosevelt. He was there, as he quickly indicated, to assert the Treasury's interest in a coordinated spending program. He demanded definitions of how much the government would spend, how fast, for what projects, and with what impact on unemployment. Unless these questions could be answered accurately, he said, the Treasury could not make plans to finance the program by taxation or by borrowing, nor could the government make progress toward a balanced budget.

Roosevelt proposed a $12 billion program over three years. This, he thought, would sufficiently prime the pump so that private industry could absorb all employables, leaving direct relief for unemployable paupers to states and localities. For the fiscal year 1936, the President contemplated a work relief and public works budget of about $5 billion. He had some general ideas about expending this sum for the elimination of slums, the building of low-cost housing, the construction of a transcontinental highway, the improvement of railways and of rivers, harbors and port facilities. He preferred self-liquidating projects. Some of these, such as a transcontinental highway and the construction of inexpensive housing, might afford the government a substantial return in tolls and rentals.

Yet neither on October 1 nor October 10 nor October 16 did Roosevelt or Hopkins or Ickes have careful estimates of costs or timetables for completion of the President's proposals. There were bound to be long delays while the government sought title to land for housing or for highways. Self-liquidating projects would entail immediate outlays which in turn would demand special financing, but no one had calculated how much. Ickes and Hopkins hoped to provide employment for six million men on useful projects by December 1935, and then gradually to be able to taper off; but they had no specific project schedules, and, like the President, could only guess that their plans would let the federal government safely abandon the dole.

Three days of discussion gave the Treasury nothing to go on. Even Roosevelt, when Hopkins and Ickes submitted their plans, pointed out that item after item was impractical. As Morgenthau saw it, Hopkins simply "yessed" everything the President said. Ickes at one point asserted that it made no difference whether the government spent $5 billion or private industry spent an equal amount. At this "classic remark" Morgenthau thought Jacob Viner "would almost pass out." The President kept reverting to his own scheme for building four cross-country highways with four north-south intersectors fed by various branches. Construction could begin where unemployment was highest, he said on October 16, and the government could build and sell houses on large plots along the completed roads. After elaborating this dream, he asked Morgenthau whether the information which the conferences had developed satisfied him.

The discussion, the Secretary replied, left him "absolutely cold."

Roosevelt said Morgenthau sounded like Russell Leffingwell, a Morgan partner who believed that large federal expenditures would retard recovery.

"I wish I had half his brains," Morgenthau answered.

In a sarcastic manner the President then asked if Morgenthau had any better suggestions. The Secretary requested reports from engineers qualified to state when projects might begin and how much they would cost. The government, he said, was contracting for public works without paying any attention to the problem of taking people off relief. He believed all public works had to be handled by one agency, directed by one man with the authority to make policy for the purpose of relieving unemployment and reducing relief rolls.

Morgenthau could tell that Roosevelt did not like this speech; and Hopkins called it unfair, arguing that Morgenthau could not reasonably expect him to come in with finished plans. After another half hour of talk, however, Roosevelt directed Ickes and Hopkins to have the Corps of Engineers submit estimates on all projects, covering costs, time schedules, and employment potentialities. He wanted a complete survey in time for a further conference to be held in Warm Springs in December. He would then, he said, take up the question of what kind of organization should run the program, and in January take his plans to Congress.

Roosevelt's concluding instructions pleased Morgenthau, who was even more encouraged by a "thrilling meeting with the President at his bedside" two days later. Roosevelt said he had tried on October 16 to catch Morgenthau's eye so that he would stop suggesting that one organization manage public works. He agreed with Morgenthau but did not want at that time to start Ickes and Hopkins fighting. Morgenthau said that Hopkins ought to keep track of the entire operation. Again Roosevelt agreed, except that he thought Ickes should be left alone to finance municipal improvements. Morgenthau questioned even this, but he left the President with a "distinct feeling of encouragement . . . that he and I were seeing absolutely eye to eye on this program."

His optimism was premature. On December 2 he and Roosevelt, Ickes, and Hopkins began at Warm Springs to review what were purported to be final plans for public works. "You could have knocked me over with a feather," Morgenthau reported in his Diary, "when Ickes pulled out of his portfolio five copies of his program. It seemed unbelievable to me that we had all been sitting around there for a couple of days and Ickes had not given any of us a chance to see the program." It was only a lot of "lump sum figures," in Morgenthau's opinion, without relevance to the need for using public works to hire the unemployed. Hopkins spoke "rather loosely" about taking four million men off relief, but Morgenthau, pleased that Roosevelt was short with Ickes, made it clear to the President that the Treasury still had nothing definite with which to calculate the dole, the projects, or the necessary financing.

Sensing again the antagonism between Ickes and Hopkins, Morgenthau that evening urged the President to put one man in charge. "In a very emphatic and rather angry tone of voice," Roosevelt shouted: "I will get a program within forty-eight hours. I am going to get my program first and I will not settle as to who is going to run it until I get my program." "I am sorry, Mr. President," Morgenthau said. "I think you are wrong."

Though the relief program remained as amorphous as it had been before the first conference about it, Roosevelt decided late in

December to ask Congress for $4 billion of new money, which Ickes and Hopkins maintained they could spend. Morgenthau told the President categorically that they could not, but he knew he was making no impression, and he realized that the actual spending was not his job. He concentrated therefore on helping Bell find unexpended funds from earlier appropriations to stretch out relief in 1935 and, if Congress consented, to supplement the $4 billion of new money for 1936.

On December 26, 1934, Roosevelt for the first time carefully considered finances for fiscal 1936. With Bell and Morgenthau at his side, he took $937 million of unobligated monies away from emergency agencies that had been sitting on their appropriations. Seeing that Roosevelt "got a kick" out of making these subtractions, Morgenthau immediately persuaded the President to dictate letters instructing the agencies to cease obligating funds until further notice.

Pressing on, Morgenthau suggested that if the 1936 deficit were less than that for 1935, the Administration could argue that it had broken the back of the depression. If, on the other hand, each year's deficit increased, he did not see how to stop Congress from forcing the Treasury to print paper money.

Roosevelt, pencil and paper in hand, tried to figure out from every angle how the Administration could make it appear that the peak of expenditures would fall in 1935, the current fiscal year. After calculating for a long time, he decided to use the estimates submitted by the departments rather than the less dramatic figures of the Bureau of the Budget which Bell felt were closer to being accurate. Bell considered this procedure "just . . . faking," but Morgenthau was pleased because he thought that at last he was making real headway in getting the President to face basic issues.

At the White House the next afternoon, however, the Secretary realized to his dismay that Roosevelt was trying to placate Ickes. Morgenthau therefore make an emphatic "stump speech" about balancing the budget except for relief and about the dangers of "paper inflation." Roosevelt swung over to his side, and between them they swept Ickes off his feet and "just left him gurgling and murmuring to himself."

After Hopkins and Ickes left, Roosevelt, "grinning all over," im-

plied that he had made it easy for Bell to take away Ickes's unexpended funds. Silently to himself, Morgenthau said: "Franklin,
old boy, you had Bell and me here to help hold your hand while
you performed the most difficult operation on Ickes and thank
God that I was there to back you up."

Out loud, the Secretary reviewed the reallocations Roosevelt had
approved. He also gave the President a draft of a budget message,
including a page written entirely by Charles Merz of the *New York
Times,* which Roosevelt accepted verbatim. That page seemed to
Morgenthau, as to Merz, essential from the standpoint of business
confidence and sound economics. Although a substantial measure
of recovery had been achieved, it said, unemployment was still
large, and increasingly the responsibility of the federal government.
Therefore the Administration could not completely balance the
budget for 1936, but the President was submitting a budget which
balanced except for expenditures for relief. This deficit, incurred as
it was to meet the emergency, would decline as rapidly as private
industry could re-employ.

At a final meeting about the budget message a few days later,
Roosevelt again approved Morgenthau's formulations. "I will most
likely never again have to face as serious a financial problem as the
one I have just gone through with the President," the Secretary
confided to his Diary, "and I now feel that I have nothing to worry
about from Congress as I do not believe that any group would have
the nerve or the backing to try to bust this budget which is balanced except for relief."

Again he was overoptimistic. Early in January Roosevelt secretly allotted Hopkins an extra $125 million. On January 21,
1935, Bell reported that Rex Tugwell had received for agricultural
rehabilitation and land reclamation $67 million from unexpended
allocations which the President had previously consented to reassign. Morgenthau at once complained, reminding Roosevelt that
they had agreed not to allot any more money before consulting
Hopkins and Ickes.

"Well," Roosevelt said, "Rex tells me he needs the money."

"He has hardly spent any that you have already given him,"
Morgenthau replied, "and you are going to need this money badly
for relief before July 1."

Roosevelt, retreating, suggested that Bell write a letter "by direction of the President" telling Tugwell he could not have the money. That took care of the immediate problem, but Morgenthau was privately unhappy about the President's unsystematic allotments. "The result," he wrote in his Diary, "is that everybody is angry and frothing at the mouth." Furthermore, while Ickes, Hopkins, Tugwell and other administrators struggled for funds for their agencies, while Roosevelt made his genial private arrangements with each of them, Morgenthau and Bell had no sure way of estimating, much less of controlling, the size or rate of federal expenditures. They had small reason to expect much improvement from the new relief bill then before Congress.

### 3. The Four Billion Eight

In April 1935 Congress passed the Emergency Relief Appropriation Act providing the funds for which Roosevelt had asked — $4 billion of new money and $880 million unused from previous appropriations. A few inflationists had advocated spending twice this amount, but the Administration received all it had asked for, the largest peacetime appropriation in American history. The law stipulated that a unified agency was to administer the work program; that the projects were to be permanent contributions to the nation; that the government was to pay a "security wage" larger than the dole but smaller than the wages paid by private industry; that preference was to be given to self-liquidating projects which directly employed labor and were located in distressed areas; and that local communities were to resume caring for unemployable paupers. These stipulations met Roosevelt's prescriptions, but the Senate complicated the administration of the Act by insisting on confirming all appointments to jobs paying more than $5000 a year and by specifying in the statute how some of the money was to be allotted. The former provision injected politics into the work program; the latter limited the Executive's flexibility.

Although the provisions of the Act did not compensate for what Morgenthau considered the inadequacies of planning for work relief, he hoped that Roosevelt would now give Hopkins unquestionable authority for the direction of expenditures. While the bill lay before Congress, the President had delayed decision about a program director; but in April, to Morgenthau's distress, he put Ickes in charge of an Allotment Division and Hopkins in charge of a Projects Division, which he was soon to reorganize as the Work Progress Administration. This separation of responsibility, Morgenthau believed, would hamstring the program. Worse still, as he put it in his Diary, the idea of Ickes as Chairman of the Allotment Division and Harry Hopkins in "some nondescript job just made me sick."

"Racking his brain" for some way to concentrate authority for the whole program and to free Hopkins from dependence upon Ickes, Morgenthau concluded that the best man in Washington for the "top job" would be Joseph P. Kennedy, a Boston Democrat then Chairman of the Securities and Exchange Commission. A successful stockbroker with frankly conservative views, Kennedy had the respect of the business community. Though he had opposed the work program at one time, he had come to support it enthusiastically.

On April 13 Morgenthau talked with Roosevelt "as one Dutchess County neighbor to another." "Please remember, Franklin," he began, "that I cannot get anything more out of politics in this life so what I am going to say to you is motivated by the desire to serve my country and you and nothing else." As it was then arranged, Morgenthau said, the "$4 billion 8" setup would surely fail, and if it did, Roosevelt would not be re-elected. He suggested the President put Kennedy in charge. Kennedy, he argued, had made an outstanding record, could handle people, and was popular with congressmen and newspapermen. Roosevelt was dubious. "The trouble with Kennedy," he said, "is you always have to hold his hand." But after further consideration, he exuberantly proposed appointing an "Assistant to the President in Charge of Public Works," who would "really run the show"; and for that job Kennedy, he thought, would be "all right."

On April 22 Roosevelt had a new plan. He would make Ickes simply senior member of an allotment board and set up a small, intermediary committee to supervise all expenditures. There Kennedy would sit at the President's side as the secretary. "I can't yet tell either Hopkins or Ickes," Roosevelt confided to Morgenthau, "that Kennedy is going to be over them. They will have to learn that gradually." But Kennedy, he said, had already accepted the appointment. Later that day, however, Kennedy told Morgenthau he was going to turn the job down, because he could not work with Ickes.

The next day, Roosevelt came up with other proposals. He would not tie up funds beyond July 1, 1936, and he would allocate them only after checking with Hopkins to see how many people in project areas were on relief rolls. Each million dollars allotted would have to provide employment for about a thousand people. The President also intended to spend at least half the money directly on wages, and he wanted to get back as much as he could in rentals and tolls, even if the length of time for repayment was longer than customary. These criteria, however, did little more than elaborate the provisions of the statute; and Roosevelt, rejecting Morgenthau's recommendations, left Ickes as Chairman of the Allotment Board and Hopkins as Administrator of the WPA.

As Morgenthau saw it, the danger was that Ickes would divert funds to projects only remotely beneficial to the unemployed, while Hopkins, disbursing what he could of what remained, would spend generously but wastefully. The Secretary therefore asked to be excused from the Allotment Board because he got "too blue at the meetings." "Some day," he noted in his Diary in July 1935, "if we keep on spending money at the rate we are and in such helter-skelter, hit and miss method, we cannot help but be riding for a fall unless we continue to decrease our deficit each year and the budget is balanced. If we are not able to do this, I do not want to be the sole goat and . . . be under terrific pressure from all the money cranks and crackpots to pull out some more white rabbits out of the hat and do some unsound economic trick in order to correct other unsound measures which the administration had taken. . . . It seems to me that we are not making any headway and the number of unemployed is staying more or less static. The unfortunate thing in this administration is that nobody seems to be trying to fit our unemployment program in with the long distant viewpoint so that we will gradually cut down on unemployment and in that manner reduce the federal expenditures to maintain the unemployed. I think that ninety-five per cent of the thinking in the administration is how to spend money and that possibly five per cent of the thinking is going toward how we can work ourselves out of our present unemployment difficulties."

Treasury statistics indicated that while employment had leveled off, the government was constantly increasing expenditures for work relief and public works. This contradicted Roosevelt's familiar assertion that he would adjust the level of spending to the level of private hiring. "It is the sort of thing which I feel it is my duty to bring to the President's attention," Morgenthau told himself. As he put it to Louis Howe, no agency getting vast sums of money should be trusted with the statistical work of charting recovery. To Harry Hopkins and Miss Perkins Morgenthau suggested a federal census of the unemployed. "Why not call a spade a spade," he said, "and admit that we have no unemployment policy. There is no one place where there is a chart showing the number of unemployed in a particular area and also showing the amount of money allotted to meet their particular needs."

Properly to fit allotments to needs, Hopkins replied, the government would have to go permanently into a great public works program. Nothing short of $10 billion would do the trick, he argued, for the $4.8 billion did not begin to strike home, particularly since it was being used for work which should have been financed out of regular appropriations. Miss Perkins thought they could make spending more efficient, but she did not see "where a census will do any good."

When Roosevelt, too, proved absolutely cold to the idea of a census, probably because it might backfire politically, Morgenthau tried another way to focus the President's attention on spending problems. At luncheon on July 23, he reported that Georgia was the only state that had returned its unemployables to community aid. Elsewhere there were almost a million unemployables on federal relief rolls. Roosevelt at once went "into a long harangue . . . how for years there had been ten families in Hyde Park, that the town had always taken care of them but now the federal government is taking care of them and that there is no reason why these ten families should not be thrown back on the town and that there must be thousands of communities who have similar situations and who could take care of their chronic unemployables."

Suddenly switching direction, but still on the side of retrench-ment, Roosevelt said he was going to tell Ickes to stop letting con-tracts for slum clearance after September 1 because heavy proj-ects, slow to start, could not be shut off.

Taking advantage of the President's mood, Morgenthau pointed out that some three and a half million people remained on work relief irrespective of improvements in private employment. He suggested that if recovery seemed likely, Roosevelt should make a speech after Congress adjourned referring to his promise to de-crease expenditures if conditions permitted, and explaining that he had been spending slowly because (and from here on Morgenthau spoke with his tongue in his cheek) he had expected recovery in the fall and did not want to waste money. "If that is not the darnedest sophistry," Morgenthau wrote in his Diary, "I do not know what sophistry is," but Roosevelt, after listening, "made a perfectly mag-nificent address right then and there and by the time he was finished, knowing my F.D.R., I believed he was fully convinced that all the ideas he had expressed were his own — which encouraged me tre-mendously because I felt I had gotten my ideas across."

Morgenthau believed he had made a real start toward keeping the deficit in the current fiscal year below $3 billion and in 1937, the next fiscal year, close to $2 billion. "This accomplishment," he wrote in his Diary, "will either be reached or not within the next sixty days and the whole thing depends upon a complete revamp-ing of the relief program."

By mid-August he had submitted to the President a number of proposals to effect the revamping. Government spending was head-ing for a peak in June 1936, when Roosevelt's political advisers would say it was "crazy" to economize with the national election pending. Morgenthau therefore considered it essential to taper off not later than March 1936. Immediately, he recommended con-centrating spending on those projects affording the most employ-ment, reducing administrative costs, and curtailing purchases of land for roads, reclamation, and resettlement. These policies could reserve $1.2 billion for use in the fiscal year 1937, but that saving depended upon cancellation of many allocations already made for rural electrification, for conservation, and especially for Ickes's

Public Works Administration. That agency, Morgenthau argued, had to be held to projects which would be completed by the end of fiscal 1936.

Because administrative overhead for spending and lending had risen about 80 per cent in fiscal 1936 over the previous year, the Secretary urged the President to reissue Lewis Douglas's old order putting all independent agencies under the supervision of the Bureau of the Budget. Finally, he asked Roosevelt to begin to liquidate the Reconstruction Finance Corporation. It planned to operate at a net deficit until 1939, including a deficit of $1.5 billion for 1936. If, however, the RFC ceased making loans at once, the Treasury could expect to receive payments of interest and principal on outstanding RFC loans which would permit a net income from that agency of $1.2 billion in 1936, and more thereafter. The various savings he advocated, Morgenthau reckoned, would reduce the deficit for 1937 to less than one billion dollars without short-changing the needy. Barring major disasters, that would guarantee a balanced budget in 1938.

Roosevelt moved cautiously in some of these directions. He registered his intention of reserving $1.2 billion for 1937. He issued an Executive Order on August 6 giving the Bureau of the Budget supervision of the administrative expenses of seven lending agencies, but leaving the spending agencies untouched — a compromise, Morgenthau suspected, designed to avoid a row with Ickes. On August 22 he ordered work on all pending or approved projects accelerated, thus hastening the flow of funds to employment and improving the prospects for completing the ongoing projects within the fiscal year. And for September 12 he called the first of several conferences on spending, work relief, and public works.

At these conferences Morgenthau again stood for unifying the direction of public works, for concentrating on assistance for the unemployed, for giving Hopkins most of the emergency appropriations and most of the voice in the relief program. Again he made little headway, though Roosevelt admitted that the data on unemployment were inaccurate and that he would have to stretch available funds.

On November 15 Hopkins told Morgenthau that he would need

at least an additional $300 million in the current fiscal year. At first "unsympathetic and cold," Morgenthau "asked him how he could go before Congress and ask for more money when so much was being wasted. He demanded to know where it was being wasted. I made the suggestion that Tugwell might be wasting it.* He said, 'Oh, it is just unbelievable the way Tugwell is throwing money away,' that the administrative setup was so terrible that in many cases people in executive positions in the field organization of Tugwell had not been paid off for so long that Hopkins had to put them on his relief rolls to take care of them. I said, 'Have you told this to the President?' No, he had not. He said a couple of hundred people were sitting around in Tugwell's Washington office with nothing to do."

Relenting, the Secretary asked Hopkins to explain his needs in writing, but Hopkins said he could venture only a guess. He did have to have a few million immediately to wind up direct relief. This report, Morgenthau told the President, disturbed him, for WPA would run out of money about April 1, but the Treasury could not ascertain how much it would have to raise. Roosevelt, who was less worried, postponed discussion of the problem after Morgenthau promised to find $3 to $5 million for direct relief.

Hopkins was grateful for this and other emergency contributions to the relief program. "No one did more than you to support that program," he wrote Morgenthau years later. "Many times when the days seemed pretty dark you were the one who helped influence a favorable decision on behalf of the millions who were out of work. . . . Never once in the long history of unemployment relief did you fail." Morgenthau was proud of this accolade, for Hopkins, he realized, had always at heart the interests of those at the bottom of the ladder. So did the Secretary. Their common humanitarian purpose transcended their disagreements about method.

Yet method, too, made a difference, for the efficient use of relief monies was as important for the unemployed as for the budget. As Morgenthau put it to his morning group on November 11, 1935, it was perfectly asinine to talk about balancing the budget immediately. It could not be balanced if decent attention were to be

* In the Resettlement Administration.

given to human needs. But relief could be put on a businesslike basis. This was his objective while he and Bell worked on the 1937 budget with Roosevelt in Warm Springs on November 26 and 27. They halved the requests of the Civilian Conservation Corps, cut down the funds for road building, and arranged to discharge rapidly the personnel engaged in winding up the affairs of the National Recovery Administration, which the Supreme Court had declared unconstitutional. Looking for another $150 million, Morgenthau suggested taking it from Ickes's Public Works Administration. To his delight, Roosevelt concurred. Weighing these and other savings against the Treasury's revised estimates of revenue, Morgenthau in December 1935 hoped to balance the 1937 budget exclusive of relief with a couple of hundred million dollars to spare.

There remained three dangers. The Supreme Court had found the Agricultural Adjustment Act unconstitutional, invalidating the processing tax which had defrayed the expenses of supporting agricultural prices. The Administration was determined to continue to support prices, but Congress had yet to provide new taxes.* Congress, furthermore, seemed ready to pay the World War I veterans their bonus but unwilling to use taxes for that purpose.† And Hopkins and Ickes, still warring with each other, had again only vague suggestions for spending the money they demanded.

Six tedious meetings with the President and his feuding spenders resembled strikingly the inconclusive sessions of the previous year. While Hopkins only "kept talking in terms of employing the people on relief rolls," Ickes "practically never opened his mouth," and neither proposed projects which the Treasury could assess for financing. Their ideas struck Morgenthau as "so fantastic and sketchy that I suggested having Admiral Peoples and his men analyze the programs . . . particularly to see what percentage of money allocated could be spent on direct labor on the job." The analysis revealed that only 28 per cent of the expenditures Ickes proposed would be for labor and Hopkins's proposals were only 2 to 12 per cent better. The only project which Morgenthau could develop for the President's consideration that would surely put a

* See pages 305–6.
† See page 258.

majority of cost in labor was for a still impracticable transcontinental highway.

Roosevelt spoke often and at length, but in Morgenthau's view
he set too many requirements. The Secretary did not believe the
money could ever be spent under the conditions Roosevelt or the
Congress had laid down. He thought it urgent for the President
to unscramble the alphabet agencies and to arrange for all remaining organizations to get their money directly from the Treasury
by way of the Director of the Budget, instead of in the existing,
slap-dash manner. "It seems almost tragic," he wrote in his Diary,
"to think that the fate of the unemployed in America is waiting to
be decided and these two men both seeking power can hold up
this whole program." While the rivalry between Ickes and Hopkins
persisted, the chances of reducing deficits would depend on "a
battle of wits between the President and myself and I hope that the
outcome will be the best for all concerned."

Good soldier that he was, Morgenthau kept these thoughts to
himself. To the public he turned a brighter face. As 1935 ended,
life in America looked much more promising than it had three
years earlier. There had been some recovery. There would be
more, Morgenthau believed, especially if the budget remained in
hand. On December 28 he gave the President a draft for the
budget message. His staff had written it, but it expressed his views.
There were three courses open to the government, it maintained.
The first was to underwrite a program of large-scale public works in
order to hasten recovery, but this was unnecessary, for steps
already taken had provided the necessary initial stimulus. A second
course of action, which critics of the Administration demanded,
called for confining expenditures to estimated revenues. This
would be disastrous, for the measure of recovery was still not great
enough to withstand government's complete relinquishment of its
role, and so long as there was substantial unemployment, government had a responsibility to assist those out of work. Eventually a
newly prosperous business community would rehire them and the
increased revenue from advancing earnings would reimburse the
government. The third course, falling between the extremes, was
to consolidate gains already made with declining expenditures for
relief. "Our policy is succeeding," said the last paragraph, which

the President used verbatim. "The figures prove it. Secure in the knowledge that steadily decreasing deficits will turn in time into steadily increasing surpluses, and that it is the deficit of today which is making possible the surplus of tomorrow, let us pursue the course that we have mapped."

Here Morgenthau had stood when Douglas resigned in August 1934, when Roosevelt began to fashion the work relief program in October 1934, when that program seemed to falter in July and August 1935. Here he still stood, for moderation, for efficiency and economy in government, but for aiding the unemployed. As 1936 began, he knew very well that the battle for efficiency in spending had yet to be won. Indeed the Congress, bent upon paying a bonus to veterans, was about to complicate the Treasury's task.

## 4. The Bonus

With the coming of depression, World War I veterans had begun agitating to collect the bonus which Congress had authorized in 1924. The Adjusted Compensation Act of that year promised them payments based upon length of service plus interest compounded from 1925 to 1945 when the bonus was to become due. The interest would make it at maturity worth two and a half times the initial value of the grant. But the veterans, working through their powerful lobbies and supported by most inflationists, asked to receive the full amount at once in cash, more than $2 billion. Over Hoover's veto Congress authorized loans on half the face value of the adjusted compensation certificates, but pressure for full payment continued, and in every year after 1929 bonus bills were introduced.

Among the opponents of the bonus, none was more dogged than Morgenthau, who viewed premature payment as an unsound, unwarranted, even immoral subsidy to a special-interest group. The issue first caught his attention in April 1935 when the House of Representatives, after considering several proposals, passed the most radical, a bill sponsored by Congressman Wright Patman, Texas Democrat, professional veteran, and cheap-money advocate. This measure called for issuing greenbacks to pay the full face value of the bonus certificates. The prospect of printing the money bothered Morgenthau even more than did the alternative of further unbalancing the budget. Like Roosevelt, he preferred paying the bonus by issuing interest-bearing bonds, but he hoped the President would not limit Executive resistance to a compromise about methods of payment. Though Jack Garner warned him that "that damn thing's got a lot of strength down in the Senate," Morgenthau thought Roosevelt could make a veto stick.

The Secretary's staff disagreed with him. In a joint memorandum, Oliphant, Gaston, Haas, and McReynolds connected the bonus with other issues. They considered a bonus inevitable, if not in 1935 then in 1936, and believed that the Treasury owed it to itself to use the issue to squeeze every possible concession out of the Senate conservatives. The enactment of a sufficiently heavy inheritance tax, they suggested, would provide the income to pay the bonus. They also argued that the appropriate time for the Treasury to borrow to pay the bonus was during a depression. The bonus was due in any case in 1945, they pointed out, and if the country then happened to be on the crest of a boom, payment might precipitate runaway inflation. In 1935 or 1936, on the other hand, the bonus would lift the lagging economy by giving a large group of consumers funds to spend. The bonus, moreover, would go out to veterans at a rate much more rapid than that at which the $4.8 billion could be expended. It would immediately expand consumption on a nation-wide basis, a condition which Morgenthau's advisers considered so important that they recommended the Secretary consider paying the bonus out of the work relief appropriations.

Most of this argument failed to convince Morgenthau. The $4.8 billion, he believed, should be used entirely to help the needy. The veterans in his opinion had no special claim upon the government. The ultimate recovery of the economy, he maintained, depended not on federal grants but on the upsurge of private enterprise. But he was taken by his advisers' comments on the inheritance tax which he, too, considered an essential instrument of social justice as well as a fruitful device for increasing federal revenues.*

Roosevelt also took a strong position initially. Meeting with

* For further discussion of the inheritance tax, see pages 298–305.

Morgenthau, Bell, and General Frank T. Hines, the head of the Veterans' Administration, the President on April 22, 1935, opposed bonus legislation on any terms. In the past, he said, the advocates of the bonus had always broken their promises. Now the veterans had a contract with the government calling for payment in 1945. If they demanded the money immediately, they should at least forego interest beyond the date of payment. Roosevelt objected to any legislation conflicting with his budget estimates or discriminating in favor of special groups. He agreed with Morgenthau that the Treasury should insist on new revenues to offset any bonus payment, and he endorsed the idea of using an inheritance tax for that purpose.

On April 23 the Secretary advocated that tax to the Senate Committee on Finance, but the committee reported out the Patman bill without incorporating the tax, and the Senate passed the bill with the provision for printing greenbacks by a vote of 55–33. The next move was the President's.

Now Roosevelt wavered. At luncheon on May 6, he told Morgenthau in strictest confidence that Garner had convinced him it was wise to get the bonus out of the way in 1935 and not have it as a political issue during the campaign the following year. He intended to veto the bill, but if he acquiesced in letting Congress override his veto, he calculated that everyone would forget about it in three or four days.

Morgenthau was dismayed, for he was sure that only strong Executive intercession would prevent Congress from overriding a veto. For ten days he marked time, but he was ready for a fight when, at Roosevelt's request, he went to the White House on the evening of May 16. There he found the President "in a very bad humor," complaining that "my sinus hurts me." Doubtless the conflict between Congress and his advisers contributed to Roosevelt's headache. In a petulant mood, he read aloud Raymond Moley's draft of a bonus veto. It was not good. He then reviewed the notes which General Hines and the Treasury staff had prepared. These lacked spirit. As Morgenthau said, only the President himself could write the veto.

Dropping his pout, Roosevelt turned to the job in hand at about a quarter to ten and dictated steadily for an hour. Occasionally Morgenthau broke in to make a suggestion. When the President had finished his dictation, Miss LeHand left, and until one in the morning Morgenthau, alone with Roosevelt, urged him to battle to the finish.

Roosevelt had dictated a great speech, Morgenthau said. He ought either to deliver it in person to Congress or, better still, to talk directly to the American people on the radio. The President thought it would be discourteous for him to speak publicly before sending the message to Congress, but Morgenthau believed that Congress would be unsympathetic, that the House would override the veto, and that a direct appeal to the people would permit the best break on publicity. As he put it in his Diary, the Secretary "kept pacing up and down in front of him making one campaign speech after another." Finally, Roosevelt's face "lit up in a great smile. He raised his two fists in the air and shook them and said, 'My god, if I win I would be on the crest of the wave!' I saw that I had convinced him and stopped arguing."

The next day Roosevelt discussed his veto with Morgenthau, Steve Early, Marvin McIntyre, and Moley, who sulked because his draft was not to be used. McIntyre argued "very heatedly" that "he guessed that Jack Garner knew more about politics" than Morgenthau did. "I do not give a whoop what Jack Garner said," Morgenthau shot back. "I think that this is the thing for the President to do." Early urged Roosevelt not to "insult" Congress by first delivering his speech to the nation. After some debate, Morgenthau agreed, Early slapped him on the back and said, "Good boy, Henry," and Roosevelt ended the discussion. Later that day he told the newspapermen his message would go to Congress May 22, and that he hoped "with all my heart that the veto will be sustained."

Encouraged by the President's announcement, Morgenthau decided to concentrate all his energy on defeating the bonus. On Saturday, May 20, he directed Steve Gibbons, the Treasury's most gifted agent in handling Congress, who was ill, to get to work on his telephone. "You know," he told Gibbons, "the President's gone right out on the end of the limb on this bonus and I'm going with him. . . . And so far as I can find, I'm the only member of the Cabinet that gives a Goddam what he's doing."

Gibbons asked whether Roosevelt thought the House could be brought to sustain the veto. "No one's thinking of it," Morgenthau replied, "but me — I'm the only fellow."

The Secretary used his own telephone to recruit support. Among others, he talked with Frank Gannett, the upstate New York publisher, William S. Paley of the Columbia Broadcasting System, Harper Sibley of the National Chamber of Commerce, Charles Michelson, the talented publicist of the Democratic National Committee, and Joseph P. Kennedy. To Roy Howard of Scripps-Howard he complained that the newspapers spent all their time talking about what the veterans wanted and not what the taxpayers needed. "America doesn't know what's happening to it," Morgenthau said. "It's just another Wayne B. Wheeler shoving prohibition down their throats."

Speaking with William H. Grimes of the *Wall Street Journal,* Morgenthau said the American businessman was "just sitting back and isn't saying a peep." Grimes replied that he had heard it would be "a veto with a wink." He felt that a good strong veto message would rally the press and the business community. Morgenthau counted on his chief. "I have been living, breathing and half sleeping on the bonus for the last three days with the President," he said at one point. ". . . The address that he's going to give to Congress is the most striking and the most forcible since his inauguration."

It was going to be a terrific fight, the Secretary believed. The enemy was "greenback printing press and greenback inflation." Therefore he was willing to enlist Jouett Shouse of the Liberty League, a turncoat Democrat bitterly opposing the New Deal, and willing also to arrange radio time for Owen D. Young, a conservative Democrat who had been a possible candidate for the Presidency. By noon of May 20 Morgenthau felt that he was making real progress in organizing the press and the radio in the President's behalf. He went to the White House exuberant, only to have his spirits dashed. Patman had called earlier with twenty-two colleagues. As Morgenthau put it in his Diary:

Had lunch with the President and told him what I was doing about the Bonus. I was rather surprised to find a sort of cool-

ness. . . . He said, "You know we may have to compromise.
. . ." I said, "What do you mean?" He said, "Well we might
have to pay the present bonus. . . ." I said, "Mr. President,
there is nothing like that in your speech. You say definitely
that you are against the bonus." He said, "Why yes, but how
can I tell what kind of a bill they may pass." He said, "Patman
asked me point-blank this morning if I was against all bonus
legislation or whether I had an open mind and I told him that
I had an open mind because how could I know what they
might pass."

I had a sort of sinking feeling and found myself sort of gradually crumpling up and I said, "If you want me to go on please
do not talk that way to me because I am building a bonfire of
support for you in your veto message." He said rather quickly
with a smile, "Let's agree that I will not talk to you about any
compromise if you will not talk to me about any bonfire." He
said, "In other words, never let your left hand know what your
right is doing." I said, "Which hand am I, Mr. President?"
And he said, "My right hand." He said, "But I keep my left
hand under the table."

This is the most frank expression of the real F.D.R. that I
ever listened to and that is the real way that he works — but
thank God I understand him.

The real F.D.R., as Morgenthau knew, also loved a good fight,
and on Sunday he trimmed again for battle. The Morgenthaus,
Rosenmans, and Roosevelts went sailing on the President's yacht.
It was a beautiful day and the President was in a grand humor.
After luncheon Morgenthau asked him for permission to keep
pressure on Congress. "Henry," Roosevelt said, "I give you carte
blanche to anything that you want."

On Monday, May 22, the President broadcast his message, which
he delivered before a joint meeting of the House and the Senate.
The federal government, he observed, had already provided veterans with insurance, hospitalization, vocational training and rehabilitation, preferential employment, the promise of a bonus in
1945, and the privilege of borrowing up to 50 per cent on their
certificates. Payment in 1936 of the debt due in 1945 would

mean appreciating the certificates $1.6 billion, expending over-
all $2.2 billion. This would violate completely the principles of
the 1924 settlement. The bill would also impede recovery. It
would weaken the federal debt structure. Furthermore, the de-
ceptively easy method of payment by printing greenbacks would
simply give rise to similar demands by other interest groups. This
could lead ultimately to uncontrollable inflation and the destruction of the value of savings. Authorizations and appropriations, the
President continued, had been and should be predicated not on mere
spending but on the sounder basis of preventing homes and farms
from bankruptcy, of restoring industrial productivity, of safeguarding bank deposits, and most important of all, of giving relief and
jobs through public works to individuals and families faced with
starvation. There were before Congress bills providing old-age and
unemployment security which would help not only veterans but all
Americans. Only this kind of general legislation truly served the
welfare of the country.

This strong speech merited the general praise which the newspapers gave it. While Roosevelt was eating breakfast the next day,
Morgenthau showed him some of the editorials. The President
seemed pleased, on the whole "very calm and quiet," but incensed
at the disparaging remarks of Father Coughlin, an impassioned
and disappointed greenbacker. If Coughlin kept it up much
longer, Roosevelt said, he was going to release the file he had on
him and perhaps even send for the three American cardinals
and the apostolic delegate to show them the attacks a priest had
made on the President and ask them how this jibed with their
theory that the Catholic Church should have an ambassador in
each country.

The generally favorable press heightened Roosevelt's joy in the
contest. Congress was considering a substitute measure authorizing
three means of financing a bonus — through greenbacks, bonds, or
out of the $4.8 billion. "If they send me the so-called three-headed
bonus bill," the President said, ". . . I am going to tell the country
that I have been forced to make my choice and I am going to pay
the bonus out of the four billion eight, which will leave about one
billion eight for relief purposes, and every man who loses his
job on relief projects can thank the veterans' lobby in Washington."

With a smile of triumph, he concluded, "What do you think of that?"

Morgenthau thought it was tremendous. "Oh, you devil," he said. Roosevelt roared.

The Senate sustained the President's veto, and the question was closed for the year. Or so Morgenthau hoped. The Patmanites, however, filed a petition making another vote on the vetoed bill mandatory in January 1936; veterans' organizations continued to agitate; and in September the American Legion passed a resolution favoring a bonus unfettered by association with greenbacks. This proposal would be hard to beat.

It was in September also that Roosevelt wavered again. Out riding with Tugwell and Morgenthau, he suddenly announced that he was going to act on the bonus before he departed on a trip through the West. Morgenthau said he was "just too tired" to discuss the issue. If Roosevelt had insisted on paying the bonus, the Secretary later wrote in his Diary, "I would have resigned on the spot."

The President did not press the matter, though he explained that if he paid the bonus after his trip, people would say he had done so because he had received a poor reception out West. This argument, Morgenthau told him, was "just pure bunk." Roosevelt was really worried, he felt, that the bonus might prove embarrassing in 1936.

On September 4 Morgenthau wrote the President a personal and confidential letter. He had "almost literally passed out," he said, when Roosevelt took up the bonus during their drive. He had been thinking of almost nothing else since, and he had come "to the very definite and positive conclusion that from the standpoint of the welfare of the country and yourself that you should not make any announcement on the bonus prior to your message to Congress in January." The President's "magnificent and courageous veto" precluded retreat. Furthermore, the Treasury was financing $1.7 billion, and an announcement about the bonus either during or after the financing might have disastrous effects on the market. Every bondholder would consider it a breach of faith on the part of the government. "Certainly any private corporation which had filed its statement with the Security Exchange

Commission and then came out with a financing and immediately after that incurred a large additional debt would be subject to the severest chastisement. . . . I fail to see any difference between this example and an announcement now that the bonus will be paid. I most strongly urge you, first as your Secretary of the Treasury and second, as one of your true and tried friends, to do nothing about the bonus for the balance of this year. My own conviction is that the bonus should not be paid until maturity, and the reasons are covered so admirably in your veto message that it would be impossible for me to add anything further. However, if you feel that politically it is necessary to do something about the bonus, then it seems that the time and the place for you to make a statement about the payment of the bonus would be in your message to Congress when it meets in January and subsequently explain how you propose to finance the bonus payment in your budget message."

This counsel prevailed. Roosevelt, it developed, had been needling his Secretary of the Treasury with the malice of fatigue. The legislative session of 1935 had been exhausting, involving as it did the $4.8 billion, the bonus, a new banking act, a difficult revenue measure, social security laws, and other reform legislation. At the end of October, after both men had had a vacation, Morgenthau found the President restored. "He and I together are almost two different men from what we were when I last saw him in September," he wrote. "You again get the feeling that he has strength and reserve power and confidence in himself and the power to inspire confidence which certainly seemed to be lacking during July, August and September. I realize how tired I was and I suppose the President was just as tired." Roosevelt admitted as much. He knew, he said, that their September conversation about the bonus had almost brought Morgenthau to tears. "After election we both must take regular vacations, irrespective of what is going on and never permit ourselves to get so tired again," Roosevelt said. ". . . I was so tired that I would have enjoyed seeing you cry or would have gotten pleasure out of sticking pins into people and hurting them."

In mid-November 1935, however, Roosevelt's state of mind counted less than did congressional sensitivity for the veterans' vote. With the campaign of 1936 approaching, some bonus bill was bound to pass. On November 16 the President discussed policy with Morgenthau, Bell and General Hines. Faced with the probability that Congress would override another veto, they concentrated on means for payment. Without dissent from the others, Morgenthau urged leaving the financing to the Treasury, for he intended, if he had to, to raise the money in an orthodox manner, by selling securities in the market. This would disturb the business and financial community less than would any alternative scheme.

Early in January 1936 the House of Representatives passed a bill authorizing full payment of the bonus without specifying the method of payment. The President, noncommittal about a veto, thought there was no chance of defeating the measure in the Senate, but he permitted Morgenthau to speak out. Testifying on January 14, the Secretary explained that the Treasury had to raise more than $9 billion before June 30, 1937. Bonus legislation would increase this to $11.3 billion. New taxes would in any case be necessary, but a bonus would make them heavier, and whatever their incidence, the Treasury would have to work hard to keep control of the money market. If there had to be a bonus, he recommended paying it in bonds bearing no coupon but accumulating interest progressively. Veterans would profit by holding them until maturity, as did all purchasers of the Treasury's "baby bonds." *

The Senate Committee on Finance pushed the bonus bill along, but modified it to adopt Morgenthau's suggestion for payment. On January 20 the Senate passed the bill, 76–16, and the House quickly concurred, 346–59.

After these votes, a veto could be only a gesture, but Morgenthau hoped Roosevelt would stand by his principles. At the White House on January 23, the Secretary noted in his Diary, "the President did not say a word but took a pencil and paper and began to write. After he had written a little while, I said to him, 'What is it, approval or veto?' and he smiled and said, 'You know perfectly well what it is. You never had any doubts what I would do,' and I said, 'Yes, I did, but I was afraid to let myself think about it!' "

The veto, which Roosevelt copied in longhand and sent to the

* See page 340.

Hill the next morning, referred Congress to the message of the previous year. Morgenthau congratulated him on his courage. Four out of five congressmen had none. Filling the veteran's pocket before asking for his vote, both houses rapidly overrode the veto. It remained only for the Treasury to print and mail the bonds, prepare to convert most of them to cash, and plan the financing this entailed.

Morgenthau had lost, but there were compensations. He took great satisfaction in seeing Roosevelt, after some equivocation, join him in a positive fight against a deplorable but seductive measure. He had succeeded, largely by influencing the President and through him the Congress, in defeating the Patman bill with its paper money clause. He had persuaded the Senate to arrange the financing of the bonus according to the Treasury's preferences. Yet the bonus in any form threatened his budgetary objectives and therefore rekindled his zeal for economy. In so far as possible, he intended to make the lenders and spenders save much of the money the veterans were to receive.

### 5. Lenders and Spenders

The resignation of Under Secretary of the Treasury T. Jefferson Coolidge on January 17, 1936, underscored Morgenthau's problems. Coolidge felt that the national emergency was over. Unstrung by the silver purchase program, he deplored the continuing outlays for relief and public works. He could not remain in office, Morgenthau told him, without supporting Roosevelt, especially in an election year. Coolidge therefore left. He had become too tense, too critical, too self-conscious to be of much help to the Secretary, but his resignation had a disturbing symbolic significance, for it was one of many episodes revealing the growing antagonism of businessmen toward Roosevelt and the New Deal.

> For a number of days [Morgenthau noted in his Diary on February 2] various articles which I have been reading plus what has been happening in Congress plus the information that naturally comes across my desk has convinced me that the Pres-

ident is extremely vulnerable to attack on his spending program. Furthermore, the whole fiscal policy of the government is at the cross-roads depending upon how we are going to pay for the new agricultural program, the bonus, etc. The final straw was Dr. Gallup's article in the Sunday paper showing that only 2 per cent of the people that he polled wanted new taxes. . . . Today I had a chance to do plenty of thinking and . . . I telephoned the White House for an appointment and got one for 5:15. . . .

The President saw me immediately and I stayed with him a little over an hour — Miss LeHand being present serving us tea. He was fixing his stamps while I talked to him. I told him that I understood from Jake Viner that the Republicans were going to concentrate on attacking him on his spending program — just the way he had attacked Hoover. "But," I said, "the Republicans have ten times as much material as you had three years ago . . ." Furthermore, that with the exception of the first six months that he was President all of the publicity that came out of the White House was "spending" and "more spending" and not a single word about economizing; that it was still time to talk and practice economy and that if he waited very much longer they would simply accuse him of doing it for the political effect. To my great surprise he sat there very quietly, nodded his head, smiled at me and said, "You are right." He never argued back at me once, except to say, "They have overlooked and misinterpreted what I said in my Message to Congress — that I pointed out that as business improved we would gradually curtail expenses." I said, "Yes, that was very nice but you have done nothing about it." Again he said, "You are right."

I have never seen him so gentle or so receptive to suggestions.

The President then said, "What would you suggest doing?" I said, "Well I, as Chairman of your Lending Committee, could call them together and possibly do something but that would not help you any. You have got to do it and let the word go out that you called a meeting in order to begin to save." He said, "Whom should we call — Missy — take this down. I suggest that Jones, Fahey, Ickes, Myers and Stewart McDonald come."* I then said, "What about Tugwell" and he said, "No, don't let's have Tugwell. He is in a sort of new business of lending to farm families in distress, and if we call him in it will start up a whole new line of thought and argument." I said, "Fine, that will make the meeting that much easier." And he let me get away with that. The President also did not want Chester Davis.†

Then, to my surprise, he said, "Let's have another meeting on Thursday and talk over the four billion eight." I said, "Frankly, I have been afraid to bring that up." He said, "Why not?" Then I told him that I did not think we would spend more than 250 million dollars in January and this seemed to surprise him greatly and he said, "At that rate Hopkins will have enough to go until July 1st, although he has been telling me that he could not last after 1st of May." (A month ago Hopkins said he could not go until the 1st of April.) The President said, "I would have gotten around to the 4 billion 8 long ago but I have been waiting for Bell to come back.‡ I made inquiries and found that Bell would not be back for a week." We both agreed that it was not necessary to wait for Bell. The President then said, "Well whom should we have to that meeting" and I said, "Ickes and Hopkins" to which the President replied, "Hopkins is away but that does not make any difference, we can have Williams§ in his place . . . and, he added, "yourself." Again I was almost speechless, at the way he let me write the whole ticket.

I then said, "I have one more suggestion to make. I think you ought to get a national figure who is a good friend of yours in whom you have confidence and who believes in you and make him Director of the Budget so that the public will know that you are really interested in trying to economize." He agreed to that. We discussed various names but could not

---

* The heads, respectively, of the Reconstruction Finance Corporation, Home Owners' Loan Corporation, Public Works Administration, Farm Credit Administration, and Federal Housing Administration.

† Then head of the Agricultural Adjustment Administration.

‡ From a brief vacation.

§ Aubrey Williams, Hopkins's Deputy Administrator.

really arrive at any conclusion. I was very much amused at
Miss LeHand seriously suggesting Bill Bullitt and the President said, quite curtly, "No, no, he is all wrapped up in international diplomacy and knows nothing about this" to which
Miss LeHand answered, "But he would like to." . . .

If the President will really go through with this program
and begin to talk and *practice* economy it may be the turning
point in his whole hold on the people because there is no
question that many many people are really worried about this
spending program because they can see no end to it.

Roosevelt struck vigorously for economy at a February 4 meeting of the Interdepartmental Loan Committee. He needed to
recover between $200 and $300 million from the lending and
spending agencies, he said. The political situation made any tax
bill unpopular with congressmen, and even if they enacted a tax
to finance the new farm program, he would still need some $200
million more than his original budget estimate. Morgenthau confirmed this figure and reported that the Bureau of the Budget
thought that fifteen emergency agencies could pare their combined estimates $17,600,000 for fiscal 1936 and $12,900,000 for
fiscal 1937. The problem, as Roosevelt put it, was where to save
the money. To get definite figures, he would go around the
room, hearing from everybody.

Jesse Jones, the President said, could reduce his authorizations
for borrowing and his administrative expenses, slow up grants of
loans, and accelerate demands for payment. Jones wriggled. Instead of reducing his authorizations to borrow, he suggested not
using the authority. Roosevelt differed. If he could tell Congress
that the Reconstruction Finance Corporation no longer needed
a $100 million authorization, Congress could repeal the authoriza-
tion, and thus remove a potential obligation on the Treasury.
That would be a real help. Jones argued that reducing his administrative costs would not aid the Treasury, since these expenditures came out of RFC profits. Morgenthau said that fifteen
agencies had economized under the supervision of the Bureau of
the Budget, and he wanted the RFC to follow suit. Roosevelt

added that a reduction in administrative expenses would also have a good psychological effect. Furthermore, any net savings improved the Treasury's position.

Still resisting, Jones said he was refusing applications for loans every day, and that he could not call in his loans to banks without weakening their capital structures. Morgenthau replied that RFC estimates of receipts and expenditures were further out of line than those of any other agency. The RFC did not spend up to its estimates, Jones snapped, because of his efficiency in holding expenses down. He was not hurting the Treasury since the Treasury discounted his estimates anyhow. It hurt the Secretary of the Treasury's heart once a month — gave him high blood pressure, Roosevelt interjected.

This quip eased tempers but recovered no money. As discussion proceeded, the group agreed that the Home Owners' Loan Corporation could not cut back its authorizations, and the Agricultural Adjustment Administration could not determine what it might save. Henry Wallace was unwilling to surrender funds for conservation and reclamation, and uncertain about how much he could recover from authorizations for cotton loans. Ickes, too, battled to keep his money. He claimed to have only $100,000 unexpended from his most recent authorizations and only $14 million from authorizations from previous fiscal years. Of the latter sum, he was holding $6 million for a new building for the War Department.

As the lenders left, Roosevelt asked them to submit calculations of possible savings to the Bureau of the Budget within a week. The meeting had settled nothing. Only Morgenthau was prepared to economize, and as he expected, the President could accomplish nothing just by talking. But Roosevelt, moving at his own pace, on February 18 slashed away. From the authorizations of RFC and its affiliates, he cut $660 million. The Farm Credit Administration lost $80 million of authorizations for crop loans. From the Federal Housing Administration and the Home Owners' Loan Corporation respectively, the President took $750 million and $805 million. Morgenthau was delighted. The savings, to be sure, were not of cash but of authorizations to borrow. Yet these savings were real. What was not borrowed constituted no obligation on the government. What was not borrowed could not be loaned or spent.

Furthermore, as he had promised Morgenthau he would, Roosevelt was reviewing the budgets of the spenders. Here the familiar difficulties remained — the rivalries of Hopkins and Ickes and Tugwell, the inadequate data on unemployment and on project costs, the unevenness, indeed the uncertainty, of economic recovery. As of January 20, 1936, Morgenthau told the President, only $1 billion 841 million of the $4.8 billion had actually been spent. Much of the rest had been allocated to slow projects. The Secretary did not think Roosevelt could ask Congress for new money for relief while Tugwell and Ickes sat on their funds. The President agreed.

Before the first session with the spenders on February 6, Roosevelt said to Morgenthau: "I must not talk too quickly or too much about saving, otherwise the impression will go out that I am afraid I am licked." Actually he was enormously confident. Morgenthau thought Hopkins would need $250 or $300 million more to carry through the end of June. "That is too big," Roosevelt said. "They will not need more than $200 million. The thing is working out just the way I thought it would and . . . on July 1 we will have left $1 billion out of the $4 billion 8."

That afternoon Roosevelt opened the conference with the spending agencies by emphasizing the need for additional funds for the WPA. The problem, he said, was to keep the existing number of people on the work relief payroll until July 1, 1936, without asking Congress for additional funds. He had told Hopkins to reduce WPA rolls as fast as possible, transferring employees to public works projects under the supervision of other agencies or to private industry as re-employment progressed. He thought Hopkins could cut back as spring weather approached. He would permit the various agencies to continue their authorized programs until about April 1 when he could more accurately estimate WPA needs for the period through June 30. He would then transfer to WPA authorizations which the other agencies did not absolutely require for fiscal 1936. After the 1937 appropriation was available, he would return to each agency whatever he had taken away.

The unobligated balances which Roosevelt thought he could transfer to Hopkins came to just short of $50 million. Within a month, he said, he expected the spenders to produce estimates for other transfers.

Roosevelt also talked economy to congressmen. It was essential to have a decreasing deficit, he told Marvin Jones, for if the deficit rose in fiscal 1937, the Treasury would be unable to market government bonds. Morgenthau, who had been taking this line for many months, noted to his Diary: "I wanted to go over in the corner and hide my face and grin but instead of that I sat back as though it was an entirely new idea to me . . . and . . . said, you are perfectly right, Mr. President. . . . If he will only keep on talking and thinking along the same lines my troubles are over."

Early in March, his confidence bolstered by Roosevelt's attitude, Morgenthau conferred with Hopkins about the relief budget for 1937. He would fight, the Secretary said, not about how many people should get work, but about preventing the use of relief funds on projects that did not help the unemployed. "There can," he emphasized, "be no more buying of $25 million worth of land."

Hopkins was naturally pleased. "The record," he said, "is always that the money is going to relief, but in reality we got only about half of the $4 billion 8 for relief. . . . I have never told anybody that I can't do this or that because we do not have the money; we have always met the thing head on, but the other fellows just keep ducking. I am getting darned sick and tired of this. The people we are handling are the people who don't eat unless we give them relief. We want to see one bill for W.P.A. and not let anybody ride on the coat tails of this bill."

Morgenthau agreed. He did not care whether the bill called for $1.5 or $2 billion as long as it stayed within the figure of $2 billion 136 million Roosevelt had used in his budget message. For the remainder of the current fiscal year, moreover, he thought Roosevelt had to transfer every bit of available cash to Hopkins.

On March 6, Morgenthau and Hopkins, supporting each other, took their case to the President, who quickly accepted their view that the 1937 relief bill should ask for money exclusively for WPA. He was less willing to accept Morgenthau's estimate, which Hopkins confirmed, that they could get by for about $2 billion. "Oh Henry," Roosevelt said, "you are going to take bread away from starving people."

"Oh I am not," Morgenthau replied. "You can't say that to me when up to date Hopkins, for relief purposes, has gotten less than half the money out of $4 billion 8."

The President seemed to be persuaded, but just as Morgenthau was ready to say three cheers, Roosevelt returned to an idea he had proposed the previous week. He would ask Congress for only $1.5 billion. That would be enough, he would say, if industry put another million men to work, but if industry did not respond, he would need to ask for more later. This scheme distressed Morgenthau. "Mr. President," he said, "you will not fool anybody with this trick because you are not saying when you come back to Congress what the amount of money will be that you are going to ask for."

Quick as a flash, Roosevelt replied: "Oh no I am not going to tie my hands and that would be spoiling my whole plea."

"Mr. President," Morgenthau continued, "you know perfectly well that industry is not going to put any such amount of people back to work and you are not fooling anybody and the only people who are going to suffer are the unemployed who will not know where they are at. Why don't you tell Congress that you want $1 billion 960 million and that if industry puts people back to work that we will use that much less money."

"No no that will not do at all," Roosevelt said, "that spoils my whole plea."

"Why not ask for enough money to last you until February 1," the Secretary suggested.

"No," Roosevelt said, "that will not do."

Morgenthau persisted until the President gave in. In his message to Congress on March 18, he used the formula the Secretary had recommended. From previous appropriations he could carry over $1 billion; the regular budget allowed $600 million for the Civilian Conservation Corps; besides this money, Roosevelt said he would need $2 billion for relief. But he asked Congress only for an initial $1.5 billion of the new money, all for the WPA. This, he explained, would be adequate if private business ab-

sorbed an increasing number of workers. The message was a
victory for Morgenthau and Hopkins. Although there was to
be a deficit, the ceiling the President proposed permitted sound
financing. By concentrating on WPA, he was making relief dollars
count most effectively toward helping the unemployed.

Roosevelt knew Morgenthau was pleased. "Wait until next year,
Henry," he said one day in April. "I'm going to be really radical."

"What do you mean?"

"I am going to recommend a lot of radical legislation," the President
said, giving Morgenthau a sort of quizzical look.

"You are going to be very careful about money spending."

"Yes, I am," Roosevelt answered.

"Well then," Morgenthau said, "I do not care how radical you
are on other matters."

The taste of victory for fiscal 1937 did not, however, resolve the
problems of fiscal 1936. In April the WPA ran out of funds. Morgenthau
tried to get some money from Tugwell. "It is a question
now," he said, "of whether we should take care of people on relief
or whether we should buy land." Tugwell, however, yielded nothing.
His conservation projects, he said, were providing jobs; he was
relocating impoverished farm families; this, he believed, was the
most fundamental kind of relief. Furthermore, he had a mandate
from Roosevelt. Morgenthau was unpersuaded, but Tugwell's last
point temporarily protected his funds.

Now Hopkins alarmed the Secretary. Desperate for money, Hopkins
proposed paying workers after July 1 for what they did in
June. He could then draw upon the appropriations for fiscal 1937.
Morgenthau begged Roosevelt not to permit this juggling. If Hopkins
had his way, he predicted, everyone would say "not only will
the billion and a half not last, but they have nicked it already. . . .
It is all a fake." Morgenthau proposed an alternative. "I have sent
a lawyer over to Tugwell," he said, "to check up and see if all of
the $48 million which he has to spend on the purchase of land has
been obligated and, if not, they should cancel the unobligated balance."
The President approved. Early in May he also, at Morgenthau's
urging, turned over to WPA five per cent of all unobligated
funds, about $30 million, enough to last through June. "I want you
to give me your word of honor," the Secretary said to Hopkins, "if

we do this, you will not come back to me and say, you must give me part of the $1 billion 500 million." Hopkins promised.

Since February Morgenthau had gained considerable ground. WPA had the funds it needed for the rest of the fiscal year. The relief budget for 1937 was manageable and most of the emergency money was earmarked for Hopkins. Roosevelt had disciplined the lenders and put the spenders under tighter scrutiny. All this brought the Administration closer to Morgenthau's objectives — a balanced budget, a coordinated spending program, an efficient policy for sustaining the unemployed. But he had no time to crow, for economy and efficiency ill suited the politics of the 1936 campaign.

### 6. The Budget and the Election

In June 1936, as the presidential campaign got under way, the Republicans increased the tempo of their attack on New Deal spending. Unbalanced budgets, they maintained, forbode disaster which only the return to power of the Grand Old Party could prevent. The assault bothered Morgenthau, for he saw how persuasive was the Republican case to bankers and other men of means whose businesses brought them regularly into contact with the Treasury. But he hoped completely to deflate the opposition by stealing its argument. On July 9 he took his morning text from an unlikely contributor to the *Saturday Evening Post,* Gertrude Stein: ". . . Who is to stop Congress from spending too much. . . . Who is to stop them?" The answer, of course, was Roosevelt, whom Morgenthau advised to make some decision that would dramatically "demonstrate to the country once and for all whether or not you really intend to curtail expenditures."

Roosevelt did not. The severe drought that had settled on the West imposed upon the federal government increasing costs for agricultural relief, seed loans, resettlement, and reclamation. These obligations made retrenchment impossible and delayed unification of relief spending, which the President in any case resisted. Furthermore, his sure political instinct told him that the Republican cult of economy was making no impact. Let the Republicans do the talking, he suggested to Morgenthau, instructing him to cancel a proposed speech on the budget.

Morgenthau nevertheless kept his staff at work on material for Roosevelt. The Research Division reckoned that, at current tax schedules, the rate of recovery would eliminate the need for relief, balance the budget and begin to retire the debt within four years. "Everybody around the President is saying the President has nothing to say," Morgenthau glowed. "Well, the above is something that he can say." Leon Henderson, then an economic adviser for the Democratic campaign and consistently an ally of the spenders, was impressed. "What you have told me," he said, ". . . is the best news I have had yet. I would like to enlist with you." Jacob Viner also thought it would be splendid if Roosevelt made the Treasury's estimates the basis of a major address, but he predicted that the President would not tie himself to any set of figures.

On August 23 Morgenthau gave Roosevelt a "swell speech" that Herbert Gaston had drafted. "We have today reached the point where we can say with real meaning, wasn't the depression awful?" it read. "We have climbed a long way out of the depths." The time had come to speak of something better than recovery, for the history of the country pointed toward new economic peaks. There would be no need for new taxes in the coming year. National productivity and therefore federal revenues would rise. This would permit not only the gradual retirement of the debt but also programs to conserve physical resources and improve national health while the country achieved a higher standard of living.

"Why," the President exclaimed, "this is political!" It was great stuff, but he simply could not use it. He would have to be much more cautious. The voters would never believe the prediction no matter how well statistics fortified it. At the most, he might say in some speech that within the next year or two federal revenues would be adequate to meet expenditures at their current levels.

Though he discarded the address Gaston had drafted, Roosevelt was at his charming best. He praised Morgenthau's effort, and he urged the Secretary to compose a speech on unemployment. This mandate gave Morgenthau the chance to develop a study he had already begun.

Early in August the Division of Procurement completed a survey of WPA rolls. It demonstrated that WPA classifications of skilled, semiskilled, and unskilled labor were misleading. A reclassification would help the government estimate the available unemployed labor supply and help, too, to single out those who were unfit for relief work because of age, infirmity, or habitual indolence. Such persons could then be classified as unemployables, subject to the care of local rather than federal agencies. Confirming WPA's report that the supply of skilled labor was inadequate for many kinds of construction projects, the survey suggested the elimination of all activities requiring more than 10 per cent skilled labor.

Regardless of cost, Morgenthau decided, a scientific monthly check of relief rolls would prove eminently justifiable. He was disturbed at the high cost of relief in the Rocky Mountain states, and he suspected that in some areas of the country the rolls were padded. Corrington Gill, one of Hopkins's top aides, admitted that careful investigation might result in reducing WPA lists about 15 per cent. He began a preliminary check in four cities and four states, intending to terminate relief in all cases where individuals had fulltime employment in private industry or in other federal agencies, had family income aggregating more than a security wage, were eligible for old-age benefits, or were inefficient.

Confident that this investigation would permit a decrease in relief expenditures, Morgenthau also believed that an independent survey would facilitate private re-employment. Many WPA workers had acquired skills that industry needed, but the Secretary had discovered that information about these new skills was not readily available. The WPA, he found, had never cooperated with the United States Employment Service.

Private employers could procure information about relief workers only from the United States Employment Service, but thousands of WPA workers were not even registered, and others were misclassified. USES, Morgenthau learned, could begin a reinterviewing and reclassifying program at once and complete it in about three months. Simultaneously the agency proposed making special efforts to place workers with private industry.

These proposals won the Secretary's immediate enthusiasm. On August 19 he took William Frank Persons, the head of USES, to the White House, and helped him explain the importance of reclassification to the President who appeared unfamiliar with the kind of work USES had done. Because Persons "seemed to have his tail between his legs," Morgenthau pressed Roosevelt for funds — $1.5 million for reclassification, $2.5 million, which the President granted much more reluctantly, for building up the service and persuading private employers to use it. During the conference Roosevelt, interested in what he was learning, asked for a "fifteen minute speech in which I can explain over the radio just how we handle the whole unemployment situation." The $4 million granted USES, he told Morgenthau when they were alone, "will answer a lot of questions which have been unanswered so far."

Hopkins, however, believed that there was some danger in overpublicizing USES. The unemployed might get the idea that they could find jobs simply by going to it. To avoid this kind of misunderstanding, Morgenthau asked Gaston to collect facts from both USES and WPA and then compose a working draft for Roosevelt. The Secretary also suggested arranging a national campaign of cooperation with the United States Chamber of Commerce, but Persons had been in touch with the Chamber and considered further publicity unwise until he could recruit and train personnel to reclassify the unemployed. It would take a month to get together the necessary staff and another two months to finish the job. If the reclassification proved successful, Hopkins suggested, it might put private employment agencies out of business. That prospect, Morgenthau replied, was okay.

As Gaston worked on, Persons became increasingly publicity-shy. He was eager to prevent Roosevelt or Morgenthau from thinking that increased grants to USES would result in any substantial increase in employment. He was especially anxious to guard against the President's conveying any such impression in a speech. Indeed if allocations were to be made with the belief that they would reduce the relief load, he thought the money should be withheld. Furthermore, Josephine Roche feared labor would misunderstand an emphasis on cooperation with employers and resent any deal with the Chamber of Commerce.

She and Persons prepared a draft which described a long-range program of assistance to workers and to industry for the purposes of obtaining better distribution of labor, speeding placement, reducing labor turnover, and increasing efficiency in production. The Employment Service, as Persons described it, was a bridge between people and jobs, a bridge steadily becoming wider and stronger, built upon public confidence which was itself founded upon understanding and experience. USES, he noted, was still in its infancy. He set a tone designed to keep a clamoring crowd from his office. Roosevelt used a much condensed version of this draft as part of a Fireside Chat delivered on the eve of Labor Day.

USES then sent out a telegram noting that $2.5 million had been allocated for improving its contacts with employers, whom it urged to act promptly. In the month to come the Service was to continue to classify and clear workers for public works projects and for WPA, and also to put workers in touch with private industry. As one Treasury memorandum observed, however, what USES could do before election day would have very little impact on the public mind. The possibility remained, moreover, that as USES accomplished more, private employment services would accomplish less, leaving the rate of re-employment unaffected.

With unemployment relatively constant, Morgenthau found it necessary during September to prevent a reduction in relief spending. While Hopkins was in California, his subordinates in Washington decided to reject applications for renewals of project funds from all federal agencies except WPA. This would have forced the dismissal of thousands of men and women on October 1, a prospect both humanly cruel and politically stupid. "You tell Corrington Gill," Roosevelt instructed Morgenthau, "that I don't give a goddam where he gets the money from but not one person is to be laid off on the first of October."

The Secretary was glad to have the chance. "For God's sake get Harry Hopkins back here," he said. "I at least do business with Harry."

In order to make ends meet, Morgenthau advised Roosevelt not to approve new projects that exceeded the amounts allotted by Congress but instead to divert WPA funds to projects which could continue only with additional financing. This advice irritated Hopkins whom Morgenthau saw on October 7. "I have a big office to run," Hopkins said, "and when I am away it must go on running.

. . . Our belief is . . . that you cannot keep these people at work by merely having approved the number of projects and the amount of dollars which the law permits. . . . Ever since I have been in this work relief game, it has been understood that we would have to get many more projects approved than we would spend money for."

"I have never interfered with you people once the money was turned over to you," Morgenthau replied, after some acrimony. ". . . As Secretary of the Treasury, I simply feel that it is my duty to see that it is pointed out to the President that he does not approve or spend more money than has been approved by Congress. . . . As man to man, can you have any difference with me as to the position I am taking?"

Without answering directly, Hopkins proposed that Roosevelt give him larger latitude for spending approved funds. Bell, Morgenthau, and Gill agreed, and together they dispatched a memorandum to the White House. Within the legal limits defined by the Comptroller General, Roosevelt accepted their recommendation. He gave Hopkins much of the latitude he had asked for and permitted him to provide funds for the continuation beyond October 1 of non-WPA projects which otherwise would have run out of money.

Roosevelt also kept Morgenthau's hand on the till. As the Secretary noted in his Diary: "The President said I should explain to Hopkins that if he allocates, for example, $2 million to Chicago through Ickes and Hopkins is already spending $10 million in Chicago, he wants Hopkins to spend only $8 million. . . . It's up to Bell to see that this is carried out. The President lays great stress on this."

Roosevelt intended to keep a ceiling on total expenditures; but as Hopkins turned over large sums of money to other administrators, WPA did not adjust to its revised expectations. The reallocations prevented layoffs on October 1 and thereby fed thousands of families for another month, precisely the month in which the election campaign was reaching its conclusion, but Hopkins operated on a hand-to-mouth basis that inevitably produced stringency a month later.

In spite of the continuing pressure for relief funds, Roosevelt took up again the theme he had put aside in July. As he had in

1932, so in 1936 he planned to deliver a speech in Pittsburgh on balancing the budget. It was an objective in which he still believed, and though he did not want to tie his hands, he hoped to contrive a formula for a persuasive address. Morgenthau first heard the speech on the evening of September 30 at the White House where he found Corcoran and Rosenman at work with the President. On October 1 he registered his impressions in his Diary:

> The President began to read draft 3 of his Pittsburgh speech. When he got through I told him I thought it was a terrible speech and I wished he wouldn't give it. He said, "I have to give it." He had no other speech and had to finish this in an hour and a half. . . . I went up to see the President, while he was in his bedroom entirely alone, and told him that I couldn't release the speech, that the President of the United States just could not make any financial mistakes and if he would trust me I would promise to get it to him sometime this morning. . . . He smiled and said that was okay. . . .

> During the discussion earlier in the evening I pointed out to the President that he made the statement that "we will balance the budget sooner than we expect" and that if he made that statement he simply would make himself the laughing stock of America. I told him that Bell and I feel that if he would be tough that he could balance the budget in '38 and still allow a billion dollars for relief. He said, "All right" and I said, "Now wait a minute" and I called on Miss LeHand to listen carefully to what I said. I said, "This decision has to be yours and no-body else's." He said, "Well I can say the Secretary of the Treasury says the budget can be balanced in '38" and I said, "*You* have to say it because nobody can balance it but *you* and both Bell and I feel it can be done."

> In the draft that came to us as draft 4 the President said, "The Treasury advises me that the budget can be balanced" and we crossed that out and wrote a very powerful statement for him to speak. . . .

> I made it clear to Tommy Corcoran that neither Bell nor I could plead with the President to make the statement "that the

budget could be balanced in '38," that the President would have to make that statement himself.

The "very powerful statement" which Morgenthau proposed committed Roosevelt to leaving "no stone unturned to balance the federal budget for the fiscal year of 1938." Bell drafted a milder alternative. He also suggested that the President, if he wanted to provide himself with a hedge, might simply say that he expected to balance the budget within a year or two.

Roosevelt settled for the hedge in his public address of October 12. "The big fellows in New York will like this," Morgenthau predicted. "This is what they have been waiting for." The Secretary, however, aware of the President's measured selection of words, discounted their significance. Bemused rather than disappointed, he joked about the speech with his staff. At their instigation he dictated a message to Jeff Coolidge: "Taking it for granted that your sense of humor is as good as it used to be, I am writing you the following personal letter. Now that Landon has come out for balancing the budget within four years and President Roosevelt has said . . . that he will balance the budget in a year or two . . . how do you feel?"

Temporarily Morgenthau relaxed. Politically "things" were "so lovely." The last fortnight of a national campaign, he knew, was an impossible time for serious discussion of fiscal matters. He was ready to resume that debate in the less charged environment following Roosevelt's overwhelming re-election.

## 7. Compassion in Practice, Prudence in Theory

"For all his ability and selflessness," Morgenthau recalled, "Hopkins did have an undeniable appetite for practical politics. He loved maneuvering, and he loved being in the know when great plans were under way. Moreover, he had supreme confidence in his own capacity for improvisation and would often embark cheerfully on huge programs without a full conception of the expense and of the difficulties involved. Harry and I got along well basically . . .

though we had occasional sharp differences . . . when he confused need with politics."

This confusion, Morgenthau concluded, had moved Hopkins to hold relief expenditures above the level of his assets during the campaign of 1936. Immediately after the election Hopkins had therefore to devise means of stretching the balance of his depleted funds. Roosevelt pointed the way. Just before leaving for Buenos Aires, the President said he hoped to have localities pay for the materials used in work relief projects. He was planning a total reorganization of the Executive establishment, including a concentration of all relief activities under one agency, and upon his return he wanted figures indicating whether or not relief appropriations would last through the fiscal year.

To make them last, Hopkins proposed to drop from his rolls in mid-December some 250,000 dirt farmers of whom about half would need direct relief, to drop also about 150,000 urban families and 25,000 administrators and supervisors. As of January 1, 1937, he intended to make localities pay for materials, thus cutting his average monthly costs per man from $65 to $50. These policies, he calculated, would permit a saving of $25 million a month.

There was no need for Hopkins to explain the implications of his plans to Morgenthau, for the Secretary saw at once that he was caught again in a "squeeze play." As he put it, Hopkins and his staff "would wait until the last minute before letting Bell and me know they were overspending. Then they would appeal to our emotions by reminding us of the plight of the jobless." Trapped by Hopkins's pre-election largess, Morgenthau had to find the money to sustain the unemployed through the winter of 1937.

"We might as well be realistic about this thing," the Secretary told Aubrey Williams. "In the first place, from the standpoint of human needs, this is not the time to make the dramatic reductions proposed; I would much rather start with a consideration for human beings. If this were put to me, I would be entirely ruthless in reclaiming funds which have been allotted but are not being actually expended. . . . I will say right now that if you try to go through with this program of rapidly reducing the number of people on your rolls, you are going to have cracked heads and state militias used. I do not think you should do it. . . . I will sweat blood for you to take care of the months of January, February and March; but you have got to help in reducing costs beginning the first of next July."

Apart from humanitarian considerations, the Administration was under pressure from the Mayors' Conference, a powerful group led by the outspoken La Guardia of New York, who protested bitterly against the proposed retrenchments. "Terribly excited," Vice President Garner and Marvin McIntyre joined Morgenthau on December 5 in cabling Roosevelt that the WPA program "for immediate reduction in relief rolls is too drastic." The President in reply instructed Morgenthau, Hopkins and Bell to find ways to avoid troublesome cuts, especially in the cities.

At the White House on December 8 Morgenthau and McIntyre hounded Hopkins, criticizing particularly Aubrey Williams's public announcement that WPA would drop 425,000 men and women. "There is something much more important to consider than you or me," Morgenthau said. "The people will blame the President. What I am trying to think of is the President's interest and the country's interest. . . . I would rather see you refuse to replace the normal turnover . . . than to see drastic cuts made at this time of the year."

The only thing the President could not defend, Hopkins replied, would be the abandonment of people who needed relief, and WPA was not going to do that. But he admitted the problem was tough.

"If you can find 150,000 people now on relief rolls who you say now are not in need of relief," Morgenthau said, "how are you going to answer the charge that you must have known before November that these people were not in need of relief? How can you explain in the month of December, two weeks before Christmas, that you can find 150,000 on the relief rolls not in need of relief, when you could not discover this excess in your rolls a month earlier?"

Hopkins, visibly annoyed, argued that the President did not have "to take the heat" until he got back. The time to cut the rolls was while he was away. "The place the budget is unbalanced is in my shop," Hopkins said. "There's going to be some headaches in the cutting, no matter when the cutting is done. If we cave in every move we make, we are never going to get anything done."

McIntyre maintained Hopkins could not carry the responsibility.

Roosevelt would have to take it. They had to find a way to avoid
the charge that they knew before the election that people had to be
taken off relief, and to avoid making a big mistake.

"It is rather unusual," Morgenthau broke in, "that I should be
here as Secretary of the Treasury pleading with you to spend
money. What I do not want to see in this country is violence and
broken heads."

"You cannot assume that I am going to do that after three and
one-half years' experience," Hopkins snapped. After further argument he agreed to explain the situation to the press. "There are
two things I do not want to say," he concluded. "The first is that
there is no money; I have never said that; I do not want to say it
now. And second, that this is being done on the President's orders;
I never tell anybody that."

At his press conference Hopkins admitted that WPA was paring
its rolls because its funds were near exhaustion. The reductions
Williams had announced, he continued, transferred 250,000 Mid-
western drought victims to the Resettlement Administration, which
would effectively put them on a federal dole. The cuts involved
too, a careful review of all nonrelief and administrative jobs within
WPA, and finally the dropping of relief workers "who . . . have
developed other sources of income." Williams had estimated that
there were 175,000 people in these brackets. Hopkins said flatly
that this figure was not definite; the cuts would be made only where
possible.

"We had quite a heated session yesterday," Morgenthau told Jack
Garner, "and . . . I think it's all right now." It would cost the federal government an extra $15 million for the month of January, but
there would be no large layoffs just before Christmas. "And then
when the boss gets back next week," he said, "we're going to have a
real talk but I mean the thing is tided over now."

Again in Washington, the President announced that he would
not need more than $500 million for relief for the balance of fiscal
1937. "Franklin," Morgenthau told him on December 22, "you certainly got yourself out on the end of a limb." Roosevelt asked if he
could get by with less. On the contrary, Morgenthau said, he had
not asked for enough. Williams thought WPA would need $900 mil-
lion; Morgenthau thought it would be at least $700 million. At a

press conference that afternoon Roosevelt had Steve Early plant a question about relief and in reply pooh-poohed the report that he had settled on $500 million. "It certainly did not take him long to climb back on safe ground," Morgenthau confided to his Diary.

The Secretary had still to find the money for Hopkins with whom he was again in full accord. As always, Ickes and Tugwell resisted any diversion of their funds — "fudging on their figures," Hopkins and Bell believed. After revising Bureau of the Budget estimates, however, Bell on December 29 reported exuberantly that the pace of recovery had resulted in unexpectedly large tax yields, regular departmental expenses were below previous predictions, and the deficit for fiscal 1937 would therefore be smaller than that for 1936 even if Congress made an additional appropriation for WPA. This news relieved the pressure for reductions in the relief program during the winter. Morgenthau was overjoyed.

The timing of the revised estimates was especially significant, for on the previous day the Secretary had discovered that the case for a balanced budget was under serious attack. At the White House on December 28 he found Roosevelt enervated by a bad cold, "fuzzy," out of sorts. Bell's draft of a budget message was terrible, the President said. He seemed to prefer a long memorandum he had received from Marriner Eccles, parts of which he read aloud. "I feel too low and my mind is not functioning to try to concentrate on the budget," Roosevelt complained. Tossing the memo to Morgenthau, he told him to take it and Bell's draft and "do something" with them.

Marriner Eccles, Chairman of the Federal Reserve Board, had been one of the first and was then one of the most influential Americans who advocated a deliberately unbalanced budget as the key instrument for recovery. A Utah Mormon, banker, and businessman, confident, self-assertive, ambitious, and energetic, Eccles first came to Washington as a special assistant to Morgenthau on housing. Quickly conscious of Eccles's large talents, Morgenthau was one of those who recommended him to Roosevelt for the Federal Reserve appointment. He helped Eccles win a long struggle for confirmation from the Senate, where Carter Glass and other conservatives opposed him. Not without friction, he and Eccles worked together to see the Banking Act of 1935 through Congress. Endowed with enlarged powers by this Act, resistant to the Treasury's increasing involvement in international and domestic monetary policy, Eccles clashed with Morgenthau over questions pertaining to the management of the national debt, interest rates on federal securities, and the disposition of inflowing gold.* Most profoundly, Morgenthau and Eccles differed about the budget.

Eccles's December memorandum on the budget advanced, in his own words and in his own spirit, the ideas which had been given their classic statement by John Maynard Keynes. An attempt to balance the budget, Eccles argued, would put the country into an economic tailspin. The popular analogy between the debt of an individual and the debt of a nation was utterly false. The crucial consideration was not the size of the deficit but the level of national income. It would be unsafe to slash federal expenditures until the expansion of private enterprise took up the whole slack of employment. Meanwhile deficit expenditures were a necessary, compensatory form of investment which gave life to an economy operating below capacity. Ultimately they would lead to restored business activity and increased national income. An attempt to balance the budget for the fiscal year 1938, Eccles maintained, would be dangerously premature, would lead to a new wave of deflation and reverse the processes of recovery thus far set in motion. This would spell doom for the Democratic party, perhaps even pave the way for totalitarianism.

Morgenthau disagreed completely with the whole drift of Eccles's thinking. Constant or increasing deficits, he believed, would impair the government's credit, force Congress to start the printing presses, precipitate runaway inflation and national disaster. Progress toward a balanced budget, on the other hand, would protect the value of government securities, win the confidence of private enterprise, and result in an upturn of private investment that would sustain a new prosperity. So Morgenthau had thought on taking office; so he believed in 1936; so, indeed, he still believed in 1959. He would not stint in caring for the needy unemployed, but he would not relax his purpose of balancing the national budget precisely as he balanced the budget for his farm.

For Morgenthau, therefore, Eccles's memorandum was a tremen-

* For discussions of these issues see Chapter VIII.

Youngest of Four—*circa* 1895

*"An only son with a father who adored him."*

At Gallipoli, 1915–1916. Henry Morgenthau, Jr., at far left

*"It was a thrilling experience."*

At Cornell, 1931

*"Friendship . . . cemented by a community of interest."*

The Cabinet aboard the *Indianapolis,* 1934

Front row: Frances Perkins, Secretary of Labor; Claude H. Swanson, Secretary of the Navy; President Roosevelt; Cordell Hull, Secretary of State; Henry Morgenthau, Jr., Secretary of the Treasury; Homer Cummings, Attorney General.

Back row: James A. Farley, Postmaster General; Daniel C. Roper, Secretary of Commerce; George H. Dern, Secretary of War; Harold Ickes, Secretary of the Interior (Henry A. Wallace, Secretary of Agriculture, absent).

*"The first man to go into the Roosevelt Cabinet who earned it."*

Baby Bonds. Henry Morgenthau, Jr., the President, James A. Farley
*"A picture of national prudence and purpose and patriotism."*

"Challenging
the Winner"
by Jerry Doyle,
in the *Record* and
New York *Post*

Mrs. Morgenthau and Mrs. Roosevelt
at a self-help cooperative in Washington, 1937
*"Doing things for people at the bottom of the ladder."*

Two of a Kind
*"That rarest of assets . . . a friend."*

"The Sour Note" by C. K. Berryman,
in the Washington *Star*, 1938

Conference with the Chinese in Washington, 1936
Front row: Ambassador Sze, Mr. Morgenthau, K. P. Chen.
Back row: Y. C. Koo, Wayne C. Taylor, P. W. Kuo, Archie Lockhead.

*"My objective . . . through finance, is world peace."*

Conference with the French in Paris, 1938
Left to right: French Minister of Finance Paul Marchandeau,
Mr. Morgenthau, Ambassador William C. Bullitt, Jacques Rueff.

Herman Oliphant

William H. McReynolds

*"Models of distinguished service"*

Herbert E. Gaston

Daniel W. Bell

Three Henry Morgenthaus

The Family at Home
Joan, Henry Morgenthau, Jr., Henry III, Mrs. Morgenthau, Robert

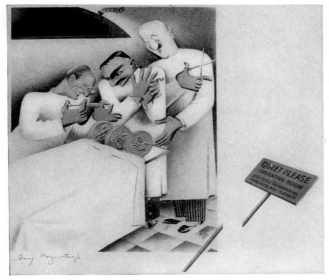

"Quiet Please"
by Garretto,
1935

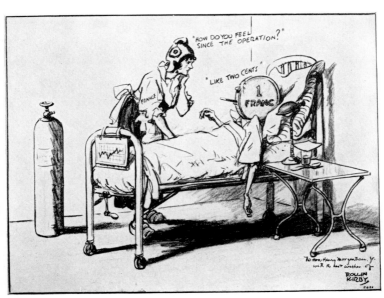

"Sick but 'Stabilized' " by Rollin Kirby,
in the New York *World-Telegram*, 1938

Harry Hopkins and Henry Morgenthau, Jr., 1935
*"Never once in the long history of unemployment relief did you fail."*

Tax Conference with Senator Pat Harrison and Roswell Magill, 1937
*"The pride of authorship is not important."*

dous challenge. If he failed to "dynamite" Eccles's point of view, he wrote, he would "find that Eccles will become the President's fiscal adviser." Bell was no less astounded and dismayed. The revised estimates of the Bureau of the Budget seemed to him and to the Secretary to constitute an overwhelming rejoinder to Eccles. The new figures, they agreed, demonstrated that recovery was well along, that the annual deficit was shrinking, that a balanced budget was in sight. "Golly," Morgenthau said on December 29, "I think we all got every reason to face the new year with the greatest of complacence and comfort."

On December 30 Morgenthau and Bell took their case to Roosevelt. Surprised by the improved figures, the President teased Bell, who, he said, had been holding out on him. The new estimates showed a gross deficit for fiscal 1936 of $3.234 billion and an anticipated gross deficit for 1937 of $1.099 billion. After doing the necessary subtraction, Roosevelt wrote out a statement in his own hand suggesting that Congress could keep the 1937 deficit below the 1936 deficit if it voted no more than $2.135 billion for relief.

If the President used that phraseology, Morgenthau said, all the hostile Republican newspapers would claim he had recommended Congress appropriate $2.135 billion. "You are right," Roosevelt said, adding that the government did not need that much. Without argument, he subscribed to the long-range fiscal program which Morgenthau and Bell advocated. Assuming a constant rate of recovery, they predicted a budget for fiscal 1938 in balance except for the cost of servicing the debt, a budget for fiscal 1939 in balance in all respects.

During the winter and early spring of 1937 Roosevelt, pleased and relieved by the prospect of decreasing deficits, stuck hard to economy, though retrenchment remained difficult. In March the governors of six industrial states protested against Hopkins's schedule for removing 600,000 people from relief rolls by the end of June. They accused the President, Morgenthau reported to his staff, "of saying for the last few years that he would take care of every hungry man. . . . He would have to live up to it. . . . Whereupon the President said, we will have another meeting and Hopkins and the Secretary of the Treasury will look it over and see what appropriations and what money we have and recommend what money we can transfer from other agencies to Hopkins. . . . Then the Governors had us for one hour afterwards and they were pretty ugly and tried to get Hopkins to say that . . . he would not lay off any more people. Hopkins said, the only person who can say that is the President."

Raiding "some of Mr. Roosevelt's pet projects," Morgenthau and Bell transferred $250 million to WPA, enough — Hopkins promised — to see him through May. Roosevelt did not object. As Hopkins remarked, he was "getting tough" about money. When the governors returned in April to fight against proposed reductions in WPA for fiscal 1938, the President was equivocal. He would stretch federal funds as far as possible, he said, but he would not make any promises about appropriations. Bad news from the Bureau of the Budget seemed only to stiffen him. For the period January 1 through March 30, 1937, revenues were off. Roosevelt responded with an Executive Order of April 7:

> It is my desire that the heads of the executive departments and independent establishments . . . will immediately . . . survey . . . expenditure requirements . . . for the remaining months of the fiscal year 1937. It is apparent at this time that the revenues of the Government . . . will be materially less than the amount estimated in my budget of last January; and, hence, the deficit will be far greater than was anticipated unless there is an immediate curtailment of expenditures.
>
> You will carefully examine the status of appropriations for your activities with a view to making a substantial saving by eliminating or deferring all expenditures which are not absolutely necessary. . . . You will report to me through the Acting Director of the Budget not later than May 1, 1937.

Morgenthau rejoiced. "I wish you'd hear the President talk about balancing the budget to Eccles," he told his morning group on April 5. "God, if he'd only say publicly what he told him, it would be marvelous." It was perhaps sufficiently marvelous that the next day Eccles, calling at the Treasury, completely reversed his earlier position. He intended to impress Roosevelt with the urgency of balancing the budget for 1938, he said, and he hoped Morgenthau would join him. With some amusement Morgenthau replied that beyond a certain point one could not press the President.

Beyond a certain point, as Morgenthau also knew, one could not hold Roosevelt too closely to any course. Time would show how frugality weighed against congressional politics, how a decline in public spending would affect the general level of economic activity, how fiscal conservatism weighed against social deprivation which the President and Secretary alike bemoaned. Even as he heard Eccles's ephemeral recantation, Morgenthau was absorbed in the economics of federal housing, in attempting simultaneously to win the battle of the budget and the battle against slums.

## 8. Formulas for Housing

For four years before April 1937, the Treasury had had a large interest in the various efforts of the New Deal to provide decent housing for the American people. The bonds of emergency corporations concerned with housing, secured as they were by the government, swelled the existing and potential national debt. The operating costs of other housing agencies constituted a substantial percentage of recovery expenditures. The housing programs had significance for recovery itself. In some cases public housing employed relief labor. In all cases, renovation or new construction produced indirect employment, created demands for steel, glass, cement, electrical and plumbing fixtures, and a multiplicity of other manufactured goods. Indeed, in the view of some economists, a sufficiently aggressive federal housing program could provide the central stimulus for recovery. Furthermore, whatever the economic implications, the nation badly needed new housing, as Morgenthau always insisted, and whatever the scope of the program, the waste and confusion occasioned by a proliferation of federal agencies worried the Treasury.

Though without immediate authority over housing, the Secretary could exercise considerable influence as chairman of the Interdepartmental Loan Committee, on which several housing agencies were represented, and through his personal avenue to the President, who supported Morgenthau's appointment within the Treasury of a succession of special assistants on housing. Ever conscious of his experience at the Henry Street Settlement, the Secretary understood the need for federal support of slum clearance. In the years 1934–36, however, his duties focused his attention upon other, though related, objectives: coordination of the housing agencies, direction of housing expenditures into channels most relevant to relief and recovery, and reliance insofar as possible upon federal sponsorship of private enterprise rather than upon direct federal spending.

Administrative laxity within the Home Owners' Loan Corporation cost that agency Morgenthau's sympathy. Established in June 1933, the corporation was designed to protect impoverished home owners from foreclosure. Deflation had hurt householders just as it hurt farmers, making their mortgaged debts excessively onerous. During 1932 more than 270,000 homes fell to the sheriff; during the first half of 1933, foreclosures occurred at a rate above one thousand a day. To arrest this process, the Home Owners' Loan Corporation, substituting its credit for that of defaulting householders, wrote new mortgages on liberal terms, consolidated multiple liens, and worked out simple schedules for monthly payments of amortization and interest. Mortgagors also benefited, for without having to scale down the debt due them, they could exchange defaulted mortgages for guaranteed government bonds. Indeed in many instances mortgagors precipitated crises in order to unload to the HOLC.

The demands upon the corporation were enormous. During the spring of 1934 more than 35,000 applications a week came in. HOLC was lending so rapidly, Morgenthau discovered, that it would pass the statutory limit on its loans by September or October. His investigations persuaded him that the existing pace was unnecessary. "I am concerned," he wrote John H. Fahey, chairman of the corporation, "over reports . . . that many of the loans . . . are being granted to mortgagors who are not in genuine distress. . . . I wish you would please send a letter, at once, to each of the State Managers, conveying to them a very definite order that they must not . . . recommend any loans other than those which they can certify to be genuine distress loans."

This chastening message helped check the runaway spirts of the agency, as did Morgenthau's intercession to protect it from patronage raids in 1935. Unless the government wanted to invite scandal or make massive foreclosures itself, he pointed out to the congressional leaders, deserving Democrats would have to yield to trained administrators. Politics had already accounted for a lot of "rotten loans," particularly in branch offices subject to the influence of real estate lobbies and local mortgage and loan companies. Ultimately about one loan in seven went bad, but before HOLC suspended lending in June 1936, it also did much good, saving over one million homes, releasing over $3 billion in frozen assets.

Morgenthau began in mid-1935 to urge the suspension of HOLC largely because he preferred the program of the Federal Housing Administration. That agency was established in 1934 chiefly for the purpose of lending money to middle-income families for the repair or modernization of old buildings or for the construction of new dwellings. The FHA did not advance credit itself but insured 80 and in some instances 90 per cent of the loans made by private lending institutions. This insurance made possible low rates of interest and long term amortizations for the many projects that met FHA's high standards for construction.

As Morgenthau continually pointed out, HOLC refinancing gave no stimulus to recovery whereas FHA loans for construction provided direct and indirect re-employment. The FHA, furthermore, mobilized private investment, whereas the housing program of the Public Works Administration entailed direct public expenditures. Morgenthau therefore in August 1935 expressed to Roosevelt his own confidence in FHA.

The Secretary realized that FHA had yet to achieve its full potentialities. The agency was bogged down, he believed, by an excessive reliance on the national mortgage associations and by inadequate promotion. It needed more and better channels for making loans; it needed to create enthusiasm for renovation and construction. To coordinate the Treasury's relations to housing activities and to push the FHA along, he appointed a new special assistant, Peter Grimm, an experienced real estate salesman and promoter from New York City.

Starting out in the field, Grimm organized a meeting in Newark, New Jersey, of representatives of the eleven federal agencies there concerned with housing. Their experience persuaded him that decentralization and coordination on the local level would bring system and energy to the federal program. The Newark investigation also confirmed his belief that more private funds, especially insurance money, could be attracted to refinancing and to new construction. Grimm soon clashed, however, with Frederick A. Delano, the President's uncle, who was also supposed to be coordinating housing, and with Harold Ickes, who resented criticism of the low-rent projects of the Public Works Administration.

Continuing jurisdictional friction accounted in large part for the diversion of Grimm's effort from coordination to promotion. Adopting a suggestion of Morgenthau, he organized a series of local exhibitions to induce householders to apply for FHA renovation loans. He also helped to plan a housing caravan that moved from city to city throughout the country, to arrange permanent housing shows in major cities, to improve FHA mortgage and debenture forms, and to train local administrators in handling the rush of applications which these activities inspired. The sluggish renovation program caught on, and by March 1937 FHA had lent a million and a quarter home owners over $500 million for improvements.

As a promoter Grimm did well, but he failed in his central mission, the preparation of a unified federal housing program. His reports of October 1935 called for divorcing the construction of low-rent housing from federal re-employment policy and for relying primarily on private enterprise and local governmental agencies to satisfy the housing shortage.

These recommendations, Morgenthau believed, reflected the influence of the powerful real estate lobby. "Our big problem," he said, speaking for the President as well as for himself, "is unemployment and how to take care of the unemployed. I do not know of any better way to get people back on the private employment rolls than through housing."

Treasury statistics, furthermore, made Grimm's faith in private industry and local government look foolish. In order to buy decent homes, the vast majority of Americans needed larger loans and lower interest rates than private lenders were prepared to offer. The states and localities lacked the resources to help. Morgenthau could only conclude that the federal program, however much it needed coordination, needed also to grow. With a sense of frustration rather than ill will, he accepted Grimm's resignation in March 1936.

Important as it was to help middle-income families to keep or buy their homes, it was even more urgent to improve the lot of the millions of Americans mired in urban slums. In 1933 approximately one-sixth of the city dwellings in the United States were unfit for habitation, ordinarily unventilated, ill-heated, without hot water or sufficient plumbing. Private capital had little to offer. Metropolitan Life, one of the most efficient private owners, set rents to yield only a modest 4 per cent on investment, but even this scale called for about $14 a room, about $50 a dwelling unit per month. Yet in 1936 approximately half the urban population earned less than $1070 a year. These people could not afford much more than $20 a month for rent. If they were to enjoy simple but decent housing, they needed federal assistance.

During Roosevelt's first Administration little was done. An appropriation for urban housing granted by the National Recovery Act of 1933 fell to the cautious Ickes whose Public Works Administration in four and a half years built or began only 49 projects containing only 24,441 residential units. Ickes suffered from lack of experience in public housing and from his own overemphasis on durability and elaborate plans. His costs were high, averaging almost $1700 a room. In Williamsburg, Brooklyn, he spent $2200 per room. "Tickled to death that the damn rotten swamp was cleaned up," Morgenthau nevertheless feared that Ickes's slow and expensive ways might destroy public and congressional confidence. The government, Morgenthau believed, needed to work out a large, inexpensive program, carefully financed but sufficiently subsidized to serve families in the lowest income groups. But the bills before Congress in the spring of 1936, he told the President, were "terrible."

Of all the measures under consideration, only that of Senator Robert F. Wagner of New York had the scope Morgenthau deemed essential. Wagner, who had grown up in the slums, detested them. He urged the establishment of a United States Housing Authority endowed with an annual subsidy for public housing. Although enthusiastic about his purpose, Morgenthau disliked his proposals for granting and borrowing funds. He therefore directed his staff to work out a bill with the proper "social slant" but also "terrific from the standpoint of finance."

Early in 1937 the Treasury planners held a series of conferences with Wagner and his assistants. They agreed completely on many principles: stimulation of the construction industry, tax exemptions on local properties purchased for new housing, restriction of federal assistance to financing and technical matters, local ownership of federally subsidized projects, safe and sanitary housing at rents slum dwellers could afford. Disagreement centered on the method of financing. The senator's bill empowered the Housing Authority to float bonds, guaranteed by the government, at a low interest rate, ordinarily 2.5 per cent. These bonds were to be amortized over sixty years with localities paying the principal. The federal government was to pay the annual interest and provide a subsidy to the community of an additional 1 per cent. Thus if the Authority undertook a billion dollar program, floating $1 billion of bonds at 2.5 per cent, the federal contribution would include the annual interest, $25 million, plus 1 per cent, $10 million. This was mighty cheap, Wagner argued, for a billion dollars worth of housing.

Morgenthau, when he first examined the formula, exclaimed: "I need a drink after seeing those figures!" At the rate of $35 million a year, the federal government would pay out $2 billion 100 million in sixty years, more than enough to cover interest and repay principal. This "sleight of hand" struck the Secretary as dreadful. It would, he maintained, "just shoot the government credit to hell." He much preferred putting the entire housing program on a "straight social basis . . . the United States will simply build so many houses, and add to its debt."

At the White House on March 2, 1937, Morgenthau maintained that the Wagner bill gave housing projects away free, with a little extra to boot. He recommended instead a direct appropriation for housing. It would strain the budget, but they could find other places to cut corners. Surely, he argued, if the government could build roads and deepen rivers, it could clear away slums. Wagner agreed in theory but insisted Congress would not provide a direct appropriation. The senator's alternative, Morgenthau said, was impossible. "Well," Roosevelt directed, "see if you can't work it out."

At luncheon on April 26 the President expounded his own theory of financing, one very like that Ickes frequently used. On a million dollar project, he explained to Morgenthau, the locality would pay for the land, probably about $200,000. That left $800,000. The federal government would provide 45 per cent in cash, $360,000, and 10 per cent in relief labor, $80,000. The locality would then have to raise the $360,000 balance on a first mortgage.

"Is that really all you are going to give them," Morgenthau asked.

"What! Henry, you and I could build on that basis and if they can't they're crazy."

"Well, they are asking for 100 per cent."

"Well, if they don't like that," Roosevelt said, "they don't get anything. They can take it and like it."

The difficulties in the President's proposal were shattering. As the Treasury's research staff pointed out, the rate of interest on a private loan for a first mortgage would be too high to permit low-cost housing. A 45 per cent federal grant would be too small to permit low rentals, but a 60 per cent grant might do, and would eliminate the need for annual subsidies.

"Out of friendship . . . for the President," Morgenthau never dared show Wagner Roosevelt's proposal, but even the Treasury's modification left the senator cold. "That looks to me like no bill . . ." he told the Secretary. "My mind isn't closed . . . but I don't want to get a housing bill that just looks like a housing bill and nothing happens."

Morgenthau thought the Treasury plan a good "transitional bill to keep things going."

Wagner said he was not a "transitionalist." The plan offered less than the President or the Democratic platform had promised. It was only "a drop in the bucket," though it might provide the spark that would "ignite the fuse." He knew what it meant to live in the slums; he did not "know why these people haven't become anarchists already. . . . They feel that the government has neglected them."

As much as did Wagner, Morgenthau wanted a bill with a heart in it, but as he told his staff, he was against "making peas jump from one shell to another." He took the senator a revised proposal calling for grants equivalent to 85 per cent of costs, but Wagner was still unhappy. Morgenthau knew he was licked. "The President asked for a financial formula," he reminded his morning group. "I have given it to him. . . . I've got a lot of other things which I'm

responsible for, which I can't do if he's going to fool around with
. . . housing. . . . We'll keep it here and mark it X — here lies the
body."

Early in June Roosevelt gave Wagner's bill his blessing, as he had
been inclined to from the start. The Act as finally passed provided
$500 million for low-cost housing loans, called upon localities to
defray 10 per cent of costs, and placed all projects under local control.

Morgenthau and Wagner had differed about means, not about
goals. A common response to human misery made them allies; the
conflict between the senator's sense of congressional politics and the
Secretary's sense of sound finance set them apart. As Wagner realized, there was nothing stingy about Morgenthau's proposals. Indeed, in the face of Bell's reports of declining revenues and Hopkins's need for extra money, the Secretary in April 1937 was prepared to strain the budget in order to house the poor. He believed,
however, that the country could have its housing and pay for it, too.
The housing program simply made it more important than ever to
curb the profligates in Washington.


### 9. A Sound Financial Foundation

In April 1937, soon after the President ordered the independent
agencies to economize, Morgenthau fought another major skirmish
in the continuing battle of the budget. Harry Hopkins was then
talking publicly of a permanent program for work relief, timed to
moderate dips in the business cycle. The Secretary, with Bell at his
side, set out to persuade Roosevelt to throw that idea, and others
involving the expenses of a large bureaucracy, "into the ash can."
He noted in his Diary:

Monday at lunch on the 12th [of April], I discussed the
Budget and Relief with the President and that night I sent him
an outline of my suggestions. The next meeting we had with
him was at two o'clock Thursday, the 15th — Bell and Aubrey
Williams being present. The President had Hopkins' suggestions, his own and Bell's. After Aubrey Williams left we got

down to the Budget Message. Bell and I had been thinking in terms of two messages — a Relief Message and a Budget Message. The President then told us that he wanted only one message and it must not be over 2000 words. He then argued with me for putting in the figure of a billion one-half instead of $1 billion to last until March 1st [1938] as stated in Bell's document. The President's argument for the billion and one half was that he thought it was a much more honest way to approach it and he kept arguing for it and, to my great surprise, I learned for the first time that he was talking about a billion one-half for the full twelve months with no qualifications.

I told him that I wanted to think it over. The reason for my wanting to think it over was that I was so surprised to find that the President was ready to commit himself for a billion and a half for twelve months. . . . I decided that the intelligent thing to do was to accept his proposition provided that he did not try to qualify the billion and a half by saying that perhaps he would have to ask for more. As a matter of fact, from that day on until the Message was finished he stuck to the billion and a half as an outside figure. . . .

We met with the President again Friday noon at the White House and Bell had another document ready. . . . I took Bell's message home with me Friday night as I had been too tired both Thursday and Friday to really get down and think. But Saturday morning, I woke up at 6:15, my sub-conscious mind having worked on this over and over and over, and I came to two conclusions. In the first place, that the Budget part of the Message was weak and not convincing. On page four I wrote in in pencil my suggestions for strengthening the message.* The second conclusion I came to was that the relief part of the message was dishwater; that the President had a

---

* As redrafted by Gaston and used by Roosevelt in his message of April 20, Morgenthau's two suggestions read: "I regard it as extremely important that we should achieve a balance of actual income and expenditure for the fiscal year 1938, and I appeal to you to join me in a determined effort to bring about that result"; and "And while I recognize many opportunities to improve social and economic conditions through federal action, I am firmly convinced that the success of our whole program and the permanent security of our people demand that we adjust all expenditures within the limits of my budget estimate."

number of times sent messages to Congress on relief and it
would be much more effective if he would simply ask for the
billion and a half and give no apologies or excuses. . . .

The President accepted these changes, it left me absolutely
breathless. . . . When the President came to the part of the
message headed, "Relief" I said, "Please wait a minute. I am
now going to suggest that you stop here and discard the rest
of your message. I got this idea at 6:15 this morning." I had
hardly had the words out of my mouth when the President
flashed at me "I got the idea in bed last night at 1:15." I
laughed and said, "Well, Mr. President, it took us just five
hours for the thought transference to work."

This experience has happened often before. When I have
an unusually good suggestion to make the President he immediately tells me that he had thought of it before and that
is a signal to me that he likes my suggestion but does not
want to give me credit for it — and I am always more interested in getting my idea over than I am in getting credit.

Aubrey Williams then started to sputter and argue about
keeping in the relief message and showed his hand when he
said, "But, Mr. President, you must say something about relief being a permanent institution." And I said, in no uncertain terms "That is just what you do not want to say, Mr.
President." . . .

About six o'clock Monday night we met with the President. . . . In looking around the room I found that Congressman Taylor of Colorado was the only Democratic leader
present who did not come from South of the Mason-Dixon
line. Every other man was a southerner — and then some
people wonder why they do not do something about slum
clearance in the cities.

The President read his Message to the crowd and the whole
argument centered on the billion and one half. Most of the
men there wanted the President to ask for one billion and
then say that he would review the situation again early next
year. Senator Jimmy Byrnes pressed the President pretty hard
and I thought, for a moment, that the President was going to
lose his temper — but he didn't. I came to his defense on the

billion and a half and in doing so made the statement that Hopkins' organization was the only emergency agency that had cut down expenditures and that we should look for savings in some of the other agencies. . . .

When the meeting broke up Senator Byrnes said to me, "Since when have you gone on Harry Hopkins' relief roll."

The meeting was unsatisfactory in this sense, that as various members of Congress raised the question as to what was to happen to their pet bill the President would not give them a clean-cut answer.

The man who made the best statement during the whole session was Senator Robinson. I got the feeling that he really wanted to save money and was not particularly interested in some pet appropriation.

Appropriations outside of the budget, which the President's message of April 20 explicitly opposed, had become Morgenthau's greatest worry. Unless Roosevelt prevented or vetoed them, the deficit would grow. But the President's proposal for a reorganization of the Supreme Court had provoked strong resistance among conservative Democrats on the Hill. To contain their growing revolt against his leadership, he apparently felt compelled to permit at least one significant departure from his message. This deviation, supported in both houses by many increasingly contrary Southern Democrats, had a worthy social purpose — the gradual elimination of farm tenancy by a program of federal loans. In any case, Roosevelt told Morgenthau on April 21, he had promised Speaker of the House Bankhead to do something about tenancy. He was in a hole, he said, but he wanted to find a way out within the budget.

Completely in sympathy with the purpose of the tenancy bill, Morgenthau nevertheless stood on principle against increasing agricultural expenses. The solution, he believed, was to reassign some of Henry Wallace's funds, which Morgenthau considered excessive. After the Supreme Court had found the processing tax unconstitutional, Congress had established a system of soil conservation payments to permit the continued control of agricultural production. Unreconciled to that program in any form, Morgenthau was

particularly unhappy about perpetuating the expense in the face
of the loss in revenue. He was grieved, too, by the advancing costs
of the Resettlement Administration, and by the budgetary inflex-
iblity imposed by a law granting 30 per cent of customs receipts to
the Department of Agriculture.

"Wallace," the Secretary told the Treasury staff on April 15, "exclusive of ever-normal granary, expects to spend in 1937, $1,267,-
000,000; in 1938, $1,176,000,000; and in 1939, $1,087,000,000. Bill
Myers comes along with a study which shows that in government
aid to Agriculture from 1934 to 1937 we have given away $2,594,-
000,000 — to Agriculture! . . . Their overhead is $130,000,000. It
costs $130,000,000 for nine months to give away $516,000,000."

These figures did not impress Wallace. "You don't understand
what we are doing," he said.

"Oh, yes I do," Morgenthau replied. "I understand it more
every day. This is ten times worse than Hopkins. Hopkins is the
only one that has cut down expenses in Washington and the one
that costs us more than anybody else is Wallace. My hat is off to
him — he is getting away with murder."

"Well," Wallace asked, "how about the farm organizations?"

"Henry," Morgenthau said, "that's your cross. You bear it."

Morgenthau's particular target was the $500 million soil con-
servation program. The Department of Agriculture was paying
farmers $10 an acre for planting trees, he complained to his staff,
whereas the same farmers had done very well during Roosevelt's
governorship when they paid the state $2 per tree. He ridiculed
the language in a Department of Agriculture bulletin offering payments for "plowing or disking under biennial or perennial legumes
from which no crop has been harvested." "If any farmer in New
York State knows what that is," Morgenthau said, "I'll eat my hat."
"Of all the boondoogling I have ever seen," he concluded, ". . . the
plan to spend the money for the so-called soil conservation takes
the prize. . . . The only thing they don't pay you to do is to plant
wood violets among the trees." Here, then, was the place to get $100
million "out of existing appropriations" for the farm tenancy bill,
"to demonstrate once and for all that the President *really* meant
what he said in his Budget Message."

"I think if we haven't got the money," Wallace protested on

April 21, "I think we'd better go along without . . . a tenancy bill."

"Yes," Morgenthau answered, "but the President told me to find the money. He wants the tenancy bill; he'll give me until tomorrow morning to find it."

Now more cooperative, the Department of Agriculture admitted that it might be able to find some unexpended funds in its appropriations for 1937. So informed, Roosevelt decided to take $15 to $25 million from balances on hand for soil conservation, but he warned Morgenthau he needed $75 million more, probably from relief moneys. Pressed to dig deeper, Wallace on April 23 reported that he could manage the tenancy program for a year for $25 to $30 million. He also suggested for the first time a $30 million cut in the expenditures for good roads which he had included in his 1938 estimates. He went even farther. If the crop insurance bill he advocated was enacted, he promised, he could administer it for a year without additional funds. Roosevelt immediately accepted these proposals. Morgenthau was "tremendously encouraged," for Wallace had conceded enough to protect the budget.

Anything less would have brought Morgenthau close to resigning. The budget was his responsibility, Jack Garner told him on April 27, and if he did not get Roosevelt's cooperation he might have to leave. Morgenthau said that he never threatened, but that if the President did not keep his promises, he would go. Garner was pleased. "Henry," he said, "frankly, I'm talking to the President through you. . . . I am your friend and I am proud of you. You can always count on me."

Morgenthau did not need Garner. Without prodding, Roosevelt on May 17 said that he was "definitely going to balance the Budget next year." The Secretary believed he meant it, and believed he could. As good as his word, Roosevelt in June 1937 ordered extensive economies for fiscal 1938. He directed all departments to reserve not less than 10 per cent of their funds, in aggregate $2.8 billion. He instructed Wallace to make every effort to reduce by $30 million his original estimate for soil conservation and Domestic Allotment. He froze $30 million — in all one kind — of the War Department's appropriation for rivers and harbors, 10 per cent of the appropriation of the Federal Housing Administration.

He requested the Reconstruction Finance Corporation to liquidate loans rapidly enough to deposit $300 million in the Treasury
— twice the deposit the 1938 Budget had initially allowed for. He
also told the Commodity Credit Corporation to deposit an extra
$20 million, and he informed the principal agencies administering
work relief that they had to live within their approved means.

These orders gave Morgenthau a sense of triumph. Without
shortchanging the unemployed, without arresting reform, the Administration had excellent prospects for balancing the budget for
fiscal 1938 except for the cost of servicing the debt. Prudence had
won over spending, perhaps largely because recovery seemed so
real, and best of all, from Morgenthau's point of view, Roosevelt
appeared to be dedicated at last to unflinching economy. "The
President," the Secretary had said in April after the budget message, "gave me . . . everything that I asked for and I told him
that I was entirely satisfied. It was a long hard trying fight but certainly at some time during the weeks that I argued with him he
must have come to the conclusion that if he wants his Administration to go forward with his reform program he must have a sound
financial foundation." Now the budget message had been made to
stick. The summer of 1937 was the sunniest season Morgenthau
had known in many years.

# VII

# *Taxation*

## *1934-1937*

## 1. Revenue and the Redistribution of Wealth

THE PROBLEMS of depression, the cost of relief, and the inequities in American society gave taxation special importance as an instrument of public policy during the 1930's. Tax schedules affected more than the government's income. They had significance, too, for national recovery and for social reform. "The primary interest of the Treasury . . . relates to . . . revenue," Morgenthau said early in his term. As long as he was Secretary, that interest was to predominate. As he also observed, however, "taxation in any form has many collateral effects . . . and . . . there is a national duty to avoid tax laws which produce undesirable social consequences and a like duty to correct evils produced by existing tax legislation."

Every tax program had to compromise among its several aims, and as changing conditions warranted a changing emphasis, Morgenthau concentrated now upon one, now upon another aspect of the tax problem. During his first months in office, while other issues absorbed him, he nevertheless set forth the principles that guided his policies. The New Deal, he told the House Ways and Means Committee late in 1933, had an overwhelming mandate to improve the position of the underdog. Wealthy individuals were in far the best position to bear additional burdens, and increases in their income and estate taxes would have the desirable effect of reducing huge disparities in economic power. Before the Senate Judiciary Committee in 1934, he recommended closing the loopholes through which rich men and corporations avoided taxes, he emphasized the need for a constitutional amendment permitting taxation of the income from federal and local securities, which were tax exempt, and he appealed for additional funds for enforcement. He could say nothing more specific, for he was under instructions from Roosevelt to leave the choice of new taxes to the Congress, and to comment only on the estimates of receipts from alternative schedules. The Revenue Act of 1934 raised slightly income, estate and gift taxes in the higher brackets, but it was at best only a beginning.

Indeed the Treasury had yet fully to develop its own policies, for the Republican Administrations of the 1920's had not recruited a staff of experts with the qualifications Morgenthau considered necessary for studying tax questions. As rapidly as he could, he put together a group of men, some permanent employees, some temporary consultants who undertook a comprehensive survey of the federal tax structure. This group included Herman Oliphant, Jacob Viner, and George Haas, who were, of course, already hard at work on many problems. Roswell Magill, a professor of tax law at Columbia University, later Under Secretary of the Treasury, gave general direction to the research. The three specialists who worked most closely and productively with Magill were Carl S. Shoup, also of Columbia, Roy Blough, a professor of economics formerly assistant director of research for Harry Hopkins, and Lawrence H. Seltzer, who in 1934 became George Haas's assistant director and chief economist. Guy Helvering, the head of the Internal Revenue Bureau, contributed useful information about tax enforcement.

By the end of the summer of 1934 Magill and his associates, who were cooperating with Congress in studying the British tax system, had reassessed the Treasury's purposes. Their reports provided Morgenthau with a series of recommendations designed to increase revenues and to dissolve dangerous concentrations of wealth. Armed with the information he needed, he was ready to try to enlist the President's support.

On December 11, 1934, Morgenthau took his proposals to the White House. The first called for a graduated inheritance tax to supplement the existing estate tax.* Such a tax would bring the

---

* An estate tax falls upon the total estate a man bequeaths; an inheritance tax, upon the individual shares of his heirs.

proportion of revenue the United States collected from estates closer to that collected by the British government. Because inheritance taxes could be in large part avoided through gifts made before death, the Treasury further suggested either raising gift taxes or taxing gifts as ordinary income.

These recommendations clearly envisaged some redistribution of national wealth, a prospect that men of means naturally found radical. Their attitude in no way deterred Morgenthau, for, as he saw it, gross economic inequities were dangerous not only in themselves but also because they seemed to justify the demands of men like Huey Long for frankly confiscatory programs. Long promised to make every man a king on $2500 a year. The aged Dr. Francis E. Townsend won thousands of followers, especially in the Far West, by proposing $200 a month for all over sixty years old. Compared to such panaceas, the Treasury's recommendations were mild. Furthermore, Morgenthau had excellent precedents. Theodore Roosevelt had supported an inheritance tax as early as 1907 and during 1934 several congressional committees had given the idea serious consideration.

The second item in the Treasury's program was an intercorporate dividend tax designed to break up holding companies. Herman Oliphant and Felix Frankfurter in particular had pressed this scheme upon the Secretary as a means of preventing a recurrence of the skulduggery which had so marked the 1920's. Adventurers owning only a minority of a corporation's stock had been able through holding company devices to control a corporation, waste its assets and manipulate its securities for their own gain. Morgenthau saw in taxation the leverage to make holding companies reorder their affairs. As things stood, only the corporation first earning income paid a tax on it. The Treasury now proposed that each corporation receiving dividends from that income should also pay taxes. This would make holding companies with several tiers of subsidiaries unduly expensive. The Treasury also recommended revising the corporate income tax so as to make business mergers unattractive. For the long run, Morgenthau suggested scaling the tax on corporations according to their size.

A third major item in the Secretary's report to Roosevelt was a tax on undistributed corporate earnings. He asked, too, for the

taxation of future issues of federal and local bonds, and for a reduction in tax exemptions for mineral depletions.

While Roosevelt, who initially considered the Treasury's recommendations premature, kept the report on his desk, the Department
had to reach a decision about social security taxes. In order to minimize deficit expenditures, Morgenthau advocated taxing employees
as well as employers for the social insurance program. In a supporting memorandum of January 1935, George Haas noted that payroll
taxes for unemployment and old-age insurance would divert funds
from current consumption to saving, but he suggested postponing
serious consideration of a less deflationary tax to a later date. Testifying before the House Ways and Means Committee, Morgenthau
in February emphasized the need for a sound financial basis for social security, the desirability of avoiding heavy taxes on future generations, and therefore the importance of a sufficient scale of contributory taxes to cover pending benefit payments. He had earlier
urged limiting the Department of Labor's original proposal for
social security coverage in order to keep initial expenditures at a
manageable level. He was in all respects a friend of old age and
unemployment insurance, but while he supported the reforms, he
tried to keep a firm hand on the budget. These were also the views
of the Congress which wrote the legislation as the Treasury had
hoped it would.

Yet Haas's memoranda raised a troublesome question. As he suggested, the contributory social security taxes would reduce the spending power of a multitude of consumers. The program Morgenthau
had taken to Roosevelt would also cut potential private spending
and private investment by its heavy levies on individual inheritances
and corporate income. This prospect bothered Marriner Eccles,
among others, and accounted for Oliphant's preference for paying
the bonus by deficit financing rather than new taxes.* Morgenthau
completely disagreed with that reasoning. The social security legislation in no way abated his zeal for increasing federal revenues as
well as for attacking corporate size and reducing inherited wealth.
Late in May 1935 he resumed his efforts to have the President adopt
the Treasury's proposals.

In spite of his disavowal of new taxation in his 1935 budget mes-

* See page 250.

sage, Roosevelt was coming gradually to Morgenthau's position. Troubled by the political challenge of Long and Townsend, he might well have hoped that intelligent liberalism in tax policy would damp the appeal of unintelligent radicalism. The President was, moreover, increasingly impatient with the "economic royalists," the men of large means who were criticizing the New Deal more and more sharply. In this situation, Morgenthau argued that, whether Congress acted on taxes or not, it was imperative for Roosevelt to state clearly where he stood on the subject.

During the first half of June the President gave continual thought to drafts of a tax message which Morgenthau and his staff and Raymond Moley and Felix Frankfurter prepared. Although Moley was expected to put the finishing touches on the document, he seriously objected to the Treasury's entire program, as to the whole recent drift of the New Deal. Frankfurter, as Morgenthau saw it, served largely as a sounding board for the Treasury's ideas.

As the work progressed, Roosevelt singled out as essential four of the recommended taxes: the tax on corporations, graduated to check the growth of monopoly; the intercorporate dividend tax; higher surtaxes on individual incomes; and the inheritance tax. He gave only incidental attention to the Treasury's other proposals. On several occasions Morgenthau urged him to say that he would use the proceeds from an inheritance tax to balance the budget, but the President resisted any reference to budget balancing.

The message Roosevelt sent to Congress on June 19, 1935, was part of a developing Administration attack on economic bigness, which the President now looked upon as a remediable evil, whereas in 1933 he had tended to consider it inevitable. The Treasury's arguments had contributed to the change of mind that his message revealed. Wealth in the modern world, Roosevelt said, resulted from a combination of individual efforts. In spite of the "great importance in our national life of the . . . ingenuity of unusual individuals, the people in the mass have inevitably helped to make large fortunes possible." The transmission of these fortunes from generation to generation, he argued, was not consistent with American ideals. Accumulations of wealth, moreover, perpetrated "great and undesirable concentration of control in a relatively few individuals over the employment and welfare of many, many others." He therefore recommended an inheritance tax, and in order to make "vast concentrations of capital . . . carry burdens commensurate with their . . . advantages," he also proposed a graduated tax on corporate income.

This unequivocal endorsement of tax reform pleased liberals in both parties. Along with the New Dealers on the Hill, progressives like Senators Borah, Norris, and La Follette supported the President, as did William Green, the head of the American Federation of Labor. The Topeka *Daily Capitol* and Philadelphia *Record* applauded the message, but most newspapers, including the New York *Herald Tribune,* the *New York Times,* and the Milwaukee *Journal* were antagonistic. The Boston *Transcript* called the President's proposals a "socialist experiment," and Raymond Moley later wrote that he felt Roosevelt was feuding with the rich. Speaking for most Republicans, Senator Vandenberg called the recommendations a "mere vagrant flirtation" with share-the-wealth ideas.

It was not at all clear, however, as Morgenthau quickly discovered, whether Roosevelt wanted Congress to act at that session or whether he would fight for more than a nominal inheritance tax. The President's intentions were obscured in his puzzling relationship with the cautious Chairman of the Senate Finance Committee, Pat Harrison of Mississippi. Harrison, a masterful parliamentarian who used his considerable power gently but effectively in the cause of fiscal conservatism, opposed the inheritance tax. Roosevelt told him, Morgenthau learned, that that tax should exempt approximately $300,000, which the Secretary considered far too much. Worse still, Morgenthau found it hard to understand the President's shifting tactics.

They changed rapidly during the week after his message. At first Roosevelt stood against having the Senate attach major taxes to the House's resolution extending nuisance taxes — excises on a variety of consumer goods. Harrison, too, apparently with the consent of the White House, spoke out for leaving major reforms to the House, where revenue legislation was supposed to originate. He also advocated postponing the inheritance tax to the following session of Congress. Led by La Follette, however, twenty-two progressive senators agreed to keep Congress in session until it adopted the President's program. Responding to this pressure, Roosevelt and the

Democratic congressional leaders announced after a conference of June 25 that they would drive for immediate action. The next day Harrison said the Senate would take the initiative. Yet a day later, the Senate returned to the original schedule, leaving the initiative with the House; Roosevelt told the press he had never intimated that Congress should push through such an important measure; and Harrison, though he was obviously surprised, remained unruffled at this sudden reversal.

These developments gave Morgenthau no indication of just what Roosevelt expected from him. Perhaps the President was not sure himself. He was involved in so many things — among others, antitrust and banking bills, social security, and a bill to regulate the bituminous coal industry — that he had inadequate time for studying revenue legislation. Without pressing him, Morgenthau tried to get his signals straight. He did not know, he told Roosevelt at luncheon on June 26, how to reply to a request from La Follette for the Treasury's working papers on the inheritance tax. Roosevelt told him to stall.

"Mr. President," Morgenthau asked, "just strictly between the two of us, do you or do you not want your Inheritance Tax program passed at this session?"

"Strictly between the two of us," Roosevelt said, "I do not know, I am on an hourly basis and the situation changes almost momentarily."

That afternoon Morgenthau told La Follette that there were a lot of things going on which he did not understand. The Secretary would not give the senator any official recommendations for taxes, but, he suggested, if La Follette, through Chairman Harrison, requested Treasury experts to bring materials to the Finance Committee, the experts would, of course, comply. This would give La Follette what he wanted, take Morgenthau out of a tough spot, and perhaps, as they saw it, keep Harrison from blocking Roosevelt's "swell message."

While La Follette worked to enlist Senate support for an inheritance tax, Morgenthau on July 8 testified before the House Ways and Means Committee. Roosevelt had again told him he would not resist a movement for adjournment before a revenue act was passed, but he had also said he wanted the Treasury to stress taxing inheritances as if they were annual personal income, a method he had earlier asked Morgenthau to "soft-pedal." This change of heart encouraged the Secretary who in his testimony emphasized the importance of the revenue that a high inheritance tax would yield. Although the Treasury felt it unwise to impose taxes that would retard recovery, he said, it considered it folly not to tap sources of taxation that would reduce the national debt without interfering with recovery. He believed that the inheritance tax fell into that category, and he suggested earmarking all revenues from it to lessen future borrowing and ultimately to pay off the debt.

The Ways and Means Committee included the inheritance tax in its bill, but the Senate, increasingly resistant, shared the skepticism of the conservative press about Morgenthau's references to balancing the budget. Roosevelt's hesitation made the Treasury's situation difficult, as did his rejection of one of Harrison's candidates for the Board of Tax Appeals. The senator now favored increasing the rates of the estate tax, which, he argued, would be easier to administer. Morgenthau and his advisers told Roosevelt that a mere increase in those rates would be inconsistent with his message, for it would not apply the principle of the ability to pay. It would take as much from an estate destined for one heir as from one destined for many. The Secretary therefore urged the application of an inheritance tax at least to large bequests.

The Treasury's determination must have impressed the President, whose attention was increasingly available as Congress passed one after another of the Administration's measures. In mid-July he was reported to be agreeable to deferring action, but a few weeks later he permitted Robert Jackson, then Assistant General Counsel of the Treasury, to speak for him as well as for Morgenthau in vigorous testimony before the Senate Finance Committee. Jackson on August 6 rehearsed the Treasury's case, gave priority to the need for revenue, but emphasized the importance of adjusting the tax structure so that it would bear most heavily on those best able to pay. He argued also for using taxes to break up large private fortunes and concentrations of corporate power, to redistribute wealth and equalize business competition. Repeating the recommendations for new taxes which Roosevelt's message had earlier made, Jackson provided the senators with a forceful reminder of the President's purpose. The testimony,

Morgenthau recalled years later, was exactly what he had hoped for.

The Revenue Act of 1935, which the Finance Committee drafted, was less satisfactory, but it was nevertheless a landmark in the history of American taxation. Though the committee in the end rejected the inheritance tax, it increased estate taxes markedly and raised individual surtax rates on incomes from 59 per cent at the top to 75 per cent. As the Treasury and the President had recommended, it imposed both a graduated corporate income tax and a tax on intercorporate dividends. The Act assured the Treasury of new revenue; less than Morgenthau had wanted but more than a less aggressive Secretary could have obtained. To his gratification, moreover, in spite of its limitations, the Act advanced the principles he and Roosevelt had advocated.

The Secretary had pursued his objectives steadily since reporting to the President in December 1934. Even if Roosevelt had joined the fight earlier, the conservatives in the Senate might not have yielded more than they did. As it was, the Treasury could measure its success by the dismay of most wealthy Americans. Roy Howard, for one, originally a supporter of Roosevelt, now wrote that businessmen were "frightened," convinced that the new law "aimed at revenge rather than revenue." This interpretation characterized the hostile thinking of those in high income brackets, whose opposition to the New Deal grew as the Treasury pressed for the adoption of significant parts of its program which the Revenue Act of 1935 omitted.

## 2. Corporate Earnings and Corporate Power

Politicians have a natural reluctance to levy new taxes in an election year. Roosevelt was no exception. Generally satisfied with existing schedules, he was also anxious to avoid another fight with Democrats on the Hill. In September 1935 and again in his annual message of January 1936, the President announced that he would request no new taxes. Three days later, however, on January 6, the Supreme Court ruled the Agricultural Adjustment Act unconstitutional, invalidated the processing tax and thereby deprived the government of $500 million of annual revenue. When, in the weeks that followed, Congress overrode the President's veto of the bonus, obligating the government to the expenditure of an additional $2 billion, neither the White House nor the Treasury was willing to tolerate the impending deficit. Election or no election, Roosevelt, like Morgenthau, considered new revenues essential.

Between January and March, Morgenthau and his assistants, often cooperating with representatives of other federal agencies, worked continually on a tax message for the President. At first Roosevelt, who doubted whether Congress would increase income taxes, advocated a general processing tax. Morgenthau objected to this proposal on several grounds. Manufacturers would pass on a processing tax by increasing prices, which would create hardships for those with low incomes. Indeed the Treasury thought federal and local consumption taxes already constituted too large a part of the total tax structure. Morgenthau was also worried because the Department of Justice believed the Supreme Court would probably find any new processing tax unconstitutional. Especially on that account, he preferred to increase taxes on personal incomes, estates and inheritances, particularly in the higher brackets.

Henry Wallace, fearing that Congress would abandon agricultural subsidies rather than pay for them by raising income taxes, favored using a processing tax even though he admitted it might be unconstitutional. As he put it to Morgenthau on January 26, the Administration would be morally culpable if it did not support such a tax.

"How much longer are we going to continue to do things that are held illegal?" Morgenthau asked.

"Better find out whether this country stands for Justice or legality," Wallace said.

"Well," replied Morgenthau, "you can have an agricultural program and be constitutional."

The Treasury also had to be political, to formulate a program that could win the enthusiasm of the President and the Congress. In this pass, Morgenthau, urged on by Oliphant, reverted to a proposal he had made in December 1934 for a tax on undistributed corporate earnings. Under the existing laws, directors of corporations who did not need larger personal incomes could leave their company's earnings in the corporation as surplus profits and thus save much of their personal income tax, especially surtaxes on high levels of income. In such cases small stockholders did not receive dividends on the full earnings of the securities they owned. A tax on a company's undistributed profits would increase the disposable income of small stockholders and penalize tax avoidance by the wealthy.

Morgenthau viewed the undistributed earnings tax primarily as a device to increase revenue by combating tax avoidance. The Treasury estimated that about $4.5 billion in corporate profits would not be distributed in 1936. If this sum were subject to an undistributed profits tax, or paid out in dividends to be taxed as personal income, the government might gain as much as $1.3 billion. Oliphant, who was for several years the foremost proponent of the tax, was more concerned with its possible bearing on recovery. Like Rex Tugwell and Marriner Eccles, he believed that the distribution of profits in dividends would increase consumer spending, which would stimulate the economy. He also thought he could write the tax so as to protect corporations which were reinvesting undistributed earnings in plant and equipment.

As they studied the tax, Oliphant and Morgenthau developed a special interest in its possibilities as an antitrust instrument — a device to force large corporations, no longer able to retain their earnings for capital expansion, to compete for new funds in the money market with their smaller competitors. Under the existing system, large corporations by retaining their surpluses could block innovation by their own subsidiaries and withhold profits from stockowners who might otherwise have invested in more venturesome enterprises. Thus the accumulation of surpluses perpetuated business oligarchy and tended to inhibit the whole investment process on which recovery depended.

On February 19 Roosevelt approved the concept of an undistributed earnings tax, for which the Treasury was to draft an appropriate message to Congress. During the ensuing discussions, both Magill and Viner, thoroughly conservative men, came to support the proposal. Magill endorsed the principles involved, though the tax was not his first choice for raising revenue. Viner disliked introducing the tax as an emergency measure, but he considered it desirable, particularly because it would give investors the right to determine what to do with their profits. Morgenthau, anticipating vigorous opposition from big business, was worried about getting the Treasury's case across to the general public. As Oliphant observed, however, there were precedents for the idea which Woodrow Wilson's Secretary of the Treasury, David Houston, had advanced in 1920, as had one of Secretary Mellon's advisers later, and a Joint Committee on Internal Revenue in 1928. Haas thought the strongest reply to any attack would be to show how rich men were avoiding the income tax. "If we have to fight," Oliphant added truculently, "we might as well fight the people who are our enemies anyway."

Influenced largely by Oliphant, the Treasury late in February made a major change in the draft for Roosevelt. It planned to substitute for all corporate taxes one undistributed earnings tax adjusted closely to ability to pay. This would eliminate the "double taxation" of business profits, first as corporation income and then, after it was paid out in dividends, as individual income. At the same time the undistributed earnings tax would provide increased revenue by practically forcing the distribution of profits to stockholders, thereby subjecting wealthy individuals who received those earnings to high surtaxes. Years later Morgenthau remarked: "I wonder what corporations today would give for such a system!"

The Treasury's completed draft provided the basis for the message Roosevelt delivered to Congress on March 3. Explaining that the AAA decision and the bonus forced the government to seek new revenue, the President recommended two temporary taxes and a graduated tax upon undistributed corporate income. The last, he said, would raise the $620 million of annual revenue which the Treasury permanently required. It would also "accomplish an important tax reform . . . and stop 'leaks' in the present surtaxes." It would equalize the tax load between profits of unincorporated and incorporated businesses. It would end the discrimination between corporate earnings that were distributed and those that were not.

The message delighted Morgenthau. Far more than he had expected, however, it excited an immediate opposition which mobilized powerful forces on the Hill. For weeks to come, the legislative struggle burdened the Secretary and his staff. As it began, Morgenthau was already under extraordinary strain. He was conducting important monetary negotiations with China, France, and England. The last stages of the bonus debate had depleted his emotional energy. In his fatigued state, he contracted a respiratory infection so severe that he had to take several weeks off. He and his wife were in Sea Island, Georgia, during much of the time in which the House of Representatives debated the tax bill, but in spite of his absence, which some journalists misinterpreted to mean a lack of sympathy with the President's proposals, the Secretary followed the course of the measure with a solicitous interest.

Oliphant carried the weight of the Treasury's case before the House Ways and Means Committee, played the pedagogue "rather brilliantly," according to reports Morgenthau received, and "did a splendid job, using just the right technique in almost every instance." The committee's bill incorporated the undistributed earnings tax, the Treasury's major objective, though it also retained in reduced form some other corporation taxes which the Department had suggested eliminating. Chairman Robert L. ("Muley") Doughton, who was convinced less by Oliphant's arguments than by his own deference to Administration policy, guided the bill through the House in just over a month.

In that period, opposition to the undistributed profits tax gained momentum. David Lawrence, one of many critical columnists, called it a tax on prudence; Arthur Krock considered it "reckless" and "bewildering"; Raymond Moley, now frankly aligned with the enemies of the New Deal, attacked the whole concept of "reform through taxation" which, he said, would strip industry of all surpluses, throw businessmen into "paroxysms of fright" and force the guiltless rich "into rags and tatters." The Republican minority of the House Ways and Means Committee agreed, asserted that the revenue bill had Communist approval, that it would lead to instability, regimentation, further waste of public money, and continuing depressions.

For the first time within their knowledge, the Republicans commented, a Secretary of the Treasury had failed to testify or to submit a statement in behalf of pending revenue legislation. This criticism raised the question of whether Morgenthau should appear before the Senate Finance Committee which began to consider the bill late in April. Cy Upham, the Secretary's administrative assistant, saw no advantage in putting his chief on the spot as a witness. Upham was a loyal but cautious counselor. He was experienced in banking and in the ways of Washington, personally skeptical about the undistributed earnings tax which he expected the Senate in any case to reject or modify, and chiefly concerned about revenue and about the Secretary's influence and prestige. He did not think Morgenthau should jeopardize his future bargaining power by seeming to decide between the two houses or by going out on a limb in favor of legislation which the Finance Committee staff considered impractical. The Secretary, whose health was still much below par, would like to have agreed with Upham, but Herbert Gaston and Oliphant thought that the Republican criticism made it urgent for him to testify, the Senate leaders insisted he should, and, most important of all, Roosevelt was anxious to have him speak.

Preparation of Morgenthau's statement revealed a disconcerting weakness in the House bill. The staff of the Ways and Means Committee, ignoring Oliphant's advice, had written schedules in a manner that prevented them from yielding their full revenue for a year. The Secretary delayed testifying until the committee could announce a correction in its estimates. These still seemed adequate, but privately Morgenthau began to worry about the capacity of the bill to produce the funds the Treasury needed. In his public appearance before Harrison's Finance Committee, he stressed the importance of new revenue which, he pointed out, the proposed taxes would yield in part in the fiscal year 1937 and in full in fiscal 1938. The undistributed earnings tax, he also said, would correct inequities in the tax system and remove an easy means of tax avoidance.

Harrison and most of his committee were obviously unconvinced. They intended, as Oliphant put it, "to mutilate our whole plan" by retaining the existing taxes on corporations and adding "a *mild* graduated tax on undistributed earnings." Morgenthau, too, on the day after he testified, began to retreat from wholesale endorsement of the House bill. He was afraid, he told his staff on May 1, that the undistributed earnings tax would handicap a man starting a new business. It might also prevent small and medium-sized corporations from building up adequate surpluses. "If there are answers," he said, "three cheers! But if there are none, let's be big enough to correct this thing. . . . The pride of authorship is not important if it is going to hurt small business."

Morgenthau was also more and more disturbed about revenue, for the Finance Committee and the parade of hostile witnesses it heard were unveiling loopholes in the measure. "You assumed the responsibility of the tax bill," the Secretary told Oliphant on May 5, "and I am willing to rely on your judgment that you have it in hand. I place my reputation in your hands. You have not abused it yet. However, as people call various things to my attention, I will bring them to you. We are gambling to the extent of $1,250,000,000 in revenue and you fellows must be triply sure that you are right. I leave it entirely to you and Haas."

Haas's staff had begun to crumble. The continuing requests of the Finance Committee for estimates of returns on a multitude of possible schedules put such pressure on Treasury statisticians that the top technician collapsed on May 5. Haste made the estimates loose, sometimes inaccurate, subject in any case to telling criticism. Morgenthau had no patience with the bombast and the laments of most witnesses before the Finance Committee, who obviously cared only about guarding their personal wealth, but he attached large significance to the testimony of George O. May of Price, Waterhouse, one of the leading accountants in New York, who on May 6 challenged the Treasury's figures.

Upham made much of that episode. May had impressed the committee, he reported, because he had said outright that Morgenthau had made a mistake. The senators were talking more and more about junking the House bill entirely and assuring increases in revenue simply by raising existing corporation taxes. According to corridor gossip only two people in Washington were for the bill, and "for the Treasury to stack Oliphant and Haas against George O. May and other business leaders is absurd." The technical staff of the Finance Committee was openly against the whole thing. "It cannot be that the whole world is wrong," Upham concluded. "Not all of us have ulterior motives to protect the rich. Isn't it possible that the people with social justice looming so big in their minds are prejudiced in their attitude? I have only two interests — to protect the Secretary and to protect the Treasury, and I am disturbed and dismayed."

So was Pat Harrison. On May 7, only a few hours after the committee concluded its hearings, he told Morgenthau categorically that approval of the House bill was out of the question. Harrison favored retaining the tax on corporate income and superimposing a small, flat tax on undistributed earnings. This solution, the senator maintained, would assure the collection of a substantial amount of revenue without violating the principles of Roosevelt's message. With only one exception, the committee and its staff were of the same view. Within the Treasury, Helvering was willing to consider a compromise, and even Haas admitted that Harrison's plan would produce the necessary revenue. Oliphant alone dissented.

On May 8 Morgenthau, without mentioning it to his staff, decided to invite George May and a few other experts to help the Treasury statisticians with their arithmetic. Roosevelt endorsed this idea. He was personally nervous, the President said, because Harrison had reported that the House bill would permit the American Telephone and Telegraph Company to pay no taxes, whereas under existing schedules the company would have to pay about $30 million.

Also on May 8 Senator Harry F. Byrd of Virginia, an anti-Administration Democrat, moved to put the Treasury on the spot. He wrote Morgenthau a letter, arranging for the newspapers to release it for publication on Monday, May 11, the same day the Secretary would receive it. The letter asked the Treasury to check the reports that the House's schedules favored wealthy corporations. As Byrd understood it, those schedules would exact no tax at all, or at best a very small tax, from a number of corporate giants, including, among others, Goodyear, General Electric, du Pont, International Harvester, A. T. and T., and R. J. Reynolds.

Though the Secretary resented Byrd's tone and tactic, he was asking himself precisely the questions that the senator raised. As he put it to his morning group on May 11, he had done a lot of thinking over the week end, and had practically concluded that the Treasury was "up against a stone wall" and needed some "alternative bill in our vest pocket." "I have come to the decision," he said, "that I cannot take the risk of giving up something that I have in hand, namely: $1,132,000,000 in revenue, for a possibility of getting roughly $1,700,000,000. It seems to me that there are too many dangers surrounding the possibilities. . . .

"I do not believe there is a living person who can guarantee that the Supreme Court will not tie up the tax bill immediately after it passes and we will be short all of our revenue. The thing is too great a risk for me to take. . . .

"You can ask me why I did not do all this two months ago. My answer is that I was sick away from the office for two months. I should have had this bright idea two months ago, but I did not. I have it now. I would rather be sorry now than be desperate a year from now."

Morgenthau also revealed that he had asked George May to help Haas on estimates for a bill incorporating Harrison's proposals. "Does anybody here want to urge me not to do what I would like to do at one o'clock," he concluded, "and that is, tell the President that I do not want to give up the revenue we have?"

Only Oliphant objected and that afternoon even he had become subdued. Harrison wanted him to defend the House bill before a private session of the Finance Committee. Oliphant refused. He would answer questions only about the legal side of the bill, he told Morgenthau. Haas would have to defend the estimates. Haas, who was tired and unsure of his figures, did not want to face the senators. Despite his doubts about the bill, Morgenthau was beside himself. Monetary negotiations were in full swing. He was in the midst of his controversies with the Department of State about the Canadian liquor cases and countervailing duties. Even without a crisis over revenue legislation, he had more to do than he could comfortably handle. Now his staff would not champion its own version of the undistributed earnings tax or even the House's modified schedules. Only Gaston, he felt, was standing by him one hundred per cent.

That evening the Secretary met with Harrison, Doughton, and Roosevelt. The President, influenced by Marriner Eccles, seemed to favor amending the House bill. "As to what happened over at the White House," Morgenthau told his staff, "I had a swell glass of orange juice. . . . Doughton kept saying, 'You can't let us down. We have gone through this thing and we wanted to change it and Oliphant and Helvering wouldn't let us. We are sick and tired of giving in to the Senate.' The President said, 'We are not trying to let you down. I want a bill which will force distribution of surplus earnings and get me the revenue.' Pat was sort of vague and . . . so when he went out I said, 'What are you going to do . . .?' and

Pat answered, 'Evidently the President is not ironclad on what he wants, but we do know that he wants a bill which will carry out his principles . . . and we are getting that, but he has . . . not definitely told us just how to do so.' I don't think that is so bad."

Later that evening Haas, who thought the President's vagueness left the Treasury "right out on a limb," threatened to resign rather than testify. When Morgenthau ordered him to join Oliphant before the Finance Committee, Haas consented, but almost wept. Oliphant was no happier. "When you were before the House Committee," the Secretary told him on May 12, "you assumed the responsibility. . . . You devoted yourself almost exclusively to this for two or three months. . . . It is up to you to go through with it."

A few hours later the Finance Committee subjected Oliphant and Haas to bitter interrogation. Byrd hammered away on the question of the taxes of the American Telephone and Telegraph Company. Couzens of Michigan disputed the contention that nondistribution of earnings cost the Treasury $620 million. Roosevelt had asked for that figure, Senator Bennett Clark of Missouri said, and "by some strange coincidence this particular tax has been stumbled on which . . . raises $620 million." "Stumbled on is right," Couzens added. Telephoning from the Hill where he was watching the performance, Upham told Morgenthau that Haas was not doing very well, but Oliphant was keeping his temper, "being forceful with a kind of strained note in his voice." On the whole, Upham reported, "it looks kind of bad for us."

That night Morgenthau once and for all gave up "the idea that we will get the bill as it passed the House." His consultants had confirmed May's findings that in that form it would result in a loss of revenue. The Secretary was now also convinced it would not give small corporations a fair chance. But he was not willing to abandon it entirely. As he put it on May 18, "We will have to reluctantly and gracefully recede." He would accept Harrison's general plan, but with important modifications. The senator, along with three other Democrats on the Finance Committee, now proposed raising the corporate income tax and adding a flat 7 per cent tax on undistributed profits. Roosevelt, however, insisted on a graduated tax on undistributed profits, as did Morgenthau and Oliphant who emphasized the importance of graduation for preventing tax dodging and for adjusting schedules to capacity to pay. All three, moreover, wanted, in so far as possible, to save the House's face.

Predisposed to resist Administration guidance, the Finance Committee seized the initiative and harassed the Treasury with requests for estimates on a plethora of possible tax schedules. The presentation and defense of these estimates was a harrowing job, for each senator tended to distrust the figures for any but his own suggestions. Haas was so weary and Oliphant so out of grace with the committee that Morgenthau called upon Larry Seltzer, a less experienced man, to represent the department. Fortunately Seltzer proved capable of mollifying senatorial sensitivities and of engaging the cooperation of the committee's self-consciously independent statisticians.

Only Morgenthau and Roosevelt, however, could evolve a strategy for compromise. On May 22 the President tentatively decided to take the issue to the people. He told Morgenthau to prepare a letter to Harrison "of not more than a page and a half or two pages" dwelling upon the importance of the principles which a graduated tax on undistributed earnings would advance. "Now, Henry," he said, "whatever you put in this letter it just can't be anything but right. . . . You just can't put anything in . . . unless you are sure."

The assignment was impossible. No short letter could be simple enough for the man on the street to understand, yet accurate enough to prevent experts from picking holes in it. Furthermore, Morgenthau feared that a public letter would infuriate Harrison and split the Democrats in the Senate, which would be embarrassing during an election year. He therefore on May 25 urged Roosevelt to forget the letter and talk with Harrison. The President instead gave Morgenthau that job, directing him to tell the senator that the Administration would conduct a fight on the floor unless the committee wrote a bill that forced the distribution of profits.

Morgenthau tried to see Harrison the next day, but the senator was ill. In any case Morgenthau thought the right man to consult was Majority Leader Joe Robinson, who was best qualified to "count noses" willing to support a minority report endorsing the Administration's program. Robinson, moreover, considered the Finance

Committee's bill a mess and was anxious to work out an alternative that would satisfy the President and the House Ways and Means Committee.

Somewhat reluctantly, Roosevelt on May 26 conferred with Robinson and the Finance Committee Democrats. The next morning the President was pleased with himself. "I do not think you realize the significance of last night's meeting," he said to Morgenthau.

"I'm afraid that I do not because I was very tired last night," Morgenthau replied.

"Well I had my nerve with me," Roosevelt said. "I tackled the lion in his own den. I went up against the majority members of the Finance Committee knowing that the majority were against me. I told them a thing or two, didn't I?"

Morgenthau thought not. "I gave him no encouragement," he reported to his staff, "and did not sit there at his feet and say what a great guy he was because I did not feel that he had done a good job . . . and I will be very much surprised if the Senate Finance Committee gives in to his wishes. The fact that I did not sit there in glowing admiration . . . put him in a bad humor and . . . he let me have it."

The Secretary's assessment of the conference was accurate. Roosevelt had not sufficiently defined his position to give his friends in the Senate anything to go on. Alben Barkley was prepared to do what he could, and Robinson would like to have bound the Democrats to Marriner Eccles's tax plan, but in the absence of instructions, they lost command of the situation. The Administration faced the possibility of a major legislative defeat from the conservative wing of its own party.

As May ended the only clear threat to Harrison's still unsatisfactory bill was a minority proposal which Senator Hugo Black advocated with the support of La Follette. Black's scheme, which was based on Eccles's suggestions, retained the corporate income tax, exempted from an additional undistributed earnings tax corporations with adjusted net incomes of $15,000 or less — about 90 per cent of all corporations — and established for other corporations a graduated rate up to 30 per cent, designed to produce $600 million in revenue. It had no chance of adoption, but as Barkley pointed out to Morgenthau on June 2, none of the Democratic leadership had been able to dissuade Black from proceeding. The President would have to intercede.

"I just got through talking with Senator Barkley," Morgenthau immediately told Roosevelt. "The situation is that he, Garner and Pat Harrison think that Black should not offer his resolution on the floor, because it will . . . get licked. Then the papers will say that this is your plan and you got licked. You have never told them just what details you wanted and that so-called Black–La Follette minority report is not close enough to the House bill to do any good. Their advice is that it is a mistake and the only person who can stop Black and La Follette is yourself."

"That is the same old buck passing," Roosevelt replied. "I think you ought to tell Barkley that I have not taken any position, and, therefore, I should not call it off. . . . It's their responsibility and not mine."

Morgenthau agreed. The President, he told Barkley, would not interfere, but he would veto the Finance Committee's bill. "Well, I'll tell you," Barkley replied. "We'll . . . take the thing up today and see how things go along."

Considering Roosevelt's lassitude, things went fairly well. Black withdrew his troublesome amendment just before the Senate voted. After three days of debate, the Senate, impatient to get away to the party conventions, approved Harrison's proposal 38–24. This vote, however, left the final decision with the conference committee where Doughton and his colleagues from the House sympathized with the Treasury. Swinging into action at last, Roosevelt overruled Garner and insisted on increasing the number of conferees from each chamber to eight, thereby assuring La Follette of a voice in the deliberations.

Barkley, the Administration's unofficial negotiator during the meetings of the conference committee, needed all the help he could get. The Senate conferees would not condone the steeply progressive undistributed earnings rates which Oliphant still recommended. The House conferees, claiming that they had acted according to the President's specifications, refused to budge from their own bill. "Your damned old tax bill," Barkley told Morgenthau on June 16 after a week of futile negotiation, was in trouble. The Democratic Senate conferees were going to submit a proposal preserving exist-

ing revenues and adding a tax on undistributed profits graduated
from 5 to 25 per cent. Their strategy was to keep the President out
of it until the last minute, but Barkley felt that if they got nowhere
that day, it would be important somehow to persuade the House to
work something out.

After the committee meeting that morning, Doughton called Morgenthau. The House conferees were pretty obstinate, he said, and
the Senate conferees would not accept the House bill or any bill that
did not carry a straight corporation tax. Obviously bending toward
the compromise plan, Doughton asked whether the Secretary believed in retaining the existing taxes. "I feel that at this stage that
we can't just throw all that overboard," Morgenthau replied.

Clearly pleased, Doughton maintained that this had been his conviction all the time. As their conversation ended, Morgenthau
turned to his staff and said confidently: "I have just settled the tax
bill."

The dénouement was rapid. On June 17 the conference committee sent the Treasury four proposals for estimates. After examining
the calculations, the committee reported out a bill that met the approval of both houses and struck Morgenthau as the best available
solution. The Revenue Act of 1936 retained the corporate income
tax, as the Senate conferees had demanded, thus insuring the revenue about which the Secretary would otherwise have worried. The
measure added a modest graduated tax on undistributed profits, as
the House conferees had insisted, thus in Morgenthau's opinion establishing the principle for which he and Oliphant had struggled
so long. This and other new schedules, the Treasury estimated,
would yield about $800 million of additional annual revenue.

The Act fell short of the ideal, but it included, Morgenthau believed, every concession the Treasury could wring from the Senate.
It protected the budget. As he saw it, it took another step toward
industrial democracy. It prevented one common form of tax dodging. The debate about the legislation, moreover, gave so much publicity to tax avoidance that the Treasury could confidently demand
the closing of other loopholes. Particularly in an election year, these
were large achievements.

Morgenthau remembered them as among the most difficult of his
career. "The undistributed profits tax," he recalled twenty years

later, "was sort of a revolution. The opposition from the conservative press and big business, and their influence in both parties on
the Hill, made a terrific impact. Nobody in the Treasury wanted to
testify. Everybody was frightened except Herbert Gaston who wrote
the statements I needed. I had to stand like a column of concrete
but I had the backing of F.D.R. He wanted to wipe out special
privilege. We both got real excitement and pleasure out of this
thing, out of laying a cornerstone for a new America. It was the
kind of thing that kept the United States from being another Rome."

### 3. In Defense of Party and Principle

New Deal revenue legislation was a prime Republican target during
the campaign of 1936. Alfred M. Landon, phrasing the sentiments
of the Liberty League in the language of the man in the street, called
the undistributed earnings tax "the most cock-eyed . . . tax . . .
ever imposed." The conservative *New York Times,* frankly dis-
pleased with Democratic policies, criticized the Revenue Act of 1936
and published a column by Arthur Krock asserting that "influential
people in business and finance" feared the trend toward radicalism
in the Treasury. By implication Krock recommended the appointment of Jesse Jones or Joseph P. Kennedy to succeed Morgenthau.

The Secretary, incensed, told Krock: "I consider this one of the
dirtiest pieces of writing . . . since I've been in Washington."
Krock said he knew Morgenthau had been "a very conservative influence" and the "best administrator the Treasury has ever had."
Why had he not said so, Morgenthau asked, instead of hitting below
the belt? Krock had no reply, but Arthur Sulzberger, the publisher
of the *Times* and an old friend of Morgenthau, explained rather ir-
relevantly that right-wing Democrats as well as Republicans disliked
the Administration's fiscal policy.

Morgenthau defended both the policy and those who had made
it. In August 1936 he fell in willingly with a scheme Roosevelt con-
trived to help Pat Harrison, who was involved in a tough primary
campaign against Theodore Bilbo, a vicious, uncouth, and impassioned opponent. The President's plan grew out of a Treasury suggestion that was nonpolitical. The Department wanted to cooper-

ate with the staff of the Joint Congressional Committee on Internal
Revenue in an investigation of problems of tax avoidance and tax
inequities. Roosevelt had Morgenthau prepare a letter on the subject, which he then made public after a conference at the White
House with Doughton and Harrison. The letter said that the Revenue Act of 1936 had strengthened the tax structure, that no new
taxes would be needed in 1937, but that the Treasury and the Joint
Committee would prepare recommendations both for removing
taxes unfair to consumers and for blocking escapes from taxes on
wealth. The identification of Harrison with a drive against tax
dodging was made to order for Mississippi politics, and the official
optimism about federal revenues countered Republican criticism
of New Deal spending and tax policies.

On October 23, with the campaign nearing its end, Morgenthau
made his major address. It was, of course, a political speech, but its
content, like that of the letter of August, was precisely what the Secretary believed. At the last minute, Roosevelt would not let him say
"that I am not going to use the printing press." Otherwise, however, the President approved the report, as Morgenthau called it,
"to . . . the stockholders of America, about the financial management of your great corporation, the United States government."

Citing statistics on the progress of recovery, the Secretary attributed it to New Deal monetary and fiscal policies. The American
people, he asserted, could not afford not to make a generous investment in their future, and they would be able to pay for it, as they
were already paying for it, out of the dividends of economic
growth. The Administration had used taxes based "upon the democratic principle of ability to pay. . . . We lowered the effective
rates of taxation on small individual incomes and on small corporation incomes, but we raised and made more fully effective the rates
of income tax on those best able to pay them. . . . Our increased
receipts already show the effect of business recovery and the great
improvement in our tax structure. . . . It took both courage and
statesmanship on the part of the President and of the Democratic
Congress to enact an important piece of revenue legislation less
than five months before a national election, but it constituted your
final assurance that the fiscal policies of this Administration are
and will continue to be sound."

Morgenthau's defense of the undistributed earnings tax could not languish after Democratic victory at the polls. Because that tax tended to return to stockholders the decision about how to spend or invest their money, it challenged the power of professional managers of large corporations. These managers, their lawyers, and accountants, in all an able, articulate, and influential group, were aggressive opponents of the tax.

There were, to be sure, a few exceptions. Thomas J. Watson, for one, the president of the International Business Machine Corporation, supported the Treasury's defeated plan for substituting a graduated undistributed profits tax for all other corporate taxes. Roosevelt and Morgenthau, though they welcomed this support, did not want to renew a futile political battle with the Senate, nor were they prepared to risk losing revenue. As Morgenthau wrote Watson, the Administration preferred to stand pat until the Treasury had at least had time to study returns under the 1936 law.

The great pressure for change came from those urging a reduction in the tax. George O. May expressed their opinion in a thoughtful speech that reached the President's desk. May argued for exempting from the tax all profits reinvested in new facilities. This, he reasoned, would lead to private spending instead of public spending as a spur to recovery. Citing John Maynard Keynes and the distinguished American economist John M. Clark, May said that savings should be used to increase capital plant rather than to pay for relief. Corporate reinvestment, he concluded, would proceed most efficiently if management controlled profits instead of having to distribute them.

In Washington perhaps the most ardent opponent of the undistributed earnings tax was Joseph B. Eastman, a member of the Interstate Commerce Commission since 1919 and from 1933 to 1936 the Federal Coordinator of Transportation. Without consulting either the Treasury or the National Emergency Council, which was supposed to coordinate Executive policy, Eastman attacked the tax in the annual report of the Interstate Commerce Commission of January 1937. The tax, he maintained, prevented the creation of sinking funds and hindered the refinancing of railway improvements.

Commenting on this report, and implicitly on some of George

May's argument, Morgenthau in a letter of January 12, 1937, pointed out that the Interstate Commerce Commission had misconstrued the Revenue Act of 1936. It specifically exempted from the undistributed earnings tax domestic corporations which were in bankruptcy, or were insolvent, or were in receivership. The ICC report failed to indicate that corporations, without paying an excessively increased tax, might accumulate reserves for improvement of property, for retiring funded debt, and for insurance against obsolescence. The report also ignored the substantial annual depreciation deductions for railroads, which were exempt from the normal corporate income tax. Finally, Morgenthau wrote, if the public interest required a federal subsidy for some of the weak railroads, he considered it wiser to grant it directly rather than in the guise of special tax favors.

Eastman was not convinced by the Secretary's letter, nor was he chastened by a scolding from Roosevelt for writing and publishing the annual report without conferring with interested Executive agencies. Interstate Commerce Commissioner Carroll Miller, however was less belligerent, and with his approval, Morgenthau directed the Treasury staff to work with the Commission on mutually acceptable recommendations for the consideration of Congress in 1938. Meanwhile the Secretary was determined, as was Miller, to keep differences of opinion within the Administration out of the press, and to prevent discussion of the undistributed earnings tax in Congress during 1937.

Indeed Morgenthau and Roosevelt, intent upon keeping their promise to ask for no new taxes, hoped to avoid any debate on the subject. Harrison, however, sensitive to the complaints of business managers, suggested amending the undistributed profits tax to provide more relief for debt-ridden corporations and to encourage companies desiring to expand plant. The senator wanted to provide a tax credit for those purposes and to grant a general exemption to all corporations for 10 or 20 per cent of undistributed earnings.

Morgenthau, speaking for himself and for Roosevelt, urged delay. Deficit financing, he told Harrison on February 15, had to stop if the government was to protect its credit. In order to eliminate the deficit, taxes would have to remain at their current levels. He preferred the risk of ruining a few people by unfair taxes, the Secretary said, to the chance of ruining the country by inviting inflation.

Harrison's advisers agreed that the provision of a full tax credit for payments on corporate debts would destroy the productivity of the undistributed earnings tax. Their estimates, like the Treasury's, also indicated that an exemption from taxation of ten per cent of undistributed earnings would result in the loss of about $167 million in revenue. These calculations persuaded Harrison to consent to waiting until after March 15, the day on which income taxes were due, before introducing any tax legislation. He could then take into account actual yields rather than estimates.

Temporarily this decision protected the undistributed earnings tax from its critics, but the possibility of preventing a full scale debate about taxes, perhaps of saving the undistributed earnings tax from repeal, depended largely upon Harrison's assessment of the yields. As it worked out, there was an unexpected truce, for the Treasury's estimates proved to be disturbingly high. Revenue fell so far below expectations that Harrison lost enthusiasm for tax reduction. He developed instead increasing sympathy for the Treasury's concern about tax loopholes.

## 4. Closing the Loopholes

Tax avoidance was an old problem that had assumed new dimensions. Probably no one ever enjoyed paying taxes, and very few deliberately paid more than they owed, but as Morgenthau put it in 1937, "tax ethics today are where business . . . ethics were in the 1890's." The Treasury could handle outright criminals like Pendergast and "Nucky" Johnson, who violated the law by falsifying their returns.* It was more difficult to deal with rich men who hired clever counsel specifically for the purpose of working out techniques for remaining within the law while avoiding taxes, for exploiting loopholes in federal revenue statutes and inventing tax-saving devices which neither Congress nor the Treasury had foreseen. Even in the 1920's the tax structure had become so complex,

* See pages 96–97.

tax questions so difficult, that adroit lawyers could often frustrate
the intention of Congress. As taxes rose during the New Deal,
wealthy taxpayers grew bolder in their maneuvering. One "economic royalist" bragged that he and his kind would continue to employ their art "as long as that bastard is in the White House."
Their success decreased revenues and threatened to demoralize
honest taxpayers who could not help but resent the ability of the
wealthy to escape their obligations.

Andrew Mellon, who personally took advantage of the law's
loopholes while he was Secretary of the Treasury, generously re-
funded or abated $3.5 billion to rich taxpayers and their corpora-
tions. Though rates during Mellon's time in office were low, he
suggested that the prevalence of tax avoidance proved the need to reduce taxes. Morgenthau, in contrast, considered the higher rates
of the 1930's eminently just, and the toleration of tax avoidance, a
crime against society. "Do not come in here with a belligerent attitude as though you were righteous," he said to the attorney of one
offender who had crossed the line of legality. "There isn't a day
passes where they don't hire some political lawyer or some shyster
who thinks he can get in the back door of the Treasury. And let me
tell you, there is no back door! . . . Who do you think the United
States Treasury is? The United States Treasury belongs to the people. . . . We are here to do our job fairly and honestly and see that
the people are protected."

In this spirit Morgenthau spurred the prosecution of criminal
charges of tax evasion which the government brought against Mellon in March 1934. The Treasury alleged that Mellon had submitted fraudulent returns and was deficient more than $3 million in
taxes and penalties. Mellon denied the charges, asserting in return that he was the victim of political persecution.

To plead the government's case before a federal grand jury in
Pittsburgh, Morgenthau recruited Robert Jackson, who reported
that the Republican press was accusing him of ruthless tactics.
"You can't be too tough in this trial to suit me," the Secretary said.

Jumping up, Jackson replied: "Thank God I have that kind of
boss."

"Wait a minute," Morgenthau went on. "I consider that Mr.

Mellon is not on trial but Democracy and the privileged rich and I want to see who will win."

In court Mellon won. The grand jury refused to indict him and the Board of Tax Appeals in 1937 ruled unanimously that he "did not file a false and fraudulent return with the purpose of evading taxes." The law, the Board observed, cloaked every man "with presumption of good faith in his business dealings." The Board also found errors in Mellon's return that made him deficient some $400,000 in taxes and interest. His attorneys and the Bureau of Internal Revenue, alike anxious to avoid further litigation, in 1938 settled out of court for slightly more than $480,000, a solution both sides interpreted as accepting the fairness of the Board's decision.

Mellon was exonerated, but as Commissioner Helvering put it, "the facts elicited and precedents set in the Mellon case have been of great importance." Indeed they constituted a kind of primer on the loopholes in the revenue laws. Mellon, while Secretary of the Treasury, had solicited from the Bureau of Internal Revenue "a memorandum setting forth the various ways by which an individual may legally avoid tax." Under oath he later admitted to using five of the ten devices the memorandum listed. These and other schemes sharply reduced his tax payments.

In Morgenthau's view, Mellon's methods revealed a serious discrepancy between legality and morality. Things that the courts approved outraged the Secretary's personal sense of justice. He could hardly contain himself as he reviewed the record. Mellon in 1931 had created a charitable trust and reported gifts to it of five paintings valued together at more than $3 million. He took a deduction for these gifts after the Treasury had disallowed certain losses he claimed on the sale of securities. Though he had not yet begun to build or to endow a gallery for the works of art which remained in his personal control, the Board of Tax Appeals found the charitable trust valid, and permitted him an income tax deduction of over $80,000.

Mellon, like most other rich men of the time, reduced his inheritance, estate, and gift taxes by passing on to his children during his lifetime the greater part of his fortune, though he retained the income from that fortune for himself. He made more dramatic savings by transfers and sales among his various personal holding companies — "incorporated pocketbooks," the Treasury called them. In 1931 and 1933, for example, he sold securities to the Ascalot Company, of which all the incorporators and directors were members of his family, claiming for income tax purposes a loss on these sales of over $500,000. At the same time the Ascalot Company sold him securities upon which it claimed a loss of almost $100,000. Payments on both sides were made simply by book entries; no cash changed hands. Oliphant could see no reason but tax avoidance for the transactions which, along with other, similar operations, the Board of Tax Appeals declared legal. Morgenthau respected the integrity of the Board, but he resented the laxness of the law.

The Secretary was both angry and alarmed because Mellon's techniques, multiplied many times by many men, slashed federal revenues. As Jackson pointed out, one of the most costly escapes was not even subtle. The rich alone could afford to invest in federal and local securities which carried low rates of interest but were entirely tax exempt. Even Mellon had called for repeal of the exemption, which Roosevelt specifically asked Congress to remove in 1936 and Morgenthau condemned annually. In 1937 tax leaks threw off the Treasury's estimates. Revenue, the President told Congress on April 20, was $600 million below predictions. Though the Republicans blamed New Deal bungling and inefficiency, Morgenthau and his associates were sure that the source of the trouble was wholesale tax avoidance. Roosevelt had planned to take the problem to Congress in November. On April 26, accelerating his schedule, he directed the Treasury to hurry its report.

The President, Morgenthau told his staff, "wants to say flatly that our estimates and our method of estimating were correct, but the citizens — that's the word he used — found a trick way of finding loopholes. And then he wants us to go into considerable detail as to what those loopholes are. . . . He wants to make a recommendation to Congress . . . that these loopholes be closed and that they be retroactive. And he said he does not want to wait until next fall and he wants particularly . . . to show the items which are held up by court action."

Delighted with this commission, Morgenthau put Magill, who had recently become Under Secretary, in charge of the preparation of materials for Roosevelt. A quick audit of individual returns in New York on incomes of $100,000 or more, of some smaller incomes, and of the deductions claimed by various corporations and personal holding companies, persuaded Magill that taxpayers had not invented any new devices for avoidance but were employing old methods more widely. The resulting threat to revenue receipts strengthened Morgenthau's preference for seeking remedial legislation at once, as Roosevelt has suggested, rather than waiting until autumn for the full report of the Joint Committee. Eager for action, the Secretary on May 17 took to the White House a memorandum by Magill on the general problem of tax avoidance and one by Oliphant on an especially flagrant case.

Without glancing at these papers, Roosevelt opened the luncheon conversation. "Henry," he said, throwing himself back in his chair, "it has come time to attack, and you have got more material than anybody else in Washington to lead the attack. Did you notice how downcast Jack Garner was at Cabinet? Well, when I saw Jack before Cabinet, rather than give him a chance to attack me, I attacked him. People like Garner, Senator Bailey, Walsh of Massachusetts, and numerous other conservative Democrats, knowingly or not, are getting prepared for a Conservative Democratic party. They won't go along with any reform measures, and they are only interested in balancing the budget. . . . Now, it's up to you to fight."

Roosevelt was so excited that Morgenthau could not help laughing. "Why are you laughing?" the President asked.

"Because you are such a wonderful showman," Morgenthau replied. "I don't know what's going to happen. I can't guess what I have got that is so useful to you."

"You and I have kept quiet while they have talked so about the Federal revenue being short five or six hundred million dollars," Roosevelt continued. "They have been unfair and lumped it altogether, not distinguishing between the money we lost through court action and the rest of the decrease in taxes. The time has come when we have to fight back, and the only way to fight back is to begin to name names of these very wealthy individuals who have found means of avoiding their taxes both at home and abroad. What do you think of it?"

Morgenthau was exceedingly happy, as he put it, to be able at that moment to produce Magill's memorandum which Roosevelt read with relish. It was just what he wanted, the President said, or it would be when he recast it with more "punch." "In the words of Theodore Roosevelt," he concluded, "my spear knows no brother. I want the Treasury to start working at once on the speech for me. I want to name names. I'm going on the air and tell this story."

Morgenthau was glad to see Roosevelt in a pugnacious mood, but as he told him, any recommendation to Congress had to be phrased so as to avoid a general debate until the Joint Committee could complete its studies. He also thought the President should be sure that Joe Robinson and others would stand by him if he opened up the issue of a new tax bill in May instead of in November. Roosevelt said he agreed one hundred per cent.

Before they could talk further, Oliphant, Magill, and Homer Cummings arrived to discuss the case on which Oliphant had written a memorandum. The Department of Justice did not want to prosecute, while the Treasury did not want to settle out of court. Taking center stage before his enlarged audience, Roosevelt read Magill's report aloud in a singsong voice, remarking at the end of each sentence that it lacked force. Morgenthau, sensing what was coming, kicked Oliphant on the shin every time the President went through his act. When he had finished, Roosevelt, smiling at Cummings, said he had in hand a better memorandum. He began then to read aloud Oliphant's report, which explained how one accomplished tax evader had persistently omitted declarations of dividends and profits, concealing his income by passing it through the hands of relations and employees, many of whom he had bribed. Halfway through the account, Roosevelt pounded his desk and asked the Attorney General why he did not prosecute the fellow. "Why don't you call him a son of a bitch," the President said, reading on with growing fervor. If he were pleading the case, he retorted when Cummings advocated a settlement, he would tell the court that the government refused to accept an offer in compromise because a moral issue was involved. He wanted the man behind bars. That would mean something to other tax violators.

"Through this whole thing," Morgenthau later wrote in his Diary, "Cummings was as white as a sheet and his eyes were as angry as

I have ever seen them. He sat there pleading for the plaintiff . . . and I hope that as long as I work for the Government that I never take a moral licking like the one Cummings took today." The tax-payer, who went to prison, took a licking, too.

Roosevelt's dudgeon, released though it was during his quarrel with Cummings, did not abate. On the evening of May 17 Morgen-thau returned to the White House to explain that his staff, particu-larly Magill, questioned the legality of making public the names of tax dodgers. The President, however, stood fast. Much impressed by his intensity, Morgenthau recaptured it the next day for his morning group: "The question is whether we are going to have a Fascist government in this country or a government of the people, whether rich men are going to be able to defy Government and re-fuse to bear their burdens. Are we going to make progress in liberal government or is it going to take a revolution finally to settle the question? The rich are getting richer in this country and the poor poorer. In France they met this problem by successive revolutions. If it had not been for the revolutions, a few men would own all France today.

"Such men as Garner, Robinson, Doughton and these men who are fighting the court plan are against the President on the real is-sues. There has got to be a fight and there has got to be a purge. . . . Let us give the President what he wants, without quibbling as to whether this or that is legal. The President is intelligent enough to decide what he can use."

Leaving the question of tactics to Roosevelt, Magill prepared a letter on tax avoidance that named names and an alternative doc-ument omitting them. The President liked the material, which Morgenthau delivered on May 21, but he asked for at least twenty-five additional names for possible inclusion in a radio address which he was considering as a supplement to a message to Congress about loopholes. He agreed, however, to delay decision about us-ing names until he had reviewed the data more carefully. Morgen-thau had concluded that the President should confine his remarks to methods of avoidance and use as his vehicle a letter to the Chair-man of the Joint Committee on Taxation. Specifying names, the Secretary thought, "would stir up class hatred unnecessarily." Any mention of them, as Magill pointed out, was bound to be discriminatory. One famous manufacturer who had incorporated his yacht might be the sole object of attack although at least twelve others followed the same practice. The depletion allowance, which saved millions of tax dollars, could not be associated with individual taxpayers. Even without names, Morgenthau believed, a letter to the Joint Committee would "have a terrific effect."

Magill's analysis of the ways around the revenue law was in itself commanding. One resident of Baltimore, for example, had established sixty-four trusts in favor of his wife and three children which saved him over $485,000 in taxes in one year. Two partners in a brokerage house in New York had forty trust funds as well as twenty-three personal holding companies that made possible innumerable transactions for the reduction of tax liabilities. Other wealthy taxpayers took their wives and children into partnership or registered stock in the names of employees and relatives subject to lower surtax rates. One man saved $50,000 in 1936 by taking four minor children into his firm.

Many taxpayers abused the privileges of pension trusts. Revenue acts for ten years had tried to encourage pension trusts for aged employees by allowing corporations special deductions for contributions to them. But clever lawyers had advised their clients to set up pension trusts and take deductions even though the only employees covered by the trusts were directors and other high officials. In one instance a corporation deducted $43,000 annually for a pension trust for the benefit of its two chief owners. One of them would retire at sixty-five with a pension of $1725 a month, the other with $1425 a month.

Another common method of avoidance was the incorporation of personal companies in foreign countries where taxes were low. One New Yorker, whose personal return showed no taxable income for 1936, owned with his two daughters a Canadian holding company which received dividends during the year in excess of $1,500,000 from American concerns. Even bolder was an American army officer who inherited the entire stock of a large business. Late in 1935 he became a Canadian citizen. Within six days he organized a corporation in the Bahamas, transferred his stock to it, and apparently planned to sell the stock through the new corporation in order to avoid the tax on capital gains. His gall unlimited, he then asked the Secretary of War whether he could continue to draw his pension from the United States Army.

Six Americans saved almost $550,000 between 1932 and 1936 by purportedly paying a large single premium for policies in a foreign insurance company in the Bahamas, immediately borrowing back most of that sum, and then claiming large tax deductions for interest on the loan, though in fact they paid no interest. However, once the Treasury found them out, they paid their back taxes.

Domestic personal holding companies became especially popular after Congress reduced their taxes for 1936. In that year one family saved $791,000 in surtaxes by manipulating its incorporated pocketbook; another man saved $322,000; still another saved more than $140,000. The creation of a number of personal holding companies by any one individual magnified the Treasury's task in administering the law. A celebrated newspaper publisher, with ninety-six companies, managed to make it almost impossible, and certainly extraordinarily expensive, for the Bureau of Internal Revenue to follow his transactions.

Many rich people incorporated their luxuries and hobbies in order to cut tax payments. One millionaire established a personal holding company which owned his yacht and $3 million in securities. It rented the yacht to him and used part of the income from the securities to pay depreciation costs, operating charges, and the wages of captain and crew. Similarly, seven Americans saved in aggregate $244,000 by incorporating their country houses. One woman carried this farce so far that she paid her husband a salary for managing her home.

The largest boons derived from deductions for percentage depletion in oil and mining. Since 1928 mining companies had been allowed from 5 to 27½ per cent of gross income as an allowance for depletion, even though they might have recovered the whole cost of their property. In such cases, the deductions were a gift from the United States which cost the government several million dollars a year. Other escapes lay in the community property laws of eight states and in the relative freedom from taxation which the Revenue Act of 1936 granted to nonresident aliens. Simplest of all methods of avoidance were the tax exempt bonds. Five wealthy men in 1937 each owned between $14 million and $32 million of those securities.

As Morgenthau saw it, the Treasury's evidence revealed a lamentable standard of tax morality which would shock the American people as soon as they were informed. Roosevelt, though he abandoned his idea of releasing names, wanted to present the case dramatically. So, too, did Senators La Follette and Black, who thought that the Treasury would conduct a much more successful public investigation than would the Joint Committee. The President agreed. "What's the name of this young fellow that's doing this investigation up in New York?" he asked Morgenthau on May 24.

"Do you mean Tom Dewey?" the Secretary replied.

"Yes," Roosevelt said. "How would he be?"

"He'd be magnificent," Morgenthau said, "but I doubt whether you could get him."

"Well," Roosevelt said, "that's the kind of fellow I want."

Dewey's name was in time to become easier for the President to remember, but the young district attorney never had a chance to go to work for the Treasury. As Magill pointed out, a departmental investigation would make the Joint Committee jealous and impede the Administration's program on the Hill. Accepting that judgment, Roosevelt set out privately to create a climate of indignation the Joint Committee could not ignore. He read aloud Magill's full report, naming names, to Jim Farley and Homer Cummings, deliberately risking or perhaps even inviting a leak to inquiring Washington columnists. That prospect bothered Herbert Gaston, but Oliphant, unperturbed, remarked: "The President knows what he's doing, doesn't he."

"No," Morgenthau replied. "I think he's feeling his way. . . . No, he doesn't know. . . . That's why I want to think about it. . . . I instinctively react to calling names — I don't know — I mean I'd like to see the evil cured, that's what I'd like to see — and the practices stopped."

Gaston suggested feeding the press a little about techniques of avoidance. This alone, he thought, would generate a demand for investigation. That was just what Roosevelt was doing, Morgenthau said, "and he's having a grand time doing it." The Secretary did not want to compete.

While moving obliquely, Roosevelt also worked directly. After consulting Senators Robinson and Black, he decided not to talk on the radio but to write a letter to Harrison and Doughton. He proposed first to reach an understanding with them for the appointment of a subcommittee to investigate tax avoidance, for which Robinson promised an appropriation of a quarter of a million dollars. Magill prepared the letter for the President, who tried to instill in Harrison and Doughton his own enthusiasm for the venture. It involved, he told them, ten million votes. They agreed to act immediately, to "expose," as Harrison later put it with unusual ardor, "the whole damn thing."

"Mr. President," Morgenthau asked, "how did you arrive at the ten million figure?"

"I don't know," Roosevelt said with a grin, "but it sounded good. . . . Everything's settled."

Essentially everything was, though Roosevelt adapted his tactics to suggestions of Democratic leaders on the Hill. On June 1 he sent a special message to Congress. He quoted a letter of May 29 from Morgenthau reporting that tax avoidance and evasion were "so widespread and so amazing both in their boldness and their ingenuity" that further action without delay seemed "imperative." The President was "indignant." The "clever little schemes" of men of wealth undermined the foundations of society and subverted the "decency of American morals." Congress, he was sure, would want to make the "present tax structure evasion-proof." As a first step, in accordance with the Administration's plan, Congress created the Joint Committee on Tax Evasion and Avoidance and empowered it to hold hearings, to subpoena witnesses, and to procure from the Treasury all the information it needed, including the names of offenders.

Roosevelt's message blew up a storm of self-righteousness. Disclosures of tax tricks, even though they were legal, were going to be unpleasant for the tricksters who attacked the President before the Joint Committee could embarrass them. Republican newspapers led the charge: Roosevelt had an "obsession against the rich"; his message was a "red herring" intended to hide the failures of the New Deal; the real evaders were not the rich but the poor, whose incomes were not subject to direct tax; the tax problem could be solved only by repeal of the unfair undistributed profits tax.

The wealthy themselves most fiercely denied the imputation of immorality. Returning from Europe, J. Pierpont Morgan said, according to several accounts: "I object strenuously to treating income tax evasion as a moral issue. . . . It is not up to us taxpayers to repair the mistakes of Congress. It is just as bad to pay too much as to pay too little." The public outcry at this candor impelled Morgan partially to retract. He had spoken, he explained, before reading Roosevelt's message or Morgenthau's letter. "I certainly have no sympathy with tax dodging . . ." he added, "and had no thought of defending such practices. What I strongly feel is that, when a tax-payer has complied with all the terms of the law, he should not be held up to obliquity for not having paid more than he owed."

This "exposition of Christianity" aroused the President's scorn. "Ask yourself," he wrote a New York lawyer, "what Christ would say about the American Bench and Bar were he to return today?" One of Roosevelt's cousins replied in a public letter condemning the New Deal and asserting the right of a taxpayer to claim every exemption the law allowed. The President's ire rose. His cousin, he said, was maintaining that because he did not agree with the laws passed by a properly elected Congress, he therefore had a right to evade taxes as long as he could get away with it. "That being your belief," Roosevelt concluded, "I do not hesitate to brand you as one of the worst anarchists in the U.S."

The rancor became more intense while the Joint Committee conducted hearings between June 17 and June 28. The committee did not employ special counsel, as Roosevelt had hoped it would, but the President assigned Thurman Arnold, a crack lawyer from the Department of Justice, to help the Treasury prepare evidence and testimony. "Everyone in tax trouble," Morgenthau told his staff, "is against Mr. Roosevelt." The investigation, he thought, was separating the sheep from the goats.

Though he was seething inwardly, the Secretary testified on the first day of the hearings with what the *New York Times* called his "characteristic reserve." There were 45,000 registered tax attorneys and accountants, he noted, the most resourceful brains in the legal world, earning large fees for finding loopholes in the revenue laws. The government had therefore continually to revise the laws before vested interests grew up in the devices of avoidance and achieved a kind of semirespectable standing. Tax ethics were thin. The popular mind confused tax avoidance, which it supposed to be proper, and tax evasion, which it supposed to be immoral. So long as a "sporting theory" of paying taxes prevailed, people would try to circumvent the law. By publicizing the general methods of avoidance, Morgenthau said, the committee would improve attitudes toward taxes while it gathered information for new legislation. In describing those methods, the Secretary put the problem in terms easy to understand. The rich man owning a racing stable called himself a horse breeder, he said, and in that character lost money which he charged off against his total income. No average taxpayer, however, thought of calling himself a golf instructor and deducting the expenses of his game because he had no pupils. The point was clear: the tax-dodgers were the well-to-do.

As the hearings continued, an "almost unbelievable tale" unfolded. Never had the wealthy looked worse to the American people. The committee's interrogation led the Treasury to name names. On June 24 Helvering listed sixty-seven "large, wealthy taxpayers who, by taking assets out of their personal boxes and transferring them to incorporated pocketbooks, have avoided paying their full share of taxes." Among those using this device, "perfectly legal" as the Treasury admitted, were Andrew W. Mellon, Thomas W. Lamont, John J. Raskob, Pierre S. du Pont, Alfred P. Sloan, Jacob Ruppert, Roy W. Howard, and William Randolph Hearst. Lamont was quoted as frowning upon paying taxes that could be avoided. Sloan, who, it developed, had also incorporated his yacht, explained that he and his wife had paid taxes on 60 per cent of their income, given half of the balance to charity, and incorporated the yacht to avoid unlimited personal liability. "No conscientious citizen," Sloan said, "desires to avoid payment of his just share of the country's burden. I do not seek to avoid mine. . . . While no one should desire to avoid payment of his share . . . neither should any one be expected to pay more than is lawfully required."

This statement, like those of Lamont and J. P. Morgan, went right to the heart of the matter. No one, not Roosevelt, not Morgenthau, not the Joint Committee, was accusing the men whose names were made public of breaking the law. On the contrary, the Administration wanted to change the law precisely because, as it stood, it enabled those men to reduce their taxes. They felt that the Administration was persecuting them because they were rich and because they were, with few exceptions, Republican. Roosevelt and Morgenthau, on the other hand, attacked as they did in order to protect federal revenues and to eliminate what they considered unethical tax behavior.

Inevitably they provoked counterattack. David Lawrence courteously identified Alfred Sloan's incorporated yacht with one of Eleanor Roosevelt's charities. With characteristic thoughtfulness, Republican Representative Hamilton Fish of New York on July 8 asked permission to present alleged evidence about tax avoidance by the Roosevelts and the Morgenthaus. The Secretary learned about Fish's maneuver over the ticker tape. At once he telephoned as many members of the committee as he could reach, announced his intention of sitting in the front row while Fish testified, and asked each member to keep the session going long enough for him to reply. Carrying audits of his tax returns, which his family bookkeeper had put in impeccable order, Morgenthau appeared in the committee room the next morning before any of the members or Fish had arrived. Fish, as the Secretary had expected, had been talking only for political effect. His accusations, such as they were, related to certain family trusts that Morgenthau's father had set up. There was nothing in the least questionable about them, or about Mrs. Roosevelt's gifts to the American Friends Service Committee, which Fish also disputed. Doughton, who presided over the session, would not even look over Morgenthau's personal returns. "Your word," he told the Secretary, "is good enough for me." Even the Republicans on the committee were annoyed by Fish's tactics. "If we had shut him off," Doughton said, ". . . he'd always claim . . . we suppressed him." As it was, Fish made himself look silly.

The episode did not obscure the real issue, the vulnerability of the tax structure. Moved by the evidence the Treasury produced, the committee reported out the Revenue Act of 1937, which both houses of Congress passed unanimously and Roosevelt signed on August 28. The new legislation taxed domestic personal holding companies at rates equivalent to the highest surtaxes on personal income. This curtailed their usefulness. The Act also limited deductions of expenses for incorporated yachts, country estates and the like. It made more difficult any artificial deductions for losses from sales or exchanges of property. It repealed a $1000 exemption allowed all trusts for the accumulation of income, thus reducing the incentives for creating multiple trusts to avoid taxes. It also radically altered the treatment of foreign personal holding companies and removed a differentiation favoring nonresident taxpayers. The Department of Justice had found a way to stop the use of foreign insurance companies for tax avoidance, but various loopholes, as the Treasury explained, remained unclosed. Congress did nothing about husband and wife or father and children partnerships, about pension trusts, about percentage depletion allowances, or about tax exempt securities, a matter which the Treasury had not chosen to raise at the hearings because no one had yet proposed a practicable and constitutional remedy. In spite of these deficiencies, the Act of 1937 saved the government between $50 and $100 million a year.

It was a significant victory for the majority of Americans who resented the habits of rich tax avoiders even though they were legal. Roosevelt and Morgenthau had consistently maintained that the wealthy should bear the increased costs of government. These costs, as Morgenthau so often said, were designed to assist those at the bottom of the economic ladder. He and the President took pride in the frankly redistributive impact of New Deal taxation. Now the government had shown that it would not brook the frustration of its purpose. Particularly because it underscored what he believed to be a major moral issue, the Revenue Act of 1937 pleased Morgenthau more than had any of its predecessors.

It contributed to the contentment he experienced in the summer of 1937. He had diverted the attack on the undistributed earnings tax and initiated the campaign against tax "chiselers." Fiscal policies were just about where he thought they should be. But even if he had not been prone to worry, as he was, the Secretary would have seen a growing shadow on the wall, for as the summer of 1937 wore on he felt more and more uneasy about the prevailing spirit of the Federal Reserve Board. He sensed a possible danger to the condition of cheap money he considered so important; he faced new problems in managing the growing debt; he began to suspect that the economic situation was not so "lovely" as he had let himself hope.

# VIII

# The Debt, the Banks,
# and the Price of Money

## 1934-1937

### 1. Managing the Federal Debt

BETWEEN 1932 and 1940, the eight years of depression preceding the beginning of the World War II defense program, the interest-bearing public debt of the United States government increased $28.7 billion. The astronomical deficits of the war and postwar periods were to make that figure seem trivial, but at the time both the Treasury and the investing public were sharply conscious of the extraordinary dimension of federal peacetime borrowing. Responsible as he was for marketing the government's securities, Morgenthau gave continuing personal attention to the manifold problems of debt management. These were more than simply technical, for debt management was a primary device of monetary policy.

Government bonds and notes held by the Federal Reserve System constituted reserves against which banks could issue currency and make loans. Any expansion of the Reserve System's portfolio therefore assisted Morgenthau's easy-money policy. He could not control that portfolio, but he could influence decisions about it. More important, he could direct the operations by which the Treasury endeavored to reduce the rate of interest on federal obligations. Under his management the rate of interest on those securities fell dramatically. In June 1932 the average yield on long-term United States government bonds was 3.76 per cent; in June 1940 it was 2.39 per cent. In September 1932 Hoover's Treas-

338

ury issued five-year notes at 3¼; in March 1940 similar notes went for ¾.

This decline in the price the Treasury had to pay to borrow money, Morgenthau believed, was a yardstick of the public's growing confidence in the government. With the decline, interest payments became a relatively lighter burden. A plentiful supply of credit also helped to silence congressional demands for the issuance of greenbacks. Most significantly, in Morgenthau's view, the drop in yields stimulated a generally low interest rate. The average rate on municipal bonds fell from 4.25 per cent to 2.6 per cent and the rate on high-grade corporate bonds from 4.25 per cent to 2.9 per cent. This made it cheaper for public authorities and private industries to borrow for construction and expansion, and that in turn spurred the economy.

Morgenthau delegated much of the responsibility for the details of debt management to Under Secretary T. Jefferson Coolidge, whom Governor Harrison of the New York Federal Reserve Bank had recommended for his competence in technical matters. In addition, both Coolidge and Morgenthau regularly consulted leading bankers in all cities with major bond markets. Perhaps most of all the Secretary leaned on the services of Randolph Burgess, who in the early 1930's was a vice president of the New York Federal Reserve Bank. Burgess attended many Treasury meetings about the marketing of public obligations and personally handled the transactions which it fell to the New York Bank to execute as the Treasury's agent. When the Department went into the market to support the price of bonds or notes, Burgess placed the necessary bids. He brought to that function both efficiency in carrying out Morgenthau's orders and a shrewd knowledge in advising the Secretary about the timing, the scope, and the price of purchases and sales.

Morgenthau guided policy and handled the most difficult marketing problems himself. The Fourth Liberty Loan bonds, scheduled to mature in 1938, yielding 4¼ per cent and involving more than $6 billion, were still outstanding when he entered office. His predecessor had issued an announcement of their redemption in October 1933, but the Treasury had not adequately prepared for the refunding, the largest of its kind ever undertaken, and the first call for the redemption was a failure. But Morgenthau's subsequent calls — four in all, which completed the refunding in October 1935 — more than realized the Department's expectations. The Treasury had to pay out less than a billion dollars in cash; the rest of the bonds were exchanged for new issues at interest rates ranging downward from 3¼ per cent to 1½ per cent. As a result the government every year saved $74 million in interest.

While directing other refundings, floating new issues, and improving the technical condition of the debt, the Secretary also strove to get a wider distribution of government securities. He wanted to reach men and women of average means, "to sell shares in America," as he put it. To that end he experimented in October 1934 with an issue of the Home Owners' Loan Corporation for which a group of dealers sought out new buyers. Although the bonds sold well, the Secretary was disappointed, for large investors bought most of them at an average unit sale of $20,000. "If the fellow has $20,000 let him go out in the open market and buy some," Morgenthau said. "No use going through all this rigmarole for that."

He was willing to go to considerable trouble, however, to accommodate people who wanted to save money regularly for investment in the government. At his instigation the Treasury developed a ten-year discount bond, the now familiar United States savings bond, which increased one third in value before maturity. A purchaser could buy this "baby bond" for $75 and ten years later collect $100. The bonds, issued in denominations of $25, $50, $100, $500 and $1000, were available only to individuals — banks, insurance companies, corporations, and investment trusts could not buy them, and no one could own more than $10,000 worth.

With the help of Jim Farley, Morgenthau arranged for the sale of the savings bonds through post offices. He started his campaign on March 1, 1935, with a newsreel of Roosevelt at the White House purchasing six baby bonds, one for himself and one for each of his five grandchildren. At first sales lagged, but they picked up gradually under the influence of the Treasury's promotional activities, to which the Secretary gave continual attention. By April 18, 1936, the Department had sold savings bonds with a maturity value of $400 million. In 1937 Morgenthau enlisted the advertising agency of Sloan and Bryan, and before the end of that year more than 1,200,000 Americans had bought approximately 4½ million bonds with a total maturity value of over $1 billion. By November of 1939 the maturity value had advanced to above $3 billion.

The first million buyers, the Treasury discovered, purchased the securities against their retirement, for emergency reserves, education, home building, estates, travel, and recreation. Skilled laborers owned the largest number of bonds, while clerks, housewives, salesmen, teachers, professional men, executives, students, and farmers followed in that order. The statistics framed a picture of national prudence and purpose and patriotism, virtues that Morgenthau esteemed. The program, moreover, achieved his objective of multiplying the number of Americans with a financial stake in their country. It also helped to create the habit of buying savings bonds, a habit on which the Treasury's vital wartime bond drives were to rely.

Other innovations had a more immediate impact. The Secretary and his staff on five different occasions in 1935 solicited competitive bids for bond issues and sold them at average prices of 100.8 to 103.1. They also standardized the timing of issues, avoiding emergency financings and instead floating securities on regular quarterly days in each year — the 15th of March, June, September, and December, which helped banks, insurance companies, and other purchasers to make their preparations.

Before each issue, Morgenthau and his associates thoroughly explored the temper of the market, holding dozens of conferences with officials of the Federal Reserve System, with other government agencies, and with bond dealers and large institutional investors. No two financings involved identical problems, but the general questions that arose had considerable similarity. The Treasury had to decide what proportion of an offering should be in notes — short-term securities — and what proportion in long-term bonds. It had to spread out maturities so that no uncomfortably large redemptions would fall in any future year or quarter. As bills and notes and bonds came due, it had to offer for conversion new securities attractive enough to encourage exchanges without giving brokers an unnecessary premium. Sometimes it was preferable to

convert for cash, but in that case, or when the Treasury had to borrow to cover deficits, the Secretary and his staff had to adjust rates
of interest to the variable tolerances of the market. If the rates
were too "thin," the securities would not "go." There had to be just
enough "gravy" to move them, but not so much that dealers could
make a quick profit by resale, for such profits in the end came out
of the pockets of taxpayers.

Diligent "homework," as Morgenthau so often called it, got results. He not only attained and preserved low interest rates but
also shifted the federal debt more and more to long-term issues.
The lengthening maturities relieved the pressure of redemptions
during depression, which in turn eased the borrowing of new
money to meet the costs of relief and the other expenses of reform
and recovery. The first bond Secretary Woodin issued, in August
1933, yielded 3¼ per cent for eight years. Morgenthau's first bond,
issued in April 1934, was a 3¼ for ten to twelve years. By 1936 he
was able to market 2¾ per cent bonds with maturities ranging from
fifteen to twenty-three years. By the end of 1938 maturities had advanced to twenty-seven years, the proportion of the total debt in
long-term bonds was growing, and the average yield was still dropping.

Morgenthau benefited, to be sure, from the decline in interest
rates that reflected the falling off of private industry's borrowings,
but his immediate predecessors had failed to exploit that condition. Unlike them, he fostered a public attitude conducive to the
successful management of the debt. In so doing, he demonstrated
that capacity for efficiency which was an indispensable adjunct to
reform.

Preserving the attitude of mind he created, however, depended
on more than homework. To manage the debt most advanta-
geously, to sustain easy money, the Secretary had either to over-
power the ordinarily uncooperative, sometimes antagonistic Federal Reserve System, or to win those controlling it to his point of
view.

## 2. Reforming the Federal Reserve

The Treasury's analysis of bond prices convinced Morgenthau soon after he entered office that the Federal Reserve Banks should increase their purchases of government securities in the open market. It was essential to prevent the market price of those securities from falling below par if the government was to be able to sell new issues. Furthermore, the market price of a bond bore a direct relationship to its yield and consequently to easy money conditions. If, for example, a bond carried a coupon of 3 per cent at par of 100, the actual yield of that bond would be considerably below 3 per cent if the market price rose to 105. Conversely, the yield would be considerably more than 3 per cent if the bond could be purchased on the open market for 95. Morgenthau had therefore to keep the market price for outstanding federal issues high, and their yields low, if he was to float new issues at gradually declining coupons, if he was to minimize the cost of servicing the debt and to gain his goal of easy money.

In this effort, the Secretary would have liked the cooperation of the Open Market Committee of the Federal Reserve System. He did not soon get it. As Roosevelt put it on October 9, 1933, "some members of the banking fraternity . . . do not want to make loans to industry. They are in a sullen frame of mind, hoping by remaining sullen to . . . force our hands." These bankers, Morgenthau later recalled, "had been the dictators of monetary policy. The large New York private banks and insurance companies dominated the Federal Reserve Board and the Open Market Committee. They were the giants in American finance and I was the first Secretary of the Treasury in this century who did not knuckle under to them."

Instead Morgenthau worked alone. During his first years in office the Open Market Committee held the Reserve System's portfolio of government bonds at a more or less constant level. It neither bought extensively when the market was falling nor sold extensively when it rose. The Secretary compensated for this inactivity by using the various trust funds in his charge, like the Postal

Savings Account and the Stabilization Fund.* As he saw it, however, the Treasury was entitled to the assistance it did not receive.
The Federal Reserve System, he believed, had public responsibilities it was not discharging. He attributed this failure to the bias of
the twelve members of the Open Market Committee, who were
elected by the boards of directors of the regional Federal Reserve
Banks and ordinarily protected the interests of the private bankers
who controlled those banks. Because he considered monetary
policy a public matter, and because that policy depended in large
part upon the control of the bond market, Morgenthau advocated
vesting the authority of the Open Market Committee in a recon-
stituted Federal Reserve Board free from the pressure of private
bankers.

The opportunity to work for that reform arose late in 1934 when
Roosevelt directed the Interdepartmental Loan Committee, of
which Morgenthau was chairman, to form a subcommittee to draft
banking legislation. At an early meeting of the subcommittee the
Secretary explained that his largest interest was in the reorganization of the Open Market Committee. He and the President, he
said, backed Marriner Eccles, the newly appointed Governor of the
Federal Reserve Board, in contending that the Board should have
both a veto over the appointments of the governors of the regional
Reserve Banks, and the authority to appoint and control the
Open Market Committee. Whatever else banking legislation might
involve, Morgenthau was going to insist on those changes.

There were a number of related issues. Some of these pertained
to the office of Comptroller of the Currency. That office had been
established in 1864 primarily for the purpose of issuing national
bank notes. It had also served other useful functions, but as Oliphant and Morgenthau had concluded, with the creation of the
Federal Reserve System in 1913 and of the Federal Deposit Insurance Corporation in 1933, most of the reasons for the existence of
the Comptroller had disappeared. His remaining functions could
easily be distributed among other agencies with resulting economies in operation and improvements in the coordination of Federal
regulation.

Morgenthau advocated the abolition of the Comptroller's Office

* See page 122.

partly because he had little use for the incumbent, J. F. T. ("Jefty") O'Connor. An affable California Democrat, O'Connor had been for five years a law partner of Senator McAdoo, who was primarily responsible for his appointment. He was also close to A. P. Giannini, the titan of West Coast banking, whom Morgenthau increasingly distrusted, and he had been a vigorous opponent of farmers' reform movements in the West.

O'Connor had done a good job in supervising those banks which the New Deal had reorganized in 1933, but he was a continuing nuisance to Morgenthau. He fought against the centralization of the legal functions of the Treasury Department of which the Comptroller's Office was one part. He also resisted the Secretary's efforts to provide a departmental clearinghouse for public statements under Herbert Gaston, whom O'Connor considered a "radical editor." He chafed, too, at the authority Morgenthau gave to McReynolds for supervision of departmental personnel, for McReynolds, a career man in government, had in O'Connor's mind the compelling disqualification of previous Republican affiliations.

Possibly O'Connor wanted Morgenthau's job. He preserved a careful intimacy with Bernard Baruch and Carter Glass, to whom he persistently berated Morgenthau and Marriner Eccles. He attempted to get to the President, too, through James Roosevelt, the President's oldest son, who became his frequent companion on weekend trips to New York.

While Morgenthau's subcommittee was considering banking legislation in 1934 and 1935, O'Connor fought to prevent any aggrandizement of the Federal Reserve System which might ultimately threaten him. Partly to frustrate Eccles, whom he intensely disliked, he opposed the changes in the Federal Reserve Board and Open Market Committee which Eccles and Morganthau advocated. He flouted the Secretary's instructions that the Interdepartmental Loan Committee should present a united front, and instead lobbied for his own objectives, which were those also of Senator Glass and his conservative subcommittee on banking. He therefore wanted to divorce legislation pertaining to his office, on which Glass smiled, from Eccles's proposed amendments to the Federal Reserve Act, to which Glass objected.

Finally, O'Connor was waging a private war with Leo Crowley, the head of the Federal Deposit Insurance Corporation. Crowley agreed with O'Connor in opposing Eccles's program and in wanting to split the banking legislation into separate bills, but in very little else. A Wisconsin Democrat and businessman, Crowley, who owed his appointment to Jim Farley, had few qualifications for his responsibilities in the Federal Deposit Insurance Corporation. In 1934 O'Connor initiated a number of telling attacks upon him, but he weathered the storm. During discussions of the banking legislation, Crowley was concerned almost exclusively with correcting deficiencies in the provisions made in 1933 for a permanent FDIC, and like O'Connor he pressed his own cause even at the risk of impeding the total program.

Crowley and O'Connor, resisting any diminution in their own power, had too many friends in Congress to be vulnerable to direct attack. Indeed it was evident by November 1934 that amendments to the Federal Reserve Act were possible only if they were part of a general statute that could command conservative support by easing the condition of bank membership in the Federal Deposit Insurance Corporation and by protecting the Office of the Comptroller from loss of authority. Roosevelt therefore suggested presenting only one bill with three or four titles. This was an obvious strategy, acceptable to Morgenthau and Eccles but anathema to Crowley and O'Connor, who endeavored with unabashed zeal to subvert it.

Morgenthau and Eccles, furthermore, had differences of their own, most significantly about the composition of the Open Market Committee. They agreed that the Secretary of the Treasury and the Comptroller of the Currency should no longer be *ex-officio* members of that committee, and after much debate, they also agreed that they would recommend a committee of three members of the Board and two representatives of the regional banks. But Eccles soon changed his mind. Testifying on March 10, 1935, he came out for making open market operations the responsibility of the Federal Reserve Board as a whole with an advisory committee of five regional governors. He defended this plan, which the House of Representatives had already adopted, on the ground that decisions about open market operations, reserve requirements, and discount rates — the three related facets of credit control — would be centralized in a single agency. Morgenthau, however, distrusted the Federal Reserve Board and therefore objected to Eccles's proposal.

Eccles's reversal, moreover, seemed to the Secretary to destroy any prospect of preserving a united front on the banking bill. With Crowley and O'Connor backbiting at every opportunity, with Eccles vacillating on the issue of prime importance for the Treasury, Morgenthau would like to have washed his hands of the whole matter. Only his mandate from Roosevelt was keeping him going when Carter Glass suggested he stop. "I am very fond of you," the senator said on March 15, "and I do not want you to get yourself into any unnecessary trouble. Don't defend this banking bill too hard. . . . I will tell you what the President told me at five o'clock on March 4. He said, 'I am only interested in two things, one to get the Federal Deposit Insurance Bill through and two to have a unified bank examination.' The President said 'I am not interested in anything else.' . . . Don't get yourself out on the end of a limb. . . . This is Eccles's bill and he doesn't know what he is talking about."

Glass had long considered unwarranted any changes in the Federal Reserve System except those he suggested himself. Proud of his role, which he vastly exaggerated, in the fashioning of the original Federal Reserve legislation of 1913, committed to preserving the degree of control over the banking system which private bankers then held, Glass had always fought proposals increasing public authority. Indeed the senator was bending every effort to prevent Eccles's confirmation as Governor of the Federal Reserve Board. Yet Morgenthau, for all his disturbance about Eccles's wobbling, believed as strongly as did Eccles that the Federal Reserve System had to be brought under public control. Glass's report therefore distressed the Secretary. As he put it in his Diary, he surmised that the President had retreated on the banking bill in exchange for the senator's private assurance of support for the $4.8 billion work relief bill.

On March 18 at the White House, Morgenthau repeated what Glass had told him. "All the color left the President's face and he said nothing for a few moments," the Secretary noted in his Diary; but in reply to Morgenthau's direct question, Roosevelt categorically denied making a deal with Glass. In January, he admitted, he had said he wanted to support only the Federal Deposit Insurance bill and unified bank examinations, but on March 4, he maintained, he had added that he was keeping his mind open about the Federal Reserve System until the picture developed further. Unconvinced, Morgenthau asked how he was to testify that week. Roosevelt told him to go up to the Hill and say that he knew nothing about banking but that he favored unified examination of banks, a permanent plan of deposit insurance, the placing of the Open Market Committee under the Federal Reserve Board in Washington, and government purchase of Federal Reserve stock.

The Secretary considered government ownership of the stock important only if there were no other way of reducing the influence of bankers. As he put it to Eccles on March 19, the Federal Reserve Board had consistently denied the Treasury cooperation and was therefore not fit to determine open market policy. He would prefer, as he had for some time, an Open Market Committee consisting of three board members and two regional governors. Alternatively, he said, the government could buy the stock of the Federal Reserve Banks and thus control their policies as well as the selection of the Open Market Committee.

The banking community opposed that alternative, but Morgenthau considered it more and more attractive as his disagreement with Eccles persisted. A change in the legislative calendar postponed the Secretary's testimony for several months, and in that time Eccles adopted as his own a recommendation of the American Bankers Association for an Open Market Committee of five board members and four governors. Still committed to a three-two ratio, the Secretary referred the issue to Roosevelt, but the President was either not ready or not willing to intercede. On May 15 Morgenthau decided to advocate government purchase of the stock. The Federal Reserve System, he told Eccles, was shot full of politics, and he wanted to make it over into a system run by independent, disinterested experts.

Two days later Morgenthau appeared before Senator Glass's subcommittee. During the previous year and a half, he said, the Open Market Committee had lacked courage, had stood pat rather than acting to the advantage of the country. The nation suffered because three different agencies, the Federal Reserve Board, the Open Market Committee, and the Treasury each had partial authority over the various methods of controlling credit. That authority should seat in a single agency, but not in the Treasury. He was therefore "in favor of the principles of Title II" of the banking bill, the section increasing the power of the Federal Reserve Board, and in favor also of government ownership of the stock of the Federal Reserve System.

"I think that the Government has got everything at stake in this," Morgenthau told Glass. "This gets right down to the whole question of credit. After all, as I understand it, the Government is the people. And we have got everything at stake. . . . I would like to see . . . that the Government owned this stock and would surround the trustees of it with every possible protection and precaution, that they should not be subjected not only to political pressure but to that of private business and banking interests as well, and that they should keep just as independent as possible, and serve the financial and business interests of the country with only one motive in mind, and that is to serve them well."

That afternoon at the President's press conference the newspapermen asked whether Roosevelt shared Morgenthau's opinion about the bank stock. Roosevelt replied off the record. During the fight between Andrew Jackson and the Second Bank of the United States, he said, one of Jackson's advisers had suggested the government obtain a majority instead of a minority interest in the Bank. Jackson had rejected the idea, but, Roosevelt went on to say, "that's a hundred years ago but it would have solved the banking situation at that time in a much more satisfactory way and probably would have prevented the era of wildcat banking during the next ten years that held sway over the country."

"Did you say the next ten years or the last ten years?" one reporter asked. Roosevelt joined in the general laughter.

Yet the President was not prepared to enter the lists for the banking bill. His neutrality helped Carter Glass's strategy of delay. Holding the measure in his subcommittee, Glass prolonged discussion while the first of July approached. On that day the temporary legislation for the Federal Deposit Insurance Corporation would expire, and unless Title I of the banking bill, which concerned that agency, had become law, many banks would have difficulty in meeting conditions for continued insurance of their deposits. In mid-June Leo Crowley began to demand the separation of Title I from Title II, precisely Glass's objective, for it would kill the latter section and defeat the Administration's proposals for changing the Federal Reserve System.

To avoid Glass's trap, the Treasury needed time and help from the Senate Banking and Currency Committee. An extension of existing regulations covering deposit insurance would provide the first; a compromise on the question of the Open Market Committee, the second. On both matters it was necessary for Morgenthau to reach agreement with Eccles.

The Secretary initially wanted to impel Congress to extend the regulations on deposit insurance by releasing a statement explaining the hardships which many banks would otherwise face. This statement, he argued, should carry his own signature and those of O'Connor, Crowley, and Eccles. O'Connor and Crowley, however, were reluctant to sign a statement that might delay or prevent the separation of the titles of the banking bill, and Eccles, supported by the Federal Reserve Board, maintained that the Federal Deposit Insurance Corporation alone had responsibility for the matter in hand. Though this opposition angered Morgenthau, he ultimately concluded that Eccles was correct. In the end the board of the FDIC had Crowley make a statement similar to the one Morgenthau had proposed, and the Secretary directed Cy Upham to join Crowley on the Hill, where on June 27 they put in an arduous day getting both houses of Congress to pass a resolution temporarily extending existing qualifications for deposit insurance. This eased the pressure which Glass had expected would force separate action on the titles of the banking bill.

Meanwhile Morgenthau had decided to mollify the bankers and their friends in the Senate in order to assure support for Title II, pertaining to the Federal Reserve System. Accordingly he dropped his demand for government purchase of Federal Reserve stock and modified his position on the Open Market Committee. Tom Smith, the St. Louis banker whom the Secretary so often consulted, advised him that the American Bankers Association and consequently those dragging their heels in the Senate would agree to an Open Market Committee composed of six members of the Federal Reserve Board and five regional governors. Eccles, however, hesitated. Though he had no objection to the ratio, he argued at a meeting of June 13 that it would not satisfy Glass. Roosevelt could take care of that, Morgenthau replied, so long as the entire group considering the matter "absolutely stick together . . . and all sing the same song."

The President, however, whom Morgenthau telephoned, refused to bargain with Glass, rejected the idea of a six–five Open Market Committee, and suggested instead a six–four ratio. Now Tom Smith objected. Having five governors rather than four, he said, would permit a better geographical representation of the regional banks. Eccles recalled that Roosevelt had earlier agreed in writing to an eight–five committee, a solution which would assure dispersed representation but also a considerable majority within the committee of members of the Federal Reserve Board. Smith was willing to consider an eight–five committee, and Roosevelt, whom Morgenthau immediately called again, approved that ratio.

So, too, at least as a basis for discussion, did James Byrnes of South Carolina and Duncan Fletcher of Florida, Chairman of the Senate Banking and Currency Committee, the parent body of Glass's subcommittee. Impatient with Glass's delay, they promised Morgenthau on June 14 to push the banking bill along. The importance of setting permanent regulations for deposit insurance gave them useful leverage, as did the fatigue of their colleagues, who were anxious to adjourn what had been an exceptionally trying session. Late in June the Senate passed the committee's bill.

On many counts it struck Eccles as pretty bad. He objected, he told Morgenthau on July 2, to a provision requiring the Federal Reserve Board to report to Congress about open-market operations. This would tend to open those operations to political influences. He particularly disliked the lack of uniformity in the different kinds of credit control functions. In the case of rediscount rates,* four members of the board of seven could initiate action; in

---

* The rates of interest which regional Federal Reserve Banks charged their member banks. These rates, of course, determined the rates which private banks charged their customers.

the case of changes in reserve requirements,* it took a vote of five; and finally, in the case of open-market operations, action was by the entire board plus five governors. Eccles also considered it unfortunate to limit members of the board to one term and to require four of them to be from one political party and three from another. So much was wrong, he believed, that he had to try to get the conference committee to improve the legislation.

Morgenthau, however, decided to abstain from interference in the bill's final stages, though he agreed with Eccles that the Senate bill was less satisfactory than the one the House had earlier approved. The Treasury, the Secretary noted in his Diary, had been carrying "the whole load of national finances, . . . without any help or interference from the Federal Reserve Board." Now the pace and the disorder of federal spending forebode trouble. If and when it came, Morgenthau wrote, "I do not want to be the sole goat and have to take the brunt of all the criticism and dissatisfaction. . . . Therefore I have been hoping and have not mentioned it to a soul that the Federal Reserve Board would be given additional powers and created more or less as a monetary authority so that they and the Treasury can share the responsibility and possibly help us in case we get into a financial jam.

"The way the Federal Reserve Board is set up now they can suggest but have very little power to enforce their will on the banks of the country. Our power has been the Stabilization Fund plus the many other funds that I have at my disposal and this power has kept the open-market committee in line and afraid of me. I prophesy that if the present bill goes into effect with the seven members of the Federal Reserve Board and the five governors of the Federal Reserve Banks forming an open market committee, that one group will be fighting the other and that consequently they will not be able to do anything constructive, and that therefore if the financial situation should go sour the chances are that the public will blame them rather than the Treasury."

The Secretary therefore left the conference committee alone, but Eccles, with some help from Roosevelt and much from Representative Thomas A. Goldsborough, succeeded in influencing the

---

* The ratio of legally acceptable bank assets to bank loans; the higher the requirements, the less banks could lend on the same assets.

committee to bring the Banking Act of 1935 closer to his own model. The new law, effective February 1, 1936, provided for a Federal Reserve Board of seven members, changed the name of the board to the Board of Governors of the Federal Reserve System, changed the name of the Governor to Chairman, and canceled the *ex officio* membership of the Secretary of the Treasury and the Comptroller of the Currency. As Morgenthau and Eccles had recommended, the law made appointments of presidents and vice presidents of the Federal Reserve Banks subject to the approval of the Board of Governors. Effective March 1, 1936, the Act established a new Open Market Committee composed of the Board of Governors and five representatives of the twelve Reserve Banks. No Reserve Bank could engage or decline to engage in open-market operations except in accordance with the regulations of the committee. The Act of 1935 also changed the rules for reserve requirements. Under the old law the Federal Reserve Board could increase or decrease reserve balances which member banks were required to maintain only in an emergency declared by an affirmative vote of five members of the board and approved by the President of the United States. Now four members of the board could change requirements in order to prevent an injurious expansion or contraction of credit. Changes were limited, however, on the lower extreme to requirements in effect on August 23, 1935, and on the upper extreme to twice the requirements effective on that date.

By and large Morgenthau was pleased with the Act. He would have liked it to merge the functions and offices of the Comptroller of the Currency and the Federal Deposit Insurance Corporation, and to unify authority for bank examinations, but he recognized the political impossibility of those objectives. As it was, the law had enhanced the authority of the Board of Governors and the Open Market Committee, bringing under increased public control the decisions which Morgenthau believed private bankers had no right to make.

Only the future could tell what private influence remained. Furthermore, although the Board of Governors was a public agency, appointed by the President with the approval of the Senate, although it now dominated the Open Market Committee, it remained to be seen whether the board and the Treasury, public agencies both, would pull together or pull apart. For the months immediately ahead, that was to depend largely upon the degree to which Eccles could influence his board and the extent to which he and Morgenthau could agree about internal monetary policy.

### 3. Easy Money: Round One

In October 1935, Morgenthau returned from a brief holiday in Europe to find many bankers and officials of the Federal Reserve worried about the possibility of unmanageable inflation. The inflow of gold from abroad had swelled the reserves of the banking system. Existing requirements called upon the banks to have approximately $2600 million in reserves, but they now had $2900 million more than that. These reserves provided the basis for a potentially enormous expansion of currency and credit. While such large excess reserves were available to banks, furthermore, the Federal Reserve could not control short term money rates.

The governors of the Federal Reserve Banks on October 23 agreed unanimously that the System should promptly take steps to absorb some of the excess reserves. It could do so by selling government securities it held, for such sales would decrease the reserves of banks as they or their depositors exchanged cash for bonds. The governors believed, however, that selling securities would shock the bond market. The public, moreover, might construe such sales as a major reversal of credit policy. An increase in legal reserve requirements therefore seemed preferable, though it was a new and untried method of controlling credit.

Morgenthau and his advisers were by no means convinced that there was need for any immediate action. There had been as yet no troubling inflation of credit or prices. Indeed the price level had yet to go as high as they thought it should. Disinclined therefore to tighten money conditions, they also feared that increasing reserve requirements would damage the bond market. Checking his own views, the Secretary on October 28 consulted Jacob Viner, Parker Gilbert of the House of Morgan, and Walter Stewart, "a bond expert and a brilliant fellow less theoretical than Viner." Their opinions confirmed his doubts. Excess reserves, as Viner put it, would melt away as recovery progressed and industry borrowed more money for new plant. The economy, as Stewart added, still needed stimulation, not contraction. Gilbert agreed. The governors of the Reserve Banks, he suggested, simply mirrored the selfish attitudes of commercial bankers who favored revising reserve requirements because that would tend to increase interest rates and therefore their profits. The burden of proof, Morgenthau concluded, lay on those who advocated constraint.

Perhaps foremost of that company was Winthrop Aldrich, president of the Chase National Bank, who in December 1935 gave the first of a series of speeches about the alleged dangers in excess reserves. He spoke the mind of the financial community which at that time and throughout 1936 was curiously terrified of inflation. Though the stock market was enjoying a minor boom, there were still nine million or more unemployed. That alone should have quieted the bankers' fears, but it did not, and their constant expression generated a kind of panic to which Marriner Eccles and the Federal Reserve Board gradually succumbed. In January 1936, Eccles said he would be satisfied if the Reserve System calculated the figure beyond which excess reserves would not be permitted to rise. This would be easier, he reasoned, than to knock them down from $4 billion. By April, however, he sided with the Open Market Committee, now reconstituted according to the provisions of the Banking Act of 1935, which favored raising reserve requirements. The committee had no definite plan, but it urged action before July 1, largely because it believed nothing could be done after that date. The bankers were too discreet to say so, but they clearly felt that it would be difficult, if not impossible, to tighten money rates during the election campaign.

Morgenthau, though he was still dubious, was willing to accept the committee's judgment but not its timetable. An increase in reserve requirements would decrease the money available for the purchase of government bonds and thus complicate the financing the Treasury had scheduled for June 15. The bankers advised moving the financing forward to May, but the Secretary, as he told Roosevelt on April 20, wanted to hold to his regular quarterly date. "Furthermore," he said, "if we could stick to this policy, which I very strongly think we should, the announcement of the financing will fall on Monday, June 1, which will be most likely the last week that Congress is in session and I am going to rely on you to tell Congress that they cannot pass a lot of cockeyed half-baked financial legislation during that week."

Roosevelt was of a similar opinion. The bankers, he said, wanted Morgenthau to advance the financing to May because they wanted to keep the Treasury from conducting a successful operation in June just before the Republican convention. The President predicted that the "main cry" of that convention would be "look at the financing, everything's wrong with the government." This argument would hold no water if the Treasury had just scored a great triumph.

Though the financing might have political value, Roosevelt was prepared to make it more difficult by permitting a tightening of money before June. He intended, he said, to show the people that the New Deal was as alive to money problems as were the bankers. He had therefore asked Eccles to raise reserve requirements in May if he was going to do it at all. That would demonstrate that the New Deal had begun to use its powers to prevent inflation and excessive speculation.

Eccles, after consulting Morgenthau, decided on April 21 to act either before May 15 or after July 1, early enough to let the market settle before the financing or well after the financing had been completed. Frankly worried about inflation, he said six days later that only a balanced budget could prevent it — a point of view Morgenthau had often advanced himself. At the same time Eccles made up his mind to do nothing about reserves until July 1. Morgenthau then turned to his June financing which was, as the *American Banker* put it, a masterly job. To Roosevelt's pleasure, it provided cash enough to carry the government through October at least.

After the end of April Eccles did not again mention reserve requirements to the Treasury. Morgenthau was therefore taken by surprise on July 15 when he picked up the morning paper and read that the Board of Governors had increased requirements 50 per cent. Furious that Eccles had not warned him about the action which so suddenly placed a strain on the bond market, he had a blistering conversation with him on the telephone for half an hour. Eccles's excuse was that Morgenthau was out of town. He thought he had cleared the matter with the Secretary the previous April, and in any case he had obtained Roosevelt's approval a week earlier. On that occasion the President had said the increase would be okay with the Treasury. But Morgenthau felt that Eccles's explanation did not ring true. When he put down the telephone, he wrote in his Diary: "I certainly put the fear of God into him and doubt if he will pull off another fast one. I can't make Eccles out unless he wants to be important and show his independence."

Though the Secretary realized that the time was as good as any for a change in reserve requirements, he could not condone Eccles's failure to alert the Treasury. Eccles had asked George Harrison to help to peg the bond market, but Treasury support was also essential. As soon as Morgenthau knew what was going on, he arranged to join Harrison in any purchases that had to be made.

By and large the market held up, but they had to intercede to keep a $150 million note issue of the Commodity Credit Corporation from flopping completely. Months later, when Eccles remarked that he had made adequate plans to protect the market in July, Randolph Burgess of the New York Federal Reserve Bank commented that only the Treasury's willingness to act had prevented serious difficulty. Morgenthau took that occasion to remind Eccles that the Treasury had borne the brunt of supporting the market ever since 1933. That entitled him, he maintained, to full information about Federal Reserve plans. Eccles promised in the future to try to supply it.

In October 1936, Morgenthau and Eccles held a succession of meetings to iron out their difficulties. Federal Reserve officials explained their need to know about the Treasury's foreign exchange transactions which so continually affected American gold holdings and therefore the whole credit base. Eccles was particularly disturbed because the New York Federal Reserve Bank seemed to learn more about the Treasury's activities than did the Board of Governors in Washington. Morgenthau, always cautious about disclosing the details of the doings of the Stabilization Fund, was willing to give weekly information about the net results of its operations. This completely satisfied Eccles, who was also reassured by the Treasury's explanation that the New York Federal Reserve Bank served only as the Department's agent, not as its partner.

The Secretary had a request of his own. He hoped the Federal Reserve would "pretty soon," perhaps shortly after the middle of December, buy or sell $50 million of government securities. He considered it important for the System to alter its portfolio of government bonds which had been constant since 1933. Someday, he observed, the Board might have to engage in open market operations, and he thought the public should become accustomed to them while there was no emergency.

After checking with his colleagues on the executive committee of the Open Market Committee, Eccles on October 27 offered to begin at once to purchase about $120 million of government securities. Burgess, he proposed, could act for both the committee and the Treasury, which was then buying heavily in order to keep its most recent bonds at 101. Morgenthau anticipated only one difficulty. Although Burgess did a splendid job, he said, he was inclined to be a little conservative, and in any event the Treasury had to make its own decisions. The Secretary therefore suggested that the Treasury buy in the open market and give the committee each day the option of taking half the purchases. Eccles accepted this solution, promised to take it up with his committee at once, and in reply to a direct question, assured Morgenthau that the Federal Reserve had in his opinion a very legitimate interest in maintaining the bond market. That afternoon he reported that his committee had found the Secretary's proposal one hundred per cent satisfactory. "Well," said Morgenthau, "now that's fine, Marriner, now we're partners."

The related problems of excess reserves and the price of government bonds were soon to test the partnership.

### 4. Hot Money

During 1936, Europeans, sensing the possibility of war, liquidated investments in their own countries, bought dollars, and then invested in American stocks and bonds. As this occurred, the gold equivalent of their purchases of dollars entered the United States. Upon acquiring it, the Treasury deposited gold certificates for its full value in the Federal Reserve System. That swelled the volume of reserves, which worried the President. His concern, as he told the Treasury in November, was twofold: first, about the expansionary effect that $7 billion of foreign funds — "hot money," he called it — might have on the domestic economy, and second, about the deflationary effect that would follow a sudden, large withdrawal of those funds. He ordered the Department and the Board of Governors to study the problem which called into question the validity of their devices for controlling the money market.

It would have been convenient to cut off "hot money" at its source by imposing a prohibitive tax on speculative investments by foreigners. This, however, proved to be impractical. Roosevelt did not want to shut out bona fide investment, which it was often impossible to distinguish from speculation, and the Department of State objected to any tax that might provoke foreign governments to retaliate against the United States. Unable therefore to keep gold from flowing in, the Administration had to concentrate on neutralizing its effect.

Eccles, who shared Roosevelt's worries, on November 17, 1936, proposed reducing the Reserve System's holding of government bonds. He had in mind, he told Morgenthau, selling $300 or $400 million, the amount by which excess reserves had advanced as a result of gold inflow since the increase in reserve requirements the previous July. Morgenthau was agreeable, but on November 19 the Open Market Committee objected. It preferred instead again to raise reserve requirements, which its members considered a better central banking technique. Accepting this judgment, Eccles now suggested another 50 per cent increase in requirements, enough to compensate for the growth of reserves during the last six months.

Morgenthau and his staff balked. The continual change of reserve requirements seemed to them to be shotgun variety of monetary control. The Treasury, moreover, had the responsibility for international monetary policy and, in its Stabilization Fund, a potentially effective instrument for moderating the impact of foreign gold movements upon the domestic economy. The question was how to proceed. Morgenthau found "the germ" of an answer in an article by Robert B. Warren, an economist with the bond house of Case, Pomeroy and an expert on British monetary practices. Warren had first presented his paper to a meeting of the American Statistical Association, and then published it in the November 13 issue of the *Annalist*. He advocated divorcing the management of the domestic monetary system from the settlement of international balances. The latter function, he suggested, could be performed by a special fund established exclusively to hold gold which it would take in or pay out in response to international trade and exchange movements.

Morgenthau, impressed by this idea, referred it on November 23 to his monetary advisers, who during the next two weeks developed it for the Treasury's use. Their plan to "sterilize" gold achieved the objective Warren had recommended and eased the problem of excess reserves. The plan was quite simple. As the Stabilization Fund accumulated gold by converting foreign exchange to bullion, the Treasury would buy the gold from the Fund with dollars but it would not deposit gold certificates with the Federal Reserve Banks. Instead, it would for an indefinite period segregate the gold in a special account in the General Fund. In this way incoming gold would be prevented from entering bank reserves and expanding the credit base. If and when gold moved out of the country, it could move out of the accumulation in the special account in the Treasury's General Fund, again without affecting bank reserves or credit levels. The Secretary could pay for the gold he segregated, or "sterilized," by marketing ninety-day bills or longer term securities. Section 8 of the Gold Reserve Act of 1934 gave him ample authority for the necessary transactions.

"I am tremendously enthusiastic over this," Morgenthau told Eccles on December 8. "It is a great weight off my shoulders." But now Eccles balked. The sterilization plan, he protested, would increase the federal debt. It would also usurp his prerogatives, for the Board of Governors, rather than the Treasury, should at certain times decide to absorb or to segregate gold. Morgenthau replied that the Treasury and the Federal Reserve could settle that question at their weekly meetings. What bothered him, the Secretary said, was that gold was "our boss," and he wanted to become "the boss of gold." Apparently assuaged, Eccles admitted that the board could not continually increase reserve requirements without driving member banks right out of the Federal Reserve System, and he was therefore delighted with the prospect of controlling reserves in some other way.

> After weeks of the most exhaustive study [Morgenthau cabled Roosevelt the next day], I have come to the conclusion that for the sake of our domestic economy it is very important that future acquisition of all gold be sterilized. We feel that the following is the most practical and satisfactory device and can be carried out under existing laws.
> 1. The Stabilization Fund would buy all imported gold.
> 2. To pay for this gold it would use funds obtained from the General Fund of the Treasury in exchange for its gold transferred to the Treasury.
> 3. The Treasury would obtain such funds by increasing the amount of Treasury bills sold to the market.
> This plan would immediately remove the pressure on excess reserves from gold flowing into the country and more important if and when gold should flow out of the country it would not act as a deflationary device.
> I have submitted the plan to Eccles and Goldenweiser* and they personally heartily approve. Eccles is submitting the plan formally to his Board for their approval.
> I recommend this plan to you for your immediate approval for many reasons. If you think well of it I would appreciate your sending me your okey.

In view of the importance of the matter Roosevelt felt unable to make any decision until he returned. In the interim Eccles changed his mind. The Treasury's proposal, he wrote in a long memorandum of December 10, though highly desirable, was untimely. The stock market was less buoyant than it had been right after the election, and reserves were likely to decline substantially before the end of the Christmas holidays. He also wondered whether the new policy should not await renewal of the Stabilization Fund by Congress. He suggested, too, that sterilization should

---

* The chief economist for the Federal Reserve Board.

not begin before the Board of Governors had exhausted the possibilities of checking reserves by raising requirements still higher,
since Congress would otherwise probably ask why the government
should pay interest for offsetting gold imports when the board could
still absorb reserves by devices which cost nothing. He further recommended using the problem of excess reserves and their relation
to gold inflow as a lever for getting legislation granting the Federal Reserve Banks new powers for controlling the internal credit
level. Concluding his memorandum, he warned that he would
endorse the Treasury plan only on two conditions. First, sterilization should be automatic, not discretionary, unless the Board of
Governors requested a change in policy. Otherwise Federal Reserve authorities would have no way of controlling a situation for
which they bore responsibility. Second, the Treasury must sell bills
up to the full amount of additions to the existing gold stock and
buy bills to offset all decreases.

Eccles's pre-emptory manner bothered Morgenthau. "I certainly think that . . . is a very impertinent statement," he told
his morning group. "I don't know whether I should let him leave
this statement with me. . . . If it stays, it becomes a part of the
Treasury records." When Eccles presented the memorandum, the
Secretary reported, he kept saying that if they ever came to a point
where the Treasury and Federal Reserve could not agree, he would
resign — a threat which Morgenthau considered ridiculous.

The Secretary's irritation rose when without warning Eccles on
December 11 canceled the arrangement whereby the Federal Reserve had been helping to support bond prices by absorbing half
of the Treasury's purchases on the open market. Doubtless Eccles
felt justified in making this decision on the ground that further acquisitions of securities intensified the problem of excess reserves,
but he may also have been trying to squeeze Morgenthau. Eccles
was admittedly jealous of his own authority. The problem of gold
and of sterilizing gold, he told one of the Secretary's assistants,
was properly a central banking function, and the Federal Reserve
"should either ask Congress to deal with it, by God . . . or the
whole duty and responsibility should be transferred to the Treasury."

"I was trying to do something to help Eccles," Morgenthau declared to his Diary on December 14. ". . . He is trading with me and I am not going to trade. I will go before the Board and tell them that what they have put up to me is impertinent. They can't show a single thing that they have done these last couple of years, except talk." The Secretary agreed with Oliphant's phrasing of the problem: "I think there is one more issue to be settled. . . . That is whether the Government through the Treasury should control . . . monetary policy . . . or whether the control should be exercised through the Federal Reserve Banks who are privately owned and dominated by individuals who are banker minded."

Sensing Morgenthau's mind, Eccles on December 15 handed him a conciliatory letter. "I don't suppose it is necessary for me to say so," he wrote, "but I want to assure you that I am in no way influenced by questions of prerogative. . . . What I feel is important above all else . . . is to make sure that everything is done to preserve the spirit of complete cooperation which has been brought about between the Treasury and the Federal Reserve Board. I have no anxieties on that score so long as you and I are here, but I am thinking ahead to the time when one or both of us may not be here, and if some of the questions involved in this important and complicated matter are left up in the air, with uncertainty as to obligations under the law and how far and for how long either the System or the Treasury is to deal with this problem, there is real danger, it seems to me, of confusion and impairment of the one thing which both of us wish to see preserved. . . . Now, Henry, if I have in any way incurred your displeasure it would certainly cause me the deepest regret. . . . I want you to know that whatever your decision may be in this matter, you will continue to have my wholehearted cooperation."

Simultaneously Eccles presented another letter saying in effect that the Board of Governors thought it unnecessary and undesirable to begin sterilizing gold. But if sterilization began against its advice, the board repeated Eccles's view that the policy should be continuous and automatic.

After reading these communications, Morgenthau stiffened. He did not like to be told "you can rape me if you want to, but I won't like it." He, too, hoped to preserve cooperation and agreement. Yet he felt there was something influencing the opinion of the Federal Reserve which Eccles was not talking about. It was not a question, the Secretary held, of whose responsibility it was or of which agency should act. It was a matter of the national interest.

Pacing the floor rapidly, Morgenthau addressed his staff and Eccles vigorously, manifesting a growing impatience with the refusal of the Federal Reserve to accept the Treasury's proposal at face value. The Secretary felt he was being backed into a corner and told that he should not interfere with domestic credit conditions. While he had not approached the problem with any intention of interfering, now that he found himself in a corner he was beginning to change his mind. Like some of his staff, he thought that a good deal of the agitation for increasing reserve requirements simply reflected a desire to tighten money rates in order to raise bank earnings.

Eccles argued back, defending points his memoranda had made, but in the end apparently satisfied with Morgenthau's motives. He would return to his board, Eccles finally suggested, and explain that the Treasury had only one purpose — not to exercise control over excess reserves as such, but to build up a fund which would insulate reserves from the effect of future inflows and outflows of gold, and thus give the Board of Governors real control over domestic credit. This statement of what had been his position from the beginning eased Morgenthau's temper, and Eccles in turn seemed willing to make an effort to bring his board around.

Two days later, however, the question was still unresolved, and Eccles and Morgenthau arranged to call on Roosevelt together in the afternoon. That morning the Secretary saw the President alone. Roosevelt had clearly thought a good deal about sterilizing gold. He gave Morgenthau to understand that he, too, believed Eccles was fighting for personal publicity, for more authority for the central bank, and for minimizing the influence of the Treasury in monetary policy. Roosevelt was ready to go ahead at once with sterilization, but Morgenthau thought he should wait until he had talked with Eccles that afternoon.

As Roosevelt asked questions at the afternoon conference, Eccles replied almost exactly as Morgenthau would have himself. He attributed the influx of gold largely to conditions abroad, especially the threat of war. He said he wanted soon to discuss the whole credit situation and steps that might be taken to control existing inflationary tendencies. The President asked what would happen to gold in case of war, to which Eccles replied that the governments involved would sequester the American securities owned by their nationals, sell them on the American market, and take home the gold thus obtained. If gold were sterilized now, he continued, it would be available for export later. There were mechanisms available to the Board of Governors which would accomplish the same purposes as sterilization, but Eccles preferred the Treasury's proposal. Most importantly, he said, the board should not yet use up its brakes. The Treasury, he concluded, intended to cooperate with the Federal Reserve; sterilization policy would be flexible enough to be stopped at any time, and the procedure could be reversed whenever there was an outflow of funds. After a little more discussion, Roosevelt authorized Morgenthau to prepare for his signature the orders necessary to begin the program.

The Secretary returned to the Treasury breathless. Eccles, he told his staff, amazed him: "In my whole experience I have never seen anything like it, and the thing that frightens me . . . is that a man can so completely reverse himself. It scares me to death; and I'm absolutely serious. Every single argument that we have pounded into that man for the last two weeks he used, and the only reason was that he felt that it was his job to think of every reason why he shouldn't and then, having exhausted that, he then took the arguments that we used." Morgenthau was none the less pleased with the outcome. Ebulliently he thanked his staff "for what you have done, for helping me. . . . I consider this one of the historic moments in the monetary history of this country."

The Treasury had still finally to establish techniques for sterilizing gold and to draft an announcement of the policy. The former issue had taken on new complexity because the Department, with Eccles's enthusiastic approval, had decided to apply the program to acquisitions not only of foreign gold but also of newly mined domestic bullion, which would otherwise have continued to expand bank reserves. The foreign transactions fell naturally to the Stabilization Fund but it had no authority to deal in domestic gold, and rather than divide those functions, Morgenthau placed all the responsibility with the General Fund, which had thereto-fore been largely a bookkeeping agency. As he then prepared to announce the program, he realized that he was unwilling to say in so many words that the accumulation of excess reserves was a bad thing. Leaving that question to Eccles, he released a brief and general statement to his press conference of December 21.

"The Secretary of the Treasury," it read, "after conferring with the Board of Governors of the Federal Reserve System, announces that he proposes, whenever it is deemed advisable in the public interest to do so, to take appropriate action with respect to net additional acquisitions or releases of gold by the Treasury Department.

"This will be accomplished by the sale of additional public debt obligations, the proceeds of which will be used for the purchase of gold, and by the purchase or redemption of outstanding obligations in the case of movements in the reverse direction."

In response to questions, Morgenthau said he would sell ninety-day bills every week to defray the cost of sterilization, trying to make the amount of the operation as uniform as possible. He refused to explain the mechanics of sterilization or to answer questions about whether the new policy gave the Stabilization Fund a status identical with the British Equalization Fund. The policy, he said, would be continuous until the Federal Reserve Board and the Treasury together agreed to abandon it. He remained on a twenty-four-hour basis.

Eccles, who attended the press conference, answered a number of other questions. Sterilization, he said, would reduce the problems of the Board of Governors, leaving them with complete freedom to adjust the amount of excess reserves that then existed. It would not solve the problem of capital flow but it would neutralize its effects.

"We got an awfully good press," Morgenthau rejoiced. The *Wall Street Journal,* the New York *Herald Tribune,* the *Journal of Commerce,* and the *New York Times* carried full and favorable stories. On December 23 sterilization began. Immediately the Treasury's daily reports indicated the volume of gold in the inactive account. The "hot money" problems that had concerned Roosevelt and Morgenthau were under control, but the future of easy money was about to trouble the Secretary much more.

## 5. Easy Money: Round Two

In November 1936, as the bond market reached a new high, long-term 2⅞'s commanded 104¹⁹⁄₃₂, but in December governments began to decline, and the descent was to continue for months. The Treasury's analysts attributed the softness to a feeling among investors that interest rates were about to rise, that credit would harden. Bondholders were worried, the analysts believed, by statements of bankers and Federal Reserve officials, including Eccles, warning against the possibility of runaway inflation. They feared also that another increase in reserve requirements was imminent and that in any case credit would become tighter as recovery progressed.

The condition of the bond market and the temper of investors forced the Treasury in January 1937 to review the decisions of the previous year and a half. Morgenthau, still committed to easy money, had not expected the sterilization program to be deflationary, for while it would keep excess reserves from growing, it would not affect the existing quantity of reserves which seemed ample for a considerable, and in his view desirable, expansion of bank lending. To the Board of Governors, however, the dimension of available reserves still seemed dangerous. Like Winthrop Aldrich and other eminent bankers, the members of the board wanted again to increase reserve requirements, thus again reducing the lending potentialities of banks, for banks, of course, could lend only against idle reserves or reserves in excess of requirements. The Board of Governors thought that there would be ample available reserves even if requirements rose another 33⅓ per cent. The Treasury was not so sure. The previous increase in requirements, Morgenthau's advisers concluded, had fallen hardest on banks in New York City which provided the principal market for Treasury bills. As those banks had less money to lend or invest, they sought higher returns, and the Treasury had to pay more interest on its bills, its securities for obtaining short-term money.

Long-term money was also becoming more expensive, as falling bond prices indicated. The demand for higher interest would not only put a strain on the Treasury's financings, but also, as it grew, retard recovery by increasing the cost of industrial borrowing for expansion. The situation disturbed the Secretary particularly because the Federal Reserve, while urging a further increase in requirements, showed no inclination to ease credit, if it became necessary, by buying bonds on the open market. Such purchases would help to sustain bond prices and also to encourage bank lending, for banks would receive cash for bonds which they or their depositors sold to the Reserve System. Yet an enlargement of its bond portfolio — an important instrument of control which could compensate for higher reserve requirements — remained anathema to the Open Market Committee. These were for Morgenthau familiar problems. As he repeatedly said, he had been living with them since 1933. None of the theory had changed. But he and his staff rehearsed it as conditions early in 1937, especially the weakness in bond prices, reminded them that the anomalous attitude of private bankers threatened easy money.

Alert to that threat Morgenthau's staff on January 27 criticized the 33⅓ per cent increase in reserve requirements which the Board of Governors was planning. It would leave less than $600 million of excess reserves, an amount which under the law would permit a further expansion of member bank deposits of only $3.5 billion. The level of business activity, however, was substantially below what was needed to bring unemployment within manageable limits, and for an improvement, low interest rates remained important, if not essential. Consequently the Secretary and his advisers preferred at least to limit the increase in requirements to 16⅔ per cent.

Eccles, his chief economist, and all the regional Reserve Banks, in contrast, thought it essential to slow down the rate of industrial advance in order to avoid soaring prices. As Eccles put it, the economy was in a position of transition that called for an effort at stabilization, a balanced budget, and a tightening of money rates. An increase of 33⅓ per cent, he argued, would still leave more excess reserves than the System had in predepression years. He therefore favored going the full distance, and Morgenthau, shrugging off his own doubts, quietly gave his approval. On January 21 the Board of Governors announced the increase, effective half on March 1, half on May 1.

March came in like a lion. In an effort to keep the bond market orderly, the Treasury spent $75 million during the three days ending the 12th. That night Morgenthau, contending that the increase in reserve requirements had hurt the market, told Eccles he thought the Federal Reserve should at once start to help by buying governments. After a long conversation, Eccles agreed, but the Secretary predicted that George Harrison and Randolph Burgess would oppose open market purchases. They did, and on the morning of the 13th there was a tremendous battle within the executive committee of the Open Market Committee.

While it raged, Morgenthau pondered. As Larry Seltzer, one of his economists, pointed out, the Treasury's sterilization of gold and public discussion of hot money had contributed to the climate of opinion that provoked the slump in bond prices. Seltzer believed the Federal Reserve should assist in easing the market, but he also proposed a policy the Treasury could mount alone — the desterilization of $300 million of gold. The suggestion attracted the Secretary who entered his response in his Diary: "The smart thing for me to do is to place the entire responsibility on the Federal Reserve Board and insist that they act to take care of this situation through open market operations. . . . I am going to keep repeating that if they do not act, I . . . will take enough of our sterilized gold, convert it into gold certificates and retire with this money an equal amount of government bonds from the market."

At a luncheon conference immediately thereafter, Eccles reported that the executive committee was willing to assume responsibility for the government bond market, but on its own terms. It would not commit itself to buying bonds; it would not define a level at which it would sustain bond prices. He personally opposed restrictive credit policies as long as there were any unemployed, but he considered interest rates still unprecedentedly low. It was not the bond market but the unbalanced budget and the rise in industrial wages and prices that disturbed him.

Frankly dissatisfied with this report, which gave the Treasury no assurance of the help it wanted, Morgenthau also considered

Eccles's analysis of current economic conditions simply a calculated diversion, designed to gloss over the unfortunate decision to raise reserve requirements. The Secretary was especially irritated because Eccles on March 16 made his views public in a statement about which he consulted neither the President nor the Treasury. On that day, too, the Open Market Committee, while authorizing the expenditure of $250 million for government bonds, left the decision to the executive committee, where Harrison and Burgess would block action.

On the 16th and 17th, during heavy trading, bond prices declined sharply. Seltzer thought the time to desterilize had come, but others within the Treasury differed, and Morgenthau found Roosevelt cautious. The President approved of the Treasury's bond purchases but left further support to the Open Market Committee. It stood pat, prices continued to fall, and the Department on March 22 just about exhausted the cash available for buying bonds in the key Postal Savings Account.

Though the market then steadied for a few days, the Secretary and his advisers were increasingly uneasy. The Research Division reported that the drop in bond prices and the sharp rise in all classes of interest rates were potentially devastating for recovery. The increase in the cost to the Treasury for its borrowings was the least significant consideration. Climbing rates of interest had already caused the indefinite suspension of a number of scheduled corporate financings and would probably cause further curtailments. They had particularly hurt railroad refunding plans but also damaged the public utilities and various major industrial groups, including steel. Furthermore, although capital goods were enjoying a pronounced revival, their level of activity was still far short of that required for full employment. Therefore low, long-term interest rates remained desirable. Yet the break in the price of bonds had been a blow to the confidence of underwriters and investors. Underwriters found their shelves full of sticky issues which they could liquidate only at a sacrifice and these losses would probably lead to an increase in underwriting charges. Substantial declines in the market prices of recently-issued, high-grade bonds made investors reluctant to take up new issues until larger coupons were available.

"Never once," the Secretary told his staff on March 19, "in any statement that Eccles has made in the last two weeks, has he mentioned . . . reserves. He's talked about everything which is my responsibility but has failed to talk about what is his responsibility. And . . . I say that the increase in the . . . requirements has thrown this bond market out, and I believe that Eccles didn't know what happened to it. . . . I think honestly that Eccles honestly wants cheap money, but I think the boy was taken for a ride. . . . I've given my life in the last three years to build up this bond market so the United States Government's credit is the highest of any in the world. Now, why should I be satisfied and sit here and keep my mouth shut?"

The Secretary's staff unanimously advised him not to make a statement, or even to leak his views to the press, but Morgenthau left for luncheon at the White House without revealing his plans. Upon returning he called his group together again. "The President is not particularly worried about the prices of bonds," he said. ". . . If anybody tells this, I'll shoot him. He said, 'Now, you take myself.' He says, 'My bonds paid off. I got $5000 in the bank. I'm not going to buy your bonds. . . . I'm going to wait until I get a better interest rate. . . . There's millions like me.'" Roosevelt had predicted that the Treasury would have to raise its rate to 2¾ or 3 per cent. "He's priceless," Morgenthau commented. He was also of a mind so similar to that of the New York bankers that the Secretary could not publicly say they had taken Eccles in.

Morgenthau made that remark privately to Eccles, however, who was nevertheless "very friendly," indeed quite apologetic about the bond market. The Federal Reserve, Eccles suggested, could facilitate the Treasury's next financings in any of three ways. It might exempt country banks from the increase in reserve requirements schedules for May 1; it might commence open-market operations; it might ask the Department to release some sterilized gold. Morgenthau appreciated the spirit behind these proposals which he and his staff assessed on April 1. They concluded that a combination of policies involving joint action by the Treasury and the Federal Reserve would serve best. The public should be made to understand, they also suggested, that the purpose of any joint action was to ease the money market, not to peg the price of

government bonds. What was needed, Morgenthau then told
Eccles, was a "big, broad stroke" — nothing "piddling" would do.
He therefore wanted to announce that the Treasury was putting
$500 million of sterilized gold into the System and that the Federal
Reserve was about to begin open-market operations. Eccles was
also "very much in favor of showing an aggressive position."

Yet the next day, April 2, discussions about phraseology for an
appropriate announcement once more disclosed significant disagreement. A sentence proposed by the Federal Reserve read: "Developments wholly unjustified by underlying financial and economic conditions have recently manifested themselves in the
markets and are adversely affecting the orderly progress of economic
recovery." Morgenthau categorically refused to let this statement
stand, for he blamed the increase in reserve requirements for the
break in the market. The sentence was neutralized by the deletion
of the words suggesting that "developments" were "wholly unjustified." The Secretary and his staff objected even more to Federal
Reserve language stating that open-market activities would begin
"if necessary." As Morgenthau put it to Eccles during a long evening of argument, open-market operations had to begin at once or
the Treasury would go ahead on its own. Eccles finally agreed
and went so far as to promise that he would personally endorse the
Treasury's statement even if the Open Market Committee ducked
out.

The next morning it did. At noon Eccles reported to Morgenthau that the committee was opposed either to cooperating with
the Treasury or to letting it go it alone. Eccles therefore wondered
whether the Treasury would hold off activating any gold and let
the Federal Reserve, after a definite announcement promising an
increase in the open market portfolio, operate independently for
the time being.

Morgenthau snapped that that would not be enough. The
Open Market Committee did not want the Treasury to act, he said,
because it would look as if the Treasury had had to step in to clean
up the mess which the increase in reserve requirements had created.
He had been playing more than fair with the Federal Reserve;
Eccles and his associates had failed to handle the situation; now the
two agencies had to move together. "I will not recede from my de-

cision of last night," the Secretary said. "I am not going to recede from it."

He could not use a club on twelve bankers, Eccles warned, and further discussion would take time. Morgenthau asked whether the statement prepared the previous evening was still agreeable to Eccles personally. It was, but Eccles, like the committee, preferred to activate no gold, and to qualify a promise of open-market operations with the controversial "if necessary" phrase. As he had understood it, Morgenthau objected, Eccles had promised to approve the Treasury's program no matter what the Open Market Committee did. Eccles, the Secretary told his staff, was weaseling, but he was going to hold his ground; only Roosevelt could persuade him to retreat.

The battle continued at the White House that afternoon. After reading the draft of the proposed statement on joint action, Roosevelt asked whether activating gold might not be interpreted as inflationary. Morgenthau admitted that it might. However, the increases in reserve requirements were largely responsible for tightening up interest rates, and if the stumbling block was that the Federal Reserve did not want the Treasury to activate gold, he was willing to withdraw the suggestion provided that the Board of Governors postponed the increase in reserve requirements scheduled for May 1. When Eccles complained that Morgenthau had not previously mentioned that possibility, the Secretary explained that it had not occurred to him. It would be a clumsy change in policy, Eccles maintained.

Roosevelt then broke in with what Morgenthau considered a "very excellent suggestion." He proposed that the Treasury give the Federal Reserve one more chance to preserve an orderly market. If that failed, the Treasury would take over. As Morgenthau reported it: "The President suggested that I should say to the Federal Reserve: 'Now Congress gave you the job of managing the money market and that is your responsibility. You muffed it. You haven't done it. You have not maintained an orderly market, and this thing is getting steadily worse. . . . Now I, Henry Morgenthau, Jr., talking for the U. S. Government, serve notice on the Federal Reserve Board that I ask you to do what Congress has given you the power to do, namely, to increase your portfolio. If you don't do it, the Treasury will step in. . . . We are putting you on notice.' "

Eccles was entirely satisfied with the President's formulation, which was substantially the policy that the Open Market Committee had recommended. Roosevelt had recast it in terms that won Morgenthau. "The President," the Secretary told his staff, "was swell. He was thinking, he wasn't rushed. . . . He just closed the door and he just concentrated on this thing, and he really was swell. I've never seen him click better than he did. And he was right, for this put the whole thing on them, and if we had gone into it, why, it would have meant 'Morgenthau's for inflation' and all this business. . . . And to show you how the President turned, he said, 'Henry, which of the bonds are selling the lowest?' I said, 'The two and a halves.' 'I think they'd be a good buy now.' He's changed; he's changed."

That evening, following Roosevelt's prescription, Morgenthau served "notice on this Open Market Committee that we hope and earnestly request that you use the machinery which you have and give us an orderly market. Now, if within reasonable time you don't or refuse to, then I'm very sorry to say — I have to say that the Government will, and that's the whole story. I'm not threatening, I'm just making a statement."

Though Eccles supported the Secretary, George Harrison and several other bankers on the committee balked. "You people," Morgenthau said, "just don't want to admit that . . . you monkeyed with the carburetor and you got the mixture too thin." For a little longer he let them stall, toy with phrasing a public statement, rehearse their doubts. But as the conversation got nowhere, he snapped that he was getting "fed up." "You give us the policy now," he demanded. "You write a policy." They had pulled apart the Treasury's decision. Now it was time for them to be constructive.

Harrison, still opposing open-market operations, asked for a little better understanding of where they wanted to go before they started to get there. "My golly, George," Eccles despaired, "if you haven't got it now, I don't know how it is possible in the English language."

Did Eccles want the Open Market Committee to go in to buy

bonds and run their prices up, Harrison asked. Yes, Eccles replied, and for psychological reasons the board had to let the country know what it was going to do. If the bond market went up of
its own accord, there would be no need for them to run it up
further, but if the market were weak, they would have to buy
vigorously. Over a period of two or three years, as prices increased
and the market worked to higher levels, interest rates would certainly rise. Cheap money was a relative thing, but the cheap
money policy now required immediate open-market purchases.

The arguments went on and on until Morgenthau, weary of
controversy, sighed: "Eccles, why don't we stop now?" As they
adjourned, Eccles, speaking quietly so that only the Secretary
could hear him, nodded toward George Harrison and said, "Damn
it, make him take some action. I'm getting tired."

Morgenthau held the group at the door just long enough to
make another plea for cooperation, to remind the Open Market
Committee again that if it did not take action, the government
would have to. This reminder, he was sure, clinched victory. The
next day, April 4, he described the session to Roosevelt. "Did you
tell him that once the United States Government stepped in
we're there for life?" the President asked. Morgenthau had not,
but he had a "distinct feeling" that Eccles and Harrison sensed
that the Federal Reserve System was on trial.

That was apparently the sense of the Open Market Committee
which announced, after a brief discussion, that it would add to its
portfolio of long-term bonds for the first time since November
1933. As Morgenthau had predicted, the committee did not have
to buy on a large scale. Its entry into the market sufficed. The
2½'s rallied, and on April 6 the market held steady enough for
the Secretary to complete *Gone with the Wind,* which had served
to divert him during his intense week of negotiations. Later in
the month, when bonds again fell off, Eccles on his initiative ordered substantial purchases, which "simply delighted" Morgenthau. He was satisfied that Eccles was now truly cooperating, even
when it involved disciplining his associates. For the time being,
at least, the Federal Reserve was really in the market. It remained
to be seen whether that would suffice to keep bonds high and
rates of interest low.

## 6. Brakes Off

The increases in reserve requirements and the sterilization of gold had grown out of the concern about inflation that agitated Washington during 1936 and the early months of 1937, but by late summer of the latter year, the picture had changed completely. Recovery had begun to falter, and what was soon to be called the recession was affecting the market for all kinds of securities, the government's not the least. Even in June 1937, though Morgenthau offered two notes on terms which the bankers on the Open Market Committee recommended, the New York press took a bearish view of the financing, except for the *Wall Street Journal* which, as the Secretary put it, "not only gave me a good story, but . . . have the courage to say the thing will be a success." It was, but in order to move the September issue, the Treasury considered it necessary to advance the rate of interest a fraction — a sure indication of the tightening in the money market as investors developed a bad case of jitters.

At Morgenthau's request, his staff on September 8 debated ways to strengthen the market. Jacob Viner, who disagreed with the others, opposed any change in the sterilization program, urging instead a reduction in reserve requirements. Morgenthau demurred. He had worn himself out twice, he said, once in putting sterilization through, once in getting the Board of Governors to begin open-market operations, and he did not want to wear himself out again. He was willing to pursue whatever policy his group advised, but he thought it should be more dramatic than just a change in reserve requirements. Viner, he continued, liked to teach pure economics, but here they were dealing with human beings, and the human element called for a dramatic public endorsement of the long-range cheap-money policy. If the Reserve Board wanted to lower requirements, he would be delighted, but in that case he wanted it announced at once. Alternatively, he would activate between $300 and $500 million of gold.

The next day, however, Eccles, while expressing a good deal of sympathy for the idea of desterilizing gold, argued that the Federal Reserve could sufficiently relieve the situation by buying bills directly from the Treasury. Except for those bills — ninety-day securities — he suggested, there was no stringency in the money market.

That analysis, Morgenthau replied, was all wrong. It was largely a matter of a state of mind. The increases in reserve requirements had left the New York banks low on reserves, and they had obtained cash by selling governments, thus precipitating a wave of sales. The bottom was not in sight, and investors knew it. The mere purchase of bills by the Federal Reserve could not restore confidence, could not demonstrate that the government intended to preserve easy money.

Eccles admitted the need for more usable reserves but resisted lowering requirements. He was all for easy money, he said, and he wanted to take a concrete proposal to his board. Just what, he asked, would Morgenthau want them to buy if they extended open-market operations? These were clearly still the remedy Eccles preferred in September as he had in April. Indeed, he gave Morgenthau to understand that he thought the only reason for desterilization would be to relieve the Treasury of some gold.

At that the Secretary exploded. "There's never any use talking to you, Marriner," he said. "I try to be nice, and then . . . you've got the audacity to put it up to me that you want . . . to know whether I want to be relieved of some gold. I say it's an insult for you to ask me a question like that. It's an insult!"

"You get irritated every time I come over here and present anything," Eccles barked back, "and I'm getting just as tired of it as anybody else. . . . Maybe the thing for me to do is get up and walk out, because I'm getting goddam sick and tired of it."

"You two fellows have got to agree whether you like it or not," Viner interrupted. "I mean there's something more important than the feelings of either of you, and that is the good of the country."

If he could not come over and talk and be peaceable without having Morgenthau jump all over him, Eccles replied, then he was damned if he was going to take it. The trouble was, Morgenthau said, that Eccles persistently and deliberately misunderstood him. The trouble was, Viner repeated, that the total economy was at stake.

Relaxing, Eccles said the question was whether to increase reserves by desterilization or by open-market operations. Morgenthau, also moving toward peace, added that he would say "God Bless you" to the Federal Reserve Board if open-market operations could produce adequate results, but he doubted the board would undertake them. Eccles thought it would oppose any action, but in that event, he said, he would personally join the Treasury in a public statement advocating desterilization.

On September 11 Eccles met with his board. They were ready to concede almost everything Morgenthau wanted, to ask the Treasury to release $200 million of gold, and simultaneously to authorize open-market purchases up to $250 million. The Secretary the next day persuaded Eccles to ask for $300 million and accepted a change of mind of the board, which now preferred not to mention the amount of money for use in the open market. Eccles asked him to be sure that the newspapers did not get the impression that the Treasury had brought any pressure on the Federal Reserve. Promising to guard against that interpretation, Morgenthau arranged to let Eccles tell the story to the press. As he put it to his Diary, he was perfectly willing to let him make it his show.

So it seemed in the statement which the Open Market Committee released on September 15. It had authorized purchases of short-term government obligations, the committee said, for the purpose of maintaining at member banks an aggregate volume of excess reserves adequate for the continuation of the System's policy of monetary ease for further economic recovery. As a means of making this policy effective, the Treasury, at the request of the Board of Governors, had released approximately $300 million of gold from the inactive account. These developments, together with recent reductions in discount rates, would enable banks to meet readily any seasonal demands for currency and credit.

The developments also, Morgenthau told his staff, corrected "a very bad situation." He thought the market should feel no further strain. But as it happened, the really rough seas were still ahead. The slump in the economy was only beginning; it had many causes, and the easing of credit could compensate for only one.

Yet even before the recession began, Morgenthau had emphasized the significance of money rates. Soon after the Treasury developed the sterilization program, he began to question its wisdom, and especially he questioned the even more stringent actions of the Board of Governors. To be sure, he came to the problem with a first responsibility for the public debt. It was his job to manage that debt as inexpensively as possible and to preserve an orderly market for government securities. But consistently, while discharging those duties effectively, he strove also to keep money cheap — which he considered vital for recovery — and to give to the government rather than to the private bankers control over decisions about money rates. He brought Eccles to Washington and he fought side by side with him to secure the reforms of the Banking Act of 1935, but he found then that he had still to struggle against the restrictive attitudes of the Federal Reserve System.

Though Morgenthau's objectives would not alone have warded off the economic downturn, he was conducting his campaign along appropriate lines. Increasing reserve requirements, as he recognized, led banks to adjust their investment portfolios, brought on a wave of selling, at first primarily of short-term government securities, but later of corporate and long-term government bonds, and ultimately of common stocks. At a time of declining public deficits and increasing wage rates, the action of the Federal Reserve had a broad and unfortunate effect on the market, bond yields, interest rates, and thus on business in general. Though monetary conditions were still relatively easy, the increase in requirements clearly contributed to the coming of the recession.

The responsibility, of course, was not unitary. The slump called upon the Administration to re-examine the whole range of federal activities, including the monetary and fiscal policies which were within the Treasury's domain. Morgenthau, as he phrased it, had "no hobbies to ride." If he found a decision wanting, he was ready to reverse it, just as he had begun to reverse his opinion of sterilization. But it was going to be hard for everyone in Washington to decide where to turn. For arduous weeks to come, Morgenthau's tasks, like those of his chief and his associates, were to be even more exacting, even more puzzling, than they had been during the first four years of the New Deal.

# IX

# *Recession*

## *1937-1938*

### 1. A Statement of Policy

HAWAII IN MIDSUMMER 1937 was a good place for relaxing. The problems of the Treasury seemed comfortably remote and in any case under control. Hopkins was following Morgenthau's prescriptions, Congress had made tax avoidance satisfyingly difficult, business conditions had not yet perceptibly slumped. Morgenthau found it easy, therefore, to enjoy his family and his leisure. Twenty years later he remembered fondly the beauty of Molokai Island and the wonderful time he had with his children sailing in Pearl Harbor. There, he also recalled, Japanese fishing vessels had unrestricted views of American naval installations — a condition the military partially corrected after he called it to their attention. Most vividly Morgenthau remembered reviewing at Hickam Field the armed forces stationed in Hawaii. Roosevelt had assigned him that duty, largely in order to emphasize the presence in the islands of the Secretary of the Treasury. "Henry," the President had explained, "as you go East you have to be more and more formal."

Parades and sunshine, the green palms, the ivory sand, the bright blue water, for all their attractions could not entirely keep Morgenthau's mind away from Washington. The plan, which he had never approved, for the reorganization of the Supreme Court, and the wave of sit-down strikes had, he thought, cost Roosevelt middle-class support during the first half of 1937. The President could regain the lost esteem, Morgenthau believed, only by balancing the budget. Committed to budget balancing on its own merits, the Secretary now had political reasons for making it his first order of business.

Warnings of a possible recession seemed to him to confirm his purpose. The satisfactory level of business activity, his advisers wrote him in August, had rested upon a backlog of unfilled orders. Unless increased buying replaced this backlog, production would fall off. Commodity prices were already tending downward and commodity futures had reached new lows. But the Research Division saw no need for collapse. Low interest rates, new residential construction, and increased purchasing power would sustain recovery unless these factors were offset by a decrease in federal spending. Here Morgenthau completely disagreed. Recovery, he believed, depended on the willingness of business to increase investments, and this in turn was a function of business confidence. In his view only a balanced budget could sustain that confidence.

Back at his desk in mid-September, Morgenthau was delighted to find Roosevelt in a frugal mood. The President struck out for a balanced cash budget for fiscal 1938, delayed the expenditure of $23 million for post office buildings, and instructed the Reconstruction Finance Corporation to make no new lending commitments. Best of all, he said he wanted to balance the budget for fiscal 1939, allowing among other things $600 million for debt retirement. He "was simply delighted" when Morgenthau on September 20 showed him how he expected to save almost $20 million previously appropriated for public buildings. Roosevelt then also agreed to review the budgets of each department.

"You know what I did in Albany," he said.

"I certainly do," Morgenthau replied, "and nobody could have been tougher." Nothing, he continued, would be more popular than if Roosevelt beat the drum for economy. That would put the country behind a balanced budget and stop Congress from spending sprees. Roosevelt said he would think it over, and meanwhile he permitted Morgenthau to see what he could do to cut down appropriations for agriculture, for the Resettlement Administration, and for the Reconstruction Finance Corporation.

The assignment exactly suited the Secretary. As he put it to his staff, "it's the biggest job I've got." He hoped to be able, before he finished, to reduce the land-buying program, to stop all Jesse Jones's lending, to recover hundreds of thousands of dollars from the road program, even to recapture funds from Ickes's Public Works Administration. His knife was out. "What you gentlemen have done in the Budget," he told Dan Bell and his associates, "— you have just scraped the barrel clean. Now, what I want to do is take the barrel apart, see? . . . I want to take the barrel apart so they can't fill it up again."

Much to Morgenthau's surprise, Harold Ickes told him on September 29 that he believed PWA should curtail its activities and had urged that policy upon the President. He was anxious, Ickes said, to balance the budget, and was sick and tired of being the whipping boy. Morgenthau was so elated that he shrugged off a report that New York investors were worried about a decline in consumer spending. That kind of talk, he said, was simply a calculated argument against balancing the budget.

The possibility of a special session of Congress posed another threat to the Secretary's resolute prudence. Roosevelt wanted quick action on two major Administration objectives, a fair labor standards bill setting minimum wages and maximum hours and an agricultural bill establishing a permanent foundation for the Agricultural Adjustment Administration's programs of crop control, conservation, and farmers' benefits. Morgenthau, however, feared that if Congress met it would authorize new expenditures. Hoping to prevent a special session, he admonished Roosevelt on October 5 against extravagance: "On the basis of present commitments and today's expectation of revenue for the fiscal year 1938–1939 we are likely to fall $275 million short of a true budget balance, including sinking fund requirements. . . . I believe that you and I are equally determined to balance the Budget for 1938–1939. . . . In order to accomplish this, it seems to me extremely important that before you obligate yourself to spend anything at all in addition to the commitments already made . . . you give . . . me an opportunity to go into this situation with you fully and examine it yourself with the utmost care." His chances of winning his way, the Secretary told his staff, were two out of three, but he was not "going to sit here another year unless we have a balanced budget."

On October 8 he urged Jim Farley to help him argue Roosevelt out of the idea of convening Congress. Reform could wait until the first of the year, Morgenthau believed; economy could not. Businessmen, he told Farley, had not been so nervous since November 1933; they might well talk themselves into a depression, and large appropriations would intensify the panic. On the other hand, he thought if businessmen knew that Roosevelt was going to devote a month to hard work on the budget, it would hearten them. Farley agreed.

At the Cabinet meeting that day Roosevelt, relying on the data Morgenthau had sent him, spoke emphatically about the need for a balanced budget, warning the departments that they would have to cut $300 million out of their combined requests for the fiscal year 1939. But the President was still resolved to call Congress into session and to get his reform legislation.

Readjusting his tactics, Morgenthau a few days later advised Roosevelt to serve notice that he would keep Congress sitting indefinitely until the budget was balanced. While the President said that the idea was a good one, he added that he would have to put it more politely than that. During the next hour and a half, however, he accepted every recommendation Morgenthau made for saving money. "I want you to tell me that I was pretty good," Roosevelt said at the end. "I think I deserve a pat on the back." Shaking his hand, Morgenthau replied: "You certainly do."

On his desk the next morning the Secretary found a statistical measure of his progress toward his goal. For the first nine months of calendar 1937, the aggregate net cash deficit of the federal government, excluding expenditures for gold and silver, amounted to only $288 million. This contrasted with $2807 million during a comparable period in 1936, $2032 million for the first nine months of 1935, and $2951 million for the same months in 1934. Indeed the total net cash deficit for the first nine months of calendar 1937 was less than the average *monthly* net cash deficit in 1936. Furthermore, the federal government would probably have a net cash surplus of about $500 million for the first half of calendar 1938.

While those figures encouraged Morgenthau, an accompanying report from the Research Division disturbed him. It noted that fifteen different indexes revealed an ominous decline in national economic activity. And over the telephone, Earle Bailie, a New York financier whose judgment Morgenthau respected, expressed alarm about the relentless selling that had plagued the stock market on October 11. Bailie felt that deflation had reached a point serious enough to affect federal revenues. There was, he said, a "lack of confidence bordering almost on disorder, or you could use the word panic, if you wanted to, but that would be putting it a little strongly." The temper of the business community he concluded, made some official expressions of optimism imperative.

To a considerable degree, the Secretary discounted Bailie. Though he was sure that things had to be watched "very, very closely," he felt that the opinion of investors and bankers was warped by their recent losses. Most of all, he believed, such men did not want Congress to enact Roosevelt's reform legislation. As Oliphant put it, those blocking reform would be satisfied with nothing short of control of the whole government. Viner, however, frankly worried about the falling pace of investment, suggested that even businessmen might be telling the truth, and suspected that the President would not heed what they said. "Roosevelt's all right . . ." Morgenthau maintained. "He's got his feet on the ground. He's absolutely all right. I've lived with the man now day in and day out for the last week, and I come out reassured."

But there was much upsetting news. The railroad situation had worsened. The roads were beset by rising costs and their financial problems were disturbing banks and insurance companies which held railroad bonds. The stock market was not absorbing new equities. Recent issues of Canada Dry and Bethlehem Steel had faltered. Perhaps most seriously, the utility industry was frozen pending the Supreme Court's decision on the constitutionality of the Act breaking up holding-company systems. Utilities were not expanding except when they could issue bonds, and this more and more impaired their capital position. In any case there was no market for their equities.

Morgenthau thought it was up to the President to clarify policy on public utilities, and at the urging of his staff, he promised to have a heart-to-heart talk with Roosevelt about that matter and perhaps also about capital markets. The Secretary's primary interest, however, remained the budget.

He had some strong allies. On October 12, 1937, Roosevelt told Congressmen Doughton and Vinson of the House Ways and Means Committee that he wanted to wipe out the $270 million deficit predicted for the fiscal year 1939. The Treasury, he said, had urged him to be rough, to insist on economy. At once Doughton and Vinson said they, too, wanted him to be rough. They would carry out a budget-balancing program if he requested it. Roosevelt said he would ask the special session at least to relieve him of an obligation to spend $170 million for roads in the coming year and $216 million the year after. As Morgenthau put it in his Diary: "The President told them with a real 'burr' in his voice that he expected to balance the Budget; that he wanted enough money to balance the Budget; that he expected to keep expenditures down so that he could balance the Budget, and that if any Committee passes an appropriation over and above his estimates he would immediately serve notice on that Committee that they must find the additional revenue."

Henry Wallace seemed also to be veering toward Morgenthau's view. Immediately after the Cabinet meeting of October 12, Wallace said, according to Morgenthau's Diary: "Mr. President, as we are now approaching a balanced budget don't you think that you ought to call some of us together and see if we can't think up some suggestions to encourage private business enterprise so that they can go ahead and take up the slack which would be left due to the government's ceasing spending." This, in Morgenthau's words, was music to his ears, and he was equally pleased by a memorandum Roosevelt sent Wallace on October 14: "During the next two or three weeks I think it is very important for you and the farm organizations to keep in touch with the Treasury in order that we may avoid a program which would unbalance the budget. As I said in Cabinet, if we adopt a farm bill for 'balanced abundance' it must balance itself financially. . . . That is why I think you and the Treasury should keep in close touch."

With Roosevelt holding checkreins on Wallace, Morgenthau

concentrated on Ickes and Jesse Jones. The best news the business community could receive, the Secretary asserted, was that the Reconstruction Finance Corporation and the Public Works Administration were through. Assistant Secretary Wayne Taylor disagreed, arguing that the government could not yet afford to cut down on lending, for there were inadequate private sources for credit. As long as Jones and Ickes were in competition with private capital, Morgenthau replied, private capital felt licked. As the government began to cut expenditures and loans, he and the President, too, expected private business to quicken, but if he weakened now, he would jeopardize all he had been working for. "Now listen," the Secretary concluded, ". . . do you mind if I go ahead, because I never, never felt that I was more right than I am now. Now, if I am wrong — I'm shooting the works, and if I'm wrong — I'm doing what I always have done since I've been Secretary; I'm willing to stick my neck out, and if I'm wrong — I'm always willing to risk my job if I think I'm right, because I think it's worth risking, and I'm perfectly willing to risk my job for this. . . . I'm willing to bet my job as Secretary of the Treasury that I'm right. . . . We're going to sweat this thing through because we think we're right."

He appeared, Morgenthau later recalled, at last to be within sight of his goal. Then on October 19, "Black Tuesday," the stock market disintegrated. Seventeen million shares changed hands while prices skidded, as Morgenthau put it, "amid an hysteria resembling a mob in a theater fire." Steve Early telephoned him from the White House to say that telegrams were pouring in asking for the closing of the exchange. The Secretary recommended keeping all exchanges open. At one-fifteen in the afternoon Roosevelt telephoned. The White House, he said, had the jitters, especially Early and Jimmy Roosevelt. "I was quite rude to them," the President added. Morgenthau said that retailing and the housing industry were as good or better than they had been. Though railroads and United States Steel were off, foreigners had bought American stocks, and there was as yet no indication of money leaving the country.

On October 20 the market recovered a little, but October 19 precipitated a policy crisis in Washington. While developments that day strengthened Morgenthau's convictions, they shook Roosevelt's faith in budget balancing and gained a hearing with him for the advocates of countercyclical spending. That policy had begun to gain currency in academic and governmental circles after the publication in 1936 of John Maynard Keynes's classic, *The General Theory of Employment, Interest and Money.* Within the Treasury itself, Oliphant, White, Seltzer, and in some degree Roswell Magill, among others, had begun to think in Keynesian terms, particularly in their analysis of taxation.* Morgenthau, as always, permitted a free expression of opinions at variance with his own, but he was unpersuaded by his associates and they were too loyal to take their views over his head to the White House.

Outside the Treasury, however, there were influential proponents of compensatory spending. Marriner Eccles, for one, had been preaching that gospel on and off for five years. Now he had capable allies who proposed, as he did, to transform spending from a temporary expedient to a permanent instrumentality of government. The economist Leon Henderson had predicted a business slump in his "Boom or Bust" memorandum of the spring of 1937. His forecast gave Harry Hopkins, for whom Henderson was then working, arguments for resuming a spending policy. Tommy Corcoran, sensitive to the play of personalities at both ends of Pennsylvania Avenue, was the political brains of the spending group, Morgenthau believed. Ben Cohen, a highly literate and imaginative liberal lawyer, and Lauchlin Currie, an energetic New Deal economist, assisted in the formation of policy, and Jimmy Roosevelt, then acting as his father's assistant, was generally sympathetic to their ideas. The decline in economic activity and the catastrophe on the market gave their case enhanced prestige. Whenever private investment fell off, they warned, only an expansion of government economic activity could maintain a satisfactory level of production and employment.

This, of course, was the antithesis of the theory which Morgenthau advanced, a theory based upon the economics of the orthodox school of which the Secretary was the most influential spokesman in Washington. Morgenthau had no doubts. He was sure that private investors would not risk their capital when economic con-

* See above, page 250, and especially below, pages 439–40.

ditions were uncertain. He was sure that federal deficits created uncertainty by causing fears of immediate inflation and future taxation. The utilities, the railroads, residential housing and other matters needed attention, he knew, but no one of them, nor indeed the combination of them all, seemed to him as important as the budget. No program had yet solved the problem of depression and unemployment — not gold buying, not the regulation of production by the NRA, not the easing of credit, not spending. It was time, he was positive, to try what the New Deal had not yet attempted, to balance the budget and see whether business could achieve recovery and full employment. As he put it twenty years later, he felt in 1937 that the Administration had to take away the crutches to test whether the patient was able to walk by himself.

Wedded to these convictions, Morgenthau continued to resist proposals for expenditures, especially on agriculture. He also advanced plans, first formulated a month earlier, to speak out in public, with the full authority of the Administration, in behalf of a balanced budget. To that end he had accepted an invitation to address the Academy of Political Science at the Hotel Astor in New York City on November 10.

Morgenthau told his staff on October 20 that he wanted his speech to emphasize that balancing the budget would be the biggest fiscal job anyone had ever faced, particularly because of the slump in business conditions. He thought he would do Roosevelt a kindness by "putting" his "own neck out" and saying it could and would be done. Herbert Gaston, who was working on the speech draft, wondered whether the Secretary was willing to say that they would balance the budget no matter what happened. Would he, for example, consent to unbalance the budget for fiscal 1939 if it were necessary to provide another $500 million for work relief? Morgenthau replied that he would not. If it came to that, there would have to be another Secretary of the Treasury:

> I won't stay and knowingly and consciously have an unbalanced budget in order to correct the mistakes made by other people. . . . We have come to a crossroad. The crossroad is when private business needed the money which the Govern-

ment has been taking up to this time, and we are at that cross-
road now. I don't see why we can't use those words. . . . The
time has come. And the only person around here who is not in
line is Wallace and Wallace wants private industry to do it.
. . . The President wants private industry to do it. . . . And
it's not balancing the budget which is putting the stock market
down. Then why the hell should we unbalance the budget to
cover up the mistakes of other people? For four years we have
carried the burden of mistakes made by other Departments.

A week later he had begun to hedge. He still felt, as he told his
staff, that the best thing he could do for his country was to devote
the first part of the speech to a discussion of why the Administration wanted a balanced budget. But then, of course, he would have
to explain the realities of the situation. Funds were still needed
for relief and for the Civilian Conservation Corps; the agricultural
program would be expensive, and $700 million were already com-
mitted to public works. He wanted his address to make it clear
that it was just as dangerous to economize too quickly as it was not
to economize at all. He wanted it just as clear (the Keynesians in
the Treasury had made their mark) that he was not yet willing
to recommend a broader tax base, even in order to balance the
budget. That would be deflationary. He intended to balance
the budget by cutting costs, not by increasing revenue, though
this might limit him to balancing his cash budget, leaving uncovered the expenses of debt retirement.

This position seemed sound to the Secretary's staff, but Jacob
Viner said categorically that he did not like the kind of advice
Morgenthau was getting. When Harry White differed, Viner asked
if he would be happy with a deficit of $1 billion. "On advice of
counsel," White said, "I refuse to answer."

Viner bridled, insisting on an answer, as did Morgenthau. White
then said that he believed the government should move in the direction of a balanced budget, to be achieved just as soon as business
conditions permitted. If they continued to turn down at the rate
of the last couple of months, however, it would be wrong to attempt to balance the budget either by increasing taxes or reducing
expenditures. Those policies would intensify deflation. Neverthe-

less, White added, the agriculture budget could be pared and those of the regular departments held to the bone.

Somewhat appeased, Viner said he did not entirely disagree with White, but he considered the whole record of the New Deal was one of deficits and broken promises. Although the time had come to make a serious effort at budget balancing, he feared Roosevelt would take no political risk. If the President were really willing to slice expenditures, then Morgenthau in his New York address could make a categorical promise, but if Roosevelt were not willing to cut back, then Viner thought the Secretary could promise nothing. Roosevelt had promised, Morgenthau said, to sit down personally with a blue pencil in hand. If he gave three afternoons a week to the budget, Morgenthau believed the chances for balancing it were good.

As the days passed, however, all business indexes suggested that the slump was developing into a full-blown depression. To Morgenthau's dismay, Roosevelt was beginning to listen to the advocates of compensatory spending. Yet though he listened, he gave no indication of the policies he intended to pursue.

This indecision, perhaps deliberate, worried Morgenthau, who believed quick action imperative. On the evening of November 2 he telephoned his chief. The country, the Secretary said, was headed into another depression, and Roosevelt should do something about it. Morgenthau proposed calling together a number of people over the week end to discuss gold, intending by this remark to suggest that desterilization would ease credit and perhaps encourage investment. The President, however, got "very excited, very dictatorial and very disagreeable." He quoted at great length a man he described as a "wise old bird" who had said that business was deliberately causing the depression in order to hold a pistol to his head and force a retreat from reform.

"A great deal depends on who this person is," Morgenthau said coldly.

"It is not necessary for you to know who that person is," Roosevelt replied.

After thinking it over, Morgenthau concluded that the "wise old bird" was the President himself. In any event, Roosevelt had been "extremely rude," as Morgenthau himself had been something less than tactful. Mrs. Morgenthau, who overheard the conversation, said to her husband that his "voice sounded like drippings of an icicle."

Before they rang off, the President said he would not raise the price of gold. The Secretary interrupted: "I never asked you to raise the price of gold." He explained that he had been referring to desterilization; and Roosevelt, laughing, admitted that he had misunderstood. The combination of the desterilization of some gold and a lowering of reserve requirements, Morgenthau continued, by reversing the steps which had, among others, led to the recession, might help to start things moving upward again.*

"Why that is entirely different," Roosevelt replied. "By all means go ahead and study those questions."

The conversation failed to satisfy Morgenthau. When Roosevelt concluded by objecting to the firm declaration for a balanced budget in the draft of the National Academy speech the Secretary had sent to the White House, Morgenthau was more worried than ever. Taking pen in hand, for him an unusual gesture, on November 3 he wrote an anguished note: "As I told you over the telephone last night I have had to come to the conclusion that we are headed right into another depression. . . . You told the newspapers that your first interest was the one-third of the nation who are ill-nourished, ill-clad, ill-housed. This part of our population is also my deep concern and therefore, I am bringing this matter again to your attention in writing. I hardly need tell you that the first to feel another depression will be this same one-third. This cruel process has already begun. Mr. President what can we do to stop it?"

Roosevelt was unmoved. At Cabinet the next day, obviously in an acid mood, he said: "Of course, I am glad to hear from the various members of the Cabinet their sad story of how bad business conditions are. Last night when I went to bed, alongside of my bed was the darnedest letter you ever saw from Henry." He grimaced. "It was just terrible." Now angry, he continued: "I am sick and tired of being told by the Cabinet, by Henry and by everybody else for the last two weeks what's the matter with the country and nobody suggests what I should do."

* See pages 376–79.

There was complete silence. Morgenthau gathered his courage: "You can do something about public utilities. You can do something about the railroads. You could do something about housing. Above all, you must do something to reassure business."

"You want me to turn on the old record," Roosevelt said.

"You asked me," Morgenthau replied. "What business wants to know is: Are we headed toward state Socialism or are we going to continue on a capitalistic basis?"

"I have told them that again and again."

"All right, Mr. President, tell them for the fifteenth time. That's what they want to know."

"That's what they want to know," Jim Farley echoed, and Wallace also backed up Morgenthau. He thought Roosevelt would be wise, too, to do something about labor.

Farley said Roosevelt should tell the country again that the Administration was going to reduce the cost of government. That was what people were interested in.

"All right, Jim; I will turn on the old record," the President said.

Farley thought it was the best Cabinet meeting they had ever had, and Morgenthau in his Diary noted: "This is the first time in my experience that the Cabinet had ever talked on a man to man basis with the President and that we did not sit back and either talk trivialities or listen to him."

His spirits high, Morgenthau resumed work on his speech. "This thing has gotten so important," he told his staff, ". . . it's a question of the whole policy being at stake now." Almost as he spoke, Marriner Eccles arrived to explain, as Roosevelt had suggested he should, his interpretation of the developing recession. One trouble, Eccles said, was the high cost of labor which was forcing prices up, particularly in the building trades. As long as this situation continued, people would not build houses and railroads would not lay track or construct new facilities. Small business, Eccles went on, needed tax relief, but the best way to stop the recession, he concluded, would be to speed up expenditures through Hopkins and Wallace.

When the Secretary showed him a draft of the speech, Eccles

called it deflationary. Frugality would have been nice a month ago, he said, but not now. Nor was he sympathetic to Morgenthau's proposal for stopping the sterilization of gold. Eccles feared Roosevelt might grab that idea as a panacea for solving all economic problems. He considered excess reserves plentiful and contended that neither desterilization nor a loosening of reserve requirements would actually ease credit. He did, however, see some merit in desterilizing gold in order to spend the funds thus obtained for relief and agricultural loans. That, he pointed out, would increase the budget without increasing the debt.

After Eccles left, Morgenthau told his staff that he thought the President wanted to sit tight, as if he were in a poker game, to see who could last longer, the advocates of spending or the advocates of balancing the budget. Meanwhile, Morgenthau said, he felt the ground was slipping from under their feet. He was afraid Roosevelt would do nothing. And in spite of Eccles's objections or Roosevelt's doubts, he did not believe his ideas were deflationary.

A balanced budget was still Morgenthau's goal when he went, on November 8, for luncheon with the President. Most of their conversation, however, took a different turn. Roosevelt was depressed. Fascism, he said, was making gains throughout the world, as the Rome-Berlin-Tokyo Pact suggested. Brazil was veering that way. Take the situation in the United States, he said. Four or five people might get together, talk it over, and decide they had to have their own man in Washington. Even though he said every so often that he wanted business to make a profit and that he believed in property rights, business did not believe him. The President thought there were about two thousand men who had reached the conclusion they had to block the New Deal, to go on strike against government. He had to decide whether to continue to go forward or do what Hoover had done and call in groups of people to try to cure particular situations one at a time in conference. He was going to see Harry Hopkins and his economists later that day, Roosevelt continued, and on the next day see another group, and then later talk with Gerard Swope, a business spokesman, and others about housing, going on from there to a discussion, again with business interests among others, about the utilities. But the

President kept reverting to the possibility that American industrialists would gradually, as their thought crystallized, conclude that they had to get their own man in the White House.

Occasionally Morgenthau interrupted to ask if there was something that Roosevelt was trying to say that he did not understand, some special point he was trying to make, but the President said no, he was just thinking out loud. He had tried to define the New Deal to his oldest son, Morgenthau said. His conception of what Roosevelt had accomplished, he had told the young man, was that "the United States has come through this terrific turmoil and that the individual in this country still had the right to think, talk and worship as he wished." Roosevelt interrupted, "And add to that the right to work."

After luncheon, in his Diary Morgenthau wrote that he did not know exactly what the President was trying to get across. He supposed Roosevelt was attempting to frighten him by waving the fascist flag. But this was not necessary. Morgenthau knew without being told how bad conditions were. On the other hand, when Roosevelt finished, Morgenthau had felt that the President was fighting like a cornered lion, that he did not want to be tamed, and yet that he did not know where to put his strength to bring about recovery. Of course, Morgenthau conceded, fascism was spreading. It was therefore vital for the United States to avoid an industrial slump because it would give the enemies of liberalism an opportunity to take solace in the failure of the world's strongest democracy.

As Morgenthau judged, Roosevelt was troubled, as yet uncertain about policy, and consequently bent upon keeping discussion open while he made up his mind. Only a few hours after his luncheon with the Secretary, the President talked with Eccles, who was temporarily cheered when Roosevelt seemed impressed with a memorandum prepared by Leon Henderson and Lauchlin Currie, among others, "indicating how a reduction in government spending had helped precipitate the recession." Eccles hoped that the spenders had carried the field, but, as he was to learn, this was not entirely the case.

The President, working over the draft of Morgenthau's speech, questioned a section reading: "This Administration is going to do everything possible to promote a continuation of recovery and to balance the budget through cutting expenditures. But I wish to emphasize that in no event will this Administration allow anyone to starve." Dissatisfied, Roosevelt added: "Nor will it abandon its broad purpose to protect the weak, to give human security and to seek a wider distribution of our national wealth."

"If you want to sound like Huey Long, I don't," Morgenthau said. The emphasis of the speech, he thought, should not be on reform but on the budget. Yet he realized that Roosevelt thought business was conspiring against him, and he knew that when the President was in that humor, nothing could change it. The Secretary would have liked a stronger statement, but even the words the President approved depressed Eccles, "baffled" him, because he was sure that the views Morgenthau expressed in New York were the antithesis of what Roosevelt had seemed to endorse in the memorandum of Henderson and Currie. He was right.

On November 10, 1937, Morgenthau arose before the meeting of the Academy of Political Science. Parker Gilbert of the House of Morgan introduced him politely to a serious and on the whole conservative audience that included some of the wealthiest businessmen of the city. The speech the Secretary was about to give had been "checked and double-checked — every word, every syllable, by the President." By and large it resembled its earliest drafts. For the four years ending June 30, 1937, Morgenthau began, the war against depression had necessitated federal expenditures $14 billion in excess of receipts.

We deliberately used an unbalanced Federal budget . . . to meet a great emergency. That policy has succeeded. The emergency . . . no longer exists. I am fully aware that many of our problems remain unsolved. I am aware that there still remains a considerable volume of unemployment; that the speculative markets have recently been under severe pressure; and that our business indices have recently shown a declining tendency. I am further aware that some persons contend that another great spending program is desirable to ward off the risk of another business depression.

I claim no prophetic insight into the future. But, after giv-

ing serious and careful consideration to all of these and other
factors, I have reached the firm conviction that the domestic
problems which face us today are essentially different from
those which faced us four years ago. Many measures are required for their solution. One of these measures but only one,
in the present juncture is a determined movement toward a
balanced budget. . . . We want to see private business expand. We believe that much of the remaining unemployment
will disappear as private capital funds are increasingly employed. . . . We believe that one of the most important ways
of achieving these ends at this time is to continue progress
toward a balance of the Federal Budget.

Someone laughed. It was probably, Morgenthau later decided,
a drunk, but there were in the audience many men who wondered
whether any Democrat could honestly say what they had just
heard. The atmosphere as much as the interruption upset the Secretary, who was always a nervous speaker, but he braced and
went on. In four fields he contemplated cutting costs: highway
construction, public works, unemployment relief, and agriculture.
But there was a point beyond which reductions were impossible
without crippling essential activities. The government could not
consider "such things as weakening our national defense, and slow-
ing up or abandoning flood control, soil erosion prevention, and
relief for the aged and the unemployed. Such a course, I believe,
would not have the approval of . . . the American people."

This sounded much more like the voice of the New Deal which
Wall Street thought it understood and knew it disliked. The
mood of the audience, as Morgenthau sensed it, was unsympathetic,
and he was increasingly tense as he came to his concluding points:
"We are definitely in a transition period between unbalanced and
balanced Federal budgets: but I firmly believe that there is just
as much danger to our economy as a whole in moving too rapidly
in this direction as there would be in not moving at all.

"Relatively few persons realize the striking fact that the net
improvement this year in the budgetary position of the Federal
Government as estimated will amount to more than $2 billion.

In other words, the net deficit this year is estimated at less than $700 million as compared with more then $2 billion 700 million last year." A pause here, an adjustment of the pince-nez, a triumphant tone: "This . . . provides the best answer to those who . . . have publicly despaired of our ability to balance the Federal budget. . . .

"This Administration is going to do everything possible to promote a continuation of recovery and to balance the budget through cutting expenditures." Another pause. Relish now for the words Roosevelt had inserted: "But I wish to emphasize that in no event will this Administration allow anyone to starve, nor will it abandon its broad purpose to protect the weak, to give human security and to seek a wider distribution of our national income."

Morgenthau had given everything he had. He had advocated precisely the policy the business community had been urging upon him, knowing as he did so that the President, by siding with Henderson and Eccles, might make him look foolish. He had hoped to inspire the confidence so important for recovery. There was, he said later to his staff, not one technical flaw in the speech, and he thanked them for their help in drafting it. The hard work, the high purpose, the great strain surrounding the occasion made the Secretary especially sensitive to the reception accorded his efforts, to the silent unbelief of the very men he was trying to help, to the disconcerting laugh that seemed to symbolize their temper. Herman Oliphant was furious. "We sit here and lose the feel of what the typical leadership of American finance is," he said, "and it's very illuminating to realize the hopelessness of trying to work with them."

This, as Morgenthau knew, was the counsel of defeat. Hurt though he was, he held on to himself and to his convictions. He had made his statement of policy, he believed in it, he would continue to defend it against its opponents in Washington. He would balance the budget and he would do whatever else he had to do to dispel the recession, to vindicate himself, his integrity, the President he loved, and the New Deal in which he saw the only hope of the democratic world.

## 2. Again the Needy

As business conditions grew worse and worse during November and December 1937, Morgenthau faced a familiar dilemma. The drop in corporate and personal income reduced federal tax revenues, making retrenchment essential if the budget was to be close to balance, but the slackening of employment increased the need for relief and therefore for federal spending. The Treasury estimated that even if there were a business upturn in 1938, tax receipts for the fiscal year 1939 would not exceed $5.919 billion, some $980 million less than Morgenthau's most optimistic prediction of expenditures. In that event the deficit would be smaller than that for the fiscal year 1938, but the Secretary admitted privately that there was no basis for optimism.

The statistics on employment accentuated his gloom. Between September 15 and December 15, approximately 1,800,000 people lost their jobs. WPA expected another 1,000,000 to be out of work by mid-January. Furthermore, there was ordinarily a lag of two or three months between the time a man was laid off and the time he applied for relief, with yet another lag before he could be certified for WPA employment.

Agency officials, Morgenthau concluded in December, were not spending enough to abate the spreading distress of unemployment. They had the funds, according to their own figures, to put 100,000 men on work relief at once, and the Secretary thought he could find money for another 80,000. He wanted to move fast in order to sustain consumer spending and keep things from getting worse, but he found it difficult, as always, to get along with anyone at WPA except Hopkins, who was ill at the Mayo Clinic during most of the late autumn.

Temporarily in Washington on December 9, Hopkins unveiled a program of his own. He was working, he told Morgenthau, to add 500,000 to his rolls. By reducing the cost per man of all WPA employees, he hoped to stay within his appropriations, but he reserved the right to ask for more money if he had to, for the pace of layoffs was "something terrible." Conditions were worst in the

Northeast, especially in Massachusetts and Rhode Island, where those on relief rolls were awaiting assignment but WPA quotas were already filled. Quotas could not be shifted from other states because they needed all the latitude they had. In the South, too, where poverty had been for long the rule, the number of those certified for relief far exceeded the quotas. Unemployment compensation helped very little, for twenty-six states had yet to establish systems for it and only about half the recently discharged workers in the other states were eligible. The picture was grim, and by the end of January it was bound to be still grimmer.

So it was, in spite of the funds Morgenthau and Hopkins found. On February 1, 1938, Aubrey Williams, directing WPA in Hopkins's continuing absence, wrote the Secretary that during the preceding six weeks the need for work relief had increased rapidly. In order to give employment to as many people as possible, Williams had authorized state administrators to swell their rolls. Consequently, if they were to stay within the budgets established in December, they would have to cut back rapidly during the last four months of the current fiscal year — March, April, May, and June. Yet it was just this eventuality which Williams and Morgenthau hoped to avoid.

Conditions were as difficult as they had been since 1933–34, the Secretary told Williams the next day, and he did not know whether or not there would be jobs in private industry in April or May. If the need arose, he would be willing in April to tell Congress that WPA had to have more money. Meanwhile he wanted to be in touch with the situation each week. Williams said that in terms of dollars, his budget was still in the black, although in terms of the numbers on relief he had gone over his expected figures. It was all a matter of how he juggled those figures.

Directly after leaving Morgenthau, however, Williams went alone to the White House, where Roosevelt later asked Morgenthau to join them. Williams had reported, the President said, that people were starving and WPA lacked the money to feed them. Morgenthau got "good and mad." Williams had just made the statement at the Treasury, he said, that WPA "had enough money"; now he said people were starving, and the Secretary wanted to know if that was true. Roosevelt, amazed though he frankly was by Williams's behavior, emphasized the emergencies in Detroit, Cleveland, and Toledo, and Morgenthau, much as he resented Williams's tactics, prepared to meet the crisis.

After reviewing the information which WPA had withheld until the tense meeting at the White House, the Secretary decided on February 3 that the agency would need another $250 million before July 1, 1938. "If $250 million will stop this downward spiral, it's cheap," he said. "The thing that bothers me here is that this is going on all over the world and the United States is dragging the world down and everytime you pull this down you are that much nearer to a world war because if the dictators get to a point where they are licked, Mussolini or Hitler, the only thing left for them to do is fight."

"Those are welcome words," Williams replied. "You are right, too."

"If we are going to do it," Morgenthau continued, "I want to shoot the works and get the maximum amount of effect and . . . I don't want to do it any phoney way. I want to borrow another $250 million cash. I want to do this with one broad sweep."

At luncheon with Roosevelt on February 8, Morgenthau recommended the additional $250 million for WPA, which would permit the agency to add 650,000 workers to its rolls. The public, he said, was holding back on buying because it felt that prices would fall further. The government had to do something to change that psychology. Purchases by workers on relief would help, and so would terminating the sterilization of gold. Roosevelt endorsed both suggestions. "I feel that at last I have made a move towards releasing the deflationary brakes," Morgenthau wrote after their conference, "and I am hopeful that this and possible other steps that we may have to take can stop the falling off in business."

At Morgenthau's suggestion, the President conferred with the congressional leaders the following day. The largest needs, Roosevelt explained, were in the major industrial sections, especially Detroit, Chicago, and Cleveland, where the decline of automobile production had resulted in particularly heavy layoffs. During the previous two months WPA had had to increase its rolls quite drastically. Unless more funds became available, they would soon have to reduce them again. The President, feeling that this could not be permitted at a time when unemployment was increasing, asked how the congressmen would respond to a request for a deficiency appropriation of $250 million.

The congressmen welcomed the prospect. Chairman Taylor of the House Appropriations Committee said he would call a hearing as soon as Roosevelt sent a message to the Hill. He thought he could report out a bill within a week, and Majority Leader Sam Rayburn said the House would give it prompt attention. Carter Glass did not anticipate any trouble in the Senate, although, he warned, speaking very much his own mind, there were still many senators who thought local communities should take over a larger share of the relief load. Nevertheless, if the House sent up an emergency appropriation bill, Glass was certain the Senate would quickly pass it. He and the others believed, however, that the President in requesting the $250 million should say that he was holding to his estimate of $1 billion for relief in fiscal 1939. Roosevelt said he was willing to stick to that figure for the time being but might have to change his estimate the following January.

On February 10 the President formally asked for the deficiency appropriation. While Congress was granting it, he instructed Morgenthau to tell Williams to spread out his funds by increasing direct relief. This meant, of course, decreasing expenditures for work relief. Williams was stunned. "Oh, my God!" he exploded to Morgenthau. But the Secretary was unsympathetic, for Roosevelt's directive made it possible for available money to help more people. That seemed more important to Morgenthau than did the commitment of WPA to work relief. Indeed Morgenthau saw no alternative to stretching funds, for he still hoped, while caring for the needy, to hold the Administration to a budget as nearly in balance as possible.

### 3. "A Different Set of Delusions"

Roosevelt, during the first weeks of 1938, was both waiting and groping — waiting to see whether the economy might right itself, delaying definition of major policy while he discussed the recession with businessmen as well as public officials. The captains of industry and finance, however, seemed to the President to have little to offer. They were not accustomed, he told the Cabinet, to thinking of the whole nation or even of businesses other than their own. Officers of corporations handling automobile installment loans had, for example, suggested that the Federal Reserve Board restrict the rediscount rate on installment notes. Amazed at their proposal "for strict government regulation," Roosevelt told them that "if such restrictions were generally applied we would not have state socialism but fascism." The President also reported that the automobile manufacturers admitted privately that they had oversold the market in 1937. He was therefore asking them, as he was asking other businesses, to work out for themselves ways to prevent extravagant production and extravagant selling.

As far as new investment went, Roosevelt felt that there were not enough opportunities for men of moderate means, nor did such men know where to get reliable advice. They had $15 billion in savings banks at nominal rates of interest although public utility bonds, he judged, were an excellent buy to yield 5 or 6 per cent. But the President saw no way to say so publicly.

He had told the businessmen that he needed confidence as much as they did. If they hit him on the chin, he said, he was going to hit them in the nose. "That was his explanation," Magill reported to Morgenthau, "of some of the December speeches. Even at that the Administration had been hit ten times for each blow it struck in return, and he thought a ratio of ten to one was big enough in this instance."

Yet the Secretary feared that the Administration was drifting. Not just unemployment but all evidence on business conditions alarmed him. On February 1 the Treasury's Research Division reported that the woolen industry was in unusually bad shape, automobile production was off, steel production had turned down, and there had been another sharp drop in construction. Morgenthau could only say: "Gosh!" He had never felt lower.

Nor had his fiscal policies ever been under sharper attack. The advocates of countercyclical spending received timely support from their intellectual mentor, John Maynard Keynes, who on February 1, 1938, wrote Roosevelt an unsolicited letter about the recession. The key to recovery, Keynes maintained, was spending. Easy short-term money and the creation of an adequate system of relief, important though they were, could not and would not in themselves suffice. Recovery depended upon large-scale recourse to public works and other investments in capital goods guaranteed by the government. The Administration, he suggested, was especially subject to criticism for its "wicked" handling of the housing problem. Housing was by far the most important aid to recovery because of the large and continuing scale of potential demand, its wide geographical distribution, and the relative independence of housing finance from the stock exchanges. Keynes therefore advised putting "most of the eggs in the housing basket," and making absolutely sure that they were hatched without delay, if necessary through the use of direct subsidies.

He also criticized the deadlock on utilities. A good deal of what was alleged about the "wickedness" of the utility holding companies, he said, was surely "wide of the mark." "The real criminals" had cleared out long ago. Personally he thought there was a great deal to be said for the ownership of all of the utilities by the government, but if public opinion was not yet ripe for this, he saw no object "in chasing utilities around the lot every other week." He considered it wise instead to "make peace on liberal terms," guaranteeing fair earnings on new investment and a fair basis of evaluation in the event of future government purchase. He spoke, too, of the railroads as potential sources of substantial demand for new capital expenditures. Nationalize them, he wrote, if the time was "ripe"; if not, "take pity" on the overwhelming problems of their management, and "let the dead bury their dead." "To an Englishman," Keynes said, "you Americans, like the Irish, are so terribly historically-minded!"

The recession, Keynes continued, was also in part psychological in origin. For this he blamed the President's attitude toward businessmen. "Businessmen," Keynes proposed, "have a different set of delusions from politicians; and need, therefore, different handling. They are, however, much milder than politicians, at the same time allured and terrified by the glare of publicity, easily persuaded to be 'patriots,' perplexed, bemused, indeed terrified, yet only too anxious to take a cheerful view, vain perhaps but very unsure of themselves, pathetically responsive to a kind word. You could do anything you liked with them, if you would treat them (even the big ones), not as wolves and tigers, but as domestic animals by nature, even though they have been badly brought up and not trained as you would wish. It is a mistake to think that they are more *immoral* than politicians. If you work them into the surly, obstinate, terrified mood, of which domestic animals, wrongly handled, are so capable, the nation's burdens will not get carried to market; and in the end public opinion will veer their way."

Morgenthau read Keynes's letter with special interest, for Roosevelt instructed him to answer it. The task was agreeable. It gave the Secretary the chance to speak for the Administration, and by a calculated silence to reject advice he disliked. He was deliberately noncommittal. "It was very pleasant and encouraging to know," he wrote, "that you are in agreement with so much of the Administration's economic program. This confirmation coming from so eminent an economist is indeed welcome. Your analysis . . . is very interesting. The emphasis you put upon . . . housing . . . is well placed."

The emphasis Keynes put upon government spending Morgenthau simply ignored. He had long since registered his disagreement. But private investment concerned him deeply, and he had begun, long before he wrote, to investigate ways to stimulate it. Like Keynes, he felt that businessmen needed reassurance, but, with Roosevelt, he questioned their benevolence. He had large sympathy for small businesses but little for some big ones. He wanted to help the utilities, but he also felt that they had to be shown how to behave. He considered housing vital, but he doubted the wisdom of direct federal expenditures for construction. He believed, as he long had, that easy money would invite private investment and that business confidence would ensure it. Allowing always for relief, he considered economy in government the surest source of that confidence. So he had believed when he addressed the Academy of Political Science in November; so he believed when he addressed Keynes three months later.

Roosevelt, accepting Morgenthau's noncommittal reply for his own signature, could have had no doubt about what it implied. Morgenthau therefore felt that he still had an opportunity to conquer the recession without capitulating to the spenders. With the President apparently still undecided about what medicine he would prescribe, the Secretary in February and March recommended a number of remedies which were intended, in one way or another, to force or to induce a degree of private spending that would make a Keynesian policy unnecessary and undesirable. Keynes and his disciples, Morgenthau insisted, had a set of delusions all of their own.

### 4. Some Shots in the Arm

At the Treasury staff meeting of February 7, 1938, Morgenthau recalled the "bust-up" of the summer of 1933. Roosevelt had then turned to him, he said, to take the shackles off his hands, when everybody else in the Administration had failed. Either because he had been courageous or young or foolhardy, Morgenthau continued, he had taken a chance. He had "read up" on Warren and Pearson, and initiated the gold-buying program. That program might not have been "profoundly important," he said, but it had its own "small importance." It was all "very nice" for people to say they wanted no more monetary tricks, but if somebody did not try to provide a "shot in the arm" for the economy, they would get instead a transcontinental highway or $8 billion of extraordinary expenses. He wanted suggestions for avoiding a major operation.

Most emphatically the Secretary's staff advised stopping the sterilization of newly mined gold, a proposal which Morgenthau, with Roosevelt's consent, put to the Federal Reserve Board. They were agreeable, but Eccles thought it important for the Treasury to set a specific figure for desterilization — he recommended $20–25 million a month — so that the Federal Reserve System would know in advance exactly how much would enter bank reserves. Roosevelt endorsed that suggestion and approved also Morgenthau's plan to consult the British before acting. The Exchequer, completely sympathetic, had two questions: How could the United States expect a monetary action to restore confidence and improve business conditions, and why was the Treasury desterilizing instead of reducing the reserve requirements that had

so recently been raised? Through his representative in England,
Morgenthau replied that they were talking to the wrong man.
They would have to ask Eccles.

British acquiescence left Morgenthau with a clear field, and on
February 14 he and Eccles announced that the Treasury, after
consultation with the Federal Reserve, would no longer sterilize
gold imports or domestic gold production unless they together exceeded $100 million in any quarter. Drawing if necessary upon
gold in the inactive account, the Treasury would add $400 million
annually to bank reserves. This policy, furthermore, was retroactive to the beginning of the year. In explaining the announcement, Eccles said it seemed appropriate at once to add to reserves
and to relieve the Treasury of having to borrow to sterilize gold.
One reporter asked whether it would help business. The newspapers could interpret it any way they wanted to, Eccles replied,
taking pains to make it clear that the Treasury and not the Federal
Reserve Board had initiated the policy. Much amused, Morgenthau claimed "the baby," as he put it, for his own.

Among possible outlets for the easier money which these policies would provide, Morgenthau gave high priority to investment
in the utilities. Oliphant hoped to encourage such investment by
having the government supervise the reorganization of a public
utilities holding company (and perhaps later also of a railroad) in
order to prove that a properly financed corporation could operate
profitably. He had in mind forcing into receivership one of the
many public utilities companies in default of taxes. Acting as
receiver, the Treasury could cooperate with the Securities and Exchange Commission to restructure the company, acquire new
capital for it in private markets, and put it on a sound business
basis.

"Bring the public utility to me," Roosevelt said when he learned
of the plan late in January. "I have lived and worked with this all
my life. In ten minutes I will show you how to reorganize it." It
was his ambition when he left the White House to reorganize a
railroad "either on constitutional or unconstitutional lines."
Meanwhile he was "crazy" about the idea. The Secretary liked it
too. "If I could prepare and develop, in all its details, the re-
organizing and refinancing of public utilities and demonstrate that

it could be done," he wrote in his Diary, "I don't know of anything that would be more helpful at this time and then if we could also do a railroad I think it would be a real help towards putting the country back on its feet because there are three things the public is talking about — Public Utilities, Railroads and Housing and, if we can get this started, it will go a long way toward putting the recovery machinery into gear."

William O. Douglas and Jerome Frank of the Securities and Exchange Commission considered Morgenthau's proposal attractive. Douglas was especially interested in simplifying capital structures and achieving a geographical integration of utility properties. He thought the Genesee Valley Gas Company of New York would provide a miniature laboratory for a combined Treasury and SEC venture. Frank, however, suggested that it would be unwise to act until the Supreme Court had passed on the validity of the holding company law. He also doubted that the reorganization of a concern as small as the Genesee Company would do business conditions any good. But Morgenthau, anxious to proceed immediately, argued that the size of the company would not matter if newspapers in the community gave the reorganization adequate publicity.

That idea struck Frank as wonderful, for the potential for exciting publicity in the Genesee case was large. A group of Philadelphia and New York promoters had gained control of a puny operating company in the Genesee Valley by erecting a series of totally unnecessary holding companies. This had imposed a capital structure on the operating company far in excess of its value. The gross annual income of the operating company was only $57,-000. It had to support a superstructure containing outstanding securities of some $2,200,000, requiring annual interest and dividends of about $130,000. Here was a classic example of a concern managed and controlled by financial interests in a remote community who were out of touch with the local situation and without interest in developing it.

The SEC wanted to reorganize the Genesee Company under local management with a simplified capital structure, including only bonds with a sinking fund and common stock. Operations of the sinking fund would eventually eliminate the bonds. This was especially important because the company's principal asset was natural gas, and gas, subject to depreciation and exhaustion, made poor collateral for bonds. The structure of the company was so top-heavy that neither the SEC nor the Treasury believed they could turn over anything of value to the common and preferred stockholders of the holding company, but Morgenthau thought that the kind of reorganization which the SEC proposed would raise the morale of most small, locally operated holding companies. He suggested announcing the appointment of a committee to advise representatives of any utility company or community with a problem similar to the Genesee's.

During February the Treasury and the SEC drew up plans for the reorganization, which they submitted to the Federal District Court. Meanwhile the commission succeeded in getting some publicity from Rochester newspapers, though less than it considered valuable. By the time the reorganization went into effect, the case of the Genesee Company had slipped from public view, and the episode, important though it was for the company and the community, never had the effect on investment that Morgenthau had hoped it would.

Yet the experiment was not without significance. Though it revealed the limitations of initiative open to the Treasury in combating a recession, it revealed also the Secretary's continuing preference for governmental activity intended to reconstruct rather than to supplant private management. Keynes had proposed socializing the utilities or leaving them alone. Morgenthau, uncomfortable with either alternative, wanted government to show the way to private salvation. He lacked the authority or the staff to reach his objective, but his instinct led him to define an area for federal participation which the SEC was to exploit fruitfully over the years.

A comparable instinct molded his thoughts about housing, another vital area for investment. The Secretary believed that the government should rely primarily upon loans to encourage private building, whereas Senator Wagner and Jimmy Roosevelt, among others, preferred direct grants and other forms of federal aid. With the President's support, Morgenthau persuaded Wagner to include in his 1938 housing bill provisions for loans to private cooperatives and limited dividend corporations. The Secretary also blocked programs Jimmy Roosevelt sponsored for using WPA labor and RFC funds to build small, low-cost, prefabricated homes, some of them on suburban land which the Farm Security Administration had acquired. These plans, Morgenthau objected, would alienate private real estate interests and businessmen, duplicate or compete with the expanding operations of the Federal Housing Administration, and run up the federal deficit perhaps as much as $7 billion. His arguments convinced the President.

As Morgenthau saw it, people were not buying houses primarily because they cost too much. He particularly admired an experiment in self-help of twelve families in Iona, Idaho, who cooperated in building their own homes. Working together, they put up houses worth $2000 apiece for cash outlays of only $700 which were readily financed for $18 a month, a rate each of the families could easily afford. The Secretary hoped the Farm Security Administration would start more self-help projects, but more immediately, and on a much broader front, he wanted drastically to reduce housing costs.

To Morgenthau, as to others in Washington, the ability of the cement, steel, and plumbing industries to sustain prices for their products while other prices were falling, seemed to impair the entire recovery effort. At Oliphant's instigation, the Secretary in mid-1937 had directed the Division of Procurement to consult the Department of Justice before accepting any bids that seemed noncompetitive. Oliphant wanted all federal agencies to adopt that procedure, and Solicitor General Robert Jackson, fully in agreement, was anxious also to prosecute the men who were destroying competition and fixing prices. The recession intensified the antitrust sentiment that had been rising within the Administration for more than a year. In December 1937, Jackson publicly blamed monopoly and big business for the country's economic ills, as did Harold Ickes. As the year turned, Leon Henderson attributed the collapse of recovery to a shortage of purchasing power which derived, he said, from a too rapid rise in prices, especially monopoly prices. "Business has convicted itself of monopoly . . ." Jackson had earlier written Roosevelt, in a vein which exactly suited Morgenthau. "The people can be made to understand this issue. I think you can seize this subject in a way that neither your economic nor political enemies can withstand."

The thought had long since occurred to the President, who in mid-February 1938, after consulting the congressional leaders, decided to make an issue of monopolistic prices. He immediately directed Morgenthau to consult the appropriate agencies and prepare a suitable statement about the problem. As discussion began, Henry Wallace, while agreeing that Roosevelt had a magnificent opportunity to speak out about prices, was afraid that the President might do some "moralizing," which would have an unfortunate effect on the psychology of the economy. He therefore proposed saying only that prices were not altogether a matter of monetary manipulation. Others, however, hoped the President would set forth a broad policy for the government to follow during the next several months, while Morgenthau thought he intended to refer only to price trends, not to positive action.

To resolve these differences of opinion, Morgenthau appointed a working committee from the staffs of the Departments of Treasury, Labor, and Agriculture, which on February 16 submitted a tentative statement about prices. Recovery, it read, depended upon a steady increase in real income. In working for that increase, the Administration had been concerned necessarily with the relation of prices of groups of commodities to each other and with the movement of the general price level. Though the price level had fallen during the last six months, some prices remained high. Those for materials used in residential construction, for example, were still above the level for 1929. The artificial maintenance of these and other monopolistic prices was accentuating the deflationary pressure on competitive prices, especially those for food and raw materials. The government, therefore, should proceed against monopoly while it also tried to raise prices that were too low. This would increase the income and thus the purchasing power of farmers, among others, before their costs of production rose further.

Wallace thought the statement excellent, but Morgenthau insisted upon adding something about the consumer in the city to balance what was said about the farmer. He and his collaborators then took their handiwork to the White House. "Well," said

Roosevelt, "this is a new kind of meeting to take place in my office. This seems to be a case where the pupils are going to tell Teacher."

"If you will pardon me, Mr. President," Morgenthau replied, "I don't think it is quite that. You will recall that you asked me to prepare some material for you on the price situation and the Administration's price policy. So, I called in all these people so that we could get together something on which we all would be united. I think they have done a first-class job. I think when you read this you will find that it is an excellent statement of your position and I think it would be very helpful indeed in the present business situation if it is used."

The President was cautious. "Well," he said after some discussion, "I don't know about a formal statement. . . . I don't often issue Presidential statements unless it is on a very unusual occasion."

As Morgenthau later put it, the President took "sometime to warm up to having us give him this program. He seemed to resent it." Roosevelt decided against giving out a direct statement and he complained that the language of the draft was rather technical. There had also, he said, to be something definite for him to tell the housewife.

The drafting committee provided that addition quickly. "The average family," they wrote, "will benefit from the business recovery which a balanced price structure will foster. Increased employment and more continuous income should more than off-set any increase in the cost of living. . . . Incomes of most families will increase while the costs of what the housewife buys should show little change."

So amended, the statement suited the President, who released it on February 18, attributing it to the heads of the three departments that had prepared it and to the Federal Reserve Board, which had endorsed it. Morgenthau "felt so good" he called Wallace "to chin." "My gosh," Wallace told him, "I feel just as good as you do." They both felt even better when prices advanced, temporarily but broadly, in response to the President's statement, the announcement of desterilization, and the publication of a letter which the Treasury had drafted for Roosevelt, requesting the Reconstruction Finance Corporation to make credit available to all deserving borrowers.

The statement on prices had a more lasting effect in providing a mandate for an attack on monopoly. On February 22 Morgenthau suggested that the Federal Trade Commission, the Department of Justice, and the Department of State could cooperate in fighting monopolistic prices. Unless the Administration moved along that line, he believed, it would never solve the building problem. Roosevelt told him to go ahead, and the next day, on the Secretary's recommendation, an interdepartmental conference appointed committees to examine the prices of building materials, the structure of the building industry, and the relationship between that industry and the business cycle.

Committee reports completed on March 8 found three categories of building prices too high: basic iron and steel products, cement, and gypsum and gypsum products. Directly or indirectly, these commodities made up roughly one-third of the total cost of materials for low-cost and moderate-cost housing. The committee members failed to agree, however, on the extent to which prices might be reduced. A reduction of about 10 per cent would lower the cost of homes only 1 or 2 per cent; a reduction of 20 per cent would affect costs from 2 to 4 per cent. But there would be other advantages in price reductions, for iron, steel, and cement were important in a large number of industries.

The reports blamed the price-fixing practices of trade associations for the excessive costs of building materials. They also blamed inefficient, complicated, and restrictive methods of distribution and a rigidity in transportation costs. There were various avenues through which the government might act. In particular, the reports called attention to the possibilities of modification of the tariff, reductions in transportation rates, investigations by the Federal Trade Commission, alterations in government purchasing policy, enforcement of antitrust legislation, and the establishment of a permanent, interdepartmental fact-finding agency.

Morgenthau was impressed, but he asked for more data on comparative prices. He also wanted to know precisely what people were involved, for he intended, he said, to send for representatives of the relevant industries, to confront them with an airtight case when they arrived, to say to "Mr. Gypsum" that either he would have to come down on his prices or the government would make him come down.

On March 9 the Division of Procurement gave the Secretary something definite to work on. In cooperation with the Federal Trade Commission, the Department of Justice, and various local citizens' committees, the Division had studied cement prices, which Oliphant had long considered exorbitant. The Bureau of Reclamation was a major purchaser of cement, and the Division of Procurement believed that if it could buy for that bureau and ultimately also for the Army Engineers, the Navy, and the Department of the Interior, the government could alter its purchasing policy so as to put pressure on cement manufacturers to reduce their prices. Morgenthau and his advisers also thought that the cement industry might be particularly sensitive to tariff changes. "I've been around this town five years now," the Secretary said, "and if you want to get something done, you've got to . . . pick one thing. . . . After all, from the day NRA was over till this day we haven't accomplished anything along those lines. So we are taking on a big job."

As the Treasury developed its plans, Robert Jackson recommended some useful modifications, and Cordell Hull, while questioning the efficacy of renegotiating cement schedules in reciprocal trade agreements, gave the general program his enthusiastic support. Not so Henry Wallace, whose department included the Bureau of Public Roads. The government, Wallace objected, had known all along the cement people were violating the law. The thing to do now was to persuade them to listen to reason. If the country did not get recovery, he continued, it would not elect a Democrat in 1940. It would therefore be a mistake to irritate big business. "This is just the kind of stuff that the President loves," Wallace warned Morgenthau. "This is red meat for the President. We mustn't give anything like that to the President at this time."

But with Hull and Jackson behind him, Morgenthau on March 21 sent the President three recommendations, which Roosevelt at once approved. First, he concentrated cement purchases for all federal agencies under the Division of Procurement. Second, he required successful bidders on contracts for cement for the federal government to make their product available at the same price to all individuals doing work under government contracts. Third, he authorized grand jury investigations of collusion in the cement industry if anything developed in the negotiation of contracts that warranted such investigations. He also directed Morgenthau to get bids on cement f.o.b. mill in order to destroy the system by which producers set prices without regard to varying costs of delivery.

Roosevelt was in no mood to heed Wallace's warning, which Morgenthau relayed. The Administration, the President said, should not get together with big business. He was not going to let the flag down for anyone.

"The first time I let it down," Morgenthau replied, "you send me home. . . . The only thing that keeps me going is the moral uplift in this thing."

Signing the cement orders, Roosevelt beamed. "Now get plenty strong," he said. ". . . We're going into training for the heavy-weight championship."

Morgenthau was delighted. The best way to stimulate building, he was sure, was to knock down building costs. And the red meat of antitrust would, he hoped, dull the President's appetite for a menu of spending.

Marriner Eccles had restated the case for spending in an un-dated memorandum for Roosevelt. Consumer demand was de-clining, Eccles wrote, and would continue to decline unless con-sumer borrowing or new capital expenditures increased or the government spent more. Current income was being used for in-stallment payments on such things as automobiles. While this went on, capital expenditures would continue to decline. More-over, with the possibilities of war abroad, American markets in Europe would shrink. Inventories were still high, and Eccles ex-pected deflationary hoarding of corporate funds, especially if the undistributed earnings tax were repealed. Yet in spite of these conditions, the federal government was making only a negligible contribution to buying power. The nation, Eccles concluded, seemed launched on a severe depression. Big business was exploit-ing the bad times to drive for the repeal of New Deal reforms. The conciliatory attitude the Administration had adopted toward business had not borne fruit in dollars or in good will. Neither business nor Congress would provide leadership; it would have to come from the White House, and it was needed if the United States was going to defeat fascism. Eccles therefore urged Roosevelt to recommend immediately an expansionary program based upon deficit spending for public works.

William O. Douglas, Chairman of the Securities and Exchange Commission, proposed another form of spending. Reviving a 1934 proposal of Adolph Berle, he suggested a permanent system of industrial banks to service the capital requirements of legitimate small business and, to a limited degree, of all business. He wanted these banks to buy preferred or common stocks as well as to make loans. He thought the banks could remedy the inadequacy of supplies of capital, that they could work in cooperation with investment bankers, and that they would displace the influence of Wall Street in parts of the United States removed from New York. Most immediately, they could absorb the equity issues which the SEC had approved but which various businesses, large and small, had thus far been unable to market.

In mid-March Roosevelt also received a proposal for helping the railroads. Joseph Eastman of the Interstate Commerce Commission called for a reorganization of railroad financial structure, a scaling down of railroad debts, and the elimination of duplicate and unnecessary facilities. This would involve, he noted, a sacrifice on the part of all interests, investors, labor, communities, and government, for the sake of the general economy. It would include the consolidation of independent carriers and the coordination of all transportation agencies for the purpose of establishing a more economical system of transportation and more equitable treatment for labor.

Roosevelt, however, was still not ready to move. "As I see it," Morgenthau said at luncheon on March 14, "what you are doing now is just treading water . . . to wait to see what happens this spring."

"Absolutely," the President replied.

Two days later Roosevelt, who was about to leave for a short vacation at Warm Springs, told Morgenthau in his absence to review the various schemes that had been proposed for industry and

the railroads. A week of studying Douglas's plan for industrial
banks left the Secretary unpersuaded. At an interdepartmental
luncheon on March 23 he spoke out against any "hurry-up," "slap-
dash" bill. The problem divided itself, he said, between emergency and long-range needs. For the long run, Morgenthau considered the banking machinery of the country in many ways defec-
tive, but a satisfactory overhaul would require at least six months
of preparation and discussion. This was a job, he believed, that
ought to be done, but he opposed setting up a parallel banking
system, such as Douglas wanted. As far as emergency needs were
concerned, he was not convinced that there was any great demand
for equity financing. He had consulted a committee of investment
bankers who had been looking around for small, solvent concerns
that wanted new capital, but had not been able to find them.
Furthermore, the Secretary said, if the government started buying
stocks in industrial concerns, the public would "land the Administration in the ashcan." He disagreed with Douglas's retort
that they were almost in the ashcan already, and he considered
Douglas's defense of his plan confusing. "All I can say," Morgenthau told Bob Wagner when the meeting was over, "as a result of
it I had acute indigestion."

The Secretary also rejected Eastman's proposal for an emergency railway authority. The Interstate Commerce Commission,
Eastman argued, was a regulatory, not a planning body, and could
not exploit the main opportunities for government help, which
lay in extending credit to the railroads and helping them to consolidate. Morgenthau sympathized with Eastman's objectives, but
he thought the Reconstruction Finance Corporation had adequate
means for lending the railways money, and he saw no point in
establishing a temporary agency. He suggested instead creating a
Department of Transportation with the power vigorously to coordinate all facilities — trucks, airlines, and waterways as well as
railways.

This was the heart of the recommendation Morgenthau gave
Roosevelt over the telephone on March 31. Some months ago,
he said, the President had considered founding a Department of
Public Works under Jesse Jones. Now Morgenthau suggested that
if Jones could get the necessary legislation through Congress, he

should be appointed Secretary of a new Department of Transportation. The President's immediate response was favorable. To head up such a department, he said, would be the most difficult job in the country, but he thought Jones would do it well.

Morgenthau immediately instructed his staff to draft an appropriate bill. Setting up a new department would cost very little, but the plan would give Roosevelt one important part of a general message for Congress on recession and recovery. It would not be enough, Morgenthau knew, but it would be a start; and during his forthcoming week of rest at Sea Island he expected to produce the balance of what the President needed. Away from the turmoil of Washington, the Secretary could mull over relief, monetary, lending, and spending policies, and on his return to his office, his mind cleared and his spirit refreshed, deliver a full program to his chief.

## 5. Stampede

On March 25, while Roosevelt was on vacation at Warm Springs, the stock market had taken another sickening dip. This, as Morgenthau later observed, was the signal for new activity on the part of the spenders. Harry Hopkins, armed with memoranda from Leon Henderson and Aubrey Williams, camped on the President's doorstep. Before Roosevelt left Georgia, he decided he had to spend his way to recovery.

Morgenthau received his first intimation of the change on April 4 when Wallace telephoned him at Sea Island. The President, Wallace said, was "rarin' to go." He had instructed Wallace and Jones to work out a program for housing, flood control, rural rehabilitation, and loans to industry. He was also planning, Morgenthau learned two days later, additional appropriations for the Civilian Conservation Corps and the Works Progress Administration.

Under Secretary Roswell Magill, who attended the Cabinet meeting of April 5 in Morgenthau's place, gave the Secretary a full account of Roosevelt's state of mind. Congressional leaders, the President had complained, were thinking of going home after passing bills on the Navy, taxes, and government reorganization.

This would be fiddling while Rome burned, he said. He had done a lot of reading at Warm Springs, and he had reports from all branches of the government. The situation was bad not only for the country but also for the Democratic party, which might lose the fall election if conditions continued as they were.

The requests for funds he had already made, Roosevelt said, would at best maintain the existing state of affairs without making possible any improvement. These requests included $1 billion 250 million for relief for the first seven months of the fiscal year 1939, $50 million to keep three hundred CCC camps going, and $300 or $400 million for the RFC. He was now thinking about what additional action to take. He contemplated at least lowering reserve requirements, desterilizing more gold, and amending the housing law so that construction could begin before localities contributed the 10 per cent required of them.

Farley recommended expanding the post office building program, but the President said that money for post offices would go mainly to country towns, where unemployment was less severe than in the cities.

Garner thought the national debt was already enormous and wondered whether the country could stand any more. He also believed that the government had to move more people out of the cities into rural areas. As between the success of the Democratic party and the success of the country, the patriotic Vice President declared for the country.

Roosevelt said he was for the country, too, but that if the Democrats were defeated in the fall, a third party might arise and the Republicans win the election of 1940. That would mean the ruin of many New Deal reforms. He wanted to spend money, he explained, in such a way as to bring it back to the Treasury ultimately; what he needed was suggestions for how to do so. He also wanted the Treasury to give him full information on reserve requirements and desterilization.

Treasury officials elected to comment on Roosevelt's whole program. On April 7 Dan Bell wrote that the recession would reduce revenues for 1939 by at least $519 million. On account of the recession, furthermore, the President had already decided to request emergency expenditures above the estimate of the previous fall by some $2.1 billion. Bell foresaw a net deficit of at least $2.719 billion, of which only a small fraction could be offset by desterilizing gold or using deposits in the unemployment insurance trust fund.

In a memorandum on April 8, the Research Division questioned the wisdom of spending for public works, which would create anxiety within the business community. Instead the memorandum recommended three moves to increase business confidence and private spending: liberal relief appropriations, desterilization of the gold remaining in the inactive fund, and restoration of reserve requirements to the level existing before the Board of Governors first raised them.

Morgenthau was less cautious than his subordinates. Knowing Roosevelt as he did, he realized he had to meet him part way. On the train from Sea Island to Washington he wrote a carefully calculated "Memorandum for the President," which he intended to deliver as soon as he arrived on the evening of Sunday, April 10. The time was propitious, Morgenthau began, for Roosevelt to present to the people a comprehensive statement of policy. He should state first his long-run objectives and describe the major legislation needed during the coming two years to attain them. That legislation should include the creation of some kind of transportation authority, appropriations for the investigation and prosecution of monopolies, a wage and hour law, and the taxation of tax-exempt bonds. Second, the program should consist of an outline of specific steps, administrative as well as legislative, which Roosevelt proposed to take in order to eliminate inefficiencies and failures in parts of the New Deal already under way. Third, Morgenthau suggested the President prepare a comprehensive government spending and lending program, coupled with measures to stimulate private re-employment. It was most important, the Secretary wrote, to put to work immediately the ten million or more unemployed. But that did not excuse waste. In formulating a program, the Administration would have to correlate expenditures with the geographical distribution of unemployment.

Obviously the recession had destroyed Morgenthau's hopes for balancing the budget in 1939. But he still favored minimizing the total deficit, relying insofar as possible on lending rather than spending, concentrating spending insofar as possible on relief and work relief rather than on large-scale public works, and making the lending and relief policies handmaidens of a central purpose to spur private investment.

Roosevelt, however, had come to quite different conclusions. On the night of April 10, Morgenthau had a long and unhappy talk at the White House with the President, Hopkins, and Jimmy Roosevelt.

"We have been traveling fast this last week and have covered a lot of ground," the President said, "and you will have to hurry to catch up."

"Mr. President," Morgenthau said, "maybe I never can catch up."

Roosevelt smiled. "Oh, yes, you can — in a couple of hours."

With that he presented his ideas. Morgenthau's heart sank. It was clear that Hopkins had "sold" the President on spending. Ickes was to be put back into the business of lending money to states and municipalities. The United States Housing Authority was to have its loan authorizations doubled. The Federal Housing Administration was to build $500 million worth of houses. A transcontinental highway was to be started. And so on. Morgenthau listened and then read his own memorandum, with its emphasis on private re-employment.

When he finished, the President asked, "You are in agreement with this?"

"What you have outlined not only frightens me but will frighten the country," Morgenthau replied. "How much is it going to cost?"

"Oh," Roosevelt said, "we have all of that . . . we have all that."

Morgenthau asked to see a list of proposed expenditures, but none was forthcoming. "Please, Mr. President," he said on departing, "don't decide on this until you sleep on it."

The Secretary arrived at the Treasury the next morning depressed and angry. "I don't mind telling you gentlemen what I heard last night," he said to his staff. "The way it was put up to me last night just scared me to death — worse than I've been scared — and the thing hasn't been thought through. And fear begets fear — I mean . . . the President's attitude . . . in 1933, was, let's be calm and do things and overcome fear, but fear begets fear. . . . They had a conference — lasted an hour before I came — in advance of my coming — and I think the whole thing is finished, and there hasn't been a single person in the Treasury that knows a single thing about this. . . . I'm awfully afraid that the cards are all stacked against us."

The new program, Morgenthau went on, would wreck the RFC before Jones had a chance to get started. If Ickes and Hopkins as well as Jones were lending to municipalities, there would be an awful mess. The spenders had carried the day and the President, too. "They have just stampeded him during the week I was away. He was completely stampeded. They stampeded him like cattle."

Morgenthau left his staff to attend a late morning conference at the White House at which Roosevelt revealed his plans to the congressional leaders. It might not be necessary, he said, to increase existing WPA rolls beyond 2,600,000 but in all probability that many people would still be on work relief through the summer and the following winter. The $1 billion allowed for WPA for the fiscal year 1939 could not suffice. Unless the sum were increased, Hopkins would have to let 500,000 or more people go. WPA needed at least $1.25 billion more, the Farm Security Administration $150 million, the National Youth Administration at least $50 million, and the Civilian Conservation Corps $50 million simply to keep the boys in CCC camps who were already there. Roosevelt said he was also studying the loan situation, and he implied that besides whatever Jones could lend, the government would have to do a lot of spending of its own on public works.

Just before the meeting adjourned, Morgenthau broke in. The congressmen, he said, might be interested to know what the budget was going to look like for the coming fiscal year. He told them he thought revenue would fall below the January estimate by $900 million; that additional expenditures, including those Roosevelt had mentioned but excluding money for lending and pump-priming, would increase the deficit for 1939 to $3.5 billion at the inside. This, as he later recalled, gave everybody quite a shock.

After the meeting Roosevelt and Morgenthau had lunch. Usually this was a gay and friendly meal, but not that day. The President said coldly that Morgenthau had no right to bring up the question of the deficit in the morning conference, that the Secretary should have spoken to him first. He was going to take care of the unemployed, Roosevelt added, no matter how much it cost. "You can call Steve Early," he said vehemently, "and he will tell you that nothing is settled. You are just jumping at conclusions."

"No use getting angry," Morgenthau said. "No use in yelling at me. It does not do any good."

What did do Morgenthau some good was the memorandum his old reliable, Herman Oliphant, presented on April 12. The President, Oliphant wrote, should avoid deficit spending. Lending would help, but Oliphant particularly recommended lowering reserve requirements and desterilizing the gold in the inactive account. If these measures proved insufficient, Roosevelt could mobilize about $425 million of silver seigniorage which had been realized but held sterile, an additional unrealized silver seigniorage of about $500 million, cash in the Treasury's working balance of about $500 million, and the deposits of the Stabilization Fund of $1.8 billion. He could also devalue gold another 10 points, which would yield $2.5 billion, and issue about $3 billion of Thomas Amendment currency. Monetary rather than fiscal action, Oliphant maintained, would lift the recession.

Morgenthau read the memorandum aloud to Eccles, Hopkins, Wallace, Jones, and Jimmy Roosevelt. Paying no attention to monetary issues, Jimmy Roosevelt argued that lending was no substitute for deficit spending. Jones disagreed, but Hopkins outlined a program for heavy public works, combining loans and grants. He proposed doubling the authority of the United States Housing Administration to incur obligations, and increasing appropriations for highways, flood control, the National Youth Administration, the Civilian Conservation Corps, and the Works Progress Administration. As Hopkins and Jimmy Roosevelt talked on, Dan Bell concluded morosely that the net federal deficit for fiscal 1939 would exceed $4 billion and perhaps even $5 billion. Although social security receipts and desterilization would provide funds to meet part of that deficit, the Treasury would still have to go into the market to raise about $3 billion.

Eccles confidently predicted the market could absorb that amount, but Morgenthau dissented vigorously. He also warned against the dangers of any plan that stimulated a quick upturn and then fell flat. He disagreed with Hopkins's contention that the program would help the Democratic party. A burst of activity during the summer followed by a slump in the fall would have far from a good political effect.

"Now at last I have heard the program," Morgenthau told Jimmy Roosevelt, "and I wish you would take the following message to your father. 'After giving the matter further consideration, I will let you know whether or not I can finance it.' "

"Well, of course you can finance it."

"I don't know, Jimmy."

As he put it later, the Secretary was deeply shaken. That evening the Federal Reserve Board agreed to desterilize gold, to liberalize their standards in making bank examinations, and to lower reserve requirements. Even that news, however, failed to hearten Morgenthau. He felt the Administration was committed to an unsound policy. With a heavy heart he went home late and tossed in bed. Sometime in the early morning he made an anguished decision. For all his loyalty to the New Deal, for all his love of Franklin Roosevelt, he could see no choice but to resign. It was the blackest hour in his entire career.

Keeping his intentions to himself, Morgenthau telephoned Roosevelt to ask for his "day in court" — half an hour to go over the whole program. He next called Cordell Hull, who also opposed spending and wished Morgenthau the best of luck. The morning group at the Treasury stood solidly behind the Secretary. Like him, they saw no point in putting Ickes back in business because they did not believe it would get results; like him, they considered all the talk about a transcontinental highway immaterial, for construction would obviously proceed too slowly to spur the economy. Like him, they preferred, if there were to be expenditures, to see them go to agencies directly helping the underprivileged. His staff meeting over, at ten-thirty that morning of the unlucky 13th Morgenthau walked sadly to the White House.

"Mr. President," he said, "I am going to say something which is one of the most difficult things that I have ever had to do, but if you insist on going through with this spending program I am seriously thinking of resigning."

Roosevelt responded with a long dissertation on the solidarity of the British cabinet — how each member was bound by the decision of the majority and how they all stood or fell together. "You just can't do this," he said. "You have done a magnificent job, and you have kept your own counsel."

"After all," Morgenthau said, "nobody in the Treasury has had time to study this program, and we have not been consulted as to whether it can or cannot be financed; furthermore, whether it will achieve the results you desire."

The President then, as Morgenthau recalled it, became excited. If the Secretary resigned it would mean the destruction of the Democratic party, the creation of a third party and the loss of the Administration program in Congress. Morgenthau, moreover, would go down in history as having quit under fire.

"The trouble with you," Roosevelt said, "is that you are piqued and sore because you have not been consulted."

"No, Mr. President," Morgenthau said, "neither of those statements is correct. You are asking your general, in charge of finances, to carry out a program when he had nothing to do with the planning."

Obviously uncomfortable, Roosevelt indicated he would like to close the discussion. "I've got Baruch waiting," he said.

"Let him wait," Morgenthau said. "This is more important."

They parted without resolving their difficulties. Roosevelt simply would not listen to the talk of resignation, and Morgenthau for the moment saw no alternative.

As he later recalled, he spent the next few hours in a gloomy daze of indecision. But gradually the relative values of the situation began to sort themselves out, and his position began to clarify itself. He and the President had differed over an issue concerning which, it was fair to say, there were, at the very least, two sides. It was also a technical rather than a moral issue; a difference about means, not ends. And it was but one of the many issues involved in the Roosevelt Administration.

Morgenthau might disagree with Franklin Roosevelt about spending, but they were in agreement on most other broad questions. They shared the same deep conviction that the first concern of government should be for the masses of the people. They shared the same deep conviction that the democracies of the world had to prepare for an impending war with the forces of aggression. Morgenthau asked himself whether he should jeopardize those common objectives, whether he should withdraw from the common struggle, because of his opposition to one phase of the President's program. He still had, he realized, a splendid opportunity to make relief efficient, to improve the banking system and tax structure, to mold a foreign economic policy helpful to the democracies. More important, was he to desert the man he admired and loved second only to his father, because of a single disagreement? At the bottom of his heart, he knew his greatest usefulness was in the service of Franklin Roosevelt, and he could not abandon him. So Morgenthau stayed on.

Roosevelt took his program to the people on April 14. For four and a half years, he said, recovery had proceeded apace, but in the previous seven months there had been a setback. The recession had not yet turned to disaster. National income, for example, was almost 50 per cent higher than in 1932. Banks were not in trouble and the federal government had accepted the responsibility for relief. Yet many people had lost their jobs. In his message to Congress during the previous session, he had said that if private enterprise did not provide jobs, government would have to take up the slack. During the last two months it had become apparent that the government had to take aggressive action.

First, he recommended appropriations to maintain the existing rate of government expenditures for work relief and similar purposes. These included additional monies for WPA, for Farm Security, for the National Youth Administration, and for the Civilian Conservation Corps, in all about $1 billion 250 million more than he had estimated the previous January. Second, to provide additional bank reserves, the Treasury would desterilize about $1 billion 400 million of gold and $1 billion of additional credit would be made available by reducing reserve requirements.

In Roosevelt's judgment these two steps, however, were insufficient to start the economy upward. He therefore needed a third kind of government action. In order to add purchasing power by providing new work, he recommended that the United States Housing Authority undertake immediately about $300 million of slum clearance projects. He also planned to renew the public works program as soon as possible to provide $1 billion of permanent public improvements, $100 million more for federal highways, $37 million more for flood control, and $25 million more for federal buildings. This, he observed, would not only help the American people but would give democracy courage the world over.

Looking back on the budget crisis of 1938 in 1947 and again in 1959, Morgenthau was not sure who had been correct. Later the huge outlays for defense and war and then for the cold war persuaded economists and thoughtful businessmen to revise "orthodox" conceptions. Certainly an unbalanced budget did not need to be an automatic disaster, as many people thought in 1938; certainly government spending could assure levels of production and employment undreamed of then. Still, as Morgenthau later put it, his position in 1938 was based on the hope that the country could get along without calling upon sustained government spending to make up for the deficiencies of private spending — on the hope that the system might run on its own power. After twenty years he still thought a balanced budget should have been given a chance.

## 6. En Garde

Morgenthau, who had consistently stressed the importance of easy credit, was pleased to have Roosevelt refer to it in his Fireside Chat about the economy. By mid-April 1938, when the President spoke, the Secretary was satisfied with the direction of monetary policy. The Treasury had ceased sterilizing gold and the Federal Reserve Board had reduced reserve requirements. Banks now had ample funds to meet any foreseeable demand for loans, and interest rates and bond yields were again falling. Morgenthau believed, however, that banks were not yet functioning as they should.

The Secretary had been worried for some time about the power of bank holding companies, especially about the Transamerica Corporation of A. P. Giannini on the West Coast. Morgenthau admitted that Giannini's huge system, like its somewhat smaller counterpart which the Eccles family had created in the mountain states, had permitted Western bankers to overcome their dependence upon

Wall Street. He argued, however, that the bankers, while saving themselves, had done very little to help farmers and home owners, and he agreed with Roosevelt that "insiders," by manipulating holding companies, could exercise a dangerous control over banks in widely scattered communities. "Tickled to death" by Morgenthau's attitude, the President in March 1937 encouraged him to draft a message to Congress expressing their views.

The Secretary to his surprise then found Cy Upham, his principal adviser on banking problems, impressed by the many virtues of bank holding companies. As Upham pointed out, they concentrated banking resources; they made possible a higher type of management; they gave greater diversification to bank investments and loans; they permitted safer and less costly operations; they provided more varied services for customers; they gave mobility to bank credit within group areas; they made possible local financing of businesses which became units of national chains; and they provided a kind of equivalent for rural bank mergers. Yet Upham also recognized arguments against such holding companies. They constituted an evasion of statutory prohibitions against interlocking bank directorates and branch banking; they permitted exploitative manipulations by management; they throve on speculative fever; they made bank examination difficult; and they did not reach the weakest element in the banking system — the very small rural banks.

Upham's inconclusive analysis left Morgenthau doubtful about the problem which he asked interested federal agencies to review. The Federal Reserve, the Federal Deposit Insurance Corporation, and the Comptroller of the Currency opposed allowing a further growth of bank holding companies, but they also opposed, as did the Reconstruction Finance Corporation, dissolving the holding companies already in being. They did not want them to expand, but they could not agree about which agency should regulate them.

Their discussions revealed a sufficient consensus to permit Oliphant to draft a section on bank holding companies for a message on economic concentration which he was composing for the President. Adapting the case Morgenthau had been advancing, Oliphant recommended gradually taking the necessary steps to break up bank holding companies, and immediately passing laws to prevent them from acquiring control of any more units and from exchanging securities with any bank in which they held stock.

Roosevelt used most of Oliphant's ideas on banking in his message to Congress of April 29, 1938, which called for a general attack on all kinds of collectivism in business. The Treasury's purchasing policies and tax program were already keyed to the spirit of the message, and the Department further advanced the President's purpose when Oliphant represented Morgenthau at a series of meetings to plan the activities of the Temporary National Economic Committee which was for several years to investigate monopoly and potential monopoly in American industry. Meanwhile the debate about bank holding companies continued, but Oliphant's recommendations for regulating them won little support outside the Treasury.

Morgenthau kept the problem of holding companies much in mind during the spring of 1938 while he and Eccles turned to another controversial matter. They had both called Roosevelt's attention to the desirability of liberalizing bank examinations and coordinating the operation of the several federal agencies that conducted them. Eccles was particularly anxious to unify the examinations under the Federal Reserve Board. Morgenthau, on the other hand, cared less about unification than about revising the criteria for classifying bank assets. Both men wanted to relax those criteria, but Morgenthau gave more thought than did Eccles to the protection of depositors. The Secretary also expected to use bank examinations to keep the directors of bank holding companies from abusing their power.

Roosevelt in April instructed the Treasury to develop plans for uniform and less restrictive examinations that he could put into effect without enabling legislation. These directions did not fit in with Eccles's ideas, for there could be no unification under the Federal Reserve System without legislation, and any uniformity achieved by cooperation among the interested agencies was bound to reflect the dominant concern for depositors which was shared by the Treasury, the Federal Deposit Insurance Corporation, and the Comptroller of the Currency. The President's order in itself almost assured Eccles's dissent.

The others quickly reached agreement and submitted their recommendations to Morgenthau on May 2. Their purpose, to which Eccles also subscribed, as did the National Association of Supervisors of State Banks, was to reclassify bank loans in a way that would discourage speculation and encourage investment in high-grade securities. Their differences with Eccles arose over method. They proposed, for example, that banks should set aside net profits from the sale of securities until they had built up adequate reserves for their securities accounts. In contrast, Eccles and other Federal Reserve officials, while insisting on adequate reserves, opposed having banks earmark individual items of profit.

Disagreement became hottest over another seemingly technical matter. The Comptroller and the FDIC favored retaining the existing classifications of bank loans as "slow," "doubtful," and "loss," but substituting for those words the Roman numerals I, II, and III, which sounded less invidious. The classifications, the argument went, were useful for protecting depositors, but the terminology was not. The Federal Reserve, however, recommended eliminating the "slow" classification entirely and replacing it with a column of "Information and Comment" where examiners might enter their thoughts about individual loans.

Morgenthau, hoping for a compromise, delayed submitting the report to the President, but Eccles stood fast, and the Secretary early in June took up the case of the majority. Bank examinations, he held, had to be strict enough to provide full protection for all depositors. Eccles contended that deposit insurance, by removing the threat of bank runs, permitted more latitude in lending. If examiners gave banks more scope, he said, it would stimulate recovery. Morgenthau thought they could achieve recovery without risking deposits which were only partially insured.

On June 6, his patience exhausted, the Secretary announced that the National Association of State Bank Examiners had agreed to the report on uniform bank examinations which the Federal Deposit Insurance Corporation and the Comptroller of the Currency were about to submit to Roosevelt. He explained that the report recommended a uniform method of classifying bond investments with Roman numerals. The first four grades would be carried on the portfolio at cost rather than market value, while other classifications would be written down to market value. An accompanying statement criticized bankers "who have forgotten that one of their primary functions is lending" and predicted that the new regulations would encourage bank loans. The *American Banker,* praising the proposed changes, agreed.

The Federal Reserve, however, for reasons which Morgenthau considered "just a lot of spinach," continued to dissent. Eccles, rumor had it, hoped there would be no agreement since it might interfere with his objective of unifying the banking agencies. Though Eccles called the rumor a "damn lie," he admitted that he hoped no agreement would be reached because it would delay more substantial reforms. Morgenthau found that explanation pretty close to the substance of the "damn lie." The Secretary also felt that Eccles erred in trying to make bank examinations vary with the business cycle, with examinations loose in bad times and strict in good times. Eccles argued that as things stood the reverse was true. He was trying to be cooperative, he said, but he was frankly amazed that Morgenthau had told the press that the proposals of the FDIC and the Comptroller were going to the President even though the Federal Reserve dissented.

In fact the Secretary had not mentioned the Federal Reserve, though that omission in itself was eloquent. It was Eccles who let the world in on the details. Responding to a request from Senator Vandenberg for an analysis of the national monetary and banking system, Eccles was deliberately indiscreet. He included in an eleven-page letter, as he later recalled, "an aside dealing with the effect bank examinations had on the flow of credit." Only in that way, he contended, could he "prudently answer the Treasury in public and point out how the Comptroller's restrictive rules . . . stopped up the ready flow of credit into productive business channels." His letter, he wrote, "was one of the few times in the New Deal years when an official of the government absolved banks from economic sins and pointed the accusing finger at the Administration itself. Needless to say, Senator Vandenberg, who at that time was freely mentioned as a likely candidate for the Republican Presidential nomination, promptly inserted" the letter in the *Congressional Record* for June 16, and the press "leaped on the passages devoted to faulty examination procedures."

The publicity made Morgenthau boil. On June 16 he announced that he was going to recommend the immediate adoption of the program without Eccles's endorsement, unless he received it within forty-eight hours. When Eccles still held back, the Secretary delayed, gave the press a rebuttal to the arguments in Eccles's letter to Vandenberg, and explained again that the Treasury had "just one thing in mind — the interest of the depositor." On June 21 Eccles at last retracted and, contrary to his own recollection of the episode, accepted the majority's scheme for classifying bank loans.

Four days later Roosevelt issued the new regulations which allowed bankers to make sound, long-term loans without criticism from examiners. Bankers might now also invest in bonds of small but trustworthy local corporations even though these securities were not quoted on stock exchanges. Previously bank examiners had classified as "slow" the majority of loans for more than nine months, which had discouraged banks from making them. Furthermore, the old practice had been to deduct from net capital part of the "slow" loans and all of the "doubtful" and "loss" classifications. The new regulations limited those deductions to 50 per cent of the "doubtful" and 100 per cent of the "loss." At the same time they discouraged speculation by penalizing rapid buying and selling of securities for quick profits.

Eccles, however, was still dissatisfied. It was one thing, he believed, to get the new rulings on paper but quite another to have them applied. He continued, therefore, though without success, to press for the unification of bank examinations, indeed for the unification of the whole banking system. He continued, too, to protect bank holding companies from increased regulation or dissolution.

But the *Wall Street Journal,* the *New York Times,* and the New York *Herald Tribune* commended Morgenthau for his stand on examinations, and the proposals he took to Roosevelt also satisfied the President. The Secretary felt confident that his recommendations safeguarded depositors and took a significant step, as the *Wall Street Journal* put it, toward the easing of credit. He was willing to concede that Eccles knew more about banking than he did, but he was in this instance uncomfortable about Eccles's motives. Morgen-

thau, as his associates constantly discovered, had a cautionary instinct that led him to keep change within bounds and thus ordinarily to make reform possible.


## 7. Waste Not, Want Not

Though he had accepted defeat in the battle of the budget, Morgenthau had not surrendered his interest in government spending.
He continued after April 1938, as before, to be the watchdog of the
public purse. And also as before, while he and Harry Hopkins were
drawn together by their common concern for relieving the suffering,
they were sometimes driven apart by their differences about the
organization and administration of the relief program.

So it was that Morgenthau interceded to prevent the allocation
of relief monies directly to the Works Progress Administration. According to the procedures that had existed since 1935, both the Bureau of the Budget and the President had a check on the use of
those funds. This permitted the Treasury and the Bureau to over-
see the bookkeeping of relief expenses, and permitted Roosevelt to
turn down projects which did not seem to him to be practical. The
revised procedure which the WPA proposed would have given it
and other agencies the authority to review their own accounting
and to pass on their own projects. Morgenthau therefore on May 5
urged the President to continue the existing system, which Roosevelt did.

The President's support encouraged Morgenthau to reopen the
question of unifying spending, an objective which Roosevelt had
previously resisted. At luncheon on May 9 Morgenthau suggested
consolidating all the money in the relief bill in a single fund for the
President to administer through one agency. The economy was still
declining, the Secretary argued, and there was a feeling throughout
the country that the Administration was not going to take care of
the situation. The management of relief would be more efficient
and public confidence in Administration policy would grow if the
President could persuade Congress to centralize federal spending.
He had fought, bled, and died on the Hopkins-Ickes problem for
four years, Morgenthau continued. They were grand fellows,

friends of Roosevelt, but the President could not give them both money and not have them fight.

To Morgenthau's surprise, Roosevelt agreed. It was, he said, too late to take up the relief bill with the House of Representatives, but Morgenthau could try his luck with the Senate. Indeed he gave the Secretary carte blanche to talk with Jimmy Byrnes. Overjoyed, Morgenthau said to Dan Bell: "We got a chance! It's worth fighting for."

There was no need to fight with Byrnes. As Morgenthau discovered that afternoon, the senator was entirely of his mind, worried about the timing of Ickes's expenditures, and fearful that divided authority and delay would work hardship on the unemployed. Harry Hopkins, whom Byrnes summoned, also believed that Ickes's public works program would start too slowly, but Hopkins did not think Congress would centralize appropriations because Ickes was popular on the Hill. Byrnes replied that Morgenthau's suggestion would appeal to Senators Harry Byrd, Carter Glass, and Bennett Clark, among others. If Hopkins would tell the Senate Appropriations Committee just what the unemployment situation was and how many additional people needed relief, Byrnes thought the Senate might rewrite the House's bill.

Hopkins's timidity disturbed Morgenthau. Back at the Treasury, he gave him, as he put it, "a piece of my mind," and asked "where was the Harry Hopkins I used to know in New York State?" Yet the events of the day were encouraging. "For the first time in a month," the Secretary told his staff, "I feel again like Henry Morgenthau, Jr. And I think if they do this thing and give everybody on the relief rolls a job — it won't cost as much as they're proposing to spend."

Byrnes, after reconnoitering, concluded that in order to make spending flexible Roosevelt had to announce his support for a unified arrangement, but for several weeks the President was silent. Meanwhile Hopkins on May 17 "pulled out the stops," as he had promised Morgenthau he would. There were 2,800,000 people on WPA rolls, Hopkins testified, but there were between 10 and 12 million unemployed. Only about a third of the funds the House had agreed to appropriate were transferable at the President's discretion. Expecting little improvement in conditions, Hopkins urged the Senate to give the President more latitude for meeting the emer-

gency. Byrnes and Jimmy Roosevelt stressed the same points in
their private conversations with Democratic senators, but on May
31 Morgenthau told the President that the relief and recovery bill
"would not do the trick" unless he intervened. Willing at last to
act, Roosevelt dictated a draft of a letter which Aubrey Williams
and Herbert Gaston later polished. Unemployment had grown,
Roosevelt said, and projects begun the next winter or spring would
not contribute to the needs of the summer or fall. To fill the gap,
he hoped the relief bill would "put no restrictions on the immediate starting of relief and public works projects," and to that end,
"flexibility of actual administration" was "essential."

Alben Barkley, acting as Roosevelt's agent, introduced an amendment to the bill giving the President discretion in the use of the
$1.425 billion for WPA. Although other funds, designated for
housing, agriculture, and large-scale public works, were unaffected
by the amendment, Morgenthau and Byrnes felt that Barkley's proposal went as far as the temper of the Senate would permit. On
June 22 Roosevelt signed the amended $3.75 billion lending and
spending bill. He disclosed at that time that Department of Commerce estimates of national income were $5 billion above what they
had been earlier in the spring. "Someone," the President said, referring to Morgenthau without using his name, had remarked that
there had been a few raindrops coming from heaven, and possibly
they would be followed by a much needed shower. The new legislation would help recovery. Three hundred and sixty million dollars
worth of public works projects would begin within sixty days. The
appropriations, moreover, permitted sizable expenditures on many
worthy forms of public assistance — for agriculture, for industry,
and for the neediest unemployed. Roosevelt was wearing his smile.

Morgenthau was also pleased, for the Act gave Roosevelt authority to spend money for direct relief, which the Secretary had been
advocating. As he had reminded the President on May 12, the
recession had been devastating in cities in the Middle West. Yet
WPA had ordinarily ignored Roosevelt's informal recommendation
of February to transfer funds to direct relief, and Morgenthau
thought the President would now want to issue explicit, official instructions. Roosevelt, however, referred him to Hopkins, who, according to Morgenthau's account, on May 13 "opposed . . . allo-

cating any money for direct relief as he said we must not do anything to keep the States . . . from allocating sufficient of their funds." But Hopkins could not long overlook the figures his own agency was compiling. Between October 1937 and May 1938, WPA rolls increased 79 per cent for the country as a whole, whereas in five cities where conditions were deplorable, the increases were much larger: 571 per cent in Flint, 434 per cent in Detroit, 197 per cent in Cleveland, 194 per cent in Toledo, 110 per cent in Chicago. With the numbers still rising, Ohio, Illinois, and Michigan had to have more federal funds. Furthermore, as Hopkins told Morgenthau on May 16, in seventeen southern states people were starving. Obviously shaken, Hopkins surrendered theory to human necessity and endorsed an amendment permitting direct relief that Byrnes added to the spending bill.

Morgenthau also succeeded in diverting, though not in recovering, some of the appropriation for agriculture. "I don't know," he wrote in his Diary in mid-May, "but I think from the day we started killing pigs there has been a curse on this Administration. The thing I am trying to do now, instead of spending $100 million to grow less wheat, I want them to buy wheat and make it up into flour for the people who need it." The farm bloc in Congress protected the money for price supports, but Morgenthau was able to revive the program which the Federal Surplus Relief Corporation* had initiated in 1933. He wrote in his Diary on May 13, "I first began to work on the President and Wallace and Hopkins to take care of the ill-fed and the ill-clothed through Surplus Commodities Corporation. Up to that time my records show that Wallace had not been buying $1 worth of flour. . . . From the date of our meeting, the President and Wallace began to take an interest in feeding the needy. I consider that date a most important one historically."

Within a week Wallace was distributing wheat in Chicago, Flint, Toledo, and Cleveland. In those and other areas, the Federal Surplus Commodities Corporation also made available beans, peas, cabbages, celery, rice, butter, dried skimmed milk, potatoes, fresh apples, and dried prunes.

The Bureau of Public Health reported, however, that children of families on relief in Chicago and elsewhere were not getting an

* In 1935 succeeded by the Federal Surplus Commodities Corporation.

adequate amount of milk. Hopkins had no money for milk, and Wallace was unable to supply it because it had not been ruled a surplus commodity. Morgenthau explained the situation to the President at luncheon on May 23, but without visible effect. He resorted then to Mrs. Roosevelt, his secret weapon. The problem, he told her, was to find some way of allocating perhaps $250,000 expressly for the purpose of distributing milk. He did not care whether it was fresh or powdered. The main thing was to get moving, for he did not want misery to spread, or some poor mother to commit suicide with her babies. "I worked awfully hard on this for ten days," Morgenthau concluded, "and I know it's out of my line, but on the other hand I don't have two glass eyes."

"They must care for them," Mrs. Roosevelt replied. ". . . I'll ask Franklin about it tonight. Not as though you said anything, but as though I were troubled."

Her intercession solved the immediate problem in Chicago, but Morgenthau hoped also to find a long-range solution for getting a balanced diet to the indigent wherever they lived. As Surgeon General Parran observed in a memorandum of May 25, dietary deficiency was high throughout the country and especially in the South. Both he and the Secretary would have liked to use surplus wheat for cattle feed and then to give out meat and dairy products to the unemployed. Wallace objected, however, that that would depress prices. As for increasing the consumption of wheat in breadstuffs, Wallace added, "well, that's out of the question." It could not be done, and in any case it was bad dietetics. In his opinion wheat was not a food which developed resistance to disease. He apparently preferred corn, largely for political reasons. If the government got people to eat more wheat, he argued, in the long run it would cause a political jam in the cornbelt. "All I could do," Morgenthau later said, "was not to just curse in his face."

Morgenthau was just as angry with Hopkins and Aubrey Williams, who opposed the distribution of any foodstuffs, even the surplus commodities that Wallace was willing to give away. If WPA began delivering food, Williams maintained at a White House conference on May 31, the public might get the impression that the Administration was switching from a works program to direct relief, and the whole problem of relief for unemployables would revert to the federal government. The preferable solution, he suggested, was to increase the wages of low income groups. That, Roosevelt replied, was out of the question for the time being. Distributing food would not replace work relief, he assured Williams, but only supplement it by stretching WPA funds. He therefore directed Wallace to go ahead.

When Wallace had disposed of the surpluses he had in hand, however, Hopkins put a stop to the program by denying it further money. He helped to subsidize Dr. Parran's continuing studies of diet, which he considered important, but he would not help to hand out groceries, as he put it, for he considered that degrading. Consequently for months agricultural surpluses again piled up while the needy remained ill-fed.

In the spring of 1938 Morgenthau tried two other approaches to the problem of surpluses. Refurbishing and expanding an abandoned project of 1933, on May 27 he suggested making a loan to China for the purchase of flour and cotton gray goods. This would dispose of a considerable quantity of wheat and cotton, he argued, and also provide employment in milling and textiles. He recommended, too, exchanging agricultural surpluses for strategic materials of which the United States was short. Hopkins and Wallace responded favorably. Wallace especially liked the idea of the loan, for it would assist the Chinese in their undeclared war with Japan. Hopkins was enthusiastic about stock-piling strategic materials, which he thought the Administration could undertake without additional legislation.

Roosevelt was more wary. The State Department would have to approve a credit for China, he said, and Congress would have to authorize any exchange of surpluses the government had acquired. As an alternative the President suggested that an American corporation, like United States Steel, might buy American cotton and use it to barter for manganese or some other commodity in short supply. Morgenthau feared that would conflict with Hull's basic philosophy of international trade, but Roosevelt said it could be taken care of on a "24-hour basis" philosophy.

At the State Department on June 1, Morgenthau found Hull "extremely sarcastic and bitter in his attitude toward the White House," pessimistic about everything, and furious with Jimmy

Roosevelt, who, he believed, had led the President to care more
about reform than recovery. This unpropitious mood did the idea
of a credit for China no good. When the United States made a similar loan in 1933, Hull said, Japan had protested. He asked what
Wallace and Morgenthau would think of finding out whether the
Japanese cared to buy more cotton or wheat. Then, if Japan turned
them down, they would be more or less free to go ahead with China.
Snippy to the end, Hull twitted Wallace about the accumulations
of cotton and wheat. "I thought," he said, "you had all of these
things under control." By June 6 he was on record against a credit
for China on any terms, for he believed it would surely antagonize
Japan and needlessly complicate American policy in the Orient.*

Morgenthau had no better luck with his idea of exchanging agricultural surpluses for strategic materials. After studying the matter, Oliphant concluded that the Surplus Commodities Corporation
could not legally arrange the exchange. Roosevelt continued to
advocate circumventing the law by working through a private corporation, but Morgenthau, whose staff investigated that possibility,
told Wallace sadly that "with all due respect to the President I
think he's all wet."

For the Secretary, the problems of spending and relief in 1938
must have had nightmarish qualities. Once again he had to struggle for a businesslike system of accounts. In that he succeeded.
Once again he had to fight alongside Hopkins for flexibility in the
use of relief monies. In that he was only partially successful. Once
again he tried but failed to reduce expenditures for the curtailment
of planting. Once again he struggled, with only limited effect, to
make surpluses available to friendly powers abroad and to the
hungry at home. In spite of all of his efforts, he believed, as he
had since 1933, that the government was not only spending too
much, but also, too often spending unwisely. Therefore the night-
mare of 1938. The problems of taxation, which consumed much of
his energy that spring, made his dreams no sweeter.

* See pages 502, 512.

## 8. Taxation in Recession

The debate over tax revision began late in the summer of 1937 when Roswell Magill presented studies of taxation which Morgenthau had commissioned. Though Magill reported before the stock market broke and Congress acted only after recession had gripped the economy, Treasury policy in that time had substantial continuity of purpose. Indeed Magill's report in many respects was itself an elaboration of principles to which the Treasury had been committed for several years. It emphasized the importance of setting schedules that would produce adequate revenue, of taxing in accordance with ability to pay, and of preventing tax avoidance.

Yet the report seriously questioned some of the assumptions on which Morgenthau had been proceeding. A year-to-year balance in federal revenues and expenditures, it asserted, would be a superficial and unrealistic aim for the tax structure. Taxes instead should be designed to yield sufficient revenues to balance expenditures over a number of years, perhaps a decade. "In periods of recession," the report explained, "such a tax structure will produce a marked decline in revenues at the very time when the financial requirements of the Government are likely to increase substantially. The result is a budgetary deficit, which is financed . . . by the sale of interest-bearing obligations. . . . The effects of the borrowing will be stimulating to the national economy.

"In the opinion of an important body of present-day economists, a business depression is characterized by a lack of balance between saving and investment. . . . The unpromising or threatening outlook causes individuals and institutions to withhold funds representing bona fide savings from current investment in concrete, durable goods; and this withholding creates a volume of unemployment of both labor and capital, corresponding to the excess of such savings over current investment. If such abortive savings are borrowed by the Federal Government and expended in the current employment of labor and capital, the effect is to increase the national income by virtually the whole of the sums so borrowed, or even more. . . .

"If, in contrast to borrowing, the Federal Government attempts to meet its current expenditures by the imposition of new taxes, such degree of success as is obtained tends to be achieved at the expense of the entire economy."

Morgenthau never accepted Magill's reasoning, which was similar to that of Keynes, but with characteristic respect for the ideas of his chosen advisers, the Secretary sent the report to the Joint Committee on Taxation. Furthermore, though he differed with some of its premises, he agreed with most of its specific recommendations. It proposed eliminating many excise taxes, reducing the allowance for mineral depletion, and increasing taxes on modest estates and on personal incomes in the medium brackets. It especially urged the repeal of some corporate taxes and the revision of others in order to make the total impact of corporate taxes proportionate to business size and business profits. Magill and his associates found the undistributed earnings tax a useful economic and social instrument, but they suggested establishing a steeper graduation, starting with a lower rate, and providing preferential treatment for small corporations.

Congressmen Doughton and Vinson of the House Ways and Means Committee had several reservations about the Treasury's program. Vinson saw no chance of reducing the allowance for mineral depletion. He also doubted the wisdom of decreasing any corporate taxes unless the undistributed earnings tax could be amended to produce more revenue. Raising personal income taxes in 1938, a congressional election year, was political poison which neither Vinson nor Doughton was willing to prescribe, yet both were too concerned about revenue to contemplate significant cuts in excise taxes.

Roosevelt, who considered Magill too conservative, had ideas of his own. In conference with Democratic congressional leaders in November 1937, he spoke emphatically in favor of retaining the undistributed earnings tax. He was amenable to reductions for corporations with incomes of $15,000 or less in order to permit them to expand plant or build up reserves, but he warned against the possibility of corporations defeating the purpose of the tax by readjusting their capital structures. Too much wealth was controlled by two hundred big corporations, the President said, as he urged the congressmen to work out a system for lowering taxes on small businesses while raising them on large ones.

On November 23 Morgenthau and Magill took Roosevelt a recommendation for putting a top tax rate of 20 per cent on net undistributed corporate profits, scaled down to 16 per cent for corporations with smaller earnings, and exempting those earning $25,000 or less. The top rate was much too low, the President said. He knew of no case of a corporation with an income of $1 million or more that had any difficulty in distributing dividends. When Magill cited Studebaker, which needed to retain earnings in order to have adequate working capital to compete with its larger rivals in the automobile business, Roosevelt scoffed. But while he was talking, Vinson's subcommittee endorsed the very rates he opposed. Magill had been keeping the committee in line, Morgenthau pointed out, but he could not continue to do so if the President forced the Treasury to adopt his views.

The Senate Finance Committee was already proceeding on its own. Unlike Vinson and Doughton, who were at least willing to listen to Roosevelt and were anxious to protect the principle of the undistributed earnings tax, Pat Harrison stood for repealing it. He had never liked the tax and now, he told Magill, Joe Kennedy had convinced him that it was forcing corporations into receivership. The senator wanted to act at once, during the special session of Congress sitting in the fall of 1937, and to press also for the repeal of the capital gains tax. He shrugged off Magill's argument for general, rather than piecemeal, revenue legislation; he chose to interpret Roosevelt as agreeable to his purpose; and he complained that taxes designed to hit big business and rich men also hit the small businesses he wanted to miss.

Harrison had powerful friends whose influence grew as the recession worsened. One of the heaviest lobbies ever to descend on Congress appeared during the last week of November to demand tax revision. Among those who testified, Kennedy, Hopkins, and Bernard Baruch advocated the immediate repeal of the undistributed profits tax. It was characteristic of Kennedy and Baruch to oppose any tax that business found distasteful, and Hopkins, according to the guesses of some columnists, itched for business support for the presidential nomination in 1940, but they all also believed that tax reduction would encourage private investment. Indeed Jesse Jones and Eccles, too, as well as a number of professional economists, called the undistributed profits tax a cause of the recession. Part of the time, Magill told Roosevelt, he did not know whether he was being shot at by his friends or by his enemies.

If Congress cut taxes hastily, the President replied, he would keep it in session until it made up all the resulting deficiencies in federal revenue. On the Hill, Alben Barkley warned his colleagues that there was no use in trying to kid the American public; Congress could not rush a tax bill through. That statement, Morgenthau thought, eased the pressure on the Administration, but privately the Secretary also admitted that Magill's report had no chance of adoption. Indifferent or opposed to most of the Treasury's program, Congress was clearly going to concentrate on corporate taxes, and Harrison, at least, had apparently enlisted with the legions of business and wealth.

The President had little choice but to accept Fred Vinson's reasonable formulation for the tax bill. At the White House early in December 1937, Vinson told Roosevelt and Morgenthau that the highest rates he could secure for the undistributed profits tax would range from 16 to 20 per cent. These rates should yield slightly less than existing schedules, but Vinson had devised an additional tax, the "third basket" tax, which would make up the loss and, more significantly, force the distribution of earnings of closely held corporations, an objective dear to the President.* With his approval and the Treasury's, Vinson's subcommittee reported out the tax plan the congressman had described. The 16–20 rate on undistributed profits applied to corporations with earnings of more than $25,000; those with less income paid between 12½ and 16 per cent; and the "third basket" tax affected only those closely held corporations with net incomes over $50,000 that distributed less than 60 per cent of their earnings.

During the hearings on the subcommittee's recommendations, a number of witnesses criticized the "third basket" tax, but none of

---

* Many closely held corporations were family corporations organized largely in order to permit the retention of earnings which, had they been distributed, would have been subject to high surtaxes on personal income.

them made a very convincing case. Their principal argument was that the tax would put family businesses at a disadvantage as compared to more widely owned corporations. But the ordinary American corporation during the previous decade had distributed on the average much more than 60 per cent of its income. If corporations continued that practice, they would not have to pay the "third basket" tax which would penalize only those corporations retaining earnings in order to allow shareholders to avoid their income taxes. Indeed the subcommittee's proposal permitted closely held corporations to retain all or any part of their earnings if their shareholders would consent to pay the taxes for which they would have been liable if those earnings had been distributed.

Perhaps the very purpose of the tax accounted for the opposition to it, which Congressman John McCormack, Massachusetts Democrat, organized within the House Ways and Means Committee. Bernard Baruch also objected to the subcommittee's bill, especially to the undistributed profits tax and the capital gains tax, and Arthur Krock, the influential *New York Times* columnist, echoed Baruch's opinions. As Morgenthau warned Roosevelt, Pat Harrison was saying in private that the Senate would rewrite the bill to conform with Baruch's recommendations. Like others in Washington, the Secretary wondered how many congressmen were indebted to Baruch for campaign contributions and other favors. Roosevelt, however, was not worried. Before the bill went to the Senate, he promised Morgenthau, he would go on the air and make it perfectly clear that he would not tolerate the reopening of loopholes that the Revenue Act of 1936 had closed. As for Baruch, who blandly assured Steve Early that his attack on the tax bill was not meant to suggest anything personal, Roosevelt considered his behavior "amusing," but also "sordid."

Roosevelt miscalculated. To the consternation of the Administration, McCormack in March 1938 mustered enough votes in the House to eliminate the "third basket" tax. The storm had been coming for some time, Doughton told Morgenthau; now he had been knocked down, rolled over and drug out. He doubted very much that he could get the House to reverse itself. In that case, Roosevelt concluded, there was no point in trying. He was probably correct, but Morgenthau considered the defeat of the "third basket" tax the worst slap the President had had to take during his entire administration.

The defeat also cut off considerable revenue which Morgenthau hoped to recapture by taxing the income from federal, state, and municipal bonds. The Treasury was drafting a speech for Roosevelt requesting Congress to remove the exemptions on those securities and thereby to close an important avenue of tax avoidance. That issue, and the fate of the rest of the bill which the House had approved, now rested with the Senate, where Harrison was striving to reduce the tax on capital gains and to substitute for the undistributed earnings tax a flat 18 per cent tax on corporate income.

In a nation-wide radio address, Harrison advocated tax reduction as an essential spur to business confidence. Roosevelt, urged on by Morgenthau, intended to answer the senator early in April, but the President was preoccupied by the spending bill, and while he delayed, the Senate accepted Harrison's schedules and the revenue bill went to conference where representatives of the two houses began to reconcile their differences. Roosevelt then asked Morgenthau to prepare a letter for the conference committee which "the man in the street" could understand.

By April 13 Magill had drafted a letter attacking the deletion of the undistributed profits tax and the weakening of the capital gains tax as repudiations of New Deal principles. He called for the retention of the House's graduated schedule on capital gains, because the Senate's flat rate was a bonanza for clever speculators. He also defended the undistributed profits tax: "Otherwise we grant a definite incentive to the avoidance of personal income tax payments through methods which are legal, but which are contrary to the spirit of the principle that every citizen should pay taxes in accordance with his means."

Jimmy Roosevelt and Steve Early suggested that the letter was politically dangerous at a time when business conditions were so bad. It would also, they argued, antagonize the Senate without accomplishing anything. Morgenthau was furious. "What about the 130,000,000 people who were under the impression that the President wants certain principles in the tax bill," he said, "and he keeps quiet and lets the thing pass without saying anything?" Roosevelt signed the letter.

The President, however, aware of his opponents' strength, told Doughton and Vinson to make the best trade they could. If the Senate did not go along with the Administration, he said, he was thinking seriously of vetoing the bill. Magill feared the Treasury would lose everything but its underwear before the trading was over. Morgenthau thought they had already lost even that. When the bargaining ended, the conference committee had retained the flat tax on capital gains and, while paying lip service to the undistributed earnings tax, made that tax so small that it was fruitless. It also ignored the message on tax-exempt securities which the President sent up on April 25, too late to have any effect in 1938.*

On May 18 Roosevelt reviewed the situation with Morgenthau and Magill. Magill reported their conference at length:

> The President . . . jokingly called attention to the fact that the Secretary of the Treasury had made no recommendation as to the President's action on the bill, but had merely asked for a conference to discuss the subject. . . . The Secretary asked whether he had not been pretty cagey in framing his letter that way. The President then asked whether we had considered that he had three possible courses of action. He could sign the bill, he could veto it or he could keep it for ten days and it would then become a law without his signature. We said we had realized that these three courses of action were open. The President said that, of course, he could not veto the bill but that at present he inclined to the third course . . . The Secretary observed that he liked that better than the President's previous suggestion of signing the bill but issuing a statement at the same time.
>
> The President started to ask me about the contents of the bill but before I could say anything proceeded to summarize the bill for himself. . . . He said that there were a large number of administrative changes which on the whole were good. . . . I verified this conclusion. . . . I told the President that the bill would yield approximately $65 millions less under present business conditions. . . . In a good year the bill would produce

---

* Borah had submitted a proposal taxing the income on future issues of federal securities, but the Treasury successfully fought it because it discriminated in favor of state and local bonds which would remain tax exempt.

around $230 millions less. . . . The bill eliminated a number of undesirable nuisance taxes. . . . The bill retained the principle of the undistributed profits tax but the differential is so small that it would probably not prevent a small group of individuals who control a profitable company from leaving the profits on their money in the company with the net result of avoiding personal income taxes which they would pay if the earnings had been distributed. . . . While the differential is lower the bill will help small business. . . .

The President said the existing rates of taxes on capital gains were too high. I interrupted to say that I did not think they were too high, the real objection to the existing law was that the treatment of capital losses was unfair. . . . The President said to put it that way. . . . Under this bill the individual with a small capital gain of $5000 would pay 15 per cent and the individual with a $500,000 capital gain would also pay 15 per cent. This was a clear violation of the principle of taxation according to capacity.

The President asked whether he could have his statement by tomorrow so that he could study it. I said we would give it to him by that time, since he had previously expressed similar views in his letter to the Conference Committee. The President said that was true but the statement to the Conference Committee was too detailed and technical, this time he wanted a short simple statement.

The Secretary said why not sign the bill promptly and issue no statement. The President seemed impatient with this suggestion. He said he wanted to take time and go over a memorandum on the subject. The Secretary said that after he had gone over the memorandum he might ask the advice of the Cabinet. For instance, it might be well to get Mr. Farley's view on the political side. The President said the question was one he had to decide for himself, that it would not be interesting to ask the Cabinet about it since he already knew what their views were.

Though Roosevelt seemed set on letting the Act become law without his signature and then explaining why he had done so, Oliphant recommended a veto. The striking fact about the Act, Oliphant maintained, was that it so obviously revealed Baruch's influence on Harrison. New Deal opponents of the bill were calling it outright the Baruch bill. Many Washington columnists interpreted it as a victory of Baruch over Roosevelt, observing also that Harrison and Jimmy Byrnes had built a fire under Doughton to force the conference committee to adopt the Senate version. Oliphant also criticized the Act on economic grounds, lamenting especially the emasculation of the undistributed earnings tax. Corporations would simply bury the earnings they withheld, he predicted, whereas shareholders would use distributed profits either to buy consumer goods or to make new investments, and the government would spend taxes it collected for public works.

Roosevelt appreciated Oliphant's spirit but hesitated to take his advice. For several days he withheld his final decision. Then, using material which the Treasury had supplied, he analyzed the Revenue Act on May 27 in a speech which neither Morgenthau nor Harrison had known he was going to deliver. It was a commencement address at the high school in Arthurdale, West Virginia, an impoverished industrial town which Mrs. Roosevelt had made a special effort to reconstruct. Though the occasion was an unlikely one, the President broadcast his speech, and Steve Early drew the attention of the press to it. It was full of fight.

For a great many years, Roosevelt said, the United States had accepted the principle that taxes ought to be levied on individuals and families in accordance with their ability to pay. The new tax bill, though it had some good features, threatened that principle. The penalty it imposed "for withholding dividends to stockholders," Roosevelt explained, "is so small . . . that it is doubtful, very doubtful, whether it will wholly eliminate the old tax avoidance practices of the past." Worse still, he said, the bill taxed "small capital profits and large capital profits at *exactly the same tax rate*. And that, my friends, *isn't right!*" Taking his audience of high school children into his company as holders of equity, the President clinched his case:

In other words, if you or I sell stocks, which we have held for a few years, at a profit of, let us say, $5000, we have to pay a tax of

15 per cent on that profit; whereas, the man who has made a profit of $500,000 on stocks he has owned is required . . . to pay a tax of only 15 per cent, just as you and I would. Nobody, by any stretch of the imagination, can say that this new provision maintains the principle of payment in proportion to ability to pay.

Some people who have favored this abandonment of principle have justified their position on the ground that one has to abandon principles once in a while when there is an emergency and that the abandonment of this particular principle will encourage many rich men to take a risk with their capital and invest it in new enterprises.

But this school of thought finds it difficult to answer the fact that almost all — about 80 per cent of all capital gains reported — are profits made in the stock market — profits made not by developing new companies, not by starting new industries . . . no, no, but by buying stocks of old companies low and selling them high, or by the still possible method of selling stocks short. . . . The abandonment of the principle of progressive tax payments in accordance with the capacity to pay may encourage a small amount of capital to go into new productive enterprises but, chiefly, it will help those who make *large profits* in buying and selling stocks.

Roosevelt was sure the audience could understand his problem: "If I sign the bill — and I have until midnight tonight to sign it — many people with some justification will think I approve the abandonment of an important principle of American taxation. If I veto the bill it will prevent many of the desirable features of it from going into effect.

"Therefore, for the first time since I have been President, I am going to take the third course which is open to me *under the Constitution*. At midnight tonight this new tax bill will automatically become law, but it will become law without my signature, without my approval."

This policy and the unexpected address announcing it infuriated Harrison. For both the speech and the decision he blamed Morgenthau, and not without some cause, for Magill and Oliphant had con-

tributed extensively to the documents on which the President based
his address. So angry was Harrison that it was months before he
was again willing to speak to the Secretary, but as Roosevelt observed, the senator had already strayed off the reservation. Whatever his mood, moreover, he had had his way on the Revenue Act.

For Morgenthau the defeat was galling. He had, in a sense, lost
the battle of the budget twice, once to the President and once to the
Senate, for the Revenue Act would reduce federal income. He had
lost, too, a battle of principle, for the Act, as Roosevelt had said,
encouraged tax avoidance and imposed inequitable schedules. All
in all, the Secretary had a dismal spring in 1938.

Discouraged, but not for long depressed, Morgenthau decided to
reconsider the arguments of those whose policies he had been opposing. Late in June, just before sailing for France, where he looked
forward to resting after the most exhausting six months he had yet
spent in Washington, he instructed his staff to review for him the
whole problem of the public debt, of public spending, and of a
compensatory budget. A number of professional economists had
put a bug in his ear, he said, and he was particularly impressed
by the writings of Gunnar Myrdal, a Swedish Keynesian. "We dis-
tinctly need a fresh viewpoint on this thing," the Secretary told his
staff. "I mean we've taken this defeatist attitude right along, that
it's something to be terribly ashamed of. Maybe it isn't. I don't
know."

The analysis that awaited him on his return from Europe, however, failed to win him to countercyclical spending. Roosevelt, too,
was still a doubter. As he and Morgenthau sat down together in the
fall of 1938 to examine prospects for the fiscal year 1940, the President "seemed quite disturbed and shocked at the figures. He . . .
indicated that what we might do from here on was to require a reduction in Hopkins's monthly expenditures as Ickes's monthly expenditures increased. He thought that possibly there was not the
same ratio of employment but that we could work out some method
to show a proportionate reduction." Back at the Treasury, Morgenthau presented the probable figures for the deficit in 1940 — figures
swollen by the needs of national defense — and asked each of his
associates if he had anything to say. "Not now," Wayne Taylor replied. "I feel awfully sick."

"I had my stomach removed about two years ago," the Secretary said. ". . . I'm not going to take 1940 for granted. I may be a damn fool, but I'm not going to do it."

He would fight the battle of the budget again, and so would Roosevelt. Neither was really reconciled to an unbalanced budget. Both, however, believed the federal government had the responsibility to relieve the distress of unemployment, indeed the responsibility to provide full employment. Roosevelt went further than did Morgenthau in advocating large-scale public works, but the Secretary differed with his chief only in degree, not in purpose. Both, furthermore, believed that government had the responsibility for preserving free enterprise. Roosevelt by the fall of 1938 counted largely on antitrust activities to do so. Morgenthau had come to rely more upon removing deterrents to private investment; had come to side with Harrison in favor of reducing taxes on business, including the shadow that was left of the undistributed profits tax. "Either we're going to fix the taxes . . . to encourage the people to risk their money . . ." he said, "or the only other alternative is more deficit finance. And while I am here I want to . . . encourage private capital."

He had always wanted to. The recession did not alter his creed, though experience persuaded him to change his tactics. Yet free enterprise was for him, as for Roosevelt, only one part of the image of a good society. As Morgenthau said in a commencement address of his own, it had been vital for the New Deal to arrest the decline in the lives and fortunes of the American people, to serve American youth, to build homes, wipe out slums, and discipline the buccaneers of the financial world. It was tragic, he observed, that abundance alarmed some Americans. There had been a short circuit between production and consumption, and this had yet fully to be repaired. But the Administration was at work on it, and he hoped the young men of Temple University would join the national effort to produce a life of plenty for everyone.

That, as he noted, had become of special importance because of the encroaching challenge of totalitarianism. The United States had to succeed, to prove that by democratic processes of free enterprise and competition, of free votes, of freedom of conscience and expression and opportunity, the nation could reach a condition of universal plenty. Not for its own sake alone, not for the sake of its people alone, but also as an example to men everywhere threatened by fascism and Communism, the United States had a mission which the New Deal was furthering.

That mission, as the Secretary interpreted it, also involved the fashioning of a foreign policy suitable to the time. In the fall of 1938, as during the previous year, the problems of the budget and the direction of reform, urgent though they were, provoked no greater anxiety than did portentous events abroad. Those developments increasingly engaged Morgenthau's attention, for like the President, he sensed that his generation all over the world had to keep its rendezvous with destiny.

# X

# The Treasury and Foreign Affairs

## 1937-1938

## 1. The Stage

DURING 1937 and 1938 Morgenthau could not rid himself of a sense of impending disaster abroad. The entire creed he had learned as a youth — democracy, the rights of man, the rights of weak nations — now trembled before the advance of totalitarianism in Europe and Asia. Like Roosevelt and most other Americans, Morgenthau knew that war was an awful prospect, but he recognized the overwhelming necessity of resisting fascism, if need be at the risk of war, indeed if need be ultimately by war itself.

It was in that respect, he later observed, that he differed most from those of his countrymen who made peace their sole objective. He differed, too, with the State Department, for he found its approach, as he put it ten years later, "timorous" and "conventional," dominated by the "foreign-office mentality"— the notion that you got things done by being a generous host at diplomatic banquets. There were, of course, exceptions to that point of view, and Morgenthau respected the realistic contributions to foreign policy of Sumner Welles, the Under Secretary of State, and Herbert Feis, Hull's economic adviser. But Secretary Hull, in Morgenthau's opinion, was obsessed by his trade agreements program and misled by the Anglophilism and the hesitancies of career diplomats. Consequently the State Department as a whole failed to realize that Japanese militarism and European fascism had released new and ugly forces which, as Morgenthau saw it, could not be controlled politely.

As Secretary of the Treasury, Morgenthau was responsible for foreign monetary policy, and before 1937 he had revealed the directions he would take. His negotiations with China about silver, and those with England and France resulting in the Tripartite Pact, had provided instruments of limited effect for stiffening democratic resistance to Germany, Italy, and Japan. During 1937 and after, he acted in his own sphere more often and more vigorously than before, and he also urged constantly upon the President a more forceful general policy than any other member of the Administration, save Harold Ickes, was yet prepared to advocate. Morgenthau's perceptions about the totalitarian threat, however, were far larger than his means to combat it, and that imbalance tormented him constantly.

It was at times difficult to know the intentions of a presumed friend. Chiang Kai-shek, to whom the Treasury had given considerable assistance, fell captive in December 1936, to Chang Ksueh Liang, "the young Marshal" of the Chinese north. Morgenthau could not believe that an old hand like Chiang had walked into a trap, and Treasury reports from China made it clear that the Generalissimo had had reason to be suspicious, for, as usual, he had powerful enemies.

Chiang had been enlarging the sway of his government. His bloodless victory over independent forces in the southwest, his moderately successful campaign against the Communists, his improved currency system, the recovery in prices and business conditions, and the fortunate accident of good crops had strengthened the authority and prestige of Nanking. The G'imo had therefore been able to take a firmer position against Japan. But the recent Japanese invasion of Suiyan, though long expected, had intensified the dissatisfaction of Chang, "the young Marshal," with Nanking's Japanese policies. Chang, who had been military governor of Manchuria in 1931 when the Japanese invaded that area, wanted to combine with all Chinese groups, including the Communists, in an immediate war against Japan. Otherwise he feared Japan would insert a wedge between China and Russia by capturing Inner Mongolia, and thus cut China off from her "one reliable ally." Chang's overt opposition to the policies of Nanking provoked Chiang Kai-shek to replace him as commander-in-chief in the northwest and to order him to move his army southwest into Kiangsi. In retaliation, Chang led a mutiny of troops at Sian while the Generalissimo was making an inspection there.

Chang then circulated a telegram to all China urging war against Japan, a military alliance with the Soviet Union, and the reorganization of the government to include Chinese Communists. Finance Minister Kung, Madame Chiang, and some of Chiang's generals advised the government at least to consider Chang's terms and, in any case, to exercise the utmost patience with the mutineers. Other generals wanted instead at once to attack Sian. If they did, Kung feared Chang might murder the G'imo and line up completely with the Communists, and in that event, the Finance Minister informed Morgenthau, Chang would be able to rally a lot of support for himself and his program.

The Chinese situation naturally disturbed Morgenthau. As he pointed out to Roosevelt, after Germany, Italy, and Japan signed the Anticomintern Pact in November 1936, the Russians had refused to sign a fishing treaty with Japan. The Japanese Minister of Foreign Affairs had then offered to resign. Now came the kidnaping. Had it not occurred, Morgenthau believed the Japanese government would have fallen. Communism and fascism were negotiating world-wide advances, each moving against and responding to the other across the entire globe. "To show you that this whole thing, I believe, goes completely around the world," Morgenthau said to the President, "take a look at Spain and see the clash there between the Russians and the Germans."

It was an importunate clash, for no matter who won, the democracies lost. Morgenthau was puzzled, he recalled twenty years later, about where Chiang Kai-shek stood. The Secretary's sense of mystery grew when on Christmas Day the Generalissimo was released without making any apparent concessions. The whole episode raised doubts about Chiang's ability to prevent civil war or to stand up to Japan. Lacking satisfactory information, Morgenthau decided to stall when the Chinese in January 1937 asked him to buy another 50 million ounces of silver. He refused, granting them instead the privilege of borrowing another $20 million against silver they held in the United States. He also promised to review their situation each month and perhaps to renew the privilege. He could do no more, he felt, until Chiang's plans were clearer. He had to wait, and while he waited, he found events in Europe as worrisome and as unmanageable as those in Asia.

## 2. Arms and the Franc

Although the Tripartite Pact of 1936 was intended primarily to facilitate the stabilization of the franc, the pound, and the dollar, Morgenthau had negotiated it with political conditions very much in mind; and the French and British, too, had from the first recognized its importance as a symbol of democratic unity. In carrying out the pact, the treasuries of the Western democracies were concentrating on monetary problems for the purpose of strengthening the will and the means of the signatories to resist totalitarianism.

As 1937 began, Vincent Auriol, the French Minister of Finance, urged the democratic nations to supplement the Tripartite Pact with further economic and political arrangements which would, among other things, open up the possibility for disarmament. In private Auriol told Merle Cochran, the Treasury's special emissary in France, that he was worried about the continuing outflow of gold. This outflow reflected a lack of confidence in the franc arising from deep-seated economic difficulties. Some of these grew out of the efforts of the Popular Front government of Leon Blum to pursue a program of reform opposed by conservative Frenchmen, including many investors. Holders of francs, furthermore, feared the enormous additional strain which the need for military preparedness imposed upon the French economy. Although Auriol maintained that there was no immediate prospect of further devaluation, the arms race was severely complicating the management of the franc.

The possibility of devaluation was larger than Auriol cared to admit even in private. By late January 1937, while negotiations were under way for a British loan to finance the French railways, the French suggested that the American Treasury buy between $5 and $10 million of francs and refrain from converting them into gold until the tourist trade of the summer gave France a larger dollar balance.

The French suggestion, Morgenthau said, made him break out in a cold sweat. It was like kiting a check, cashing it on a Saturday against deposits which were to be made the following Monday. If the transaction became public it would embarrass the Treasury, for it came close to being the kind of loan which the Johnson Act of 1934, with its ban against American loans to governments in default on their war debts, specifically forbade. The congressional leaders who had written the law, including isolationist watchdogs like Borah of Idaho, would certainly look with disfavor upon the French proposal, which Herbert Feis called typically French, a small maneuver that would accomplish nothing. Morgenthau without hesitation turned the French down, a decision Roosevelt fully endorsed.

London bankers from whom the French were seeking a loan asked the National City Bank of New York whether it would care to participate. Gordon Rentschler of the National City in turn asked Morgenthau whether participation would violate the Johnson Act. After talking with Roosevelt, Morgenthau on January 26, 1937, told Rentschler: "If it is a question of the purchase of foreign exchange against the delivery of gold, it is okay, but outside of that it is against the spirit of the Johnson Act." As the Secretary later added, participation by American bankers would in any case fail to cure the French troubles.

Meanwhile, at the urgent request of the French government, British Chancellor of the Exchequer Neville Chamberlain had privately informed the Bank of England that he would be glad if the French got a railway loan. The money, however, would have to come from private sources, for neither the British government nor the Bank of England would put it up. Chamberlain had taken the exceptional step of encouraging a loan — exceptional because if investors lost their money they would blame him for his intercession — only in order to help the French avoid exchange control and thus remain within the Tripartite Pact. The French succeeded in borrowing £250 million, which pleased Morgenthau, who considered Leon Blum the only one of their leaders who was truly committed to social reform and opposition to fascism.

Roosevelt agreed. The British, he said, "are showing some sanity. It is very important to keep Blum in."

Yet the loan was at best a makeshift, and on February 6 Chamberlain in a confidential message to Morgenthau described the increasing difficulties of the Blum government. The Secretary, as he noted in his Diary, immediately telephoned Roosevelt:

I said I thought the most significant thing about it was that Chamberlain sent me a message more than what was in it. The President said every time the French have a crisis they seem a little worse off. I said we were only talking about what we would *do in case of war,* but were doing nothing to try and *stop war.* I said I . . . wanted to talk to him about the plan he had mentioned to me about . . . going possibly to Holland and try and call in various leaders from various countries and try and talk sense to them. (He mentioned this to me maybe a year ago.) What I *did not say* is that I feel the only way to stop war is to try and stop this mad race to arm that is going on in Europe. After all we would have nothing to lose and everything to gain. Everything points towards war in Europe and surely sooner or later we will be dragged into it. I am having prepared by Haas figures to show how much the ten leading countries have been spending to arm themselves during the last five years. The cost of arming is what is breaking down the Treasuries of the World. I hope the President will let me help him work this out. I don't believe that Hull and Norman Davis* ever will. They just don't have guts enough. The President has the courage and I hope to be able to convince him that if the world is to be saved the next move is up to him.

On February 9, with Haas's memorandum in hand, Morgenthau lunched with Roosevelt. "The world is just drifting rapidly towards war," the Secretary said. "We patch up the French situation every so often but with the constant increased percentage of

---

* Norman Davis was a veteran diplomat, internationalist, and advocate of disarmament, on whom Hull leaned. Morgenthau considered Davis an "unimpeachable gentleman" but an overcautious counselor.

their budget going for war purposes we really cannot help them. The European countries are gradually going bankrupt through preparing for war. You are the only person who can stop it."

With a smile on his face, Roosevelt replied: "I feel like throwing either a cup and saucer at you or the coffeepot."

"Or throw both, but why?"

"Well," Roosevelt continued, "I had Hull, Norman Davis to lunch and Davis said, the only person who can save the situation is Roosevelt and then I said to Davis how, and Davis said by sending a secret envoy to Europe." Roosevelt paused. "Another Colonel House."

"Hull's philosophy," the President went on, "is that through his trade treaties he would increase world trade and take up the slack of unemployment as the individual countries gradually disarm."

"I am not in disagreement with Hull," Morgenthau said, "but his policies will take five years to feel the full effect. He may only have five months before we have a world war and if we do and it lasts two or three years you can be sure we will be drawn into it. Would you have any objection to my sending a secret confidential message by word of mouth through Bewley, who is returning to England, to Neville Chamberlain asking him if he has any suggestions to make as to how we can keep the world from going financially broke due to constant increased cost of armaments?"

After thinking a moment, Roosevelt said: "No, that will be all right."

"Are you sure?" Morgenthau asked.

"Yes, I am sure."

"You know my idea," Morgenthau said, "is that if there are any negotiations to be conducted it is to do them here not send anybody abroad."

"That is right," the President replied.

"I certainly had a most interesting and constructive lunch," Morgenthau recorded in his Diary, "and if I can be helpful in doing something to get the world to disarm I will die happy."

Two days later, on February 11, Morgenthau gave Kenneth Bewley, the Exchequer's representative in Washington, a message for Chamberlain, a communication "from one finance minister to another." Only Roosevelt, the Secretary explained, knew about the message, which Morgenthau asked Bewley to deliver personally as soon as he could, even though he would have to postpone his vacation to do so. The Secretary put nothing in writing; instead he asked Bewley to say to Chamberlain that "the thing that is breaking down the credit of the big countries . . . is armaments. That affects your Treasury and . . . is the basis of the French troubles, the Japanese troubles, and looking at it as a financial matter and not as a diplomatic has he any suggestions to make to me whereby he and I might make some start to stop the arming that is going on all over the world."

Chamberlain would not be able to answer without discussing the message with the Cabinet, Bewley pointed out. As long as Chamberlain got the message directly, Morgenthau said, it was up to him to discuss it with anyone he wished. England, Bewley noted in departing, was doing her best to moderate the arms race. The prime offender was Germany.

The basic question was how to stop Germany; the immediate question, how to help France. Morgenthau tried to answer both while he awaited a reply from Chamberlain. On February 16 the Secretary again suggested a disarmament conference of the major powers. Roosevelt, who seemed favorable to the idea, said that if he called a conference, he would invite just about half a dozen countries. He would tell their delegates that the problem was theirs, and send them to some other building to work out a solution and come back with it. He would offer no advice about political issues, the President added, but he would try to get disarmament started at an accelerating pace over a five year period. Any nation refusing to comply with the majority rule, he said, should then be hit by an economic boycott imposed by the others at the conference.

Dumfounded though he was by Roosevelt's rapid and elaborate response, Morgenthau did not expect any quick developments from his chief's musings. They excited the Secretary's imagination, but his sense of the practical led him to propose that the United States at once recommend another 8 per cent devaluation of the franc, which the Tripartite Pact and French legislation of 1936 permitted. People were expecting devaluation, he believed, and when it came, especially if it were accompanied by a reorganization of the Bank of France, the act of devaluation might arouse confidence in future stability. "This French thing is just about as bad as it can be," he told his morning conference on February 26, ". . . and if the French fail, why, there goes our Tripartite Agreement."

The Secretary maintained that someone had to shock France into facing the issue, to tell the French they were a bankrupt, fourth-class power. He was not worried about hurting their feelings, and unlike some of his staff, he was unwilling to make them a loan. The Johnson Act forbade a loan; and even if, as Harry White suggested, Morgenthau could draw upon the Stabilization Fund to extend the French a credit, the Secretary would not, "because it is just flowing money into the Atlantic Ocean." Devaluation, he thought, would provide a stopgap until Roosevelt could summon a disarmament conference; indeed he thought the President might say just that to the French. When White again urged a loan, Morgenthau replied: "My whole upbringing, my whole background, rises up in protest against making a loan against French paper. I can't do it."

Though the British were willing to have France devalue another 8 per cent, Roosevelt did not want Morgenthau to recommend that step unless he could be sure the French would not reveal that the initiative had come from the United States. The Secretary could not be sure, and in any event Premier Blum was not ready to devalue.

Stymied, Morgenthau wondered whether he could solve the French problem by bringing Soviet Russia into the Tripartite Pact. "With their large holdings of gold," he wrote in his Diary on March 3, "it might make just the sufficient difference to tide the French across the present crisis." Speaking for the State Department, Herbert Feis saw no merit in that idea, which, as Morgenthau put it to his staff, had "not crystallized itself in my mind as yet." He foresaw, he added pessimistically, little chance of improvement unless Franco-German tensions eased. "It is like a fight between two drunken men," he said, "— which will die of exhaustion first."

On March 5 Blum tried to re-establish confidence in the franc by reducing governmental expenditures and establishing a free gold market, accompanying his announcements of these policies with a statement that he planned neither devaluation nor exchange control. He hoped that he had done enough to bring gold out of hoarding.

"It is just a cockeyed scheme," Morgenthau told Roosevelt, "which will not work." To French Ambassador Georges Bonnet, a man experienced in finance, he expressed sympathy for France's predicament, but suggested that she had not yet taken the necessary steps to protect herself. When the United States devalued, the Secretary pointed out, the government took the resulting profit from the increase in the price of gold, whereas the French in 1936 had permitted much of that profit to accrue to holders of gold. France had gone only halfway, he said, and should now devalue another 8 per cent. Bonnet pleasantly disagreed.

On March 6 Morgenthau learned that the French intended to float a large defense loan with a foreign exchange guarantee. They needed pounds and dollars, but Herman Oliphant, who interpreted the Johnson Act to prohibit Americans from purchasing the new French bonds, ruled that no officer of the United States government could publicly approve any measure designed to encourage such purchases.

Oliphant had no more than made that point when the United Press reported a French announcement to the effect that Morgenthau had told Blum that American banks might invest in the French loan without violating the Johnson Act. "The nice thing about the French is," the Secretary said, "they never wait for your answer. They are sweet people."

"It's their imagination," George Harrison agreed, "which has made such progress in Art."

After reviewing the situation with Roosevelt, Attorney General Cummings, and Oliphant, Morgenthau personally wished the French government great success in its loan, but his official communique rejected their scheme: "While the Treasury cannot, of course, express either its approval or disapproval of the proposal of the French government to issue a loan payable either in francs, pounds, or dollars at the option of the holder, nevertheless in response to your specific inquiry, and in view of American legislation, it does envisage objections to the appointment of an agent in

New York for the purpose of making such payment in dollars."

The French proposal alarmed American isolationists who applauded Senator Borah's forceful speech of March 8 attacking it. So agitated was the Congress that Morgenthau had to go to the Hill to reassure Senators Robinson and Pittman and Speaker of the House Bankhead. The Secretary showed them his exchange with the French which Robinson then disclosed in a public statement mollifying the sponsors and supporters of the Johnson Act.

March 8 was a trying day. The British, Morgenthau learned, had also refused the French request for the appointment of an agent to service the loan, since they considered the convertibility provision objectionable, liable to embarrass all the partners to the Tripartite Pact. Yet French Minister of Finance Auriol, refusing to accept these negative responses, informed Morgenthau through Ambassador Bonnet that in his opinion it would not be contrary to the Johnson Act, or any other American law, for the French to designate an American bank to pay the coupons on the loan in dollars. The success of the loan, Auriol added, depended on the decision of the American government.

"That is not fair," Morgenthau replied to Bonnet. "That isn't fair and I don't like it. . . . The success of your loan depends upon the confidence . . . of the French investor . . . and not on the decision whether he is going to get paid in dollars or sterling. . . . I may also say to Mr. Vincent Auriol that . . . when it comes to interpreting the Johnson Act I think he is pressing a little bit hard. . . . I also have a little temperament, so you understand that it is not only the French citizens who have temperament . . . and I get excited because . . . I think your Government is making a great mistake. Now, I very seriously and very politely in my note pointed out that we could not do this . . . and that note . . . had the full backing of the entire Administration. . . . This request . . . we feel would be contrary to the Johnson Act — not maybe, but absolutely contrary to the Johnson Act.

"Now, here is Senator Borah. He made a speech in the Senate today. . . . My dear Mr. Ambassador, the more your Government pushes this, the more, every hour, France is losing friends here. . . . This . . . disturbs me very much."

The French had also disturbed Chamberlain who did not see

how the Tripartite Agreement could continue in the spirit of cooperation that inspired it if, in matters so crucial as the loan,
France acted with so little consideration of the views of the other
parties involved. Chamberlain's basic objection was to the terms
of the loan, but Morgenthau was more worried about the domestic
reaction to the publicity the French government had given the
question of appointing an American agent. Both agreed that the
French Treasury had tried to protect itself by forcing the British
and American hands. "It's been," Morgenthau sighed, "a great
disillusionment."

Neither the loan, which faltered, nor the establishment of a free
gold market, nor Blum's efforts to reduce normal government expenditures kept the franc from continuing its decline. As Blum
retrenched, militant elements in the French Left feared that he
might delay social reforms indefinitely, and the unions and the
Communists provoked a wave of strikes and riots that again shook
confidence in the government, the nation, and its currency. In
April Blum had to devalue the franc the full 8 per cent permitted
by French law, just the move that England and the United States
had been urging. France's persisting social unrest and unfavorable balance of trade made further devaluation and the collapse of
the Blum government imminent.

This, of course, was precisely what Morgenthau hoped some
progress toward European disarmament might prevent. French
ineptness in the management of the franc and French maladroit-
ness in inter-treasury communication would not have disturbed
the Secretary for long if he had felt that the possibilities for disarmament were real. Clearly, however, they were not. Recognizing this, Roosevelt had made no gesture toward summoning a
conference. And whatever hopes Morgenthau had dared nourish
were dashed when on March 26 he received Neville Chamberlain's
reply to his query about disarmament.

Chamberlain had received the message, he wrote Morgenthau,
with great interest, and discussed it with both Prime Minister
Baldwin and Foreign Secretary Eden. He wanted to say "how
warmly they all three appreciate this evidence of Mr. Morgenthau's and — as they understand — the President's earnest desire
to find some way in which the United States — possibly in con-

junction with the United Kingdom — could help in preventing the outbreak of another war. Beset as they are with the difficulties and risks inherent in the present political situation in Europe, the Chancellor and his colleagues had given their most anxious consideration to this message."

In order to gauge the possibilities of averting war, Chamberlain continued, it was necessary first to consider where the menace lay and what the causes were that kept it alive. "These causes are both political and economic," he wrote, "and it is sometimes difficult to disentangle them . . . but Mr. Morgenthau is undoubtedly right in saying that the needs of armament programs are responsible for a good deal of the economic troubles in Europe and these programs are in turn the result of political considerations." Yet, Chamberlain observed, the main source of fear of war was Germany. "No other country, not Italy, since she has her hands full with the task of consolidating her Abyssinian conquest, not Russia with all her military preparations, certainly not France, England or any of the smaller Powers, is for a moment credited with any aggressive designs. But the fierce propaganda against other nations continually carried on by the German Press and wireless . . . the intensity and persistence of German military preparations, together with the many acts of the German Government in violation of treaties, cynically justified on the ground that unilateral action was the quickest way of getting what they wanted, have inspired all her neighbors with a profound uneasiness. Even these islands which could be reached in less than an hour from German territory by an airforce equipped with hundreds of tons of bombs cannot be exempt from anxiety."

Germany's aggressiveness, Chamberlain believed, arose from her desire to make herself so strong that no one would venture to withstand whatever demands she might make for European or colonial territories. "With this intention in her heart she is not likely to agree to any disarmament which would defeat her purpose. The only consideration which would influence her to a contrary decision would be the conviction that her efforts to secure superiority of force were doomed to failure by reason of the superior force which would meet her if she attempted aggression."

England was rearming, to the gratification of many nations.

The British government, moreover, had "no doubt whatever that the greatest single contribution which the United States could make at the present moment to the preservation of world peace would be the amendment of the existing neutrality legislation. Under this legislation an embargo would be imposed on the export from the United States of arms and munitions, irrespective of whether a country is an aggressor or the victim of an aggression. It is obvious that the existing neutrality law and . . . any extension of it to include raw materials, suits the requirements of a country contemplating an aggression, which can and would lay up large stores of war materials with the knowledge that its intended victim will, when the time comes, be precluded from obtaining supplies from one of the greatest world markets. The legislation in its present form constitutes an indirect but potent encouragement to aggression, and it is earnestly hoped that some way may be found of leaving sufficient discretion with the Executive to deal with each case on its merits."

Chamberlain realized that the question, apart from its international aspects, was a matter of domestic controversy within the United States, and that it might well be impossible for the American government to take the step he recommended even if the Administration so desired, but in view of Morgenthau's request for his opinions, Chamberlain was expressing them "without reserve." In this mood he turned to a related issue:

Japan . . . is another Power with far-reaching ambitions which affect the interests of this country . . . not with the same intensity as those which touch her very existence, but in highly important respects. The strain upon our resources is therefore seriously aggravated by the necessity of providing for the protection of our Far Eastern and Pacific interests, especially as the most favorable moment for any enterprise in that region injurious to our position there would be precisely when we were engaged in hostilities in Europe. The conclusion of the recent German-Japanese agreement is an indication, if one were needed, that if we were seriously involved in Europe we could not count even on the neutrality of Japan. Anything therefore which would tend to stabilize the position in the Far East would . . . ease our position there and safeguard us against added embarrassment in the event of trouble in Europe.

Even if the Japanese were to change their attitude, Chamberlain went on, the British would welcome an exchange of views with the United States "on the possibility of taking this opportunity to try to put relations between the United States of America, Japan and Great Britain on a footing that would ensure harmonious cooperation for the protection and development of their respective interests." Chamberlain concluded by expressing his earnest trust that "some form of collaboration" might be possible between the United States and Great Britain, since he was "profoundly convinced that almost any action common to them both would go far to restore confidence to the world and divert the menace which . . . threatens it."

There it was. The British government saw no chance for disarmament. Reading Hitler and his purposes more accurately than he was to read them later, Chamberlain in effect asserted the futility of attempting to negotiate. Morgenthau had hoped that the prestige and strength of the United States, personified in Roosevelt, might bring the Germans to see the impossibility of an arms race and of aggression. Chamberlain shared this hope, but what he urged was not a move for disarmament but a basic change in the structure of American neutrality legislation.

Morgenthau sympathized with the Chancellor's recommendation. The Neutrality Act embargoed the shipment of arms to all belligerents; before 1937 was over, it was amended to permit the President to embargo also other commodities he chose to list. In this manner the Congress expected to insulate the United States from hostilities overseas. The result, as Chamberlain said, and as Morgenthau and a minority of Americans recognized, was a backhanded invitation to aggressors. But the Senate's response to the French loan proposal argued powerfully that Congress was not likely to do what the Chancellor advocated.

Nor, given the posture of the Department of State, could Morgenthau begin to follow the Chancellor's prescription in the Orient. It was not that Chamberlain was wrong, but rather that Morgenthau had no way to operate within the boundaries of action that Chamberlain defined.

As Secretary of the Treasury, Morgenthau had available but one recourse — to make what he could of his monetary negotiations, using them further to cement Anglo-American cooperation, to make that cooperation a buttress for a failing France, perhaps thus in some small degree to postpone catastrophe while those with larger powers sought some means to prevent it. He would have liked to enlarge the partnership opposing Hitler, and to that end he began tentatively to sound out the Russians.

### 3. Russian Gold

During the spring of 1937 Morgenthau conducted a brief and unsuccessful negotiation with the Russians about gold policy. Monetary cooperation, he hoped, might provide a basis for bringing them into a circle of powers working for peace by standing against fascist aggression. His immediate and lesser purpose was to ease the temporary decline in the international value of gold that occurred in April 1937. The Soviet Union and the British Empire were the greatest gold-producing states in the world. Moreover Russia was systematically converting nonmonetary gold into foreign exchange in order to protect her ability to purchase war materials abroad. Morgenthau therefore wanted to effect either a reduction in Russian gold production or a regularization of her sales of the metal. Either objective depended upon establishing a degree of mutual understanding beyond anything that existed.

Thus it was that Morgenthau was cautiously receptive to overtures from Russian Ambassador Troyanovski and his associate Constantin A. Oumansky. Late in April they approached the Treasury about opening an account for the Russian State Bank with the New York Federal Reserve Bank. This prospect quite alarmed George Harrison who feared that it might result in Russian inclusion in the Tripartite Agreement. His alarm, however, was premature. No one in the Treasury proposed to make hasty decisions about the Russians, or, indeed, to make any decisions at all without the approval of the State Department. In fact, assaults of Communist rhetoric kept the Treasury very much on its guard.

At luncheon with Assistant Secretary Wayne Taylor on April 29, Oumansky delivered himself of a standard Marxist diatribe on the inevitability of collapse under capitalism, asserting that another downswing would come perhaps as early as 1939 (a prediction which proved a little optimistic) and would lead to political disasters and international war among capitalist nations. Yet Oumansky also said that Russia wished to cooperate with peace-loving nations. She needed certain American products, particularly machinery for mass production, and he suggested the possibility of doing a good deal of business if Russia could find some way to pay for what she bought by direct exchange, by selling gold, or by obtaining special credits.

Neither Taylor nor Morgenthau took this statement at face value. The Treasury's Research Division noted that the principal objective of Soviet trade was the accumulation of foreign exchange, which the Russians could achieve only by exporting gold or other commodities. That would be possible, however, only with some increased austerity in Russian domestic consumption. The analysis, like Oumansky's rhetoric, made Morgenthau wary about Soviet intentions.

Yet politically and economically there seemed too much at stake for the Secretary immediately to close the door on the Russians. Before proceeding he discussed the problem with the State Department. The Russians, he said, were anxious to obtain credits from the United States, but these could be granted under the Johnson Act only if they made some settlement of the debt incurred by the pre-Soviet government during World War I. Feis doubted the feasibility of debt settlement. "I am thinking of it in connection with the whole question of gold," Morgenthau reassured him. ". . . I don't know yet whether I want to do it and I certainly don't want to do it unless Mr. Hull would be entirely satisfied (and of course it goes without saying, if the President wants me to do it). . . . You have seen me go into these things before. I want a free hand, keeping your Department advised through you step by step, just as I have. You have seen me work often enough, but I haven't yet made up my mind to do it. You see, a number of times the Russians have tried their best to come see me. . . . Each time I asked the President and each time the President said no, so I dropped it. . . . The President may say no and that ends it, but I think it's a big thing."

It was also an extraordinarily complicated thing, as Morgenthau learned by reviewing Soviet-American negotiations since 1933. Had the Russians been willing to repay some $100 million of their World War I debt, Roosevelt would in turn have agreed to extend them a generous credit for the purchase of American goods. During Russian-American discussions of recognition, however, Maxim Litvinov would not commit the Soviet Union to a satisfactory settlement of the debt, nor would he accept a credit. He held out instead for an outright loan of dollars which would have permitted the Russians to purchase what they wanted in any market, instead of confining them to the United States.

Thereafter American Ambassador William Bullitt was unable to advance the matter in Moscow, and by late 1935 the State Department had concluded that nothing could be accomplished. The history of the affair persuaded Morgenthau that Bullitt had irritated the Russians, but he also decided that it would be stupid for him to raise the question of war debts again. He had, he reminded himself, conducted the negotiations leading to the Tripartite Pact without reference to war debts, and in dealing with the Russians his best course seemed to be to confine himself to gold.

Morgenthau reached this decision on May 19, 1937. A few days later the French called his attention to the importance of Russian gold to them, for they hoped to buy it with francs and thereby acquire additional backing for their currency. In the past, the Russians had converted their francs too quickly to permit the French to profit much from their gold purchases, but it was hoped that now they would hold the French currency longer. The British, anxious in any case to see the franc steadied, made no proposals about Russia, but late in May they officially noted their concern about the falling price of gold on the London market. From this message the Secretary could infer that England would welcome an agreement limiting sales of Russian gold if he could arrange one with the Soviets.

As he prepared to talk with the Russians, he had to reckon with their secretiveness. The Treasury would need to know how much gold Russia had in hand, Harry White pointed out, and how much she was producing, information which he did not believe would be disclosed, for past experience had not led Americans to expect much Russian candor. The Soviet Union, moreover, was apt to be especially sensitive about the production of gold, for much of it depended on forced labor. Yet White thought it important "that we ask . . . the specific question."

The Russians proved as elusive as he had predicted. When Morgenthau met Oumansky and Troyanovski on May 26, the Secretary warned that he was going to talk very frankly. "The two governments," he said, "are not getting any closer together."

"Uh-huh," Troyanovski replied.

He would not have tried to discuss finances, Morgenthau said, without the consent of the President and the Department of State. "I am only interested in the financial end," he explained, "the monetary end. I am not interested in trade treaties or anything like that." Moving on to his central subject, he pointed out that both Russia and the United States would suffer if people in all nations lost their interest in gold. "We are like squirrels," he said, "we take it out of one hole and put it in another. . . . What I am leading up to is this: if we could have a free exchange of information . . . and we could work out together mutual problems on this thing . . . I should think it would be most useful to both Governments."

"I don't know," Troyanovski replied. "At the present time nobody knows what production of gold we have. Maybe if it is published fact, maybe it will be . . . some disturbance."

"No," Morgenthau said. "The worst thing is the lack of knowledge. I don't care how big your production of metals is, it's the unknown factor that worries people." Much good, he continued, would come from the two governments gaining sufficient confidence in each other to exchange information. The Treasury, he assured the Russians, like their own government, could keep things secret.

"But maybe you don't know," Troyanovski said. "We have four aces. You have interest in the game. But once you know—"

"I don't know that you have four aces," Morgenthau interrupted, "but I don't know how many chips you have got. . . . I don't know whether they are ten cent chips or dollar chips. And this is finance. It's the biggest game in the world. And up to now England has always played it alone and London has always dictated. . . . Whether this thing fits into the picture looking four or five years ahead, your Government knows. I don't. But frankly, talking for myself, it seems that we are less close today than we were before we had recognition. There have been some misunderstandings."

"I can't tell," Troyanovski said, "because the atmosphere is more favorable generally now than before. We can talk. We can look for a solution of certain problems. . . . You are talking about reserves and it's more advantageous for you."

"You produce more gold than we do," Morgenthau replied.

"Oh, yes."

"At least," Morgenthau continued, "we think you do. We think you do. We don't know. We have more but we think you produce more." Yet Russia could only use gold to buy things. He wondered whether Troyanovski would like to ask him a question.

Troyanovski asked again whether the United States would keep secret statistics about Soviet production. Again Morgenthau promised to do so, adding that it was not just data he wanted. It was rather that the British Empire, Russia, and the United States could pretty well control gold if they could cooperate. The Secretary thought this was important for peace: "We are interested in peace. The reason they didn't have a war in Europe last fall, in my belief, was because we saved France." The Tripartite Pact was "an instrument of peace," Morgenthau added, and the Treasury's monetary diplomacy had also "saved China."

The ambassador said the Russian army had contributed a little. They agreed, however, that a weak China meant trouble for both Russia and the United States.

"I may not always say a thing very diplomatically," the Secretary continued, "but my objective . . . through finance, is world peace."

"Yes," Troyanovski said. "Of course, if you can cooperate; have some contact, it will be helpful for world peace and can better the general situation. . . . Of course, we are in strong position in the world affairs, but still we are ready to cooperate."

"You are in a very strong position," Morgenthau said, "and I think you will get stronger as time goes on and I recognize that. I think it would be stupid not to recognize that."

"I will convey the message," the ambassador replied, departing, "and maybe something come out."

Almost three weeks later, on June 15, Troyanovski returned. Moscow wanted to know, he said, whether the Americans had in mind a special agreement about gold or only an exchange of information. Morgenthau told him that for the moment he was thinking of an exchange of information, but this might later lead to an agreement. Moscow considered the gold market the important side of the problem, Troyanovski said. Russia could rigidly regulate all the gold she exported, and was ready to talk about her exports in terms of the market, but that had nothing to do with production as far as she was concerned. Production was a domestic problem.

He would have to think that over, Morgenthau replied, but he considered the message on the face of it an encouraging one.

The Soviet position, a State Department memorandum indicated, was consistent with her policy on timber and sugar. The Russians appeared willing enough to participate in agreements with other countries about the regulation of exports, but they would not undertake any commitment affecting the operation of their internal economy.

Nor would they change their ways, and their reticence about production cooled Morgenthau's enthusiasm for the whole project. As experience with the French and British had amply demonstrated, international monetary cooperation without free communication was impossible. The Secretary therefore quietly let the conversations trail off.

In the end his efforts resulted only in the establishment of direct relations between the Russian State Bank and the Federal Reserve

Bank of New York, which facilitated sales of Russian gold in transit to the United States. Yet two decades later Morgenthau believed the venture had also educated the participants. "The Russians were children about international finance," he recalled. "I used to call them American Indians. They dumped commodities like quicksilver and killed their markets. Oumansky even had to be briefed about how a central bank worked. And George Harrison was horrified at the thought of dealing with them. But when they learned, they knew what they were doing, and they learned fast, and while I was in office they lived up to their financial agreements."

## 4. The Franc Floats

The monetary distress of China* and France had lent extra urgency to the inconclusive Russian negotiations. In early June 1937, a Spanish Loyalist attack on a German man-of-war provoked German retaliation. Heightened European tensions sent the teetering franc plunging. With another monetary crisis brewing, Anglo-American cooperation was essential. Yet just at this time a change in the British government made it harder than it had been for Morgenthau to communicate with his English counterpart.

At the end of May, following the resignation of Stanley Baldwin, Neville Chamberlain became Prime Minister. Chamberlain had been always official and at times abrupt in dealing with Morgenthau; he had never invited any intimacy. Still, he had often been helpful, and in his last years as Chancellor of the Exchequer increasingly candid and reassuringly stiff in the face of developments on the Continent. When he ascended to the Prime Ministry he conveyed to Morgenthau his sincere appreciation "of the spirit of cordial collaboration" between the two treasuries. He said also, as he had to, that he was sure Morgenthau would find his successor as Chancellor of the Exchequer no less anxious than he had been for full cooperation.

Yet Morgenthau, like others in Washington, had grave reservations about Chamberlain's successor, Sir John Simon. Conserva-

* See pages 479 ff.

tive in thought and manner as well as in politics, Simon had a poor reputation in America because of his role as Foreign Secretary during the Manchurian crisis in 1931. Henry Stimson, at that time American Secretary of State, had tried to persuade Britain to join in a reassertion of the Nine-Power Treaty of Washington of 1921 which Japan had violated by her invasion of Manchuria. During five crucial transatlantic telephone conversations, Simon had evidently approved of Stimson's plan in principle, but, as the American later recalled, "in practice . . . held back." There were understandable reasons for this hesitancy, but to Stimson, Simon's course seemed "a tacit admission that aggression in Manchuria was less reprehensible than aggression in an area where there were extensive British interests." Stimson, furthermore, had expressed his views in his book on the Manchurian crisis, and his frank displeasure with Simon created serious doubts in the United States, by no means without substance, about Simon's strength of mind.

In mid-June 1937, the pressure on the franc tested both Simon and Morgenthau. As Morgenthau put it to Roosevelt, "La belle France still has her virtue, but not much gold!" The French Equalization Fund was nearly drained of its resources and the Paris markets were nervous. Premier Blum, exhausted after months of contest with a fractious opposition, told Ambassador Bullitt with a gesture of weariness and disgust: "I have had enough! Everything that I have attempted to do has been blocked."

On June 14 Blum demanded from the French parliament full powers to regulate all financial matters by executive decree. He intended at once to stabilize the franc, no matter what it cost, and to forbid the export of French capital. The French Senate, however, rejected his proposal, although the Chamber passed the bill by a majority of more than 100 votes, and on June 21 the Blum government fell.

Fully expecting this development, much as he deplored it, Morgenthau on June 18 had asked his morning group whether it was worth preserving the Tripartite Agreement if the French found it necessary to devalue again. Oliphant was the first to reply: "A bulwark against fascism is worth preserving, and that's the thing lying back of the Tripartite Agreement." The Pact had saved France temporarily from fascism, Morgenthau agreed, but he did not know what was going to happen if the French began to make false statements, or if they ceased to have a liberal government, or would no longer cooperate on financial matters.

In France the new government of Camille Chautemps, in which Ambassador Bonnet was to be Finance Minister, stood to the right of Blum's coalition. Chautemps and Bonnet on June 29 told Merle Cochran they planned to reduce the budget, to seek a credit for the Bank of France, and to abandon the stated limits within which the French Stabilization Fund was charged with managing the franc. Some devaluation might be necessary, but the French assured Cochran they would seek no competitive advantages in international exchange. Rather, they needed a cheaper franc, they said, because of the increased charges on the French economy resulting from Blum's social legislation. They wanted very much to adhere to the Tripartite Agreement, and they intended to avoid exchange controls.

Shortly after Morgenthau heard this news, Simon, who considered decisions about the Tripartite Pact too important to reach hastily, promised for the while to tell Parliament only that the French government had assured him it was not seeking any exchange advantage. He had privately sent the French a commentary on their plans. He was awaiting, he told them, information about how they were eliminating their budget deficit, because in the British experience, deficits impaired confidence. He had also recorded his regret that the French were temporarily letting the franc float.* If that continued, it would have serious consequences for the Tripartite Pact.

In Morgenthau's view, Simon was scolding the French. He telephoned the Chancellor at once to say that he felt the French were still in the Tripartite Pact. They had given the American Treasury a buying rate and a selling rate for the franc, as well as the right freely to convert francs into gold. The franc was floating — its value might change — but it was not adrift.

The United States had no promise from the French that they would hold to this arrangement in the future, Simon replied. Furthermore, he had not received comparable assurances. Morgenthau therefore agreed to withhold any public statement until France

---

* That is, not managing the value of the franc within stated limits or "points") quoted in dollars and pounds.

had set a buying and selling rate in London, and until the two English-speaking nations could settle on an identical draft, but he made it clear that he preferred a more friendly tone than Simon was employing.

The next day, June 30, Morgenthau, who was admittedly distracted, attended the wedding of Ethel du Pont and Franklin Roosevelt, Jr., in Wilmington. After the ceremony he joined Mrs. Roosevelt, who was racing to a radio broadcast in Washington. Squeezed into the front seat of a three-year-old Chevrolet between the driver and a state trooper, with the First Lady in the back, the Secretary feared that upon returning to his office he would find the "currency club" disbanded. Instead he discovered that Simon had said he would continue the Tripartite Pact so long as the French kept the franc relatively steady, but he did want to know before July 1 precisely how far they planned to let the franc fall.

There was word also from Paris. The French had previously managed the franc between 4.35 and 4.65 cents. Now they had in mind going to 3.80 or 3.96. They were, in effect, notifying the United States of their plans and asking for a reply, but Bonnet had not, in the full meaning of the word, consulted the American Treasury. The French were going to do things their way, it seemed, whether the United States liked it or not.

Yet, as Oliphant put it, the French had conceded as much as sovereignty permitted, and Morgenthau fully agreed. He therefore proposed telling Simon that although he shared British apprehensions about an undervalued or unduly fluctuating franc, he believed international danger could best be minimized by avoiding any suggestion of a lack of confidence in France's future. He trusted Simon would agree that even at some cost and risk, confidence in the future of democracy needed to be preserved by a demonstration that the three powers could continue to work in mutual trust.

While the Treasury staff put the Secretary's words into official language, Morgenthau called the White House to ask whether the President, who had returned from his son's wedding, wanted to be interrupted. The Secretary told Mrs. Roosevelt that he could make up his own mind, and that there was no need to bother the President if he was terribly tired. Returning to his staff, he said that if the Exchequer insisted on being wishy-washy, or on telling the French they had to balance their budget or establish a 44- instead of a 40-hour week, then he did not want to be put in the position of seeming to agree. To avoid such an eventuality, he thought his note to Simon had to support the French clearly and boldly.

Shortly after 11 P.M. on June 30, Marvin McIntyre, Roosevelt's secretary, called the Treasury to say that the President knew all about the international monetary situation and that it was all right for Morgenthau to go ahead. "Well," Morgenthau said, "if he knows all about it, he must be clairvoyant. . . . I'll just assume the responsibility and go ahead and do what I think is best."

By midnight the Secretary had discussed his completed draft on the transatlantic telephone with Cochran in Paris, who warmly approved of it. Morgenthau then dispatched it to London. Great Britain and the United States, he told Simon, could most effectively reduce the dangers of further French devaluation by avoiding "any move on our part which might add to any lack of confidence in the future of the franc. In the present juncture of world affairs, I trust you will agree with me that it is of prime importance to preserve the beneficial effects which resulted from the Tripartite Declaration. . . . In view of all these considerations, it is my conviction that every reasonable effort should be made to make it possible for France to continue as a participant. . . . It is therefore my sincere hope . . . that you and I may present to M. Bonnet similar messages somewhat along the following lines: Now that the French Ministry of Finance has been given the powers which it sought . . . I look forward to a continuation of close cooperation between our Treasuries under the Tripartite Declaration. May I express to you the sincere hope that France will soon emerge from the temporary difficulties with which she is now confronted."

Simon immediately replied that he was sending Bonnet a message in the terms Morgenthau had suggested. He was also going to tell Bonnet confidentially that cooperation depended on keeping the franc relatively stable at a reasonable rate.

As Morgenthau prepared to cable his statement to Paris and to release it to the American press, Herbert Feis suggested he omit any reference to world affairs. Feis thought it would be wiser to treat the matter as exclusively monetary. Although Harry White differed, Morgenthau accepted the suggestion. "At least," he added, "we have kept Sir John from going off half-cocked."

"You have done a magnificent job," Feis replied. "It's too bad to save Sir John." He hoped the Secretary did not feel he had been too abrupt about asking for a change in phraseology. "I asked you to come over . . ." Morgenthau answered, "and when you wanted something I was more than satisfied to give you the veto power."

On July 1 Bonnet received the American message, "shook his head rather sadly" at the mention of France's "temporary difficulties," and expressed his appreciation for Morgenthau's assistance and good wishes. Unhappy that the British had pressed for exact figures on devaluation, Bonnet did not yield to the request, though he offered to visit London to consult Simon. The French parliament removed statutory limits to exchange movements and the floating franc began its difficult career. French gold holdings were revalued at 4.3 cents to the franc, and the profit was utilized to support the market for government securities.

During July the franc declined to about 3.8 cents. Its future depended on how well the Chautemps government could manage its domestic labor problems and how severe European tensions might become. For the time being, the floating franc had a fair chance while the tourist season brought in foreign exchange and while parliament was in recess. Though no one was wholly optimistic about the autumn, Bonnet had the opportunity to do what he could technically to stabilize the currency. There was the possibility, at least, that the mood of conservative French investors would brighten.

The immediate crisis had ended with the exchange of cables of July 1. Though French developments had strained the Tripartite Pact, it survived the difficulty, and in spite of the State Department's unwillingness to have Morgenthau refer to world affairs, continuing monetary cooperation had, as before, obvious political significance. Though not without friction, the treasuries of the three Western democracies were still working together, in part because Morgenthau had fortified Simon's faltering spirit. He had succeeded just in time, for developments in the Orient were shaking the world.

## 5. War in China

In May 1937, H. H. Kung, the Chinese Minister of Finance, had cabled Morgenthau to ask whether the Treasury would buy 50 million ounces of silver which China had in New York. Kung, who was then attending the coronation of George VI, had failed to negotiate a loan in London. He needed foreign exchange to preserve his currency reforms,* and he hoped to sell his silver during his forthcoming visit to the United States.

Morgenthau was at first reluctant to make the purchase. The Treasury, he told Chinese Ambassador Sze, had already done everything possible for China. "If and when Dr. Kung comes here," the Secretary said, "I will go out of my way with great pleasure to tell him that you got the last penny that anybody could have gotten and no one else could have done so well!" When Kung arrived on June 30, Morgenthau, still preoccupied by the troubles of the franc, said at once that he was considering no change in his silver policy, which in his view provided China with adequate credits each month, but he promised to review the situation.

Almost immediately the Secretary softened. With Chiang Kai-shek again putting his affairs in order, Roosevelt wanted to treat the Chinese "extra nice." Morgenthau, moreover, deemed it appropriate to save Kung's face, to give him something to take home. He therefore decided to purchase 12 million ounces of silver, which China had in San Francisco, provided that Kung used the proceeds to increase China's gold reserves. "I am inclined not to give them the whole cherry at the first bite," the Secretary said to his staff. "They are great traders. Start with the 12 million and be very reluctant about the 50 million." After further reflection, however, he made up his mind to take all 62 million ounces at 45 cents an ounce.

On July 8 Morgenthau gave Kung the good news, explaining that Roosevelt had instructed the Treasury to do everything it could to keep China strong. Frankly pleased, Kung commended

* See page 227.

the American point of view, since a "strong China" meant security and peace in the Far East. What Kung was trying to say, one of his associates explained, was that Morgenthau was a great statesman.

"Listen, Dr. Kung," Morgenthau replied, "I bought all your silver; you don't have to give me anything more."

"Well," said Kung, "I sold the silver to you cheap. I bought your surplus gold."

The meeting closed with laughter, but at an ironic time, for Kung had remarked on peace and stability in the Far East in ignorance of the news which had yet to reach Washington: Japanese and Chinese troops had clashed at the Marco Polo Bridge near Peking. The undeclared Sino-Japanese War began just before the conference reached its conclusion. Henceforth keeping China strong was to prove more difficult than ever. Henceforth, indeed, the Treasury was to be unable to confine its negotiations to the monetary aspects of diplomacy.

The undeclared war immediately raised questions about American policies. At Cabinet meetings of August 6 and 13, Vice President Garner urged the withdrawal of American troops in the Peking area, a policy also demanded by a resolution then before the Congress. Roosevelt agreed that there should have been no troops in Peking, explaining that the complete transfer of the embassy to Nanking had been delayed three years earlier at the recommendation of Stanley Hornbeck, the Chinese expert in the State Department. Roosevelt and Hull had accepted his advice which, in retrospect, the President judged unfortunate. Roosevelt also reminded Garner that American troops, as well as those of other countries, were in China in order to maintain a sufficient total complement of foreign components to protect all Westerners. This policy rested on a gentlemen's agreement which in present circumstances the United States could not very well violate. The Chinese situation, Hull added, was extremely complicated. An orderly withdrawal in agreement with other nations would be given one interpretation, whereas the Japanese would consider a scuttling departure to signify a complete retreat of the United States from the Pacific. This would mean giving up American influence and damaging American trade in approximately half the world. With the last point Admiral Leahy completely agreed.

When Garner then objected to risking war for the sake of business, Hull replied that he believed all the major powers should gradually withdraw from China, and he planned if necessary to take the lead in doing so. The only purpose of the American troops, he repeated, was to protect American nationals from irresponsible mobs. Roosevelt, who was also reassuring, told Garner the Administration was basing its policies in the Far East "on the hope of Japanese disaster, which could be produced by a rise in the strength of Russia and China and a revolt on the part of the Japanese population against militarism." The Cabinet then decided to inform American residents in China that ships would be held in readiness to take away all women and children who wished to leave. Those who remained would stay at their own risk.

The President had to make an even more difficult decision about whether to recognize a state of war between China and Japan. On the advice of the State Department, he did not. A proclamation of a state of war, the Department argued, would lessen the possibility of composing the differences between the belligerents, and increase the chances of American involvement, which might follow hard on a Japanese invocation of belligerent rights to restrict neutral commerce.

So long as the war was undeclared and officially unrecognized, the Neutrality Act did not apply, and both China and Japan were free to make purchases in the American market insofar as they had available funds and reasonable expectations of delivery. In both respects, the Treasury believed, Japan had an advantage, for her finances were far stronger than the Chinese, and whereas there was no problem in shipping materials to Japanese ports, the Japanese fleet blocked access to China. Nevertheless some material got through, and there would be more if the Chinese were able to work out overland transportation from Burma and other areas outside of Japanese control.

Morgenthau's predisposition to help China was confirmed by the political analyses he received from his Research Division in September. In the long run, the Division believed, a Japanese victory would greatly increase the chance of general world war, if only by encouraging other fascist nations to aggression. Germany was quite prepared to fish in troubled waters; and should

Japan achieve success, the probability of a German move against Czechoslovakia would become great. Moreover, if Japan won a clear and decisive victory, the moment might be propitious for a joint German-Japanese attack on Russia. The peace of the world, as the Treasury saw it, was tied up to China's ability to prolong resistance.

During the fall of 1937, however, various diplomatic efforts failed to assist the Chinese. At their request, the League of Nations investigated the undeclared war. A League report of October 6, which the United States endorsed, blamed Japan for the hostilities. The previous day Roosevelt, speaking in Chicago, had compared world lawlessness to an epidemic. "When an epidemic . . . starts to spread," he said, "the community . . . joins in a quarantine of the patients . . . to protect the health of the community against the spread of the disease. . . . There must be positive endeavors to preserve peace." Just what the President implied has never been clear, and probably was not entirely clear to him, but he did not, he later explained, have sanctions in mind, and as isolationists attacked his message, he obscured his purpose behind a vague discussion of the importance of peace. He also did not, it developed, intend to pursue a policy of collective security against aggressors, at least not yet. At the Brussels Conference of November 1937, the United States and the European democracies reaffirmed their concern for the territorial integrity of China, but took no significant action against Japan. On their part the Japanese, defying both the conference and the League report of October, indicated that they would tolerate no outside interference with their China policy.

There was little in these developments to sustain Chinese resistance. Cordell Hull offered nothing more. Though he continually remarked the importance of international treaties and international law, he avoided the question of China's integrity, thus giving Japan an implied invitation to negotiate with the United States to settle the Chinese war. China had reason to wonder whether she had any friend.

Morgenthau, resolved to be friendly, did not know how far the State Department would tolerate his monetary diplomacy, but he responded as generously and as freely as he could to China's overtures. On November 29 he began to consider a request for a bid on 10 million more ounces of silver. He wanted to tell the Chinese that he would buy 50 million ounces from them during the next ten weeks. He also wanted to extend for another year the agreement permitting China to borrow foreign exchange against gold on deposit within the United States. But before proceeding toward either of those goals, he asked Roosevelt for advice.

The President on December 2 instructed him to consult the Secretary of State. He would personally tell Hull, Roosevelt added, that he was inclined to go along with both of Morgenthau's proposals, but that both might be affected by any future proclamation of American neutrality. In the absence of such a proclamation (and Roosevelt said he would issue none unless the Japanese or Chinese declared war), the United States, the President believed, should continue its friendly policy just as if there were no hostilities.

The State Department had no official comment to make about Treasury purchases of Chinese silver. Informally, however, Hull advised Morgenthau to keep free of any commitments he would have to follow through should there be either a declaration of war or an application of the neutrality legislation. The customary rules of international law did not pertain to loans to belligerent governments, but Hull's legal adviser held that the purchase of silver from China would be against those customary rules if there were a formal declaration of war. He was not prepared to say whether this would be so if a commitment to purchase predated the declaration of war.

The State Department's indirect but nonetheless clear opposition to the proposed silver purchase led Morgenthau to change his rhetoric and restate his case entirely apart from its bearing on conditions in the Orient. The purchase of 50 million ounces of Chinese silver, he suggested, had as its real purpose the stabilization of the dollar, for China would be able to buy dollars by selling the gold she received for her silver. This kind of transaction was a tested device for improving the regulation of foreign exchange, specifically for maintaining the parity between the yuan and the dollar. The State Department, however, in a memorandum of December 6, 1937, expressed reservations about the Treasury plan. Since the Treasury said that the transactions in question could not be regarded as a loan or credit, and since the Treasury had made similar agreements with countries other than China, the State Department did not see how the arrangements could properly be considered as rendering the United States unneutral. But since the transaction was of a somewhat novel character, the State Department suggested retaining some freedom of action. It recommended that the Treasury include a provision making future extensions contingent on "any possible questions of neutrality that may arise." The Treasury might also tell the Chinese that, in the present judgment of the Department of State, such contingencies would not in fact arise.

After reading and rereading the memorandum, Morgenthau said he could not understand whether the State Department was telling the Treasury yes or no. He therefore turned to Roosevelt, who on December 8 called the memorandum "the most stupid . . . I have ever read. When they recommend that we add to the agreement to give China a foreign exchange loan a statement 'This may be cancelled in case of a Neutrality Proclamation,' this would be playing into the hands of somebody like Senator Nye."

"Or the Japanese," Morgenthau added.

"Fix up an agreement with them right away in writing," the President directed.

Despite the hesitations of the Department of State, the Treasury bought the Chinese silver and extended to China for six months the privilege of procuring dollar credits against gold held in the United States. These policies, conveniently redefined as ventures in monetary stabilization, were in fact efforts, however modest, to help the Chinese to purchase the materials of war which they desperately needed. They were soon to require much more help, but Morgenthau had given them at least the psychological lift which Hull's timid advisers would have denied them. Morgenthau had found a way around, and Roosevelt had stood behind him.

Franklin Roosevelt — the President — sensitive, perhaps to a fault, to the isolationist sentiment in the country and on Capitol Hill, buried the concept of quarantines beneath the caution of the State Department. Franklin Roosevelt — the man — indignant at Japan's brazen aggression, rejoiced in the uninhibited response of

his like-minded friend, the Secretary of the Treasury. If Cordell
Hull was Roosevelt's book of rules, Morgenthau, as Mrs. Roosevelt
often said, was her husband's conscience.


## 6. The *Panay*

On December 12, 1937, Japanese military airplanes bombed and
sank the United States gunboat *Panay* and destroyed three Standard Oil Company tankers twenty miles up the Yangtze River
from Nanking. They machine-gunned the survivors of the American
ships as they escaped, killing three and wounding others. Japanese
army motorboats also machine-gunned the *Panay,* and Japanese
personnel boarded that vessel although they could plainly see the
American markings on the ship, including the large ensign she flew
and two large flags painted on her upper deck.

Roosevelt, "deeply shocked," told the State Department to ren-
der a protest to the Japanese Emperor, and Hull on his own account also instructed the American ambassador in Tokyo to impress upon the Japanese government "the gravity of the situation
and the imperative need to take every precaution against further attacks on American vessels and personnel." Yet neither Hull nor his
advisers believed that the United States was in a position to send
sufficient naval forces to the Orient to require the Japanese to behave. Furthermore, the Department of State was acutely conscious
of persisting pressures from the American people for the withdrawal of American troops from the Far East, and of persistent opposition to the tone of the President's quarantine speech. Hull
therefore proposed to confine American policy to demanding an
apology, indemnities, and punishment of the officers who had directed the attack, as well as assurances that similar incidents would
not again occur.

The Japanese ambassador on December 13 described those requests as "wholly reasonable," and the Japanese Foreign Minister
called on the American ambassador in Tokyo to deliver "a profound apology." There was no question but that the Japanese government would repudiate the deliberate but unauthorized action of

their army on the Yangtze. Consequently Hull apparently never even considered the possibility that the attack on the *Panay* might lead to a rupture in diplomatic relations or to war.

Roosevelt, who was more bellicose, told Morgenthau on December 14 that there were lots of ways of declaring war. In the old days, he said, sinking an American naval vessel would have in itself constituted a cause of war. Now it was not considered such, but Roosevelt wanted Morgenthau to find out what authority he needed as President to take possession of all the belongings of the Japanese government and its citizens in the United States, and hold them against payment for the damages the Japanese had done. If he lacked authority to do this, he wanted to know how he could do it anyhow, and what anyone could do to him for having taken matters into his own hands.

A quick review of the available figures led the Treasury on December 15 to conclude that Japan and her citizens held about $72 million in short-term funds and something between $55 and $125 million in long-term securities, as well as merchandise, ships, and real estate valued between $25 and $50 million. The grand total ranged between $152 and $247 million, most of which the Japanese, if warned, could convert into pounds sterling within a few hours. Yet Herman Oliphant, with his customary resourcefulness, proposed a plan for sequestering Japanese funds if Roosevelt found that necessary. As Oliphant explained in a detailed memorandum, under a 1933 amendment to the Trading with the Enemy Act, the President could proclaim a national emergency and issue regulations prohibiting or restricting exchange transactions. The proclamation could be drawn in general terms, reciting the necessity for forestalling events which might plunge the country into war, for quarantining the war situation, and consequently for providing a basis for indemnity as well as for protection against future acts. On that basis the President could expressly prohibit banking and foreign exchange transactions and monetary exports in which the Japanese government was directly or indirectly interested.

Surprised and delighted by Oliphant's memo, Roosevelt exclaimed: "My God, I completely forgot about it." He also directed Morgenthau to examine the scheme further.

Treasury experts, discussing the plan on December 17, pointed out that at the first intimation of government action, the Japanese would begin to convert all their assets. The only way to stop this was to issue a proclamation making all transactions subject to licensing, and then to delay issuing the licenses. It might also be necessary to persuade the British to cooperate in preventing the conversion of dollars to pounds, and even so Germany and Italy might act as agents for Japan. To these objections Oliphant replied: "We have a doctrine of *'secit per alia secit per se'* which, being rendered, means you're stuck if you act through an agent."

As a first step toward Oliphant's plan, Morgenthau proposed sounding out Sir John Simon on the transatlantic telephone, but Assistant Secretary Wayne Taylor thought the plan was too vague for presentation to the British. For what circumstances, he asked, would the United States impose the rules, and for how long would they apply? That would be up to Roosevelt, Morgenthau replied; the rules would be removed when the Japanese agreed to be "good boys." "You know," he added, as the conversation continued, "this is the kind of thing I get a great kick out of. I enjoy this because I love to come through on something for the President like this, when he's in a tough spot."

The Secretary thought a telephone call would stiffen the British. It would be "a bombshell to Simon," Harry White agreed, but Taylor was not yet satisfied. If, for example, Italy sent Japan material she had been stockpiling and later attempted to replenish her stockpiles from the United States, it would be hard to prevent. Oliphant admitted that if there were a piece of paper from Il Duce saying "this is for my account," it would not be possible to say to Il Duce, "you son of a bitch, you're a liar," but they could do a lot of stalling. If the regulations were 75 per cent effective, Morgenthau interrupted, then they were wonderful.

Now Taylor asked whether the President was willing to go beyond the proposed regulations to war. If necessary, Morgenthau answered, the United States would fight. After all, he continued, "they've sunk a United States battleship and killed three people. . . . You going to sit here and wait until you wake up here in the morning and find them in the Philippines, then Hawaii, and then in Panama? Where would you call a halt?"

Taylor said he would wait quite a while.

Morgenthau, disagreeing "1000 per cent," said that economically, psychologically and financially, the country was ready for a war basis. He could see no reason for waiting for the Japanese to strike again.

"Well," Taylor replied, "of all the cockeyed things in the world that we can do that would be more cockeyed than the last World War we got into, this would be it."

"Now listen, Wayne," the Secretary said, "I am under great strain; I can't always stand having you do this to me. . . . I have yet to find you come in and say, well, Henry, I'll help you on this thing. But when you say that . . . what the President wants is cockeyed, I object."

Taylor replied that he had said that to get into war would be cockeyed.

Morgenthau still objected: "Has anybody said we were going to get into war? I say to you this is what the President wants. I think it's all right. I'm going to do what he asked me to do. . . . Now, be reasonable. . . . I'm only a human being, Wayne."

"I think that this particular thing we have to think through, and I don't think we have," Taylor answered.

"Well, I'm very sorry," Morgenthau said, "but this is what the President wants. Personally, I think it's a marvelous idea. . . . For us to let them put their swords into our insides and sit there and take it and like it, and not do anything about it, I think is unAmerican and I think that we've got to begin to inch in on those boys, and that's what the President is doing. . . . How long are you going to sit there and let these fellows kill American soldiers and sailors and sink our battleships?"

"A helluva a while," Taylor said.

Even Hull didn't feel that way, Morgenthau said, and Oliphant assured Taylor that they had been over the legal side of the problem. The Constitution gave to Congress the power to declare war, but American legal precedent was reasonably clear that the Executive had the authority to resist violence. That was all very pretty, Taylor replied, but if in the circumstances the particular move under discussion led to war, he was absolutely opposed to it.

"We are," Oliphant protested, "in a situation where not acting is just as fraught with consequences as acting."

Taylor was not so sure. "There is no reflection on the President," he said to Morgenthau, "and there's no reflection on you. I'm talking about the possibilities . . . of going through with this thing, and where do you go?"

Morgenthau explained again that he was acting as Roosevelt's agent. He had been told to explore the matter. And he thought the time had come for the United States to tell the Japanese to behave, because otherwise "it's only a matter of five or ten years before we'll have them on our necks."

"Well," Taylor said, "that's where I disagree."

At this point, Morgenthau had to go off to a Cabinet meeting. When he returned he reported that Roosevelt had pulled out Oliphant's memorandum, without explaining what it was, and said, "We want these powers to be used to prevent war. . . . After all, if Italy and Japan have evolved a technique of fighting without declaring war, why can't we develop a similar one?"

Vice President Garner thought that only real force would have any effect on the Japanese. Roosevelt, however, believed that economic sanctions could be made effective. "We don't call them economic sanctions; we call them quarantines. We want to develop a technique which will not lead to war. We want to be as smart as Japan and as Italy. We want to do it in a modern way."

After concluding his account of the Cabinet meeting, Morgenthau, frankly excited by Roosevelt's enthusiasm for sanctions for peace, put in his telephone call to Sir John Simon. He was calling, the Secretary said, with the knowledge and the approval of the President. He was operating through the Treasury rather than through diplomatic channels, and his message was for Simon and Chamberlain alone.

Simon interrupted to say that in England foreign affairs had to be conducted through regular channels. He was nevertheless sure that Chamberlain would consider the call all right, and he was agreeable to discussing it with as few people as possible.

Morgenthau then explained that while the United States was awaiting a Japanese reply to the American note about the *Panay,* the Administration was exploring various methods for handling an unsatisfactory answer. Under the Trading with the Enemy Act, the President had the authority to declare a national emergency

and "under such an act the idea would be to keep this nation quar-
antined against a war." That would involve complete exchange
control, including control both of bank credits and gold movements. Unless the United States had cooperation in such a policy,
however, it would not be very useful, and Morgenthau wondered
whether Simon might not like to think the problem over.

"Yes," Simon said. "Now, look here, Dr. Henry Morgenthau,
thank you very much for even consulting me. I do appreciate your
speaking about a rather technical thing. . . . And, of course,
when you use a long-distance telephone, it's hardly possible to
grasp details . . . and I am certain that if we are going to do this
we must really have the opportunity of looking at this act you
speak of and considering it in some detail." He suggested Morgenthau have the British ambassador cable the Foreign Office.

"Frankly," Morgenthau said, "we didn't want to put it in writing."

Simon replied that in the past he had not found that long-distance telephone calls were always understood. In England they
tried to discuss business as far as possible through their offices. He
was at dinner, his soup was getting cold, and he could not send a
note to the Prime Minister until the following day. "I don't want it
to be said hereafter," Simon continued, "that a suggestion was
made to us and I didn't understand and the consequence is that if
they had only acted differently something else would have happened. You know what happened in the case of Stimson. And I
don't want there to be any misunderstanding."

"I didn't know how you felt about telephone calls," Morgenthau
said.

"I don't think well of them," Simon said, "for this sort of purpose, to tell you the truth because I can't make a proper record.
. . . I want to do everything that is helpful and frankly it is very
difficult — our own methods in this country are rather the mode
of our habits."

Morgenthau replied that it was an American habit to use the
telephone freely; and Simon, laughing, said that he knew it, but
England was a small country, and "we have a system that is completely confidential."

So did Roosevelt. Following new instructions from him, Mor-

genthau cabled Simon on December 18: "In pursuance my telephone conversation with you it is obvious that the subject is corol-
lary to but an essential part of naval conversations and studies
about to be made. The British Ambassador and your Foreign Office have been advised. With full concurrence of Secretary of State
Hull we are asking the American officer who will shortly arrive in
London to see you and obtain your views on the economic phase
which I discussed with you by telephone Friday evening."

The President had decided to send Captain R. E. Ingersoll of the
United States Navy to London to investigate "with the British
Admiralty . . . what we could do if the United States and England would find themselves at war with Japan." Roosevelt was
still interested in Oliphant's memorandum, and he wanted the
Treasury to draft regulations governing foreign exchange, but he
was not in as great a hurry as he had been. Though he was uncertain about Japan's assurances of friendship, he had, as Morgenthau
put it, cooled off a bit.

By December 21, when the regulations were ready, the White
House gave no indication of wanting them. That afternoon, furthermore, Morgenthau heard from Simon. He had given Morgenthau's complete message of December 17 to Prime Minister
Chamberlain and Foreign Secretary Eden. He was pleased that
Ingersoll was coming to England. But the British, lacking powers
similar to those of the American Trading with the Enemy Act,
could not cooperate in monetary action against Japan without requesting special legislation from Parliament, and without first
consulting the dominions.

Most important, Simon said that study and experience had convinced the Chamberlain government that all aspects of such a problem as the Japanese crisis had to be considered together, and no
separate decisions could be made about economic, political or
strategic factors. Simon himself believed that long-range economic
pressure would not produce immediate results, and was therefore
hardly worth while. The application of immediate and drastic
pressure was, in his view, indistinguishable from other forceful devices. Though he did not say so explicitly, Sir John implied that
such forceful methods were not yet in order. The Treasury understood him to be saying "no," indirectly, politely, but emphatically.

There was, as it developed, no occasion for action. The Japanese government made a full apology, promised to pay the reparations the United States had requested, gave firm assurances that the episode would not be repeated, and agreed to punish the officers at fault. On December 23, to the delight of the Japanese, the United States officially accepted their apology, and the matter was closed. Hull had never expected any other resolution, and though Roosevelt had contemplated retaliation, Japan's apology made it unnecessary as well as unwise.

The episode was nonetheless revealing. It showed that the President was prepared, albeit only emotionally and momentarily, to force the issue in the Far East. It showed that Morgenthau favored a tougher policy than did either Hull or Roosevelt. Some of those within the Treasury, like Oliphant, were ready to go along with the Secretary, indeed ready to urge him on, whereas others, like Wayne Taylor, endeavored to restrain him. Yet whatever his own instincts, Morgenthau was less susceptible to pressure from his associates than he was to changes in the President's mood. It was while he had Roosevelt's encouragement that he pressed Oliphant's plan for freezing Japanese assets. It was after Roosevelt backed off that Morgenthau, in any case inhibited by the British response, turned the negotiation over to Ingersoll, Roosevelt's special agent, and to Hull who moved within regular diplomatic channels.

As it worked out, Ingersoll did not meet Simon. At Morgenthau's direction, he left it to the Chancellor to ask for an interview, which Simon did not do. Ingersoll talked with Eden and with the British Admiralty, but he did not discuss Oliphant's proposal, which remained where Roosevelt had put it, in the drawer of his desk, a memento, in a sense, of a difference of opinion within the Administration that had resulted in no conflict of policy. That difference of opinion was to persist, but in the early months of 1938 the Japanese apology eased tensions, and Morgenthau's concerns in monetary diplomacy focused again on Europe and on the western hemisphere.

## 7. Gold, Silver, and Oil

Fascism, as Morgenthau knew, endangered the Americas as well as Europe and Asia, for Germany was intent upon cultivating the friendships of the indigenous (and often corruptible) dictatorships south of the Rio Grande whose peoples were frequently anti-Yankee. Roosevelt countered this threat by striving to preserve and enhance hemispheric solidarity. So it was in 1937 that he hid his personal distaste for General Getulio Vargas, Brazil's political chieftain, and promised him American assistance in setting up a central bank. On that account Morgenthau, in spite of his distrust of Vargas, agreed to sell the Brazilians up to $60 million of gold over a period of five years, to furnish foreign exchange against that gold, and to provide technical aid and advice to the Brazilian treasury. This arrangement helped to keep Vargas a Pan-American.

By 1937 Mexico worried Morgenthau more than did Brazil. Barter agreements were bringing to Germany Mexican cotton, rice, and minerals, and the Germans had their eyes also on Mexican oil. Equally significantly, while the Mexican government persisted in its program of economic reform, the conservative opposition, consisting of wealthy landowners and others in the social elite, applauded German intervention in behalf of the Spanish fascists. Morgenthau was anxious, therefore, as was Roosevelt, to strengthen democratic tendencies in Mexico.

The depletion of the Mexican gold reserve presented an opportunity to act in December 1937. The Mexicans wanted to exchange silver for American gold, and Morgenthau asked Roosevelt for permission to negotiate without reference to the Department of State. The President, however, instructed him to avoid any conflict of policy between the two departments.

This was a serious limitation, for the State Department contemplated a general rather than a piecemeal settlement of Mexican problems. A crisis had been reached in the department's conversations about oil and land rights. Unable to obtain concessions from the Mexicans on wage scales in oil fields where British and

American companies were operating, the State Department had also failed to get compensation for owners of lands the Mexican government had expropriated. Consequently Hull opposed any softness toward Mexico.

In conference with Minister of Finance Suarez on December 13, 1937, Morgenthau followed Hull's prescription and refused to buy 35 million ounces of Mexican silver* or to lend dollars without gold or silver as collateral. But on reflection, the Secretary decided that the democratic regime in Mexico needed immediate help. "We're just going to wake up," he said to the President on December 15, "and find inside a year that Italy, Germany, and Japan have taken over Mexico. . . . It's the richest — the greatest store of natural resources close to the ocean of any country in the world. . . . They've got everything that those three countries need." He urged the President, therefore, to persuade the State Department to let the Treasury proceed independently.

The way to treat Mexico, Morgenthau proposed to Roosevelt several days later, was "the way you would reorganize . . . the Missouri Pacific Railroad or any big public utility, and we'll have to do an all-inclusive job." He suggested that Roosevelt invite the Mexican President to the United States, or alternatively send Sumner Welles to Mexico. "Fine," Roosevelt replied, but as the days passed he reported to Morgenthau no change in policy.

The Secretary proceeded informally on his own. On December 22, at a dinner party he gave for Minister of Finance Suarez and his shrewd companion, Ambassador Najera, Morgenthau said that applying adhesive plaster for a small scratch would fail to cure a patient suffering from a serious illness. The general conditions in Mexico, he thought, called for thorough examination. President Cardenas was the doctor in charge. If he cared to have help in attempting a real cure, he would find the United States receptive to examining the patient and willing to delay any payment of the fee.

The next morning the Mexican ambassador rushed over to the State Department to say that Morgenthau's proposal was a marvelous thing, but Hull was of just the opposite opinion, and the Treasury could do nothing for the Mexicans except buy their silver. "I

---

* In addition to the regular monthly purchases of silver, which were continuing, see page 203.

have about made up my mind," the Secretary recorded in his Diary on December 29, "that all these long negotiations with Mexico are the bunk. . . . It seems to me that the thing we ought to do is to buy whatever silver the Mexican Government has for sale and help them out *now* and let the State Department do their own horse-trading. There are too many angles to this situation that I do not understand and they do not smell good, and, therefore, I would rather confine myself to the strictly confidential end of the deal and let the State Department do its own negotiating."

Pressed by Morgenthau, Sumner Welles differentiated between short and long term aspects of the Mexican problem and assented to the Treasury's purchase of 35 million ounces of silver. On December 30 he reported an encouraging message from President Cardenas. The oil question was going to the Mexican supreme court, and Welles felt that he was making satisfactory progress on water rights. He also said that the Mexicans were overwhelmed with appreciation for the silver purchase.

Buying the silver was not entirely altruistic, for the Mexicans could always have sold it on the open market where consequent falling prices would have embarrassed the Treasury. But the gesture was more important than the cash, and the Treasury offered a good price. Morgenthau was sure he was right, as he put it, because "with any kind of sympathetic treatment, intelligent treatment, we may be able to help them pull through and have a friendly neighbor to the south of us. And I think it's terribly important to keep the continents of North and South America from going fascist."

Further developments came rapidly. The Mexican supreme court on March 1, 1938, supported previous decisions against foreign companies engaged in disputes with the Mexican union of oilworkers. On March 18, Cardenas expropriated the properties of these companies. Hull immediately began negotiations to obtain a reconsideration of the decision and expropriation, and on March 24 Herbert Feis told Morgenthau that the State Department was embarrassed because the Treasury was continuing to subsidize the Mexicans by buying their silver every month.

From the Treasury's point of view, Morgenthau answered, the monthly silver purchases were a monetary matter, not a political weapon. When Feis suggested he read the State Department's protests against Mexican policy, the Secretary blew up. He did not want to see the blankety-blank cables, he said. "The Treasury position is a monetary one and we stand on that ground. I don't want to be influenced. I don't want to know about the political thing. . . . They ask us and we do what they ask us, but from the monetary standpoint I think we ought to continue to buy silver." Mexico's problems, he added, could bring on a repetition of the Spanish situation. But reluctantly, in spite of all his feelings, he admitted that if American foreign policy was at stake, he had to accede to the State Department, though he would insist on a formal request.

On March 25 Feis delivered a statement of policy which constituted a formal request. Welles had drafted it and expected Morgenthau to use it. "In view of the decision of the Government of the United States," it read, "to re-examine certain of its financial and commercial relationships with Mexico, the Treasury will defer continuation of the monthly silver purchase arrangements with Mexico until further notice." To Morgenthau's surprise, Senators Pittman and McNary stood with the Department of State. The Secretary had no choice but to add his own reluctant endorsement, subject only to Roosevelt's approval.

To his further dismay, moreover, the State Department handled publicity about the decision in a manner that made the Treasury seem responsible for it. They notified the Mexicans before Roosevelt endorsed the statement and before an announcement of the new silver policy had been made in Washington. Mexican press releases attributed the decision to Morgenthau and in reporting the Mexican story, American newspapers spoke of "reprisals" and "retaliation." Cordell Hull, also pointing to Morgenthau, announced "that the suspension of Treasury Mexican silver purchases is primarily a Treasury function." Justifiably irate, Morgenthau demanded a correction, and Hull later explained that suspension was the decision of "the government."

Tensions eased on March 30 when Hull announced that the United States did not question Mexico's right to exercise its sovereign power by expropriating properties within its jurisdiction. The problem, he said, was one of indemnification. Some settlement now seemed possible, for the Mexicans wanted American friendship, and in May the Treasury proposed making a generous loan against their silver. Roosevelt encouraged Morgenthau to go ahead, but the Department of State objected on the grounds that the Mexican government was irresponsible and too backward industrially to be permitted to control its own oil fields. The State Department also feared making any gesture that might provoke other expropriations in Latin America, and argued further that the American public would consider the proposed loan a device to bail out the American oil companies.

Hull blocked the loan but made no progress in his own negotiations. Furthermore, after British and American oil companies embargoed Mexican oil exports, the fascist nations dickered with Cardenas for the oil they needed so badly. Though Cardenas entered into no arrangements, Hull was unrelenting. In July he asked Morgenthau to lower the price of silver about a cent. "We are having lots of trouble in Mexico," Hull said, "and you know the President and Daniels* have given the Mexicans the impression that they can go right ahead and flaunt everything in our face. . . . I have to deal with these communists down there, I have to carry out international law." But Morgenthau would not change the price of silver without a valid reason, and he felt Hull had not presented one.

Meanwhile Roosevelt, in spite of pressures upon him from Hull, from American oil interests, and from the American press, continued a good neighbor to Mexico. Quietly he permitted the Treasury during the summer to resume silver purchases on a new and informal basis. Without guaranteeing the Mexican government specific quotas or prices, the Treasury bought silver regularly and thus helped Cardenas replenish his diminishing foreign exchange. Morgenthau would have liked to do more, but he could not budge the Department of State, and Cardenas ultimately had no alternative to trading for German goods.

* Josephus Daniels, United States Ambassador to Mexico, where he was consistently a patient friend.

## 8. Another French Crisis

In September 1937, Sir Frederick Phillips, the permanent Under Secretary of the Exchequer and the head of the British civil service, came to Washington for conversations with the Treasury. Austere, laconic, sometimes imperious, Phillips cultivated the reputation of a man of mystery. His characteristic tactic, Morgenthau was warned, was to make those dealing with him reveal their purpose so that he could then maneuver them to his own ends. At their first meeting Morgenthau therefore sat silently until, after what seemed to be almost an hour, his visitor "broke down and talked first."

The British, Phillips said, expected the franc repeatedly to slip and rally but on the whole to fall gradually. They were willing nevertheless to keep France within the Tripartite Pact unless she imposed exchange controls, which in England's view would violate the agreement and lead to a retrogression everywhere.

Morgenthau had to answer circumspectly, for while his primary concern was for France's political future, the State Department had enjoined him to discuss only monetary matters. He would not, he said, commit himself to any hypothetical situation. Though he also opposed exchange controls, he was reluctant to make any irrevocable decision. In particular he did not value "things written on a piece of paper." He cared about "the human equation," and he was therefore anxious to continue his free exchange of information with the Exchequer. "Sooner or later," he said, "your Government and mine have got to carry the whole burden of stable exchange and when that happens we want to have enough confidence in each other so that we can stand shoulder to shoulder."

Very soon — in February 1938 — a new French crisis tested this rapport. For some weeks the American Stabilization Fund and the British Equalization Fund helped to control the decline of the franc, but both English-speaking countries observed with consternation the inability of French politicians to construct a stable government or to agree upon economic and financial policies. Furthermore, Prime Minister Chamberlain's conciliatory disposition toward Italy led early in March to the resignation of his Foreign Secretary, Anthony Eden. This in turn cost the Chamberlain government prestige among those, like Morgenthau, who believed that Eden, more than any other member of the British cabinet, stood for opposition to fascism. Hard on Eden's resignation there followed Hitler's occupation of Austria. Der Führer was also demanding the annexation of the Sudeten area of Czechoslovakia.

In France the Chautemps government, which had long been tottering, now fell. The British believed that only a nonpartisan, coalition government could succeed in France, but the French Socialists, who had precipitated Chautemps' fall, obtained authorization for Leon Blum to try to construct a Popular Front cabinet.

While Blum was so engaged, Morgenthau on March 14 told Roosevelt that he wanted to recommend that the French immediately impose exchange controls. They had tried just about everything else, he said, and only this move would now prevent further outflow of gold. Later they could gradually relax the controls in order to encourage commercial transactions. When Roosevelt made his approval subject to British consent, Morgenthau warned him that the Chamberlain government did not like Blum. Yet the Treasury would try to develop a persuasive plan. "Hitler goes and bluffs his way through Europe," the Secretary said, "and if the French showed a little strength they would find England quickly rallying to their side. This way they have no friends at all."

Later that day, reviewing the plight of the French with his staff, Morgenthau said that Chamberlain, who feared socialism anywhere, did not want Blum to succeed; the Czechs, Rumanians, and Yugoslavs were a liability to France; Russia was "not going outside of Russia to help anybody." The Secretary therefore wanted France to know the United States would stand behind her, and tentatively even Hull had agreed to indicating that exchange controls would be acceptable. "All we are going to say to France," Morgenthau explained, "is if you think this is a good move for you to make we are willing to sit behind and see you make it."

The State Department, like the President, thought Morgenthau should consult the British before acting, but he got Hull's consent to ask the French informally whether the question of exchange controls was worth putting to England. On the afternoon of March 14 he called Merle Cochran in Paris. He was prepared to have

France stretch the Tripartite Pact, the Secretary said, "twice as far as she was ever supposed to." He had a confidential message for Cochran to deliver orally to Blum: "We assume that in view of the foreign exchange developments of the past few days you have explored the possibility of imposing exchange control. If you feel that your internal situation can best be stabilized by the temporary imposition of exchange restrictions which will control capital movements, we are prepared to discuss immediately with you and the British Treasury to the end that every effort be made by our three Governments to cooperate under the Tripartite Agreement with your efforts to stabilize your internal situation by the imposition of certain exchange restrictions."

Morgenthau's proposal, Blum replied through Cochran, was a great source of personal comfort and relief. The Premier wanted to preserve the Tripartite Pact, which he had helped to draft, and he intended to make every effort to avoid exchange controls, but he was not certain that he or anyone else could do so. Furthermore, he said, France might be on the eve of war. The internal value of the franc was not important if war should come, whereas gold and credit were vital. He did not, therefore, want to see the gold reserves in the Bank of France used endlessly and hopelessly to maintain the exchange value of the franc. He was studying means for checking the flight of French capital, but he had no preconceived plan and consequently he did not want an official approach yet to be made to him or to the British about exchange control. If circumstances later warranted such an exploration, he would let the Secretary know. For the present, he would not even tell his own colleagues about Morgenthau's message.

Blum's mind was much on the possibility of war. He considered the news from Spain dreadful. The imminent collapse of the Loyalist forces would give the fascist dictators another victory. Chamberlain, he believed, was taking a weak position about threatening German aggression in Czechoslovakia. Indeed the Czechs themselves seemed inclined to accept Nazi assurances too readily, though Blum had given them almost a categorical promise that if Germany attacked them, France would fulfill her obligations of military assistance. He thought Russia would also aid Czechoslovakia, and he considered Russian aviation the most powerful in the world. He believed, too, that if France fought, Great Britain would have to cooperate. Yet he was greatly disappointed about the failure of the French center to support his appeals for a national government, and he was pessimistic about the immediate future.

So also, Morgenthau learned, was the British Exchequer. London predicted an international arms race, oppressive taxation, perhaps a general war in which Great Britian, for the first time in her history, would be menaced in three areas of the world by totalitarian states in a position to take the initiative. The Exchequer considered the new Blum government doomed to a very brief term in office.

Roosevelt was also glum. On March 16 he told Morgenthau that he thought Germany would take Czechoslovakia in stride. He had thought so for three months, he said. He felt that Hitler had made a deal with Mussolini by which Germany had a free hand in Central Europe and Italy in the Mediterranean. And as if this were not devastating enough, Morgenthau heard from the Treasury's representative in London the following day that Chamberlain had publicly admitted his dissatisfaction with the progress of the British economy and prophesied that the depression would get worse. Never, it seemed, had British opinion showed so little cohesion in the face of decisive issues.

Nor was there cohesion in France where former Finance Minister Bonnet and other self-styled moderates considered Blum and the Socialists too extreme in their reform program and too susceptible to Russian influence in foreign affairs. France, they held, should aid Czechoslovakia in the event of a German attack only if Great Britain promised to join them, and France could not in their view afford to intercede in Spain where the civil war was ending rapidly. These attitudes proved dominant, at least for the time. Increasing public dismay at the possibility of war, increasing resentment toward strikes which the Blum government was unable to prevent, led early in April to the fall of that government. Under Daladier, a center and right coalition came into office for the first time since mid-1936. The Socialists refused to participate, and by the middle of the month it was clear that Daladier was moving in directions with which Blum and his associates could not sympathize. As Cochran reported from Paris, French bankers were developing confidence in the franc not because the strain on the French economy had ceased, but because of the increasing rapprochement between Paris and Rome and between London and Berlin. Daladier and his Finance Minister Marchandeau had also put the brakes on domestic reform.

Morgenthau, of course, had no way to check the mounting influence of the French Right. During the weeks between mid-March and mid-April 1938, moreover, he was virtually overwhelmed by his own domestic problems, by the difficulties of the recession, and by the President's decision to forego economy for deliberate deficit spending. Yet while events at home preoccupied him and events in France saddened him, he was not yet ready to write off the possibility of French resurgence. And whatever the political complexion of the French government, he did not see how France could retain her gold assets unless she imposed stringent restrictions on capital movements.

The British still disagreed. On April 25 Ambassador Joseph P. Kennedy wrote a scolding letter from London. He thought that Morgenthau, by telling Blum the United States would not object to the imposition of exchange controls, had come close to playing "dirty ball" against the British. In Paris Ambassador Bullitt was also critical, for he had been persuaded that the franc should be permitted to seek its own level. This prospect worried Morgenthau, who predicted that the Tripartite Pact would not survive a franc depreciated from 160 to the pound, the prevailing ratio, to 200; and the Exchequer, too, according to advice from London on April 29, would not tolerate a deliberate depreciation of that dimension. Yet short of exchange controls, Morgenthau could not see how France could prevent it.

On May 2 France informed the United States that she could no longer continue the expensive effort to maintain the value of the franc. Forced to choose between exchange control and further depreciation, the Daladier government had decided to let the franc drop to 175 to the pound, with the intention of restoring the existing ratio as soon as economic improvements permitted. Meanwhile the French hoped the United States would consider their course acceptable within the meaning of the Tripartite Agreement.

Morgenthau hesitated. As he said to his staff, he did not know whether the French could pull themselves out, but he hated to be a party to giving them a death blow, especially since he had nursed them along for so many years. Yet, as he put it to Sumner Welles, he was sure that French bankers had known the change was coming and had speculated against it, which "smells bad." The Secretary still believed the French would do better to control capital movements, but the State Department, opposing controls, argued that the United States could take a franc at 175 to the pound if England could. Undecided, Morgenthau said he was afraid of making the Tripartite Pact a laughingstock. At the very least, he needed more time. He also needed the President's advice. Roosevelt, who considered France's plan weak, thought supervision of capital movements would offer a more permanent solution. If that failed, he would favor more drastic exchange controls.

American policy was still unsettled on the morning of May 3 when Morgenthau received the draft of the reply which Chancellor of the Exchequer Simon planned to send the French. Simon regretted that the French government had concluded it could no longer defend the current franc rate. The British were prepared not to take exception to the French proposal, but they did not think existing circumstances justified it. Explaining his draft to Morgenthau, Simon noted that this would be the first time one of the Tripartite countries had deliberately depreciated as an instrument of policy. There was no blinking the fact, the Chancellor observed, that that contravened the provisions of the Pact.

Morgenthau had no more than read the cable when Ambassador Kennedy telephoned from England. He had seen Chamberlain and Simon, who were "just as sore" as Morgenthau was, but did not believe in exchange controls because they felt they would be the beginning of the end. Furthermore, the British were worried about the diplomatic situation. Hitler was going to be in Rome that day, and might "bust" the whole world open. The French action, Chamberlain had argued, was not in fact going to cost anybody any money, but with Hitler on the move, the breakup of the Tripartite Pact would be a calamity. Depreciation, if it hurt at all, would hurt England more than the United States. Yet the British were willing to accept it, rather than face the collapse of the pact, which would knock "the hell out of the market in England" and give Hitler and Mussolini just what they wanted. Chamberlain had told Kennedy that so long as they were working on the problems in hand, the worst had not yet happened, but if they let all agreements go, why "to hell with everything." The Prime Minister wanted to preserve the Pact and to go on from there. If people became fatalistic about the impossibility of making any deal in Europe, he had said, there was no hope for the world.

Morgenthau told Kennedy his report was a big help. When the French and British got together to discuss what to do in case of war, the Secretary hoped a French general would be in charge of the armies but an Englishman in charge of the two banks. But joking aside, Kennedy's message was troubling. The Secretary was afraid Chamberlain intended only to let things drift as the British had in Ethiopia, Spain and the Far East. On the other hand, the last thing Morgenthau wanted to do was to throw the French out of the currency club.

As the day waned, he came slowly to the British position. A cable from Paris reported that only the Communists favored exchange controls, which Daladier would simply not impose. In that case, Morgenthau remarked, for him to ask Daladier to initiate exchange controls would be like the French asking Roosevelt to give up Hull's trade treaties. His delay, the Secretary felt, had scared "hell" out of the French. Now that they knew the United States and England were irritated, he was willing to retreat. As he recognized, he had no choice. Daladier opposed exchange controls and the British Exchequer, defining its views in a message of May 3, held that a system of controls would bring on the worst of both worlds — autarchy and depreciation.

Late in the afternoon of May 3, supported by Cordell Hull, Morgenthau told the French ambassador* that if his government said it was executing a carefully thought out plan, the United States Treasury would accept it. A franc at 175 to the pound would not affect the American economy, he continued, but it would set a bad example. He wished he could convince himself that by letting the franc drop France could poise to snap back again, for his central interest was in international financial stability. He would announce

* At that time Count R. D. de Saint-Quentin.

his support of the French after he studied the official decrees.

Cochran reported those decrees that evening. Among other things, they called for an increase of 8 per cent in all taxes except customs duties, which was expected to produce an additional 3 billion 200 million francs. In order to increase production, the government was also going to adjust the 40-hour law and give financial benefits to those industrialists making capital improvements. The next day, May 4, Minister of Finance Marchandeau urged Morgenthau to support depreciation at once, for the Daladier government needed public assurances from the United States in order to solidify its position at home.

Morgenthau, though still dubious, was ready to help. "Consequent upon the consultation which the French Government has carried on with the American and British Governments," he replied, "as provided by the Tripartite accord, this government regards the accord as continuing in full operation." Simultaneously the British, while officially regretting the French decision, accepted the word of the French government that it sought no competitive trade advantage and considered the depreciation final. In these circumstances and after consulting the United States, Simon was prepared, he said, to regard the French proposal as "not inconsistent" with the Tripartite Pact.

So once again the United States and England, as Morgenthau put it, "held their nose and went along." As Chamberlain had said, there was no alternative, for Hitler and Mussolini would have rejoiced at any democratic discomfort. But on several counts Morgenthau was unhappy about the solution. Without exchange controls, the Secretary believed, the French would be unable, no matter what government was in power, to arrest the flight of capital. Still more distressing was the French abandonment of reform and retreat from Leon Blum's resistance to the Nazis. And had the Secretary only known, Chamberlain had struck the most ominous note of all. The Treasury interpreted his emphasis on preserving agreements to pertain to the currency club. In fact, however, the Prime Minister had apparently already decided to make new, more portentous arrangements. This decision, though Morgenthau at the time did not realize it, was soon further to shake the world.

## 9. Spain

Determined to help the opponents of fascism help themselves, Morgenthau in 1938 found a way in which to assist the Spanish Loyalists. The Neutrality Act prevented lending them money, but there was nothing in the Act to keep Morgenthau from purchasing old coins and other silver which Loyalist Ambassador Fernando de los Rios proposed selling to the Treasury. In January 1938 the ambassador broached that possibility, and in March he offered the Treasury 55 million ounces of silver in the form of peseta coins. Though the Treasury ordinarily purchased only silver bars, Morgenthau agreed to accept 5000 ounces of the coins in a trial shipment.

The Loyalists consigned the shipment to the Federal Reserve Bank of New York as the Treasury's agent, but when it arrived on May 30, the bank also received an adverse claim against it from Sullivan and Cromwell, the law firm representing General Franco and the fascist faction in Spain. Leaving the silver temporarily aboard the ship on which it had come, the Treasury studied the legal problem which Franco's claim created. On May 31 Herman Oliphant advised Morgenthau that there were two ways of proceeding. One was to execute the contract, which would involve the United States government in possible liabilities, for the contract had not been drawn in such a manner as to preclude the claims Franco had entered. Alternatively, the Treasury could refuse to pay for the silver until the Loyalists had cleared up their title to it. As Oliphant pointed out, however, this latter course, while it would be safer legally, would give no help to the Loyalists.

Morgenthau agreed that there were possible liabilities in executing the contract, but he believed that he and the President had the right to rely upon the representations of Ambassador de los Rios, who was the accredited agent of a legally recognized government. The Secretary therefore decided that the Treasury would accept the silver and pay the Ambassador. Oliphant prepared papers to relieve the Federal Reserve Bank of New York of any liability on its part, and the Treasury had the silver unloaded and moved directly to the Assay Office. The Department also sent a check to the Spanish ambassador for just a little over $2 million. On June 3, de los Rios accepted the check, endorsed it, and cashed it in Washington. On June 4, Sullivan and Cromwell served the Federal Reserve Bank of New York with a summons.

If Franco's lawyers intended the summons to inhibit Morgenthau from purchasing more silver, they miscalculated their antagonist. The Secretary immediately contracted for a second shipment of 5000 ounces and upon its arrival for a third. He hoped ultimately to purchase 10 million ounces a month from Spain and 20 million from China, he told his staff. "Work it out on a population basis," a colleague suggested. "No," Morgenthau replied, "on the basis of direct hits by bombs." He also, with Roosevelt's consent, called Henry Stimson, Hoover's Secretary of State, to ask him to represent the Treasury and the New York Federal Reserve Bank in the suit which Franco had brought. Stimson, whom Morgenthau considered one of America's most distinguished statesmen, accepted the assignment, remarking that he always preferred to support the side with which he could sympathize. His firm gave the Treasury legal advice on the succession of cases arising out of the continuing purchases. (The United States in later years finally won three of those cases and settled the others by compromise.)

On several counts the silver purchases were difficult to complete. Morgenthau had to help the Loyalists find counsel for their part in the law suits which the Franco faction continued to bring. Franco's legal maneuvers made American steamship companies wary about transporting the metal, and Oliphant had to make a special appeal to the president of the United States Lines in order to get a reliable carrier. Most distressing, the Department of State proved uncooperative. In September 1938 the Spanish ambassador asked the State Department for diplomatic immunity for Gonzala Zabala, a Loyalist officer of the Bank of Spain, who was in the United States on business. John Foster Dulles of Sullivan and Cromwell had subpoenaed Zabala in connection with the silver suit. The State Department, although fully informed about the Treasury's interest in the suits and in Zabala, refused diplomatic immunity. This particularly irritated Morgenthau, because the State Department had neglected even to consult the Treasury before making the decision, and thereafter would not reverse it.

In spite of these problems Morgenthau during 1938 bought 35 million ounces of Loyalist silver, taking five different shipments, and paying over to the Loyalists some $14 million. The amount of war materials which the Loyalists could buy with that sum was trivial, but the friendship of the United States Treasury was surely heartening at a black hour in their failing days. It was heartening in turn to Morgenthau that in the face of Franco's legal opposition and the clear disapproval of the Department of State, Roosevelt from first to last supported his efforts to sustain the Loyalists.

## 10. The Immobile Mr. Hull

Fascist gains in Europe made Morgenthau increasingly anxious to extend to the Chinese all possible assistance. At Kung's request, he continued his purchases of Chinese silver, buying 50 million ounces in March and April 1938. He also then for the first time permitted China to use the proceeds from the purchases for purposes other than the stabilization of currency. Nevertheless the Chinese, even though the Treasury in May agreed to take 50 million more ounces in biweekly installments, were desperately short of dollars to pay for military supplies. Ambassador Wang therefore began to explore the possibilities of negotiating a cash loan either from the American government or on the American market. Though Sumner Welles and Morgenthau both discouraged him, the Department of State was at least willing to discuss the possibility, which in earlier years it had preferred not even to contemplate.

Discussion, however, stopped short of action. When in June Morgenthau and Henry Wallace attempted to arrange a loan to China for the purchase of flour and cotton goods, Hull insisted that they could proceed only if they made an identical offer to Japan. Left once again with only one way to help the Chinese, Morgenthau contracted for another 50 million ounces of silver.

Kung was grateful, as he wrote on June 21, but he would not minimize the urgency of China's problems or the menace of Japanese aggression to all democratic nations. American neutrality laws, he observed, would not in the end protect the United States from fascism. Furthermore, he argued, since he believed 90 per cent of the American people were in sympathy with China, it behooved the American government to increase her capacity to resist Japan.

Wellington Koo, the Chinese ambassador to France, made the same case to William Bullitt, who urged a credit for China for the purchase of flour and grain. Without such a credit, he contended, Chiang Kai-shek would soon lack the means and the will to fight. The French, moreover, had intimated that if the United States extended some sort of credit to China, they and the British would act simultaneously though not jointly. The French did not believe that this would provoke a serious Japanese reaction, for they considered the Japanese too fearful of Russian attack to proceed against the Western powers.

Bullitt's advice provoked Roosevelt to instruct the Treasury to consult the Departments of State and Agriculture and, if necessary, the Reconstruction Finance Corporation, Commodity Credit Corporation, and Export-Import Bank in order to push to completion a loan for the Chinese. While these discussions were underway, J. Lossing Buck, the Treasury's special representative in China, reported that Chinese youth was joining the ranks of the Communists in large numbers in the belief that only Russia would help China against Japan. As K. P. Chen had put it to Buck, "the present generation of leaders in China will have to make drastic changes if this trend is to be averted." One remedy was American assistance, and Colonel Joseph Stilwell of the United States Army, the "Vinegar Joe" whose heroic efforts were to form a bold chapter in World War II, recommended that the United States help the Chinese finance the purchase of military equipment. This, Stilwell said, would be the cheapest possible way to buy national defense.

Morgenthau, who fully agreed, at Roosevelt's request discussed the possibility of a loan with Chinese Ambassador Wang early in September. The ambassador had the impression from a previous interview with the President that he could at once arrange for a $25 million loan for medical supplies, cattle, gray goods, and flour. Morgenthau, however, did not believe that anything was settled.

The State Department had yet to agree to any form of assistance. The President at one time had considered having the Chinese repay the United States in kind, whereas Ambassador Wang wanted a dollar loan repayable in dollars, as did Morgenthau. The Secretary in the end could only tell Wang that the Treasury had been in favor of the loan for two months and would approve it as soon as the President and the State Department did.

On September 6, a few days after talking with Wang, Morgenthau asked Roosevelt about the loan. The President said he had made no promises, but he was "enthusiastic to do something." So was Morgenthau, who told an interdepartmental conference that afternoon that an American gesture would probably "break the ice" and get the French and British going, too. Even a small loan for limited materials had important psychological value. He himself wrote off every dollar he lent the Chinese, he said, but with a battleship costing $80 million, the United States had to risk losing money in China. "Do we want to show these people our friendship and do we want to do it in a substantial way?" Morgenthau asked. "Personally, I do, not as Secretary of the Treasury, but as a member of this Administration. I am very keen to do it." But Hull was still unwilling, as he indicated on September 8, and when K. P. Chen arrived in Washington two weeks later to negotiate a loan, the entire issue was as confused as it had been since the previous June.

As Morgenthau saw it, this confusion had become intolerable, for the Sudeten crisis in Europe* made him almost desperate to demonstrate that the United States would aid those who withstood fascist aggression. "After all," the Secretary said in exasperation, "we might just as well recognize that the democratic form of Government in my lifetime is finished. There is a bare chance we may still keep a democratic form of Government in the Pacific, but only a bare chance, and . . . the Chen mission is our last opportunity and . . . this has been in Mr. Hull's lap since June or July and the responsibility is entirely his."

Jacob Viner, however, suggested on September 22 that the record was not that clear. Morgenthau, he said, had agreed only to a wheat and cotton loan which the Chinese now said they could not use. Was the Secretary willing to go further than that?

---

* See pages 513–22.

Indeed Morgenthau was. He would, he said, buy every dollar of silver China had as fast as Chen could ship it. He would also take any tung oil Chen could transport. He would invite American oil executives to confer with Chen about Chinese transportation. He would endorse a $100 million credit for exports to China of any variety. "I am willing," the Secretary continued. "I don't think that on the tung oil you'd get anywhere because . . . by the time you organize the transportation system Confucius will come back to this earth." The Chinese, he thought, needed a competent middleman to conduct their business for them, "a buying company which is on the level. If we give them $25 million for their silver, I would like to know where every dollar of that goes."

Minutes later he said as much to K. P. Chen. He was moving forward ten days, he told Chen, the execution of the biweekly Treasury contract for Chinese silver, and he was prepared to purchase 20 million additional ounces. "We are going to try to do everything we can to assist you," Morgenthau went on. "It's very difficult. But we are going to do everything we can. I, in turn, have to explain what I do to my Congress. It has to make sense." The Chinese, he suggested, should form a kind of corporation with which they could deposit proceeds of the silver sales and through which they could buy whatever they needed. The time had come to be practical. Only by creating an efficient corporation within the United States could the Chinese avoid using funds for the payment of interest on miscellaneous debts or in other ways which would not help the war effort. He wanted Chen to come back and propose to him just what he had proposed, but as if it were Chen's idea. "This is business," the Secretary said, "not diplomacy."

It was, of course, also diplomacy, and, as it happened, at best a difficult business. Shortly after Chen left, Morgenthau received a cable from London noting that the British would oppose intervening in the Orient if the Sudeten crisis worsened. He also discovered that before the Chinese could produce the 20 million ounces of silver which he was ready to buy, they would have somehow to divorce it from loans they had made in Europe against it. Almost everything China had was pledged or otherwise tied up. But Roosevelt gave Morgenthau the encouragement he needed. "Well," the the President said on September 26, "if there's war in Europe we'll give them the credit." After reflecting a moment, he added: "If there isn't maybe we'll do it anyway."

As a beginning Roosevelt approved the purchase of the unpledged Chinese silver, and he favored lending the Chinese money to buy American wheat for resale wherever they wanted. But Hull wanted to think that possibility over, and Wallace feared the repercussions on the world market if China dumped the wheat. Hull also opposed dumping, and on September 30 he argued further that a wheat loan would involve the United States in the Sino-Japanese conflict by giving China definite economic support. The State Department, he said, had been preaching strict neutrality. The Japanese were certain to find out about the transaction and it would be hard to anticipate how they might retaliate. He was also hesitant to act in any way contrary to the wishes of Congress. Though the decision, of course, was up to the President, he considered it his duty to advise Roosevelt "that this proposal would conflict with the neutrality policy."

The burden of defending a wheat loan would be on his shoulders, Hull continued. His own personal feelings were with the Chinese, but he wanted to avoid entanglements in the Far Eastern war. The Department of State was already taking a stiffer line with the Japanese. He had been able to stop shipping American planes to Japan and he had protested the aerial bombings by the Japanese in which some American citizens had been hurt. These actions, he felt, had hindered Japan's war effort. They had been possible, he believed, only because he could offer a plausible explanation for them to the American people, and only because they were part of a general policy that might be applied against any nation whose use of war planes involved American citizens. He opposed the wheat loan to the Chinese because by contrast it was not part of a general policy, nor was it a policy which he could in his own mind defend to neutrality-minded Americans or to an irritated Japan. He admitted that there was a difference of opinion among his advisers. Feis supported the loan, but others opposed it on the grounds that it was out of proportion to the damage it might cause. So, obviously, did Hull.

Senator Key Pittman, whom Morgenthau consulted, had still another approach to the problem. As always, Pittman, in spite of his alleged interest and competence in foreign affairs, steered his course toward the highest possible price of silver. If it were legal, he said, he would lend China enough money to win the war, but this was impossible. The only alternative he saw was to pay China $1.29 an ounce for her silver. With the proceeds, vastly larger than they would be at the market price, China could buy American products. In this way the increased cost of the silver to the Treasury would constitute a bonus to American exporters. Then Pittman came to his central point. If the Chinese received $1.29 for their silver, the Treasury would have, of course, to purchase American production at the same price. What Pittman recommended would have helped the silver-mining corporations of Nevada far more than Chiang Kai-shek.

For the time being Morgenthau could give the Chinese only ideas. Chen had already begun to set up a purchasing corporation, and now the Secretary persuaded several executives of American oil companies to advise him about a program for improving Chinese roads and highway equipment. This had the incidental merit of pleasing Roosevelt who, as Morgenthau knew, had told Chen that "the most important thing is to get your transportation organized." Perhaps progress on that front brought the President closer to over-ruling Hull, but Morgenthau was not to have his way about the loan until the resolution of the Sudeten crisis had accentuated the peril of the free world.

## 11. Munich

During July and August 1938, while Morgenthau was in France, general war in Europe seemed more imminent than at any time since 1914. Hitler's frenzied demands for the Sudeten area of Czechoslovakia, supported as they were by German mobilization near the Czech border, provoked the Czechs to mobilize in turn. The Nazis, invoking their mad logic, made Czech mobilization the occasion for further protest and new demands. France was committed to go to war with Germany if Hitler invaded Czechoslovakia, and in that case Great Britain might be drawn in. But in Paris and London official opinion wanted to resolve the crisis short of war by devising a settlement acceptable to Hitler.

Morgenthau had no leverage for strengthening the will of the Western powers to resist the Nazis. French devaluation had already weakened the Tripartite Pact, and France now had new monetary problems. As the French Minister of Finance, Paul Marchandeau, put it, the growing — and inevitable — military budget could only further strain the government's credit. He could not hold the franc at its existing level for long without new support from the United States. Rumors of an impending devaluation exacerbated his difficulties, he said, and he hoped that Morgenthau would make some public statement jointly with France and Great Britain indicating the steadfastness of three-power cooperation in monetary policy.

Morgenthau, who doubted the usefulness of words, preferred the possibility of using the American Stabilization Fund to buy francs for future delivery, which would provide the French fund with dollars for sustaining the "spot" (or immediate) value of its currency. Merle Cochran had proposed that scheme at the suggestion of the French, but he and they, after further reflection, were not sure it would help, and the British Exchequer, whose participation Morgenthau considered essential, lacked authority to deal in futures. The Secretary therefore fell back on words and on August 24, boarding the *Normandie* for his voyage home, announced, as he had so often before, his desire to be a friend to France.

As the Sudeten crisis mounted, France and England needed a friend. The public statements of Roosevelt and Hull gave them small comfort. Both the President and the Secretary of State had reminded the American people in mid-August of the need for international cooperation to check lawlessness and preserve peace, but both had stopped far short of advocating foreign commitments. Roosevelt's caution may have reflected a conviction that Chamberlain was bent on appeasing Hitler. In any case, the declared American opposition to entanglements surely intensified the Prime Minister's trepidations.

Privately the President was beginning to look for devices short of entanglements that would help the British and the French, and perhaps also restrain the Germans. To this end he asked Morgenthau on August 30 to have his staff think about setting up a special fund for French and English gold, "just for safekeeping." Roosevelt thought it would help psychologically to indicate to the world that the democracies had gold resources in a safe haven. He also wanted the Treasury to consider plans for expending that gold for arms and ammunition.

On August 31 Morgenthau, calculating the odds on war as no better than 50–50, gave his staff half a day to prepare the plans Roosevelt had requested, and to complete arrangements for the imposition of exchange controls on one hour's notice. That afternoon they offered him three possibilities. Wayne Taylor proposed that the Export-Import Bank open special accounts for the governments of England and France, and operate in effect as their agent for converting their gold into dollars for the purpose of making purchases of war materials. Oliphant favored arrangements under the Tripartite Pact permitting Great Britain and France at any time freely to withdraw or to export any gold which they held under earmark in the United States. The United States, moreover, would agree for twelve months to purchase earmarked gold at $35 an ounce. Since the price of gold had been theoretically subject to change, a commitment to $35 for a year was, as Morgenthau noted, "really something new." Harry White favored a third plan which called upon the President once again to apply countervailing duties, and perhaps ultimately an embargo, against Germany.*

At 4:15 P.M. on August 31, Taylor, Oliphant, and Morgenthau conferred with Roosevelt. "I gave you the germ of an idea," the President said, obviously pleased, "and you come back with three golden kernels." At first he particularly liked the Taylor proposal for the Export-Import Bank because he considered it more dramatic than the other plans. He wanted also to be told immediately how, if Germany went to war, he could impound every German ship in American ports. Because time was short, he said, Morgenthau should at once go over to the Department of State and show all the plans to Hull. In "a very meek voice," Morgenthau asked Roosevelt if he would mind telephoning Hull first. After the President put the call in, Morgenthau again "meekly suggested" that

* See pages 149–54.

Roosevelt ask Hull to come to the White House. Roosevelt, nod-
ding, said to the Secretary of State: "I have hatched a chicken. Do
you want to come over and look at it?"

After Hull arrived, Roosevelt read aloud Oliphant's plan for
utilizing the Tripartite Pact, stressing as he went along the advantage of action before war. Hull said he would have to sleep on it.
He said also that he thought there was such a thing as doing too
much at that time. Roosevelt's recent speech about the need for
international cooperation, the pending trade treaty with the British, and then the proposed expansion of the Tripartite Agreement,
Hull argued, were apt together to "get the American people up on
their toes" over the European situation. As an alternative to the
Treasury plans, Hull preferred one of his own — "to put the heat"
on the Austrians for payment of their debt to the United States,
and thus, perhaps, to embarrass the Germans.

The advantage of the Treasury approach, Morgenthau suggested, was that the decision about the Austrian debt rested exclusively with the Germans, whereas the decision about the Tripartite
Pact rested with the United States.

Roosevelt emphasized the importance of taking steps at once in
order to show the German government exactly where American
sympathies lay. He then took a stronger line on the question of
countervailing duties. He said he thought Hull should send for the
German ambassador and tell him the United States might apply
the duties if Germany went into Czechoslovakia. No, Roosevelt
mused, he would send for the German himself. He might put it
this way: "It's a hundred to one shot that I will do this if you go
into Czechoslovakia." Or he might phrase it instead: "I hope you
won't force my hand."

As Hull, still resistant, got up to leave, Roosevelt told him not
to show the Treasury memoranda to anyone in the Department of
State. This was a Treasury matter, the President said, and the State
Department, except for the Secretary, was not supposed to know
about it.

Back at his office, Morgenthau opened his mind to his staff: "My
own feeling is that if we are going to do anything, the time to do
it is in the next 48 hours, as I think that the offer we are making
under the Tripartite would be most reassuring to the British and

the French and I think if the President decided to do both, that it would give the German general staff and Dr. Schact something to think about, and if this is a 50–50 question everything that we can add on the score for peace is just that much to the good. But time is the essence! And it ought to be out in the papers . . . and the President ought to send for the German diplomatic representative."

The President did not. Either his own reflections or Hull's opposition persuaded him to put the Treasury plans aside. They were, of course, of limited value for resolving Europe's crisis. Hitler, for one, was probably not of a mind to be restrained by embargo, and Chamberlain, for another, had probably passed the point where an easy convertibility of gold to munitions was sufficient to bolster his spirit. But in the awful days of September 1938, the Treasury proposals had at least one indisputable asset. Had the President chosen to adopt them, had he chosen to put himself publicly on record as prepared to do as much as the law permitted to aid the democracies, he might have given heart to the thousands of Englishmen and Frenchmen who needed desperately every potion of courage which the United States could provide.

There was, after all, a moral as well as a political reason for speaking out. It was this that Morgenthau so clearly understood. Unlike the President, the Secretary was not responsible for foreign policy; unlike the President, he was not the elected representative of the whole American people. Except for public opinion, Roosevelt might have gone along with his Secretary of the Treasury; except for the influence he supposed Hull to have with the Congress, he might not have been so moved by the reservations of his Secretary of State. As it was, however, he could not see his way clear to following the path which the Treasury had cut at his instigation. Because Morgenthau realized all this, he kept his faith in his chief, but he could not help but feel the pain of helplessness, the anguish of what Henry Stimson once called a "policy of amoral drift."

The Secretary, as he told Roosevelt, was particularly disturbed by reports from London. Chamberlain had told Ambassador Kennedy that if the issue were one simply between the Czechs and the Sudeten Germans, an amicable settlement might be possible. The Prime Minister feared that England might be forced into a war, but he definitely would not go unless forced. Some of his colleagues,

Chamberlain added, thought Hitler had to be stopped now or never, but he himself rejected that thesis. If Hitler struck, Chamberlain would influence the French to stay out, and even if France went in, some time would elapse before the British followed.

Though Ambassador Bullitt in Paris believed the British would respond more courageously, Roosevelt was worried. The British press said that Lord Halifax, the Foreign Secretary, had asked Kennedy what the United States would do if Great Britain did fight. As Roosevelt put it: "It is a nice kettle of fish." The President, angry that Kennedy had not berated the British press for inaccurate reporting, also suspected that the Ambassador was deliberately leaking information. Roosevelt considered Chamberlain "slippery," giving one story to the French and another to the Germans; he thought Halifax's inquiry was designed to put Washington on the spot, and he concluded that the Prime Minister was trying to place the blame for fighting or not fighting on the United States. The President was especially perturbed over Kennedy's apparent preference for appeasement. The ambassador had submitted for clearance a speech he planned to deliver in Scotland in which he intended to say: "I can't for the life of me understand why anybody would want to go to war to save the Czechs" — a sentence the State Department promptly struck out. "Who would have thought that the English could take into camp a red-headed Irishman?" Roosevelt said to Morgenthau. "The young man needs his wrists slapped rather hard." The Treasury's plans were in his middle drawer, the President concluded, and he could always get them out in a minute.

As Hull again recommended, however, the United States did nothing. French Foreign Minister Bonnet, who rivaled Chamberlain as an advocate of avoiding war at any price, proposed on September 8 that, if the need arose, Roosevelt act as arbiter, and on September 12 that the United States urge Hitler not to use force. Still Washington stood pat. By September 13 war seemed so close that Morgenthau took steps to send American gold in London back to the United States on American naval vessels. He acted, he told the President, to avoid the possibility of the destruction of the gold in an air raid, but even this small gesture disturbed Hull who objected when he discovered that the Navy was stationing a battleship at

Gravesend until further notice. He withdrew his objection only after Morgenthau assured him that "that battleship is being held at my request" for the purpose of removing gold, not of showing the flag.

On September 15 Chamberlain flew to Berchtesgaden for the first of what were to be his three conferences with Hitler. Hopes for peace briefly rose in London and Paris, but Hitler's renewed denunciations of the Czechs, and Czechoslovakia's show of resistance, left matters still boiling.

On September 19 Morgenthau had a chance to talk frankly with the President, who thought the Czechs would fight. Morgenthau agreed. Roosevelt thought he ought to get word to the French that, if they became involved, they should stay behind the Maginot Line and with other countries surrounding Germany conduct a defensive war, shut off German supplies on land and sea, and thus bring the Germans to their senses. Again Morgenthau agreed. A defensive war, he believed, if properly executed, had a 60–40 chance of bringing Germany around. "If the various countries should attack Germany," Roosevelt added, "they only have a 40–60 chance of being successful."

The President gave Morgenthau the feeling that he was ready to go rather far in demonstrating American sympathy for a defensive war. As to the existing crisis, not yet a war, he said: "The time has passed for speeches on my part." Morgenthau asked him how he was going to get his messages to England and France. "That is my worry," Roosevelt said. ". . . I guess my best bet is the old boy up at the British Embassy." * If he acted at all, the President continued, it would be that afternoon.

Pressing his luck, Morgenthau criticized Hull more openly than he ever had before. "You know Mr. Hull," he said to Roosevelt, "as represented to the public, is about 100 per cent different from the real Mr. Hull." After the President "agreed readily," Morgenthau went on: "You know last June or July you put up to him the question of assisting the Chinese and he followed his usual policy by trying to wear all of us out and then do nothing."

"That is right."

"You know, Mr. President," Morgenthau added, "if we don't

* British Ambassador to the United States, Sir Ronald Lindsay.

stop Hitler now he is going right on to the Black Sea — then what? The fate of Europe for the next 100 years is settled."

The following day, September 20, the prospects for the fate of Europe seemed grim indeed. According to analyses Morgenthau received, the British and French cabinets both accepted the Chamberlain plan for solving the Sudeten problem by permitting Germany to annex those areas in which a preponderantly German population lived. The British and French people were deeply chagrined by this surrender to the diplomacy of intimidation, but at the same time relieved to escape the immediate consequences of war to which their own military weakness had rendered them vulnerable. The Czechs, however, were extremely bitter, and it would require great sagacity on the part of the Czech government to get the people to accept the concessions.

"War is probably avoided," Leon Blum remarked, "but under such conditions that I, who have never ceased to fight for peace and for many years have dedicated my life to peace, cannot feel joy and that my emotions are divided between a cowardly relief and shame." Democrats everywhere felt the same way.

In further conferences with Chamberlain on September 22 and 23, Hitler made new and bolder demands on Czechoslovakia. This produced a spurt of resistance in France where Chautemps deserted the peace party, and Bonnet almost alone stood for peace at any price. There seemed an increasing chance that the Czechs would reject the German terms. In that case France and Britain would have to confront the war they had tried so hard to avoid. Morgenthau, without influence on the direction of events, exercised his available authority and informed the French that if they decided to go ahead with exchange controls, he would be glad to cooperate with them.

On September 24 Bullitt recommended that if the British and French rejected the German demands, the President should urge England, France, Germany, Italy and Poland to confer about ways and means of preserving peace, and offer to send an American representative to such a conference. Roosevelt liked the suggestion, but Hull argued that the Germans were armed to the teeth, bent on aggression. Only a display of force, he thought, could deter them.

In any event Roosevelt abandoned Bullitt's idea for fear, as Sumner Welles explained it, that it might have "untoward domestic effects." Instead, early in the morning of September 26 the President sent messages to Hitler, to President Benes of Czechoslovakia, to Chamberlain and Daladier, reminding them of the dangers of a rupture and urging them to continue negotiations toward a "peaceful, fair, constructive settlement."

At this point in the crisis, Morgenthau, in spite of his earlier support of a stronger policy, could see no alternative to Roosevelt's move. As he put it to his staff, the Secretary could not bring himself "in the middle of the Munich crisis" to advocate a boycott of Germany. Economic pressure, he said, would not keep Germany from going into Czechoslovakia. A boycott, furthermore, might give Hitler an excuse to tell the German people that a Jewish Secretary of the American Treasury was trying to strangle their nation economically and that they would have to fight. This was too big a risk, Morgenthau believed, for the limited good which a boycott might bring. But he still thought that a gesture of resistance was in order, and he was quite prepared not only to extend a credit to the Chinese but also to consider a boycott against Japan, for in the Pacific, he felt, such action was less likely to precipitate war.

Meanwhile the State Department invited all governments to support Roosevelt's appeal for negotiations in Europe, and the President personally asked Mussolini to work to that end. In a second message to Hitler on September 27, Roosevelt asked again for a peaceful settlement of existing differences. The use of force, he said, might lead to a general war "as unnecessary as it is unjustifiable." Still sensitive to American opinion, however, the President added: "The Government of the United States has no political involvements in Europe, and will assume no obligations in the conduct of the present negotiations. Yet in our own right we recognize our responsibility as a part of a world of neighbors."

Neither Roosevelt's appeal, nor his careful self-exclusion from the conversations he urged, influenced Hitler's decision to call the Munich conference. Hitler was willing to talk only because he knew Chamberlain and Bonnet were prepared to give him what he wanted. By the time of Roosevelt's appeal, the question was whether the Nazis would take the Sudetenland by force or without it. The

President apparently believed that postponing war might give France and England a chance to work out with Germany "a new order based on justice and law." Though Morgenthau had no such optimism, he still felt relieved that for the moment war had been averted. When the tickertape at the Treasury reported that Hitler had agreed to a conference, the Secretary called Roosevelt and said, "I want to be the first to congratulate you."

The settlement at Munich was as bad as Morgenthau had feared it might be, almost as bad as war. The Czechs yielded the Sudetenland and all their vital fortresses to Germany. In return Czechoslovakia received French and British guarantees of her new frontiers, guarantees which, considering the events of the previous months, seemed peculiarly unreassuring. Some observers spoke hopefully of Chamberlain's broad vision and tireless patience, and of the importance for the democracies to appreciate the need for correcting maladjustments growing out of the Treaty of Versailles. This last was exactly Hitler's line. More astute analysts recognized that the brutal debate in the British Parliament about the Munich conference made it clear that Chamberlain had had to make a virtue of necessity. Great Britain and France were physically and morally unprepared to face the Germans and had therefore agreed to terms which Hitler dictated. It was still too early to judge whether Chamberlain was a sentimentalist expecting an era of peace which would depend on Hitler's willingness to be moderate, or a realist who had avoided an initial disaster in order to prepare a stronger resistance.

The latter possibility provided the only solace Morgenthau could find in the Munich settlement. In spite of its many demerits, he believed, it gave the United States a chance to put itself in a position where it would never have to make a virtue of necessity, never have to submit to the dictation of the Nazis. Late in October he therefore made it his business, for the first time since he had been in Washington, to investigate the state of American preparedness. He began occasionally to lunch with officials in the War Department, to learn from them about American plans for aircraft production, and to learn also from their files about German aircraft and tank production. He was to become probably the best informed and most ardent advocate of preparedness in the Administration. Simultaneously he sought ways in which to make the diplomacy within the authority of the Treasury a formidable instrument of moral and economic support for antifascist governments in the Orient and the Americas. That mission led him irrevocably to demand what was, in effect, a "cold war" against Germany, Italy, and Japan.

## 12. Postlude to Munich

In the days after Munich, the Treasury had under consideration three ways in particular of strengthening democratic resistance to fascism — a credit to China; a program of economic aid to nations of the Western Hemisphere; and a program of increasing duties on German, and possibly also Japanese, imports. This last possibility appealed to the Secretary, who urged White and Oliphant to prepare a case for it which he could take to the President. Oliphant believed the argument was simple. If Roosevelt wanted to know why to increase duties on Japanese products 50 per cent, the answer was "because it would be decisive in the war of China against Japan. And I would do it in the case of Germany because it might very well be decisive in the struggle between that grisly thing in Europe and the sort of institutions we know about."

"It's a waste of my time to walk across the street to tell the President of the United States to do this in the case of Germany and Japan because we don't like their type of government," Morgenthau replied. Roosevelt would agree that the Japanese method of warfare and conduct of government were outrageous, but Hull would argue in return that the imposition of duties was unneutral. "What I had hoped you'd say," Morgenthau explained, remembering his previous experience with countervailing duties, "what I'm begging you to say, is that it's illegal for the President not to act. See? Now if it's just a question of judgment . . . I can't get anywhere. But if you say to me that as Secretary of the Treasury the law directs me . . . to act . . . I've got something to work with."

Harry White suggested repeating the Treasury's proposal of a month earlier.* Morgenthau said that would not do: "That was before the President made his statement . . . in which he inferred

* Page 515.

that we weren't interested in doing anything about Europe. I mean . . . everything he asked us to do was to give him weapons, which we did. Then . . . he makes this statement. . . . Now we've been all over that, and Czechoslovakia is gone, and for me to walk over there now with not only the horse gone but the barn gone. . . ." He could only trail off in despair. He had only so much influence with Roosevelt, Morgenthau continued, and if he brought up countervailing duties again, Roosevelt would only say to him, "go over and get Hull . . . to agree to this." Hull might be thinking about a trade treaty with Germany, Morgenthau feared. But with the right approach, the Secretary added, he could persuade Roosevelt to act. The President was becoming impatient. Recently when they were alone, Roosevelt had turned to him and said: "Henry, these trade treaties are just too goddamned slow. The world is marching too fast. They're just too slow."

The best way to speed things along, Morgenthau and Oliphant agreed, was to urge the President to approve the credit for China. Harry White had drafted a letter on that subject which Morgenthau considered "swell." The Secretary felt that the draft needed polishing, however, and he also believed it should incorporate the case for loans to Latin America, for a "financial Monroe Doctrine." He outlined his ideas to White, asked Oliphant to help rewrite the draft, and instructed White to keep working until the letter was just right. "I'd rather work on this than anything else I have," White replied.

The letter was ready for the Secretary's signature on October 17. In sending it to the President, Morgenthau made the strongest statement on foreign policy he had yet ventured. "The events of the past weeks have brought home to all of us the increasing effectiveness of the forces of aggression," the letter began. "Since 1931 we have seen, succeeding each other with briefer and briefer intervals between, the fall of Manchuria and the invasion of China, the conquest of Ethiopia, fomented unrest in Latin America and in the Near East, armed intervention in Spain, the annexation of Austria, and the dismemberment of Czechoslovakia — all in seven short years."

There was no reason to expect the aggression to stop. Japan at first had wanted only Manchuria, then north China. "Now," the argument continued, "she will not be content with less than the whole of China. Italy wanted only Ethiopia; and now she wants control of North Africa. Germany wanted only equality in armaments, then the remilitarization of the Rhineland, then Austria, then Czechoslovakia, now Poland. The current claim of an aggressor power is always its last — until the next one."

With grim clarity the Secretary forecast the future: "So well have the aggressor nations mastered the tactics of aggression that a victory in one part of the world is followed by outbursts of aggression elsewhere." The history of the last seven years taught an obvious lesson. "Let us not repeat the short-sighted mistakes of Britain and France," Morgenthau wrote. "The impact of the aggressor nations upon American life and American interests has so far, to be sure, been more insidious than overt but it will be too late if we wait until the effects are obvious. Who in France as late as 1930 would have dreamt that in less than a decade that great democratic nation was to become a second-rate power, shorn of influence in central Europe, dependent upon a grudging and demanding ally for security? Who would have expected that Great Britain's might would be challenged in the Mediterranean, that her economic interests would be brushed aside in China, and that the Premier of England would hurry to Hitler to plead that he be not too demanding or impatient, and to plead, moreover, in humble tones lest the dictator take umbrage and demand more?"

What then was the United States to do? "Let us *while we can peacefully do so* try to check the aggressors. Let us not be placed in the position of having to compound with them. Let it not be necessary for the President of the United States to fly to Tokyo and in humble manner plead with the Mikado that he be content with half the Philippines rather than wage war for the whole. Such a possibility may seem ridiculous now, but no more ridiculous than Chamberlain's flight to Berlin would have seemed seven years ago."

Long before most Americans, Morgenthau had read the words of the great champion of the cause of freedom. As his letter to the President put it: "In March of this year Winston Churchill called upon England to act, saying 'if we do not stand up to the dictators now, we shall only prepare the day when we shall have to stand up to them under far more adverse conditions. Two years ago it was safe, three years ago it was easy, and four years ago a mere dispatch might have rectified the position. . . . Now the victors are the vanquished, and those who threw down their arms in the field and sued for an armistice are striving on to world mastery.' The basis for the present humiliation of England was laid in 1931, when England failed to join the United States in disapproval of Japanese aggression in Manchuria. The basis of either humiliation or war for the United States is being laid today by a foreign policy that shuts its eyes to aggression and withholds economic support from those who resist."

Appealing to the Franklin Roosevelt he knew, his old friend, and not to "the President" taking counsel from the Department of State, Morgenthau went on: "I know you are firmly convinced, as I am firmly convinced that the forces of aggression must be stopped. By whom if not by us? I believe that we are the only country in the world now in a position to initiate effective steps to stop aggression by peaceful means. Once the United States takes the lead in developing an effective program, democratic forces in all countries — even those now submerged in the aggressor nations — will take heart. In England and in France groups within the government and without will be stimulated and encouraged to press for parallel action.

"To use our great financial strength to help safeguard future peace for the United States, and to make your 'Good Neighbor' policy really effective, we should introduce at once a program of peaceful action on two fronts — in the Far East and in Latin America. In these two areas we can move most effectively and with the least complications."

The Latin American nations needed capital to develop their resources free from foreign intervention: "Unless we assist them, they will become a helpless field for political and economic exploitation by the aggressor nations. Already some inroads have been made in that direction. Now, after the Munich agreement, we may expect that Germany, Italy, and Japan will become bolder and more effective in their attempts to establish areas of economic and political support to the south of us. We can stop that penetration by an intelligent use of a small proportion of our enormous gold and silver holdings."

More even than Latin America, China needed American assistance. "It is yet possible for such aid to be of decisive help," Morgenthau argued. "Sanguine as I desire to be, I am forced to the view that without substantial financial aid given promptly the Chinese resistance may soon disintegrate. By risking little more than the cost of one battleship we can give renewed vitality and effectiveness to the Chinese. We can do more than that. By our action we can further the struggle of democracy against aggression everywhere.

"I am pleading China's cause with special urgency because you have on numerous occasions told me to proceed with proposals for assistance to China. All my efforts to secure immediate substantial aid for China have proved of no avail against the adamant foreign policy of doing nothing which could possibly be objected to by an aggressor nation. I need not tell you that I respect the integrity and sincerity of those who hold the belief that a course of inaction is the right one, but the issues at stake go beyond any one of us and do not permit me to remain silent. What greater force for peace could there be than the emergence of a unified China?" Morgenthau's reasoning was conclusive. Largely because of his continuing agitation, China in December got $25 million from the Export-Import Bank to purchase American agricultural and industrial goods. This was less than Morgenthau asked for, but it was a start. It boded well for the future.

As Morgenthau's letter to Roosevelt had said, "the measures we may adopt can be developed as the specific occasions requiring assistance may arise." It was first necessary, he noted, for the United States to accept in principle "the need for *positive action*." To that principle the Secretary was fully committed. After Munich, no matter what domestic issues arose, his constant preoccupation was with American defense and foreign policy. In a sense, he had gone to war. When war actually came, it simply increased the tempo of his work. His letter to Roosevelt of October 17 marked for him and for his department a major turning point. "Dr. New Deal," to use the President's phrase, gave way within the Treasury to "Dr. Win the War."

The years since 1933 had been years of preparation as well as years of achievement. Morgenthau's battle against waste in government was to be as significant after Munich as it had earlier been. The instruments of taxation useful in a time of depression were to be just as useful in a time of war. So also with credit policy which could help to control inflation just as it helped to inspirit prosperity.

The successful internal administration of the Treasury, depending as it did upon the recruiting of talent and the reorganization which Morgenthau accomplished, provided him with the staff to direct any effort. That staff, moreover, working under his direction, had devised the techniques of foreign economic policy which permitted him to influence national foreign policy. That influence, of course, depended upon the support of the President.

Central to the years ahead, as it had been central to the years behind, was the friendship of Roosevelt and Morgenthau, their mutual confidence, their shared view of the good life. This, their years together in New York had developed, their years together in Washington, tested and strengthened. They had differed about details and they were to differ again. That was unimportant. They had stood side by side in their large purpose, to help those in need, and side by side they would stand to erase fascism from the world.

# Notes
# and Index

# *Notes*

THE NOTES that follow are intended only to indicate the immediate sources of the quotations and other materials on which this book is based. I have made no effort to list all the sources I consulted, for they consist of the manuscripts, government documents, newspapers, serials, memoirs, biographies, and special studies available to any student of the period. I have, however, referred specifically to those books and articles which particularly helped me to understand the men and the issues with which I had to deal. My brief references to those works cannot, of course, adequately reveal the large debt I owe to their authors.

All manuscripts cited are in the Franklin D. Roosevelt Library at Hyde Park, New York, and all, except where I have otherwise indicated, are in the Morgenthau Manuscripts. The notes refer to the Morgenthau Diaries for the years in which Mr. Morgenthau was in the Treasury as Diary. Volume numbers precede the colon; page numbers or dates follow the colon. The notes describe other diaries of Mr. Morgenthau by name, for example, "Diary for 1930," or "FCA Diary." Material derived from conversations between Mr. Morgenthau and me is cited as conversations. The "Press Conferences of Henry Morgenthau, Jr.," are referred to as "Press Conferences."

### CHAPTER I. ONE OF TWO OF A KIND

1. The Land and the People, pp. 1–6

The descriptions of Morgenthau's mother and father, of his

responses to his jobs, and of his decision to go into farming are based on conversations. The long quotations of Elinor Morgenthau are from Diary 1:55–84; the material on Exeter, from "Diary for 1905," n.p.; the comment of Miss Wald, from Lillian D. Wald to Josephine Roche, Nov. 16, 1934. There is excellent background material for this section and other sections of this chapter in the records and drafts for a biography prepared for Mr. Morgenthau by Joseph Gaer, and in two articles of Geoffrey Hellman, "Any Bonds Today," *The New Yorker,* Jan. 22 and 29, 1944.

2. A Good Start, pp. 6–9

The comment on the German ambassador is from Henry Morgenthau, Jr., to Elinor Fatman, Dec. 20, 1915; that on Christmas Eve, from conversations; that on "Elly Fatman," from Henry Morgenthau, Jr., to Henry Morgenthau, Sr., Oct. 9, 1914; that of the manager of the herd, from the *Dairymen's League News,* March 3, 1935. Other quotations are from the Gaer records and drafts.

3. New Friendships, New Vistas, pp. 10–15

This section is based largely on correspondence between Morgenthau and his father. A letter of Sept. 5, 1914, treats the Saratoga Conference; the comments on Al Smith and on the Houston Convention are in letters of March 23, 1924; July 6, 1928; and July 23, 1928. The remarks of Roosevelt and his mother are from letters in the Franklin D. Roosevelt MSS, Roosevelt to John E. Mack, June 23, 1915; Sarah D. Roosevelt to Roosevelt, July 21, 1918; Roosevelt to Louis Howe, Aug. 2, 1918; Roosevelt to Morgenthau, June 18, 1937.

4. A Program for Agriculture, pp. 15–21

Morgenthau's statements to the press are in the *New York Times,* Jan. 7, 16, 1929. The letters quoted in this section are Morgenthau to Roosevelt, April 19, May 8, 1929, and May 6, July 25, 1930, and Roosevelt to Morgenthau, April 16, 24, May 13, 1929, and May 20, July 29, 1930. The section is based largely on a "Diary for 1930," n.p., especially entries for Feb. 13, 18, 20, 25, 26, 27, March 3, 5, 6, 10, 11, 12, 17, April 22, Oct. 18–25. Of the many accounts of Roosevelt's governorship and candidacy for nomination and election as President in 1932, three were especially helpful: James M. Burns,

*Roosevelt: The Lion and the Fox* (New York, 1956); Frank Freidel, *Franklin D. Roosevelt: The Triumph* (Boston, 1956); Arthur M. Schlesinger, Jr., *The Crisis of the Old Order* (Boston, 1957).

5. Conservation Commissioner, pp. 21–27
The bulk of this section is based upon papers collected as "Files of the Conservation Commissioner"; on interviews Gaer held and recorded with Morgenthau's subordinates, which are especially amusing on the Legge affair; and on the *New York Times* for Dec. 8, 1930; Jan. 19, Feb. 6, 20, 24, March 25, May 26, Dec. 3, 1931; Feb. 7, June 3, July 8, 25, 1932 — the reporting about the referendum of 1931 and the reforestation program in 1932 was conveniently full. Elinor Morgenthau's letter to Roosevelt was dated Dec. 14, 1930; her comments about her husband's "philosophy" are in Diary 1:79. For Edward J. Flynn's remark, see his *You're the Boss* (New York, 1947). It was in conversation with me that Mr. Morgenthau referred to the Bear Mountain trains.

6. Roosevelt and Morgenthau, pp. 27–34
The letter about Pinchot was dated June 12, 1931. Data on the western trip are from "Notebook on 1932 Trip," n.p., in "Files of the Conservation Commissioner." Those files also contain letters about the drafts of the Topeka speech, and letters endorsing Morgenthau for Secretary of Agriculture. In a quotation in the *New York Times* of May 13, 1932, and a letter to Roosevelt, May 5, 1932, Roosevelt MSS, Morgenthau predicted Republican defections in the farm belt. Roosevelt's letter of gratitude for Morgenthau's services was dated December 27, 1932; the senior Morgenthau's remark about his son's future is in a letter of Feb. 6, 1933. For Mrs. Roosevelt's comments, see her *This Is My Story* (New York, 1937), p. 347, and *This I Remember* (New York, 1949), p. 5. The material on the Roosevelt-Morgenthau jokes is from Diary 1:7, Diary 10:140; Roosevelt to Morgenthau, March 25, 1935, and Aug. 2, 1937.

CHAPTER II. "THE COURAGE TO EXPERIMENT"

1. The Agricultural Crisis, pp. 35–42
The first sentence in this section is from conversations; the gen-

eral discussion of the agricultural problem is based upon Murray R. Benedict, *Farm Policies of the United States, 1790–1950* (New York, 1953), Chs. 10, 11, and the more incisive account in Arthur M. Schlesinger, Jr., *The Coming of the New Deal* (Boston, 1958), Ch. 2. The material on the farm conferences is from the full reports about them of William J. Myers, "Washington Conferences on Farm Legislation, December 1932–February, 1933." See also Henry Morgenthau, Jr., "The Morgenthau Diaries: The Paradox of Poverty and Plenty," *Collier's,* Oct. 25, 1947.

2. The Farm Credit Administration, pp. 42–50

For Morgenthau's early sales and his conference with Bennett, see *New York Times,* March 8, April 30, May 11, 1933, and Morgenthau to Roosevelt, Jan. 21, 1933; H. H. Wrong to Morgenthau, Jan. 27, 1933, both Roosevelt MSS. On the organization of FCA, see Benedict, *Farm Policies; Congressional Digest* 12:184–85; Ernest K. Lindley, *The Roosevelt Revolution* (New York, 1933), p. 108. Morgenthau's "FCA Diary" is of capital importance for this section and the rest of the chapter. On FCA salaries, see entries for May 29, June 5, 12, 1933; on patronage, see entries for May 12, 17, 22, July 30, 1933, and also Morgenthau to Morgenthau, Sr., June 9, 1933. On the mortgage problem, see "FCA Diary," May 9, 15, July 10, 1933; *New York Times,* May 6, 12, 13, July 9, Aug. 2, Sept. 13, 20, 1933; and Morgenthau, "The Morgenthau Diaries: The Paradox of Poverty and Plenty." The last reports Garner's comment. The farmers' letters are with FCA material in the Morgenthau MSS; Myers's assessment is in his letter to Morgenthau of April 12, 1934.

3. Prescriptions for "Galloping Palsy," pp. 50–60

For the conference on and discussions of the AAA, see "FCA Diary," May 3, 4, 5, 15, 1933. For the loan to China, see "FCA Diary," May 15, 17, 26, 1933; much of the same material is in Morgenthau, "The Morgenthau Diaries: The Paradox of Poverty and Plenty," and "The Morgenthau Diaries: How F.D.R. Fought the Axis," *Collier's,* Oct. 25, 11, 1947. The last deals with the Russian negotiation, but I have relied primarily upon "FCA Diary," May 2, 9, 13, Aug. 16, Sept. 26, 27, Oct. 19, 23, 27, Nov. 6, 16, 1933. There is also useful material on the Russian negotiation in Cordell Hull,

*The Memoirs of Cordell Hull* (2 v., New York, 1948), I, Ch. 22, and in Jesse H. Jones and Edward Angly, *Fifty Billion Dollars* (New York, 1951), Ch. 18. For the wheat purchases, see "FCA Diary," Sept. 26, Oct. 16, 17, 27, 28, Nov. 4, 1933.

4. The Price of Gold, pp. 61–68

There is an excellent account of Warren's ideas and influence, and of public opinion about gold policy, in Joseph E. Reeve, *Monetary Reform Movements* (Washington, 1943), especially Chs. 4, 5, 16; there is also an admirable analysis of the gold problem in Schlesinger, *Coming of the New Deal*. Those books, and G. F. Warren and F. A. Pearson, *Gold and Prices* (New York, 1935), supply indispensable background material for this and the next section. Pearson's memorandum to Morgenthau, quoted in the first paragraph, was undated, *ca.* May 1933. Morgenthau wrote editor Eastman of the *American Agriculturist* on May 12, 1933. Morgenthau's father wrote him from London on June 9, 1933; Morgenthau's statement that he really had nothing to do with Roosevelt's message to London is from conversations; Warren's letters prodding Morgenthau and the President were dated Oct. 16, 1933. The Attorney General's written opinion is in Cummings to Roosevelt, Nov. 17, 1933, Roosevelt MSS. There is an account of the gold-buying question written from a point of view rather hostile to Morgenthau in Jones and Angly, *Fifty Billion Dollars*, Ch. 20, and a discussion of Acheson's role in Philip Hamburger, "Mr. Secretary," *The New Yorker*, Nov. 19, 1949. This section rests primarily, however, on the rich material in "FCA Diary," May 16, June 29, 30, July 2, 10, Aug. 14, 16, Sept. 26, Oct. 1, 18, 19, 22, 23, 1933. See also Morgenthau, "The Morgenthau Diaries: The Paradox of Poverty and Plenty."

5. Gold Buying, pp. 69–77

The references listed for the previous section provided useful background material here, too, but the account in this section is based almost exclusively on "FCA Diary," Oct. 23, 25, 27, 28, 29, 30, Nov. 1, 2, 4, 1933. Lippmann's column was published on Jan. 3, 1934. O'Neill of the Farm Bureau and R. E. Wood of the Committee for the Nation wrote Roosevelt respectively on Nov. 20 and 16, 1933, Roosevelt MSS. The statistics about the effect of gold buying are from FCA analyses deposited with the Morgenthau MSS. In interpreting them, I have profited from the astute work of G. Griffith Johnson, Jr., *The Treasury and Monetary Policy, 1933–1938* (Cambridge, 1939), especially Ch. I. The quotation about the courage to experiment is from the *New York Times,* May 28, 1933; the quotation about swimming and not sinking, from "Press Conferences," II, June 25, 1934. Howe's statement appears in Morgenthau, "The Morgenthau Diaries: The Paradox of Poverty and Plenty."

CHAPTER III. MISCELLANY OF OFFICE

1. The Department of the Treasury, pp. 78–83

The description of Morgenthau's routine, based on a general familiarity with the Diaries, depends especially upon the text of two of Morgenthau's speeches: a radio address of March 4, 1935, Diary 4:34, and "A Day in the Treasury," Jan. 31, 1940, filed with miscellaneous papers. For the remarks to the college students, see Diary 47:334–41. On press relations, see the *New York Times,* Nov. 21, 22, 23, 25, 28; also Reports of Staff Meetings, Nov. 29, Dec. 18, 1933. On Morgenthau's attitudes in recruiting a staff, see Diary 2:187; Diary 14:21; Washington *Herald,* Aug. 19, 1935. For the remark about Republicans, see Report of Staff Meeting, Nov. 29, 1933. On patronage, see Eleanor Roosevelt, *This I Remember* (New York, 1949), p. 6; on the Philadelphia case, Civil Service Commission to Morgenthau, June 12, 1934; Roosevelt to Alvin F. Fix, June 12, 1934; Fix to Farley, June 21, 1934; Fix to Morgenthau, June 25, 1934; Morgenthau to Fix, June 28, 1934.

2. Public Health, pp. 83–86

There is a file of material about Miss Roche in the Morgenthau MSS. Particularly important within it are Frances Perkins to Josephine Roche, April 23, 1936, and Eleanor Roosevelt to Josephine Roche, Nov. 4, 1937. For the episode of the state public health officers, see Diary 2:289; Diary 13:36. The telegram to McIntyre is in Diary 2:72–73, Sept. 12, 1934. The material on Dr. Parran, a hospitable as well as a great doctor, is based partly upon an interview with him on April 19, 1956. The quotation is from the *New York*

*Times,* Sept. 26, 1937. The *Times* continually carried detailed accounts, too numerous to cite, of Dr. Parran's work, especially in fighting VD. The material on Dr. Parran, Morgenthau, and Roosevelt is from Diary 109:114, 205; Diary 110:129; Diary 111:92.

3. The Division of Procurement, pp. 87–91

There is general material on the division in Box 41, Official File, Roosevelt MSS. On the episode of the Interior Department building, all data are from the Ickes File in Morgenthau MSS; see especially Roosevelt memoranda to Ickes and Morgenthau, Oct. 19, 1934. The account of the New York Post Office Annex is based partly on conversations, largely on Diary 3:307 ff.; Diary 4:36 ff.; Diary 7:153 ff. For another point of view, see Harold L. Ickes, *The Secret Diary of Harold L. Ickes: The First Hundred Days* (New York, 1953), especially pp. 294–300. The quotations in the last two paragraphs are from Diary 10:143; Diary 15:54.

4. The Treasury Art Program, pp. 91–94

Of the many accounts of the Treasury art program, the following were most useful for background for this section: Edward Bruce and Forbes Watson, *Mural Designs, 1934–1936,* Vol. I of *Art in Federal Buildings* (Washington, 1936), especially Bruce's preface; Federal Arts Projects, *Federal Art in New England* (Washington, 1938), especially the introduction by Francis H. Taylor; "Critics Evaluate Federal Murals," *Art Digest,* May 15, 1940. Conversations with Morgenthau also helped. For Oliphant's role, I used the Bruce file in the Morgenthau MSS. There is also important material, including that quoted directly in Diary 45:156–58; Diary 145:376 ff.

5. Let the Chips Fall, pp. 94–100

The statistics in the first paragraph are from Horack to Morgenthau, Nov. 26, 1934; see also W. C. John, "The Department of the Treasury," *School Life,* Jan. 1940. For the woman smuggler, see Diary 121:105–6, and the file "Confidential Reports on People." On informers, see "Press Conferences," XXIII, 319–21. On wiretapping, see Diary 130:122 ff. On reorganization, see Diary 107: 52–57; this includes the quotations from Gaston. On the Intelligence Unit and its tax work, there is much of importance in Elmer L. Irey and William J. Slocum, *The Tax Dodgers* (New

York, 1948). I also used the file "Confidential Reports on People."
For Huey Long and the Louisiana cases, with which Irey's book
deals at some length, the Diary is vital. My material, including the
quotations, is from: Diary 3:284; Diary 4:9, 143; Diary 8:47, 191;
Diary 9:8; Diary 10:183; Diary 11:163; Diary 13:295; Diary 23:200–
208; Diary 24:254–60; Diary 25:62 ff.; Diary 31:158.

6. T-Men at Work, pp. 100–105

On the Buffalo customs house and Gorman, see Diary 11:179,
181; Diary 12:23–24, 51. On Moran, Wilson, and the Secret Service,
see Diary 3:438; Diary 4:34; Diary 29:132; Diary 30:228, 234–50,
265; Diary 31:101, 102, 145 ff., 170. On the reorganization of Secret
Service, see Diary 130:328–38. This covers counterfeiting, too, as do
the files on Wilson and on Secret Service in the Morgenthau MSS.
On jurisdictional problems in the enforcement of the narcotics law,
see Anslinger and the Bureau of Narcotics files. These include reports of staff meetings on Feb. 21 and June 20, 1935, bearing on the
steamship problem, which is covered also in Diary 3:436. On the
reorganization plan for the enforcement agencies, and trouble with
the State Department about that question, see Diary 17:187, 193 ff.,
237; Diary 18:8–9; Diary 30:3–6; Diary 61:179 ff.; Diary 62:21.
Thompson's report is in Diary 63:166–67. The material on the
West Coast roundup is in Diary 30:338–41, and in the Narcotics file,
especially Melvin Hanks to T. J. Gorman, March 9, 1938.

7. Postlude to Prohibition, pp. 105–10

In the preliminary drafts of a biography prepared for Mr. Morgenthau there are detailed studies of all the issues treated in this
section. For the background to the problem, see Diary 1:85 ff.;
Diary 2:9; Diary 19:88 ff.; see also Item G, Morgenthau MSS, Klaus
Report of Nov. 26, 1934. On Morgenthau, Congress, and McKellar,
see Diary 4:5 ff., 53 ff., 83, 109, 229. On bulk sales, see Diary 6:59,
75; Diary 7:35–62, 143–56. The quotation about the "people . . .
at the Waldorf" is from conversations. On the problem of supervising the retail trade, see Diary 3:212 ff., 273 ff., 318 ff., and the Helvering and McReynolds files. On smuggling, see Diary 3:318, 366–67;
Diary 14:319 ff.; Diary 25:14–15, 140; Diary 55:460–64; Diary 56:56–
57, 233; Diary 58:248.

8. Retributive Justice, pp. 110–19

For this section, too, there are useful preliminary studies prepared more than a decade ago for Mr. Morgenthau. For the Schultz episode, I relied upon Diary 2:145 ff., 240; Diary 9:71; also memorandum of Nov. 8, 1934, Irey to Morgenthau, Irey File. The Klaus Report is Item G in the Morgenthau MSS. The material on the Canadian issue is in Diary 5:55 ff., 78 ff.; Diary 9:118 ff.; Diary 11:62, 117; Diary 15:72–73, 140–41; Diary 19: *passim,* but especially 73 ff., 135–41, 164–258; Diary 20:1, 2, 7, 13, 14, 26, 66–73, 185–93, 200–201, 218–58; Diary 21:23, 169–71, 192–98; Diary 22:55–56; Diary 23:6–8, 26–27, 117–19; Diary 24:57, 127, 132.

## CHAPTER IV. THE DOLLAR AT HOME AND ABROAD

1. The Gold Reserve Act, pp. 120–25

For background information and for monetary theory for this section and the rest of this chapter, I have again relied heavily upon both G. Griffith Johnson, Jr., *The Treasury and Monetary Policy, 1933–1938* (Cambridge, 1939), and Joseph E. Reeve, *Monetary Reform Movements* (Washington, 1943). Viner's report to Morgenthau was Nov. 21, 1933. Morgenthau's comment about the British is from conversation, but the data of 1933 bear out its spirit; on the attitudes of Roosevelt and Morgenthau toward the British, and on Harrison's maneuver and Mills's alleged activities, see Private Memorandum of Roosevelt, Dec. 16, 1933; Harrison to Roosevelt, Dec. 12, 1933; Morgenthau to Roosevelt, Jan. 31, 1934 (all Roosevelt MSS), and Diary 1:6; Diary 3:23. Morgenthau's statement on the need for a stabilization fund is quoted in Johnson, *The Treasury,* p. 31; his statement about what the new standard was is from "Press Conferences," I, Feb. 1, 1934.

2. The Supreme Court and the Gold Clause, pp. 125–31

One characteristic letter of Warren to Morgenthau was that of May 16, 1934. The proclamations for use if the Court decided against the government are in Diary 3:330 ff. Oliphant's memorandum on the gold cases was of Jan. 14, 1935. For Morgenthau's unpleasant luncheon with Roosevelt and Cummings, and its aftermath, see Diary 3:98 ff. For the Stabilization Fund's operations, see Diary 3:104 ff., 136 ff., 156, 177, 189–90, 206, 221, 285, 287–93; Diary 6:13. Morgenthau's statement about the international speculators is from Diary 3:138. Data on the gathering to receive the Court's opinion is from Diary 3:327 ff.

### 3. Invitation to Stabilization, pp. 131–34

Viner's report was March 6, 1935. For Oliphant's ideas, see Diary 4:142 ff. For the question of the French credit, see Diary 4:10–20, 25–28, 67–71, 159, 164–70, 182. The last entry pertains to Morgenthau's conversation with the French ambassador about stabilization. For Roosevelt's view on that subject, see Diary 4:205; the data on the Treasury-State Department difference are in Diary 4:210 ff., 227, 244, 250; also Morgenthau to Hull, April 17, 1935, and Hull to Morgenthau, April 20, 1935. For Morgenthau's speech, its drafting, and its effect, see Diary 4:226 ff.; Diary 5: Part II; also Morgenthau to Roosevelt, May 14, 1935, Roosevelt MSS.

### 4. First Aid for France, pp. 134–38

This section is based upon Diary 5:135–87; Diary 6:1–7, 11–21, 28, 39; Diary 7:3, 9, 73–95; Diary 8:100–101.

### 5. Rapport with England, pp. 138–49

For Morgenthau's conversations in France, see State Department memorandum on that subject, Oct. 14, 1935. For White's report, see White to Haas, June 13, 1935. For Harrison's views, see Diary 10:29; Diary 11:170 ff.; Diary 12:1–2. Morgenthau's "big brother" remark is from "Press Conferences," VI, 19. For Morgenthau's attitude in April 1936, see Diary 21:21, 128–32, 172. His conversation with Roosevelt on April 29 is in Diary 22:138, 155–56; see also Diary 22:187, 194 ff. The talks with Bewley are in Diary 22:146–48; Diary 23:70 ff.; Diary 24:185 ff.; Diary 26:22 ff. For the American response to Chamberlain, see Diary 26:15, 16, 23–27, 51 ff. Roosevelt's "long harangue" of June 3 is in Diary 26:81 ff.; the events and conversations of June 4, in Diary 26:115–21. For the American offer, the French rejection, and the Anglo-American response through the rest of June, see especially Diary 26:149–60, 172, 219; Diary 27:22. Some of this material provided the basis for three good articles about the Stabilization Agreement and its background: Joseph Alsop and Robert Kintner, "Henny Penny: Farmer at the Treasury," "The Great World Money Play," "The Secret Finale," *Saturday Evening Post*, April 1, 8, 15, 1939.

## 6. Countervailing Duties, pp. 149–55

For the emergence of this issue in 1935, see Diary 12:136, 151–58, 160; Diary 14:179. The Memorandum of the Executive Committee on Commercial Policy, which states but differs from the Treasury's reasoning, is in Diary 19:169–88. Hull's letter is in Diary 20:20–22; Treasury discussion about it, in Diary 20:103 ff., 202–3; Diary 21:1–14. For Morgenthau's luncheon of April 14 with Roosevelt, see Diary 21:146–47; consequent Treasury discussions are in Diary 21:150–65. The Bell Memorandum is in Diary 22:157–69. The material on Treasury-State Department conflict, in Diary 21:173, 177, 270; Diary 22:140, 151–52; Diary 23:40. For Morgenthau's talks with Roosevelt of May 12 and 22, see Diary 24:126; Diary 25:23–24, 59. The meeting of May 29 and Roosevelt's response are reported in Diary 25:161–66, 188. For the Treasury directives and the German response, see Diary 25:167–80, 189. For negotiations with Germany, see Diary 26:19, 28–29, 80–82, 94–111, 119, 142, 179; Diary 27:4, 13–16, 50–58, 118–19, 125–29, 159–67, 200; Diary 28:98–99; Diary 29:9–10, 22–23, 130, 185, 216, 221–24, 232. The quotation in the last paragraph is from Henry Morgenthau, Jr., "The Morgenthau Diaries: How F.D.R. Fought the Axis," *Collier's*, Oct. 11, 1947.

## 7. The Monick Mission, pp. 155–59

For Monick's conversations with Morgenthau and Roosevelt, see Diary 27:148 ff., 176 ff., 178 ff., 201 ff. For Oliphant's statement and Morgenthau's rejoinder, see Diary 30:167 ff.

## 8. The Tripartite Pact, pp. 159–73

There is a useful chronology of the negotiation of the Pact in Diary 30:1 ff. For Morgenthau's remark to the British embassy, see Diary 31:105. The French draft received on Sept. 9 is in Diary 32:48–53. For the American conferences that followed, see Diary 32:54–58, 65–68, 74–75. The American reply is in Diary 32:59–61; Morgenthau's telephone talk of Sept. 9 with Roosevelt, in Diary 32:84. The French draft of Sept. 17 and the American discussions of it are in Diary 32:269 ff., 289–301. For the developments of Sept. 18, see Diary 33:8 ff. (8a–8z, 8aa–8zz), which includes, among other things, the conversation in German between Morgenthau and Cochran. For the drafting of the Treasury's proposal for the Pact, see Diary 33:18 ff., 28 ff., 147. For the Vandenberg matter, see Diary 33:117–31, 147. On the question of cross-rates, see Diary 33:152–62. For the completion of the negotiation, see Diary 33:172–190, 220–26, 246–53, 276 ff.; Diary 34:10 ff., 84–134. Cochran's own account of the entire negotiation fills Diary 43. Auriol's letter is in Diary 46:15–16; for other responses to the Pact, see Diary 34:161 ff., 312 ff. For Lippmann's comment, *Literary Digest*, Oct. 10, 1936. Orders implementing the Pact are in Diary 35:1 ff.

9. A Bearish Interlude, pp. 173–76
     Material for this section is from Diary 34:285–98, 390; Diary 35:12, 52 ff., 62 ff.; Diary 36:163.

10. The Currency Club, pp. 177–82
     The discussions of Oct. 5 are in Diary 37:197–201, 208, 212, 219, 221, 229, 238–48, 256–71, 321. The British-American discussions of gold policy run throughout Diary 38. For Morgenthau's press conference of Oct. 12, see Diary 39:1–8, 28–40. On the Belgian question, and the completion of negotiations, see especially Diary 40:53–57, 237–40; Diary 41:181; Diary 42:1–9, 28–37, 102, 118–50; Diary 44:60–77, 120 ff., 154–56; Diary 45:30–63; see also, particularly for its explanations of technical and theoretical issues, Johnson, *The Treasury*. The quotations in the last paragraph are from Diary 38:354 ff.

CHAPTER V. STATECRAFT FOR SILVER

1. "Something for Silver," pp. 183–88
     For the background and enactment of the Silver Purchase Act, I relied constantly upon G. Griffith Johnson, Jr., *The Treasury and Monetary Policy, 1933–1938* (Cambridge, 1939), Ch. VI; Joseph E. Reeve, *Monetary Reform Movements* (Washington, 1943), Chs. V,

IX, X, XV; and Allan S. Everest, *Morgenthau, the New Deal, and Silver* (New York, 1950), Ch. III. Everest, who used the Diaries, wrote in detail, accurately, and astutely about the various issues covered in this section and in the rest of this chapter. There is also a discerning account of the enactment of the Silver Purchase Act in Arthur M. Schlesinger, Jr., *The Coming of the New Deal* (Boston, 1958), Ch. 14. The *New York Times* reported legislative developments fully and continually; particularly important are the issues of March 16, 18, 20, April 24, 25, 26, 27, 29, May 8, 9, 10, 11, 12, 26, 27, 1934. For Morgenthau's remarks of March 15, see "Press Conferences," I, 237; for his exchange with Ashurst, see Diary 56:33; for his comment about preventing speculators from "cleaning up," see "Press Conferences," II, 118. On the publication of the list of silver speculators and the congressional reaction, see Diary 1:46–49 and the file "Upham Reports," particularly for April 24, 1934. On the negotiations between Congress and the President, see "Upham Reports," April 27, May 8, 18, 22, 23, June 13, 1934; Diary 1:51.

2. Executing the Mandate, pp. 188–99

There is important material for this section in Everest, *Morgenthau*, pp. 46–50. On Coolidge's role, see Coolidge to Morgenthau, July 12, 1934; Diary 2:3, 6, 14, 19. On nationalization and the steps leading to it, see Diary 2:3, 14–19; *New York Times*, Aug. 12, 1934. For Oliphant's proposal to put the price of silver at $1.29, and for Roosevelt's reaction, see Oliphant to Morgenthau, Dec. 15, 1934; also Diary 4:178, 205. The best material on the events of April 1934 is in a long memorandum quoting Oliphant's diary for that period in Oliphant to Morgenthau, Aug. 19, 1935. This covers Morgenthau's conference with the five senators, on which see also King to Morgenthau, April 26, 1935; and see also Diary 5:18–25. For Coolidge's threatened resignation and Morgenthau's response, see Diary 5:61–63; also Coolidge to Morgenthau, May 2, 1935. On Morgenthau's sales of May, 1935, see Diary 5:63, 78, 89, 90. For the McCarran-Morgenthau exchange, see Diary 6:50–56, 97. The reporter's analysis of July 1935 is in Diary 8:65; Pittman's advice against fixing the price, in Diary 8:60. For the developments of August, see Diary 9:32–39, which includes the negotiations with LeBlanc. The Diary entry of Dec. 8 is in Diary 13:89 ff. The material on the decision to drop the price, and the effects of that decision is in Diary 13:92–97, 105, 112, 120–24, 132 ff., 155 ff., 221 ff., 291 ff.; Diary 14:42–43, 145 ff., 180, 199 ff., 212. Morgenthau's remark of Dec. 12 is in Diary 13:225. Roosevelt's "forbidden subject" is in Diary 59:136; his conversation with Morgenthau about an index, in Diary 101:70.

3. Repercussions in Mexico, pp. 199–204

There is an excellent treatment of this issue in Everest, *Morgenthau,* pp. 79–84. The material in this section for the period before April 23, 1935, is from Diary 4:225, 245, 250. For Morgenthau's offer of April 23, see Diary 5:1, 2. For the discussions Morgenthau had with Roosevelt, the Mexicans, and Hull during the rest of April, see Diary 5:18–25, 28–44. For the conversations with Lockett in December and the events surrounding them, see Diary 13:119–217. For the discussions preceding the meetings with Suarez, see Diary 14:301 ff.; those meetings and attending developments are reported in Diary 14:314–20; Diary 15:1–3, 6–7, 10, 17, 29, 43–45. For the Canadian agreement, see Diary 19:34.

4. Repercussions in China, pp. 204–11

Using most of the data I used, but from a somewhat different point of view, Everest, in *Morgenthau,* pp. 101–19, discusses the events treated in this section and the rest of this chapter. For Kung's notes of Oct. and Dec. 1934 and for the State Department's attitude and conversations with the Treasury in that period, *Foreign Relations of the United States, 1934: III, The Far East* (Washington, 1950), pp. 499, 455, 456, 457, 834 is absolutely indispensable. In interpreting them and other materials about China, I have profited from the advice of Dorothy Borg. On Hull's views in Oct. 1934, see also his memorandum to Morgenthau of Oct. 3, 1934, and Haas to Morgenthau, Oct. 25, 1934; for the developments in December, see Diary 2:294–301, 338, 345, 346. Pittman's views are in Diary 3:1; the following exchanges among Morgenthau, Hull, Roosevelt, and the Chinese, in Diary 3:53–57, 84, 200, 247–53. For the events and discussions of mid-February 1935, see *Foreign Relations of the United States, 1935: III, The Far East* (Washington, 1953), pp. 533–42; also Diary 3:296–306, 328. For the intelligence reports, see file "Department of State, 1935," especially reports of Jan. 23, March 21,

April 30, May 15. For the British mission and conflicting Treasury-State Department attitudes toward it, see *Foreign Relations* . . . *1935*, pp. 542–49, 570, 596 ff.; see also Diary 7:66–72; and file "Department of State, 1935," reports on Leith-Ross mission. Morgenthau's remark to Sze, quoted in the next to last paragraph in this section, is from Diary 9:14. For Buck's report about Chiang's views, see Diary 8:192.

5. The Yuan and the Dollar, pp. 211–20

For the conversations of Oct. 28 and 29, see Diary 10: 180–81. For Morgenthau's conversations with Sze, and with Roosevelt about the proposals of Sze and Kung, see Diary 11:5–13, 17–25, 29–31, 50, 58–60, 159. The long White House conference of Nov. 9 about silver policy is reported in Diary 11:63–79. Morgenthau's talks of Nov. 13 with Sze and Roosevelt are reported in Diary 11:155–57. Morgenthau's talk with Bewley is in Diary 12:13–19; and see, too, Diary 12:70, 116–22. Morgenthau's reports from Buck and conversations of mid-December with Sze are in Diary 14:77–80, 83. Sze's lament about the State Department, Morgenthau's suggestion about a mission, and the consequent negotiations with and remarks about Hull are in Diary 15:90 ff., 125, 147. The material on Chen is from Diary 16:118; Diary 17:174–77, 179.

6. The Chen Mission, pp. 220–28

Kung's cables and other information Morgenthau received about China, and his responses to the data, are in Diary 19:122; Diary 20:18–19, 36–45, 132–54. The material about private debts is in Diary 18:164–66; Diary 19:32, 130; Diary 20:74–76. The meeting with Chen of April 8 is reported in Diary 20:92–97. The Haas-White report of April 9 is Diary 20A; Morgenthau's meeting with Chen of April 9 is in Diary 20:111–30. For the developments of April 12 and 13, see Diary 21:34–55, 146. White's memorandum of April 17 is in Diary 21:186–91, 215–25. For Morgenthau's "test" of the Chinese, and for the Morgenthau-Chen meeting of April 20, see Diary 21:226–35, 274. On the meeting with Tomito, see Diary 22:41–47. On negotiations between the Chinese and the Treasury during early May, see Diary 23:1–3, 21, 112–14. The concluding conversations of May 12, and the draft and text of the agreement,

along with the attending press releases, are in Diary 24:114–24, 157–
60, 195–212. For the initial American and British reception of the
announcement of the agreement, see Diary 24:217–36.


CHAPTER VI. ESSENTIAL SPENDING

1. A Difficult Job, pp. 229–33
    This section is based upon Diary 2:18–19, 60–62, 68–72, and
Henry Morgenthau, Jr., "The Morgenthau Diaries: The Fight to
Balance the Budget," *Collier's,* Sept. 27, 1947. The article provided
useful background material for the entire chapter, as did also the
excellent accounts of early New Deal relief and public works policies
and their administrators in Arthur M. Schlesinger, Jr., *The Coming
of the New Deal* (Boston, 1958), Chs. 16, 17.

2. Search for a Program, pp. 233–40
    Morgenthau's remark about Ickes is from the article cited above.
The conferences about a program of Oct. 1, 10, and 16 are reported
in detail in Diary 2:82–111; Morgenthau's meeting "with the President at his bedside" is from Diary 2:112. For the Warm Springs discussions, see Diary 2:246; for the meetings about the budget at the
end of Dec. 1934, see Diary 3:4–8. Morgenthau's conversation with
Roosevelt of Jan. 21, 1935, is in Diary 3:200.

3. The Four Billion Eight, pp. 240–49
    There is a good account of the legislation and its history in
James M. Burns, *Roosevelt: The Lion and the Fox* (New York, 1956),
pp. 220–21. For Morgenthau's reflections about the organization of
work relief, and his conversations of April 1935 with Roosevelt on
that subject, see Diary 4:206–8, 249, 252. For Morgenthau's feelings
and comments in July, see Diary 7:151; Diary 8:15, 51–52. The discussion with Hopkins and Miss Perkins is from Diary 8:93–95.
Roosevelt's "harangue" about relief, and Morgenthau's "sophistry,"
are from Diary 8:108–10. For the recommendations Morgenthau
made in August, and for Roosevelt's responses, see Diary 9:1, 8–10,
20–21, 33–34, 41, 53–63, 117–22. For Hopkins's talk with Morgenthau on Nov. 15, see Diary 12:9; Hopkins's accolade is in his letter

to Morgenthau of Sept. 6, 1940, Hopkins MSS. For the Treasury staff meeting of Nov. 11, see Diary 11:112; for the budget discussions of late November in Warm Springs, see Diary 13:1–2. The six meetings with the "feuding spenders" are discussed in Diary 14:176–78. For the draft of the budget message, see Diary 14:216–53.

### 4. The Bonus, pp. 249–59

Garner's warning about the strength of the bonus bill is in Diary 4:169d. The Treasury staff memorandum is in the folder "Bonus"; Morgenthau's reaction and his conference of April 22, 1935, with Roosevelt, in Diary 4:251; the Secretary's testimony is in Diary 4:253d; Diary 5:6. The material on the developments of May 1935 is all in Diary 5:109–19, 128–33; for the material on September and October, see Diary 10:12–14, 108. The discussion of Nov. 16 is from Diary 12:125. For the developments of Jan. 1936, see Diary 15:70–71, 103, 126, 157; Diary 16:50–54.

### 5. Lenders and Spenders, pp. 259–68

The discussion of Coolidge's resignation is based upon conversations. The Diary entry of Feb. 2, 1936, is from Diary 17:1–3. The Feb. 4 meeting of the Interdepartmental Loan Committee is reported in Diary 17:27–37; for the resulting budget cuts of Feb. 18, see Diary 18:17–28. Roosevelt's statements to Morgenthau of Feb. 6 are in Diary 17:98; the meeting of that date with the spending agencies is reported in Diary 17:100–110. For Morgenthau's comment about Roosevelt's remark to Marvin Jones, see Diary 17:181. Morgenthau's early March meeting with Hopkins is reported in Diary 19:26–30; their session with Roosevelt of March 6, in Diary 19:36–38. Roosevelt's comment about being "really radical," and Morgenthau's reply, are from Diary 21:276. For Morgenthau's conversation with Tugwell, see Diary 23:44-56. The material on Hopkins's "juggling" and Morgenthau's response is from Diary 23:58–61, 67, 131.

### 6. The Budget and the Election, pp. 268–75

Morgenthau took Gertrude Stein as his text for reaching Roosevelt, Diary 28:96. The President ordered Morgenthau to cancel plans for a speech, Diary 29:133, but for the material the Secretary put together, and the responses to it of Henderson and Roosevelt, see Diary 29:162–63; Diary 30:149–66. The material about the survey of WPA rolls is from Diary 29:48–54, 234–37; Diary 30:116–17. The discussion of USES and the preparation of a speech about it is based upon Diary 30:82–100, 168–72, 313–26; Diary 31:119–27. Roosevelt's statement that Gill was to lay off no one, and Morgenthau's reply, are in Diary 36:103–8. For Morgenthau's talk with Hopkins on Oct. 7, 1936, see Diary 38:133–36; the President's directive about allocations is in Diary 38:286. For the material on the drafting of the Pittsburgh speech, and on its reception, see Diary 37:34–36; Diary 39:153.

7. Compassion in Practice, Prudence in Theory, pp. 275–83

The first paragraph of this section is from Morgenthau, "The Morgenthau Diaries: The Fight to Balance the Budget." The material on the problem of cutting the relief rolls as that issue developed during Nov. and Dec. 1936 is from Diary 44:148–49; Diary 46:169–71; Diary 47:133–43, 177, 245, 283–89. For the President's announcement and Morgenthau's response of Dec. 22, see Diary 49:238. The remark about "fudging on their figures" is from a conference of Dec. 29, reported in Diary 49:321–30. For Bell's report, and for the Eccles memorandum and the conversations pertaining to it, see Diary 49: 266–68, 272–92, 315. The draft of the budget message fills Diary 50. On Roosevelt and the state governors in March 1937, see Diary 58:249, 311. For the transfer of funds to Hopkins, see Diary 59:198. The President's Executive Order of April 7 is in Diary 63:195. For the Secretary's conversations with his staff and with Eccles on April 5 and 6, see Diary 63:3–13, 123–26.

8. Formulas for Housing, pp. 283–90

The discussion of HOLC is based upon Diary 1:44; Diary 3:24–31, 61–66, 124, 132, 180, 236–42; Diary 4:184, 234, 248; also Morgenthau to Fahey, May 9, 1934. There is extensive material on the appointment and work of Peter Grimm, and on his report and Morgenthau's response to it; see especially the folders, "Housing," and "Grimm"; also Diary 9:7–8, 16–17, 25, 31; Diary 10:117, 152, 159, 164–67, 179, 184, 185, 188, 196–98; Diary 16:98, 146; Diary 17:186, 208–16; Diary 19:124–29. The last reference especially also contains significant data on slum clearance, introducing the question of the

Wagner bill. My discussion of the Treasury's work on that bill is based upon Diary 20:24j; Diary 23:198–99; Diary 55:5–8, 448 ff., 254 ff.; Diary 57:62–102, 124, 135–39; Diary 70:300–309; Diary 71: 67 ff., 111–35; Diary 72:69–87, 99, 103. I profited also from the study of the housing issue prepared for Mr. Morgenthau by Professor Allan Nevins and his associates.

9. A Sound Financial Foundation, pp. 290–96

The "into the ashcan" comes from Diary 65:174. For the long quotation beginning "Monday at lunch," see Diary 65:61, 268–72. See also Diary 65:324–30 for Bell's memorandum on the same issues. The material on the tenancy bill, Wallace and his discussions with Morgenthau is from the previous two references and Diary 64:179 ff., 205 ff.; Diary 65:10–11, 165-67, 273–323; Diary 66:9–13. For Morgenthau's April 27 conversation with Garner, see Diary 66:88. Roosevelt's remark of May 17 is from Diary 68:240; his economies are reported in Diary 77:101–2; Diary 78:43–45. The closing quotation is from Diary 65:272.

### CHAPTER VII. TAXATION

1. Revenue and the Redistribution of Wealth, pp. 297–305.

Randolph E. Paul, *Taxation in the United States* (Boston, 1954), provided indispensable background material for this chapter; Paul was for many years the General Counsel for the Treasury Department. Also indispensable was a perceptive analysis of the impact of federal fiscal policy by E. Cary Brown, "Fiscal Policy in the 'Thirties: A Reappraisal," *American Economic Review*, XLVI (Dec. 1956) 857–79. Also useful were the preliminary studies of tax policy prepared for Mr. Morgenthau by Professor Allan Nevins and his associates, and Mr. Morgenthau's review of his purposes in *Summary Report of the Secretary of the Treasury, 1945* (Washington, 1945), pp. 3–44. The quotations in the first paragraph are from the last citation and from the Secretary's testimony reported in the second paragraph, for which see Diary 1:2, 21; Diary 3:74. For Roosevelt's instructions to leave the method of new taxes to Congress, see Roosevelt to Morgenthau, April 2, 1934, Howe MSS. For Magill's studies

and reports of 1934, see Diary 2:204 and the folder "Roswell Magill."
The report given Roosevelt on Dec. 11, 1934, is in Diary 2:275 ff. On
the influence upon it of Oliphant and Frankfurter, see folder "Oliphant" and also Diary 2:332. In writing about social security taxes,
I profited from the account in Arthur M. Schlesinger, Jr., *The Coming of the New Deal* (Boston, 1958), Ch. 18; my data about the Treasury's role is from Diary 2:336; Diary 3:37–50, 58–60, 278, 397, 412,
417–18; Diary 4:248. On the preparation of Roosevelt's message of
June 1935, see Diary 6:81; Diary 7:1 ff., 10, 15a, 29, 96–105, 119, 138–
41. On the legislative history of the inheritance tax and the other
recommendations of that message, see Diary 7:146, 156, 161, 163, 170;
Diary 8:1, 7, 8, 38–41, 112; Diary 9:28–30, and also *New York Times*,
June 19–27, 1935. Morgenthau's warm approval of Robert Jackson's
testimony is from conversation.

2. Corporate Earnings and Corporate Power, pp. 305–19
       In this section I have again drawn heavily on Paul, *Taxation*,
pp. 188–98, though our accounts differ where I had access to manuscript materials he did not see. There is another significant analysis
of the undistributed earnings tax, which reflects the author's point of
view, in Marriner S. Eccles, *Beckoning Frontiers* (New York, 1951),
256–65. The material on the preparation of the President's tax message during the winter of 1936 is from Diary 16:47, 51, 56–68, 86–96
(a report of a conference which included the exchange between Morgenthau and Wallace), 141–46; Diary 17:14–18, 80–83, 91–92; Diary
18:15–16. For the material on the undistributed earnings tax and
Roosevelt's approval of it on Feb. 19, 1936, see Diary 18:33–37, 40–41,
43, 60–74, 92–96, 114–19 (a report of a meeting which included Oliphant's truculent statement). Morgenthau's comment about eliminating double taxation is from conversation. For the final draft of
the message Roosevelt delivered on March 3, see Diary 19:1–13. For
the progress of the revenue bill in the House, see Diary 19:46m, 166,
190 ff.; Diary 20, which consists of relevant hearings; also Upham to
Morgenthau, April 6, 14, 23, 1936; also Paul, *Taxation*. Arguments
in favor of having the Secretary speak, and his testimony, are in
Diary 21:15, 173–74; Diary 22:21–27, 68–129, 205 ff. For the developments through May 22, my material is from Oliphant to Morgenthau, April 27, 1936; Upham to Morgenthau, May 1, 4, 5, 6, 12, 13,

15, 17, 1936; Diary 23:5 (including "the pride of authorship" comment), 13–24, 35, 70d (including the "you must be triply sure" remark), 148 ff., 156–61, 166–77, 185; Diary 24:3–8, 12–18 (a report of the May 11 staff meeting), 21–41, 44–53, 55–57 (including the long quotation beginning "I had a swell glass of orange juice"), 63–78 (Eccles's memoranda), 97–103 (the Secretary's insistence that Haas and Oliphant testify), 104 ff. (their testimony), 109–12, 140–49, 162–71, 270–76 (the last three groups of pages contain extensive data on estimates and strategy). On the letter Roosevelt asked Morgenthau to write, and the resulting conferences and discussions through May 26, see Diary 25:31, 34, 41–45, 69–79, 96–98, 103–5, 125–27, 150. For Morgenthau's talks with Barkley, Roosevelt, and Doughton, and the resulting denouement, see Diary 26:4–5, 7–9, 11b–11c, 18, 22, 76, 83–87, 123; Diary 27:1a–1h, 45, 151 ff. The quotation in the last paragraph is from conversation.

3. In Defense of Party and Principle, pp. 319–23

For Landon's remark, see Paul, *Taxation,* p. 192. The Morgenthau-Krock exchange is from Diary 31:7–14, 128–31. The material on the plan to help Harrison is from Diary 29:83–84, 87–90, 134, 145–60, 186–205. On the Secretary's October speech, see Diary 40: 16–23, 205 ff., 251–55, 283–87; Diary 41:1 ff., 19–21, 108–12, 172, 175–76. The material on Watson and May is from Diary 59:297 ff. and Diary 64:208–10, 213. On the ICC matter, see Diary 51:215–20, 374–76, 394; Diary 53:66–78, 213, 321; Diary 54:253–54, 300–302, 401. For Morgenthau's dealings with Harrison, see Diary 55:1, 104–5.

4. Closing the Loopholes, pp. 323–37

There is an excellent account of the Revenue Act of 1937, on which I relied often, in Paul, *Taxation,* pp. 199–208. Morgenthau's remark about "shysters" is from Diary 25:128–39; his exhortation to Jackson, from Diary 5:80. For material on the Mellon case, see Diary 3:384–86; Diary 61:184–94; Diary 126:340; Diary 128:123; and also letters and memoranda of Jackson to Morgenthau of May 1, July 16, 1935, Feb. 13, 1936; and also the *New York Times,* Dec. 8, 1937; March 25, June 22, 1938. The conferences about tax avoidance, and Magill's memoranda and drafts on that subject, are in Diary 67:173–76; Diary 68:193–201, 235–51; Diary 69:3 ff., 11–12, 46–53, 197–220,

255–59, 280–89. For the President's message and strategy, the public discussion of the issue, and the developments in Congress, see Diary 70:264–69, 281 ff.; Diary 71:92–98, 101–2; Diary 72:17 ff., 235; Diary 73:47, 50–51, 179–94; Diary 78:11, 38–40, 69–76, 98–99, 292–95; and also the *New York Times*, June 18, 25, July 1, 2, 14, 1937.

## CHAPTER VIII. THE DEBT, THE BANKS, AND THE PRICE OF MONEY

1. Managing the Federal Debt, pp. 338–42

The Diaries contain an extraordinary volume of material pertaining to the debt and to each of the Treasury's financings. That material provided the bases for the general remarks about those issues in this section which rests also on the data in the *Annual Reports* of the Secretary of the Treasury. In writing this section, I profited also from the preliminary studies of debt management prepared for Mr. Morgenthau and from the instructive analysis of debt management in Seymour E. Harris, *The National Debt and the New Economics* (New York, 1947). No two financings involved identical problems, but the financing of the winter of 1936 particularly engaged the Secretary's attention and consequently especially revealed his methods and objectives; much of Diary 18 pertains to it. There is rich material on baby bonds in the folders devoted to them in the Morgenthau MSS; and also in Diary 2:353; Diary 3:373; Diary 4:2; Diary 10:85, 147, 182; Diary 12:12; Diary 16:15; Diary 18:24; Diary 22:67 ff.; Diary 28:93 ff.; Diary 66: 289; Diary 101:267–70.

2. Reforming the Federal Reserve, pp. 343–54

There is an excellent description and analysis of the tensions between the New Deal and the banking community in Arthur M. Schlesinger, Jr., *The Coming of the New Deal* (Boston, 1958), pp. 423–45; there is an important account of the genesis and legislative history of the Banking Act of 1935, written from the point of view of the author, in Marriner S. Eccles, *Beckoning Frontiers* (New York, 1951), pp. 165–248. The letter of Oct. 9, 1933, is in the

Roosevelt MSS; Morgenthau's comment in extenuation is from conversation. For Morgenthau's ideas about banking legislation as they developed during 1934, and for conferences about that subject in that period, see Diary 2:189, 195, 221, 229, 265, 320 ff., 348 ff.; and also Morgenthau to Roosevelt, Nov. 2, 1934, Roosevelt MSS. On Morgenthau and O'Connor, see O'Connor to Morgenthau, Jan. 14, 1938; and also Diary 23:128; and also Diary of J. F. T. O'Connor, O'Connor MSS, especially Jan. 13, 22, 23, 31, Feb. 23, May 3, July 2, Aug. 18, 29, Sept. 3, 4, 7, 8, 9, 21, 25, Oct. 9, 11, Dec. 6, 10, 1934; March 21, July 21, 30, 1935; May 14, 16, 1936; and also the folder "O'Connor," which contains data too about the O'Connor-Crowley rivalry. That subject is clarified in Diary 1:16, 71; Diary 2:113 ff.; Diary 3:11–21, 67–69, 98, 105–23, 132–34; Diary 24:52, 135, 239; Diary 25:16–20, 22; Diary 27:3 ff.; Diary 28:92–93. On the Morgenthau-Eccles discussions of the banking bill during Jan.–March 1935, see Diary 3:91 ff., 153 ff., 268 ff.; Diary 4:118 ff.; and also Coolidge to Morgenthau, Feb. 1, 4, 7, 13, 14, 1935. For Morgenthau's response to Eccles's testimony, and his conversations in March with Glass and Roosevelt, see Diary 4:5, 109, 114. On the issue of stock ownership, and Morgenthau's testimony, see Coolidge to Morgenthau, March 18, 1935; Upham to Morgenthau, April 9, 1935; and also Diary 5:46–53, 90–91, 91b ff. Roosevelt's comments on Jackson are in Diary 5:92. On the tactics of Glass and of the Treasury during June, and the resulting legislation, see Eccles, *Beckoning Frontiers,* and Diary 6:61–74, 77–80, 82–86; Diary 7:132–37, 176–78, 180; Diary 8:13–15.

3. Easy Money: Round One, pp. 354–58

For attitudes toward excess reserves during the fall of 1935, including those of the Treasury staff, see Diary 10:87, 91, 118–30, 142, 146, 168–76, 195; Diary 11:142–53. For Aldrich's comments, see the *New York Times,* Dec. 12, 1935, April 3, Dec. 9, 1936, Jan. 4, 13, Oct. 15, 1937. The ideas of Eccles and his board, and the Treasury's responses, Jan.–April 1936, are recorded in Diary 15:30 ff.; Diary 21:126–27. For Morgenthau's meeting with Roosevelt of April 20, see Diary 21:275. For Eccles's decision of April 21, see Diary 22:32–40. On the Morgenthau-Eccles conversations in July

1936, see Diary 28:98–99. The October meetings and conversations are reported in Diary 39:117–26, 253–55; Diary 44:23–25, 232, 242–46, 260–62.

### 4. Hot Money, pp. 358–66

Roosevelt's order for a study of the problem is in Diary 44:48–50. There is a great quantity of material on the question of using a tax to control "hot money," but see especially Diary 54:168–203; Diary 56:247 ff. For the Treasury-Federal Reserve discussions of Nov. 1936, see Diary 45:136–40, 236–54, 269–88. For Morgenthau's use of Warren's article during his staff meeting of Nov. 23, see Diary 46:137–40; for the working out of the sterilization plan, see Diary 46:119–213; Diary 47:63–65, 237–55. The Morgenthau-Eccles conversation of Dec. 8 and Morgenthau's cable to Roosevelt are in Diary 47:306–27, 386–89. For the developments during the rest of December, including the conversations and memoranda quoted, see Diary 48:16–20, 57–58, 140–45, 169–70, 174–79, 227–29, 235–54, 262; Diary 49:111–14, 119–51, 158–76, 186–93, 204–20, 242.

### 5. Easy Money: Round Two, pp. 367–75

The Treasury-Federal Reserve attitudes and conversations of Dec. 1936–Jan. 1937 are reported in Diary 49:106 ff., 245–61; Diary 51:269–74, 323–24; Diary 52:91–93; Diary 53:132–57, 165–78, 185–86, 215, 327–31. The events and conversations of March 12, 13, 16, and 17 are reported in Diary 59:377–83; Diary 60:7–25, 33, 45–48, 60–79, 80–87, 98, 100–105, 116, 119, 168–69. The Research Division's analysis of the market is in Diary 61:156–63; the March 29 staff meetings in Diary 61:204 ff., 250–55. Eccles was apologetic and "very friendly," Diary 61:287. The tense developments and less friendly conversations of April are reported fully in Diary 62:27–60, 229–34, 237, 240–56, 266–326; Diary 63:3–13, 22–23, 29–38, 123–26; Diary 64:136–42, 151–56, 315–19, 326–27. Morgenthau was again "simply delighted" by April 26, Diary 66:49.

### 6. Brakes Off, pp. 376–79

The quotation in the first paragraph is from a meeting reported in Diary 72:12–21. For the discussions of Sept. 8 and 9, see Diary 87:310–33, 421–55. For the drafting and release of the statement of the

Open Market Committee, see Diary 88:9–10, 12–20, 63–66. For an astute analysis of the relationship between the Federal Reserve's tight-money policy and the coming of the recession, see Kenneth D. Roose, *The Economics of Recession and Revival* (New Haven, 1954), especially Chs. 6, 7. There is quite a different point of view in Eccles, *Beckoning Frontiers,* especially pp. 287 ff. Morgenthau's remark about hobbies is from conversation.

CHAPTER IX. RECESSION

1. A Statement of Policy, pp. 380–97

The material on Hawaii is from conversation; Morgenthau's evaluation of the Supreme Court issue and the sit-down strikes, from Diary 88:253; the Aug. 1937 report of the Research Division, from Diary 80:82 ff. For one good statement of the Secretary's attitude about the budget, and for general background for this chapter, see Henry Morgenthau, Jr., "The Morgenthau Diaries: The Struggle for a Program," *Collier's,* Oct. 4, 1947. For the President's economies in Sept. 1937, his talk with Morgenthau of Sept. 20, and Morgenthau's response, see Diary 88:188–89, 213–14, 244–51; Diary 89:50–52, 255–64. The remark about the barrel is from a meeting reported in Diary 90:33–64; Ickes's cooperative gesture, from Diary 90:180. For the letter of Oct. 5 and Morgenthau's remark about it, see Diary 91:68 ff. For the discussions of Oct. 8 through 11, see Diary 91:208, 212–16, 231. The talk with Bailie and about the market is from Diary 92:18–22, 112–17 (which includes the remark about Roosevelt's feet being on the ground), 135–60 (on the economy, equities, and the utilities). For the developments of Oct. 12 through 14, see Diary 92:25, 43–44, 57, 130. The argument between Morgenthau and Taylor is from Diary 92:163–75. For Roosevelt's remark of Oct. 19, see Diary 92:230. The remark about taking away the crutches to test the patient is from conversation. On the preparation and delivery of the speech before the Academy of Political Science, see Diary 95:39–56, 129–33, 134–65, 295–331, 470–97; Diary 96:75–82; Diary 97:270–97; Diary 98:35, 110, 116. For Morgenthau's dealings with Roosevelt on Nov. 2, 3, 8 and the Cabinet meeting of Nov. 4, see Diary 94:47–53, 152–54. For a different view of the

Academy speech, as well as of the onset and significance of the recession, see Marriner S. Eccles, *Beckoning Frontiers* (New York, 1951),
especially pp. 303–4.

2. Again the Needy, pp. 398–401

For Hopkins's plan to add 500,000 to WPA, see Diary 101:174–
75. On Morgenthau's dealings with Williams and Roosevelt in Feb.
1938, see Diary 108:142–43, 167–76, 213–15, 290–97; Diary 109:40–
57, 60, 77–78, 146–50, 157–59, 255; Diary 110:16–18.

3. "A Different Set of Delusions," pp. 401–5

The data in this section is from a memorandum of Magill to
Morgenthau about the Cabinet meeting of Jan. 21, and from Diary
108:35 ff.; Diary 112:309–17.

4. Some Shots in the Arm, pp. 405–17

For the staff meeting of Feb. 7 and the next week's developments in gold policy, see Diary 108:340–67; Diary 109:136–42, 268–
343, 350–62, 380; Diary 110:55, 68–82, 95–110. The data and quotations on the reorganization of the utilities, especially the Genesee
Valley Gas Company, are from Diary 107:92 ff., 134, 136, 229–46,
294; Diary 108:146–63, 185, 187, 191–98, 307; Diary 109:383; Diary
112:269. The discussion of housing is based upon Diary 105:236 ff.,
317, 319, 335; Diary 110:119–23, 232–33, 288; Diary 111:21–23, 70;
Diary 113:99–127, 225. Jackson's remark about monopoly is from
Diary 89:271 — a Diary volume full of important background material on the Treasury's concern about monopoly. For the discussions of Feb. 1938, leading to the statement about prices, see Diary
110:83, 183 ff.; Diary 111:28–54, 95–116, 121–25, 169, 181–83, 204–8.
For the investigations and discussions of March, leading to the cement order, see Diary 112:40–63, 113–26, 142; Diary 114:44–56,
78–105, 387–400; Diary 115:48–75, 103, 109, 110, 157–58, 403–12;
Diary 116:1–2, 33, 46 ff., 144–53, 195–96, 336 ff., 361–63; Diary
121:215. Eccles's and Douglas's plans appear respectively in Diary
113:3–5 and 16 ff. Roosevelt admitted to a policy of wait-and-see in
Diary 114:295. For Morgenthau's studies and conversations about
the proposals, see Diary 115:40–47, 345–47; Diary 116:276–93, 307–
13; Diary 117:94–95, 256–58. The fullest statement of the Eastman

proposal, which Morgenthau considered more or less concurrently, is in Dairy 117:100–189. Morgenthau remarked to Wagner about his "indigestion" in Diary 116:385; his recommendations to Roosevelt are in Diary 117:447–48, 458.

5. Stampede, pp. 417–26

Parts of this section appeared in Morgenthau, "The Morgenthau Diaries: The Struggle for a Program." For Taylor's report of April 4, see Diary 118:45, 176–80; for Magill's of the next day, Diary 118:125–28; the Treasury analyses of April 7 and 8 are in Diary 118:211–12, 225–33; for Morgenthau's memorandum, see Diary 118:247–50. The conversations of April 10, 11, and 12 are in Diary 118:266–86, 296–99, 304–5, 316, 319, 326–28, 343–48. The account of the resignation and the reflections about deficit spending are from "The Struggle for a Program" and conversations.

6. En Garde, pp. 426–32

The discussion of bank holding companies is based upon Diary 105:78–82, 317; Diary 106:201–15, 274, 277–82; Diary 107:59, 188, 193–94, 251; Diary 108:209–12, 381–84; Diary 109:177–79; Diary 112:231; Diary 115:113–21, 293. The discussion of the problem of bank examinations is based upon Diary 120:151, 280–88, 291–92; Diary 122:1–2, 4–5, 247–62; Diary 128:352–61; Diary 130:50–64, 177–248; Diary 132:*passim,* and also a volume of newspaper clippings dated 1938 and entitled "Uniform Bank Examinations"; but for another view, see Eccles, *Beckoning Frontiers,* pp. 266–86.

7. Waste Not, Want Not, pp. 432–38

The material, including quotations, pertaining to the lending and spending bill is from Diary 123:343–47; Diary 124:23–24, 28–36, 102 ff., 346, 356–59, 362, 452; Diary 125:52–65, 165; Diary 126:298, 309 ff., 346; Diary 127:40–41, 137. The discussion of the appropriations for agriculture and the problem of food surplus and distribution is based upon Diary 125:134, 69, 163, 166, 330, 446 ff.; Diary 126:32, 124–25, 128, 170–80, 318 ff.; Diary 128:295–96; Diary 130:123–30; Diary 131:39–48. For the material on the Chinese credit and on exchanging surpluses for strategic supplies, see Diary 126:170–80, 257 ff., 273–84, 318 ff.; Diary 127:109–10, 176, 300–308; Diary 128:430–31.

8. Taxation in Recession, pp. 439–51

There is an excellent discussion of the Revenue Act of 1938 in Randolph E. Paul, *Taxation in the United States* (Boston, 1954), pp. 208–20. A summary of Magill's report fills Diary 81; the full report, Diaries 82 through 86. For the responses of Vinson and Doughton, see Diary 90:107–8; Diary 92:39–42; for Roosevelt's views, see Diary 92:228–30, 249; Diary 94:153, 192–94. For the events of Nov. 23, see Diary 99:8–10, 22. On Harrison and the Senate Finance Committee, see Diary 99:143–53, 157–58. For the President's negotiations with Magill, Harrison, and Vinson, leading to the Administration's support of Vinson's formula and the third-basket tax, see Diary 99:199–200, 232–36; Diary 101:69–70, 75, 167–72, 263–65; Diary 104:109–22; Diary 105:108–10. The discussion of the opposition to the third-basket tax is based upon Diary 107:256–58; Diary 113:97–98; Diary 114:154–79. On Harrison's radio speech and the developments during April 1938, including discussions of Administration strategy, see Diary 118:40, 274–75, 317, 353–54, 376–81, 398; Diary 119:278–79, 291–94; Diary 121:287–93, and also Oliphant to Morgenthau, May 10, 1938. The conference of May 18 is reported in Magill to Morgenthau, May 18, 1938. For Oliphant's views, see Diary 126:73–75 and also Oliphant to Magill, June 2, 1938. On the Arthurdale speech and the responses to it, see Diary 126:347–48 and two volumes entitled "Revenue Act of 1938," which include the text of the speech and the letters of Oliphant and of Magill cited above. Morgenthau asked for "a fresh viewpoint" in Diary 133:18–20 but rejected a Keynesian view again in Diary 142:231–37. The President's shock at the prospects for fiscal 1940 is reported in Diary 145:78–80, and Taylor and Morgenthau expressed their dismay in Diary 145:99–145. The Temple commencement address is in Diary 129:297 ff.

### CHAPTER X. THE TREASURY AND FOREIGN AFFAIRS

1. The Stage, pp. 452–55

There is useful material for this section and the rest of this chapter in Henry Morgenthau, Jr., "The Morgenthau Diaries: How F.D.R. Fought the Axis," *Collier's*, Oct. 11, 1947; the quotations in the second paragraph of this section are from the article which also contains a fraction of the data in this chapter pertaining to disarmament. About the kidnaping of Chiang Kai-shek very little is known. There is, however, a disingenuous account in Mei-ling Suong Chiang (Madame Chiang Kai-shek), *General Chiang Kai-shek: The Account of the Fortnight in Sian When the Fate of China Hung in the Balance* (Garden City, N.Y., 1937). For the comments and proposals Morgenthau made about the affair, see Diary 48:167–68, 260–62; Diary 52:148–51, 285–87. The recollection noted in the last paragraph is from conversation; the material on the monetary arrangement, from Diary 53:164.

2. Arms and the Franc, pp. 455–67

On the French efforts of Jan. 1937 to negotiate a loan, and the messages and discussions pertaining to those efforts, see Diary 52:90, 133–35, 138, 200–207, 265–70; Diary 53:43–46, 50–55, 59, 93, 104, 241–84. Morgenthau's conversations with Roosevelt on Feb. 6 and 9 are reported in Diary 54:125–27, 303–4; his talk with Bewley of Feb. 11 is in Diary 54:360–62; that with Roosevelt on Feb. 16, in Diary 55:330–31. The Feb. 26 staff meeting about French devaluation is from Diary 56:281–305. For the French and British responses to the devaluation proposal, see Diary 57:49–54, 196–206. Roosevelt hesitated in Diary 57:233; Morgenthau's remarks of March 3 are in Diary 57:281–83; his criticisms of Blum's policy, in Diary 58:1–3, 10–19. For discussions of the Johnson Act and the French loan proposal, see Diary 58:157–62, 200–202, 267, 273, 401–10, 417, 418 ff. The long message from Chamberlain which Morgenthau received on March 26 is in Diary 62:176–81.

3. Russian Gold, pp. 467–73

There is a useful analysis of the gold problem of the spring of 1937 in G. Griffith Johnson, Jr., *The Treasury and Monetary Policy, 1933–1938* (Cambridge, 1939), pp. 122–24. The Taylor-Oumansky luncheon is reported in Diary 66:263–65; the Research Division's analysis of Russian objectives is in Diary 66:368 ff. Morgenthau's remark to Feis is from a conference reported in Diary 67:242–55. For Morgenthau's attitude toward Soviet-American negotiations, see Diary 69:113. French views about Russian gold are reported in Diary 70:64–66; 253–63. White's memorandum about Russian gold is in Diary 70:108–9; Morgenthau's conversation with the Russians on May 26, in Diary 70:110–18; that of June 15, in Diary 73:24–28. The State Department memorandum on Soviet timber and sugar policies is in Diary 73:77–80. The quotation in the last paragraph is from conversation.

### 4. The Franc Floats, pp. 473–78

Chamberlain's message quoted in paragraph two is from Diary 70:298–99. For Stimson's view of Simon, see Henry L. Stimson and McGeorge Bundy, *On Active Service in Peace and War* (New York, 1948), pp. 247–48. Morgenthau's remark about France's virtue is from Diary 72:331; Blum's remark to Bullitt, from Diary 72:368–73. The staff meeting of June 18 is reported in Diary 73:224–83. Diary 76 consists of Cochran's full and informative report of the French crisis of June and July and of Anglo-American negotiations pertaining thereto. For the developments of June 30–July 1, besides Diary 76, see Diary 75:14–25, 152–98, 210–11, 225–26; Diary 77:6–14, 23–45, 81, 86–89, 92–96, 186–91.

### 5. War in China, pp. 479–85

Chinese-American monetary diplomacy during 1937 and 1938 is treated with accuracy and discernment in Allan S. Everest, *Morgenthau, the New Deal, and Silver* (New York, 1950), pp. 117–22; the account there, like the account in this chapter, rests upon the material in the Diaries. Morgenthau's conversation of May 11, 1937, with Sze is reported in Diary 67:257–60. The "extra nice" and "they are great traders" comments are from a staff meeting of July 6 reported in Diary 77:171–72; the July 8 meeting with Kung is in Diary 78:12–37. Taylor's reports of the Cabinet meetings of Aug. 6 and 13 are in memoranda he sent Morgenthau on Aug. 9 and 17; see also his memorandum of Aug. 28. There is a good analysis of the State Department's case for not recognizing a state of war in Cordell Hull, *The Memoirs of Cordell Hull* (2 v., New York, 1948), Ch. 39. The Treasury Research Division's analysis is in Diary 87:156–78, 383–89; see also Diary 87:274–82. The Chinese silver offer of Nov. 29 is reported in Diary 99:207; the written exchanges and discussions that followed, Dec. 2–8, among the Treasury and State Departments and Roosevelt, are in Diary 100:141, 154–62, 189, 311, 317–19, 394–95; Diary 101:14–16, 70. Mrs. Roosevelt, during an interview with me, several times remarked that Henry Morgenthau was her husband's conscience; that remark she has made often also to Mr. Morgenthau.

### 6. The *Panay*, pp. 485–92

For the State Department's point of view about the *Panay* crisis, see Hull, *Memoirs,* Ch. 39, which contains also a good narrative of the events of the crisis. For what Roosevelt told Morgenthau on Dec. 14, see Diary 102:2. The Treasury's research on Japanese assets is in Diary 102:41, 226; for Oliphant's memorandum and Roosevelt's response, see Diary 103:20 ff. The staff meeting of Dec. 17, including Morgenthau's argument with Taylor, is reported in Diary 103:21–58, and continued, after Morgenthau's return from a Cabinet meeting, in 59–62. Morgenthau's conversation with Simon follows, see Diary 103:63–74. The Dec. 18 cable is in Diary 103:84; Roosevelt seemed to have "cooled off" according to comments at a conference reported in Diary 103:88–94. For Simon's Dec. 21 message, see Diary 103:225–38. On Ingersoll's mission, see his testimony, Feb. 12, 1946, *Hearings before the Joint Committees on the Investigation of the Pearl Harbor Attack* (Washington, 1946), IX, 4273–78.

### 7. Gold, Silver, and Oil, pp. 493–97

The subject matter of this section is covered fully in Everest, *Morgenthau,* pp. 84–93, an account based on the data in the Diaries. On Brazilian-American monetary negotiations, see Diary 68:97–103, 159–60; Diary 78:89–97, 204–37, 242–75, 277, 281–307; Diary 79:30–41, 49–50. For the conference with Suarez of Dec. 13 and the preliminaries to it, see Diary 101:52, 55–58, 70, 292–300. Morgenthau's discussions with Roosevelt are in Diary 102:96; Diary 103:79. For the dinner party of Dec. 22 and the discussions the next morning, see Diary 104:32, 64–70. The State Department's attitude is reported in Diary 102:177–80; Diary 104:163 ff. For Morgenthau's reflection of Dec. 29, see Diary 104:202. Treasury-State negotiations of Dec. 30–31 are reported in Diary 104:276–78, 283–87. The Treasury-State discussions of March 24–25, 1938, and the controversial statement to the press, appear in Diary 116:400–408; Diary 117:25,

26, 75, 331, 333, 345–61. For the Treasury's proposal of May, see Diary 125:262. Morgenthau's conversation with Hull in July is reported in Diary 134:164 ff.

### 8. Another French Crisis, pp. 498–505

The quotation in the first paragraph is from conversation. The Morgenthau-Phillips meetings are reported in Diary 89:10–12, 16–17, 18–20, 35–37. Morgenthau's March 14 conversation with Roosevelt is reported in connection with a Treasury staff meeting of that day in Diary 114:277–94, which includes the other material quoted from that date. The call to Cochran and Blum's reply through Cochran are in Diary 114:341, 365, 377–80. The predictions from London are in Diary 115:23–26, 315–17; Roosevelt's comments of March 16 in Diary 115:27. Cochran's mid-April report of growing confidence within France is in Diary 119:347–50; Kennedy's April 25 letter, in Diary 120:362–63; Bullitt's views and Morgenthau's response, in Diary 121:78–79; the April 29 cable from London, in Diary 121:317–20. For the events, exchanges, and discussions of May 2, 3, and 4, see Diary 122:29–31, 33–67, 73–110, 112–58, 168–77, 185–97, 206–15, 230–35; Diary 123:243, 436.

### 9. Spain, pp. 506–8

Everest, in *Morgenthau*, pp. 125–31, covers the subject matter of this section and carries the account of the law suits beyond 1938. The data pertinent to the events of that year covered in this section are from Diary 127:177, 203, 312–17; Diary 128:17–19 (Morgenthau's conversation with Stimson); Diary 134:209–10 (the "direct hits by bombs" remark); Diary 139:11, 49, 73 ff. On the Zabala matter, see Diary 141:116, 158; Diary 142:166–67, 218–19.

### 10. The Immobile Mr. Hull, pp. 508–13

On the silver purchases of the early spring of 1938, see Diary 117:424; Diary 121:195–204. Kung's letter of June 21 is in Diary 130:171–72; Roosevelt's instructions, in Diary 135:132; see also Diary 135:181; Diary 138:109–10. Buck's reports of the views of Chen and Stilwell are in Diary 138:167–68, 171–72, 176, 187–88. For Morgenthau's report of his conversation with Wang, for his conversation with Roosevelt on Sept. 6, and for the interdeparmental discussion that followed, see Diary 138:205–24; the State Department's attitude of Sept. 8 was revealed in a meeting reported in Diary 139:22 ff. It was on Sept. 22 that Morgenthau made his remarks about "the democratic form of government," the tung oil, and a buying company, and then talked with Chen about "business, not diplomacy" — see Diary 142:175–98. Roosevelt's statement of Sept. 26 was noted at a meeting reported in Diary 142:352 ff. For the discussions Morgenthau then had with Hull, Wallace, and Pittman, see Diary 143:27–45, 54–55, 272–85; Diary 144:106–8. On the Chinese purchasing corporation, see Diary 144:177, 199–205, 279–300, 306–9; Diary 145:248–51. Roosevelt's remark about transportation was repeated during a conference reported in Diary 145:386–93.

11. Munich, pp. 513–23

In writing this section I relied often on the trenchant account of the genesis, development, and significance of the Czech crisis in William L. Langer and S. Everett Gleason, *The Challenge to Isolation* (New York, 1952), Ch. I, especially pp. 32–35. For the Morgenthau-Marchandeau talks, see Diary 135:79–84. On the possibility of the Treasury's buying future francs, and Morgenthau's statement upon sailing, see Diary 135:159 ff., 216–21, 266–91. Roosevelt's request of Aug. 30 and the resulting Treasury studies and the discussions of Aug. 31 are reported in great deail in Diary 137:87–88, 165–68, 214–43. For the responses to Kennedy's attitudes, see Diary 138:20–21, 33 ff. Morgenthau's statement about "the battleship" is from Diary 139:220; his talk with Roosevelt on Sept. 19 is reported in Diary 141:115. For Blum's Sept. 20 statement, see Diary 141:225. Morgenthau reconsidered a boycott at the staff meeting of Sept. 26, reported in Diary 142:338–43; he was "the first to congratulate" Roosevelt in Diary 143:142. On Morgenthau's early investigation of preparedness, see Louis Johnson to Morgenthau, Oct. 29, 1938; Roosevelt to Johnson, Oct. 31, 1938.

12. Postlude to Munich, pp. 523–28

For Morgenthau's conversation with Oliphant and White, see Diary 145:259–93; the resulting letter was Morgenthau to Roosevelt, Oct. 17, 1938, Roosevelt MSS.

# Index